CRIMIN

CRIMINOLOGY
SECOND EDITION

Freda Adler

Gerhard O. W. Mueller

William S. Laufer

McGraw-Hill, Inc.
New York St. Louis San Francisco Auckland
Bogotá Caracas Lisbon London Madrid Mexico City
Milan Montreal New Delhi San Juan Singapore
Sydney Tokyo Toronto

Criminology

Photo Credits and Illustration and Text Credits appear on pages 525–530 and on this page by reference.

This book is printed on acid-free paper.

34567890 VNH VNH 9098765

ISBN 0-07-000471-4

This book was set in Palatino by Ruttle, Shaw & Wetherill, Inc.
The editors were Phillip A. Butcher, Jeannine Ciliotta, and Bob Greiner;
the design was done by Initial Graphic Systems, Inc.;
the production supervisor was Annette Mayeski.
The photo editor was Barbara Salz.
Von Hoffmann Press, Inc., was printer and binder.

Library of Congress Cataloging-in-Publication Data

Adler, Freda.
   Criminology / Freda Adler, Gerhard O. W. Mueller, William S. Laufer.
—2d ed.
     p.   cm.
   Includes bibliographical references and index.
   ISBN 0-07-000471-4
   1. Criminology.   I. Mueller, Gerhard O. W.   II. Laufer, William
S.   III. Title.
HV6025.A35   1995
364—dc20   94-15931

About the Authors

FREDA ADLER is Distinguished Professor of Criminal Justice at Rutgers University, School of Criminal Justice. She received her B.A. in sociology, her M.A. in criminology, and her Ph.D. in sociology from the University of Pennsylvania. Teaching since 1968, Dr. Adler's subjects include criminology, statistics, research methods, and international and comparative criminology. She has served as criminological advisor to the United Nations, as well as to federal, state, and foreign governments. Her published works include eight books as author or co-author, eight books as editor, and over sixty journal articles. She has served on the editorial boards of the *Journal of Research in Crime and Delinquency, Criminology,* and the *Journal of Criminal Justice.* Presently, Dr. Adler serves as editorial consultant to the *Journal of Criminal Law and Criminology* and is co-editor of *Advances in Criminological Theory.* She has been elected President of the American Society of Criminology (November 1994-95).

GERHARD O. W. MUELLER is distinguished Professor of Criminal Justice at Rutgers University, School of Criminal Justice. He studied law and sociology in Europe and America, earning his J.D. degree from the University of Chicago. He went on to receive the L.L.M. degree from Columbia University. He was awarded the degree of Dr. Jur. (h.c.) by the University of Uppsala, Sweden. His teaching in criminal law, criminal procedure, criminology, criminal justice, and comparative criminal justice, begun in 1953, was partially interrupted between 1974 and 1982, when, as Chief of the United Nations Crime Prevention and Criminal Justice Branch, he was responsible for all of the United Nations' programs dealing with problems of crime and justice worldwide. Professor Mueller has been a member of the faculties of the University of Washington, West Virginia University, New York University, and of the National Judicial College, with visiting appointments and lectureships at universities and institutes in the Americas, Western and Eastern Europe, Africa, Asia and Australia. His published works include some 50 authored or edited books and 250 scholarly articles.

WILLIAM S. LAUFER is Anheuser-Busch Term Assistant Professor of Legal Studies at the Wharton School of the University of Pennsylvania. Dr. Laufer received the B.A. in social and behavioral sciences at The Johns Hopkins University, the J.D. at Northeastern University School of Law, and the Ph.D. at Rutgers University School of Criminal Justice. Teaching since 1987, his subjects include criminological theory, corporate and white collar crime, and business ethics. Dr. Laufer's research has appeared in law reviews and a wide range of criminal justice, legal, and psychology journals, such as the *Journal of Research in Crime and Delinquency, Law and Human Behavior,* and the *Journal of Personality and Social Psychology.* He is co-editor of the *Handbook of Psychology and Law, Personality Moral Development and Criminal Behavior,* and *Crime, Values and Religion.* Dr. Laufer is co-editor of *Advances in Criminological Theory,* with Freda Adler.

To our children and grandchildren

Mark J. Adler and Susan B. Weinstock-Adler with David S. Adler and
   Daniel Adler

Jill E. Adler-Donkersloot and Willem H.F.A. Donkersloot

Nancy D. Adler-Knijff and Robert F. Knijff

Mark H. Mueller and Constance Sobol Mueller with Nicolai
   Alexander Mueller

Marla L. Mueller and Lawrence Frederick Bentley

Monica R. Mueller

Matthew A. Mueller and Martha Sullivan Mueller with Lauren
   Elizabeth, Stephen William, and Anna Lisette Mueller

Hannah Laufer

Contents in Brief

Contents

List of Special Features

Preface

Criminology is a young discipline—the term "criminology" is barely a century old. But in those hundred years criminology has emerged as a major social and behavioral science. Criminology's contributions are essential for dealing with a crime problem in our society that many people consider intolerable. Problems as vital and urgent as those addressed in this book are also challenging and exciting. We invite teachers and students to join us in traveling along criminology's path, exploring its domain and mapping out its future in the twenty-first century, which is just about upon us.

THE SECOND EDITION

The first edition of this book was so well received by students and professors that we have made no major changes in the second. There is of course much updating, necessitated by rapid developments in the field, and we have tried to make everything as current as possible. Explanations include examples which are fresh in the minds of readers, covering events that occurred as late as 1994. Statistical information, research literature, and policy changes are current to the moment the book went to press.

A new chapter (Chapter 14) on comparative criminology covers this important and growing area.

New full-page boxes contain discussion questions and source materials and can be used as learning tools in class discussion or for research or group assignments.

Full-color photo essays describe and illustrate topics of special interest today: Criminology's focus and rapid social change; America's changing ethnic gangs; the drug problem today and tomorrow; and the range of police work today, from shootouts to social service.

ORGANIZATION

This book has four parts. Part I presents an overview of criminology and describes the vast horizon of this science. It explains techniques for measuring the characteristics of criminals, crime, and victims. It also traces the history of criminological thought through the era that witnessed the formation of the major schools of criminology: classicism and positivism (eighteenth and nineteenth centuries).

Part II explains criminal behavior on the basis of the various theories developed in the twentieth century. Among the subjects covered are theories that offer biological, psychological, sociological, sociopolitical, and integrated explanations. The most recent theoretical developments, including new psychological factors and genetics, and the newly constructed "general theory of crime" are included. Coverage of research by radical, socialist, and feminist criminologists has been updated.

Part III takes an innovative approach by explaining the types of crime not only from a legal-historical perspective, but also on the basis of the contemporary theories of rational choice and routine activities. This approach permits an assessment of the motivations and activities of offenders, as well as the prevalence and distribution of crime. The familiar street crimes, such as assault and robbery, are assessed, as are criminal activities that have been highlighted by researchers only in recent years. We have added a new chapter to Part III: Comparative Criminology. While our approach has always been international and we included comparative material throughout the book in the first edition, a separate chapter that explains the meaning, purpose, significance, and scientific dimensions of comparative criminology seems warranted in this edition, since this is a growing research area in the field. It is also an area that will have more and more practical and policy implications in the future.

Part IV, "A Criminological Approach to the Criminal Justice System," includes an explanation of the component parts and the functioning of the system, and it explains contemporary criminological research on how the people who run the system operate it, the decision-making processes of all participants, and the interaction of all the system components.

SPECIAL FEATURES

In our effort to provide the student with a pleasurable learning experience and the instructor with a teaching tool that is at once dynamic and effective, we have included a number of special features:

- *Explaining Criminal Behavior:* We highlight the evolution and interrelationships of theories that explain criminal behavior to make them part of students' own experience rather than an academic exercise.

- *Theory to Practice:* We demonstrate the interrelatedness of theory, policy, and practice. The theory chapters, for example, include "Theory to Practice" sections that enable the student to appreciate the practical significance of theoretical work. In the criminal justice chapters, we present the system within the context of contemporary theory and research.

- *Boxes:* Every chapter contains three boxes, one on each of three themes,

  Criminological Focus
  At Issue
  Window to the World

  Each box has the same full-page format, with text, illustrations, tables, discussion questions, and sources. *Focus* boxes provide an intensive analysis of selected cases and research studies within the topics covered in the particular chapter. *At Issue* boxes contain selected problems that constitute new or continuing challenges to the criminologist. *Window to the World* boxes highlight the international dimensions of crime and criminological study.

- *Global Focus:* To cover the dramatic impact of the globalization of society on contemporary crime, we highlight global and international material and examples throughout the text, in the Window to the World boxes, and in the new chapter on comparative criminology.

- *Victimology:* Additional emphasis is given to another new constituent area of criminology, victimology, which also has a global aspect today, when once again entire ethnic groups have become victims of genocide.

- *Looking to the Future:* The topics and examples we have chosen for the boxes, for the photo essays, for the chapter openings, and for the text itself are all current developments, new discoveries, or continuing problems. They range from the significance of fairy tales in understanding crime historically to the emerging illicit global market in human body parts. They include the criminological significance of the recent discovery of Oetzi, the 5,500-year-old ice man, as well as the development of electronic devices for tracking stolen motor vehicles. They reach as far as the Amazon, where an ancient and synnomic culture is being threatened with extinction, to Yugoslavia, where violence has replaced multiculturalism, to Europe and America, where neo-Nazi skinheads are a violent and growing threat to democracy.

Photo Essays: Full-color photo essays in each part highlight and document major issues that relate to each part:

I *Criminology: A World of Constant Change and Challenge* depicts criminology's vast horizon

II *America's Changing Ethnic Gangs* explores the new ethnic-based groups with which criminologists and criminal justice officials have to contend today

III *Drugs: A Continuing Problem* tracks the world's drug problem as it manifests itself in the United States today in social problems and human suffering

IV *Police Activities: From Shootouts to Social Service* details the range of modern police activities and the new challenges that confront law enforcement agencies

As in the first edition, we have endeavored not only to reflect developments and change, but to anticipate them on the basis of trend data. The authors look forward to the challenges of the twenty-first century, when those who study criminology with this text may be decision-makers, researchers, or planners of a future as free from crime as possible.

TWO VERSIONS

Recent developments in the criminology curriculum have created a need for two books, not just one; so for this edition we have two versions of the text: the full version and a shorter one. Many schools retain the traditional criminology course, which includes criminological coverage of criminal justice. For such programs, **Criminology,** Second Edition, is the ideal text. For schools that have expanded their offerings by adding an introductory course in criminal justice, thus freeing instructors from having to cover this subject matter in a criminology course, **Criminology: The Shorter Version** is more appropriate, since it omits Part IV (A Criminological Approach to the Criminal Justice System). We hope these two verions will make using the text easier for instructors, and we would appreciate their comments and suggestions.

PEDAGOGICAL AIDS

Working together closely and cooperatively, the authors and the editors have developed a format for the text that is both readable and attractive: Photographs, tables, and figures, in addition to the boxes and the photo essays, highlight and amplify the text coverage. Chapter outlines, lists of key terms, chapter review sections, and the Glossary help make the book user-friendly. As before, the instructor's manual and test file (both IBM and Mac versions) have been prepared by Marie Henry, respected and experienced instructor of criminology at Sullivan County Community College.

IN APPRECIATION

We greatly acknowledge the assistance and support of a number of dedicated professionals. We thank Professor Marvin E. Wolfgang, Director of the Sellin Center of the University of Pennsylvania, for his helpful and generous suggestions and comments. At Rutgers University, the librarian of the N.C.C.D./Criminal Justice Collection, Phyllis Schultze, has been most helpful in patiently tracking and tracing sources. We thank Professor Sesha Kethineni, Illinois State University, for her tireless assistance on the first edition, and Deborah Leiter-Walker for her help on the second. Joan Schroeder has done a superb job of word processing on both editions; we could not have produced the manuscript without her. Among those to whom we are grateful for their work on the first edition are former Rutgers University School of Criminal Justice research assistants Susanna Cornett, Dory Dickman, Lisa Maher, Susan Plant, and Mangai Natarajan.

We owe a special debt to the team at McGraw-Hill. Executive editor Phil Butcher orchestrated the planning of this new edition, as he did the first. Development editor Jeannine Ciliotta's many ideas and suggestions helped shape this new edition and realize that plan. Editing supervisor Bob Greiner's keen judgment and devotion to **Criminology** through two editions deserve very special appreciation. Safra Nimrod, photo editor, and Barbara Salz, photo researcher, deserve thanks for giving the book its visual appeal. Writer Carolyn Kroehler helped make our new boxes truly outstanding. We are also grateful to Howard Leiderman, the designer; to Susan Gottfried, who copyedited the manuscript; and to production manager Annette Mayeski for keeping the project on schedule.

Many academic reviewers (listed facing title page) offered invaluable help in planning and drafting chapters. We thank them for their time and thoughtfulness and for the wisdom they brought from their teaching and research.

A combined total of over seventy years of teaching criminology provides the basis for the writing of **Criminology,** Second Edition. We hope the result is a text that is intellectually provocative, factually rigorous, and scientifically sound and that gives the student a stimulating learning experience.

Freda Adler
Gerhard O. W. Mueller
William S. Laufer

Understanding Criminology

Criminology is the scientific study of the making of laws, the breaking of laws, and society's reaction to the breaking of laws. Sometimes these laws are arrived at by consensus; sometimes they are imposed by those in power. In ancient times, laws expressed the common interest of small groupings of people: clans, tribes, and kingdoms. Today, the people of the entire world have certain common interests. As a result, criminological research and crime-prevention strategies are becoming globalized, even though the reach of laws may not yet be global (Chapter 1).

Criminologists have adopted methods of study from all the social and behavioral sciences. Like all scientists, criminologists measure. They assess crime over time and place, and they measure the characteristics of criminals, of crimes, and of victims (Chapter 2).

Throughout history thinkers and rulers have written about crime and criminals and the control of crime. Yet the term "criminology" is little more than a century old, and the subject has been of scientific interest for only two centuries. Two schools of thought contributed to modern criminology: the classical school, associated predominantly with Cesare Beccaria (eighteenth century), which focused on crime, and the positivist school, associated with Cesare Lombroso, Enrico Ferri, and Raffaele Garofalo (nineteenth and early twentieth centuries), which focused on criminals (Chapter 3). Contemporary American criminology owes much to these European roots.

1

An Overview of Criminology

KEY TERMS
communal consensus model
conflict model
crime
crimes against the peace and security of
mankind
criminology
customs

ost people think criminology deals only with crimes like murder, robbery, car theft, burglary, or perhaps shoplifting. Not so. Of course criminologists are greatly concerned with such crimes, but their interest reaches much further: to the boardrooms where banking decisions are made, to ships moving people and goods around the world, to streets where children cannot play safely, to places where ethnic interests collide.

The case of millionaire financier and banker Charles H. Keating, Jr. is one example. For a millionaire his court appearance was an unusual one: Keating was being sentenced to 12 years and 7 months in prison. U.S. district court judge Mariana R. Pfaelzer explained why such a severe sentence was called for: Keating, in concert with nine associates, had swindled thousands of small investors in his Lincoln Savings and Loan Association out of their life savings, at an astounding cost to American taxpayers of $2.5 billion. With his ill-gotten gains—more than all the pickpockets of America together could amass—Keating maintained an extraordinarily extravagant lifestyle.

Criminologists also study an area known as white-collar crime. Much research has been conducted to understand why middle- and upper-class people commit crimes that affect broad sectors of the population. Criminologists are called upon by industry and government to measure, describe, and explain white-collar and corporate crime, to assist in devising strategies to curb it, and thus to save taxpayers' money.

On June 6, 1993, the Taiwan-registered "rust bucket" freighter *Golden Venture* grounded on the beach at Rockaway in New York City. The ship's captain and 12-man crew, with 281 "passengers," jumped overboard in 6-foot swells, as the ship creaked and rolled in the surf. Six died in the effort to swim ashore. Most of the others were rounded up by officials of the U.S. Coast Guard, the Immigration and Naturalization Service, and the New York City police.

By now the Coast Guard has identified or intercepted 40 of the many "rust-bucket" ships that ferry an estimated 100,000 illegal Chinese immigrants to U.S. shores every year, for fees of between $20,000 and $50,000, which the "lucky ones" must pay off to enforcers of the gangs through years of slavery in sweatshops or massage parlors. Chinese gang killings keep increasing.

Scholars of many disciplines are concerned with the causes and control of illegal migrations. Criminologists are expert at studying the criminal exploitation of human desires and ambitions, the organizational structure of the large and pervasive syndicates which resort to many kinds of crimes in order to enrich themselves at the expense of individual victims and the public at large. They also study the links between alien, drug, arms, and contraband smuggling, and their impact on social structure and, indeed, world peace.

Neil Maddox, age 11, died young. He happened to get in the way of a drive-by shooting in his Chicago neighborhood. In the slang of the drug gangs the child is just another "mushroom," like the mushrooms of the Super Mario Brothers' Nintendo game, who pop up, seemingly out of nowhere, in the line of fire. But the human mushrooms are either innocent bystanders, caught in a crossfire, or individuals simply wiped out for fun or revenge. Figures are hard to come by, since crime statistics do not record "mushroom killings." Prior to 1985 the term "mushroom children" did not exist. By 1989

it is estimated that there were 28, and by now well over 100 such children have been killed. And the number keeps rising.

Criminologists are interested in the vast, intertwined problems of drug-related crime and violence, of the causes of addiction within society, and of the impact of drug abuse on the quality of life. They are attempting to sort out the ramifications of the drug culture in search of feasible and socially acceptable solutions, inside and outside the criminal justice system.

In 1989, news photographs depicted the supertanker *Exxon Valdez* aground in Prince William Sound, Alaska, exuding oil through a rupture in its hull. This caused North America's largest ecological disaster. The captain was eventually convicted on a misdemeanor charge. But criminologists have many questions. How can we avoid such disasters in the future? Should negligent captains be held liable for more serious crimes? Should corporations be held liable for the acts of their employees? Are there better remedies than those of the criminal law? While criminologists are searching for answers, tankers keep running aground and polluting the shorelines.

Criminologists study the criminal sanctions used against individuals and corporations. How can human and corporate behavior be controlled to safeguard the environment? Are new laws likely to provide greater protection against negligence and error? How much will new measures cost, and are they cost-beneficial? To do such studies, criminologists develop research questions, select the most appropriate methods, and then assemble and analyze the results carefully.

Every day, photographs show the terrible evidence of a civil war. Atrocities occur daily in the heart of Europe, the former Yugoslavia, where a civil war is raging with a criminal violence most thought had ended in 1945 with the Holocaust. Yet once again an ethnic group, the Muslims living in Bosnia-Herzegovina, is being driven to extinction by "ethnic cleansing" on the part of Serbs and Croats who want to enlarge their territories and have them free of Muslims. Commissions of the U.N. Security Council, of the European Community, of the Red Cross, and of many other organizations have investigated and recorded the facts: there are at least 21,000 murder victims (and over 5000 murderers), there have been tens of thousands of reported rapes, whole towns have been destroyed, and hundreds of thousands of refugees have no future.

For criminologists, this is one of the most vital tasks: the prevention of genocide, of wars of aggression, of crimes against humanity, and of war crimes. The search is on for solutions: for conflict resolution instead of war, and for tolerance instead of atrocities. The blueprints for dealing with **crimes against the peace and security of mankind** have been drawn, yet international power politics continues to get in the way of criminologically sound solutions.

Some other examples demonstrating the scope of criminology are: the end of apartheid in South Africa, the destruction of Pan Am 103 by a terrorist bomb, and the great flood of 1993 in the American Midwest.

In early April 1993, Nelson Mandela, leader of the black majority of South Africa's population, and F. W. de Klerk, the president of South Africa, received the Liberty Medal from President Bill Clinton, in front of Liberty Hall in Philadelphia. Mandela had been imprisoned for 27 years under the apartheid policies of de Klerk's government. Yet in a remarkable change of policy it was de Klerk who ended apartheid—a crime under international law. Mandela and de Klerk now seek to steer the country toward peaceful coexistence of all races. Many South Africans are full of distrust, and extremists on both sides continue a policy of murder and intimidation.

Criminologists are interested in such questions as how criminal laws are created, who has the power to create them, what the purpose of such laws is, how they are enforced, and what role ethnicity plays with respect to crime and the criminal justice system.

In the early months of 1989, investigators from many jurisdictions picked through the debris of a plane crash. But this was no ordinary crash: Pam Am flight 103 was destroyed over Lockerbie, Scotland, on December 21, 1988, by a terrorist bomb. Police investigations extending to 50 countries led to federal indictment of two alleged Lybian terrorists. As yet, despite a judgment by the International Court of Justice against Lybia, and sanctions imposed by the U.N. Security Council, Lybia has refused to extradite the sus-

pects for trial either in the United States or Scotland. A U.S. court has awarded $300 million in damages in favor of the victims' families, to be paid by defunct Pan Am's insurers.

Terrorism poses a particular challenge to criminologists. Who are the terrorists? What prompts them to commit what types of terrorist crimes against whom, and when? What measures can be adopted to prevent terrorism, a crime that can virtually cripple an economy and destroy a government? What international strategies can be adopted to deal with this form of crime?

By virtually any measure the monstrous inundation of the American Midwest, along the routes of the Mississippi and its tributaries, is an unprecedented disaster. More land then ever before (17,000 square miles) is under water, and even before the flood receded, damage was estimated at a staggering $10 billion.

Why is a natural catastrophe of interest to criminologists? Criminologists are very much interested in human behavior under stress, including catastrophic stress. Their studies show that during the "sandbagging" phase of a disaster, there is a great deal of social cohesion. Unfortunately, when the flood waters recede, social cohesion often breaks down, and certain forms of criminality, such as price gouging for necessities like drinking water or kerosene and, under certain conditions, looting, may occur. During the subsequent recovery phase yet another form of criminality happens: vastly inflated or fabricated insurance claims are filed—to the detriment of the real victims of the disaster. Studies done by criminologists form the basis for preventing disaster-related criminality.

Having surveyed the universe of the criminologist's interests, it is now necessary to define criminology, to delineate its place among the sciences, and to describe its major areas of concern: the making of laws, the breaking of laws, and society's reaction to the breaking of laws. We turn first to history.

WHAT IS CRIMINOLOGY?

In the Middle Ages human learning was commonly divided into four areas: law, medicine, theology, and philosophy. Universities typically had four faculties, one for each of these fields. Imagine a young person in the year 1392—a hundred years before Columbus came ashore in America—knocking at the portal of a great university with the request: "I would like to study criminology. Where do I sign up?" A stare of disbelief would have greeted the student, because the word had not yet been coined. Cautiously the student would explain: "Well, I'm interested in what crime is, and how the law deals with criminals." The university official might smile and say: "The right place for you to go is the law faculty. They will teach you everything there is to know about the law."

The student might feel discouraged. "That's a lot more than I want to know about the law. I really don't care about inheritance laws and the law of contracts. I really want to study all about crime and criminality. For example, why are certain actions considered wrong or evil in the first place, and . . ." The official would interrupt: "Then you must go to the faculty of theology. They know all there is to know about good and evil, heaven and hell." The student might persist. "But could they teach me what it is about the human body and mind that could cause some people and not others to commit crime?" "Oh, I see," the official would say; "you really should study medicine." "But, sir, medicine probably is only part of what I need to know, and really only part of medicine seems relevant. I want to know all there is to know about . . ." And then would come the official's last attempt to steer the student in the right direction: "Go and study philosophy. They'll teach you all there is to know!"

For centuries, all the knowledge the universities recognized continued to be taught in these four faculties. It was not until the eighteenth and nineteenth centuries that the natural and social sciences became full-fledged disciplines. In fact, the science of criminology has been known as such for only a little more than a century.

In 1885 the Italian law professor Raffaele Garofalo coined the term "criminology" (in Italian, *criminologia*).[1] The French anthropologist Paul Topinard used it for the first time in French (*criminologie*) in 1887.[2] "Criminology" aptly described and encompassed the scientific concern with the phenomenon of crime. The term immediately gained acceptance all over the world, and criminology became a subject taught at universities. Unlike their predecessors in 1392—or even in 1892—today's entering students will find that teaching and learning are distributed among 20 or 30 disciplines and departments. And criminology or criminal justice is likely to be one of them.

Criminology is a science, an empirical science. More particularly, it is one of the social, or behavioral, sciences. It has been defined in various ways by its scholars. The definition provided in 1934 by Edwin H. Sutherland, one of the founding scholars of American criminology, is widely accepted:

> **Criminology** is the body of knowledge regarding crime as a social phenomenon. It includes within its scope the process of making laws, of breaking laws, and of reacting toward the breaking of laws. . . . The objective of criminology is the development of a body of general and verified principles and of other types of knowledge regarding this process of law, crime, and treatment or prevention.[3]

This definition suggests that the field of criminology is narrowly focused on crime yet broad in scope. By stating as the objective of criminology the "development of a body of general and verified principles," Sutherland mandates that criminologists, like all other scientists, collect information for study and analysis in accordance with the research methods of modern science. As we shall see in Chapter 3, the first persons who conducted serious investigations into criminal behavior, in the eighteenth century, were not engaged in empirical research, although they based their conclusions on factual information. It was only in the nineteenth century that criminologists systematically gathered facts about crime and criminals and then evaluated their data in a scientific manner.

Among the first researchers to analyze empirical data (facts, statistics, and other observable information) in a search for the causes of crime was Cesare Lombroso (1835–1909) of Italy (see Chapter 3). His biologically oriented theories influenced American criminology at the turn of the twentieth century. At that time the causes of crime were thought to rest within the individual: criminal behavior was attributed to feeblemind-

Crime-resistant housing design. This new low-income housing in East New York, Brooklyn, incorporates features that help promote resident security and prevent crime, such as good lighting, good visibility, and controlled access.

edness and "moral insanity." From then on, psychologists and psychiatrists played an important role in the study of crime and criminals.

By the 1920s other scholars saw the great influx of immigrants, with their alien ways of behaving, as the cause of crime. The search then moved to cultural and social interpretations. Crime was explained not only in terms of the offender but also in terms of social, political, and economic problems.

In increasing numbers, sociologists, political scientists, legal scholars, and economists have entered the arena of criminology. Architects too have joined the ranks of criminologists in an effort to design housing units that will be relatively free from crime. Engineers are working to design cars that are virtually theftproof. Pharmacologists play a role in alleviating the problem of drug addiction. Satellites put into space by astrophysicists can help control the drug trade. Specialists in public administration work to improve the functioning of the criminal justice system. Educators have been enlisted to prepare children for a life as free from delinquency as possible.

Economists and social workers are needed to help break the cycle of poverty and crime. Biologists and endocrinologists have expanded our understanding of the relationship between biology and deviant behavior. Clearly, criminology is a discipline composed of the accumulated knowledge of many other disciplines. Criminologists acknowledge their indebtedness to all contributing disciplines, but they consider theirs a separate science.

In explaining what is meant by Sutherland's definition—"making laws," "breaking laws," and "reacting toward the breaking of laws"—we will use a contemporary as well as an historical perspective on these processes, and a global as well as a local focus.

THE MAKING OF LAWS

Until a few years ago, whenever a man entered an elevator anywhere in the United States, he would take his hat off. Just conjure up the picture of an elevator crowded with people, and all the men holding their hats in their hands. Then, at the next floor, another man enters the elevator and does not take his hat off. Stares from all those aboard warn the newcomer that he is in violation of a socially accepted practice, or custom. Embarrassed, he takes his hat off. Today we could not witness such a scene. Most American men do not wear hats any more, and the few who do rarely take them off in elevators.

Customs, social conventions carried on by tradition, are a gentle way of regulating human conduct. Customs—whatever their origin—come and go. Criminologists are interested in the study of customs. They study the emergence of customs, reactions to violations of customs, and success or failure in inducing compliance. They are also interested in what society does when customs no longer regulate conduct perceived as undesirable. New Yorkers' concern over the problem of dog droppings provides an example.

Disciplined city dwellers had always observed the custom of curbing their dogs. Street signs exhorted them to do this. But as more and more dog owners failed to comply, New Yorkers decided that the cleanliness of the sidewalks was an important issue. Laws were enacted making it an offense not to clean up after one's dog. In Beijing, China, and Reykjavik, Iceland, dogs have been banned altogether.

The Concept of Crime

A **crime** is any rational human conduct that violates a criminal law and is subject to punishment. What leads a society to designate some wrongs as crimes and leave other wrongs to be settled in private? For centuries, "natural law" philosophers, believing in the universal rightness and wrongness of certain human behaviors, have held the view that some behaviors are innately criminal and that all societies condemn them equally. Homicide and theft were thought to be among these behaviors.

This notion is no longer supported. Raffaele Garofalo, who gave our discipline its name, defended the concept of "natural crime," by which he meant behavior that offends basic moral sentiments, such as respect for the property of others and revulsion against infliction of suffering. Nevertheless, he admitted that

although we might think such crimes as murder and robbery would be recognized by all existing legal systems, "a slight investigation seems to dispel this idea."[4]

Neither the Roman Law of the Twelve Tables (451–450 B.C.) nor the Babylonian Code of Hammurabi (about 1750 B.C.) lists homicide or ordinary theft among crimes. Nor can we find them among the listings of crimes of other very early legal systems. On the contrary, homicides appear to have been in a category of wrongs that could be righted by compensation or by the surrender of the perpetrator to the injured clan as a substitute worker for the slain victim. Theft was not a problem in societies that had not developed the concept of property, and it was a minor problem in societies that had little property to be concerned about or in which the few items of property in existence—a hammer, an ox, or a hoe—could be easily replaced or exchanged. In such societies, people resolved their problems by private arrangements rather than by resorting to legal systems. Clearly the socioeconomic circumstances of a society determine which behaviors that society considers serious enough to be controlled by law.

The overriding need of every society is to protect its own existence. Let us look at the story of Romulus and his brother Remus, the legendary founders of Rome. Romulus killed his brother after Remus had jumped over the protective city wall Romulus and his workers had just constructed around the town that was to become Rome. Rather than being condemned for killing his brother, Romulus became a revered figure among his people, who named their city after him. Why? Romulus had not killed Remus without just cause. By jumping over a certain part of the city wall, Remus had shown the town's enemies where the wall was most vulnerable to attack. That was treason, the one offense that threatens the existence of a society. It is also the only crime that all societies share.

All the earliest legal systems also recognized some other wrongs as crimes subject to punishment. To discover the types of behavior that societies have outlawed for self-preservation, we have to look at the economic, social, and environmental conditions of specific societies. Among the pre-Columbian Incas of Peru, for example, one of the most serious wrongs was the destruction of a bridge. In a country crisscrossed by ravines and canyons, bridges were the only means of communication. Among North American Plains Indians, theft of a horse or of a blanket was one of the most serious public wrongs. A person without a horse or a blanket was in danger of death. Among the ancient Germanic tribes, theft of a beehive was one of the most serious public wrongs. Beehives provided honey, which was the only source of sugar for food and drink.

To study the emergence of the earliest concepts of crime, which is part of Sutherland's inquiry into the making of laws, criminologists employ the research methods of anthropologists, ethnologists, and historians. Cross-cultural and historical comparison can teach us much about the making of laws in contemporary society.

The Development of Early Legal Systems

When we say that certain acts were considered to be crimes, we may seem to be saying that early societies actually had legal systems. Early societies had no legal systems in the contemporary sense of the term. But they had ways of solving problems of wrongdoing. The information we have is sketchy, for many societies left no written records. Yet we do have some reports about preliterate societies by observers from more sophisticated cultures.

Germanic Criminal Law

In the first century A.D. the Roman writer Tacitus described crime control among the barbarian tribes living in what is now Germany. Their approach was the forerunner of what ultimately became Anglo-Saxon and Anglo-American law. One way of dealing with wrongdoing, Tacitus wrote, was to institute a feud between the clans of the victim and the offender. Other wrongdoing could be settled by compensation. Finally, according to Tacitus:

> It is also possible to make accusations and apply for the infliction of the death penalty before the assembly. The differences of penalties depend on the [nature of the] crime. Traitors and deserters they hang on trees, cowards, war objectors and people

bodily disgraced they drown in mud and swamps, even throwing wattlings on top.[5]

There are also records of a Germanic tribe, the migrant Goths, of the fourth century A.D. When their first native Christian bishop, Ulfilas, attempted to translate the Bible into Gothic, he could find no equivalent for the biblical text "They shall condemn him to death" (Mark 10:33). So he rendered it in Gothic as "They shall declare him to be a wolf." Among the Goths, the most serious punishment for a public wrong was a "wolf declaration." This punishment was tantamount to a sentence of death because the person so sentenced was, like the wolf, banished from the campfire and forced to flee into the forest.

Roman Criminal Law

There are two good reasons for examining early Roman criminal law. Not only are its sources well preserved, but it influenced most of the world's legal systems. By the time Tacitus wrote his report about the primitive Germanic approach to crime and justice, the Roman legal system was highly developed. But it, too, had humble beginnings. The earliest written form of Roman law was the Law of the Twelve Tables (451–450 B.C.). Here are some of its precepts:

> If anyone sings or composes an incantation that can cause dishonor or disgrace to another . . . he shall suffer a capital penalty.

> If anyone has broken another's limb there shall be retaliation in kind unless he compounds for compensation with him.

> If one commits an outrage against another the penalty shall be twenty-five asses.

> If a thief commits a theft by night, if the owner kills the thief, the thief shall be killed lawfully.

> Whoever is convicted of speaking false witness shall be flung from the Tarpeian Rock [on the Capitoline Hill in Rome].[6]

The laws in the Twelve Tables had existed for centuries as unwritten law. To a large extent, however, they were kept secret by the ruling patrician class. The subjugated class, the plebeians, was nevertheless expected to conform to those laws.[7] The plebeians finally demonstrated their objection to this situation by gathering in protest on the holy mountain outside the city

CRIMINOLOGICAL FOCUS
Fairy Tales and Crime

Have you ever wondered about the wolf who accosts Little Red Riding Hood as she makes her way through the forest to her grandmother's house? Later he devours both Grandma and Little Red Riding Hood. Who is that wolf who speaks like a man?

The Wolf-Outlaw

Scholarly research suggests that he is a wolf of the two-legged variety—a convicted criminal banished to the woods. Fairy tales embody ancient folk wisdom and law. Before there were written legal codes, law was transmitted orally from generation to generation. The Red Riding Hood fairy tale reflects a time when the punishment for the most serious crimes was *to be a wolf*. Like the four-legged variety, the offender was banished from human society and condemned to the forest, there to live or die among the four-legged wolves, shunned or hunted like one of them.

The ancient European tribes, ever on the move, could not rely on prisons as punishment for offenders. Outlawry seemed to be the perfect solution, and the wolf provided a model.

Imprisonment as a punishment for crime does not appear in any of the Grimms' fairy tales, another accurate reflection of historical fact: German principalities began to use imprisonment only in the fourteenth century, and the tales collected by the Grimm brothers generally predated that period.

Catalogs of Crime and Punishment

Fairy tales are rich in criminological lore. Every category of crime and the punishments that were in vogue in the early Middle Ages appear in the Grimms' tales. Death by fire was the punishment of choice for witchcraft, as in "Hansel and Gretel," where the witch is incinerated in her own stove. Mur-

derers were drowned, burned, or banished to the forest, and grand larceny was punished by hanging, as in the fairy tale "The Master-Thief" (although the ruler commuted the sentence). Petty larceny was punished corporally, and impersonation and involuntary servitude, as in "Cinderella," were punished by blinding, a penalty German tribes regarded as very severe. Tarring also appeared as a punishment for serious crimes, both in the fairy tales and in law documents from the period.

In the fairy tale "The Twelve Brothers," perverting justice and attempting to cause an innocent person to be executed was punished by being boiled in oil into which vipers were thrown, the most unusual penalty that appears in the Grimms' collection. But it, too, reflects historical fact; a similar punishment is recorded in early Roman law.

Psychological Treatises

These tales can tell us about more than just types of crimes and punishments. The author of a research report entitled "The Criminal Element in German Folk Tales," published in 1910, used a criminological

psychology approach to analyze the Grimms' tales and those collected by others. This report uncovered "every conceivable criminal motivation, from base greed to the grossest form of psychopathology." Perhaps fairy tales would be useful "required reading" for students of criminology.

Source: Gerhard O. W. Mueller, "The Criminological Significance of the Grimms' Fairy Tales," in Fairy Tales and Society: Illusion, Allusion, and Paradigm, ed. Ruth B. Bottigheimer (Philadelphia: University of Pennsylvania Press, 1986), pp. 217–227.

Questions for Discussion

1. What might be the modern equivalent of fairy tales in terms of an unofficial recording of the types of crimes and punishments in use today?
2. The Grimms' fairy tales provide information about European crime and punishment. Is there any similar source of information about early forms of crime and punishment in North America?

walls. Since the plebeians were the artisans and workers, the life of Rome was brought to a standstill. The plebeians demanded a written code of law spelling out their duties, rights, and expectations. The result was the first codification of Roman law. That law was written on twelve wooden tablets, which were prominently displayed in the Forum; hence the name, Law of the Twelve Tables.

In this code there are three groups of wrongs. In the first group are wrongs that were not considered criminal, such as battery (hitting another person). These were civil wrongs, for which the wrongdoer had to compensate the victim. In the second group are wrongs for which the wrongdoer had to pay a fine in the amount of a multiple (double or triple) of the value of the injury inflicted. Only in the third group do we find crimes, offenses against the security of the state or the welfare of the people as a whole. These wrongs could be vindicated only by a purely criminal sanction, such as capital punishment.

This category of wrongs was considered so heinous that the offender could not make amends by any kind of material compensation. The Romans called them sacral crimes, and they included treason, conspiracy, removal of sacred boundary stones, and perjury.[8]

Other Early Legal Systems

Many early cultures had legal codes, among them Babylon, with its Code of Hammurabi (about 1750 B.C.); the Israelites, with the Mosaic Code (1200 B.C.); Greece, with the Draconian Code (seventh century B.C.); India, with the Hindu Code of Manu (fifth century B.C.); and the Islamic societies, with the Koran (seventh century A.D.). When looked at closely, these codes show that the development of criminal laws generally followed the same pattern among all people everywhere. All codes began with the recognition of some acts as wrong. All cultures regarded some law violations as minor and subject to private compensation. And all, according to the earliest records, considered some wrongs to be so serious that material compensation was not considered sufficient as a punishment or effective as a deterrent.

The Code of Hammurabi, king of Babylonia, is the oldest intact legal code to have been discovered. The 8.2-foot diorite monument was found in Iran in 1902 and is now on display in the Louvre in Paris. A replica can be found in the United Nations building in New York City.

The Influence of Early Legal Systems on Contemporary Systems

The Code of Hammurabi had little influence on the later law of the Persians, but some of its principles, such as the government's duty to compensate victims of crime, live on. The Draconian Code of the Greeks had a great influence on later Greek laws, such as those formulated by Solon in 403 B.C. These laws in turn influenced Roman law, most directly the Law of the Twelve Tables. Early Roman laws formed the basis for the highly sophisticated legal system of the Roman Empire. With the collapse of the Roman Empire in the West in A.D. 476, the Roman codes were lost until the twelfth century, when they were rediscovered by accident. Thereafter they had a profound impact on the legal systems that developed all over continental Europe, and on criminal justice within those systems.

From these legal systems the Roman (so-called civil) law system spread over a great part of the world. Today all of continental Europe, all of Latin America, most of the countries of Africa that once were French, Belgian, Spanish, or Portuguese colonies, the countries of Asia that once were Dutch colonies, and Japan, China, and—to some extent South Africa—are the heirs of the Greco-Roman system of law and justice.

Even the Anglo-American system of justice derived some benefit from the Greco-Roman system, though its foundation remains the Germanic (Anglo-Saxon) heritage of law and justice. The Anglo-Saxon (now called Anglo-American or common law) system of law and justice continues to be applied in all English-speaking countries with the exception of Scotland and—to some extent—South Africa.

India's Code of Manu lives on only in history and in some customs. The British imposed Anglo-Saxon law on India, with modifications to meet local conditions. The Koran continues in full force in Iran and Saudi Arabia (where it has been extended by regulatory legislation) and survives in large part in the legal systems of other Islamic countries, including Pakistan (otherwise a common law country), Sudan, several Persian Gulf states, and the countries of Africa north of the Sahara.

In this book we are primarily concerned with crime and justice in the United States, which is a common law nation. Our historical references therefore deal primarily with the common law experience of justice and crime.

The Consensus and Conflict Views of Law and Crime

In the traditional interpretation of the historical development of legal systems, and of criminal justice in particular, lawmaking is a smooth accommodation of interests in a society, whether that society is composed of equals (as in a democracy) or of rulers and ruled (as in absolute monarchies), so as to produce a system of law and enforcement to which everybody basically subscribes. This is the **communal consensus model.** According to this view, certain acts are deemed so threatening to the society's survival that they are designated crimes. If the vast majority of a group shares this view, we can say the group has acted by consensus.

The model assumes that members of society by and large agree on what is right and wrong and that law is the codification of social values, a mechanism of control that settles disputes which arise when some individuals stray too far from what is considered to be acceptable behavior. In the words of the famous French sociologist Émile Durkheim, "We can . . . say that an act is criminal when it offends strong and defined states of the collective conscience."[9] Consensus theorists view society as a stable entity in which laws are created for the general good. Laws function to reconcile and to harmonize most of the interests that most of us accept, with the least amount of sacrifice.

Some criminologists view the making of laws in a society from a different theoretical perspective. In their interpretation, known as the **conflict model,** the criminal law expresses the values of the ruling class in a society, and the criminal justice system is a means of controlling the lower classes. Conflict theorists claim that a struggle for power is a far more basic feature of human existence than is consensus. It is through power struggles that various interest groups manage to control lawmaking and law enforcement. Accordingly, the appropriate object of criminological investigation is not the violation of laws but the conflicts within society.

Traditional historians of crime and criminal justice do not deny that throughout history there have been conflicts that needed resolution. Traditionalists claim that differences have been resolved by consensus, while conflict theorists claim that the dominant group has ended the conflicts by imposing its will. This difference in perspective marks one of the major criminological debates today, as we shall see in Chapter 8. It also permeates criminological discussion of who breaks the criminal laws and why.

THE BREAKING OF LAWS

Sutherland's definition of criminology includes the task of investigating and explaining the process of breaking laws. This may seem simple if viewed from a purely legal perspective. A prosecutor is not interested in the fact that hundreds of people are walking on Main Street. But if one of those hundreds grabs a woman's purse and runs away with it, the prosecutor is interested, provided the police have brought the incident to the prosecutor's attention. What alerts the prosecutor is the fact that a law has been broken, that one of those hundreds of people on Main Street has turned from a law-abiding citizen into a lawbreaker. This event, if detected, sets in motion a legal process which ultimately will determine that someone is indeed a lawbreaker.

Who Commits Crime (Breaks Laws)?

Sutherland, in saying that criminologists have to study the process of lawbreaking, had much more in mind than determining whether or not someone has violated the criminal law. He was referring to the process of breaking laws. That process encompasses a series of events, perhaps starting at birth or even earlier, which result in the commission of crime by some individuals and not by others.

Let us analyze the following rather typical scenario: In the maximum security unit of a midwestern penitentiary is an inmate we will call Jeff. He is one of three robbers who held up a check-cashing establishment. During the rob-

bery, another of the robbers killed the clerk. Jeff has been sentenced to life imprisonment, which in his case means he will have to serve at least another 25 years on a felony murder conviction.

Born in an inner-city ghetto, Jeff was the third child of an unwed mother. He had a succession of temporary "fathers." By age 12 he had run away from home for the first time, only to be brought back to his mother, who really did not care much whether he returned or not. He rarely went to school because, he said, "all the guys were bigger." At age 16, after failing two grades, Jeff dropped out of school completely and simply hung around the streets of his deteriorated, crime-ridden neighborhood. He had no job. He had no reason to go home, since usually no one was there.

One night he was beaten up by members of a local gang. He joined a rival gang for protection and soon began to feel proud of his membership in one of the toughest gangs in the neighborhood. Caught on one occasion tampering with parking meters and on another trying to steal a car radio, he was sentenced to 2 months in a county correctional institution for boys. By the age of 18 he had moved from petty theft to armed robbery.

Many people reading the story of Jeff would conclude that he deserves what is coming to him and that his fate should serve as a warning to others. Other people would say that with his background, Jeff did not have a chance. Some may even consider Jeff a folk hero who managed to survive for a while in a very tough world.

To the criminologist, popular interpretations of Jeff's story do not explain the process of breaking laws in Sutherland's terms. Nor do these interpretations explain why people in general break a certain law. Sutherland demanded scientific rigor in researching and explaining the process of breaking laws. As we will see later in the book (Parts II and III), scientists have thoroughly explored the stories of Jeff and of other lawbreakers. Some have researched the question of why people who are inclined to break laws engage in particular acts at particular times. They have demonstrated that opportunity plays a great role in the decision to commit a crime. Opportunities are suitable targets inadequately protected. In these circumstances, all that is required for a crime to be committed is a person

AT ISSUE
A Portrait of Crime: Television Docu-Drama

The NBC special on the 1993 standoff between federal agents and the Branch Davidians, a religious cult headquartered in Waco, Texas, set a new speed record for turning real-life crime into television drama. As *Newsweek* reported, it was "the first docu-drama about a horrific disaster filmed while the disaster was still unfolding."(1) Federal agents raided the cult's compound on February 28, and the television deal was closed the next day. A replica of the compound was constructed in Oklahoma, and filming began almost immediately. But the dramatization was just one of many such disaster shows in the making that year; the television deal for a docu-drama on the World Trade Center bombing was completed within 10 days of the event, and Hurricane Andrew's devastation was slated to become TV drama 5 days after the storm.

Americans spend nearly half their free time watching television, and—if the networks know their audience—crime is a favorite subject. In 1990 nearly 25 percent of prime-time programming related to crime and law enforcement, up from 4 percent in the 1950s, and *docu-drama*—the dramatization for TV of real-life crime—has become big business. The Amy Fisher story, about a teenage girl who shot her adult lover's wife, was dramatized by all three major networks, and the three movies were watched by 100 million Americans.(2)

Docu-Drama Lessons
What are Americans learning about crime from such shows? According to Ray Surette, a Florida International University professor, the answer is not much—at least, not much that's true. In his book *Media, Crime, and Criminal Justice: Images and Realities,* Surette states:

> The offenses that are most likely to be emphasized on television are those that are least likely to occur in real life, with property crime underrepresented and violent crime overrepresented. Media portraits of crime also greatly overemphasize individual acts of violence . . . . A large difference exists between what viewers are likely to experience in reality and what they are likely to be exposed to in the media.(3)

But surely docu-drama, which is based on real events, should provide a more realistic picture of crime? Not necessarily. Docu-dramas, like most television shows, deal only with "exciting" crimes, so the portrayal of crime in America will still be misleading. Jeff Sagansky, the president of CBS Entertainment, says that whether docu-drama is useful depends on the show:

> True-crime dramas are always going to be done. The question is, are they going to be good? Some of the most riveting dramas of the last five years have come in this form. The question is, do these true-crime stories, beyond the fact that they're recounting the events, contain any sort of insight into either the criminal mind or social issues? Those are the ones that I think really rise above the genre.(4)

The real Amy Fisher faces the media.

Preempting the News
The speed with which the docu-dramas are being produced calls their value into question even more. The NBC production of the Waco disaster was finished before the disaster was over, spawning complaints from critics. "Dramatizing such events before they're fully resolved can be irresponsible," said an ABC senior vice president. "In a way, it almost preempts the news."

Newsweek reporter Harry Waters used the Waco disaster to illustrate some general flaws of docu-drama. "It isn't just their odor of exploitation or their penchant for selling fiction as fact," he commented. "What's less obvious is the genre's habit, exacerbated by haste, of reducing a complex story to the simplest, most viewer-friendly terms."(1)

Sources
1. Harry F. Waters, "Racing the News Crews," *Newsweek,* May 24, 1993, p. 58.
2. Georgina Henry, "The Primest Time for Infotainment," *Guardian,* May 3, 1993, p. 15.
3. Ray Surette, *Media, Crime, and Criminal Justice: Images and Realities* (Pacific Grove, Calif.: Brooks/Cole, 1992), pp. 31–35.
4. Tom Feran, "NBC Winds Up Trio of Tragedies Tonight," *Plain Dealer,* May 26, 1993, p. 6F.

Questions for Discussion
1. Television programming is shaped by the public's desires. What makes crime docu-drama so appealing to Americans?
2. Do you think television networks should do anything to provide a more realistic picture of crime in America? Why or why not?

motivated to offend. These claims are made by criminologists who explain crime in terms of two perspectives, called routine activities and rational choice. In our discussion of the many types of crime (Chapters 10 to 13), we use both a rational-choice and a routine-activities framework.

Criminologists have also researched another fundamental question: Why are some people prone to commit crime and others are not? There is no agreement on the answer, because researchers have approached the question from different perspectives. Some have examined delinquents (juvenile offenders) and criminals from a biological perspective in order to determine whether some human beings are constitutionally more prone to yield to opportunities to commit criminal acts. Are genes to blame? Hormones? Diet? Others have explored the role played by the mind and the emotions. What kind of mental or emotional makeup makes a person prone to commit crime? (Both approaches are discussed in Chapter 4.)

Most contemporary criminologists look to such factors as economic and social conditions, which can produce strain among social groups and lead to lawbreaking (Chapter 5). Others point to subcultures committed to violent or illegal activities (Chapter 6). Yet another argument is that the motivation to commit crime is simply part of human nature. So some criminologists examine the ability of social groups and institutions to make their rules effective (Chapter 7). The findings of other researchers and scholars tend to show that lawbreaking depends less on what the offender does than on what society, including the criminal justice system, does to the offender (Chapter 8). This is the perspective of the labeling, conflict, and radical theorists, who have had great influence on criminological thinking since the 1970s.

Rule Breaking: Deviance

Society also governs itself by sets of norms that are totally unrelated to penal codes. And while some scholars have argued that criminology is concerned only with lawmaking, lawbreaking, and reactions to lawbreaking, as Sutherland's definition seems to imply,[10] the overwhelming majority believe that criminology is concerned with the making and breaking of all norms and with society's reactions to these activities.

Criminological scholars have good reason for taking the latter position. The difference between law and custom is subject to constant change, and it may vary from one state or country to another and from one time to another. What yesterday was only distasteful or morally repugnant may today be illegal. Criminologists are therefore interested in all norms that regulate conduct. Making something that is distasteful into a crime may be counterproductive and detrimental to the social order. If everything *deviant* (inconsistent with the majority's norms) were to be made criminal, society would become very rigid. The more rigid a society, the more deviance, or behavior defined as violating social norms, is prohibited by law.

Jack D. Douglas and Frances C. Waksler have presented the continuum of deviance as a funnel (Figure 1.1). This funnel consists of definitions ranging from the broadest (a feeling that something is vaguely wrong, strange, peculiar) to the narrowest (a judgment that something is absolutely evil). Somewhere between these two extremes, deviant behavior becomes criminal behavior. But the criminologist's interest in understanding the process begins at the earliest point—when a behavior is first labeled deviant.[11]

SOCIETY'S REACTION TO THE BREAKING OF LAWS

Criminologists' interest in understanding the process of breaking a law or a social norm is tied to understanding society's reaction to deviance. The study of reactions to lawbreaking demonstrates that society has always tried to control or prevent norm breaking.

In the Middle Ages, the wayfarer entering a city had to pass the gallows, on which the bodies of criminals swung in the wind. Wayfarers had to enter through gates in thick walls, and the drawbridges were lowered only during the daylight hours; at nightfall the gates were closed. In front of the town hall, stocks and pillory warned dishonest vendors and pickpockets. Times have changed, but perhaps less than we think. Today penitentiaries and jails dot the countryside.

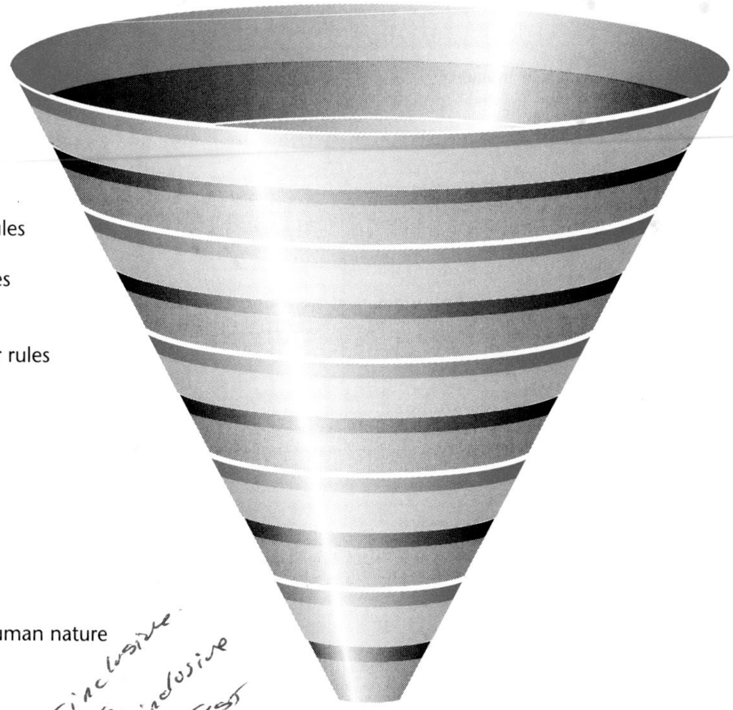

Most inclusive

I. Feeling that something is
   vaguely wrong, strange, peculiar

II. Feelings of dislike, repugnance

III. Feeling that something violates values or rules

IV. Feeling that something violates moral values
    or moral rules

V. Judgment that something violates values or rules

VI. Judgment that something violates moral
    values or moral rules

VII. Judgment that something violates morally
     legitimate misdemeanor laws

VIII. Judgment that something violates morally
      legitimate felony laws

IX. Judgment that something violates moral human nature

X. Judgment that something is absolutely evil

Least inclusive

FIGURE 1.1   The funnel of deviance

Source: Adapted from Jack D. Douglas and Frances C. Waksler, *The Sociology of Deviance* (Boston: Little, Brown, 1982), p. 11.

Teams of work-release convicts work along highways under guard. Signs proclaim "Drug-Free School Zone," and decals on doors announce "Neighborhood Crime Watch." Police patrol cars are as visible as they are audible.

These overt signs of concern about crime provide us with only a surface view of the apparatus society has created to deal with lawbreaking; they tell us little of the research and policy making that have gone into the creation of the apparatus. Criminologists have done much of the research on society's reaction to the breaking of laws, and the results have influenced policy making and legislation aimed at crime control. The research has also revealed that society's reaction to lawbreaking has often been irrational, arbitrary, emotional, politically motivated, and counterproductive.

Research on society's reaction to the breaking of laws is more recent than research on the causes of crime. It is also more controversial. For some criminologists, the function of their research is to

assist government in the prevention or repression of crime. Others insist that such a use of science only supports existing power structures that may be corrupt. The position of most criminologists is somewhere between these extremes. Researchers often discover inhumane and arbitrary practices and provide the data base and the ideas for a humane, effective, and efficient criminal justice system.

Criminal Justice and Criminology

The term "criminal justice system" is relatively new. It became popular only in 1967, with the publication of the report of the President's Commission on Law Enforcement and Administration of Justice, *The Challenge of Crime in a Free Society.* The discovery that various ways of dealing with lawbreaking form a system was itself the result of criminological research. Research into the functioning of the system and its component parts, as well as into the work of functionaries

WINDOW TO THE WORLD
The New Terrorism

For years Americans who feared terrorism just stayed home. The United States had not been a major terrorist target in the past, but terrorist attacks against U.S. citizens and installations had taken place in other countries. The February 1993 bombing of the World Trade Center in New York City, followed by the discovery of a plot to bomb the United Nations headquarters, the Holland and Lincoln tunnels, and the New York offices of the FBI, changed all that. These two events electrified the public and drove home a serious message: the United States is no longer safe from attacks by foreign terrorists.

The New Vulnerability

The extent of the vulnerability was unclear. But the plots served as catalysts to those involved in combating terrorism. A meeting of more than 200 counterterrorism experts and Pentagon officials held in mid-1993 focused on the new threats to public safety. A report on the conference noted:

[The participants] concluded that the proliferation of ethnic and regional conflicts will spawn new radical movements, leading inevitably to new terrorism. "We're going to see a global increase in anarchy," says one Defense Department analyst. Some at the meeting worried about what they term "mass terrorism," like the ethnic cleansing rife in Bosnia. Others were more concerned about what they are calling "single issue" terrorism, attacks by radicals who share no ideology, only the hatred for a particular enemy."(1)

The investigations of the two terrorist conspiracies—both the one that resulted in a bombing and the one that was averted—uncovered a complex web of additional conspiracies involving an Egyptian Islamic fundamentalist group: suspected plots to assassinate Egypt's president, the secretary-general of the

United Nations, and two New York legislators. A simple mix of fertilizer pellets and fuel oil that was to have blown up the targets was found.

On March 4, 1994, one year after the World Trade Center bombing, all four conspirators were found guilty of all charges.

International Cooperation

Richard Ward, the director of the Office of International Criminal Justice, says:

Developing a broader interpretation of terrorist activity might allow economy in resources . . . and greater ability to link the activities of the more traditional terrorist groups with criminal activities of groups with a "profit" motive. . . . Currently, investigative efforts involving broad intelligence and information requirements are frequently split by type of activity: terrorism, drug trafficking, organized crime, street gangs and hostile government spying. The structure does not provide . . . an ability to cross-filter information for timely use.(2)

Ward says that the establishment of terrorist task forces in the United States, with representatives from

Terrorism comes home; the view from ground zero at the World Trade Center, February 1993.

local, state, and federal levels, has been successful and might be a good model for the international cooperation he sees as necessary to combat terrorism. Sam Perry, a specialist in counterterrorism, also calls for a new approach, citing new terrorism problems:

Terrorists are far more mobile than ever. They are taking full advantage of a worldwide breakdown in border security. . . . Despite tough U.S. anti-smuggling programs, sophisticated weaponry is finding its way into some very unfriendly hands. . . . The link-up between well-structured terrorist factions, organized crime and arms merchants is downright scary.(3)

The need for coordinated approaches to counterterrorism all over the world is growing. "Ultimately, the threat of terrorist attacks from a broad range of groups is likely to increase," says Ward. "Government's inability to meet the threat undermines public confidence and creates an environment which strikes at the economic and social fabric of a community."(2)

Sources

1. Douglas Waller, "Counterterrorism: Victim of Success?" *Newsweek,* July 5, 1993, pp. 22–23.
2. Richard Ward, "The Changing Face of Terrorism," *CJ International,* **9** (May–June 1993): 1, 4.
3. Sam Perry, "Terrorism and the Public: Message and Massage," *CJ The Americas,* **6** (June–July 1993): 1, 4.

Questions for Discussion

1. International terrorism is a criminal activity that can involve an almost limitless number of specific crimes, individuals, and countries. How would you devise a strategy to combat it at the national and international levels?
2. How would you go about studying trends in terrorism and its impact on society and the economy?

within the system, has provided many insights over the last few decades.

Scientists who study the criminal justice system are frequently referred to as criminal justice specialists. This terminology suggests a separation between criminology and criminal justice. In fact, the two fields are closely interwoven. Their origins, however, do differ. Criminology has its roots in European scholarship, though it has undergone refinements, largely under the influence of American sociology. Criminal justice is a recent American innovation. Scholars of both disciplines use the same scientific research methods. They have received the same rigorous education, and they pursue the same goals. Both fields rely on the cooperation of many other disciplines, including sociology, psychology, political science, law, economics, management, and education.

The two fields are distinguished by a difference in focus. Criminology generally focuses on scientific studies of crime and criminality, whereas criminal justice focuses on scientific studies of decision-making processes, operations, and such justice-related concerns as the efficiency of police, courts, and corrections systems, the just treatment of offenders, the needs of victims, and the effects of changes in sentencing philosophy.

The United States has well over 50 criminal justice systems—those of the 50 states and of the federal government, the District of Columbia, Puerto Rico, Guam, the U.S. Virgin Islands, American Samoa, the Commonwealth of the Northern Mariana Islands, Palau, the Panama Canal Zone, and the military. They are very similar: all are based on constitutional principles and on the heritage of the common law. All were designed to cope with the problem of crime within their territories, on the assumption that crime is basically a local event calling for local response. Crimes that have an interstate or international aspect are under the jurisdiction of federal authorities, and such offenses are prosecuted under the federal criminal code.

The Global Approach to the Breaking of Laws

Until fairly recently there was rarely any need to cooperate with foreign governments, as crime had few international connections. This situation has changed drastically: crime, like life itself, has become globalized, and responses to lawbreaking have inevitably extended beyond local and national borders. In the first three and a half decades after World War II, from 1945 until the late 1970s, the countries of the world gradually became more interdependent. Commercial relations among countries increased. The jet age brought a huge increase in international travel and transport. Satellite communications facilitated intense and continuous public and private relationships.

Beginning in the 1980s, the internationalization of national economies accelerated sharply, and with the collapse of Marxism in Eastern Europe in the 1990s, a global economy is being created. These developments, which turned the world into what has been called a "global village," have also had considerable negative consequences. As everything else in life became globalized, so did crime. Transnational crimes, those that violate the laws of more than one country, suddenly boomed. Among these are drug trafficking, commercial fraud, environmental offenses, and the smuggling of aliens. Then there are the truly international crimes—those which are proscribed by international law—such as crimes against the peace and security of mankind, genocide, and war crimes. But even many apparently purely local crimes now have international dimensions, whether they be local drug crime or handgun violence. In view of the rapid globalization of crime, we devote an entire chapter (14) to the international dimensions of criminology. In addition, a "Window to the World" box in each chapter explores the international implications of various topics.

■ REVIEW

Very little happens on earth that does not concern criminology. Yet criminology, as a science, is only a century old. Edwin H. Sutherland provided the most widely accepted definition: "the body of knowledge regarding crime as a social phenomenon. It includes within its scope the process of making laws, of breaking laws, and of reacting toward the breaking of laws."

In reviewing the history of some of the earliest criminal laws, it becomes clear that custom often becomes law. In analyzing history, it is necessary to distinguish between two conflicting views of the history of criminal law: the consensus view, which regards lawmaking as the result of communal agreement as to what is to be prohibited, and the conflict view, according to which laws are imposed by those with power on those without power.

The breaking of laws (the subject to which much of this book is devoted) is not merely a formal act that may lead to arrest and prosecution but an intricate process by which some people violate some laws under some circumstances. Many disciplines contribute to understanding the process of breaking laws or other norms, but as yet there is no consensus on why people become criminals. Society has always reacted to lawbreaking, although the scientific study of lawbreaking is of very recent origin. Today criminologists analyze the methods and procedures society uses in reacting to crime; they evaluate the success or failure of such methods; and on the basis of their research, they propose more effective and humane ways of controlling crime.

Most important, criminologists have discovered that the various organizations society has created to deal with lawbreaking constitute a system which, like any other system, can be made more efficient. Research on the system depends on the availability of a variety of data, especially statistics. The gathering and analysis of statistics on crime and criminal justice are among the primary tasks of criminologists. The effectiveness of their work depends on reliable data.

The province of criminology today is the entire world: every aspect of life, including crime, has become increasingly globalized in recent years as a result of rapid advances in technology and of economic integration.

■ NOTES

1. Raffaele Garofalo, *Criminologia* (Naples, 1885), published in English as *Criminology,* trans. Robert W. Millar (Boston: Little, Brown, 1914; rpt., Montclair, N.J.: Patterson Smith, 1968).
2. Paul Topinard, "L'Anthropologie criminelle," *Revue d'anthropologie,* **2** (1887).
3. Edwin H. Sutherland, *Principles of Criminology,* 2d ed. (Philadelphia: Lippincott, 1934), originally published as *Criminology,* 1924.
4. Garofalo, *Criminologia,* p. 5.
5. Tacitus, *Germania* (first century A.D.), as quoted in Gerhard O. W. Mueller, "Tort, Crime and the Primitive," *Journal of Criminal Law, Criminology, and Police Science,* **43** (1955): 303–332, at p. 310.
6. Allan Chester Johnson, Paul Robinson-Norton, and Frank Card Bourne, *Ancient Roman Statutes* (Austin: University of Texas Press, 1961), pp. 9–13.
7. Mueller, "Tort, Crime and the Primitive," p. 311.
8. Ibid., p. 312. In classical Roman law, wrongs which were not subject to compensation but required punishment were covered by *fas* - sacral criminal law. The remainder of wrongs, subject to compensation or even punitive damages (a multiple of the injury caused) were covered by *jus* - secular law.
9. Émile Durkheim, *Rules of Sociological Method,* trans. S. A. Solaway and J. H. Mueller (Glencoe, Ill.: Free Press, 1958), p. 64.
10. Paul W. Tappan, *Crime, Justice and Correction* (New York: McGraw-Hill, 1960). See also Jerome Michael and Mortimer J. Adler, *Crime, Law and Social Science* (New York: Harcourt Brace, 1933).
11. Jack D. Douglas and Frances C. Waksler, *The Sociology of Deviance* (Boston: Little, Brown, 1982).

2

Measuring Crime and Criminal Behavior Patterns

KEY TERMS
aging-out phenomenon
birth cohort
case study
crimes against property
crimes against the person
criminal careers
data
experiment
field experiment
hypothesis
index crimes
longitudinal study
nonparticipant observation
participant observation
population
primary data
random sample
sample
secondary data
self-report surveys
survey
theory
variables
victimization surveys
victimology

In one of many versions of Aesop's fable about the three blind men and the elephant, a circus comes to town, and the residents of a home for the blind are invited to "experience" an elephant. When one blind man is led to the elephant, he touches one of its legs. He feels its size and shape. Another man happens to touch the tail, and still another feels the trunk. Back at their residence they argue about the nature of the beast. Says the first man, "An elephant is obviously like the trunk of a tree." "No," says the second, "it's like a rope." "You're both wrong," says the third. "An elephant is like a big snake." All three are partly right, for each has described the part of the animal he has touched.

Assessment of the nature and extent of crime often suffers from the same shortcomings as the three blind men's assessments of the elephant.

Researcher A may make assessments on the basis of arrest records. Researcher B may rely on conviction rates to describe crime. Researcher C may use the number of convicts serving prison sentences. None of the researchers, however, may be in a position to assess the full nature and extent of crime; each is limited by the kinds of data he or she uses.

Questions about how crime is measured and what those measurements reveal about the nature and extent of crime are among the most important issues in contemporary criminology. Researchers, theorists, and practitioners need information in order to explain and prevent crime and to operate agencies that deal with the crime problem. It is extremely difficult, however, to gather accurate information. Because of these difficulties, it is necessary for students of criminology to understand how data are collected, what they mean, and whether they are useful. After we look at the objectives and methods of collecting information, we will consider the limitations of the three information sources criminologists most frequently use to estimate the nature and extent of crime in the United States. We then explore measurement of the characteristics of crimes, criminals, and victims.

MEASURING CRIME

There are three major reasons for measuring characteristics of crimes, criminals, and victims. First of all, researchers need to collect and analyze information in order to test theories about why people commit crime. One criminologist might record the kinds of offenses committed by people of different ages; another might count the number of crimes committed at different times of the year. But without ordering these observations in some purposeful way, without a **theory,** a systematic set of principles that explain how two or more phenomena are related, scientists would be limited in their ability to make predictions from the data they collect.

The types of data that are collected and the way they are collected are crucial to the research process. Criminologists analyze these data and use their findings to support or refute theories. In Part II we examine several theories (including the

one outlined briefly here) that explain why people commit crime, and we will see how these theories have been tested.

One theory of crime causation, for example, is that high crime rates result from wide disparity between people's goals and the means available to them for reaching those goals. Those who lack legitimate opportunities to achieve their goals try to reach them through criminal means. To test this theory, researchers might begin with the **hypothesis** (a testable proposition that describes how two or more factors are related) that lower-class individuals engage in more serious crimes and do so more frequently than middle-class individuals. (See "Social Class and Crime," later in this chapter.) Next they would collect facts, observations, and other pertinent information—called **data**—on the criminal behavior of both lower-class and middle-class individuals. A finding that lower-class persons commit more crimes would support the theory that people commit crimes because they do not have legitimate means to reach their goals.

The second objective of measurement is to enhance our knowledge of the characteristics of various types of offenses. Why are some more likely to be committed than others? What situational factors, such as time of day or type of place, influence the commission of crime? Experts have argued that this information is needed if we are to prevent crime and develop strategies to control it (Part III deals with this subject).

Measurement has a third major objective: criminal justice agencies depend on certain kinds of information to facilitate daily operations and to anticipate future needs. How many persons flow through county jails? How many will receive prison sentences? Besides the questions that deal with the day-to-day functioning of the system (number of beds, distribution and hiring of personnel), other questions affect legislative and policy decisions. For instance, what effect does a change in law have on the amount of crime committed? Consider legislation on the death penalty. Some people claim that homicides decrease when a death penalty is instituted. Others claim that capital punishment laws make no difference. Does fear of crime go down if we put more police officers in a neighborhood? Does drug smuggling move to another entry point if old access routes are cut off? These and other potential changes need to be evaluated—and evaluations require measurement.

Methods of Collecting Data

Given the importance of data for research, policy making, and the daily operation and planning of the criminal justice system, criminologists have been working to perfect data collection techniques. Through the years these methods have become increasingly more sophisticated.

Depending on what questions they are asking, criminologists can and do collect their data in a variety of ways: through survey research, experiments, observation, and case studies. One of the most widely used methods is survey research, which is a cost-effective method of measuring characteristics of groups. Experimental studies are difficult and costly to conduct and for this reason they are used infrequently. But they have been, and still are, an important means of collecting data on crime. Participant observation involves the direct participation of the researcher in the activities of the people who are the subjects of the research. A variation of this technique is nonparticipant observation, in which the researcher collects data without joining in the activity. Another way to collect information about crime, and especially about criminal careers, is to examine biographical and autobiographical accounts of individual offenders (the case-study method).

Data can be found in a wide variety of sources, but the most frequently used sources are statistics compiled by government agencies and private foundations. Familiarity with the sources of data and the methods used to gather data will help in understanding the studies we discuss throughout this book. The facts and observations researchers gather for the purpose of a particular study are called **primary data.** Those they find in government sources, or data that were previously collected for a different investigation, are called **secondary data.**

Surveys

Most of us are familiar with surveys—in public opinion polls, marketing research, and election-prediction studies. Criminologists use surveys to obtain quantitative data. A **survey** is the systematic collection of respondents' answers to questions asked in questionnaires or interviews; interviews may be conducted face-to-face or by telephone. Generally, surveys are used to gather information about the attitudes, characteristics, or behavior of a large group of persons who are called the **population** of the survey. Surveys conducted by criminologists measure, for example, the amount of crime, attitudes toward police or toward the sentencing of dangerous offenders, assessment of drug abuse, and fear of crime.

Instead of interviewing the total population under study, most researchers interview a representative subset of that population—a **sample.** If a sample is carefully drawn, researchers can generalize the results from the sample to the population. A sample determined by random selection, whereby each person in the population to be studied has an equal chance of being selected, is called a **random sample.**

Surveys are a cost-effective method, but they have limitations. If a study of drug use by high school students was done one time only, the finding of a relationship between drug use and poor grades would not tell us whether drug use caused bad grades, whether students with bad grades turned to drugs, or whether bad grades and drug taking result from some other factor, such as family ties.

Experiments

The **experiment** is a technique used in the physical and biological sciences, and in the social sciences as well. An investigator introduces a change into a process and makes measurements or observations in order to evaluate the effects of the change. Through experimentation, scientists test hypotheses about how two or more **variables** (factors that may change) are related. The basic model for an experiment involves changing one variable, keeping all other factors the same (controlling them, or holding them constant), and observing the effect of that change on another variable. If you change one variable while keeping all other factors constant and then find that another variable changes as well, you may safely assume that the change in the second variable was caused by the change in the first.

Most experiments are done in laboratories, but

WINDOW TO THE WORLD
Measuring World Crime

Crime problems do not stop at national borders. The first effort to measure world crime was based on the idea that effective international cooperation is necessary to solve global crime problems and that such cooperation is impossible without reliable data. In the mid-1970s, United Nations officials prepared questionnaires about the extent of crime, grouping offenses into a few very broad categories, and sent them to the governments of all countries. Three world crime surveys now have been published, with responses increasing with each survey. Ninety-five governments responded to the third survey (1981–1985), and 78 replies, representing half of the world's countries, were analyzable.(1)

Increasing Participation

One researcher has tried to ascertain why some countries do not participate in crime surveys.(2) He discovered that crime statistics are being kept by countries accounting for the greater part of the world's population but that 64 of these countries did not participate in any of the world crime surveys. Since many of the nonparticipating countries, including China, do keep crime statistics, why do they not respond to requests for information?

Some are so small that their administrative staffs may not be able to cope with the requests; others are embroiled in wars, civil strife, and changes in government. They cannot keep track of crime problems. Some countries simply will not participate, perhaps because of the notion that the incidence of crime reflects negatively on their standing as a nation, or because it may affect the tourist trade, or because crime rates contradict a philosophy that crime disappears with the achievement of national goals. Others cannot participate because there are no criminal justice statisticians to count crimes.

Different Cultures, Different Crimes

Researchers also face problems in the interpretation of world crime statistics. Reported crime rates may reflect "real" rates of crime, or they may reflect the efficiency and veracity with which crimes are detected, reported, and recorded in a particular country. But these problems are almost trivial in comparison to the problem of the very real cultural and political differences among countries.

Despite all the caveats, researchers have been able to determine some very general trends in broad categories of crimes—thefts, homicides, assaults, and drug-related crimes, for example. The third U.N. world crime survey, released in 1990, has been used to project a doubling of the overall world crime rate from 1985 to the year 2000 (from 4000 per 100,000 to 8000 per 100,000).(3) Of course, national and international efforts to curb crime may be able to prove that prediction incorrect.

Sources

1. U.N. Committee on Crime Prevention and Control, *The United Nations and Crime Prevention* (New York: United Nations, 1991).
2. G. O. W. Mueller, *World Survey on the Availability of Criminal Justice Statistics* (Newark, N.J.: Rutgers University, 1992).
3. *Third United Nations Survey of Crime Trends, Operations of Criminal Justice Systems and Crime Prevention Strategies* (New York: United Nations, 1990).

Questions for Discussion

1. Give an example (from a newspaper, magazine, or history book) of an act that is seen as a crime in one society and not in another. Is the disparity caused by political or normative differences? Explain.
2. Countries may base their published crime rates on a variety of sources: crimes reported to the police, arrest rates, conviction rates, or imprisonment figures. Which of these data sets is most reliable, and how could countries be persuaded to report on a unified standard?

Replies to Three U.N. Surveys of Crime Trends

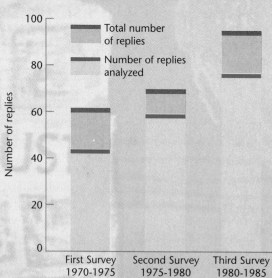

it is possible to do them in real-world, or field, settings (hence the name **field experiment**). A field experiment was done at New Jersey's Rahway State Prison to test the hypothesis that if youngsters were shown the horrors of prison, they would not commit crimes. (The object was to scare young people out of crime; hence the project became known as "Scared Straight!") Several agencies were asked to propose male juveniles for the experiment. All were given a series of tests to determine their attitudes toward crime, punishment, prison, the police, and so forth. Afterward some of the juveniles were randomly assigned to the experimental group, which would actually go to the prison. The rest were assigned to a control group, which would not go.

After the experimental group had participated in the program, both groups were again given the same attitude tests to find out if the prison experience had changed the attitudes of the experimental group. Six months later the juvenile records of the two groups were checked to find out how many of the youths in both groups had committed crimes during the 6-month period. Had fewer of the youngsters who had supposedly been "scared straight" been arrested than those who had not made the prison visit? No, according to James Finckenauer's analysis. In fact, many more of the boys in the experimental group had been arrested than boys in the control group.[1]

Experiments in the real world are costly and difficult to carry out, but they have the advantage of increasing scientists' ability to establish cause and effect.

Participant and Nonparticipant Observation

Researchers who engage in participant and nonparticipant observation have different goals. These methods provide detailed descriptions of life as it actually is lived—in prisons, gangs, and other settings.

Observation is the most direct means of studying behavior. Investigators may play a variety of roles in observing social situations. When they engage in **nonparticipant observation,** they do not join in the activities of the groups they are studying; they simply observe the activities in everyday settings and record what they see. Investigators who engage in **participant observation** take part in many of the group's activities in order to gain acceptance, but they generally make clear the purpose of their participation. Anne Campbell, a criminologist who spent 2 years as a participant observer of the lifestyles of girl gang members, explains:

Possible subjects for observation: The girl gang formally named the "Tiny Diablas of the South Side Grape Street Watts" or (in Spanish) the "Watts Varrio Grapes (WVG)" often shortened to the "Grapes" pose in front of a wall of their graffiti. Their gang color is purple, and their hand signal is similar to a sign language "g".

My efforts to meet female gang members began with an introduction through the New York City Police Department's Gang Crimes Unit. Through one of their plain-clothes gang liaison officers, John Galea, I was introduced first to the male gang members of a number of Brooklyn gangs. On being reassured that I "only" wanted to talk to the female members, the male leaders gave their OK and I made arrangements to meet with the girls' leaders or "godmothers." At first they were guarded in their disclosures to me. They asked a lot about my life, my background and my reasons for wanting to hang out with them. Like most of us, however, they enjoyed talking about themselves and over the period of six months that I spent with each of three female gangs they opened up a good deal—sitting in their kitchens, standing on the stoops in the evenings or socializing at parties with allied gangs.[2]

Observations of groups in their natural setting afford the researcher insights into behavior and attitudes that cannot be obtained through such techniques as surveys and experiments.

✱ Case Studies

A **case study** is an analysis of all pertinent aspects of one unit of study, such as an individual, an institution, a group, or a community. The sources of information are documents like life histories, biographies, diaries, journals, letters, and other records. A classic demonstration of criminologists' use of the case-study method is found in Edwin Sutherland's *The Professional Thief*, which is based on interviews with a professional thief.

Sutherland learned about the relationship between amateur and professional thieves, how thieves communicate, how they determine whether to trust each other, and the process of networking. From discussions with the thief and an analysis of his writings on topics selected by the researcher, Sutherland was able to draw several conclusions that other techniques would not have yielded. For instance, a person is not a "professional thief" unless he is recognized as such by other professional thieves. Training by professional thieves is necessary for the development of the skills, attitudes, and connections required in the "profession."[3] One of the drawbacks of the case-study method is that the information given by the subject may be biased or wrong and by its nature is limited. For these reasons it is difficult

to generalize from one person's story—in this instance, to all professional thieves.

Using Available Data in Research

Besides collecting their own data, researchers often depend on secondary data collected by private and public organizations. The police, the courts, and corrections officials, for example, need to know the number of persons passing through the criminal justice system at various points in order to carry out day-to-day administrative tasks and to plan for the future. It is not always feasible to collect new data for a research project, nor is it necessary to do so when such vast amounts of relevant information are already available.

To study the relationship between crime and such a variable as income or a single-parent family, one might make use of the Uniform Crime Reports (national police statistics, discussed below), together with information found in the reports of the Bureau of the Census. Various other agencies, among them the Federal Bureau of Prisons, the Drug Enforcement Agency, the Treasury Department, and the Labor Department, are also excellent sources of statistics useful to criminologists. At the international level, United Nations world crime surveys contain information on crime, criminals, and criminal justice systems in countries on all continents.

Researchers who use available data can save a great deal of time and expense. However, they have to exercise caution in fitting data not collected for the purpose of a particular study into their research. Many official records are incomplete or have been collected in such a way as to make them inadequate for the research. It is also frequently difficult to gain permission to use agency data that are not available to the public because of a concern about confidentiality.

Ethics and the Researcher

In the course of their research, criminologists encounter many ethical issues. Chief among such issues is confidentiality. Consider the dilemma faced by a group of researchers in the late 1960s. In interviewing a sample of 9954 boys born in 1945, the team collected extensive self-reported criminal histories of offenses the boys had committed before and after they turned 18. Among the findings were 4 unreported homicides and 75 rapes. The researchers were naturally excited about capturing such interesting data: these findings supported the hypothesis of "hidden" delinquency (discussed below). More important, the researchers had feelings of grave concern. How should they handle their findings?

Should the results of these interviews be published?

Could the failure of the research staff to disclose names be considered the crime of "obstructing justice"?

Does an obligation to society as a whole to release the names of the offenders transcend a researcher's obligation to safeguard a subject's confidentiality?

What is the best response to a demand by the police, a district attorney, or a court for the researcher's files containing the subjects' names?

Should criminologists be immune to prosecution for their failure to disclose the names of their subjects?

Is it possible to develop a technique that can ensure against the identification of a subject in a research file?[4]

Such questions have few clear-cut answers. When researchers encounter these problems, however, they can rely on standards for ethical human experimentation. Human-experimentation review committees at most universities and government agencies check all proposals for research projects to ensure the protection of human subjects. In addition, researchers are required to inform their subjects about the nature of the study and to obtain written and informed agreement to participate.

Despite heightened awareness of the ethical issues involved in human experimentation—particularly in correctional institutions, where coercion is difficult to avoid—the field of criminology has not yet adopted a formal code of ethics. Some members of the discipline are arguing in favor of one. Frank Hagan, for example, has suggested that the code include guidelines on honoring commitments made to respondents, avoiding procedures that might harm subjects, exercising

integrity in the performance and reporting of research, and protecting confidentiality.[5] In the end, however, as Seth Bloomberg and Leslie Wilkins have noted, "the responsibility for safeguarding human subjects ultimately rests with the researcher. . . . A code of ethics may provide useful guidelines, but it will not relieve the scientist of moral choice."[6]

THE NATURE AND EXTENT OF CRIME

As we have seen, criminologists gather their information in many ways. The methods they choose depend on the questions they want to answer. To estimate the nature and extent of crime in the United States, they rely primarily on the Uniform Crime Reports, data compiled by the police; on the National Crime Victimization Survey, which measures crime through reports by victims; and on various self-report surveys, which ask individuals about criminal acts they have committed, whether or not these acts have come to the attention of the authorities.

Official statistics gathered from law enforcement agencies provide information available on the crimes actually investigated and reported by these agencies. But not all crimes appear in police statistics. In order for a criminal act to be "known to the police," the act first must be *perceived* by an individual (the car is not in the garage where it was left). It must then be *defined*, or classified, as something that places it within the purview of the criminal justice system (a theft has taken place), and it must be *reported* to the police. Once the police are notified, they classify it and often *redefine* what may have taken place before *recording* the act as a crime known to the police (Figure 2.1). Information about criminal acts may be lost at any point along this processing route, and many crimes are never discovered to begin with.

Police Statistics

In 1924 the director of the Bureau of Investigation, J. Edgar Hoover, initiated a campaign to make the bureau responsible for gathering national statistics. With support from the American Bar Association (ABA) and the International

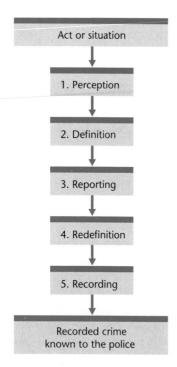

FIGURE 2.1 The process of bringing crime to the attention of police

Source: R. F. Sparks, H. G. Genn, and D. J. Dodd, *Surveying Victims: A Study of the Measurement of Criminal Victimization, Perceptions of Crime, and Attitudes to Criminal Justice* [Chichester, England: Wiley, 1977], p. 6.

Association of Chiefs of Police (IACP), the House of Representatives in 1930 passed a bill authorizing the bureau (later renamed the Federal Bureau of Investigation, or FBI) to collect data on crimes known to the police. These data are compiled into reports called the Uniform Crime Reports (UCR). At present approximately 16,000 city, county, and state law enforcement agencies, which cover 97 percent of the total population, voluntarily contribute information on crimes brought to their attention. If the police verify that a crime has been committed, that crime goes into the report, whether or not an arrest has been made. Each month, reporting agencies send data on offenses in 29 categories.

Part I and Part II Offenses

The UCR divide offenses into two major categories: Part I and Part II. Part I offenses include eight crimes, which are aggregated as **crimes against the person** (criminal homicide, forcible

rape, robbery, and aggravated assault) and **crimes against property** (burglary, larceny-theft, motor vehicle theft, and arson). Collectively, Part I offenses are called **Index crimes.** Because they are serious, these crimes tend to be reported to the police more reliably than others and therefore can be used in combination as an index, or indicator, of changes over time. All other offenses, except traffic violations, are Part II crimes. Its 21 crimes include fraud, embezzlement, weapons offenses, vandalism, and simple assaults.

Crime Rates

To analyze crime data, experts frequently present them as crime rates. Crime rates are computed by the following formula:

$$\text{Crime rate} = \frac{\text{number of reported crimes}}{\text{total population}} \times 100,000$$

Crime rates may be computed for groups of offenses (such as the Index crimes or crimes against the person) or for specific offenses (such as homicide). If we say, for example, that the homicide rate is 10.2, we mean that there were 10.2 homicides for every 100,000 persons in the population under consideration (total U.S. population, say, or all males in the United States). Expressing the amount of crime in terms of rates shows whether an increase or a decrease in crime results from a change in population or a change in the amount of crime committed.

In addition to data on reported crimes, the UCR include the number of offenses "cleared by arrest." Crimes may be cleared in one of two ways: by the arrest, charging, and turning over to the courts of at least one person for prosecution, or by disposition of a case when an arrest is not possible, as when the suspect has died or fled the jurisdiction. Besides reported crimes and crimes cleared by arrest, the reports contain extensive data on characteristics of crimes (such as geographical location, time, and place), characteristics of criminals (such as gender, age, and race), and distribution of law enforcement personnel. We shall look at what these statistics reveal about the characteristics of crime and criminals in more detail later, but first we must recognize their limitations.

AT ISSUE
Stalking: An Unrecorded Crime

Linda has bouncy auburn hair, a petite build, a shy smile, and a handgun in her purse.

She always carries the gun, even though it's illegal, just in case "he" shows up again.

It's been five years since the young, attractive, blond man stopped stalking her. She still flinches whenever she sees a pickup truck in her rearview mirror.

The man's brown truck triggered a recurring nightmare for Linda. He stalked her in it every week, and sometimes daily, for 1½ years. He followed her to work . . . and back home again.

He parked next to her car while she shopped and waited until she came out.

Always, he stared at her with the same impassive, unsmiling look.(1)

The measurement of crime rests on a society's definitions of crime; acts cannot be recorded as crime until they have been defined as crime. In Texas in the mid-1980s, Linda's stalker was breaking no law. But by 1993, 31 states had made stalking a crime. Most of the laws define *stalking* as "willful, malicious and repeated following and harassing of another person, where there is a credible threat of violence against the victim or a member of the victim's family."(2) While stalkers can be strangers, those who work with victims of stalkers say that most stalking cases grow out of "intimate relationships that have soured."(2)

Stalking and Domestic Violence

Indeed, the practice of stalking may have evolved primarily in response to laws against domestic violence, some experts feel. Restraining orders don't provide women with enough protection from abusive boyfriends or husbands, says an attorney for the National Battered Women's Law Project in New York,

and before stalking was recognized as a crime, men could harass women with impunity. But now, at least in much of the United States, such harassment is a crime, yet "many of these guys know what the definition of domestic violence is and officially avoid it," the attorney explains.(3)

Defining stalking as a crime gives police a tool to use to prevent more serious crimes. When no law defines stalking as a crime, the police can do nothing about stalking complaints except ask the stalker to stop. The problem with that, says David Beatty of the National Victim Center, is that stalking often escalates from phone

States with Laws against Stalking

Alabama
California
Colorado
Connecticut
Delaware
Florida
Hawaii
Idaho
Illinois
Iowa
Kansas
Kentucky
Louisiana
Massachusetts
Michigan
Mississippi
Nebraska
New Jersey
New York
North Carolina
Ohio
Oklahoma
Rhode Island
South Carolina
South Dakota
Tennessee
Utah
Virginia
Washington
West Virginia
Wisconsin

Source: "National Conference of State Legislatures," *The New York Times,* Feb. 8., 1993, p. B10.

calls and messages to rape, assault, or homicide. While no one knows how many of the victims had been stalked, 30 percent of the women murdered in 1990 were killed by husbands or boyfriends—the men most likely to be involved in stalking cases. Stalking laws, according to Beatty, are intended to allow the police to intervene before violence occurs.(2)

Stalking and Women's Experience

The definition of stalking as a crime, advocates of women's rights say, is part of the evolution of law to reflect women's problems. "Over the last 25 years . . . we have begun . . . reshaping the law in ways that are more responsive to women's experience, of giving things names, and defining them as part of a cultural pattern," comments Elizabeth Schneider, who teaches at Brooklyn Law School. "That's what happened with sexual harassment, with battering and now with stalking."(2)

Sources

1. Cheryl Laird, "Laws Confront Obsession That Turns Fear into Terror and Brings Nightmares to Life," *Houston Chronicle,* May 17, 1992, p. 1.
2. Tamar Lewin, "New Laws Address Old Problem: The Terror of a Stalker's Threat," *New York Times,* Feb. 8, 1993, p. A1.
3. Elizabeth Ross, "Problem with Men Stalking Women Spurs New Laws," *Christian Science Monitor,* June 11, 1992, p. 6.

Questions for Discussion

1. Some civil rights advocates protest that stalking laws will violate the rights of investigative reporters who have to follow people as a part of their jobs. Do you agree? Explain your position.
2. Just as new crimes may be defined, acts that were once considered to be crimes may become "noncrimes" as society changes. Give an example of something that once was criminal but is no longer considered to be so.

Limitations of the Uniform Crime Reports

Despite the fact that the UCR are among the main sources of crime statistics, their research value has been questioned. The criticisms deal with methodological problems and reporting practices. Some scholars argue, for example, that figures on reported crime are of little use in categories such as larceny, in which a majority of crime is not reported. The statistics present the amount of crime known to law enforcement agencies, but they do not reveal how many crimes have actually been committed. Another serious limitation is the fact that when several crimes are committed in one event, only the most serious offense is included in the UCR; the others go unreported. At the same time, when certain other crimes are committed, each individual act is counted as a separate offense. If a person robs a group of six people, for example, the UCR list one robbery. But if a person assaults six people, the UCR list six assaults. UCR data are further obscured by the fact that they do not differentiate between completed acts and attempted acts.

Police reports to the FBI are voluntary and vary in accuracy. In a study conducted on behalf of the Police Foundation, Lawrence Sherman and Barry Glick found that while the UCR require that arrests be recorded even if a suspect is released without a formal charge, all 196 departments surveyed recorded an arrest only after a formal booking procedure.[7] In addition, police departments may want to improve their image by showing that their crime rate has either declined (meaning the streets are safer) or risen (justifying a crackdown on, say, prostitution).[8] New record-keeping procedures can also create significant changes (the New York robbery rate appeared to increase 400 percent in 1 year).[9] Many fluctuations in crime rates may therefore be attributable to events other than changes in the actual numbers of crimes committed.

Finally, the UCR data suffer from several omissions. Many arsons go unreported because not all fire departments report to the UCR.[10] Federal cases go unlisted. Most white-collar offenses are omitted because they are reported not to the police but to regulatory authorities, such as the Securities and Exchange Commission and the Federal Trade Commission.[11]

To deal with the limitations of the UCR, in 1986 the International Association of Chiefs of Police, the National Sheriffs' Association, and the state-level UCR programs joined forces with the FBI. A new reporting system was developed, called the National Incident-Based Reporting System (NIBRS). Reporting to the NIBRS is voluntary and coexists with the UCR. Each offense is considered an "incident," and information is recorded about the offender, victim, property, and so forth. There are 52 items of information about 22 types of crimes.[12] The implementation of NIBRS depends on the resources and abilities of law enforcement agencies. Thus far 6 states contribute data in the NIBRS format, 15 states are testing the system, and 19 states are in various planning stages.

The NIBRS is a major attempt to improve the collection of crime data. But it deals only with crimes that come to the attention of the police. What about crimes that remain unreported? For what is called the "dark figure of crime," we have to rely on victimization data and self-report studies.

Victimization Surveys

Victimization surveys measure the extent of crime by interviewing individuals about their experiences as victims. The Bureau of the Census, in cooperation with the Bureau of Justice Statistics, collects information annually about persons and households that have been victimized. The report is called the National Crime Victimization Survey (NCVS). Researchers for the NCVS estimate the total number of crimes committed by asking respondents from a national sample of approximately 60,000 households, representing 135,000 persons over the age of 12 (parental permission is needed for those below 14 years old), about their experiences as victims during a specific time period. Interviewers visit (or sometimes telephone) the homes selected for the sample. Each housing unit remains in the sample for 3 years. Every 6 months 10,000 households are rotated out of the sample and replaced by a new group.

The NCVS measures the extent of victimization by rape, robbery, assault, larceny, burglary, and motor vehicle theft. Note that two of the

TABLE 2.1   HOW DO THE UNIFORM CRIME REPORTS AND THE NATIONAL CRIME SURVEY DIFFER?

	Uniform Crime Reports	*National Crime Survey*
Offenses measured:	Homicide Rape Robbery (personal and commercial) Assault (aggravated) Burglary (commercial and household) Larceny (commercial and household) Motor vehicle theft Arson	Rape Robbery (personal) Assault (aggravated and simple) Household burglary Larceny (personal and household) Motor vehicle theft
Scope:	Crimes reported to the police in most jurisdictions; considerable flexibility in developing small-area data	Crimes both reported and not reported to police; all data are for the nation as a whole; some data are available for a few large geographic areas
Collection method:	Police department reports to FBI	Survey interviews; periodically measures the total number of crimes committed by asking a national sample of (originally) 60,000 households representing 135,000 persons over the age of 12 about their experiences as victims of crime during a specified period
Kinds of information:	In addition to offense counts, provides information on crime clearances, persons arrested, persons charged, law enforcement officers killed and assaulted, and characteristics of homicide victims	Provides details about victims (such as age, race, sex, education, income, and whether the victim and offender were related to each other) and about crimes (such as time and place of occurrence, whether or not reported to police, use of weapons, occurrence of injury, and economic consequences)
Sponsor:	Department of Justice Federal Bureau of Investigation	Department of Justice Bureau of Justice Statistics

Source: U.S. Department of Justice, Bureau of Justice Statistics, *Report to the Nation on Crime and Justice*, 2d ed. (Washington, D.C.: U.S. Government Printing Office, 1988). p. 11.

UCR Part I offenses—criminal homicide and arson—are not included (see Table 2.1).[13] Homicide is omitted because the NCVS covers only crimes whose victims can be interviewed. The designers of the survey also decided to omit arson, a relative newcomer to the UCR, because measuring it with some validity by means of a victimization survey was deemed to be too difficult. Part II offenses have been excluded altogether because many of them are considered victimless (prostitution, vagrancy, drug abuse, drunkenness) or because victims are willing participants (gambling, con games) or do not know they have been victimized (forgery, fraud).

The survey covers characteristics of crimes such as time and place of occurrence, number of offenders, use of weapons, economic loss, and time lost from work; characteristics of victims, such as gender, age, race, ethnicity, marital status, household composition, and educational attainment; perceived characteristics of offenders, such as age, gender, and race; circumstances surrounding the offenses and their effects, such as financial loss and injury; and patterns of police reporting, such as rates of reporting and reasons for reporting and for not reporting. Recently questions have been added that encourage interviewees to discuss family violence.

Limitations of Victimization Surveys

While victimization surveys give us information about crimes that are not reported to the police, these data, too, have significant limitations. The NCVS covers crimes in a more limited way than the UCR; the NCVS includes only 6 offenses, whereas there are 8 offenses in Part I of the UCR and an additional 21 in Part II. Although the NCVS is conducted by trained interviewers, some individual variations in interviewing and recording style are inevitable, and as a result the information recorded may vary as well.

Since the NCVS is based on personal reporting, it also suffers from the fact that memories may fade over time, so some facts are forgotten while others are exaggerated. Moreover, some interviewees may try to please the interviewer by fabricating crime incidents.[14] Respondents also have a tendency to telescope events—that is, to move events that took place in an earlier time period into the time period under study. Like the UCR, the NCVS records only the most serious offense committed during an event in which several crimes are perpetrated.

Self-Report Studies

Another way to determine the amount and types of crime actually committed is to ask people to report their own criminal acts in a confidential interview or, more usually, on an anonymous questionnaire. These investigations are called **self-report surveys.**

Findings of Self-Report Studies

Self-reports of delinquent and criminal behavior have produced several important findings since their development in the 1940s. First, they quickly refuted the conventional wisdom that only a small percentage of the general population commits crimes. The use of these measures over the last several decades has demonstrated very high rates of law-violating behavior by seemingly law-abiding people. Almost everyone, at some point in time, has broken a law.

In 1947, James S. Wallerstein and Clement J. Wyle questioned a group of 1698 individuals on whether or not they had committed any of 49 offenses that were serious enough to require a maximum sentence of not less than 1 year. They found that over 80 percent of the men reported committing malicious mischief, disorderly conduct, and larceny. More than 50 percent admitted a history of crimes including reckless driving and driving while intoxicated, indecency, gambling, fraud, and tax evasion. The authors acknowledged the lack of scientific rigor of their study. No attempt was made to ensure a balanced or representative cross section of the individuals surveyed.[15] However, these findings do suggest that the distinction between criminals and non-criminals may be more apparent than real.

Studies conducted since the 1940s have provided a great deal more information. They suggest a wide discrepancy between official and self-report data as regards the age, race, and gender of offenders.[16] Unrecorded offenders commit a wide variety of offenses, rather than specializing in one type of offense.[17] It also appears that only one-quarter of all serious, chronic juvenile offenders are apprehended by the police. Moreover, an estimated 90 percent of all youths commit delinquent or criminal acts, primarily truancy, use of false identification, alcohol abuse, larceny, fighting, and marijuana use.[18]

Limitations of Self-Report Studies

Self-report studies have taught us a great deal about criminality. But they, like the other methods of data collection, have drawbacks. The questionnaires are often limited to petty acts, such as truancy, and therefore do not represent the range of criminal acts that people may commit. Michael

Hindelang, Travis Hirschi, and Joseph Weis argue that researchers who find discrepancies with respect to gender, race, and class between the results produced by official statistics and those collected by self-report methods are in fact measuring different kinds of behavior rather than different amounts of the same behavior. They suggest that if you take into account the fact that persons who are arrested tend to have committed more serious offenses and to have prior records (criteria that affect decisions to arrest), then the two types of statistics are quite comparable.[19]

Another drawback of self-report studies is that most of them are administered to high school or college students, so the information they yield applies only to young people attending school. And who can say that respondents always tell the truth? The information obtained by repeated administration of the same questionnaire to the same individuals might yield different results. Many self-report measures lack validity; the data obtained do not correspond with some other criterion (such as school records) that measures the same behavior. Finally, samples may be biased. People who choose not to participate in the studies may have good reason for not wanting to discuss their criminal activities.

Each of the three commonly used sources of data—police reports, victim surveys, self-report studies—adds a different dimension to our knowledge of crime. All of them are useful in our search for the characteristics of crimes, criminals, and victims.

MEASURING CHARACTERISTICS OF CRIME

Streets in Charlotte, North Carolina, with tranquil names—Peaceful Glen, Soft Wind, Gentle Breeze—have recently become killing lanes.[20] The city that had hoped to displace Atlanta as the "Queen City of the South" had 115 homicides in 1992, more than double the number it had 6 years earlier.[21] More recent figures suggest that the situation continues to grow worse and that the homicide rate is increasing at an even faster rate. Experts tie the mounting murder rate in Char-

lotte to drugs and the growing number of swap shops and flea markets that serve as unregulated outlets for buying guns. Most of the murders have taken place in a 26-square-mile area made up primarily of low-income black families.

These statistics tell us a good deal about the crime problem in Charlotte. They reveal not only a problem of drugs and illegal use of handguns but also the number of homicides that have resulted, the changes in the homicide rate over time, the high-risk areas, and the racial and economic composition of those areas. Criminologists use these kinds of data about crimes in their research. Some investigators, for example, may want to compare drug use to crime in major cities. Others may want to explain a decrease or an increase in the crime rate in a single city (Charlotte), in a single neighborhood (the impoverished inner city), or perhaps in the nation as a whole.

Crime Trends

One of the most important characteristics of any crime is how often it is committed. From such figures we can determine crime trends, the increases and decreases of crime over time. The UCR show that more than 14.4 million Index crimes (excluding arson) were reported to the police in 1992 (Figure 2.2). Of the total number of Index crimes, violent crimes make up a small portion—13 percent—with a murder rate of 9.3 per 100,000. Most Index crimes are property offenses (87 percent), and 63 percent of these property offenses are larcenies.

The 1992 NCVS presents a somewhat different picture (Figure 2.2). Though the data presented in the NCVS and the UCR are not entirely comparable because the categories differ, the number of crimes reported to the police and the number reported in the victimization survey are clearly far apart. According to the NCVS, there were nearly 34 million victimizations. Indeed, the NCVS reports almost as many personal thefts as the total number of UCR Index offenses taken together.

According to UCR data, the crime rate increased slowly between 1930 and 1960. After 1960 it began to rise much more quickly. This

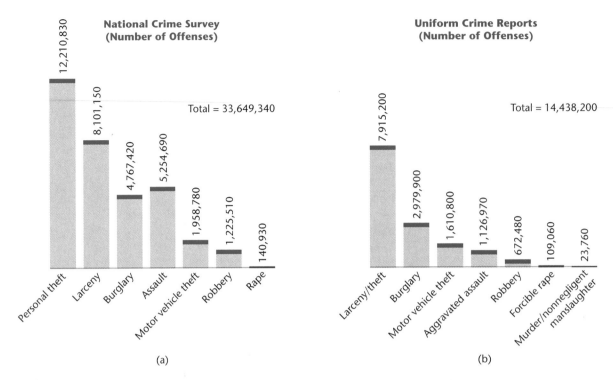

FIGURE 2.2 National Crime Survey and Uniform Crime Reports: A comparison of number of crimes reported [a] National Crime Victimization Survey: Total number of victimizations, 1992 [b] Uniform Crime Reports: Total number of index offenses, 1991

Source: [a] Adapted from U.S. Department of Justice, Bureau of Justice Statistics, *Highlights from 20 Years of Surveying Crime Victims,* Washington D.C.: U.S. Government Printing Office, 1993, p. 6. [b] Adapted from U.S. Department of Justice, Federal Bureau of Investigation, *Crime in the United States, 1992* [Washington D.C.: U.S. Government Printing Office, 1993], p. 58.

trend continued until 1980 (Figure 2.3), when the crime rate rose to 5950 per 100,000. From that peak the rate steadily dropped until 1984, when there were 5031.3 crimes per 100,000. After that year the rate rose again until 1990. Then it decreased to 5660.2.[22] The NCVS also shows that the victimization rate peaked from 1979 to 1981. These data, however, show a consistent decline since the early 1980s.[23]

The gradual decline in the crime rate after 1980 is an important phenomenon that requires a bit more analysis. One important factor is the age distribution of the population. Given the fact that young people tend to have the highest crime rate, the age distribution of the population has a major effect on crime trends. After World War II, the birthrate increased sharply in what is known as

the baby boom. The baby-boom generation reached its crime-prone years in the 1960s, and the crime rate duly rose. As the generation grew older, the crime rate became more stable and in the 1980s began to decline. Some researchers claim that the children of the baby boomers may very well once again expand the ranks of the crime-prone ages and that crime will once again increase.

During the period when the baby-boom generation outgrew criminal behavior, U.S. society was undergoing other changes. We adopted a get-tough crime-control policy, which may have deterred some people from committing crimes. Mandatory prison terms permitted judges less discretion in sentencing, and fewer convicted felons were paroled. In addition, crime-preven-

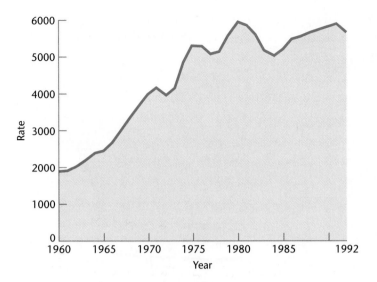

FIGURE 2.3 Uniform Crime Reports: Rate of all index crimes per 100,000 population, 1960–1992

Source: U.S. Department of Justice, Federal Bureau of Investigation, *Crime in the United States, 1975; 1980; 1992* (Washington D.C.: U.S. Government Printing Office, 1976, 1981, 1993), pp. 41, 49, 58.

tion programs, such as Neighborhood Watch groups, became popular. These and other factors have been suggested to explain why the crime rate dropped, but we have no definitive answers.

Locations and Times of Criminal Acts

Statistics on the characteristics of crimes are important not only to criminologists who seek to know why crime occurs but also to those who want to know how to prevent it. Two statistics of use in prevention efforts are those on where crimes are committed and when.

Most crimes are committed in large urban areas rather than in small cities, suburbs, or rural areas (Figure 2.4). This pattern can be attributed to a variety of factors—population density, age distribution of residents, stability of the population, economic conditions, and the quality of law enforcement, to name but a few. The statistics for Charlotte, North Carolina, for example, show that most arrests took place in the poverty-ridden ghetto areas. The fact that the majority of those arrests were made in neighborhoods where drug dealers were visibly present on the streets fits the

national picture, for almost half of all crimes occur outdoors. NCVS data tell us that the safest place to be is inside one's home; according to victims' reports, 8 percent of robberies and 11 percent of assaults were committed in their homes. The only crime that shows a significantly different pattern is rape: 27 percent of such attacks occurred in the victim's home or lodging.[24]

As for the times when crimes are committed, NCVS data reveal that over 58 percent of all violent crimes involving strangers are committed at night, between 6 P.M. and 6 A.M. Household crimes follow the same pattern: of crimes committed within a known period, 70 percent of household larcenies and 75 percent of motor vehicle thefts are committed at night. Most personal thefts, however, are committed during the day.[25]

Nationwide crime rates also vary by season. Personal and household crimes are more likely to be committed during the warmer months of the years, perhaps because in summer people spend more time outdoors, where they are more vulnerable to crime.[26] People often leave doors and windows open when they go out in warm weather.

In what counties is crime most likely to occur?

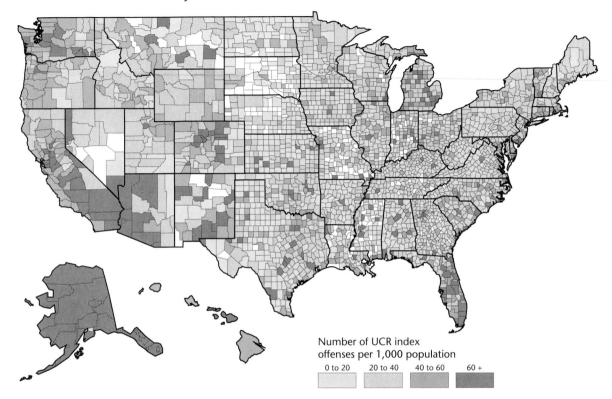

Number of UCR index
offenses per 1,000 population

| 0 to 20 | 20 to 40 | 40 to 60 | 60 + |

FIGURE 2.4   Number of UCR index offenses per 1,000 population, by county

Source: U.S. Department of Justice, Bureau of Justice Statistics, *Report to the Nation on Crime and Justice,*
2d ed. (Washington, D.C.: U.S. Government Printing Office, 1988), p. 18.

Severity of Crime

We have seen that crime rates vary by time and place. They also vary in people's perception of their severity. To some extent legislation sets a standard of severity by the punishments it attaches to various crimes. But let us take a critical look at such judgments.

Do you believe that skyjacking an airplane is a more serious offense than smuggling heroin? Is forcible rape more serious than kidnapping? Is breaking into a home and stealing $1000 more serious than using force to rob a person of $10? A yes answer to all three questions conforms with the findings of the National Survey of Crime Severity, which in 1977 measured public percep-

tions of the seriousness of 204 events, from planting a bomb that killed 20 people to playing hooky from school.[27]

The survey, conducted by Marvin E. Wolfgang and his colleagues, found that individuals generally agree about the relative seriousness of specific crimes (Table 2.2). In ranking severity, people seem to base their decisions on such factors as the ability of victims to protect themselves, the amount of injury and loss suffered, the type of business or organization from which property is stolen, the relationship between offender and victim, and (for drug offenses) the types of drugs involved. Respondents generally agreed that violent crime is more serious than property crime. They also considered white-collar crimes, such as

TABLE 2.2   HOW DO PEOPLE RANK THE SEVERITY OF CRIME?

Severity Score	Ten Most Serious Offenses	Severity Score	Ten Least Serious Offenses
72.1	Planting a bomb in a public building. The bomb explodes and 20 people are killed.	1.3	Two persons willingly engage in a homosexual act.
52.8	A man forcibly rapes a woman. As a result of physical injuries, she dies.	1.1	Disturbing the neighborhood with loud, noisy behavior.
43.2	Robbing a victim at gunpoint. The victim struggles and is shot to death.	1.1	Taking bets on the numbers.
39.2	A man stabs his wife. As a result, she dies.	1.1	A group continues to hang around a corner after being told to break up by a police officer.
35.7	Stabbing a victim to death.	0.9	A youngster under 16 years old runs away from home.
35.6	Intentionally injuring a victim. As a result, the victim dies.	0.8	Being drunk in public.
33.8	Running a narcotics ring.	0.7	A youngster under 16 years old breaks a curfew law by being out on the street after the hour permitted by law.
27.9	A woman stabs her husband. As a result, he dies.	0.6	Trespassing in the backyard of a private home.
26.3	An armed person skyjacks an airplane and demands to be flown to another country.	0.3	A person is a vagrant. That is, he has no home and no visible means of support.
25.8	A man forcibly rapes a woman. No other physical injury occurs.	0.2	A youngster under 16 years old plays hooky from school.

Source: Adapted from Marvin E. Wolfgang, Robert Figlio, Paul E. Tracey, and Simon I. Singer, National Survey of Crime Severity (Washington, D.C.: U.S. Government Printing Office, 1985).

engaging in consumer fraud, cheating on income taxes, polluting, and accepting bribes, to be as serious as many violent and property crimes.

MEASURING CHARACTERISTICS OF CRIMINALS

Information on the characteristics of crimes is not the only sort of data analyzed by criminologists. They also want to know the characteristics of the people who commit those crimes.

Behind each crime is a criminal or several criminals. Criminals can be differentiated by age, ethnicity, gender, socioeconomic level, and other criteria. These characteristics enable us to group criminals into categories, and it is these cate-

gories that researchers find useful. They study the various offender groups to determine why some people are more likely than others to commit crimes or particular types of crimes. It has been estimated that 14 million arrests were made in 1992 for all criminal offenses except traffic violations. Figure 2.5 shows how these arrests were distributed among the offenses. During the 10 years between 1983 and 1992, the number of arrests rose 16.9 percent. Let us take a close look at the characteristics of the persons arrested.

Age and Crime

Six armed men who have been called the "over-the-hill gang" were arrested trying to rob an elegant bridge and backgammon club in midtown

PART I OFFENSES

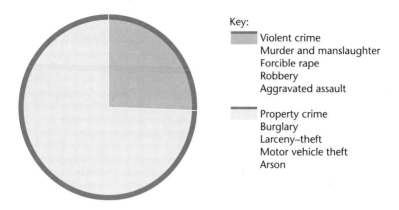

Key:

▮ Violent crime
    Murder and manslaughter
    Forcible rape
    Robbery
    Aggravated assault

▬ Property crime
    Burglary
    Larceny–theft
    Motor vehicle theft
    Arson

PART II OFFENSES

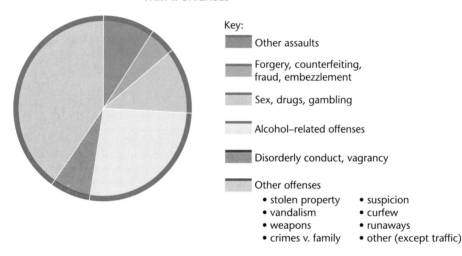

Key:

▮ Other assaults

▬ Forgery, counterfeiting,
    fraud, embezzlement

▬ Sex, drugs, gambling

▬ Alcohol–related offenses

▮ Disorderly conduct, vagrancy

▬ Other offenses
    • stolen property   • suspicion
    • vandalism   • curfew
    • weapons   • runaways
    • crimes v. family   • other (except traffic)

FIGURE 2.5   Distribution of total number of arrests, 1992 (estimated)

Source: U.S. Department of Justice, Federal Bureau of Investigation, *Crime in the United States, 1992*
[Washington D.C.: U.S. Government Printing Office, 1993], p. 217.

New York City. The robbery began at 10:25 P.M. when the men, wearing rubber gloves and ski masks and armed with two revolvers, a shotgun, and a rifle, forced the customers and employees to lie down in a back room while they loaded a nylon bag with wallets, players' money, and the club's cash box. A club worker slipped out a side door to alert police, who arrived within minutes. They surprised and disarmed one member of the gang, a 48-year-old, whom they found clutching a .22-caliber revolver. They took a .38-caliber revolver from another gang member, 41 years old.

During the scuffle with the officers, one suspect tried to escape, fell, and broke his nose. The officers then found and arrested a 40-year-old man standing in the hallway with a 12-gauge Winchester shotgun. Meanwhile, the other gang members abandoned their gloves and masks and lay down among the people they had robbed. One of the suspects, aged 72, who wore a back brace, complained of chest and back pain as police locked handcuffs on him. He was immediately hospitalized.[28]

This gang is extraordinary for at least two reasons. First, in any given year approximately half of all arrests are of individuals under the age of 25; and second, gang membership is ordinarily confined to the young. Though juveniles (young people under 18) constitute about 8 percent of the population, they account for almost one-third of the arrests for Index crimes. Arrest rates begin to decline after age 30 and taper off to about 2 percent or less from age 50 on.[29] This decline in criminal activities with age is known as the **aging-out phenomenon.** The reasons for it have sparked a lively scientific debate. Michael Gottfredson and Travis Hirschi contend there is a certain inclination to commit crimes which peaks in the middle or late teens and then declines throughout life. This relationship between crime and age does not change, "regardless of sex, race, country, time, or offense."[30]

Crime decreases with age, the researchers add, even among people who commit frequent offenses. Thus differences in crime rates found among young people of various groups, such as men and women or lower class and middle class, will be maintained throughout the life cycle. If lower-class youths are three times more likely to commit crimes than middle-class youths, for instance, then 60-year-old lower-class persons will be three times more likely to commit crimes than 60-year-old middle-class persons, though crimes committed by both lower-class and middle-class groups will constantly decline.[31] According to this argument, all offenders commit fewer crimes as they grow older because they have less strength, less mobility, and so on.

James Q. Wilson and Richard Herrnstein support the view that the aging-out phenomenon is a natural part of the life cycle.[32] Teenagers may become increasingly independent of their parents yet lack the resources to support themselves; they band together with other young people who are equally frustrated in their search for legitimate ways to get money, sex, alcohol, and status. Together they find illegitimate sources. With adulthood, the small gains from criminal behavior no longer seem so attractive. Legitimate means open up. They marry. Their peers no longer endorse lawbreaking. They learn to delay gratification. Petty crime is no longer adventurous.[33] It is at this time that the aging-out process begins for most individuals. Even the ones who

continue to commit offenses will eventually slow down with increasing age.[34]

The opposing side in this debate argues that the decrease in crime rates after adolescence does not imply that the number of crimes committed by all individual offenders declines. In other words, the frequency of offending may go down for most offenders, but some chronic active offenders may continue to commit the same amount of crime over time. Why might this be so? Because the factors that influence any individual's entrance into criminal activity vary, the number and types of offenses committed vary, and the factors that eventually induce the individual to give up criminal activity vary.[35]

According to this argument, the frequency of criminal involvement, then, depends on such social factors as economic situation, peer pressure, and lifestyle; and it is these social factors that explain the aging-out phenomenon. A teenager's unemployment, for example, may have very little to do with the onset of criminal activity because the youngster is not yet in the labor force and still lives at home. Unemployment may increase an adult's rate of offending, however, because an adult requires income to support various responsibilities. Thus the relationship between age and crime is not the same for all offenders. Various conditions during the life cycle affect individuals' behavior in different ways.

To learn how the causes of crime vary at different ages, Alfred Blumstein and his colleagues suggest that we study **criminal careers,** a concept that describes the onset of criminal activity, the types and amount of crime committed, and the termination of such activity.[36] **Longitudinal studies** of a particular group of people over time should enable researchers to uncover the factors that distinguish criminals from noncriminals and those that differentiate among criminals in regard to the number and kinds of offenses they commit.

Those who are involved in research on criminal careers assume that offenders who commit 10 crimes may differ from those who commit 1 or 15. They ask: Are the factors that cause the second offense the same ones that cause the fourth or the fifth? Do different factors move one offender from theft to rape or from assault to shoplifting? How many persons in a **birth cohort** (a group of people born in the same year) will become criminals? Of those, how many will become career criminals (chronic offenders)?

Starting in the 1960s, researchers at the Sellin Center of the University of Pennsylvania began a search for answers. Their earliest publication, in 1972, detailed the criminal careers of 9945 boys (a cohort) born in Philadelphia in 1945. Marvin Wolfgang, Robert Figlio, and Thorsten Sellin obtained their data from school records and official police reports. Their major findings were that 35 percent of the boys had had contact with the police before reaching their eighteenth birthday; of those boys, 46 percent were one-time offenders and 54 percent were repeat offenders. Eighteen percent of those with police contact had committed five or more offenses; they represented 6 percent of the total. The "chronic 6 percent," as they are now called, were responsible for more than half of all the offenses committed, including 71 percent of the homicides, 73 percent of the rapes, 82 percent of the robberies, and 69 percent of the assaults.[37]

Research continued on 10 percent of the boys in the original cohort until they reached the age of 30. This sample was divided into three groups: those who had records of offenses only as juveniles, those who had records only as adults, and those who were persistent offenders with both juvenile and adult records. Though they made up only 15 percent of the follow-up group, those who had been chronic juvenile offenders made up 74 percent of all the arrests. Thus chronic juvenile offenders do indeed continue to break laws as adults.[38]

The boys in the original cohort were born in 1945. Researchers questioned whether the same behavior patterns would continue over the years. Criminologist Paul Tracy and his associates found the answer in a second study, which examined a cohort of 13,160 males born in 1958. The two studies show similar results. In the second cohort, 33 percent had had contact with the police before reaching their eighteenth birthday, 42 percent were one-time offenders, and 58 percent were repeat offenders. Chronic delinquents were found in both cohorts. The chronic delin-

quents in the second cohort, however, accounted for a greater percentage of the cohort—7.5 percent. They also were involved in more serious and injurious acts than the previous group.

The 1945 cohort study did not contain females, so no overall comparisons can be made over time. But comparing women to men in the 1958 cohort, we see significant gender differences. Of the 14,000 females in the cohort, 14 percent had had contact with the police before age 18. Sixty percent of the female delinquents were one-time offenders, 33 percent were repeat offenders, and 7 percent were chronic offenders. Overall, female delinquency was less frequent and less likely to involve serious charges.[39]

In another longitudinal study, researchers followed about 4000 youngsters in Denver, Pittsburgh, and Rochester, New York, for 5 years, 1988 through 1992. By the age of 16, over half the youngsters admitted to committing violent criminal acts. According to Terence P. Thornberry, the principal investigator in Rochester, chronic offenders also accounted for a high percentage of all violent offenses: 15 percent of the youths in the sample were responsible for 75 percent of the acts.[40]

The policy implications of such findings are clear. If a very small group of offenders is committing a large percentage of all crime, the crime rate should go down if we incarcerate those offenders for long periods of time. Many jurisdictions around the country are developing sentencing policies to do just that, but such policies are quite controversial.

Gender and Crime

Except for such crimes as prostitution, shoplifting, and welfare fraud, males traditionally commit more crimes than females at all ages. According to the UCR for 1992, the arrest ratio is typically about 5 male offenders to 1 female offender.[41] The NCVS of 1992 reports a wider gap: for personal crimes of violence involving a single offender, 85 percent of victims perceived the gender of the offender as male.[42]

Since the 1960s, however, there have been some interesting developments in regard to gender and crime data. In 1960 females accounted for

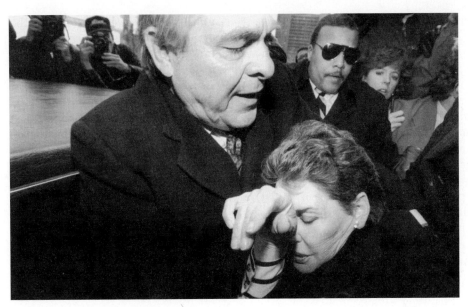

Hotel queen Leona Helmsley collapses after being resentenced to four years in a federal prison for tax evasion.

11 percent of the total number of arrests across the country. They now account for 19 percent. And while the female arrest rate is still much lower than that of males, the rate of increase for women has risen faster than the rate for men.[43]

Self-report studies, which show more similarities in male and female criminal activity than official reports do, find that males commit more offenses than females. However, several of these studies suggest that gender differences in crime may be narrowing. They demonstrate that the patterns and causes of male and female delinquent activity are becoming more alike.[44] John Hagan and his associates agree, but only with respect to girls raised in middle-class egalitarian families in which husband and wife share similar positions of power at home and in the workplace. They argue that girls raised in lower-class, father-dominated households grow up in a "cult of domesticity" that reduces their freedom and thus the likelihood of their delinquency.[45] Researchers Merry Morash and Meda Chesney-Lind disagree. In a study of 1427 adolescents and their caretakers, they found gender differences in delinquency between girls and boys regardless of the type of family in which the youngsters were raised.[46]

Because traditionally women have had such low crime rates, the scientific community and the mass media have generally ignored the subject of female criminality. Both have tended to view female offenders as misguided children who are an embarrassment rather than a threat to society. Only a handful of the world's criminologists have deemed the subject worthy of independent study. Foremost among them was Cesare Lombroso (whom we shall meet again in Chapter 3). His book *The Female Offender*, which appeared in 1895, detailed the physical abnormalities that would predestine some girls to be criminal from birth.[47] Lombroso's findings on male criminals, however, have not stood the test of later scientific research, and his portrayal of the female criminal has been found to be similarly inaccurate.

A little over a generation later, in the 1930s, Sheldon and Eleanor Glueck launched a massive research project on the biological and environmental causes of crime, with a separate inquiry into female offenders. Their conclusions were decidedly sociological. They said, in essence, that in order to change the incidence of female criminality, there would have to be a change in the social circumstances in which females grow up.[48]

Otto Pollack shared the Gluecks' views on sociological determinants. In 1952 he proposed that female crime has a "masked character" that keeps it from being properly recorded or otherwise noted in statistical reports. Protective attitudes toward women make police officers less willing to arrest them, make victims less eager to report their offenses, make district attorneys less enthusiastic about prosecuting them, and make juries less likely to find them guilty. Moreover, Pollack noted that women's social roles as homemakers, child rearers, and shoppers furnish them with opportunities for concealed criminal activity and with victims who are the least likely to complain and/or cooperate with the police. He also argued that female crime was limited by the various psychological and physiological characteristics inherent in the female anatomy.[49]

A quarter of a century after Pollack's work, two researchers, working independently, took a fresh look at female crime in light of women's new roles in society. In 1975 Freda Adler posited that as social and economic roles of women changed in the legitimate world, their participation in crime would also change. According to this argument, the temptations, challenges, stresses, and strains to which women have been increasingly subjected in recent years cause them to act or react in the same manner in which men have consistently reacted to the same stimuli. In other words, equalization of social and economic roles leads to similar behavior patterns, both legal and illegal, on the part of both men and women. To steal a car, for example, one needs to know how to drive. To embezzle, one needs to be in a position of trust and in control of funds. To get into a bar fight, one needs to go to a bar. To be an inside trader on Wall Street, one needs to be on the inside.[50]

Rita Simon has taken a similar position. She, too, has argued that female criminality has undergone changes. But these changes, according to Simon, have occurred only in regard to certain property crimes, such as larceny/theft and fraud/embezzlement. Women are becoming more involved in these crimes because they have more opportunities to commit them. Simon hypothesizes that since the propensity of men and women to commit crime is not basically different, as more women enter the labor force and work in a much broader range of jobs, their property crime rate will continue to go up.[51]

Some criminologists have challenged the views of Adler and Simon. Many questions have been asked about the so-called new female criminal. Does she exist? If so, does she commit more crimes than the old female criminal did? What types of crimes? Is she still involved primarily in offenses against property, or has she turned to more violent offenses? Researchers differ on the answers. Some contend that the extent of female criminality has not changed through the years but that crimes committed by women are more often making their way into official statistics simply because they are more often reported and prosecuted. In other words, the days of chivalry in the criminal justice system are over.[52]

Others argue that female crime has indeed increased, but they attribute the increase to nonviolent, petty property offenses that continue to reflect traditional female sex roles.[53] Moreover, some investigators claim, the increased involvement in these petty property offenses suggests that women are still economically disadvantaged, still suffering sexism in the legitimate marketplace.[54] Other researchers support the contention of Adler and Simon that female roles have changed and that these changes have indeed led women to commit the same kinds of crimes as men, violent as well as property offenses.[55]

Though scholars disagree on the form and extent of female crime, they do seem to agree that the crimes women commit are closely associated with their socioeconomic position in society. The controversy has to do with whether or not that position has changed. In any case, the association between gender and crime has become a recognized area of concern in the growing body of research dealing with contemporary criminological issues.[56]

Social Class and Crime

Researchers agree on the importance of age and gender as factors related to crime, but they disagree strongly as to whether social class is related to crime. First of all, the term "class" can have many meanings. If "lower class" is defined by income, then the category might include graduate students, unemployed stockbrokers, pensioners, welfare mothers, prison inmates, and many others who have little in common except low income. Furthermore, "lower class" is often defined by the low prestige associated with blue-collar occupations. Some delinquency studies determine the class of young people by the class of their fathers, even though the young people may have jobs quite different from those of their fathers.

Another dispute focuses on the source of statistics used by investigators. Many researchers attribute the relatively strong association between class and crime found in arrest statistics to class bias on the part of the police. If the police are more likely to arrest a lower-class suspect than a middle-class suspect, they say, arrest data will show more involvement of lower-class people in criminality whether or not they are actually committing more crimes. When Charles Tittle, Wayne Villemez, and Douglas Smith analyzed 35 studies of the relationship between social class and crime rates in 1978, they found little support for the claim that crime is primarily a lower-class phenomenon. In an update of that work, which evaluates studies done between 1978 and 1990, Charles Tittle and Robert Meier again found no pervasive relationship.[57]

Many scholars have challenged such conclusions. They claim that when self-report studies are used for analysis, the results show few class differences because the studies ask only about trivial offenses. Delbert Elliott and Suzanne Ageton, for example, looked at serious crimes among a national sample of 1726 young people ages 11 to 17. According to the youths' responses to a self-report questionnaire, lower-class young people were much more likely than middle-class young people to commit such serious crimes as burglary, robbery, assault, and sexual assault.[58] In a follow-up study, Elliott and David Huizinga concluded that middle-class and lower-class youths differed significantly in both the nature and the number of serious crimes they committed.[59]

Controversies remain about the social class of people who commit crimes. There is no controversy, however, about the social class of people in prison. The probability that a person such as Ivan Boesky, a Wall Street tycoon convicted of insider trading, will get a prison sentence is extremely low. Boesky does not fit the typical profile of the hundreds of thousands of inmates of our nation's jails and prisons. He is educated. Only 28 percent of prison inmates have completed high school.[60] His income was in the millions. The average income of jail inmates who work is $5600. He had a white-collar job. Eighty-five percent of prison inmates are blue-collar workers. He committed a white-collar offense. Only 18 percent of the persons convicted of such offenses go to prison for more than 1 year, whereas 39 percent of the violent offenders and 26 percent of the property offenders do.[61] Finally, Ivan Boesky is white in a criminal justice system where blacks are disproportionately represented.

Race and Crime

Statistics on race and crime show that while blacks constitute 12 percent of the population, they account for 30 percent of all arrests for Index crimes.[62] Other statistics confirm their disproportionate representation in the criminal justice system. Fifty percent of black urban males are arrested for an Index crime at least once during their lives, compared with 14 percent of white males. The likelihood that any man will serve time in jail or prison is estimated to be 18 percent for blacks and 3 percent for whites. Moreover, the leading cause of death among young black men is murder.[63]

These statistics raise many questions. Do blacks actually commit more crimes? Or are they simply arrested more often? Are black neighborhoods under more police surveillance than white neighborhoods? Do blacks receive differential treatment in the criminal justice system? If blacks commit more crimes than whites, why?

Some data support the argument that there are more blacks in the criminal justice system because bias operates from the time of arrest through incarceration. Other data support the argument that racial disparities in official statistics reflect an actual difference in criminal behavior. Much of the evidence comes from the statistics of the NCVS, which are very similar to the statistics on race found in arrest data. When interviewers asked victims about the race of offenders in violent crimes, 28 percent identified the assailants as black.[64] Similarly, while self-report data demonstrate that less serious juvenile offenses are about equally prevalent among black and white youngsters, more serious ones are not: black youngsters report having committed many more Index crimes than do whites of comparable ages.[65]

If the disparity in criminal behavior suggested by official data, victimization studies, and self-reports actually exists, and if we are to explain it, we have to try to discover why people commit crimes. A history of hundreds of years of abuse, neglect, and discrimination against black Americans has left its mark in the form of high unemployment, residence in socially disorganized areas, one-parent households, and negative self-images.[66]

In 1968, in the aftermath of the worst riots in modern American history, the National Advisory Commission on Civil Disorders alluded to the reasons blacks had not achieved the successes accomplished by other minority groups that at one time or another were discriminated against as well. European immigrants provided unskilled labor needed by industry. By the time blacks migrated from rural areas to cities, the U.S. economy was changing and soon there was no longer much demand for unskilled labor. Immigrant groups had also received economic advantages by working for local political organizations. By the time blacks moved to the cities, the political machines no longer had the power to offer help in return for votes. Though both immigrants and blacks arrived in cities with little money, all but the very youngest members of the cohesive immigrant family contributed to the family's income. As slaves, however, black people had been forbidden to marry, and the unions they formed were subject to disruption at the owner's convenience and tended to be unstable. We will have more to say about the causal factors associated with high crime rates and race in Chapters 5 and 6.

The data reviewed here show that crime is an activity disproportionately engaged in by young people, males, and minorities. The characteristics of victims of violent crime tend to show a similar pattern.

MEASURING CHARACTERISTICS OF VICTIMS: THE SCIENCE OF VICTIMOLOGY

After a night at the theater, Caroline Isenberg headed home alone. The 23-year-old aspiring actress entered the darkened lobby of her apartment house on New York's Upper West Side. Inside, Emmanuel Torres, son of the building superintendent, lurked in the shadows. At knifepoint he forced Isenberg into the elevator. On the roof he tried to rape and rob her. When she resisted, Torres stabbed her nine times. She screamed, "He's going to kill me! I'm bleeding to death!" Neighbors called police, who found the victim. She died 5 hours later at St. Luke's Hospital.[67] The story of Caroline Isenberg appeared in the national news media. It was newsworthy because the victim was so different from most victims of violent crime: she was white, female, a Harvard graduate. Victims of violent crimes are typically black males from lower-income families.[68]

In ancient law, the victim played a role in the criminal event equal to that of the perpetrator. Then, for a thousand years, the victim was all but forgotten. Now the pendulum has swung back again with the emergence of "victimology" 50 years ago. It was the scientist Hans von Hentig, a victim of Nazi persecution, who focused our attention on the significance of the victim in criminal activity. People knew, for example, that tourist resorts were attractive to criminals who wanted to prey on unsuspecting vacationers. But von Hentig actually gathered such information systematically. Indeed, his book *The Criminal and His Victim*, published in 1948, may be said to have founded the criminological subdiscipline of **victimology,** which examines the role played by the victim in a criminal incident.

Today the process of gathering information about victims and the analysis of victim–offender relationships has become much more sophisticated with the creation of victimization surveys. We now know that the characteristics of victims of violent offenses differ from those of victims of theft. As we have noted, victims of violent offenses are predominantly black, male, and poor, whereas theft victims are primarily white

Department of Justice (Washington, D.C.: U.S. Government Printing Office, September 1985), pp. 5–11.

40. Terence P. Thornberry, "What's Working and What's Not Working in Safeguarding Our Children and Preventing Violence," Safeguarding Our Youth: Violence Prevention for Our Nation's Children, speech presented at Department of Education, Washington, D.C., July 20, 1993. For a discussion of the significance of age of onset and the desistance in the Pittsburgh sample, see Rolf Loeber, Magda Stouthamer-Loeber, Welmoet Van Kammen, and David Farrington, "Initiation, Escalation and Desistance in Juvenile Offending and Their Correlates," *Journal of Criminal Law and Criminology, 82* (1991): 36–82.

41. Uniform Crime Reports, 1992, p. 234.

42. U.S. Department of Justice, *Highlights from 20 Years of Surveying Crime Victims,* pp. 23, 59.

43. U.S. Department of Justice, *Report to the Nation on Crime and Justice,* 2d ed. (Washington, D.C.: U.S. Government Printing Office, 1988), p. 230.

44. Rosemary Sarri, "Gender Issues in Juvenile Justice," *Crime and Delinquency, 29* (1983): 381–397; Delbert Elliott and Suzanne Ageton, "Reconciling Race and Class Differences in Self-Reported and Official Estimates of Delinquency," *American Sociological Review, 45* (1980): 95–110; Hindelang et al., *Measuring Delinquency;* Stephen A. Cernkovich and Peggy C. Giordano, "Delinquency, Opportunity, and Gender," *Journal of Criminal Law and Criminology, 70* (1979): 145–151; Francis T. Cullen, Kathryn M. Golden, and John B. Cullen, "Sex and Delinquency: A Partial Test of the Masculinity Hypothesis," *Criminology, 17* (1979): 301–310.

45. John Hagan, John Simpson, and A. R. Gillis, "Class in the Household: A Power Control Theory of Gender and Delinquency," *American Journal of Sociology, 92* (1987): 788–816. See also Simon I. Singer and Murray Levine, "Power-Control Theory, Gender, and Delinquency: A Partial Replication with Additional Evidence on the Effects of Peers," *Criminology, 26* (1988): 627–647; and Gary F. Jensen, John Hagan, and A. R. Gillis, "Power-Control vs. Social Control Theories of Common Delinquency: A Comparative Analysis," in *New Directions in Criminological Theory,* ed. Freda Adler and William S. Laufer (New Brunswick, N.J.: Transaction, 1993), pp. 363–398.

46. Merry Morash and Meda Chesney-Lind, "A Reformulation and Partial Test of the Power Control Theory of Delinquency," *Justice Quarterly, 8* (1991): 347–377.

47. Cesare Lombroso and William Ferrero, *The Female Offender* (London: T. Fisher Unwin, 1895).

48. Sheldon Glueck and Eleanor T. Glueck, *Five Hundred Delinquent Women* (New York: Knopf, 1934).

49. Otto Pollack, *The Criminality of Women* (Philadelphia: University of Pennsylvania Press, 1950).

50. Freda Adler, *Sisters in Crime* (New York: McGraw-Hill, 1975), pp. 6–7.

51. Rita Simon, *The Contemporary Woman and Crime* (Rockville, Md.: National Institute of Mental Health, 1975).

52. Meda Chesney-Lind, "Female Offenders: Paternalism Reexamined," in *Women, the Courts, and Equality,* ed. Laura Crites and Winifred Hepperle (Newbury Park, Calif.: Sage, 1987).

53. Darrell J. Steffensmeier, "Crime and the Contemporary Woman: An Analysis of Changing Levels of Female Property Crimes, 1960–1975," *Social Forces, 57* (1978): 566–584; Darrell J. Steffensmeier, "Organization Properties and Sex-Segregation in the Underworld: Building a Sociological Theory of Sex Differences in Crime," *Social Forces, 61* (1983): 1024–1025; Darrell J. Steffensmeier and Renée Hoffman Steffensmeier, "Trends in Female Delinquency: An Examination of Arrest, Juvenile Court, Self-Report, and Field Data," *Criminology, 18* (1980): 62–85; Susan K. Datesman and Frank R. Scarpitti, "The Extent and Nature of Female Crime," in *Women, Crime, and Justice,* ed. Datesman and Scarpitti (New York: Oxford University Press, 1980); Lee H. Bowker, *Women, Crime, and the Criminal Justice System* (Lexington, Mass.: Heath, 1978). For a discussion of "masculine" characteristics and reported delinquency, see Stephen Norland, Randall C. Wessel, and Neal Shover, "Masculinity and Delinquency," *Criminology, 19* (1981): 421–433. For a description of the typical female offender (young, black, poorly educated, unskilled, unemployed, unmarried), see Nancy T. Wolfe, Francis T. Cullen, and John B. Cullen, "Describing the Female Offender: A Note on the Demographics of Arrests," *Journal of Criminal Justice, 12* (1984): 483–492. For a social-psychological discussion of the female offender, see Cathy Spatz Widom, "Female Offenders: Three Assumptions about Self-Esteem, Sex Role Identity, and Feminism," *Criminal Justice and Behavior, 6* (1979): 365–382.

54. Mary E. Gilfus, "From Victims to Survivors to Offenders: Women's Routes of Entry and Immersion into Street Crime," *Women and Criminal Justice, 4* (1992): 63–89; Joseph Weis, "Liberation and Crime: The Invention of the New Female Criminal," *Crime and Social Justice, 6* (Fall 1976): 17–27; Carol Smart, *Women, Crime, and Criminology: A Feminist Critique* (London: Routledge & Kegan Paul, 1977); E. Miller, "International Trends in the Study of Female Criminality: An Essay Review," *Contemporary Crisis, 7* (1983): 59–70; Jane Chapman, *Economic Reality and the Female Offender* (Lexington, Mass.: Lexington Books, 1980); Steven Box and Chris Hale, "Liberation/ Emancipation, Economic Marginalization, or Less Chivalry," *Criminology, 22* (1984): 473–497. For a discussion of the internalization of gender roles by female prisoners, see Edna Erez, "The Myth of the New Female Offender: Some Evidence from Attitudes toward Law and Justice," *Journal of Criminal Justice, 16* (1988): 499–509; and Meda Chesney-Lind, "Girls' Crime and Woman's Place: Toward a Feminist Model of Female Delinquency," *Crime and Delinquency, 25* (1989): 5–29.

55. Nanci Koser Wilson, "The Masculinity of Violent Crime—Some Second Thoughts," *Journal of Criminal Justice*, **9** (1981): 111–123; Josefina Figueira-McDonough, "A Reformulation of the 'Equal Opportunity' Explanation of Female Delinquency," *Crime and Delinquency*, **26** (1980): 333–343; Ronald L. Simons, Martin G. Miller, and Stephen M. Aigner, "Contemporary Theories of Deviance and Female Delinquency: An Empirical Test," *Journal of Research in Crime and Delinquency*, **17** (1980): 42–57; Roy Austin, "Women's Liberation and Increase in Minor, Major, and Occupational Offenses," *Criminology*, **20** (1982): 407–430.

56. For a discussion of a unisex theory of crime, see Coramae Richey Mann, *Female Crime and Delinquency* (Tuscaloosa: University of Alabama Press, 1984). For an analysis of the relation of both gender and race to crime, see Vernetta D. Young, "Women, Race, and Crime," *Criminology*, **18** (1980): 26–34; Gary D. Hill and Elizabeth M. Crawford, "Women, Race, and Crime," *Criminology*, **28** (1990): 601–626; and Sally S. Simpson, "Caste, Class, and Violent Crime: Explaining Differences in Female Offending," *Criminology*, **29** (1991): 115–136. For a discussion of female crime in countries around the world, see Freda Adler, ed., *The Incidence of Female Criminality in the Contemporary World* (New York: New York University Press, 1984). See also Freda Adler and Rita James Simon, eds., *The Criminology of Deviant Women* (Boston: Houghton Mifflin, 1979).

57. Charles Tittle, Wayne Villemez, and Douglas Smith, "The Myth of Social Class and Criminality: An Empirical Assessment of the Empirical Evidence," *American Sociological Review*, **43** (1978): 643–656; Charles R. Tittle and Robert F. Meier, "Specifying the SES/Delinquency Relationship," *Criminology*, **28** (1990): 271–299.

58. Elliott and Ageton, "Reconciling Race and Class Differences."

59. Delbert Elliot and David Huizinga, "Social Class and Delinquent Behavior in a National Youth Panel: 1976–1980," *Criminology*, **21** (1983): 149–177.

60. The data on socioeconomic factors come from U.S. Department of Justice, *Report to the Nation on Crime and Justice*, pp. 48–49; Tittle et al., "Myth of Social Class and Criminality"; James Short and F. Ivan Nye, "Reported Behavior as a Criterion of Deviant Behavior," *Social Problems*, **5** (1958): 207–213; Jay Williams and Martin Gold, "From Delinquent Behavior to Official Delinquency," *Social Problems*, **20** (1972): 209–229.

61. U.S. Department of Justice, Bureau of Justice Statistics, *Annual Report, Fiscal 1986* (Washington, D.C.: U.S. Government Printing Office, April 1987), p. 39.

62. Uniform Crime Reports, 1992, p. 235. See also Gary La Free, Kriss A. Drass, and Patrick O'Day, "Race and Crime in Postwar America: Determinants of African-American and White Rates, 1957–1988," *Criminology*, **30** (1992): 157–188.

63. Joan Petersilia, "Racial Disparities in the Criminal Justice System: A Summary," *Crime and Delinquency*, **31** (1985): 15–34.

64. U.S. Department of Justice, *Highlights from 20 Years of Surveying Crime Victims*, p. 23.

65. Delbert Elliott and Harwin Voss, *Delinquency and Dropout* (Lexington, Mass: Lexington Books, 1974); Elliott and Ageton, "Reconciling Race and Class Differences."

66. Robert J. Sampson, "Urban Black Violence: The Effect of Male Joblessness and Family Disruption," *American Journal of Sociology*, **93** (1987): 348–382; Charles Silberman, *Criminal Violence, Criminal Justice* (New York: Random House, 1979).

67. *Newsweek*, Dec. 17, 1984, p. 52.

68. U.S. Department of Justice, *Highlights from 20 Years of Surveying Crime Victims*, p. 18.

69. U.S. Department of Justice, *Report to the Nation on Crime and Justice*, p. 29. See also Keith D. Parker, "Criminal Victimization among Black Americans," *Journal of Black Studies*, **22** (1991): 186–195. For a discussion of juvenile victimization, see Finn-Aage Esbensen and David Huizinga, "Juvenile Victimization and Delinquency," *Youth and Society*, **23** (1991): 202–228; and Janet L. Lauritsen, Robert J. Sampson, and John H. Laub, "The Link between Offending and Victimization among Adolescents," *Criminology*, **29** (1991): 265–292. See also Kevin M. Fitzpatrick, Mark E. La Gory, and Ferris J. Ritchey, "Criminal Victimization among the Homeless," *Justice Quarterly*, **10** (1993): 353–368.

70. U.S. Department of Justice, *Highlights from 20 Years of Surveying Victims*, p. 19. See also Bonnie Fisher, "A Neighborhood Business Area Is Hurting: Crime, Fear of Crime, and Disorders Take Their Toll," *Crime and Delinquency*, **37** (1991): 363–373.

71. U.S. Department of Justice, *Highlights from 20 Years of Surveying Crime Victims*, pp. 14, 16.

72. For a discussion of fear among the elderly, see Ronald L. Akers, Anthony J. La Greca, Christine Sellers, and John Cochran, "Fear of Crime and Victimization among the Elderly in Different Types of Communities," *Criminology*, **25** (1987): 487–505. See also Vincent J. Webb and Ineke Haen Marshall, "Response to Criminal Victimization by Older Americans," *Criminal Justice and Behavior*, **16** (1989): 239–259; and Mark Warr, "Fear of Victimization and Sensitivity to Risk," *Journal of Quantitative Criminology*, **3** (1987): 29–46. For a discussion of the elderly as victims of homicide, see James Alan Fox and Jack Levin, "Homicide against the Elderly: A Research Note," *Criminology*, **29** (1991): 317–327.

73. Elizabeth A. Stanlev, "The Case of Fearful Women: Gender, Personal Safety and Fear of Crime," *Women and Criminal Justice*, **4** (1992): 117–135. See also Mark Warr, "Altruistic Fear of Victimization in Households," *Social Science Quarterly*, **73** (1992): 723–736; M. Dwayne Smith and Ellen S. Kuchta, "Trends in Violent Crime against Women, 1973–89," *Social Science Quarterly*, **74** (1993): 28–45; and Chris E. Marshall,

"Fear of Crime, Community Satisfaction and Self-Protective Measures: Perceptions from a Midwestern City," *Journal of Crime and Justice,* **14** (1991): 97–121.

74. U.S. Department of Justice, *Report to the Nation on Crime and Justice,* p. 32.

75. For an alternative approach to victimology, see Marilyn D. McShane and Frank P. Williams III, "Radical Victimology: A Critique of the Concept of Victim in Traditional Victimology," *Crime and Delinquency,* **38** (1992): 258–271.

3

Schools of Thought throughout History

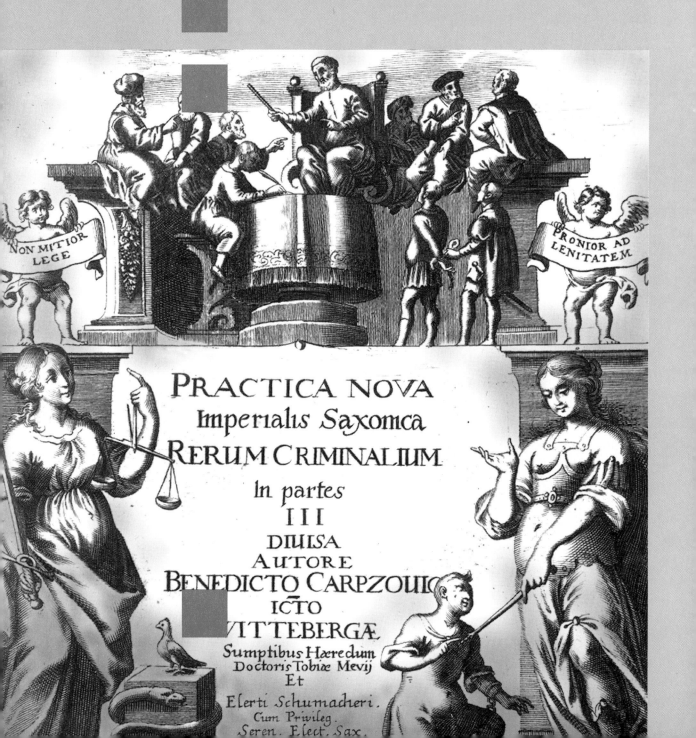

NON MITIOR LEGE

PRONIOR AD LENITATEM

PRACTICA NOVA
Imperialis Saxonica
RERUM CRIMINALIUM
In partes
III
DIUISA
AUTORE
BENEDICTO CARPZOUIO
ICTO
VITTEBERGÆ
Sumptibus Hæredum
Doctoris Tobiæ Mevij
Et
Elerti Schumacheri.
Cum Privileg.
Seren. Elect. Sax.

KEY TERMS
anomie
atavistic stigmata
born criminal
classical school of criminology
eugenics
laws of imitation
phrenology
physiognomy
positivist school of criminology
somatotype school of criminology
utilitarianism

Children now love luxury. They have bad manners, contempt for authority. They show disrespect for elders. They contradict their parents, chatter before company, cross their legs and tyrannize their teachers.

The ideal condition would be, I admit, that men should be right by instinct; but since we are all likely to go astray, the reasonable thing is to learn from those who can teach.

When there is an income tax, the just man will pay more and the unjust less on the same amount of income.[1]

Criminologists traditionally consider that their field has its origins as a science in the eighteenth century, when Cesare Beccaria established what came to be known as the classical school of criminology. But when we look at what some much earlier thinkers had to say about crime, we may have to reconsider this assumption. Look again at the quotations above. The first may appear to be a modern description of delinquent youth, but Socrates made this observation over 2300 years ago. The second quotation, about instinct and learning and their association with criminality, was an observation made by Sophocles, who lived almost 2500 years ago. The final quotation, about income tax fraud, is not taken from a study of American white-collar crime: Plato voiced this insight, in his treatise *The Republic,* in the fourth century B.C.

Scholars, philosophers, and poets have speculated about the causes of crime and possible remedies since ancient times, and modern criminology owes much to the wisdom the ancient philosophers displayed. The philosophical approach culminated in the middle of the eighteenth century in the **classical school of criminology.** It is based on the assumption that individuals choose to commit crimes after weighing the consequences of their actions. According to classical criminologists, individuals have free will. They can choose legal or illegal means to get what they want; fear of punishment can deter them from committing crime; and society can control behavior by making the pain of punishment greater than the pleasure of the criminal gains.

The classical school did not remain unchallenged for long. In the early nineteenth century great advances were made in the natural sciences and in medicine. Physicians in France, Germany, and England undertook systematic studies of crimes and criminals. Crime statistics became available in several European countries. There emerged an opposing school of criminology, the **positivist school.** This school posits that human behavior is determined by forces beyond individual control and that it is possible to measure those forces. Unlike classical criminologists, who claim that people rationally choose to commit crime, positivist criminologists view criminal behavior as stemming from biological, psychological, and social factors.

The earliest positivist theories centered on biological factors, and studies of these factors dominated criminology during the last half of the nineteenth century. In the twentieth century, biological explanations were ignored (and even targeted as racist after World War II). They did not surface again until the 1970s, when scientific advances in psychology shifted the emphasis from defects in criminals' bodies to defects in their minds. Throughout the twentieth century, psychologists and psychiatrists have played a major role in the study of crime causation. A third area of positivist criminology focuses on the relation of social factors to crime. Sociological theories, developed in the second half of the nineteenth century and advanced throughout the twentieth, continue to dominate the field of criminology today.

An understanding of the foundations of modern criminology helps us to understand contemporary developments in the field. Let us begin with the developments that led to the emergence of the classical school.

CLASSICAL CRIMINOLOGY

In the late eighteenth to the mid-nineteenth centuries, during what is now called the neoclassical period, the classical culture of the ancient Mediterranean was rediscovered. This was also a period of scientific discoveries and the founding of new scholarly disciplines. One of these was criminology, which developed as an attempt to apply rationality and the rule of law to brutal and

WINDOW TO THE WORLD
Stone Age Crime and Social Control

On a fine Thursday afternoon in September 1991, vacationers from Germany, on an alpine hiking trip, spotted a head protruding from the glacial ice. They hurried to a nearby guest house and reported their find to the innkeeper, who promptly called both the Italian and the Austrian police. It became immediately apparent that this corpse was no ordinary mountain casualty. Rather, this was an ancient mountain casualty. Experts were brought in from Austrian universities, and the body was freed from its icy embrace. It was dubbed "Oetzi," after the Oetztal Alps of the discovery.

Oetzi is 5300 years old, a robust young man, 25 to 30 years old at the time of his death. Completely mummified, he was found in the position in which he had placed himself, in a crevice, probably to escape a snowstorm. He was fully dressed, in an unlined fur robe. Originally fashioned with great skill, the robe was badly repaired with sinew and plant fiber, suggesting that he could not have relied on the services of his wife or the vil-lage seamstress for some time. Oetzi had placed his equipment by his side, most of it of the best Stone Age craftsmanship. What is surprising is that he did not carry with him a ready-to-shoot bow.

Investigators determined that Oetzi was an outdoor type, a shepherd who sought refuge in the crevice, froze to death, and was preserved for 5 millennia by permafrost and glacial ice. But what was Oetzi doing at 3210 meters (nearly 10,000 feet) above sea level on a fall day? He was far above the grazing range of a herd. Nor was he a trader trying to cross the Alps in Fall. So what was he doing up there, where nothing grows and where it is hard to breathe? There is one possibility which suggests itself on the basis of all the evidence available so far. Oetzi may have been an outlaw.

Oetzi was a Late Stone Age (Neolithic) man, likely to have come from a herding community of at most 200 persons. Robert Carneiro of the American Museum of Natural History has figured out that a community of 200 produces 20,000 one-on-one disagreement possibilities. The tasks of social control even within such a small community stagger the imagination.

Any interpersonal problems Oetzi's people had could have been similar to those experienced by contemporary Stone Age people. Fighting could erupt within a community or among communities. Jealousy could be engendered as to who deserves more respect as the best hunter, the best storyteller, the best healer, or the wisest person. Disputes could happen over the distribution of food or the sharing of tools. The evidence about past and present Neolithic society permits us to conclude that such societies had or have no institution which we could compare to modern criminal justice, although they had problems which today might be referred to a criminal justice system. How were such problems solved? Minor problems were dealt with by shaming the offender, by dispute resolution, by compensation, and by sacrifices. Major unforgivable offenses led to casting out the wrongdoer: he would be declared an outlaw. The person had to leave camp instantly, without gathering his weapons, and flee to the wilderness. Oetzi fits the description of such an outlaw, literally a person cast outside the protection of the laws, the customs, and the protection of his group, to take to the wilderness and perhaps to die there. If Oetzi was a criminal banished from his village, the punishment clearly was effective.

Source: Adapted from Gerhard O. W. Mueller and Freda Adler, "The Emergence of Criminal Justice: Tracing the Route to Neolithic Times," in Festskrift till Jacob W. F. Sundberg, ed. Erik Nerep and Wiweka Warnling Nerep (Stockholm: Juristförlaget, 1993), pp. 151–170.

Questions for Discussion

1. For purposes of improving modern crime-control techniques, can we learn anything from Stone Age societies?
2. What crimes do you think might result in the banishment of one of the members of such a community?

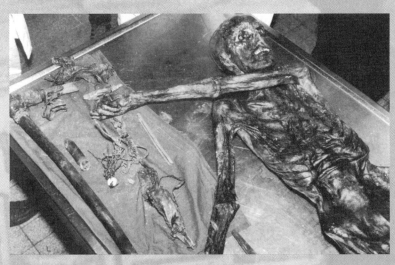

Oetzi, who was preserved in the glacial crevice in which he died.

arbitrary criminal justice processes. The work of criminology's founders—scholars like Cesare Beccaria and Jeremy Bentham—became known as "classical" criminology.

The Historical Context

Classical criminology grew out of a reaction against the barbaric system of law, punishment, and justice that existed before the French Revolution of 1789. Until that time, there was no real system of criminal justice in Europe. There were crimes against the state, against the church, and against the crown. Some of these crimes were specified; some were not. Judges had discretionary power to convict a person for an act not even legally defined as criminal.[2] Monarchs often issued what were called in French *lettres de cachet,* under which an individual could be imprisoned for almost any reason (disobedience to one's father, for example) or for no reason at all.

Many criminal laws were unwritten, and those that had been drafted, by and large, did not specify the kind or amount of punishment associated with various crimes. Arbitrary and often cruel sentences were imposed by judges who had unbounded discretion to decide questions of guilt and innocence and to mete out punishment. "Due process" in the modern sense did not exist. While there was some general consensus on what constituted crime, there was no real limit to the amount and type of legal sanction a court could command. Punishments included branding, burning, flogging, mutilation, drowning, banishment, and beheading.[3] In England a person might receive the death penalty for any of more than 200 offenses, including what we today call petty theft.

Public punishments were popular events. When Robert-François Damiens was scheduled to be executed on March 2, 1757, for the attempted murder of Louis XV, so many people wanted to attend the $1^z\backslash x$-hour spectacle that window seats overlooking the execution site were rented for high prices. Torture to elicit confessions was common. A criminal defendant in France might be subjected to the *peine forte et dure,* which consisted of stretching him on his back and placing over him an iron weight as heavy as

he could bear. He was left that way until he died or spoke. A man would suffer these torments and lose his life in order to avoid trial and therefore conviction so that his lands and goods would not be confiscated and would be preserved for his family. This proceeding was not abolished until 1772.[4]

Even as Europe grew increasingly modern, industrial, and urban in the eighteenth century, it still clung to its medieval penal practices. With prosperity came an increasing gulf between the haves and the have-nots. Just before the French Revolution, for example, a Parisian worker paid 97 percent of his daily earnings for a 4-pound loaf of bread.[5] Hordes of unemployed people begged by day and found shelter under bridges by night. One of the few ways in which the established upper class could protect itself was through ruthless oppression of those beneath it, but ruthless oppression created more problems. Social unrest grew. And as crime rates rose, so did the brutality of punishment. Both church and state became increasingly tyrannical, using violence to conquer violence.

The growing educated classes began to see the inconsistency in these policies. If terrible tortures were designed to deter crime, why were people committing even more crimes? There must be something wrong with the underlying reasoning. By the mid-eighteenth century, social reformers were beginning to suggest a more rational approach to crime and punishment. One of them, Cesare Beccaria, laid the foundation for the first school of criminology—the classical school.

Cesare Beccaria

Cesare Bonesana, Marchese di Beccaria (1738–1794), was rather undistinguished as a student. After graduating with a law degree from the University of Pavia, he returned home to Milan and joined a group of articulate and radical intellectuals. Disenchanted with contemporary European society, they organized themselves into the Academy of Fists, one of many young men's clubs that flourished in Italy at the time. Their purpose was to discover what reforms would be needed to modernize Italian society.

In March 1763 Beccaria was assigned to pre-

Cesare Bonesana, Marchese di Beccaria, 1738–1794.

pare a report on the prison system. Pietro Verri, the head of the Academy of Fists, encouraged him to read the works of English and French philosophers—David Hume (1711–1776), John Locke (1632–1704), Claude Adrien Helvétius (1715–1771), Voltaire (1694–1778), Montesquieu (1685–1755), and Jean-Jacques Rousseau (1712–1778). Another member of the academy, the protector of prisons, revealed to him the inhumanities that were possible under the guise of social control. Beccaria learned well. He read, observed, and made notes on small scraps of paper. These notes, Harry Elmer Barnes has observed, were destined to "assure to its author immortality and would work a revolution in the moral world" upon their publication in July 1764 under the title *Dei delitti e delle pene (On Crimes and Punishment)*.[6] Beccaria presented a coherent, comprehensive design for an enlightened criminal justice system that was to serve the people rather than the monarchy.

The climate was right: with the publication of this small book, Cesare Beccaria became the "father of modern criminology." The controversy between the rule of men and the rule of law was at its most heated. Some people defended the old order, under which judges and administrators made arbitrary or whimsical decisions. Others fought for the rule of law, under which the decision making of judges and administrators would be confined by legal limitations. Beccaria's words provided the spark that ultimately ended medieval barbarism.

According to Beccaria, the crime problem could be traced not to bad people but to bad laws. A modern criminal justice system should guarantee all people equal treatment before the law. Beccaria's book supplied the blueprint. That blueprint was based on the assumption that people freely choose what they do and are responsible for the consequences of their behavior. Beccaria proposed the following principles:

- *Laws should be used to maintain the social contract:* "Laws are the conditions under which men, naturally independent, united themselves in society. Weary of living in a continual state of war, and of enjoying a liberty, which became of little value, from the uncertainty of its duration, they sacrificed one part of it, to enjoy the rest in peace and security."

- *Only legislators should create laws:* "The authority of making penal laws can only reside with the legislator, who represents the whole society united by the social compact."

- *Judges should impose punishment only in accordance with the law:* "[N]o magistrate then, (as he is one of the society), can, with justice inflict on any other member of the same society punishment that is not ordained by the laws."

- *Judges should not interpret the laws:* "Judges, in criminal cases, have no right to interpret the penal laws, because they are not legislators. . . . Every man hath his own particular point of view, and, at different times, sees the same objects in very different lights. The spirit of the laws will then be the result of the good or bad logic of the judge; and this will depend on his good or bad digestion."

- *Punishment should be based on the pleasure/pain principle:* "Pleasure and pain are the only springs of actions in beings endowed with sensibility. . . . If an equal punishment be ordained for two crimes that injure society in different degrees, there is nothing to deter men from committing the greater as often as it is attended with greater advantage."

■ *Punishment should be based on the act, not on the actor:* "Crimes are only to be measured by the injuries done to the society. They err, therefore, who imagine that a crime is greater or less according to the intention of the person by whom it is committed."

■ *The punishment should be determined by the crime:* "If mathematical calculation could be applied to the obscure and infinite combinations of human actions, there might be a corresponding scale of punishments descending from the greatest to the least."

■ *Punishment should be prompt and effective:* "The more immediate after the commission of a crime a punishment is inflicted, the more just and useful it will be. . . . An immediate punishment is more useful; because the smaller the interval of time between the punishment and the crime, the stronger and more lasting will be the association of the two ideas of crime and punishment."

■ *All people should be treated equally:* "I assert that the punishment of a nobleman should in no wise differ from that of the lowest member of society."

■ *Capital punishment should be abolished:* "The punishment of death is not authorized by any right; for . . . no such right exists. . . . The terrors of death make so slight an impression, that it has not force enough to withstand the forgetfulness natural to mankind."

■ *The use of torture to gain confessions should be abolished:* "It is confounding all relations to expect . . . that pain should be the test of truth, as if truth resided in the muscles and fibres of a wretch in torture. By this method the robust will escape, and the feeble be condemned."

■ *It is better to prevent crimes than to punish them:* "Would you prevent crimes? Let the laws be clear and simple, let the entire force of the nation be united in their defence, let them be intended rather to favour every individual than any particular classes. . . . Finally, the most certain method of preventing crime is to perfect the system of education."[7]

Perhaps no other book in the history of criminology has had so great an impact. Beccaria's ideas were so advanced that Voltaire, the great French philosopher of the time, who wrote the commentary for the French version, referred to Beccaria as "brother."[8] The English version appeared in 1767; by that time, 3 years after the book's publication, it had already gone through six Italian editions and several French editions.

After the French Revolution, Beccaria's basic tenets served as a guide for the drafting of the French penal code, which was adopted in 1791. In Russia, Empress Catherine II (the Great) convened a commission to prepare a new code and issued instructions, written in her own hand, to translate Beccaria's ideas into action. The Prussian King Friedrich II (the Great) devoted his reign to revising the Prussian laws according to Beccaria's principles. Emperor Joseph II had a new code drafted for Austria-Hungary in 1787—the first code to abolish capital punishment. The impact of Beccaria's treatise spread across the Atlantic as well: it influenced the first ten amendments to the U.S. Constitution (the Bill of Rights).

Jeremy Bentham's Utilitarianism

Legal scholars and reformers throughout Europe proclaimed their indebtedness to Beccaria, but none owed more to him than the English legal philosopher Jeremy Bentham (1748–1832). Bentham had a long and productive career. He inspired many of his contemporaries, as well as criminologists of future generations, with his approach to rational crime control.

Bentham devoted his life to developing a scientific approach to the making and breaking of laws. Like Beccaria, he was concerned with achieving "the greatest happiness of the greatest number."[9] His work was governed by utilitarian principles. **Utilitarianism** assumes that all human actions are calculated in accordance with their likelihood of bringing happiness (pleasure) or unhappiness (pain). People weigh the probabilities of present and future pleasures against those of present and future pain.

Bentham proposed a precise pseudo-mathematical formula for this process, which he called "felicific calculus." According to his reasoning, individuals are "human calculators" who put all the factors into an equation in order to decide whether or not a particular crime is worth committing. This notion may seem rather whimsical today, but at a time when there were over 200 capital offenses, it provided a rationale for reform of the legal system.[10] Bentham reasoned that if prevention was the purpose of punishment, and if punishment became too costly by creating more harm than good, then penalties needed to be set just a bit in excess of the pleasure one might derive from committing a crime, and no higher. The law exists in order to create happiness for the community. Since punishment creates unhappiness, it can be justified only if it prevents greater evil than it produces. Thus, Bentham suggested, if hanging a man's effigy produced the same preventive effect as hanging the man himself, there would be no reason to hang the man.

Sir Samuel Romilly, a member of Parliament, met Jeremy Bentham at the home of a mutual friend. He became interested in Bentham's idea that the certainty of punishment outweighs its severity as a deterrent against crime. On February 9, 1810, in a speech before Parliament, he advocated Benthamite ideas:

> So evident is the truth of that maxim that if it were possible that punishment, as the consequence of guilt, could be reduced to an absolute certainty, a very slight penalty would be sufficient to prevent almost every species of crime.[11]

Although conservatives prevented any major changes during Romilly's lifetime, the program of legislative pressure he began was continued by his followers and culminated in the complete reform of English criminal law between 1820 and 1861. During that period the number of capital offenses was reduced from 222 to 3: murder, treason, and piracy. Gradually, from the ideals of the philosophers of the Age of Enlightenment and the principles outlined by the scholars of the classical school, a new social order was created, an order that affirmed a commitment to equal treatment of all people before the law.

The Classical School: An Evaluation

Classical criminology had an immediate and profound impact on jurisprudence and legislation.

The rule of law spread rapidly through Europe and the United States. Of no less significance was the influence of the classical school on penal and correctional policy. The classical principle that punishment must be appropriate to the crime was universally accepted during the nineteenth and early twentieth centuries. Yet the classical approach had weaknesses. Critics attacked the simplicity of its argument: the responsibility of the criminal justice system was simply to enforce the law with swiftness and certainty and to treat all people in like fashion, whether the accused were paupers or nobles; government was to be run by the rule of law rather than at the discretion of its officials. In other words, the punishment was to fit the crime, not the criminal. The proposition that human beings had the capacity to choose freely between good and evil was accepted without question. There was no need to ask why people behave as they do, to seek a motive or to ask about the specific circumstances surrounding criminal acts.

During the last half of the nineteenth century, scholars began to challenge these ideas. Influenced by the expanding search for scientific explanations of behavior in place of philosophical ones, criminologists shifted their attention from the act to the actor. They argued that people did not choose of their own free will to commit crime; rather, factors beyond their control were responsible for criminal behavior.

POSITIVIST CRIMINOLOGY

During the late eighteenth century, significant advances in knowledge of both the physical and the social world influenced thinking about crime. Auguste Comte (1798–1857), a French sociologist, applied the modern methods of the physical sciences to the social sciences in his six-volume *Cours de philosophie positive (Course in Positive Philosophy)*, published between 1830 and 1842. He argued that there could be no real knowledge of social phenomena unless it was based on a positivist (scientific) approach. Positivism alone, however, was not sufficient to bring about a fundamental change in criminological thinking. Not until Charles Darwin (1809–1882) challenged the doctrine of creation with his theory of the evolution of species did the next generation of criminologists have the tools with which to challenge classicism.

The turning point was the publication in 1859 of Darwin's *Origin of Species*. Darwin's theory was that God did not make all the various species of animals in 2 days, as proclaimed in Genesis 1:20–26, but rather that the species had evolved through a process of adaptive mutation and natural selection. The process was based on the survival of the fittest in the struggle for existence. This radical theory seriously challenged traditional theological teaching. It was not until 1871, however, that Darwin publicly took the logical next step and traced human origins to an animal of the anthropoid group—the ape.[12] He thus posed an even more serious challenge to a religious tradition which maintained that God created the first human in his own image (Genesis 1:27).

The scientific world would never be the same again. The theory of evolution made it possible to ask new questions and to search in new ways for the answers to old ones. New biological theories replaced older ones. Old ideas that demons and animal spirits could explain human behavior were replaced by knowledge based on new scientific principles. The social sciences were born.

The nineteenth-century forces of positivism and evolution moved the field of criminology from a philosophical to a scientific perspective. But there were even earlier intellectual underpinnings of the scientific criminology that emerged in the second half of the nineteenth century.

BIOLOGICAL DETERMINISM: THE SEARCH FOR CRIMINAL TRAITS

Throughout history a variety of physical characteristics and disfigurements have been said to characterize individuals of "evil" disposition. In the earliest pursuit of the relationship between biological traits and behavior, a Greek scientist who examined Socrates found his skull and facial features to be those of a person inclined toward alcoholism and brutality.[13] The ancient Greeks and Romans so distrusted red hair that actors portraying evil persons wore red wigs. Through the ages cripples, hunchbacks, people with long

hair, and a multitude of others were viewed with suspicion. Indeed, in the Middle Ages laws indicated that if two people were suspected of a crime, the uglier was the more likely to be guilty.[14]

The belief that criminals are born, not made, and that they can be identified by various physical irregularities is reflected not only in scientific writing but in literature as well. Shakespeare's Julius Caesar states:

> Let me have men about me that are fat;
> Sleek-headed men, and such as sleep o' nights.
> Yond Cassius has a lean and hungry look;
> He thinks too much: such men are dangerous.

Although its roots can be traced to ancient times, it was not until the sixteenth century that the Italian physician Giambattista della Porta (1535–1615) founded the school of human **physiognomy,** the study of facial features and their relation to human behavior. According to Porta, a thief had large lips and sharp vision. Two centuries later Porta's efforts were revived by the Swiss theologian Johann Kaspar Lavater (1741–1801).[15] They were elaborated by the German physicians Franz Joseph Gall (1758–1828) and Johann Kaspar Spurzheim (1776–1832), whose science of **phrenology** posited that bumps on the head were indications of psychological propensities.[16] In the United States these views were supported by the physician Charles Caldwell (1772–1853), who searched for evidence that brain tissue and cells regulate human action.[17] By the nineteenth century, the sciences of physiognomy and phrenology had introduced specific biological factors into the study of crime causation.

Lombroso, Ferri, Garofalo: The Italian School

Cesare Lombroso (1835–1909) integrated Comte's positivism, Darwin's evolutionism, and the many pioneering studies of the relation of crime to the body. In 1876, with the publication of *L'uomo delinquente (The Criminal Man)*, criminology was permanently transformed from an abstract philosophy of crime control through legislation to a modern science of investigation into causes. Lombroso's work replaced the concept of free

CRIMINOLOGICAL FOCUS
The Mismeasure of Man

In 1981 historian, biologist, and writer Stephen Jay Gould published *The Mismeasure of Man*, a study of biased science and its social abuse. One of its reviews begins as the book itself does—with a quote from Gould's earlier work on Cesare Lombroso's 1876 *The Criminal Man*:

"Perhaps because its bold thesis seemed so clear, simple and impeccably scientific—criminals are ignorant apes with small brains as well as a brutish physical appearance—Lombroso's book won wide assent, despite its paltry data. At criminal trials for years afterward, a 'sinister look' signaled an incorrigible miscreant. 'Theoretical ethics,' declared Lombroso, 'passes over these diseased brains, as oil does over marble, without penetrating it.'"

In *The Mismeasure of Man*, Gould discusses the methodology used to "support" the ideas of many noted figures such as Lombroso. The review presents a brief summary: Gould brings back to life an astonishing rogues' gallery of once-eminent scientists, most of them committed to racial purity, a privileged elite, and the theory that class rule rests on immutable biological differences. Besides Lombroso, there is Francis Galton, a pioneer of modern statistics and the first apostle of "eugenics," a term he invented for the brave new science of breeding; Paul Broca, the French surgeon who spent a lifetime weighing brains and juggling figures to prove the superior heft of the European mind; and Samuel George Morton, a Philadelphia patrician who collected more than 1,000 skulls from all over the world, meticulously used BB's to measure the volume of each one, and then fudged the results to show that whites had bigger skulls than blacks.

Craniometry—the science of measuring skulls—seems the quaint vestige of a bygone era. Aptitude tests, by contrast, still determine educational opportunity in our own society. Gould shows precisely how . . . scholars gathered data to suit their own assumptions. R. M. Yerkes . . . tested immigrants for "innate" intelligence by asking them multiple-choice questions like, "Crisco is a: Patent medicine, disinfectant, toothpaste, food product." H. H. Goddard, another crusading advocate of IQ testing and scientific breeding, doctored photographs of "morons"—he coined the term—to make them look demented. And then there is the case of the late Sir Cyril Burt, the doyen of British mental testing, who palmed off faked data, "patent errors and specious claims," for more than 50 years.

Gould concedes that IQ testing can, in certain contexts, become a tool "for enhancing potential through proper education." But when prejudice passes for science and bigots wield IQ as a measure of innate human limits, the results are often tragic. Between 1924 and 1972, the state of Virginia secretly sterilized more than 7,500 people—simply because they scored low on one of [these] dubious tests.

Source: Jim Miller, Book Review: "The Mismeasure of Man," Newsweek, Nov. 9, 1981, p. 106.

Questions for Discussion

1. Alfred Binet, who first devised aptitude tests, viewed his work with caution and said that test scores should not be used as if they recorded "a fixed faculty." Why and how did IQ tests come to be misused?
2. Do you think a thesis such as that put forth by Lombroso would be accepted by the public today?

Part of the frontispiece to the atlas of Lombroso's *The Criminal Man*. Group A are German murderers; B are swindlers; C are those who declared themselves bankrupt fraudulently.

(a)

(b)

(c)

will, which had reigned for over a century as the principle that explained criminal behavior, with that of determinism. Together with his followers, the Italian legal scholars Enrico Ferri (1856–1929) and Raffaele Garofalo (1852–1934), Lombroso developed a new orientation, the Italian or positivist school of criminology, which seeks explanations for criminal behavior through scientific experimentation and research.

Cesare Lombroso

After completing his medical studies, Cesare Lombroso served as an army physician, became a professor of psychiatry at the University of Turin, and later in life accepted an appointment as professor of criminal anthropology. His theory of the "born criminal" states that criminals are a lower form of life, nearer to their apelike ancestors than noncriminals in traits and dispositions. They are distinguishable from noncriminals by various **atavistic stigmata**—physical features of creatures at an earlier stage of development, before they became fully human.

He argued that criminals frequently have huge jaws and strong canine teeth, characteristics common to carnivores who tear and devour meat raw. The arm span of criminals is often greater than their height, just like that of apes, who use their forearms to propel themselves along the ground. An individual born with any five of the stigmata is a **born criminal.** This category accounts for about a third of all offenders.

The theory became clear to Lombroso "one cold grey November morning" while he pored over the bones of a notorious outlaw who had died in an Italian prison:

> This man possessed such extraordinary agility, that he had been known to scale steep mountain heights bearing a sheep on his shoulders. His cynical effrontery was such that he openly boasted of his crimes. On his death . . . I was deputed to make the post-mortem, and on laying open the skull I found . . . a distinct depression . . . as in inferior animals.

Lombroso was delighted by his findings:

> This was not merely an idea, but a revelation. At the sight of that skull, I seemed to see all of a sudden, lighted up as a vast plain under a flaming sky the problem of the nature of the criminal–an atavistic being who reproduces in his person the ferocious instincts of primitive humanity.[18]

Criminal women, according to Lombroso, are different from criminal men. It is the prostitute who represents the born criminal among them:

> We also saw that women have many traits in common with children; that their moral sense is different; they are revengeful, jealous, inclined to vengeance of a refined cruelty. . . . When a morbid activity of the psychical centres intensifies the bad qualities of women . . . it is clear that the innocuous semi-criminal present in normal women must be transformed into a born criminal more terrible than any man. . . . The criminal woman is consequently a monster. Her normal sister is kept in the paths of virtue by many causes, such as maternity, piety, weakness, and when these counter influences fail, and a woman commits a crime, we may conclude that her wickedness must have been enormous before it could triumph over so many obstacles.[19]

To the born criminal Lombroso added two other categories, insane criminals and criminoloids. *Insane criminals* are not criminal from birth; they become criminal as a result of some change in their brains which interferes with their ability to distinguish between right and wrong.[20] *Criminoloids* make up an ambiguous group that includes habitual criminals, criminals by passion, and other diverse types.

Lombroso's "born criminal" man and woman. Sculptures by an unknown Italian artist; commissioned by the Italian Ministry of Justice in the 1920s and now at the United Nations Interregional Crime and Justice Research Institute, Rome.

Psychiatrist Dr. Cesare Lombroso, 1836–1909, the first criminologist to use physical measurements in the search for the causes of crime and criminality.

Most scientists who followed Lombroso did not share his enthusiasm or his viewpoint. As happens so often in history, his work has been kept alive more by criticism than by agreement. The theory that criminals were lodged on the lower rungs of the evolutionary ladder did not stand up to scientific scrutiny. But the fact that Lombroso measured thousands of live and dead prisoners and compared these measurements with those obtained from control groups (however imperfectly derived) in his search for determinants of crime changed the nature of the questions asked by the generations of scholars who came after him.

His influence continues in contemporary European research; American scientists, as the criminologist Marvin Wolfgang says, use him "as a straw man for attack on biological analyses of criminal behavior."[21] Thorsten Sellin has noted: "Any scholar who succeeds in driving hundreds of fellow-students to search for the truth, and whose ideas after half a century possess vitality, merits an honorable place in the history of thought."[22] At his death, true to his lifetime pursuits, Lombroso willed his body to the laboratory of legal medicine and his brain to the Institute of Anatomy at the University of Turin, where for so many years the father of empirical criminology had espoused biological determinism.[23]

Enrico Ferri

The best known of Lombroso's associates was Enrico Ferri (1856–1929). Member of Parliament, accomplished public lecturer, brilliant lawyer, editor of a newspaper, and esteemed scholar, Ferri had published his first major book by the time he was 21. By age 25 he was a university professor. Although Ferri agreed with Lombroso on the biological bases of criminal behavior, his interest in socialism led him to recognize the importance of social, economic, and political determinants.

Ferri was a prolific writer on a vast number of criminological topics. His greatest contribution was his attack on the classical doctrine of free will, which argued that criminals should be held morally responsible for their crimes because they must have made a rational decision to commit these acts. Ferri believed criminals could not be held morally responsible because they did not choose to commit crimes but, rather, were driven to commit them by conditions in their lives. He did, however, stress that society needed protection against criminal acts and that it was the purpose of the criminal law and penal policy to provide that protection.

Although he advocated conventional punishments and even the death penalty for individuals he assumed would never be fit to live in society, he was more interested in controlling crime through preventive measures—state control of the manufacture of weapons, inexpensive housing, better street lighting, and so forth.

Ferri claimed that strict adherence to preventive measures based on scientific methods would eventually reduce crime and allow people to live together in society with less dependence on the penal system. Toward the end of his life he proudly admitted that he was an idealist, a statement with which generations of scholars have agreed. Though his prescription for crime reduction was overly optimistic, Ferri's importance to the development of modern criminology is undisputed. "When Enrico Ferri died on April 12, 1929," writes Thorsten Sellin, "one of the most colorful, influential figures in the history of criminology disappeared."[24]

Raffaele Garofalo

Another follower of Lombroso was the Italian nobleman, magistrate, senator, and professor of law Raffaele Garofalo (1852–1934). Like Lombroso and Ferri, Garofalo rejected the doctrine of free will and supported the position that the only way to understand crime was to study it by scientific methods. Influenced by Lombroso's theory of atavistic stigmata, in which he found many shortcomings, Garofalo traced the roots of criminal behavior not to physical features but to their psychological equivalents, which he called "moral anomalies." According to this theory, natural crimes are found in all human societies, regardless of the views of lawmakers, and no civilized society can afford to disregard them.[25]

Natural crimes, according to Garofalo, are those that offend the basic moral sentiments of probity (respect for the property of others) and piety (revulsion against the infliction of suffering on others). An individual who has an organic deficiency in these moral sentiments has no moral constraints against committing such crimes. Garofalo argued that these individuals could not be held responsible for their actions. But, like Ferri, he also emphasized that society needed protection and that penal policy should be designed to prevent criminals from inflicting harm.[26]

Influenced by Darwinian theory, Garofalo suggested that the death penalty could rid society of its maladapted members, just as the natural selection process eliminated maladapted organisms. For less serious offenders, capable of adapting themselves to society in some measure, other types of punishments were preferable: transportation to remote lands, loss of privileges, institutionalization in farm colonies, or perhaps simply reparation. Clearly, Garofalo was much more interested in protecting society than in the individual rights of offenders.

Challenges to Lombrosian Theory

Although Lombroso, Ferri, and Garofalo did not always agree on the causes of criminal behavior or on the way society should respond to it, their combined efforts marked a turning point in the development of the scientific study of crime. These three were responsible for developing the positivist approach to criminality, which influences criminology to the present day. Nevertheless, they had their critics. By using the scientific method to explore crime causation, they paved the way for criminologists to support or refute the theories they had created. The major challenge to Lombrosian theory came from the work of Charles Buckman Goring.

From 1901 until 1913 Charles Buckman Goring (1870–1919), a medical officer at Parkhurst Prison in England, collected data on 96 traits of more than 3000 convicts and a large control group of Oxford and Cambridge university students, hospital patients, and soldiers. Among his research assistants was a famous statistician, Karl Pearson. When Goring had completed his examinations, he was armed with enough data to refute Lombroso's theory of the anthropological criminal type. Goring's report to the scientific community proclaimed:

> From a knowledge only of an undergraduate's cephalic [head] measurement, a better judgement could be given as to whether he were studying at an English or Scottish university than a prediction could be made as to whether he would eventually become a university professor or a convicted felon.[27]

This evaluation still stands as the most cogent critical analysis of Lombroso's theory of the born criminal. But though Goring rejected the claim that specific stigmata identify the criminal, he was convinced that poor physical condition plus a defective state of mind were determining factors in the criminal personality.

A Return to Biological Determinism

After Goring's challenge, Lombrosian theory lost its academic popularity for about a quarter of a century. Then in 1939 Ernest Hooten (1887–1954), a physical anthropologist, reawakened an interest in biologically determined criminality with the publication of a massive study comparing

American prisoners with a noncriminal control group. He concluded:

> in every population there are hereditary inferiors in mind and in body as well as physical and mental deficients. . . . Our information definitely proves that it is from the physically inferior element of the population that native born criminals from native parentage are mainly derived.[28]

Like his positivist predecessors, Hooten argued for the segregation of those he referred to as the "criminal stock," and he recommended their sterilization as well.[29]

The Somatotype School

In the search for the source of criminality, other scientists, too, looked for the elusive link between physical characteristics and crime. The **somatotype school of criminology,** which related body build to behavior, became popular during the first half of the twentieth century. It originated with the work of a German psychiatrist, Ernst Kretschmer (1888–1964), who distinguished three principal types of physiques: (1) the asthenic—lean, slightly built, narrow shoulders; (2) the athletic—medium to tall, strong, muscular, coarse bones; and (3) the pyknic—medium height, rounded figure, massive neck, broad face. He then related these physical types to various psychic disorders: pyknics to manic depression, asthenics and athletics to schizophrenia, and so on.[30]

Kretschmer's work was brought to the United States by William Sheldon (1898–1977), who formulated his own group of somatotypes: the *endomorph,* the *mesomorph,* and the *ectomorph.* Sheldon's father was a dog breeder who judged animals in competition, and Sheldon worked out a point system of his own for judging humans. Thus one could actually measure on a scale from 1 to 7 the relative dominance of each body type in any given individual. People with predominantly mesomorph traits (physically powerful, aggressive, athletic physiques), he argued, tend more than others to be involved in illegal behavior.[31] This finding was later supported by Sheldon Glueck (1896–1980) and Eleanor Glueck (1898–1972), who based their studies of delinquents on William Sheldon's somatotypes.[32]

By and large, studies based on somatotyping have been sharply criticized for methodological flaws, including nonrepresentative selection of their samples (bias), failure to account for cultural stereotyping (our expectations of how muscular, physically active people should react), and poor statistical analyses. An anthropologist summed up the negative response of the scientific community by suggesting that somatotyping was "a New Phrenology in which the bumps on the buttocks take the place of the bumps on the skulls."[33] After World War II, somatotyping seemed too close to **eugenics** (the science of controlled reproduction to improve hereditary qualities), and the approach fell into disfavor. During the 1960s, however, the discovery of an extra sex chromosome in some criminal samples (see Chapter 4) revived interest in this theory.

Inherited Criminality

During the period when some researchers were measuring skulls and bodies of criminals in their search for the physical determinants of crime, others were arguing that criminality was an inherited trait passed on in the genes. To support the theory, they traced family histories. Richard Dugdale (1841–1883), for example, studied the lives of more than a thousand members of the family he called "Jukes." His interest in the family began when he found six related people in a jail in upstate New York. Following one branch of the family, the descendants of Ada Jukes, whom he referred to as the "mother of criminals," Dugdale found among the thousand of them 280 paupers, 60 thieves, 7 murderers, 40 other criminals, 40 persons with venereal disease, and 50 prostitutes.

His findings indicated, Dugdale claimed, that since some families produce generations of criminals, they must be transmitting a degenerate trait down the line.[34] A similar conclusion was reached by Henry Goddard (1866–1957). In a study of the family tree of a Revolutionary War soldier, Martin Kallikak, Goddard found many more criminals among the descendants of Kallikak's illegitimate son than among the descendants of his son by a later marriage with "a woman of his own quality."[35]

These early studies have been discredited primarily on the grounds that genetic and environmental influences could not be separated. But in the early twentieth century they were taken quite seriously. On the assumption that crime could be

AT ISSUE
Somatotyping: A Physique for Crime?

In 1949 the physician William H. Sheldon reported that 200 boys living in Boston's Hayden Goodwill Inn had body builds significantly different from a control group of 4000 college students.

Sheldon's Body Types

Sheldon classified physiques into three categories: mesomorphs, ectomorphs, and endomorphs. A mesomorph tends to be muscular, strong, heavy-boned, and firm; an ectomorph is fragile, thin, and delicate; and an endomorph has a predominance of soft roundness throughout the body. Sheldon used his classifications to show that body types were related to behavior, temperament, and even life expectancy.

Sheldon's 200 young males included alcoholics, mental defectives, and psychopaths, nondelinquents and criminals. He found that the criminal types were more mesomorphic.

A follow-up study of these 200 youths 30 years later identified 14 "primary criminals," individuals who had felony convictions as adults. These persistent criminals were relatively mesomorphic, compared with the others.

Somatotyping: Pro and Con

In *Crime and Human Nature* (1985), James Q. Wilson and Richard J. Herrnstein evaluated a number of studies relating physique to delinquency, including Sheldon's. They stated: "[T]he main conclusions have been confirmed wherever they have been tested, despite the initial skepticism of criminologists."(1)

Somatotyping is not without its critics. In an extensive review of Wilson and Herrnstein's conclusions, Leon J. Kamin ridicules their presentation of the topic, claiming that they completely ignore a number of studies that have appeared since 1949.(2)

Wilson and Herrnstein themselves present information that raises questions about the value of somatotyping to criminology. They cite studies in which, while the tendency toward the mesomorphic was clear, "mesomorphs could be found among the nondelinquents and ectomorphs among the delinquents." And they emphasize the difference between correlation and causation, stating clearly, "Physique does not cause crime."(1)

The Continuing Questions

If physique *is* correlated with crime, what does that mean? Kamin warns against drawing illogical conclusions and compares searching for a genetic basis to crime via somatotyping studies to finding a genetic link to unemployment on the basis of race:

> This kind of logic asserts that should it turn out that people with black skin make up a disproportion of the unemployed, we are on the trail of a genetic correlate of unemployment—just because black skin has a genetic basis. . . .(2)

Psychologists today list impulsivity, inability to defer gratification, and fearlessness as characteristics of the criminal personality. Could there be a link between physique and personality that explains the correlation between physique and crime? With the current interest in genetic explanations of criminal behavior, perhaps somatotyping will be examined again and the questions surrounding it resolved.

Sources

1. James Q. Wilson and Richard J. Herrnstein, *Crime and Human Nature* (New York: Simon & Schuster, 1985), p. 87.
2. Leon J. Kamin, "Crime and Human Nature," *Scientific American* 254: 22, February 1986.

Questions for Discussion

1. What makes the search for a genetic basis to crime such a sensitive issue?
2. If criminals were shown conclusively to be "skewed toward the mesomorph," what use might crime prevention strategists make of such information?

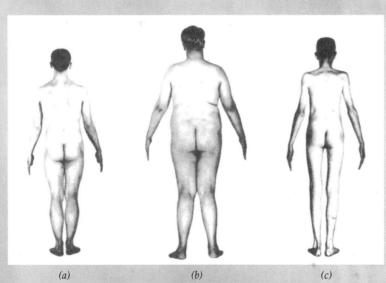

(a)   (b)   (c)

Sheldon's body types: (A) mesomorphic, (B) endomorphic, (C) ectomorphic.

controlled if criminals could be prevented from transmitting their traits to the next generation, some states permitted the sterilization of habitual offenders. Sterilization laws were held constitutional by the U.S. Supreme Court in a 1927 opinion written by Justice Oliver Wendell Holmes, Jr., which included the following well-known pronouncement:

> It is better for all the world, if instead of waiting to execute degenerate offspring for crime, or to let them starve for their imbecility, society can prevent those who are manifestly unfit from continuing their kind. . . . Three generations of imbeciles are enough.[36]

Clearly the early positivists, with their focus on physical characteristics, exerted great influence. They were destined to be overshadowed, though, by investigators who focused on psychological characteristics.

PSYCHOLOGICAL DETERMINISM

On the whole, scholars who investigated criminal behavior in the nineteenth and early twentieth centuries were far more interested in the human body than in the human mind. During that period, however, several contributions were made in the area of psychological explanations of crime. Some of the earliest contributions came from physicians interested primarily in the legal responsibility of the criminally insane. Later on, psychologists entered the field and applied their new testing techniques to the study of offenders (see Chapter 4).

Pioneers in Criminal Psychology

Isaac Ray (1807–1881), acknowledged to be America's first forensic psychiatrist, was interested throughout his life in the application of psychiatric principles to the law. He is best known as the author of *The Medical Jurisprudence of Insanity*, a treatise on criminal responsibility that was widely quoted and influential.[37] In it he defended the concept of "moral insanity," a disorder first described in 1806 by the French humanitarian and psychiatrist Philippe Pinel (1745–1826).[38] "Moral insanity" was a term used

to describe persons who were normal in all respects except that something was wrong with the part of the brain that regulates affective responses. Ray questioned whether we could hold people legally responsible for their acts if they had such an impairment, because such people committed their crimes without an intent to do so.

Born in the same year as Lombroso, Henry Maudsley (1835–1918), a brilliant English medical professor, shared Ray's concerns about criminal responsibility. According to Maudsley, some people may be considered either "insane or criminal according to the standpoint from which they are looked at." He believed that for many persons crime is an "outlet in which their unsound tendencies are discharged; they would go mad if they were not criminals."[39] Most of Maudsley's attention focused on the borderline between insanity and crime.

Psychological Studies of Criminals

Around the turn of the twentieth century, psychologists used their new measurement techniques to study offenders. The administering of intelligence tests to inmates of jails, prisons, and other public institutions was especially popular at that time, because it was a period of major controversy over the relation of mental deficiency to criminal behavior. The new technique seemed to provide an objective basis for differentiating criminals from noncriminals.

In 1914 Henry H. Goddard (1866–1957), research director of the Vineland, New Jersey, Training School for the Retarded, examined some intelligence tests that had been given to inmates and concluded that 25 to 50 percent of the people in prison had intellectual defects that made them incapable of managing their own affairs.[40] This idea remained dominant until it was challenged by the results of intelligence tests administered to World War I draftees, whose scores were found to be lower than those of prisoners in the federal penitentiary at Leavenworth. As a result of this study and others like it, intelligence quotient (IQ) measures largely disappeared as a basis for explaining criminal behavior.

SOCIOLOGICAL DETERMINISM

During the nineteenth and early twentieth centuries, some scholars began to search for the social determinants of criminal behavior. The approach had its roots in Europe in the 1830s, the time between Beccaria's *On Crimes and Punishment* and Lombroso's *The Criminal Man.*

Adolphe Quételet and André Michel Guerry

The Belgian mathematician Adolphe Quételet (1796–1874) and the French lawyer André Michel Guerry (1802–1866) were among the first scholars to repudiate the classicists' free-will doctrine. Working independently on the relation of crime statistics to such factors as poverty, age, sex, race, and climate, both scholars concluded that society, not the decisions of individual offenders, was responsible for criminal behavior.

The first modern criminal statistics were published in France in 1827. Guerry used those statistics to demonstrate that crime rates varied with social factors. He found, for example, that the wealthiest region of France had the highest rate of property crime but only half the national rate of violent crime. He concluded that the main factor in property crime was opportunity: there was much more to steal in the richer provinces.

Quételet did an elaborate analysis of crime in France, Belgium, and Holland. After analyzing criminal statistics, which he called "moral statistics," he concluded that if we look at overall patterns of behavior of groups across a whole society, we find a startling regularity of rates of various behaviors. According to Quételet:

> We can enumerate in advance how many individuals will soil their hands in the blood of their fellows, how many will be frauds, how many prisoners; almost as one can enumerate in advance the births and deaths that will take place.[41]

By focusing on groups rather than individuals, he discovered that behavior is indeed predictable, regular, and understandable. Just as the physical world is governed by the laws of nature, human behavior is governed by forces external to the individual. The more we learn about those forces, the easier it becomes to predict behavior. A major goal of criminological research, according to Quételet, should be to identify factors related to crime and to assign to them their "proper degree of influence."[42] Though neither he nor Guerry offered a theory of criminal behavior, the fact that both studied social factors scientifically, using quantitative research methods, made them key figures in the subsequent development of sociological theories of crime causation.

Gabriel Tarde

One of the earliest sociological theories of criminal behavior was formulated by Gabriel Tarde (1843–1904), who served 15 years as a provincial judge and then was placed in charge of France's national statistics. After an extensive analysis of these statistics, he came to the following conclusion:

> The majority of murderers and notorious thieves began as children who had been abandoned, and the true seminary of crime must be sought for upon each public square or each crossroad of our towns, whether they be small or large, in those flocks of pillaging street urchins who, like bands of sparrows, associate together, at first for marauding, and then for theft, because of a lack of education and food in their homes.[43]

Tarde rejected the Lombrosian theory of biological abnormality, which was popular in his time, arguing that criminals were normal people who learned crime just as others learned legitimate trades. He formulated his theory in terms of **laws of imitation**—principles that governed the process by which people became criminals. According to Tarde's thesis, individuals emulate behavior patterns in much the same way that they copy styles of dress. Moreover, there is a pattern to the way such emulation takes place: (1) individuals imitate others in proportion to the intensity and frequency of their contacts; (2) inferiors imitate superiors—that is, trends flow from town to country and from upper to lower classes; and (3) when two behavior patterns clash, one may take the place of the other, as when guns largely replaced knives as murder weapons.[44]

Tarde's work served as the basis for Edwin Sutherland's theory of differential association, which we shall examine in Chapter 5.

Émile Durkheim

Modern criminologists take two major approaches to the study of the social factors associated with crime. Tarde's approach asks how individuals become criminal. What is the process? How are behavior patterns learned and transmitted? The second major approach looks at the social structure and its institutions. It asks how crime arises in the first place and how it is related to the functioning of a society. For answers to these questions, scholars begin with the work of Émile Durkheim (1858–1917).

Of all nineteenth-century writers on the relationship between crime and social factors, none has more powerfully influenced contemporary criminology than Durkheim, who is universally acknowledged as one of the founders of sociology. On October 12, 1870, when Durkheim was 12 years old, the German army invaded and occupied his hometown, Epinal, in eastern France. Thus at a very early age he witnessed social chaos and the effects of rapid change, topics with which he remained preoccupied throughout his life. At the age of 24 he became a professor of philosophy, and at 29 he joined the faculty of the University of Bordeaux. There he taught the first course in sociology ever to be offered by a French university.

By 1902 he had moved to the University of Paris, where he completed his doctoral studies. His *Division of Social Labor* became a landmark work on the organization of societies. According to Durkheim, crime is as normal a part of society as birth and death. Theoretically, crime could disappear altogether only if all members of society had the same values, and such standardization is neither possible nor desirable. Furthermore, some crime is in fact necessary if a society is to progress:

> The opportunity for the genius to carry out his work affords the criminal his originality at a lower level. . . . According to Athenian law, Socrates was a criminal, and his condemnation was no more than just. However, his crime, namely, the independence

of his thought, rendered a service not only to humanity but to his country.[45]

Durkheim further pointed out that all societies have not only crime but sanctions. The rationale for the sanctions varies in accordance with the structure of the society. In a strongly cohesive society, punishment of members who deviate is used to reinforce the value system—to remind people of what is right and what is wrong—thereby preserving the pool of common belief and the solidarity of the society. Punishment must be harsh to serve these ends. In a large, urbanized, heterogeneous society, on the other hand, punishment is used not to preserve solidarity but rather to right the wrong done to a victim. Punishment thus is evaluated in accordance with the harm done, with the goal of restitution and reinstatement of order as quickly as possible. The offense is not considered a threat to social cohesion, primarily because in a large, complex society criminal events do not even come to the attention of most people.

The most important of Durkheim's many contributions to contemporary sociology is his concept of **anomie,** a breakdown of social order as a result of a loss of standards and values. In a society plagued by anomie (see Chapter 5), disintegration and chaos replace social cohesion.

HISTORICAL AND CONTEMPORARY CRIMINOLOGY: A TIMELINE

Classical criminologists thought the problem of crime might be solved through limitations on governmental power, the abolition of brutality, and the creation of a more equitable system of justice. They argued that the punishment should fit the crime. For over a century this perspective dominated criminology. Later on, positivist criminologists influenced judges to give greater consideration to the offender than to the gravity of the crime when imposing sentences. The current era marks a return to the classical demand that the punishment correspond to the seriousness of the crime and the guilt of the offender. Table 3.1 presents a chronology of all the pioneers in criminology we have discussed.

TABLE 3.1 PIONEERS IN CRIMINOLOGY: A CHRONOLOGY

Classical Criminology	Positivist Criminology		
Free Will	Biological Determinism	Psychological Determinism	Social Determinism
Cesare Beccaria (1738–1794) Wrote first coherent comprehensive design for an enlightened criminal justice system based on law rather than arbitrary decisions.	Johann Kaspar Lavater (1741–1801) Early biological approach to crime causation. Developed phrenology, the study of the relationship between bumps on the brain's outer surface and psychological traits.		
Jeremy Bentham (1748–1832) Developed utilitarian principles of punishment based on the amount of happiness (pleasure) or unhappiness (pain) any given act will bring to the actor.	Franz Joseph Gall (1758–1828) Early biological approach to crime causation. Further developed phrenology.		
	Johann Kaspar Spurzheim (1776–1832) Early biological approach. Continued studies of phrenology.		
			Adolphe Quételet (1796–1874) Made early attempt to repudiate free-will doctrine of classicists. Studied social determinants of behavior.
			August Comte (1798–1857) Brought modern scientific methods of the physical sciences into the social sciences.
		Isaac Ray (1807–1881) Questioned whether people who were "morally insane" could be held legally responsible for their acts.	André Michel Guerry (1802–1866) Made early attempt to repudiate free-will doctrine of classicists. Related crime statistics to social factors.

TABLE 3.1 (Continued)

Classical Criminology	Positivist Criminology		
Free Will	Biological Determinism	Psychological Determinism	Social Determinism
	Charles Darwin (1809–1882) Formulated theory of evolution, which challenged theological teaching and changed explanations of human behavior.		
	Cesare Lombroso (1835–1909) Replaced free will with determinism as the explanatory factor in criminal behavior. Posited the "born criminal." Shifted attention from act to actor. Father of modern criminology.	**Henry Maudsley** (1835–1918) Pioneered criteria for legal responsibility.	
	Richard Dugdale (1841–1883) Related criminal behavior to inherited traits (Jukes family).		**Gabriel Tarde** (1843–1904) Explained crime as learned behavior.
	Raffaele Garofalo (1852–1934) Traced roots of criminal behavior to "moral anomalies" rather than to physical stigmata.		
	Enrico Ferri (1856–1929) Produced first penal code based on principles of positivism. Replaced "moral responsibility" with social accountability.	**Henry H. Goddard** (1866–1957) Related criminal behavior to intelligence levels (Kallikak family).	**Émile Durkheim** (1858–1917) A founder of sociology. Developed theory of anomie, idea that crime is "normal" in all societies, relation between social change and behavior, etc.

TABLE 3.1   (Continued)

Classical Criminology		Positivist Criminology		
Free Will	Biological Determinism	Psychological Determinism	Social Determinism
			Charles Buckman Goring (1870–1919)
			Used empirical research to refute Lombroso's theory of criminal types.
	Ernest Hooten (1887–1954)		
	Related criminality to hereditary inferiority.		
	Ernst Kretschmer (1888–1964)		
	Introduced the somatotype (body build) school of criminology.		
	William Sheldon (1898–1977)		
	Related body types to illegal behavior.		

As modern science discovered more and more about cause and effect in the physical and social universes, the theory that individuals commit crimes of their own free will began to lose favor. The positivists searched for determinants of crime in biological, psychological, and social factors. Biologically based theories were popular in the late nineteenth century, fell out of favor in the early part of the twentieth, and emerged again in the 1970s (see Chapter 4) with studies of hormone imbalances, diet, environmental contaminants, and so forth. Since the studies of criminal responsibility in the nineteenth century centering on the insanity defense and of intelligence levels in the twentieth, psychiatrists and psychologists have continued to play a major role in the search for the causes of crime, especially after Sigmund Freud developed his well-known theory of human personality (Chapter 4). The sociological perspective became popular in the 1920s and has remained the predominant approach of criminological studies. (We will examine contemporary theories in Chapters 5 through 8.)

■ REVIEW

In the history of criminology from ancient times to the early twentieth century, its many themes at times have clashed and at times have supported one another. There is no straight-line evolutionary track that we can follow from the inception of the first "criminological" thought to modern theories (see Table 3.1). Some scholars concentrated on criminal law and procedure, others on criminal behavior. Some took the biological route, others the psychological, still others the sociological, and the work of some investigators has encompassed a combination of factors. Toward the end of the nineteenth century a discipline began to emerge.

Tracing the major developments back in time helps us to understand how criminology grew into the discipline we know today. Many of the issues that appear on the intellectual battlefields as we approach the twenty-first century are the same issues our academic ancestors grappled with for hundreds, indeed thousands, of years. With each new clash, some old concepts died, but most were incorporated within competing doctrinal boundaries, there to remain until the next challenge. The controversies of one era become the foundations of knowledge for the next. As societies develop and are subjected to new technologies, the crime problem becomes ever more complex. So do the questions it raises. In Part II we will see how twentieth-century theorists have dealt with them.

■ NOTES

1. First quote: attributed to Socrates by Plato, wording unconfirmed by researchers; see *Respectfully Quoted*, ed. Suzy Platt (Washington, D.C.: Library of Congress, 1989), p. 42. Second quote: Sophocles, *Antigone*, I, 720. Third quote: Plato, *The Republic*, I, 343 d.

2. Leon Radzinowicz, *Ideology and Crime* (New York: Columbia University Press, 1966), p. 2; Marc Ancel, Introduction to *The French Penal Code*, ed. G. O. W. Mueller (South Hackensack, N.J.: Fred B. Rothman, 1960), pp. 1–2.

3. Thorsten Sellin, *Slavery and the Penal System* (New York: Elsevier, 1976); Thorsten Eriksson, *The Reformers: An Historical Survey of Pioneer Experiments in the Treatment of Criminals* (New York: Elsevier, 1976).

4. Marcello T. Maestro, *Cesare Beccaria and the Origins of Penal Reform* (Philadelphia: Temple University Press, 1973), p. 16.

5. George Rude, *The Crowd in the French Revolution* (New York: Oxford University Press, 1959), appendix.

6. Harry Elmer Barnes, *The Story of Punishment: A Record of Man's Inhumanity to Man*, 2d ed. (Montclair, N.J.: Patterson Smith, 1972), p. 99.

7. Cesare Beccaria, *On Crimes and Punishment*, 2d ed., trans. Edward D. Ingraham (Philadelphia: Philip H. Nicklin, 1819), pp. 15, 20, 22–23, 30–32, 60, 74–75, 80, 97–98, 149, 156. For a debate on the contribution of Beccaria to modern criminology, see G. O. W. Mueller, "Whose Prophet Is Cesare Beccaria? An Essay on the Origins of Criminological Theory,"

Advances in Criminological Theory, **2** (1990): 1–14; Graeme Newman and Pietro Marongiu, "Penological Reform and the Myth of Beccaria," *Criminology*, **28** (1990): 325–346; and Piers Beirne, "Inventing Criminology: The 'Science of Man,' in Cesare Beccaria's *Dei delitti e delle pene*," *Criminology*, **29** (1991): 777–820.

8. Marcello T. Maestro, *Voltaire and Beccaria as Reformers of Criminal Law* (New York: Columbia University Press, 1942), p. 73.

9. Jeremy Bentham, *A Fragment on Government and an Introduction to the Principles of Morals and Legislation*, ed. Wilfred Harrison (Oxford: Basil Blackwell, 1967), p. 21.

10. Barnes, *The Story of Punishment*, p. 102.

11. Quoted in Leon Radzinowicz, *A History of English Criminal Law and Its Administration from 1750*, vol. 1 (New York: Macmillan, 1948), p. 330.

12. Charles Darwin, *Origin of Species* (1854; Cambridge, Mass.: Harvard University Press, 1859); Charles Darwin, *The Descent of Man and Selection in Relation to Sex* (1871; New York: A. L. Burt, 1874).

13. Havelock Ellis, *The Criminal*, 2d ed. (New York: Scribner, 1900), p. 27.

14. Christopher Hibbert, *The Roots of Evil* (Boston: Little, Brown, 1963), p. 187.

15. Arthur E. Fink, *The Causes of Crime: Biological Theories in the United States, 1800–1915* (Philadelphia: University of Pennsylvania Press, 1938), p. 1.

16. Hermann Mannheim, *Comparative Criminology* (Boston: Houghton Mifflin, 1965), p. 213.

17. George B. Vold, *Theoretical Criminology* (New York: Oxford University Press, 1958), pp. 44–49.

18. Gina Lombroso Ferrero, *Criminal Man: According to the Classification of Cesare Lombroso*, with an Introduction by Cesare Lombroso (1911; Montclair, N.J.: Patterson Smith, 1972), pp. xxiv–xxv.

19. Cesare Lombroso and William Ferrero, *The Female Offender* (New York: Appleton, 1895), pp. 151–152.

20. Cesare Lombroso, *Crime, Its Causes and Remedies* (Boston: Little, Brown, 1918).

21. Marvin Wolfgang, "Cesare Lombroso," in *Pioneers in Criminology*, ed. Hermann Mannheim (London: Stevens, 1960), p. 168.

22. Thorsten Sellin, "The Lombrosian Myth in Criminology," *American Journal of Sociology*, **42** (1937): 898–899. For Lombroso's impact on American anthropological criminology, see Nicole Hahn Rafter, "Criminal Anthropology in the United States," *Criminology*, **30** (1992): 525–545.

23. Wolfgang, "Cesare Lombroso."

24. Thorsten Sellin, "Enrico Ferri: Pioneer in Criminology, 1856–1929," in *The Positive School of Criminology: Three Lectures by Enrico Ferri*, ed. Stanley E. Grupp (Pittsburgh: University of Pittsburgh Press, 1968), p. 13.

25. Raffaele Garofalo, *Criminology*, trans. Robert Wyness Millar (Montclair, N.J.: Patterson Smith, 1968), pp. 4–5.

26. Marc Ancel, *Social Defense: The Future of Penal Reform* (Littleton, Colo.: Fred B. Rothman, 1987).

27. Charles B. Goring, *The English Convict: A Statistical Study* (London: His Majesty's Stationery Office, 1913), p. 145. For a critique of Goring's work, see Piers Beirne, "Heredity versus Environment," *British Journal of Criminology*, **28** (1988): 315–339.

28. E. A. Hooten, *The American Criminal* (Cambridge, Mass.: Harvard University Press, 1939), p. 308.

29. E. A. Hooten, *Crime and the Man* (Cambridge, Mass.: Harvard University Press, 1939), p. 13.

30. Ernst Kretschmer, *Physique and Character* (New York: Harcourt Brace, 1926).

31. William H. Sheldon, *Varieties of Delinquent Youth: An Introduction to Constitutional Psychiatry* (New York: Harper, 1949). See also Emil M. Hartl, Edward P. Monnelly, and Ronald D. Elderkin, *Physique and Delinquent Behavior: A Thirty-Year Follow-Up of William H. Sheldon's* Varieties of Delinquent Youth (New York: Academic Press, 1982).

32. Eleanor Glueck and Sheldon Glueck, *Unraveling Juvenile Delinquency* (Cambridge, Mass.: Harvard University Press, 1950). See also Sheldon Glueck and Eleanor Glueck, *Of Delinquency and Crime* (Springfield, Ill.: Charles C. Thomas, 1974), p. 2. For a recent reanalysis of the Gluecks' data, see John H. Laub and Robert J. Sampson, "Unravelling Families and Delinquency: A Reanalysis of the Gluecks' Data," *Criminology*, **26** (1988): 355–380. For a study of constitutional variables, see Juan B. Cortes and Florence M. Gatti, *Delinquency and Crime: A Biopsychosocial Approach* (New York: Seminar Press, 1972).

33. S. L. Washburn, Book Review: "*Varieties of Delinquent Youth, An Introduction to Constitutional Psychiatry*," *American Anthropologist*, **53** (1951): 561–563.

34. Richard L. Dugdale, *The Jukes: A Study in Crime, Pauperism, Disease, and Heredity*, 5th ed. (New York: Putnam, 1895), p. 8.

35. Henry H. Goddard, *The Kallikak Family: A Study in the Heredity of Feeble-Mindedness* (New York: Macmillan, 1912), p. 50.

36. *Buck v. Bell*, 274 U.S. 200, 207 (1927).

37. Isaac Ray, *The Medical Jurisprudence of Insanity* (Boston: Little, Brown, 1838).

38. Philippe Pinel, *A Treatise on Insanity* (1806; New York: Hafner, 1962). See also Jean Etienne Dominique Esquirol, *Mental Maladies: A Treatise on Insanity*, (1845; facs. ed. New York: Hafner, 1965), pp. 320–321; and James Cowles Prichard, *A Treatise on Insanity and Other Disorders Affecting the Mind* (New York: Arno, 1973).

39. Peter Scott, "Henry Maudsley," in *Journal of Criminal Law, Criminology, and Police Science*, **46** (March–April 1956): 753–769.

40. Henry H. Goddard, *The Criminal Imbecile* (New York: Macmillan, 1915), pp. 106–107.

41. Adolphe Quételet, *A Treatise on Man*, facs. ed. of 1842 ed., trans. Salomon Diamond (1835; Gainesville, Fla.: Scholars Facsimiles and Reprints, 1969), p. 97. For a discussion of the historical significance of Quételet, see Piers Beirne, "Adolphe Quételet and the Origins of Positivist Criminology," *American Journal of Sociology*, **92** (1987): 1140–1169.

42. Quételet, *A Treatise on Man*, p. 103. See also George von Mayr, as quoted in Gustav Aschaffenburg, *Crime and Its Repression* (Boston: Little, Brown, 1913), p. 106. For Quételet's influence on modern scholars, see Derral Cheatwood, "Is There a Season for Homicide?" *Criminology*, **26** (1988): 287–306.

43. Gabriel Tarde, *Penal Philosophy*, trans. R. Howell (Boston: Little, Brown, 1912), p. 252. On the ancient and widespread practice of abandoning children, which still flourished in the nineteenth century, see John Boswell, *The Kindness of Strangers* (New York: Pantheon, 1988).

44. Gabriel Tarde, *Social Laws: An Outline of Sociology* (New York: Macmillan, 1907).

45. Émile Durkheim, *The Rules of Sociological Method*, ed. George E. G. Catlin (Chicago: University of Chicago Press, 1938), p. 71.

Explanations of Criminal Behavior

Having explored the history of criminology, the early explanations of criminal behavior, and the scientific methods used by criminologists, we turn now to contemporary theories and research. Current explanations of criminal behavior focus on biological, psychological, social, and economic factors. Biological and psychological theories assume that criminal behavior results from underlying physical or mental conditions that distinguish criminals from noncriminals (Chapter 4). These theories yield insight into individual cases, but they do not explain why crime rates vary from place to place and from one situation to another.

Sociological theories seek to explain criminal behavior in terms of the environment. Chapter 5 examines strain and cultural deviance theories, which focus on the social forces that cause people to engage in criminal behavior. Both theories assume that social class and criminal behavior are related. Strain theorists argue that people commit crime because they are frustrated by not being able to achieve their goals through legitimate means. Cultural deviance theorists claim that crime is learned in socially disorganized neighborhoods where criminal norms are transmitted from one generation to the next. In Chapter 6 we examine subcultures that have their own norms, beliefs, and values, which differ significantly from those of the dominant culture. Chapter 7 explains how people remain committed to conventional behavior in the face of frustration, poor living conditions, and other criminogenic factors. Finally, in Chapter 8 we discuss three theoretical perspectives that focus on society's role in creating criminals and defining them as such.

4

Psychological and Biological Perspectives

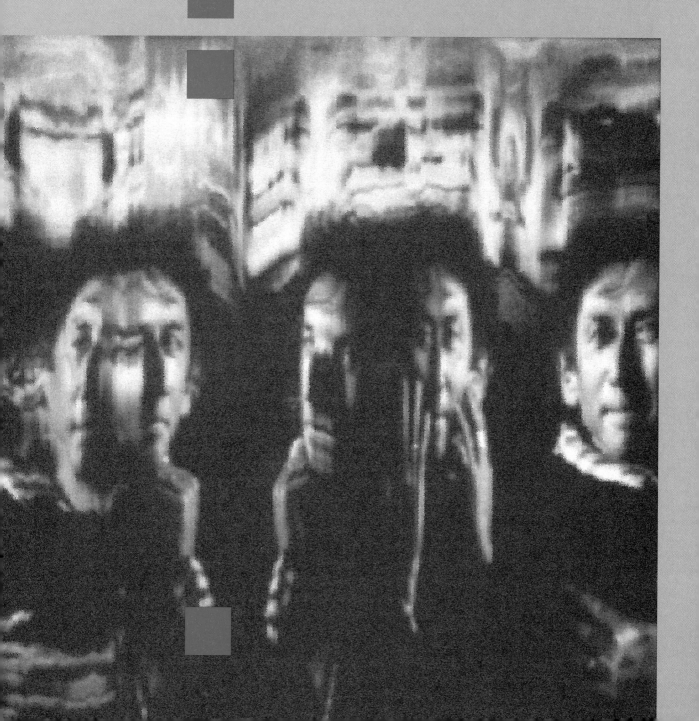

John W. Hinckley, Jr., began to withdraw from social relationships in adolescence. He found it difficult to establish and maintain friendships with anyone other than his family. As a young adult, while attending Texas Tech, he spent most of his day listening to music, reading, watching television, and playing the guitar. After less than 3 years of college, John dropped out. He moved to Hollywood with the hope of becoming a songwriter. It was in Hollywood that he developed a fascination with the movie *Taxi Driver* and one of its characters, Iris—a fascination that led him to see the film about 15 times. The movie had a complex plot, one that involved an alienated, lonely, and socially inept taxi driver who ends up planning to kill a presidential candidate over a failed relationship with one of the candidate's workers.

Early in 1979 Hinckley's outlook on life deteriorated. He was depressed over his parents' perceptions that he had failed to achieve his goals. He did not seem to have a purpose in life. In August 1979 he purchased a gun and later played Russian roulette. He complained of sleeplessness, weakness, and headaches.

In the latter part of 1980, John Hinckley went to New Haven, Connecticut, to visit Jodie Foster, the young actress who portrayed Iris in *Taxi Dri-*

ver. His goal was to establish a relationship with her. Over the next several months, he developed an obsession with Foster and considered the possibility of assassinating President Ronald Reagan. He wrote Foster love notes and also described his plan to assassinate the president. On March 30, 1981, as the nation watched television coverage of Reagan leaving a meeting, John Hinckley made his attempt: he shot and wounded the president, White House press secretary James Brady, a secret service agent, and a Washington police officer.

In the United States, explanations of criminal behavior have been dominated by sociological theories. These theories focus on lack of opportunity and the breakdown of the conventional value system in urban ghettos, the formation of subcultures whose norms deviate from those of the middle class, and the increasing inability of social institutions to exercise control over behavior. Criminological texts have treated psychological and biological theories as peripheral, perhaps because criminology's disciplinary allegiance is to sociology. When psychological theories were first advanced to explain criminal behavior, their emphasis was largely psychoanalytic, so they may have seemed not quantitative enough to some criminologists.[1] Others may have considered the early work of Lombroso, Goring, and Hooten too scientifically naive to be taken seriously.

Sociological theories focus on crime rates of groups that experience frustration in their efforts to achieve accepted goals, not on the particular individual who becomes a criminal. Sociological theories cannot explain how a person can be born in a slum, be exposed to family discord and abuse, never attend school, have friends who are delinquents, and yet resist opportunities for crime, while another person who grows up in an affluent suburban neighborhood in a two-parent home can end up firing a gun at the president. In other words, sociologists do not address individual differences.[2] Psychologists and biologists are interested in finding out what may account for individual differences.

It is clear that psychological, biological, and sociological explanations are not competing to answer the same specific questions. Rather, all three disciplines are searching for answers to dif-

ferent questions, even though they study the same act, status, or characteristic. We can understand crime in a society only if we view criminality from more than one level of analysis: why a certain individual commits a crime (psychological and biological explanations) and why some groups of individuals commit more or different criminal acts than other groups (sociological explanations).

Sociological theory and empirical research often ignore such factors as personality and human biology, almost as if they were irrelevant. And psychological theory often focuses on the individual with little regard for the fact that while each one of us comes into the world with certain predispositions, from the moment we are born we interact with others in complex situations that influence our behavior.

PSYCHOLOGY AND CRIMINALITY

Psychologists have considered a variety of possibilities to account for individual differences—defective conscience, emotional immaturity, inadequate childhood socialization, maternal deprivation, poor moral development. They study how aggression is learned, which situations promote violent or delinquent reactions, how crime is related to personality factors, and the association between various mental disorders and criminality.

Psychological Development

The **psychoanalytic theory** of criminality attributes delinquent and criminal behavior to a conscience so overbearing that it arouses feelings of guilt or so weak that it cannot control the individual's impulses and to a need for immediate gratification. Consider the case of Richard. Richard was 6 when he committed his first delinquent act: he stole a comic book from the corner drugstore. Three months before the incident his father, an alcoholic, had been killed in an automobile accident, and his mother, unable to care for the family, had abandoned the children.

For the next 10 years the county welfare agency moved Richard in and out of foster homes. During this time he actively pursued a

John W. Hinckley, Jr. holds a pistol to his head in this self-portrait. One of his letters to actress Jodie Foster was introduced as evidence to support his insanity defense.

life of crime, breaking into houses during daylight hours and stealing cars at night. By age 20, while serving a 10-year prison sentence for armed robbery, he had voluntarily entered psychoanalysis. After 2 years Richard's analyst suggested three reasons for his criminality:

1. Being caught and punished for stealing made him feel less guilty about hating his father and mother for abandoning him.
2. Stealing did not violate his moral and ethical principles.
3. Stealing resulted in immediate gratification and pleasure, both of which Richard had great difficulty resisting.

Sigmund Freud (1856–1939), the founder of psychoanalysis, suggested that criminality may result from an overactive conscience. In treating patients, Freud noticed that those who were suffering from unbearable guilt committed crimes in order to be apprehended and punished.[3] Once they had been punished, their feelings of guilt were relieved. Richard's psychoanalyst suggested that Richard's anger over his father's death and his mother's abandonment created unconscious feelings of guilt, which he sought to relieve by committing a crime and being punished for it.

The psychoanalyst also offered an alternative explanation for Richard's persistent criminal activities: his conscience was perhaps not too strong but too weak. The conscience, or **superego,** was so weak or defective that the **ego** (which acts as a moderator between superego and id) was unable to control the impulses of the **id** (the part of the personality that contains powerful urges and drives for gratification and satisfaction). Because the superego is essentially an internalized parental image, developed when the child assumes the parents' attitudes and moral values, it follows that the absence of such an image may lead to an unrestrained id and thus to delinquency.[4]

Psychoanalytic theory suggests yet another explanation for Richard's behavior: an insatiable need for immediate reward and gratification. A defect in the character formation of delinquents drives them to satisfy their desires at once, regardless of the consequences.[5] This urge, which psychoanalysts attribute to the id, is so strong that relationships with people are important only so long as they help to satisfy it. Most analysts view delinquents as children unable to give up their desire for instant pleasure.

The psychoanalytic approach is still one of the most prominent explanations for both normal and asocial functioning. Despite criticism,[6] three basic principles still appeal to psychologists who study criminality:

1. The actions and behavior of an adult are understood in terms of childhood development.

2. Behavior and unconscious motives are intertwined, and their interaction must be unraveled if we are to understand criminality.

3. Criminality is essentially a representation of psychological conflict.

Despite their appeal, psychoanalytic treatment techniques devised to address these principles have been controversial since their introduction by Freud and his disciples. The controversy has involved questions about improvement following treatment and, perhaps more important, the validity of the hypothetical conflicts the treatment presupposes.

Moral Development

Consider the following moral dilemma:

> In Europe, a woman is near death from a special kind of cancer. There is one drug that the doctors think might save her. It is a form of radium that a druggist in the same town has recently discovered. The drug is expensive to make, and the druggist is charging ten times that cost. He paid $200 for the radium and is charging $2,000 for a small dose of the drug. The sick woman's husband, Heinz, goes to everyone he knows to borrow the money, but he can get together only $1,000. He tells the druggist that his wife is dying and asks him to sell the drug more cheaply or to let him pay later. The druggist says, "No, I discovered the drug and I'm going to make money from it." Heinz is desperate and considers breaking into the man's store to steal the drug for his wife.[7]

This classic dilemma sets up complex moral issues. While you may know that it is wrong to steal, you may believe that this is a situation in which the law should be circumvented. Or is it always wrong to steal, no matter what the circumstances? Regardless of what you decide, the way you reach the decision about whether or not to steal reveals much about your moral development.

The psychologist Lawrence Kohlberg, who pioneered moral developmental theory, has found that moral reasoning develops in three phases.[8] In the first, the *preconventional level*, children's moral rules and moral values consist of dos and don'ts to avoid punishment. A desire to avoid punishment and a belief in the superior power of authorities are the two central reasons for doing what is right. According to the theory, until the ages of 9 to 11, children usually reason at this level. They think, in effect, "If I steal, what are my chances of getting caught and being punished?"

Adolescents typically reason at the *conventional level*. Now individuals believe in and have adopted the values and rules of society. Moreover, they seek to uphold these rules. They think, in effect, "It is illegal to steal and therefore I should not steal, under any circumstances." Finally, at the *postconventional level*, individuals examine customs and social rules according to their own sense of universal human rights, moral principles, and duties. They think, in effect, "One must live within the law, but certain universal ethical principles, such as respect for human rights and for the dignity of human life, supersede the written law when the two conflict." This level of moral reasoning is generally seen in adults after the age of 20. (See Table 4.1.)

According to Kohlberg and his colleagues, most delinquents and criminals reason at the preconventional level. Low moral development or preconventional reasoning alone, however, does not result in criminality. Other factors, such as the presence or the absence of significant social bonds, may play a part. Kohlberg has argued that basic moral principles and social norms are learned through social interaction and role playing. In essence, children learn how to be moral by reasoning with others who are at a higher level of moral development.[9]

Students of Kohlberg have looked at practical applications of his theory. What would happen, for instance, if delinquents who were poor moral reasoners were exposed to individuals who reasoned at a higher level? Joseph Hickey, William Jennings, and their associates designed programs for Connecticut and Florida prisons and applied them in school systems throughout the United States. The "just-community intervention" approach involves a structured educational curriculum stressing democracy, fairness, and a sense of community. Above all, the focus is on the growth and development of moral reasoning. A series of evaluations of just-community programs has revealed significant improvement in moral development.[10]

Maternal Deprivation and Attachment Theory

In a well-known psychological experiment, infant monkeys were provided with the choice between two wire "monkeys." One, made of uncovered cage wire, dispensed milk. The other, made of cage wire covered with soft fabric, did not give milk. The infant monkeys in the experiment gravitated to the warm cloth monkey, which provided comfort and security even though it did not provide food. What does this have to do with criminality? Research has demonstrated that a phenomenon important to social development takes place shortly after the birth of any mammal: the construction of an emotional bond between the infant and its mother. The strength of this emotional bond, or **attachment,** will determine, or at least materially affect, a child's ability to form attachments in the future. In order to form a successful attachment, a child needs a warm, loving, and interactive caretaker.

Studies of Attachment

The psychologist John Bowlby has studied both the need for warmth and affection from birth onward and the consequences of not having it. He has proposed a theory of attachment with seven important features:

- *Specificity:* Attachments are selective, usually directed to one or more individuals in some order of preference.
- *Duration:* Attachments endure and persist, sometimes throughout the life cycle.
- *Engagement of emotion:* Some of the most intense emotions are associated with attachment relationships.
- *Ontogeny* (course of development): Children form an attachment to one primary figure in the first 9 months of life. That principal attachment figure is the person who supplies the most social interaction of a satisfying kind.
- *Learning:* Though learning plays a role in the development of attachment, Bowlby finds that attachments are the products not of rewards or reinforcements but of basic social interaction.

- *Organization:* Attachment behavior follows a developmental organization from birth onward.
- *Biological function:* Attachment behavior has a biological function—survival. It is found in almost all species of mammals and in birds.[11]

Bowlby contends that a child needs to experience a warm, intimate, and continuous relationship with either a mother or a mother substitute in order to be securely attached. When a child is separated from the mother or is rejected by her, anxious attachment results, and the capacity to be affectionate and to develop intimate relationships with others is reduced. Habitual criminals, it is claimed, typically have an inability to form bonds of affection:

> More often than not the childhoods of such individuals are found to have been grossly disturbed by death, divorce, or separation of the parents, or by other events resulting in disruption of bonds, with an incidence of such disturbance far higher than is met with in any other comparable group, whether drawn from the general population or from psychiatric casualties of other sorts.[12]

Considerable research supports the relationship between anxious attachment and subsequent behavioral problems:

- In a study of 113 middle-class children observed at 1 year and again at 6 years, researchers noted a significant relationship between behavior at age 6 and attachment at age 1.[13]
- In a study of 40 children seen when they were 1 year old and again at 18 months, it was noted that anxiously attached children were less empathetic, independent, compliant, and confident than securely attached children.[14]
- Researchers have noted that the quality of one's attachment correlates significantly with asocial preschool behavior—being aggressive, leaving the group, and the like.[15]

Family Atmosphere and Delinquency

Criminologists also have examined the effects of the mother's absence, whether because of death, divorce, or abandonment. Does her absence cause delinquency? Empirical research is

TABLE 4.1   KOHLBERG'S SEQUENCE OF MORAL REASONING

Level	Stage	Sample Moral Reasoning	
		In Favor of Stealing	*Against Stealing*
Level 1: Precon-ventional morality. At this level, the concrete interests of the individual are considered in terms of rewards and punishments.	*Stage 1: Obedience and punishment orientation.* At this stage, people stick to rules in order to avoid punishment, and there is obedience for its own sake.	If you let your wife die, you will get in trouble. You'll be blamed for not spending the money to save her, and there'll be an investigation of you and the druggist for your wife's death.	You shouldn't steal the drug because you'll be caught and sent to jail if you do. If you do get away, your conscience will bother you, thinking how the police will catch up with you at any minute.
	Stage 2: Reward orientation. At this stage, rules are followed only for one's own benefit. Obedience occurs because of rewards that are received.	If you do happen to get caught, you could give the drug back and you wouldn't get much of a sentence. It wouldn't bother you much to serve a little jail term, if you have your wife when you get out.	You may not get much of a jail term if you steal the drug, but your wife will probably die before you get out, so it won't do much good. If your wife dies, you shouldn't blame yourself; it wasn't your fault she had cancer.
Level 2: Conventional morality. At this level, moral problems are approached as a member of society. People are interested in pleasing others by acting as good members of society.	*Stage 3: "Good boy" morality.* Individuals at this stage show an interest in maintaining the respect of others and doing what is expected of them.	No one will think you're bad if you steal the drug, but your family will think you're an inhuman husband if you don't. If you let your wife die, you'll never be able to look anybody in the face again.	It isn't just the druggist who will think you're a criminal; everyone else will too. After you steal it, you'll feel bad, thinking how you've brought dishonor on your family and yourself; you won't be able to face anyone again.
	Stage 4: Authority and social-order-maintaining morality. People at this stage conform to society's rules and consider that "right" is what society defines as right.	If you have any sense of honor, you won't let your wife die just because you're afraid to do the only thing that will save her. You'll always feel guilty that you caused her death if you don't do your duty to her.	You're desperate and you may not know you're doing wrong when you steal the drug. But you'll know you did wrong after you're sent to jail. You'll always feel guilty for your dishonesty and lawbreaking.

equivocal. Perhaps the most persuasive evidence comes from longitudinal research conducted by Joan McCord, who has investigated the relationship between family atmosphere (such as parental self-confidence, deviance, and affection) and delinquency.

In one study, she collected data on the childhood homes of 201 men and their subsequent

TABLE 4.1 KOHLBERG'S SEQUENCE OF MORAL REASONING (Continued)

Level	Stage	Sample Moral Reasoning	
		In Favor of Stealing	*Against Stealing*
Level 3: Postconventional morality. People at this level use moral principles which are seen as broader than those of any particular society.	*Stage 5: Morality of contract, individual rights, and democratically accepted law.* People at this stage do what is right because of a sense of obligation to laws which are agreed upon within society. They perceive that laws can be modified as part of changes in an implicit social contract.	You'll lose other people's respect, not gain it, if you don't steal. If you let your wife die, it will be out of fear, not out of reasoning. So you'll just lose self-respect and probably the respect of others too.	You'll lose your standing and respect in the community and violate the law. You'll lose respect for yourself if you're carried away by emotion and forget the long-range point of view.
	Stage 6: Morality of individual principles and conscience. At this final stage, a person follows laws because they are based on universal ethical principles. Laws that violate the principles are disobeyed.	If you don't steal the drug, if you let your wife die, you'll always condemn yourself for it afterward. You won't be blamed and you'll have lived up to the outside rule of the law, but you won't have lived up to your own standards of conscience.	If you steal the drug, you won't be blamed by other people but you'll condemn yourself because you won't have lived up to your own conscience and standards of honesty.

Source: Adapted from Robert S. Feldman, Understanding Psychology (New York: McGraw-Hill, 1987), p. 378.

court records in order to identify family-related variables that would predict criminal activity. Such variables as inadequate maternal affection and supervision, parental conflict, the mother's lack of self-confidence, and the father's deviance were significantly related to the commission of crimes against persons and/or property. The father's absence was not by itself correlated with criminal behavior.[16]

Other studies, such as those by Sheldon and Eleanor Glueck and the more recent studies by Lee N. Robins, which were carried out in schools, juvenile courts, and psychiatric hospitals, suggest a moderate to strong relation between crime and childhood deprivation.[17] However, evidence that deprivation directly causes delinquency is lacking.[18]

So far we have considered psychological theories that attribute the causes of delinquency or criminality to unconscious problems and failures in moral development. Not all psychologists agree with these explanations of criminal behavior. Some argue that human behavior develops through learning. They say that we learn by observing others and by watching the responses to other people's behavior (on television or in the movies, for instance) and to our own. Social learning theorists reject the notion that internal functioning alone makes us prone to act aggressively or violently.

AT ISSUE

Parricide: Abused Children Strike Back

Mark Martone was 16 when he shot his father to death. [He] remembers abuse back to age five, when he told his dad he was scared of the dark. "Oh, Jesus Christ," said the parent in disgust. Then he led the terrified boy down to the cellar, handcuffed his arms over a rafter, turned off the light and shut the door. Mark dangled in silence for hours. When Mark was nine, his father held the boy's hand over a red-hot burner as punishment for moving a book of matches on a bureau. And when he was 15, his dad, angered by a long-distance phone bill, stuck a gun in his son's mouth and "told me he was going to blow my brains out."[1]

An estimated 5.7 million children in the United States are physically, mentally, and sexually abused by their parents annually, and the problem is not lessening. Of those millions of children, maybe a few hundred each year fight back with the ultimate weapon: they kill the abusive parent. In the past such children were regarded as particularly evil, and the law reserved the most terrible forms of capital punishment for parricides. With the growing understanding of the horrors of child abuse, however, these youths are being treated with increasing sympathy. "They know what they're doing is wrong," comments a psychologist at the University of Virginia. "But they are desperate and helpless, and they don't see alternatives."[1]

The typical case involves a 16- to 18-year-old from a white middle-class family. Sons are more likely than daughters to commit murder, and the victim is more likely to be a father than a mother. While children who kill nonabusive parents usually display some sign of mental disorder, the killers of abusive parents generally are seen as well adjusted.[2]

The increasing sympathy for these teenagers has led to verdicts of not guilty by reason of self-defense or guilty of reduced charges (for example, manslaughter instead of first-degree murder). A "battered-child-syndrome" defense sometimes is successful, but the killings do not usually fit the typical idea of self-defense: most happen when the parent is in a vulnerable position instead of in the middle of an attack on the child. But mental-health experts think that treatment is more appropriate than punishment for children who kill their abusive parents. "These kids don't need to be locked up for our protection," says one attorney and psychologist. "Some may benefit in the sense that they've been able to atone and overcome some guilt. But beyond that, it's really Draconian."[1]

Sources

1. Hannah Bloch and Jeanne McDowell, "When Kids Kill Abusive Parents," *Time*, Nov. 23, 1992.
2. Kathleen M. Heide, *Why Kids Kill Parents* (Columbus: Ohio State University Press, 1992), pp. 40–41.

Questions for Discussion

1. If you were on a jury, would you be willing to consider that what appears to be "cold-blooded murder" might have been a form of self-defense for a battered child?
2. An attorney specializing in parricide feels that such cases "open a window on our understanding of child abuse." How would you go about determining which of millions of child abuse cases are likely to lead to parricide for which a standard defense should be recognized?

Characteristics Associated with Adolescent Parricide Offenders

1. Patterns of family violence (parental brutality and cruelty toward child and/or toward one another).
2. Adolescent's attempts to get help from others fail.
3. Adolescent's efforts to escape family situation fail (e.g., running away, thoughts of suicide, suicide attempts).
4. Adolescent is isolated from others/fewer outlets.
5. Family situation becomes increasingly intolerable.
6. Adolescent feels increasingly helpless, trapped.
7. Adolescent's inability to cope leads to loss of control.
8. Prior criminal behavior minimal or nonexistent.
9. Availability of gun.
10. Homicide victim as alcoholic.
11. Evidence to suggest dissociative state in some cases.
12. Victim's death perceived as relief to offender/family; initial absence of remorse.

Source: Excerpted from Kathleen M. Heide, Why Kids Kill Parents (Columbus: Ohio State University Press, 1992), table 3.1, pp. 40–41.

Learning Aggression and Violence

Social learning theory maintains that delinquent behavior is learned through the same psychological processes as any other behavior. Behavior is learned when it is reinforced or rewarded; it is not learned when it is not reinforced. We learn behavior in various ways: observation, direct exposure, and differential reinforcement.

Observational Learning

Albert Bandura, a leading proponent of social learning theory, argues that individuals learn violence and aggression through **behavioral modeling:** children learn how to behave by fashioning their behavior after that of others. Behavior is socially transmitted through examples, which come primarily from the family, the subculture, and the mass media.[19]

Psychologists have been studying the effects of family violence (Chapter 10) on children. They have found that parents who try to resolve family controversies by violence teach their children to use similar tactics. Thus a cycle of violence may be perpetuated through generations. Observing a healthy and happy family environment tends to result in constructive and positive modeling.

To understand the influence of the social environment outside the home, social learning theorists have studied gangs, which often provide excellent models of observational learning of violence and aggression. They have found, in fact, that violence is very much a norm shared by some people in a community or gang. The highest incidence of aggressive behavior occurs where aggressiveness is a desired characteristic, as it is in some subcultures.

Observational learning takes place in front of the television set and at the movies, as well. Children who have seen others being rewarded for violent acts often believe that violence and aggression are acceptable behaviors.[20] And today children can see a lot of violence, as Table 4.2 shows. The psychologist Leonard Eron has argued that the "single best predictor of how aggressive a young man would be when he was 19 years old was the violence of the television programs he preferred when he was 8 years old."[21]

There is, of course, another side to the issue of television violence. Researchers conducted a longitudinal study to assess the association between children's aggressive behavior and exposure to violence on television. Questionnaire data were collected on 3718 subjects in four time periods between 1970 and 1973. Responses were coded by exposure time and "violence weights" (Table 4.3). Responses were then compared with self-reports of violent behavior. The findings indicate that exposure to violence on television is statistically unrelated to self-reported violent behavior. The question remains open.[22]

Direct Experience

What we learn by observation is determined by the behavior of others. What we learn from direct experience is determined by what we ourselves do and what happens to us. We remember the past and use its lessons to avoid future mistakes. Thus we learn through trial and error. According to social learning theorists, after engaging in a given behavior, most of us examine the responses to our actions and modify our behavior as necessary to obtain favorable responses. If we are praised or rewarded for a behavior, we are likely to repeat it. If we are sub-

TABLE 4.2 ONE DAY'S BODY COUNT

BETWEEN THE HOURS OF 6 A.M. AND MIDNIGHT ON APRIL 2, 1992, ABC, CBS, NBC, PBS, FOX, WDCA-WASHINGTON, TURNER, USA, MTV AND HBO COMBINED AIRED THE FOLLOWING CARNAGE:

Act	Number of Scenes	Percent of Total
Serious assaults (without guns)	389	20
Gunplay	362	18
Isolated punches	273	14
Pushing, dragging	272	14
Menacing threat with a weapon	226	11
Slaps	128	6
Deliberate destruction of property	95	5
Simple assault	73	4
All other types	28	1

Source: Harry F. Waters, "Networks under the Gun," Newsweek, July 12, 1993, p. 65.

TABLE 4.3 VIOLENCE WEIGHTS ATTACHED TO POPULAR TELEVISION SHOWS, 1970–1973

Television Show	Violence Weights
FBI	7
Hawaii 5-0	7
Mannix	7
Mod Squad	7
Mission Impossible	6
Bonanza	5
Wrestling	5
Adam-12	4
Monday Night Football	4
Then Came Bronson	4
Laugh-in	1
Medical Center	1
Room 222	1
Andy Williams Show	0
Bewitched	0
Bill Cosby Show	0
Carol Burnett Show	0
The Odd Couple	0

Source: J. Ronald Milavsky, H. H. Stipp, R. C. Kessler, and W. S. Rubens, Television and Aggression: A Panel Study (New York: Academic Press, 1982).

jected to verbal or physical punishment, we are likely to refrain from such behavior. Our behavior in the first instance and our restraint in the second are said to be "reinforced" by the rewards and punishments we receive.

The psychologist Gerald Patterson and his colleagues examined how aggression is learned by direct experience. They observed that some passive children at play were repeatedly victimized by other children but were occasionally successful in curbing the attacks by counteraggression. Over time, these children learned defensive fighting, and eventually they initiated fights. Other passive children, who were rarely observed to be victimized, remained submissive.[23] Thus children, like adults, can learn to be aggressive and even violent by trial and error.

While violence and aggression are learned behaviors, they are not necessarily expressed until they are elicited in one of several ways. Albert Bandura describes the factors that elicit behavioral responses as "instigators." Thus social learning theory describes not only how aggression is acquired but also how it is instigated. Consider the following instigators of aggression:

- ■ *Aversive instigators:* physical assaults, verbal threats, and insults; adverse reductions in conditions of life (such as impoverishment) and the thwarting of goal-directed behavior

- ■ *Incentive instigators:* rewards, such as money and praise

- ■ *Modeling instigators:* violent or aggressive behaviors observed in others

- ■ *Instructional instigators:* observations of people carrying out instructions to engage in violence or aggression

- ■ *Delusional instigators:* unfounded or bizarre beliefs that violence is necessary or justified.[24]

Differential Reinforcement

In 1965 the criminologist C. Ray Jeffery suggested that learning theory could be used to explain criminality.[25] Within 1 year Ernest Burgess and Ronald Akers combined Bandura's psychologically based learning theory with Edwin Sutherland's sociologically based differential association theory (Chapter 5) to produce the theory of **differential association–reinforcement,** which states that the persistence of criminal behavior depends on whether or not it is rewarded or punished. The most meaningful rewards and punishments are those given by groups that are important in an individual's life—the peer group, the family, teachers in

In some countries, television violence is strictly controlled because of a concern that children will learn aggressive behavior from watching it.

WINDOW TO THE WORLD
Censoring TV Violence

In early 1994, U.S. television networks announced plans to set up a committee to devise a rating system for levels of violence on TV shows. What prompted this unprecedented move? Many Americans had for some time been concerned about the ever-increasing amount of violence on television and its effects on children.(1)

Social Control versus Censorship

While many people saw the networks' plans for ratings as a disappointingly small contribution to a big problem, others began worrying about freedom of expression. Representative Edward J. Markey pushed for a plan that would require "V-block" computer chips in all new TV sets—the chip would allow parents to block all V-rated (violent) shows. "'That's getting awfully close to censorship,' frets Peggy Charren, founder of Action for Children's Television."(1)

If such warnings and "zappings" do constitute censorship, the United States is way behind other countries. In Egypt, both radio and television are owned by the state, and all broadcasts are supervised by the government.(2) In Singapore, television also is state-controlled, but a 1991 revamp of the country's film classification system was going to allow movie audiences to see for the first time "a little more sex, nudity and violence."(3) India, despite being open to satellite-dish broadcasting, was still using its government-run network in 1992 to censor the violence that occurred during religious riots across the country.(4) Indonesia's government announced in 1993 that censoring all materials citizens could watch on private and foreign networks had become "too onerous a task" for its National Film Censorship Board; it stated that the people themselves should judge what to watch and should avoid "morally unsuitable" programs, such as those containing pornography and violence.(5)

The Chinese Example

Perhaps China provides the most prominent example of the use of television for social control: "In the hands of Chinese media experts, TV is both an instrument to instill terror and obedience and an educational tool," wrote Newsday reporter Thomas Collins after the Tiananmen Square protests. "The . . . important thing was to control and limit what a billion Chinese people would believe had happened."(6) According to Collins, the event was portrayed as follows:

> Rather than a demonstration for democratic reforms involving millions of people throughout the country, the protests were the work of a handful of "counterrevolutionaries" and "hoodlums."

A study of the 1991–1992 television season shows that children's programming actually features more violence than prime time shows.

	CHILDREN'S PROGRAMS	PRIME TIME
Violent acts per hour	32	4
Violent characters	56%	34%
Characters who are victims of violence	74%	34%
Characters who are killers or who get killed	3.3%	5.7%
Characters involved in violence as perpetrators or victims	79%	47%

Source: Harry F. Waters, "Networks under the Gun," Newsweek, July 12, 1993, p. 64.

Instead of the massacre of hundreds, possibly thousands of students and workers, the Chinese populace is being told that the only casualties were soldiers. No students were killed.

Sources
1. Harry F. Waters, "Networks under the Gun," Newsweek, July 12, 1993, pp. 64–66.
2. "Middle East Watch Report," Middle East News Network, Nov. 17, 1991.
3. "Singapore: Opening Up to a Little Sex and Nudity," Inter Press Service, Apr. 15, 1991.
4. Molly Moore, "Satellite TV Shows Asia a World Beyond Reach of State Censors," Washington Post, Apr. 10, 1993, p. A12.
5. "Indonesia to Revamp Film Censorship," Straits Times, Apr. 29, 1993, p. 13.
6. Thomas Collins, "In China, the Carnage That Never Was," Newsday, June 14, 1989, p. 67.

Questions for Discussion
1. Research suggests an association between children's exposure to TV violence and the likelihood that they will resolve their own conflicts by violent means. Are we then justified in censoring TV violence?
2. Suppose censorship were imposed. How could we then measure the impact of censorship on rates of violent crime?

school, and so forth. In other words, people respond more readily to the reactions of the most significant people in their lives. If criminal behavior elicits more positive reinforcement or rewards than punishment, it will persist.[26]

Social learning theory helps us understand why some individuals who engage in violent and aggressive behavior do so: they learn to behave that way. But perhaps something within the personality of a criminal creates a susceptibility to aggressive or violent models in the first place. For example, perhaps criminals are more extroverted, irresponsible, or unsocialized than noncriminals. Or perhaps criminals are more intolerant and impulsive or have lower self-esteem.

Personality

Four distinct lines of psychological research have examined the relation between personality and criminality.[27] First, investigators have looked at the differences between the personality structures of criminals and noncriminals. Most of this work has been carried out in state and federal prisons, where psychologists have administered personality questionnaires such as the Minnesota Multiphasic Personality Inventory (MMPI) and the California Psychological Inventory (CPI) to inmates. The evidence from these studies shows that inmates are typically more impulsive, hostile, self-centered, and immature than noncriminals.[28]

Second, a vast amount of literature is devoted to the prediction of behavior. Criminologists want to determine how an individual will respond to prison discipline and whether he or she will avoid crime after release. The results are equivocal. At best, personality characteristics seem to be modest predictors of future criminality.[29] Yet when they are combined with such variables as personal history, they tend to increase to the power of prediction significantly.[30]

Third, many studies examine the degree to which normal personality dynamics operate in criminals. Findings from these studies suggest that the personality dynamics of criminals are often quite similar to those of noncriminals. Social criminals (those who act in concert with others), for example, are found to be more sociable, affiliative, outgoing, and self-confident than solitary criminals.[31]

Finally, some researchers have attempted to quantify individual differences between types and groups of offenders. Several studies have compared the personality characteristics of first-time offenders with those of repeat or habitual criminals. Other investigators have compared violent offenders with nonviolent offenders and murderers with drug offenders. In addition, prison inmates have been classified according to personality type.[32]

In general, research on criminals' personality characteristics has revealed some important associations. However, criminologists have been skeptical of the strength of the relationship of personality to criminality. A review of research on that relationship published in 1942 by Milton Metfessel and Constance Lovell dismissed personality as an important causal factor in criminal behavior.[33] In 1950 Karl Schuessler and Donald Cressey reached the same conclusion.[34] Twenty-seven years later, Daniel Tennenbaum's updated review agreed with earlier assessments. He found that "the data do not reveal any significant differences between criminal and noncriminal psychology. . . . Personality testing has not differentiated criminals from noncriminals."[35]

Despite these conclusions, whether or not criminals share personality characteristics continues to be debated. Are criminals in fact more aggressive, dominant, and manipulative than noncriminals? Are they more irresponsible? Clearly, many criminals are aggressive; many have manipulated a variety of situations; many assume no responsibility for their acts. But are such characteristics common to all criminals? Samuel Yochelson and Stanton Samenow addressed these questions. In *The Criminal Personality*, this psychiatrist–psychologist team described their growing disillusion with traditional explanations of criminality.

From their experience in treating criminals in the Forensic Division of St. Elizabeth's Hospital in Washington, D.C., they refuted psychoanalysts' claims that crime is caused by inner conflict. Rather, they said, criminals share abnormal "thinking patterns" that lead to decisions to commit crimes. Yochelson and Samenow identified as many as 52 patterns of thinking common to the criminals they studied. They argued that criminals are "angry" people who feel a sense of superiority, expect not to be held accountable for their acts, and have a highly inflated self-image. Any perceived attack on their glorified self-image elicits a strong reaction, often a violent one.[36]

Other researchers have used different methods to study the association between criminality and personality. William Laufer and his colleagues conducted a review of the findings of a large sample of studies that had used the California Psychological Inventory. Their research revealed a common personality profile: the criminals tested showed remarkable similarity in their deficient self-control, intolerance, and lack of responsibility.[37]

Though studies dealing with personality correlates of criminals are important, some psychologists are concerned that by focusing on the personalities of criminals in their search for explanations of criminal behavior, investigators may overlook other important factors, like the complex social environment in which a crime is committed.[38] A homicide that began as a barroom argument between two intoxicated patrons who backed different teams to win the Super Bowl, for example, is very likely to hinge on situational factors that interact with their personalities.

Eysenck's Conditioning Theory

For over 20 years Hans J. Eysenck has been developing and refining a theory of the relationship between personality and criminality that considers more than just individual characteristics.[39] His theory has two parts. First, Eysenck claims that all human personality may be seen in three dimensions—psychoticism, extraversion, and neuroticism. Individuals who score high on measures of **psychoticism** are aggressive, egocentric, and impulsive. Those who score high on measures of **extraversion** are sensation-seeking, dominant, and assertive. High scorers on scales assessing **neuroticism** may be described as having low self-esteem, excessive anxiety, and wide mood swings. Eysenck has found that when criminals respond to items on the Eysenck Personality Questionnaire (EPQ), they uniformly score higher on each of these dimensions than do noncriminals.

The second part of Eysenck's theory suggests that humans develop a conscience through **conditioning.** From birth on we are rewarded for social behavior and punished for asocial behavior. Eysenck likens this conditioning to training a dog. Puppies are not born house-trained. You have to teach a puppy that it is good to urinate and defecate outside your apartment or house by pairing kind words and perhaps some tangible reward (such as a dog treat) with successful outings. A loud, angry voice will convey disapproval and disappointment when mistakes are made inside.

In time most dogs learn and, according to Eysenck, develop a conscience. But as Eysenck also has noted, some dogs learn faster than others. German shepherds acquire good "bathroom habits" faster than basenjis, who are most difficult to train. It is argued that the same is true of humans; there are important individual differences. Criminals become conditioned slowly and appear to care little whether or not their asocial actions bring disapproval.

Eysenck has identified two additional aspects of a criminal's poor conditionability. First, he has found that extraverts are much more difficult to condition than introverts and thus have greater difficulty in developing a conscience. Youthful offenders tend to score highest on measures of extraversion. Second, differences in conditionability are dependent on certain physiological factors, the most important of which is **cortical arousal,** or activation of the cerebral cortex.

The cortex of the brain is responsible for higher intellectual functioning, information processing, and decision making. Eysenck found that individuals who are easily conditionable and develop a conscience have a high level of cortical arousal; they do not need intense external stimulation to become aroused. A low level of cortical arousal is associated with poor conditionability, difficulty in developing a conscience, and need for external stimulation.

MENTAL DISORDERS AND CRIME

It has been difficult for psychiatrists to derive criteria that would help them decide which offenders are mentally ill. According to the psychiatrist Seymour L. Halleck, the problem lies in the evolving conceptualization of mental illness. Traditionally the medical profession viewed mental illness as an absolute condition or status—you are either afflicted with **psychosis** or you are not. Should such a view concern us? Halleck suggests that it should. "Although this kind of thinking is not compatible with current psychiatric knowledge," he writes, "it continues to exert considerable influence upon psychiatric practice. . . . As applied to the criminal, it also leads to rigid dichotomies between the 'sick criminal' and the 'normal criminal.'"[40]

Halleck and other psychiatrists, such as Karl Menninger, conceptualize mental functioning as a process.[41] Mental illness may not be considered apart from mental health—the two exist on the same continuum. At various times in each of our lives we move along the continuum from health toward illness.[42] For this reason, a diagnosis of "criminal" or "mentally ill" may overlook potentially important gradations in mental health and mental illness. This issue is perhaps no more apparent than in the insanity defense, which calls for proof of sanity or insanity and generally does not allow for gradations in mental functioning (see Chapter 9).

Estimates vary, but between 20 and 60 percent of state correctional populations suffer from a

The image of serial killer Theodore "Ted" Bundy peering out of a TV monitor, prior to his execution in Florida in 1989.

type of mental disorder that in the nineteenth century was described by the French physician Philippe Pinel as *manie sans délire* ("madness without confusion"), by the English physician James C. Prichard as "moral insanity," and by Gina Lombroso Ferrero as "irresistible atavistic impulses." Today such mental illness is called *psychopathy, sociopathy,* or *antisocial personality*—a personality characterized by inability to learn from experience, lack of warmth, and absence of guilt.

The psychiatrist Hervey Cleckley views psychopathy as a serious illness even though patients may not appear to be ill. According to Cleckley, psychopaths appear to enjoy excellent mental health; but what we see is only a "mask of sanity." Initially they seem free of any kind of mental disorder and appear to be reliable and honest. After some time, however, it becomes clear that they have no sense of responsibility whatsoever. They show a disregard for truth, are insincere, and feel no sense of shame, guilt, or humiliation. Psychopaths lie and cheat without hesitation and engage in verbal as well as physical abuse without any thought. Cleckley describes the following case:

A sixteen-year-old boy was sent to jail for stealing a valuable watch. Though apparently . . . untouched by his situation, after a few questions were asked he began to seem more like a child who feels the unpleasantness of his position. He confessed that he had worried much about masturbation, saying he had been threatened and punished severely for it and told that it would cause him to become "insane."

He admitted having broken into his mother's jewelry box and stolen a watch valued at $150.00. He calmly related that he exchanged the watch for 15 cents' worth of ice cream and seemed entirely satisfied with what he had done. He readily admitted that his act was wrong, used the proper words to express his intention to cause no further trouble, and, when asked, said that he would like very much to get out of jail.

He stated that he loved his mother devotedly. "I just kiss her and kiss her ten or twelve times when she comes to see me!" he exclaimed with shallow zeal. These manifestations of affection were so artificial, and, one would even say, unconsciously artificial, that few laymen would be convinced that any feeling, in the ordinary sense, lay in them. Nor was his mother convinced.

A few weeks before this boy was sent to jail he displayed to his mother some rifle cartridges. When asked what he wanted with them he explained that they would fit the rifle in a nearby closet. "I've tried them," he announced. And in a lively tone added, "Why, I could put them in the gun and shoot you. You would fall right over!" He laughed and his eyes shone with a small but real impulse.[43]

Psychologists also have found that psychopaths, like Hans Eysenck's extraverts, have a low internal arousal level; thus psychopaths constantly seek external stimulation, are less susceptible to learning by direct experience (they do not modify their behavior after they are punished), are more impulsive, and experience far less anxiety than nonpsychopaths about any adverse consequences of their acts.[44] Some psychiatrists consider "psychopathy" to be an artificial label for an antisocial personality.[45] To Eysenck and others, it is a major behavioral category that presents significant challenges. Eysenck sums up this view by writing that the psychopath poses the riddle of delinquency. If we could solve the riddle, then we would have a powerful weapon to fight the problem of delinquency.[46]

BIOLOGY AND CRIMINALITY

Within the last two decades, biologists have followed in the tradition of Cesare Lombroso, Raffaele Garofalo, and Charles Goring in their search for answers to questions about human behavior. Geneticists, for example, have argued that the predisposition to act violently or aggressively in certain situations may be inherited. In other words, while criminals are not born criminal, the predisposition to be violent or commit crime may be present at birth.

To demonstrate that certain traits are inherited, geneticists have studied children born of criminals but reared from birth by noncriminal adoptive parents. They wanted to know whether the behavior of the adoptive children was more similar to that of their biological parents than to that of their adoptive parents. Their findings play an important role in the debate on heredity versus environment. Other biologists, sometimes called biocriminologists, take a different approach. Some ask whether brain damage or inadequate nutrition results in criminal behavior. Others are interested in the influence of hormones, chromosomal abnormalities, and allergies. They investigate interactions between brain and behavior and between diet and behavior.

Modern Biocriminology

Biocriminology is the study of the physical aspects of psychological disorders. It has been known for some time that adults who suffer from depression show abnormalities in brain waves during sleep, experience disturbed nervous system functioning, and display biochemical abnormalities. Research on depressed children reveals the same physical problems; furthermore, their adult relatives show high rates of depression as well. In fact, children whose parents suffer from depression are more than four times more likely than the average child to experience a similar illness.[47] Depression appears to be an inherited condition that manifests itself in psychological and physical disturbances. The important point is that until only recently, physicians may have been missing the mark in their assessment and treatment of depressed children and adults by ignoring the physiological aspects.

Criminologists who study sociology and psychology to the exclusion of the biological sciences may also be missing the mark in their efforts to discover the causes of crime. Recent research has demonstrated that crime does indeed have psychobiological aspects similar to those found in studies of depression—biochemical abnormalities, abnormal brain waves, nervous system dysfunction. There is also evidence that strongly suggests a genetic predisposition to criminality.[48]

The resurgence of interest in integrating modern biological advances, theories, and principles into mainstream criminology began two decades ago. The sociobiological work of Edward Wilson on the interrelationship of biology, genetics, and social behavior was pivotal.[49] So were the contributions of C. Ray Jeffery, who argued that a biosocial interdisciplinary model should become the major theoretical framework for studying criminal behavior.[50]

Criminologists once again began to consider the possibility that there are indeed traits that predispose a person to criminality and that these traits may be passed from parent to child through the genes. Other questions arose as well. Is it possible, for instance, that internal biochemical imbalances or deficiencies cause antisocial behavior? Could too much or too little sugar in the bloodstream increase the potential for aggression? Or could a vitamin deficiency or some hormonal problem be responsible? We will explore the evidence for a genetic predisposition to criminal behavior, the relationship between biochemical factors and criminality, and neurophysiological factors that result in criminal behavior.

Genetics and Criminality

Today the proposition that human beings are products of an interaction between environmental and genetic factors is all but universally accepted. We can stop asking, then, whether nature or nurture is more important in shaping us; we are the products of both. But what does the interaction between the two look like? And what concerns are raised by reliance on genetics to the exclusion of environmental factors? Consider the example of the XYY syndrome.

The XYY Syndrome

Chromosomes are the basic structures that contain our genes—the biological material that makes each of us unique. Each human being has 23 pairs of inherited chromosomes. One pair determines gender. A female receives an X chromosome from both mother and father; a male receives an X chromosome from his mother and a Y from his father. Sometimes a defect in the production of sperm or egg results in genetic abnormalities. One type of abnormality is the XYY chromosomal male. The XYY male receives two Y chromosomes from his father rather than one. Approximately 1 in 1000 newborn males in the general population has this genetic composition.[51] Initial studies done in the 1960s found the frequency of XYY chromosomes to be about 20 times greater than normal XY chromosomes

among inmates in maximum security state hospitals.[52] The XYY inmates tended to be tall, physically aggressive, and frequently violent.

Supporters of these data claimed to have uncovered the mystery of violent criminality. Critics voiced concern over the fact that these studies were done on small and unrepresentative samples. The *XYY syndrome,* as this condition became known, received much public attention because of the case of Richard Speck. Speck, who in 1966 murdered eight nurses in Chicago, initially was diagnosed as an XYY chromosomal male. However, the diagnosis later turned out to be wrong. Nevertheless, public concern was aroused: Were all XYY males potential killers?

Studies undertaken since that time have discounted the relation between the extra Y chromosome and criminality.[53] Although convincing evidence in support of the XYY hypothesis appears to be slight, it is nevertheless possible that aggressive and violent behavior is at least partly determined by genetic factors. The problem is how to investigate this possibility. One difficulty is separating the external or environmental factors, such as family structure, culture, socioeconomic status, and peer influences, from the genetic predispositions with which they begin to interact at birth.

A particular individual may have a genetic predisposition to be violent but be born into a wealthy, well-educated, loving, and calm familial environment. He may never commit a violent act. Another person may have a genetic predisposition to be rule-abiding and nonaggressive yet be born into a poor, uneducated, physically abusive, and unloving family. He may commit violent criminal acts. How, then, can we determine the extent to which behavior is genetically influenced? Researchers have turned to twin studies and adoption studies in the quest for an answer.

Twin Studies

To discover whether or not crime is genetically predetermined, researchers have compared identical and fraternal twins. Identical, or **monozygotic (MZ)**, twins develop from a single fertilized egg that divides into two embryos. These twins share all their genes. Fraternal, or **dizygotic (DZ),**

CRIMINOLOGICAL FOCUS
The Roots of Controversy: Violence and Genes

At the same time that advances in genetics and biochemistry are providing new avenues for research into biological bases of violence, attacks on such research are calling its usefulness into question. Government-sponsored research plans have been called racist, a conference on genetics and crime was canceled after protests, and a session on violence and heredity at the 1993 American Association for the Advancement of Science meeting became "a politically correct critique of the research."(1)

Looking for a Link

Few involved in such research expect to find a "violence gene"; rather, researchers are looking for a biological basis for some of the behaviors associated with violence. As one explanation put it:

> Scientists are . . . trying to find inborn personality traits that might make people more physically aggressive. The tendency to be a thrill seeker may be one such characteristic. So might "a restless impulsiveness, an inability to defer gratification." A high threshold for anxiety or fear may be another key trait. . . . such people tend to have a "special biology," with lower-than-average heart rates and blood pressure."(2)

No one yet has found any direct link between genes and violence. In fact, Sarnoff Mednick, the psychologist who conducted adoption studies of criminal behavior in Denmark (see p. **94**), found no evidence for the inheritance of violence. "If there were any genetic effect for violent crimes, we would have picked it up," says Mednick, whose study included 14,427 men.(2)

The Ethical Question

The controversy over a genetic basis for violent behavior seems to deal less with actual research findings than with the implications of such findings. For example, Harvard psychologist Jerome Kagan predicts that in 25 years biological and genetic tests will make it possible to identify the 15 children in every 1000 who may have violent tendencies. Of those 15, only 1 will actually become violent. The ethical question, then, is what to do with this knowledge. "Do we tell the mothers of all 15 that their kids might be violent?" he asks. "How are the mothers then going to react to their children if we do that?"(1)

A 1992 National Academy of Science (NAS) report on violence recommended finding better ways to intervene in the development of children who could become violent, and it listed risk factors statistically linked to violence: hyperactivity, poor early grades, low IQ, fearlessness, and an inability to defer gratification, for example.(3)

What frightens those opposed to biological and genetic research into the causes of violence is the thought of how such research could be used by policy makers. If a violent personality can be shown to be genetically determined, crime-prevention strategies might try to identify "potential criminals" and to intervene before their criminal careers begin—and before anyone knows if they would ever have become criminals. "Should genetic markers one day be found for tendencies . . . that are loosely linked to crime," explains one researcher, "they would probably have little specificity, sensitivity or explanatory power: most people with the markers will not be criminals and most criminals will not have the markers."(2) On the other hand, when environment—poverty, broken homes, and other problems—is seen as the major cause of violence, crime prevention takes the shape of improving social conditions rather than labeling individuals.

A middle road is proposed by those who see biological research as a key to helping criminals change their behavior. "Once you find a biological basis for a behavior, you can try to find out how to help people cope," says one such scholar. "Suppose the link is impulsivity, an inability to defer gratification. It might be you could design education programs to teach criminals to readjust their time horizon."(2)

Sources

1. Hannah Bloch and Dick Thompson, "Seeking the Roots of Violence," *Time,* April 19, 1993, pp. 52–53.
2. Daniel Goleman, "New Storm Brews on Whether Crime Has Roots in Genes," *New York Times,* Sept. 15, 1992, p. C1.
3. Fox Butterfield, "Study Cites Biology's Role in Violent Behavior," *New York Times,* Nov. 13, 1992, p. A7.

Questions for Discussion

1. If, in fact, we could positively identify those few among each 1000 youngsters who are biologically disposed to become violent criminals, should we design interventions for them early in life?
2. What research would you suggest to determine the role of social forces in the outcomes of those who are biologically disposed to become criminal?

twins develop from two separate eggs, both fertilized at the same time. They share about half of their genes. Since the prenatal and postnatal family environments are, by and large, the same, greater behavioral similarity between identical twins than between fraternal twins would support an argument for genetic predisposition.

In the 1920s a German physician, Johannes Lange, found 30 pairs of same-sex twins—13 identical and 17 fraternal pairs. One member of each pair was a known criminal. Lange found that in 10 of the 13 pairs of identical twins, both twins were criminal; in 2 of the 17 pairs of fraternal twins, both were criminal.[54] The research techniques of the time were limited, but Lange's results were nevertheless impressive.

Many similar studies have followed. The largest was a study by Karl Christiansen and Sarnoff A. Mednick which included all twins born between 1881 and 1910 in a region of Denmark, a total of 3586 pairs. Reviewing serious offenses only, Christiansen and Mednick found that the chance of there being a criminal twin when the other twin was a criminal was 50 percent for identical twins and 20 percent for same-sex fraternal twins.[55] Such findings lend support to the hypothesis that some genetic influences increase the risk of criminality.[56] A more recent American study conducted by David C. Rowe and D. Wayne Osgood reached a similar conclusion.[57]

While the evidence from these and other twin studies looks persuasive, we should keep in mind the weakness of such research. It may not be valid to assume a common environment for all twins who grow up in the same house at the same time. If the upbringing of identical twins is much more similar than that of fraternal twins, as it well may be, that circumstance could help explain their different rates of criminality.

Adoption Studies

One way to separate the influence of inherited traits from that of environmental conditions would be to study infants separated at birth from their natural parents and placed randomly in fos-

Separated at birth, the Mallifert twins meet accidentally.

ter homes. In such cases we could determine whether the behavior of the adopted child resembled that of the natural parents or that of the adoptive parents, and by how much. Children, however, are adopted at various ages and are not placed randomly in foster homes. Most such children are matched to their foster or adoptive parents by racial and religious criteria. And couples who adopt children may differ in some important ways from other couples. Despite such shortcomings, adoption studies do help us to expand our knowledge of genetic influences on human variation.

The largest adoption study conducted so far was based on a sample of 14,427 male and female adoptions in Denmark between 1924 and 1947. The hypothesis was that criminality in the biological parents would be associated with an increased risk of criminal behavior in the child. The parents were considered criminal if either the mother or the father had been convicted of a felony. The researchers had sufficient information on more than 4000 of the male children to assess whether or not both the biological and the adoptive parents had criminal records. Mednick and his associates reported the following findings:

- Of boys whose adoptive and biological parents had no criminal record, 13.5 percent were convicted of crimes.
- Of boys who had criminal adoptive parents and noncriminal biological parents, 14.7 percent were convicted of crimes.
- Of boys who had noncriminal adoptive parents and criminal biological parents, 20 percent were convicted of crimes.
- Of boys who had both criminal adoptive parents and criminal biological parents, 24.5 percent were convicted of crimes.[58]

These findings support the claim that the criminality of the biological parents has more influence on the child than does that of the adoptive parents. Other research on adopted children has reached similar conclusions. A major Swedish study examined 862 adopted males and 913 adopted females. The researchers found a genetic predisposition to criminality in both sexes, but an even stronger one in females. An American study of children who were put up for adoption by a group of convicted mothers supports the Danish and Swedish findings on the significance of genetic factors.[59]

Results of adoption studies have been characterized as "highly suggestive" or "supportive" of a genetic link to criminality. But how solid is this link? There are significant problems with adoption studies. One is that little can be done to ensure the similarity of adopted children's environments. Of even greater concern to criminologists, however, is the distinct possibility of mistaking correlation for causation. In other words, there appears to be a significant correlation between the criminality of biological parents and adopted children in the research we have reviewed, but this correlation does not prove that the genetic legacy passed on by a criminal parent causes an offspring to commit a crime.

So far research has failed to shed any light on the nature of the biological link that results in the association between the criminality of parents and that of their children. Furthermore, even if we could identify children with a higher-than-average probability of committing offenses as adults on the basis of their parents' behavior, it is unclear what we could do to prevent these children from following the parental model.

The IQ Debate

A discussion of the association between genes and criminality would be incomplete without paying at least some attention to the debate over IQ and crime. Is an inferior intelligence inherited, and if so, how do we account for the strong relationship between IQ and criminality?

The Research Background

Nearly a century ago scientists began to search for measures to determine people's intelligence, which they believed to be genetically determined. The first test to gain acceptance was developed by a French psychologist, Alfred Binet. Binet's test measured the capacity of individual children to perform tasks or solve problems in relation to the average capacity of their peers.

Between 1888 and 1915 several researchers administered intelligence tests to incarcerated criminals and to boys in reform schools. Initial studies of the relationship between IQ and crime revealed some surprising results. The psychologist Hugo Munsterberg estimated that 68 percent of the criminals that he tested were of low IQ. Using the Binet scale, Henry H. Goddard found that between 25 and 50 percent of criminals had low IQs.[60] What could account for such different results?

Edwin Sutherland observed that the tests were poor and there were too many variations among the many versions administered. He reasoned that social and environmental factors caused delinquency, not low IQ.[61] In the 1950s the psychologist Robert H. Gault added to Sutherland's criticism. He noted particularly that it was "strange that it did not occur immediately to the pioneers that they had examined only a small sample of caught and convicted offenders."[62]

For more than a generation the question about the relationship between IQ and criminal behavior was not studied, and the early inconsistencies remained unresolved. Then in the late 1970s the debate resumed.[63] Supporters of the view that inheritance determines intelligence once again began to present their arguments. The psychologist Arthur Jensen suggested that race was a key factor in IQ differences; Richard J. Herrnstein, a geneticist, pointed to social class as a factor.[64] Both positions spurred a heated debate in which criminologists soon became involved. In 1977 Travis Hirschi and Michael Hindelang evaluated the existing literature on IQ and crime.[65] They cited the following three studies as especially important:

■ Travis Hirschi, on the basis of a study of 3600 California students, demonstrated that the effect of a low IQ on delinquent behavior is more significant than that of the father's education.[66]

■ Marvin Wolfgang and associates, after studying 8700 Philadelphia boys, found a strong relation between low IQ and delinquency, independent of social class.[67]

■ Albert Reiss and Albert L. Rhodes, after an examination of the juvenile court records of 9200 white Tennessee schoolboys, found IQ to be more closely related to delinquency than is social class.[68]

Hirschi and Hindelang concluded that IQ is an even more important factor in predicting crime than either race or social class. They found significant differences in intelligence between criminal and noncriminal populations within like racial and socioeconomic groups. A lower IQ increases the potential for crime within each group. Furthermore, they found that IQ is related to school performance. A low IQ ultimately results in a youngster's associating with similar nonperformers, dropping out of school, and committing delinquent acts. Hirschi and Hindelang's findings were confirmed by James Q. Wilson and Richard Herrnstein but rejected by criminologist Deborah Denno, who conducted a prospective investigation of 800 children from birth to age 17.[69] Her results failed to confirm a direct relationship between IQ and delinquency.

The Debate: Genetics or Environment?

The debate over the relationship between IQ and crime has its roots in the controversy over whether intelligence is genetically or environmentally determined. IQ tests, many people believe, measure cultural factors rather than the innate biological makeup of an individual.[70] Studies by psychologists Sandra Scarr and Richard Weinberg of black and white adopted children confirmed that environment plays a significant role in IQ development. They found that black children adopted by white parents had IQs comparable to those of white adopted children and performed just as well.[71] With evidence of cultural bias and environmental influence, why not abandon the use of intelligence tests? The answer is simple: they do predict performance in school and so have significant utility. It appears that this debate will be with us for a long time to come.

Biochemical Factors

Biocriminologists' primary focus has been on the relationship between criminality and biochemical and neurophysical factors. Biochemical factors include food allergies, diet, **hypoglycemia,** and hormones. Neurophysical factors include brain lesions, brain wave abnormalities, and minimal brain dysfunction.

Food Allergies

Jerome was not a typical sixth-grader. He frequently engaged in fights with other teenagers. His teachers found him disruptive, angry, moody, and rude. His mother complained that he had no friends and spent a good deal of time alone in his room crying. His father characterized him as irritable, unhappy, restless, aggressive, and hostile. Jerome had trouble falling asleep. He had other physical ailments as well.

Treatment with drugs and psychotherapy had failed. He was transferred to a private school, where the psychologist designed an individual study program for him. That, too, failed. Then the school nutritionist placed Jerome on a diet that contained no food dyes, milk, eggs, corn, cocoa, sugar, or wheat. Within a day he was a bit better. Within a week he was sleeping well, doing his homework, and making friends. And after 6 months, Jerome was a normal sixth-grader. But this is not the end of the story. After 8 months, Jerome tested the waters. "What harm could a couple of eggs do?" he reasoned. For lunch he ate one fried-egg sandwich on wheat bread with corn on the cob and a large glass of artificial lemonade. Within minutes Jerome's eyes became dilated and glassy, his face turned red, and he screamed without restraint. His violent and aggressive behavior returned more quickly than it had disappeared.[72]

Over the last decade researchers have investigated the relation between food allergies and antisocial behavior. In fact, since 1908 there have been numerous medical reports indicating that various foods cause such reactions as irritability, hyperactivity, seizures, agitation, and behavior that is "out of character."[73] Investigators have identified the following food components as substances that may result in severe allergic reactions:

Phenylethylamine (found in chocolate)

Tyramine (found in aged cheese and wine)

Monosodium glutamate (used as a flavor enhancer in many foods)

Aspartame (found in artificial sweeteners)

Xanthines (found in caffeine)

Each of these food components has been associated with behavioral disorders, including criminality.

Diet

Other investigations link criminality to diets high in sugar and carbohydrates, to vitamin deficiency or dependency, and to excessive food additives. Criminologist Stephen Schoenthaler conducted a series of studies on the relation between sugar and the behavior of institutionalized offenders. In these investigations inmates were placed on a modified diet that included very little sugar. They received fruit juice in place of soda and vegetables instead of candy. Schoenthaler found fewer disciplinary actions and a significant drop in aggressive behavior in the experimental group.[74] Some individuals charged with crimes have used this finding to build a defense—like Dan White.

In 1979, San Francisco city supervisor Dan White was on trial for the murder of his fellow supervisor, Harvey Milk, and Mayor George Moscone. White defended himself with testimony on the impact of sugar on his behavior. The testimony showed that when White was depressed, he departed from his normal, healthy diet and resorted to high-sugar junk food, including Twinkies, Coca-Cola, and chocolates. Thereafter, his behavior became less and less controllable. The jury found White guilty of manslaughter, rather than murder, due to diminished capacity. White served 5 years in prison and committed suicide after his release. His defense was promptly dubbed the "junk-food defense," "Dan White's defense," or the "Twinkie defense."

Most subsequent attempts to use the junk-food defense have failed. In a 1989 Ohio case *(Johnson)*, it was ruled that the defense may not be used to establish diminished capacity. In 1990, a Cape Cod man was unsuccessful when he defended himself on a charge of stealing (and eating) 300 candy bars *(Callanan)*. Nor did this defense (Twinkie and soda pop) succeed in a

In center, at arrow: Ex-supervisor Dan White, whose "Twinkie defense" reduced his murder charge to a manslaughter conviction for the 1978 killing of San Francisco's Mayor George Moscone and Supervisor Harvey Milk.

murder case in Ohio (*McDonald*, 1988). But in a 1987 Florida case, a defendant (*Rosenthal*) was acquitted of drunk-driving charges on evidence that consumption of chocolate mousse after half a glass of sherry caused an unusual blood sugar reaction.

Other researchers have looked for the causes of crime in vitamin deficiencies. One such study found that 70 percent of criminals charged with serious offenses in one Canadian jurisdiction had a greater-than-normal need for vitamin B_6.[75] Other studies have noted deficiencies of vitamins B_3 and B_6 in criminal population samples.

Some investigators have examined the effects of food additives and food dyes on behavior. Benjamin Feingold has argued that between 30 and 60 percent of all hyperactivity in children may be attributable to reactions to food color-

ing.[76] There is additional support for this hypothesis.[77] Some studies have suggested that a diet deficient in protein may be responsible for violent aggression.

Let us look at the association between the consumption of tryptophan, an amino acid (a protein building block), and crime rates. Tryptophan is a normal component of many foods. Low levels of it have been associated with aggression and, in criminal studies, an increased sensitivity to electric shock. Anthony R. Mawson and K. W. Jacobs reasoned that diets low in tryptophan would be likely to result in higher levels of violent crime, particularly violent offenses such as homicide.

They hypothesized that because corn-based diets are deficient in tryptophan, a cross-national comparison of countries should reveal a positive relationship between corn consumption and homicide rates. Mawson and Jacobs obtained homicide data from the United Nations and the mean per capita corn intake rates of 53 foreign countries from the U.S. Department of Agriculture. They discovered that countries whose per capita rates of corn consumption were above the median had significantly higher homicide rates than countries whose diets were based on wheat or rice.[78]

Hypoglycemia

Another biochemical factor related to criminality may be **hypoglycemia,** a condition that occurs when the level of sugar in the blood falls below an acceptable range. The brain is particularly vulnerable to hypoglycemia, and such a condition can impair its function. Symptoms of hypoglycemia include anxiety, headache, confusion, fatigue, and even aggressive behavior. As early as 1943 researchers linked the condition with violent crime, including murder, rape, and assault. Subsequent studies found that violent and impulsive male offenders had a higher rate of hypoglycemia than noncriminal controls.

Consider the work of Matti Virkkunen, who has conducted a series of studies of habitually violent and psychopathic offenders in Finland. In one such study done in the 1980s he examined the results of a glucose tolerance test (used to determine whether hypoglycemia is present) administered to 37 habitually violent offenders with antisocial personalities, 31 habitually violent offenders with intermittent explosive disorders, and 20 controls. The offenders were found to be significantly more hypoglycemic than the controls.[79]

Hormones

Experiments have shown that male animals are typically more aggressive than females. Male aggression is directly linked to male hormones. If an aggressive male mouse is injected with female hormones, he will stop fighting.[80] Likewise, the administration of male hormones to pregnant monkeys results in female offspring who, even 3 years after birth, are more aggressive than the daughters of noninjected mothers.[81]

While it would be misleading to equate male hormones with aggression and female hormones with nonaggression, there is some evidence that abnormal levels of male hormones in humans may prompt criminal behavior. Several investigators have found higher levels of testosterone (the male hormone) in the blood of individuals who have committed violent offenses.[82] Some studies also relate the premenstrual syndrome (PMS) to delinquency and conclude that women are at greater risk of aggressive and suicidal behavior before and during the menstrual period. After studying 156 newly admitted adult female prisoners, Katherina Dalton concluded that 49 percent of all their crimes were committed either in the premenstrual period or during menstruation.[83] Recently, however, critics have challenged the association between menstrual distress and female crime.[84]

Neurophysiological Factors

In England in the mid-1950s, a father hit his son with a mallet and then threw him out of a window, killing him instantly. Instead of pleading insanity, as many people expected him to do, he presented evidence of a brain tumor, which, he argued, resulted in uncontrollable rage and violence. A jury acquitted him on the grounds that the brain tumor had deprived him of any control over or knowledge of the act he was committing.[85] Brain lesions or brain tumors have led to violent outbursts in many similar cases. Neurophysiological studies, however, have not focused exclusively on brain tumors; they have included a wide range of investigations: brain wave studies, clinical reports of minimal brain dysfunction, and theoretical explorations into the relationship between the limbic system and criminality.[86]

EEG Abnormalities

The *electroencephalogram (EEG)* is a tracing made by an instrument that measures cerebral functioning by recording brain wave activity with electrodes placed on the scalp. Numerous studies that have examined the brain activity of violent prisoners reveal significant differences between the EEGs of criminals and those of noncriminals. Other findings relate significantly slow brain wave activity to young offenders and adult murderers.[87] When Sarnoff A. Mednick and his colleagues examined the criminal records and EEGs of 265 children in a birth cohort in Denmark, they found that certain types of brain wave activity, as measured by the EEG, enabled investigators to predict whether convicted thieves would steal again.[88]

When Jan Volavka compared the EEGs of juvenile delinquents with those of comparable nondelinquents, he found a slowing of brain waves in the delinquent sample, most prominently in those children convicted of theft. He concluded that thievery "is more likely to develop in persons who have a slowing of alpha frequency than in persons who do not."[89]

Minimal Brain Dysfunction

Minimal brain dysfunction (MBD) is classified as "attention deficit hyperactivity disorder."[90] MBD produces such asocial behavioral patterns as impulsivity, hyperactivity, aggressiveness, low self-esteem, and temper outbursts. The syndrome is noteworthy for at least two reasons. First, MBD may explain criminality when social theories fail to do so; that is, when neighborhood, peer, and familial associations do not suggest a high risk of delinquency. Second, MBD is an easily overlooked diagnosis. Parents, teachers, and clinicians tend to focus more on the symptoms of a child's psychopathology than on the possibility of brain dysfunction, even though investigators have repeatedly found high rates of brain dysfunction in samples of suicidal adolescents and youthful offenders.[91]

CRIME AND HUMAN NATURE

The criminologist Edward Sagarin has written:

> In criminology, it appears that a number of views
> . . . have become increasingly delicate and sensitive,
> as if all those who espouse them were inherently
> evil, or at least stupidly insensitive to the conse-
> quences of their research. . . . In the study of crime,
> the examples of unpopular orientations are many.
> Foremost is the link of crime to the factors of genes,
> biology, race, ethnicity, and religion.[92]

Criticisms of Biocriminology

What is it about linking biology and criminality
that makes the subject delicate and sensitive?
Why is the concept so offensive to so many people? One reason is that biocriminologists deny
the existence of individual free will. The idea of
predisposition to commit crimes fosters a sense
of hopelessness. But this criticism seems to have
little merit. As Diana H. Fishbein has aptly noted,
the idea of a "conditioned free will" is widely
accepted.[93] This view suggests that individuals
make choices in regard to a particular action
within a range of possibilities that is "preset" yet
flexible. When conditions permit rational
thought, one is fully accountable and responsible
for one's actions. It is only when conditions are
somehow disturbed that free choice is con-
stricted. The child of middle-class parents who
has a low IQ might avoid delinquent behavior.
But if that child's circumstances changed so that
he lived in a lower-class, single-parent environment, he might find the delinquent lifestyle of the
children in the new neighborhood too tempting
to resist.

Critics have other concerns as well. Some see a
racist undertone to biocriminological research. If
there is a genetic predisposition to commit crime
and if minorities account for a disproportionate
share of criminal activity, are minorities then predisposed to commit crime? In Chapter 2 we
learned that self-reports reveal that most people
have engaged in delinquent or criminal behavior.
How, then, do biocriminologists justify their
claim that certain groups are more prone than
others to criminal behavior? Could it be that the
subjects of their investigations are only criminals
who have been caught and incarcerated? And is
the attention of the police disproportionately
drawn to members of minority groups?

How do biocriminologists account for the fact
that most criminologists see the structure of our
society, the decay of our neighborhoods, and the
subcultures of certain areas as determinants of
criminality? Are biocriminologists unfairly
deemphasizing social and economic factors? (In
Chapters 5 through 8 we review theories that
attribute criminality to group and environmental
forces.)

These issues raise a further question that is at
the core of all social and behavioral science: Is
human behavior the product of nature (genetics)
or nurture (environment)? The consensus among
social and behavioral scientists today is that the
interaction of nature and nurture is so pervasive
that the two cannot be viewed in isolation.

Supporters of biocriminology also maintain
that recognizing a predisposition to crime is not
inconsistent with considering environmental factors. In fact, some believe that predispositions are
triggered by environmental factors. Even if we
agree that some people are predisposed to commit crime, we know that the crime rate would be
higher in areas that provide more triggers. In
sum, while some people may be predisposed to
certain kinds of behavior, most scientists agree
that both psychological and environmental factors shape the final forms of those behaviors.

An Integrated Theory

In recent years the debate has found a new forum
in integrated biocriminological theories, such as
the one proposed by James Q. Wilson and
Richard Herrnstein. These scholars explain
predatory street crime by showing how human
nature develops from the interplay of psychological, biological, and social factors. It is the interaction of genes with environment that in some
individuals forms the kind of personality likely
to commit crimes. The argument takes into
account such factors as IQ, body build, genetic
makeup, impulsiveness, ability to delay gratification, aggressiveness, and even the drinking and
smoking habits of pregnant mothers.

According to Wilson and Herrnstein, the
choice between crime and conventional behavior
is closely linked to individual biological and psy-

If the correctional officer was not in the background, would you be able to tell that this was a group of convicted felons on the basis of their body types?

chological traits and to such social factors as family and school experiences. Their conclusion is that "the offender offends not just because of immediate needs and circumstances, but also because of enduring personal characteristics, some of whose traces can be found in his behavior from early childhood on."[94] In essence, they argue that behavior results from a person's perception of the potential rewards and/or punishments that go along with a criminal act. If the potential reward (such as money) is greater than the expected punishment (say, a small fine), the chance that a crime will be committed increases.

■ REVIEW

When psychologists have attempted to explain criminality, they have taken four general approaches. First, they have focused on failures in psychological development—an overbearing or weak conscience, inner conflict, insufficient moral development, and maternal deprivation, with its concomitant failure of attachment. Second, they have investigated the ways in which

aggression and violence are learned through modeling and direct experience. Third, they have investigated the personality characteristics of criminals and found that criminals tend to be more impulsive, intolerant, and irresponsible than noncriminals. Fourth, psychologists have investigated the relation of criminality to such mental disorders as psychosis and psychopathy.

Biocriminologists investigate the biological correlates of criminality, including a genetic predisposition to commit crime. The XYY syndrome, though now generally discounted as a cause of criminality, suggests that aggressive and violent behavior may be at least partly determined by genetic factors. Studies of the behavior of identical and fraternal twins and of the rates of criminality among adopted children with both criminal and noncriminal biological and adoptive parents tend to support this hypothesis. Investigators have also found a strong correlation between a low IQ and delinquency.

Biocriminologists' most recent and perhaps most important discovery is the relation of criminal behavior to biochemical factors (food allergies, dietary deficiencies, hormonal imbalances) and neurophysiological factors (EEG abnormalities and minimal brain dysfunction). Most scientists agree that if some people are biologically predisposed to certain behaviors, both psychological and environmental factors shape the forms of those behaviors.

■ NOTES

1. See Ronald Blackburn, *The Psychology of Criminal Conduct: Theory, Research, and Practice* (Chichester, England: Wiley, 1993); and Hans Toch, *Violent Men: An Inquiry into the Psychology of Violence*, rev. ed. (Washington, D.C.: American Psychological Association, 1992).

2. See, e.g., Cathy Spatz Widom, "Cycle of Violence," *Science*, **244** (1989): 160–165; and Nathaniel J. Pallone and J. J. Hennessey, *Criminal Behavior: A Process Psychology Analysis* (New Brunswick, N.J.: Transaction, 1992).

3. See, e.g., Sigmund Freud, *A General Introduction to Psychoanalysis* (New York: Liveright, 1920); and Sigmund Freud, *The Ego and the Id* (London: Hogarth, 1927).

4. August Aichhorn, *Wayward Youth* (New York: Viking, 1935).

5. Kate Friedlander, *The Psycho-Analytic Approach to Juvenile Delinquency* (New York: International Universities Press, 1947).

6. See Hans Eysenck, *The Rise and Fall of the Freudian Empire* (New York: Plenum, 1987).

7. Lawrence Kohlberg, "The Development of Modes of Moral Thinking and Choice in the Years Ten to Sixteen," Ph.D. dissertation, University of Chicago, 1958.

8. Lawrence Kohlberg, "Stage and Sequence: The Cognitive-Developmental Approach to Socialization," in *Handbook of Socialization Theory and Research*, ed. David A. Goslin (Chicago: Rand McNally, 1969).

9. Carol Gilligan has studied moral development in women—extending Kohlberg's role-taking theory of moral development. She found that moral reasoning differed in women. Women, according to Gilligan, see morality as the responsibility to take the view of others and to ensure their well-being. See Carol Gilligan, *In a Different Voice: Psychological Theory and Women's Development* (Cambridge, Mass.: Harvard University Press, 1982).

10. William S. Jennings, Robert Kilkenny, and Lawrence Kohlberg, "Moral Development Theory and Practice for Youthful Offenders," in *Personality Theory, Moral Development, and Criminal Behavior*, ed. William S. Laufer and James M. Day (Lexington, Mass.: Lexington Books, 1983). See also Daniel D. Macphail, "The Moral Education Approach in Treating Adult Inmates," *Criminal Justice and Behavior*, **16** (1989): 81–97; Jack Arbuthnot and Donald A. Gordon,

"Crime and Cognition: Community Applications of Sociomoral Reasoning Development," *Criminal Justice and Behavior*, **15** (1988): 379–393; and J. E. LeCapitaine, "The Relationships between Emotional Development and Moral Development and the Differential Impact of Three Psychological Interventions on Children," *Psychology in the Schools*, **15** (1987): 379–393.

11. John Bowlby, *Attachment and Loss*, 2 vols. (New York: Basic Books, 1969, 1973). See also Bowlby's "Forty-four Juvenile Thieves: Their Characteristics and Home Life," *International Journal of Psychoanalysis*, **25** (1944): 19–52.

12. John Bowlby, *The Making and Breaking of Affectional Bonds* (London: Tavistock, 1979). See also Michael Rutter, *Maternal Deprivation Reassessed* (Harmondsworth, England: Penguin, 1971).

13. Michael Lewis, Candice Feiring, Carolyn McGuffog, and John Jaskir, "Predicting Psychopathology in Six-Year-Olds from Early Social Relations," *Child Development*, **55** (1984): 123–136.

14. L. Sroufe, "Infant Caregiver Attachment and Patterns of Adaptation in Preschool: The Roots of Maladaptation and Competence," in *Minnesota Symposium on Child Psychology*, vol. 16, ed. Marion Perlmutter (Hillsdale, N.J.: Erlbaum, 1982).

15. Alicia F. Lieberman, "Preschoolers' Competence with a Peer: Influence of Attachment and Social Experience," *Child Development* **48** (1977): 1277–1287.

16. Joan McCord, "Some Child-Rearing Antecedents of Criminal Behavior," *Journal of Personality and Social Psychology*, **37** (1979): 1477–1486; Joan McCord, "A Longitudinal View of the Relationship between Paternal Absence and Crime," in *Abnormal Offenders, Delinquency, and the Criminal Justice System*, ed. John Gunn and David P. Farrington (London: Wiley, 1982). See also Scott W. Henggeler, Cindy L. Hanson, Charles M. Borduin, Sylvia M. Watson, and Molly A. Brunk, "Mother-Son Relationships of Juvenile Felons," *Journal of Consulting and Clinical Psychology*, **53** (1985): 942–943; and Francis I. Nye, *Family Relationships and Delinquent Behavior* (New York: Wiley, 1958).

17. Sheldon Glueck and Eleanor T. Glueck, *Unraveling Juvenile Delinquency* (New York: Commonwealth Fund, 1950); Lee N. Robins, "Aetiological Implications in Studies of Childhood Histories Relating to Antisocial Personality," in *Psychopathic Behaviour*, ed. Robert D. Hare and Daisy Schalling (Chichester, England: Wiley, 1970); Lee N. Robins, *Deviant Children Grow Up* (Baltimore: Williams & Wilkins, 1966).

18. Joan McCord, "Instigation and Insulation: How Families Affect Antisocial Aggression," in *Development of Antisocial and Prosocial Behavior: Research Theories and Issues*, ed. Dan Olweus, Jack Block, and M. Radke-Yarrow (London: Academic Press, 1986).

19. Albert Bandura, *Aggression: A Social Learning Analysis* (Englewood Cliffs, N.J.: Prentice-Hall, 1973); Albert Bandura, "The Social Learning Perspective: Mechanism of Aggression," in *Psychology of Crime and Criminal Justice*, ed. Hans Toch (New York: Holt, Rinehart & Winston, 1979).

20. Leonard D. Eron and L. Rowell Huesmann, "Parent-Child Interaction, Television Violence, and Aggression of Children," *American Psychologist, 37* (1982): 197–211; Russell G. Geen, "Aggression and Television Violence," in *Aggression: Theoretical and Empirical Reviews*, vol. 2, ed. Russell G. Geen and Edward I. Donnerstein (New York: Academic Press, 1983); Leonard D. Eron and L. Rowell Huesmann, "Adolescent Aggression and Television," *Annals of the New York Academy of Sciences, 347* (1980): 319–331.

21. Leonard D. Eron and L. Rowell Huesmann, "The Control of Aggressive Behavior by Changes in Attitudes, Values, and the Conditions of Learning," in *Advances in the Study of Aggression*, vol. 1, ed. Robert J. Blanchard and D. Caroline Blanchard (Orlando, Fla: Academic Press, 1984).

22. J. Ronald Milavsky, H. H. Stipp, R. C. Kessler, and W. S. Rubens, *Television and Aggression: A Panel Study* (New York: Academic Press, 1982).

23. See Gerald R. Patterson, R. A. Littman, and W. Brickler, *Assertive Behavior in Children: A Step Toward a Theory of Aggression*, monograph of the Society for Research in Child Development, no. 32 (1976).

24. Bandura, *Aggression*.

25. C. Ray Jeffery, "Criminal Behavior and Learning Theory," *Journal of Criminal Law, Criminology and Police Science, 56* (1965): 294–300.

26. Ernest L. Burgess and Ronald L. Akers, "A Differential Association–Reinforcement Theory of Criminal Behavior," *Social Problems, 14* (1966): 128–147. See also Reed Adams, "Differential Association and Learning Principles Revisited," *Social Problems, 20* (1973): 458–470.

27. See D. W. Andrews and J. Stephen Wormith, "Personality and Crime: Knowledge Destruction and Construction in Criminology," *Justice Quarterly 6* (1989): 149–160.

28. William S. Laufer, Dagna K. Skoog, and James M. Day, "Personality and Criminality: A Review of the California Psychological Inventory," *Journal of Clinical Psychology, 38* (1982): 562–573.

29. Richard E. Tremblay, "The Prediction of Delinquent Behavior from Childhood Behavior: Personality Theory Revisited," in *Facts, Frameworks, and Forecasts: Advances in Criminological Theory*, vol. 3, ed. J. McCord (New Brunswick, N.J.: Transaction, 1992).

30. Michael L. Gearing, "The MMPI as a Primary Differentiator and Predictor of Behavior in Prison: A Methodological Critique and Review of the Recent Literature," *Psychological Bulletin, 36* (1979): 929–963.

31. Edwin I. Megargee and Martin J. Bohn, *Classifying Criminal Offenders* (Beverly Hills, Calif.: Sage, 1979); William S. Laufer, John A. Johnson, and Robert Hogan, "Ego Control and Criminal Behavior," *Journal of Personality and Social Psychology, 41* (1981): 179–184; Edwin I. Megargee, "Psychological Determinants and Correlates of Criminal Violence," in *Criminal Violence*, ed. Marvin E. Wolfgang and Neil A. Weiner (Beverly Hills, Calif.: Sage, 1982): Edwin I. Megargee, "The Role of Inhibition in the Assessment and Understanding of Violence," in *Current Topics in Clinical and Community Psychology*, ed. Charles Donald Spielberger (New York: Academic Press, 1971); Edwin I. Megargee, "Undercontrol and Overcontrol in Assaultive and Homicidal Adolescents," Ph.D. dissertation, University of California, Berkeley, 1964; Edwin I. Megargee, "Undercontrolled and Overcontrolled Personality Types in Extreme Antisocial Aggression," *Psychological Monographs, 80* (1966); Edwin I. Megargee and Gerald A. Mendelsohn, "A Cross-Validation of Twelve MMPI Indices of Hostility and Control," *Journal of Abnormal and Social Psychology, 65* (1962): 431–438.

32. See, e.g., William S. Laufer and James M. Day, eds. *Personality Theory, Moral Development, and Criminal Behavior* (Lexington, Mass.: Lexington Books, 1983).

33. Milton Metfessel and Constance Lovell, "Recent Literature on Individual Correlates of Crime," *Psychological Bulletin, 39* (1942): 133–164.

34. Karl E. Schuessler and Donald R. Cressey, "Personality Characteristics of Criminals," *American Journal of Sociology, 55* (1950): 476–484.

35. Daniel J. Tennenbaum, "Personality and Criminality: A Summary and Implications of the Literature," *Journal of Criminal Justice, 5* (1977): 225–235. See also G. P. Waldo and Simon Dinitz, "Personality Attributes of the Criminal: An Analysis of Research Studies, 1950–1965," *Journal of Research in Crime and Delinquency, 4* (1967): 185–202; and R. D. Martin and D. G. Fischer, "Personality Factors in Juvenile Delinquency: A Review of the Literature," *Catalog of Selected Documents in Psychology*, vol. 8 (1978), ms. 1759.

36. Samuel Yochelson and Stanton Samenow, *The Criminal Personality* (New York: Jason Aronson, 1976).

37. Laufer et al., "Personality and Criminality"; Harrison G. Gough and Pamela Bradley, "Delinquent and Criminal Behavior as Assessed by the Revised California Psychological Inventory," *Journal of Clinical Psychology, 48* (1991): 298–308.

38. See Anne Campbell and John J. Gibbs, eds., *Violent Transactions: The Limits of Personality* (Oxford: Basil Blackwell, 1986); Lawrence A. Pervin, "Personality: Current Controversies, Issues, and Direction," *Annual Review of Psychology, 36* (1985): 83–114; and Lawrence A. Pervin, "Persons, Situations, Interactions: Perspectives on a Recurrent Issue," in Campbell and Gibbs, *Violent Transactions*.

39. See Hans J. Eysenck, *Crime and Personality* (London: Routledge & Kegan Paul, 1977); Hans J. Eysenck, "Personality, Conditioning, and Antisocial Behavior," in Laufer and Day, *Personality Theory*; Hans J. Eysenck, "Personality and Criminality: A Dispositional Analysis," in *Advances in Criminological Theory*, vol. 1, eds. William S. Laufer and Freda Adler (New Brunswick, N.J.: Transaction, 1989); and Hans J. Eysenck and Gisli H. Gudjonnson, *The Causes and Cures of Crime* (New York: Plenum, 1990).

40. Seymour L. Halleck, *Psychiatry and the Dilemmas of Crime* (New York: Harper & Row, 1967); Nicholas N. Kittrie, *The Right to Be Different: Deviance and Enforced Therapy* (Baltimore: Md.: Johns Hopkins Press, 1971).

41. Karl Menninger, *The Crime of Punishment* (New York: Viking, 1968).

42. See Daniel L. Davis et al., "Prevalence of Emotional Disorders in a Juvenile Justice Institutional Population," *American Journal of Forensic Psychology*, **9** (1991): 5–17.

43. Hervey Cleckley, *The Mask of Sanity* (St. Louis: Mosby, 1980), pp. 56–57.

44. Ibid., p. 57; Robert D. Hare, *Psychopathy: Theory and Research* (New York: Wiley, 1970); M. Philip Feldman, *Criminal Behavior: A Psychological Analysis* (New York: Wiley, 1978); William McCord and Joan McCord, *Psychopathy and Delinquency* (New York: Wiley, 1956).

45. The American Psychiatric Association's *Diagnostic and Statistical Manual of Mental Disorders*, 3rd rev. ed. *(DSM III-R)* (Washington, D.C., 1987), classifies psychopathy as "antisocial personality." See Benjamin Karpman, "On the Need of Separating Psychopathy into Two Distinct Clinical Types: The Symptomatic and the Idiopathic," *Journal of Criminal Psychopathology*, **3** (1941): 112–137.

46. Eysenck and Gudjonsson, *The Causes and Cures of Crime*. See also Robert D. Hare, "Research Scale for the Assessment of Psychopathology in Criminal Populations," *Personality and Individual Differences*, **1** (1980): 111–119.

47. J. Puig-Antich, "Biological Factors in Prepubertal Major Depression," *Pediatric Annals*, **12** (1986): 867–878.

48. See, e.g., Guenther Knoblich and Roy King, "Biological Correlates of Criminal Behavior," in McCord, *Facts, Frameworks, and Forecasts*; Diana H. Fishbein, "Biological Perspectives in Criminology," *Criminology*, **28** (1990): 17–40; David Magnusson, Britt af Klinteberg, and Hakan Stattin, "Autonomic Activity/Reactivity, Behavior, and Crime in a Longitudinal Perspective," in McCord, *Facts, Frameworks, and Forecasts*; Frank A. Elliott, "Violence: The Neurologic Contribution: An Overview," *Archives of Neurology*, **49** (1992): 595–603; L. French, "Neuropsychology of Violence," *Corrective and Social Psychiatry and Journal of Behavior Technology Methods and Therapy*, **37** (1991): 12–17; and Elizabeth Kandel and Sarnoff A. Mednick, "Perinatal Complications Predict Violent Offending," *Criminology*, **29** (1991): 519–530.

49. Edward O. Wilson, *Sociobiology: The New Synthesis* (Cambridge, Mass.: Harvard University Press, 1975).

50. C. Ray Jeffery, *Biology and Crime* (Beverly Hills, Calif.: Sage, 1979).

51. See Sarnoff A. Mednick, Terrie E. Moffitt, and Susan A. Stack, *The Causes of Crime: New Biological Approaches* (New York: Cambridge University Press, 1987).

52. A. A. Sandberg, G. F. Koepf, and T. Ishihara, "An XYY Human Male," *Lancet* (August 1961): 488–489.

53. Herman A. Witkin et al., "Criminality, Aggression, and Intelligence among XYY and XXY Men," in *Biosocial Bases of Criminal Behavior*, eds. Sarnoff A. Mednick and Karl O. Christiansen (New York: Wiley, 1977).

54. Johannes Lange, *Verbrechen als Schicksal* (Leipzig: Georg Thieme, 1929).

55. Cf. Gregory Carey, "Twin Imitation for Antisocial Behavior: Implications for Genetic Environment Research," *Journal of Abnormal Psychology*, **101** (1992): 18–25.

56. See Karl O. Christiansen, "A Preliminary Study of Criminality among Twins," in Mednick and Christiansen, *Biosocial Bases of Criminal Behavior*.

57. David C. Rowe and D. Wayne Osgood, "Heredity and Sociological Theories of Delinquency: A Reconsideration," *American Sociological Review*, **49** (1986): 526–540; David C. Rowe, "Genetic and Environmental Components of Antisocial Behavior: A Study of 256 Twin Pairs," *Criminology*, **24** (1986): 513–532.

58. Sarnoff A. Mednick, William Gabrielli, and Barry Hutchings, "Genetic Influences in Criminal Behavior: Evidence from an Adoption Court," in *Prospective Studies of Crime and Delinquency*, eds. K. Teilmann et al. (Boston: Kluwer-Nijhoff, 1983).

59. These and other studies are reviewed in Mednick et al., *The Causes of Crime*.

60. Hugo Munsterberg, *On the Witness Stand* (New York: Doubleday, 1908); Henry H. Goddard, *Feeble-Mindedness: Its Causes and Consequences* (New York: Macmillan, 1914).

61. Edwin H. Sutherland, "Mental Deficiency and Crime," in *Social Attitudes*, ed. K. Young (New York: Henry Holt, 1931).

62. Robert H. Gault, "Highlights of Forty Years in the Correctional Field—and Looking Ahead," *Federal Probation*, **17** (1953): 3–4.

63. Arthur Jensen, *Bias in Mental Testing* (New York: Free Press, 1979).

64. Ibid.; Richard J. Herrnstein, *IQ in the Meritocracy* (Boston: Atlantic–Little, Brown, 1973).

65. Travis Hirschi and Michael J. Hindelang, "Intelligence and Delinquency: A Revisionist Review," *American Sociological Review*, **42** (1977): 571–586.

66. Travis Hirschi, *Causes of Delinquency* (Berkeley: University of California Press, 1969).

67. Marvin E. Wolfgang, Robert F. Figlio, and Thorsten Sellin, *Delinquency in a Birth Cohort* (Chicago: University of Chicago Press, 1972).

68. Albert J. Reiss and Albert L. Rhodes, "The Distribution of Juvenile Delinquency in the Social Class Structure," *American Sociological Review*, **26** (1961): 720–732.

69. James Q. Wilson and Richard Herrnstein, *Crime and Human Nature* (New York: Simon & Schuster, 1985); Deborah W. Denno, "Sociological and Human Developmental Explanations of Crime: Conflict or Consensus?" *Criminology*, **23** (1985): 711–740. See also Deborah W. Denno, "Victim, Offender, and Situational Characteristics of Violent Crime," *Journal of Criminal Law and Criminology*, **77** (1986): 1142–1158.

70. "Taking the Chitling Test," *Newsweek*, July 15, 1968.

71. Sandra Scarr and Richard Weinberg, "I.Q. Test Performance of Black Children Adopted by White Families," *American Psychologist*, **31** (1976): 726–739.

72. See Doris J. Rapp, *Allergies and the Hyperactive Child* (New York: Simon & Schuster, 1981).

73. Diana H. Fishbein and Susan Pease, "The Effects of Diet on Behavior: Implications for Criminology and Corrections," *Research on Corrections,* **1** (1988): 1–45.

74. Stephen Schoenthaler, "Diet and Crime: An Empirical Examination of the Value of Nutrition in the Control and Treatment of Incarcerated Juvenile Offenders," *International Journal of Biosocial Research,* **4** (1982): 25–39.

75. Abram Hoffer, "The Relation of Crime to Nutrition," *Humanist in Canada,* **8** (1975): 2–9.

76. Benjamin F. Feingold, *Why Is Your Child Hyperactive?* (New York: Random House, 1975).

77. James W. Swanson and Marcel Kinsbourne, "Food Dyes Impair Performance of Hyperactive Children on a Laboratory Test," *Science,* **207** (1980): 1485–1487.

78. Anthony R. Mawson and K. W. Jacobs, "Corn Consumption, Tryptophan, and Cross-National Homicide Rates," *Journal of Orthomolecular Psychiatry,* **7** (1978): 227–230.

79. Matti Virkkunen, "Insulin Secretion during the Glucose Tolerance Test among Habitually Violent and Impulsive Offenders," *Aggressive Behavior,* **12** (1986): 303–310.

80. E. A. Beeman, "The Effect of Male Hormones on Aggressive Behavior in Mice," *Physiological Zoology,* **20** (1947): 373–405.

81. D. A. Hamburg and D. T. Lunde, "Sex Hormones in the Development of Sex Differences," in *The Development of Sex Differences,* ed. Eleanor E. Maccoby (Stanford, Calif.: Stanford University Press, 1966).

82. L. E. Kreuz and R. M. Rose, "Assessment of Aggressive Behavior and Plasma Testosterone of a Young Criminal Population," *Psychosomatic Medicine,* **34** (1972): 321–332; R. T. Rada, D. R. Laws, and R. Kellner, "Plasma Testosterone Levels in the Rapist," *Psychosomatic Medicine,* **38** (1976): 257–268.

83. Katharina Dalton, *The Premenstrual Syndrome* (Springfield, Ill.: Charles C. Thomas, 1971).

84. Julie Horney, "Menstrual Cycles and Criminal Responsibility," *Law and Human Behavior,* **2** (1978): 25–36.

85. *Regina v. Charlson,* 1 All. E.R. 859 (1955).

86. Lee Ellis, "Monoamine Oxidase and Criminality: Identifying an Apparent Biological Marker for Antisocial Behavior," *Journal of Research in Crime and Delinquency,* **28** (1991): 227–251.

87. H. Forssman and T. S. Frey, "Electroencephalograms of Boys with Behavior Disorders," *Acta Psychologica et Neurologia Scandinavica,* **28** (1953): 61–73; H. de Baudouin et al., "Study of a Population of 97 Confined Murderers," *Annales medico-psychologique,* **119** (1961): 625–686.

88. Sarnoff A. Mednick, Jan Volavka, William F. Gabrielli, and Turan M. Itil, "EEG as a Predictor of Antisocial Behavior," *Criminology,* **19** (1981): 219–229.

89. Jan Volavka, "Electroencephalogram among Criminals," in Mednick et al., *The Causes of Crime.*

90. *DSM III-R,* 314.01. See also Michael Rutter, "Syndromes Attributed to 'Minimal Brain Dysfunction' in Children," *American Journal of Psychiatry,* **139** (1980): 21–33.

91. Lorne T. Yeudall, D. Fromm-Auch, and P. Davies, "Neuropsychological Impairment of Persistent Delinquency," *Journal of Nervous and Mental Disorders,* **170** (1982): 257–265; R. D. Robin et al., "Adolescents Who Attempt Suicide," *Journal of Pediatrics,* **90** (1977): 636–638.

92. Edward Sagarin, "Taboo Subjects and Taboo Viewpoints in Criminology," in *Taboos in Criminology,* ed. Sagarin (Beverly Hills, Calif.: Sage, 1980), pp. 8–9.

93. Diana H. Fishbein, "Biological Perspectives in Criminology," *Criminology,* **28** (1990): 27–40.

94. Wilson and Herrnstein, *Crime and Human Nature.* Infants develop attachment to mothers, or mother substitutes, for comfort, security, and warmth.

5

Strain and Cultural Deviance Theories

KEY TERMS
anomic suicide
conduct norms
cultural deviance theories
cultural transmission
culture conflict theory
deviance
differential association theory
social disorganization theory
strain theory

The early decades of the twentieth century brought major changes to American society. One of the most significant was the change in the composition of the populations of cities. Between 1840 and 1924, 45 million people—Irish, Swedes, Germans, Italians, Poles, Armenians, Bohemians, Russians—left the Old World; two-thirds of them were bound for the United States.[1] At the same time, increased mechanization in this country deprived many American farmworkers of their jobs and forced them to join the ranks of the foreign-born and the black laborers who had migrated from the South to northern and midwestern industrial centers. During the 1920s large U.S. cities swelled with 5 million new arrivals.[2]

Chicago's expansion was particularly remarkable: its population doubled in 20 years. Many of the new arrivals brought nothing with them except what they could carry. The city offered them only meager wages, 12-hour working days in conditions that jeopardized their health, and tenement housing in deteriorating areas. Chicago had other problems as well: in the late 1920s and early 1930s it was the home of major organized crime groups, which fought over the profits from the illegal production and sale of liquor during Prohibition (as we shall see in Chapter 12).

Teeming with newcomers looking for work, corrupt politicians trying to buy their votes, and bootleggers growing more influential through sheer firepower and the political strength they controlled, Chicago also had a rapidly rising crime rate. The city soon became an inviting urban laboratory for criminologists, who began to challenge the then-predominant theories of crime causation, which were based on biological and psychological factors. Many of these criminologists were associated with the University of Chicago, which has the oldest sociology program in the United States (begun in 1892). By the 1920s these criminologists began to measure scientifically the amount of criminal behavior and its relation to the social turmoil Chicago was experiencing. Since that time sociological theories have remained at the forefront of the scientific investigation of crime causation.

THE INTERCONNECTEDNESS OF SOCIOLOGICAL THEORIES

The psychological and biological theories of criminal behavior (Chapter 4) share the assumption that such behavior is caused by some underlying physical or mental condition that separates the criminal from the noncriminal. They seek to identify the kind of person who becomes a criminal and to find the factors that caused the person to engage in criminal behavior. These theories yield insight into individual cases, but they do not explain why crime rates vary from one neighborhood to the next, from group to group, within large urban areas, or within groups of individuals. Sociological theories seek the reasons for differences in crime rates in the social environment. These theories can be grouped into three general categories: strain, cultural deviance, and social control.[3]

The strain and cultural deviance theories formulated between 1925 and 1940 and still popular today focus on the social forces that cause people to engage in criminal activity. These theories laid the foundation for the subcultural theories we discuss in Chapter 6. Social control theories (Chapter 7) take a different approach: they are based on the assumption that the motivation to commit crime is part of human nature. Consequently, social control theories seek to discover why people do *not* commit crime. They examine the ability of social groups and institutions to make their rules effective.

Strain and cultural deviance theories both assume that social class and criminal behavior are related, but they differ as to the nature of the relationship. **Strain theory** argues that all members of society subscribe to one set of cultural values—that of the middle class. One of the most important middle-class values is economic success. Since lower-class persons do not have legitimate means to reach this goal, they turn to illegitimate means in desperation. **Cultural deviance theories** claim that lower-class people have a different set of values that tend to conflict with the values of the middle class. Consequently, when lower-class persons conform to their own value system, they may be violating conventional or middle-class norms.

ANOMIE THEORY: ÉMILE DURKHEIM

Imagine a clock with all its parts finely synchronized. It functions with precision. It keeps perfect time. But if one tiny weight or small spring breaks down, the whole mechanism will not function properly. One way of studying a society is to look at its component parts in an effort to find out how they relate to each other. In other words, we look at the structure of a society to see how it functions. If the society is stable, its parts operating smoothly, the social arrangements are functional. Such a society is marked by cohesion, cooperation, and consensus. But if the component parts are arranged in such a way as to threaten the social order, the arrangements are said to be dysfunctional. In a class-oriented society, for example, the classes tend to be in conflict.

The Structural-Functionalist Perspective

The structural-functionalist perspective was developed by Émile Durkheim (1858–1917) before the end of the nineteenth century.[4] At the time, positivist biological theories, which relied on the search for individual differences between criminals and noncriminals, were dominant. So at a time when science was searching for the abnormality of the criminal, Durkheim was writing about the normality of crime in society. To him, the explanation of human conduct, and indeed human misconduct, lies not in the individual but in the group and the social organization. It is in this context that he introduced the term *anomie*, the breakdown of social order as a result of the loss of standards and values.[5]

Throughout his career, Durkheim was preoccupied with the effects of social change. He believed that when a simple society develops into a modern, urbanized one, the intimacy needed to sustain a common set of norms declines. Groups become fragmented, and in the absence of a common set of rules, the actions and expectations of people in one sector may clash with those of people in another. As behavior becomes unpredictable, the system gradually breaks down, and the society is in a state of anomie.[6]

Anomie and Suicide

Durkheim illustrated his concept of anomie in a discussion not of crime but of suicide.[7] He suggested several reasons why suicide was more common in some groups than in others. For our purposes, we are interested in the particular form of suicide he called **anomic suicide.** When he analyzed statistical data, he found that suicide rates increased during times of sudden economic change, whether that change was major depression or unexpected prosperity. In periods of rapid change people are abruptly thrown into unfamiliar situations. Rules that once guided behavior no longer hold.

Consider the events of the 1920s. Wealth came easily to many people in those heady, prosperous years. Toward the end, through July, August, and September 1929, the New York stock market soared to new heights. Enormous profits were made from speculation. But on October 24, 1929, a day history records as Black Thursday, the stock market crashed. Thirteen million shares of stock were sold. As more and more shares were offered for sale, their value plummeted. In the wake of the crash, a severe depression overtook the country and then the world. Banks failed. Mortgages were foreclosed. Businesses went bankrupt. People lost their jobs. Lifestyles changed overnight. Many people were driven to sell apples on street corners to survive, and they had to stand in mile-long breadlines to feed their families. Suddenly the norms by which people lived were no longer relevant. They became disoriented and confused. Suicide rates rose.

It is not difficult to understand rising suicide rates in such circumstances, but why would rates also rise at a time of sudden prosperity? According to Durkheim, the same factors are at work in both situations. What causes the problems is not the amount of money available but the sudden change. Durkheim believed that human desires are boundless, an "insatiable and bottomless abyss."[8] Since nature does not set such strict biological limits to the capabilities of humans as it does to those of other animals, he argued, we have developed social rules that put a realistic cap on our aspirations. These regulations are incorporated into the individual conscience

WINDOW TO THE WORLD
A Social System Breaks Down

In mid-1993, three young members of the Yanomami, an ancient Amazon tribal people, committed suicide—an unprecedented remedy for life's problems in a culture that forbids even talking about death. But the man and two women who took their own lives are among more than 1500 Yanomami who have died from the effects of the invasion of their lands—and culture—by gold miners.(1)

The "gold rush" began in 1987 when prospectors began cutting through swaths of the rainforest where the Yanomami have lived for perhaps 40,000 years, according to one theory. Miners built airstrips, extracted tons of gold, polluted the rivers with metal silt, and left behind "the dubious gifts of the 20th century: disease, prostitution, weapons, alcohol, denuded forests and befouled rivers."(2) While most of the deaths of the Yanomami have resulted from malaria, the tribe also has suffered from flu, venereal disease, measles, tuberculosis, and mercury poisoning from the fish they catch in the now-polluted rivers of their lands. Others have died in direct clashes with miners. In August 1993, for example, there were allegations of a massacre in Brazil of up to 73 tribal members, including at least 10 children, by wildcat gold miners.(3)

Operation Free Jungle

Attempts have been made to protect the Yanomami. In 1990, Operation Free Jungle employed soldiers and police to destroy airstrips, remove mining equipment, and expel prospectors. The Brazilian government created a 37,000-mile reservation for its 9000 members of the Yanomami tribe, but the 11,000 tribe members on the Venezuelan side of the border have no such reservation. In 1993, in a second major attempt to protect the tribe, Brazilian police and military evacuated 3000 miners, and Venezuelan troops seized gold miners who crossed the border into the Venezuelan Amazon region.(4)

A Poor Prognosis

But the chances that the Yanomami will be able to withstand the attack on their land and culture are slim. The land contains large deposits of gold, diamonds, tin, and other minerals, and the miners typically are impoverished Brazilians fiercely determined to continue prospecting. Even if the government wants to continue its attempts to protect the area, funds to enforce protective measures are limited. "It's not enough to create a reserve when, inside, you have riches and, outside, marginalized people," says Sidney Possuelo, who is charged with protecting Brazil's indigenous peoples.(5) Already outnumbered by the miners, the Yanomami have lost 20 percent of their tribe members since this battle began; 200 people died in 1992. And their traditional way of life has been disrupted: hunting and fishing are increasingly difficult; alcohol and prostitution are taking their toll; miners have raped women and shot children from trees.

The problems of the Yanomami are far from unique. Brazil's Indian population has fallen from 5 million to 220,000 since 1500, and the pattern has repeated itself in virtually every industrializing country. "As the pressure for minerals and timber increases, indigenous groups become more vulnerable to armed attack," stated an Amnesty International report on the Yanomami.(2)

Sources

1. Lynne Wallis, "Quiet Genocide: Miners Seeking Precious Metals Are Causing Deaths of the Yanomami," *Ottawa Citizen*, June 28, 1993, p. A6.
2. "Aid for an Ancient Tribe," *Newsweek*, Apr. 9, 1990, p. 34.
3. "Genocide in the Amazon," *Newsweek*, Aug. 30, 1993, p. 61.
4. James Brooke, "Brazil Evicting Miners in Amazon to Reclaim Land for the Indians," *New York Times*, Mar. 8, 1993, p. A4.
5. Christina Lamb, "Extermination in Eden: A Visit to Amazonia Where the Lust for Gold Threatens the Last Stone Age Tribe," *Financial Post*, Feb. 27, 1993, p. 47.

Questions for Discussion

1. As the Yanomami culture is destroyed, how would you expect the tribe's traditional ways of dealing with crime to be affected? Explain.
2. What measures might be effective in protecting indigenous peoples in all parts of the world from suffering a fate similar to that of the Yanomami?

A Yanomami man with the trappings of modern civilization.

The wake of a Moscow policeman shot in one of many violent confrontations with criminals. There has been a significant rise in organized crime and gang violence in the new Russia.

and thus make it possible for people to feel fulfilled.

But with a sudden burst of prosperity, expectations change. When the old rules no longer determine how rewards are distributed among members of society, there is no longer any restraint on what people want. Once again the system breaks down. Thus, whether sudden change causes great prosperity or great depression, the result is the same—anomie.

STRAIN THEORY

A few generations after Durkheim, the American sociologist Robert Merton (1910–   ) also related the crime problem to anomie. But his conception differs somewhat from Durkheim's. The real problem, Merton argued, is created not by sudden social change but by a social structure that holds out the same goals to all its members without giving them equal means to achieve them. This lack of integration between what the culture calls for and what the structure permits, the former encouraging success and the latter preventing it, can cause norms to break down because they no longer are effective guides to behavior.

Merton borrowed the term "anomie" from Durkheim to describe this breakdown of the normative system. According to Merton:

It is only when a system of cultural values extols, virtually above all else, certain common symbols of success for the population at large while its social structure rigorously restricts or completely eliminates access to approved modes of acquiring these symbols for a considerable part of the same population, that antisocial behavior ensues on a considerable scale.[9]

Disparity between Goals and Means

Merton argued that in a class-oriented society, opportunities to get to the top are not equally distributed. Very few members of the lower class ever get there. His anomie theory emphasizes the importance of two elements in any society: (1) cultural aspirations, or goals that people believe are worth striving for; and (2) institutionalized means or accepted ways to attain the desired ends. If a society is to be stable, these two elements must be reasonably well integrated; in other words, there should be means for individuals to reach the goals that are important to them. Disparity between goals and means fosters frustration, which leads to strain.

From this perspective, the social structure is the root of the crime problem (hence the approach Merton takes is sometimes called a *structural* explanation). Strain theory, the name given by contemporary criminologists to Merton's explanation of criminal behavior, assumes that people are law-abiding but when under great pressure will resort to crime. Disparity between goals and means provides that pressure.

Merton's theory explains crime in the United States in terms of the wide disparities in income among the various classes. Statistics clearly demonstrate that such disparities exist. The poorest fifth of American families received less than 4 percent of all income in 1990, while the highest fifth received 46.4 percent of all income—more than ten times as much.[10] A summary of Americans' incomes in 1991 shows that the median income for white families was $37,793, for black families $21,548, and for hispanic families $23,895.[11] It is not, however, solely wealth or income which determines people's position on a social ladder that ranges from the homeless to the very, very rich who live on great estates. Other attributes of social class are education, prestige, power, and even language.

The United States

In our society opportunities to move up the social ladder exist, but they are not equally distributed. A child born to a single, uneducated, 13-year-old girl living in a slum has practically no chance to move up, whereas the child of a middle-class family has a better-than-average chance of reaching a professional or business position. Yet all people in the society share the same goals. And those goals are shaped by billions of advertising dollars spent each year to spread the message that everyone can drive a sports car, take a well-deserved Caribbean vacation, and record the adventure on videotape.

The mystique is reinforced by instant lottery millionaires, superstar athletes, the earnings of Wall Street traders, and rags-to-riches stories of such people as Ray Kroc. Kroc, a high school dropout, believed that a 15-cent hamburger with a 10-cent bag of French fries could make dining out affordable for low-income families; his idea spread quickly through the United States—and to 29 other countries that now have McDonald's restaurants with the familiar golden arches. Though Merton argued that lack of legitimate means for everyone to reach material goals like these does create problems, he also made it clear that the high rate of deviant behavior in the United States cannot be explained solely on the basis of lack of means.

India

The world has produced class systems that are more rigid than our own, and societies that place much stricter limitations on people's ability to achieve their goals, without causing the problems the United States faces. In the traditional society of India, for example, the untouchables at the bottom of the caste system are forbidden by custom (although no longer by law) even to enter the temples and schools used by those above them, while those at the top enjoy immense privileges.

All Hindu castes fall within a hierarchy, each one imposing upon its members duties and prohibitions covering both public and private life. People of high status may give food to people of lower status, for example, but may not receive food from them. One may eat in the home of a person of lower status, but the food must be cooked and served by a person of equal or higher status. Members of such a rigid system clearly face many more restraints than we do. Why, then, does India not have a very high crime rate?

The answer lies in the fact that Indians learn from birth that all people do not and cannot aspire to the same things. In the United States, the egalitarian principle denies the existence of limits to upward mobility within the social structure.[12] In reality, everyone in society experiences some pressures and strains, and the amounts are inversely related to position in the hierarchy: the lower the class, the higher the strain.

Modes of Adaptation

To be sure, not everyone who is denied access to a society's goals becomes deviant. Merton outlined five ways in which people adapt to society's goals and means. Individuals' responses (modes of adaptation) depend on their attitudes toward the cultural goals and the institutional means of attaining those goals. The options are conformity, innovation, ritualism, retreatism, and rebellion (see Table 5.1).

Merton does not tell us how any one individual chooses to become a drug pusher, for example, and another chooses to work on an assembly line. Instead, he explains why crime rates are high in some groups and low in others.

Conformity

Conformity is the most common mode of adjustment. Individuals accept both the culturally defined goals and the prescribed means for achieving those goals. They work, save, go to

TABLE 5.1   A TYPOLOGY OF MODES OF INDIVIDUAL ADAPTATION

Modes of Adaptation	Culture Goals*	Institutionalized Means*
Conformity	+	+
Innovation	+	–
Ritualism	–	+
Retreatism	–	–
Rebellion	±	±

*+ = acceptance; – = rejection; ± = rejection and substitution.

Source: Robert K. Merton, Social Theory and Social Structure (New York: Free Press, 1957), p. 140.

school, and follow the legitimate paths. Look around you in the classroom. You will see many children of decent, hardworking parents. After college they will find legitimate jobs. Some will excel. Some will walk the economic middle path. But all those who are conformists will accept (though not necessarily achieve) the goals of our society and the means it approves for achieving them.

Innovation

Individuals who choose the adaptation of innovation accept society's goals, but since they have few legitimate means of achieving them, they design their own means for getting ahead. The means may be burglary, robbery, embezzlement, or a host of other crimes. Youngsters who have no parental attention, no encouragement in school, no way to the top—no future—may scrawl their signatures on subway cars and buildings and park benches in order to achieve recognition of a sort. Such illegitimate forms of innovation are certainly not restricted to the lower classes, as evidenced by such crimes as stock manipulation, sale of defective products, and income tax evasion.

Ritualism

People who adapt by ritualism abandon the goals they once believed to be within reach and resign themselves to their present lifestyles. They play by the rules; they work on assembly lines, hold middle-management jobs, or follow some other safe routine.[13] Many workers have been catching a bus at the same street corner at the same hour every day for 20 years or more. They have long forgotten why, except that their jobs are where their paychecks come from. Their great relief is a 2-week vacation in the summer.

Retreatism

Retreatism is the adaptation of people who give up both the goals (can't make it) and the means (why try?) and retreat into the world of drug addiction or alcoholism. They have internalized the value system and therefore are under internal pressure not to innovate. The retreatist mode allows for an escape into a nonproductive, nonstriving lifestyle. Some members of the antiwar movement of the 1960s opted to drop out

entirely. The pressure was too great; the opportunities were unacceptable. They became addicts or followers of occult religions.

Rebellion

Rebellion occurs when both the cultural goals and the legitimate means are rejected. Many individuals substitute their own goals (get rid of the establishment) and their own means (protest). They have an alternate scheme for a new social structure, however ill-defined. In 1981, when youths of conservative Zurich, Switzerland, grew frustrated over the establishment's rejection of their demands for a "youth house," they took to the streets, stripped naked, and threw eggs at the operagoers and at the opera house itself.

Merton's theory of how the social structure produces strain that may lead to deviant behavior is illustrated in Figure 5.1. His theory has challenged researchers for half a century.

Tests of Strain Theory

Merton and his followers (Chapter 6) predict that the greatest proportion of crime will be found in the lower classes because lower-class people have the least opportunity to reach their goals legitimately. Many research studies designed to test the various propositions of strain theory focus on the association between social class and delinquency (an association that evokes considerable controversy). Some studies report a strong inverse relationship: as class goes up, crime rates go down. Others find no association at all between the two variables (Chapter 2).

Social Class and Crime

The controversy over the relationship between social class and crime began when researchers, using self-report questionnaires, found more serious and more frequent delinquency among lower-class boys.[14] In Chapter 2 we saw that other researchers seriously questioned those findings.[15] When Charles Tittle and his colleagues attempted to clarify the relationship by analyzing 35 empirical studies, they concluded that "class is not now and has not been related to criminality in the recent past."[16] Among the researchers who continued to question the asso-

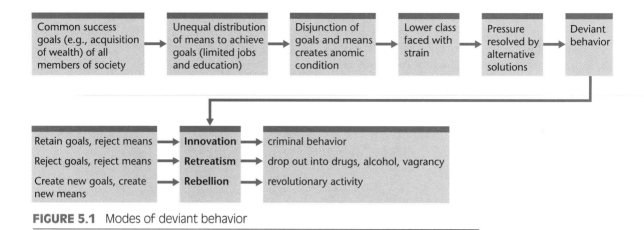

FIGURE 5.1 Modes of deviant behavior

ciation was Travis Hirschi, who commented: "If socioeconomic status is unrelated to delinquency, then consistency requires that 'socioeconomic status' be removed from the dictionary of delinquency theory and research."[17]

Once again there was a critical reaction. A summary of more than 100 projects concluded that "lower-class people do commit those direct interpersonal types of crime which are normally handled by the police at a higher rate than middle-class people."[18] But if low social status creates frustration that pushes people to commit crime, why don't all the people in the lowest class commit crimes, or drop out into the drug world, or become revolutionaries? Since they clearly do not, there must be some limitations to the causal relationship between crime and social class.

Terence Thornberry and Margaret Farnworth have tried to address this limitation by explaining that the problem arises with studies that make a simple connection between class and crime. The relationship, they say, is highly complex; it involves race, seriousness of the offense, education of family and offender, and many other factors.[19]

According to a number of researchers, we may be able to learn more about the relationship between social class and crime if we look closely at specific types of offenses rather than at aggregate crime (or delinquency) rates.[20] Take homicide, for example: In two large cross-national studies, two teams of Canadian researchers explored the relationship between income inequality and national homicide rates.[21] Both teams reported results that support strain theory. When opportunities or means for success are not provided equally to all members of society (as indicated by crime rates), pressure is exerted on some members of that society to engage in deviant behavior (in this case, homicide). Further analyses by one of the teams showed that the effects of inequality on homicide may be even more pronounced in more democratic societies. The researchers commented: "Income inequality might be more likely to generate violent behavior in more democratic societies because of the coexistence of high material inequality and an egalitarian value system."[22]

David Brownfield also related social class to specific offenses, in this instance to fistfights and brawls among teenagers.[23] His information came from two sources: the Richmond Youth Study, conducted at the University of California at Berkeley, and the Community Tolerance Study, done by a team of researchers at the University of Arizona. Brownfield's analysis of questionnaires completed by 1500 white male students in California and 1300 white male students in Arizona suggests a very strong relation between poverty—as measured by unemployment and welfare assistance—and violent behavior. He concluded that the general public expresses much hostility against the "disreputable poor," a term used by David Matza to describe people who remain unemployed for a long time, even during periods of full employment.[24] In fact, Brownfield suggests, many people hold them in contempt. (He cites a *New York Times*/CBS poll which found that over half of all the respondents believed that most people on welfare could get along without it if they only tried.) This hostility causes the disreputable poor to build up frustration, which is made worse by the lack of such fundamental necessities as food and shelter. Such a situation breeds discontent—and violence.

Race and Crime

Yet another question that relates to strain theory concerns the relationship between racial inequality and violent crime. Judith and Peter Blau studied data from 125 metropolitan areas in the United States.[25] Their primary finding was that racial inequality—as measured by the difference in socioeconomic status between whites and nonwhites—is associated with the total rate of violent crime. The conclusion fits well with Merton's theory.

The Blaus argued that in a democratic society which stresses equal opportunities for individual achievement but in reality distributes resources on the basis of race, there is bound to be conflict. The most disadvantaged are precisely those who cannot change their situation through political action. In such circumstances, the frustrations created by racial inequalities tend to be expressed in various forms of aggression, such as violent crime. Several researchers have supported these findings.[26] But not all researchers are in agreement.

John Braithwaite examined Uniform Crime Report statistics for a sample of 175 American cities. He compared the rates of violent crime with racial inequality, as measured by the incomes of black families and the incomes of all other families in his sample cities. He concluded that racial inequality does not cause specific crime problems.[27] Other researchers confirm his finding.[28] Perhaps the crucial point is not whether one actually has an equal chance to be successful but rather how one perceives one's chances. According to this reasoning, people who feel the most strain are those who have not only high goals but also low expectations of

reaching them. So far, however, research has not supported this contention.[29]

Evaluation: Strain Theory

The strain perspective developed by Merton and his followers has influenced both research and theoretical developments in criminology.[30] Yet, as popular as this theory remains, it has been questioned on a variety of grounds. By concentrating on crime at the lower levels of the socioeconomic hierarchy, for example, it neglects crime committed by middle- and upper-class people. Radical criminologists (see Chapter 8), in fact, claim that strain theory "stands accused of predicting too little bourgeois criminality and too much proletarian criminality."[31]

Other critics believe there is some question as to whether a society as heterogeneous as ours really does have goals on which everyone agrees. Some theorists argue that American subcultures have their own value systems (Chapter 6). If that is the case, we cannot account for deviant behavior on the basis of Merton's cultural goals.[32] Other questions are asked about the theory. If we have an agreed-upon set of goals, is material gain the dominant one? If crime is a means to an end, why is there so much useless, destructive behavior, especially among teenagers?

No matter how it is structured, each society defines goals for its members. The United States is far from being the only society in which people strive for wealth and prestige. Yet, while some people in other cultures have limited means for achieving these goals, not all these societies have high crime rates. Two such societies—Japan and Switzerland—are among the most developed and industrialized in the world. Although the United States has quite a bit in common with them, it does not share their very low crime rates.[33]

Despite the many critical assessments, strain theory, represented primarily by Merton's formulation of anomie, has had a major impact on contemporary criminology. For one thing, it appeals to common sense. Its propositions seem to be borne out by everyday observations. Generations of scholars have tried to figure out how crime is related to the problem created by inequalities in a society that prides itself on its egalitarian principles. The theory has also had practical significance.

From Theory to Practice

Strain theory has helped us develop a crime-prevention strategy. If, as the theory tells us, frustration builds up in people who have few means for reaching their goals, it makes sense to design programs that give lower-class people a bigger stake in society.

Head Start

In the 1960s, President Lyndon Johnson inaugurated the Head Start program as part of a major antipoverty campaign. The goal of Head Start is to make children of low-income families more socially competent, better able to deal with their present environment and their later responsibilities. The youngsters get a boost (or a head start) in a 1-year preschool developmental program that is intended to prevent them from dropping out of society. Program components include community and parental involvement, an 8-to-1 child/staff ratio, and daily evaluation and involvement of all the children in the planning of and responsibility for their own activities.

Since a 1-year program could not be expected to affect the remainder of a child's life, Project Follow Through was developed in an effort to provide the same opportunities for Head Start youngsters during elementary school. What began as a modest summer experience for half a million preschool children has expanded into a year-round program that provides educational and social services to millions of young people and their families. This, then, is a program clearly intended to lower stress in the group most likely to develop criminal behavior.

Some research findings do indicate that the program has had a certain measure of success.[35] Yet successes of individual Head Start programs are unevenly distributed over the country, depending largely on program and staff quality. President Clinton, in his 1993 State-of-the-Union Message, promised to increase Head Start's $2.8 billion annual budget by an additional $10 billion over the next 4 years. But even supporters warn that Head Start's success rates can improve only if these funds are carefully aimed at program improvement, rather than enlargement.[36]

Perry Preschool Project

Another program that tried to ameliorate the disparity between goals and means in society was the Perry Preschool Project, begun in 1962 on the south side of Ypsilanti, Michigan. Its purpose was to develop skills that would give youngsters the means of getting ahead at school and in the workplace, thereby reducing the amount and seriousness of delinquent behavior. Overall, 123 black children 3 and 4 years old participated for 2 years, 5 days a week, $2^1/_2$ hours a day. The program provided a teacher for every five children, weekly visits by a teacher to a child's home, and a follow-up of every child annually until age 11 and thereafter at ages 14, 15, and 19.

There is little doubt about the effectiveness of the project. By age 19, the participants did better in several areas than a group that had not participated:

- Employment rates doubled.
- Rates of postsecondary education doubled.
- Teenage pregnancy was cut in half.
- The high school graduation rate was one-third higher.
- Arrest rates were 40 percent lower.[37]

Job Corps

Yet another survivor of President Johnson's War on Poverty is the federal Job Corps program. It aims at "the worst of the worst," as Senator Orrin Hatch of Utah said.[38] The program enables neglected teenagers—otherwise headed for juvenile detention or jail—to master work habits that they did not learn at home. In 1992, 62,000 young people were serving in the Job Corps. Most of them had enlisted on the basis of recruitment posters, like those distributed by the armed forces. The average length of stay in the corps is just short of a year, at an annual cost of $18,831. That sounds expensive, but juvenile detention costs $29,600—and residential drug treatment centers cost $19,000.

Over two-thirds of former Job Corps members get jobs, and 17 percent go on to higher education. Research has shown that the Job Corps returns $1.46 for every dollar spent, because of

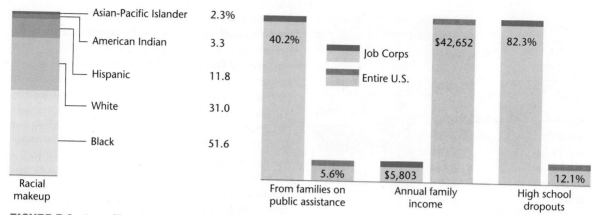

FIGURE 5.2 A profile of Job Corps members
Job Corps figures are for members from July 1, 1990, to June 30, 1991.
72.8 percent of Job Corps members were never employed in full-time jobs before
they entered the program.

Source: Jane Gross, "Remnant of the War on Poverty, Job Corps Is Still a Quiet Success," *New York Times,* Feb. 17, 1992, p. A14.

increased tax revenue and decreased cost of welfare, crime, and incarceration. Over two-thirds of Job Corps members come from minorities; less than one-third have a low-income white background (see Figure 5.2).

CULTURAL DEVIANCE THEORIES

The programs that emanate from strain theory attempt to give lower-class children ways to achieve middle-class goals. Programs based on cultural deviance theories concentrate on teaching middle-class values.

Strain theory attributes criminal behavior in the United States to the striving of all citizens to conform with the conventional values of the middle class, primarily financial success. Cultural deviance theories attribute crime to a set of values peculiar to the lower class. Conformity with the lower-class value system, which determines behavior in slum areas, causes conflict with society's laws. Both strain and cultural deviance theories locate the causes of crime in the disadvantageous position of those at the lowest stratum in a class-based society.

Scholars who view crime as resulting from cultural values that permit, or even demand, behavior in violation of the law are called cultural deviance theorists. The three major cultural deviance theories are social disorganization, differential association, and culture conflict. **Social disorganization theory** focuses on the development of high-crime areas in which there is a disintegration of conventional values caused by rapid industrialization, increased immigration, and urbanization. **Differential association theory** maintains that people learn to commit crime as a result of contact with antisocial values, attitudes, and criminal behavior patterns. **Culture conflict theory** states that different groups learn different conduct norms (rules governing behavior) and that the conduct norms of some groups may clash with conventional middle-class rules.

All three theories contend that criminals and delinquents in fact do conform—but to norms that deviate from those of the dominant middle class. Before we examine the specific theories that share the cultural deviance perspective, we need to explore the nature of cultural deviance.

The Nature of Cultural Deviance

When you drive through rural Lancaster County, Pennsylvania; Holmes County, Ohio; or Elkhart and Lagrange counties, Indiana, in the midst of

(a)

(b)

(c)

Nonconformists all: An Amish farmer in Pennsylvania whose vehicle obviously doesn't need gas (a); a gang of bikers running on a lot of gas (b); and Pentecostalists who include serpent handling among their rituals (c).

fertile fields and well-tended orchards, you will find isolated villages with prosperous and well-maintained farmhouses but no electricity. You will see the farmers and their families traveling in horse-drawn buggies, dressed in homespun clothes, and wearing brimmed hats. These people are Amish. Their ancestors came to this country from the German-speaking Rhineland region as early as 1683 to escape persecution for their fundamentalist Christian beliefs. Shunning motors, electricity, jewelry, and affiliation with political parties, they are a *nonconformist* community within a highly materialistic culture.

Motorcycle gangs made their appearance shortly after World War II. The Hell's Angels were the first of many gangs to be established in slum areas of cities across the country. To become a member of this gang, initiates are subjected to grueling and revolting degradations. They are conditioned to have allegiance only to the gang. Contacts with middle-class society are usually antagonistic and criminal. Motorcycle gangs finance their operations through illegal activities such as dealing drugs, running massage parlors and gambling operations, and selling stolen goods. The members' code of loyalty to one another and to their national and local groups makes the gangs extremely effective criminal organizations.

The normative systems of the Amish and the bikers are at odds with the conventional norms of the society in which they live. Both deviate from middle-class standards. Sociologists define **deviance** as any behavior that members of a social group define as violating their norms. As we can see, the concept of deviance can be applied to noncriminal acts that members of a group view as peculiar or unusual (the lifestyle of the Amish) or to criminal acts (behavior that society has made illegal). The Hell's Angels fit the expected stereotype of deviance as negative; the Amish culture demonstrates that deviance is not necessarily bad, just different.

Cultural deviance theorists argue that our society is made up of various groups and subgroups, each with its own standards of right and wrong. Behavior considered normal in one group may be considered deviant by another. As a result, those who conform to the standards of cultures considered deviant are behaving in accordance with their own norms but may be breaking the law—the norms of the dominant culture.

You may wonder whether the Hell's Angels are outcasts in the slum neighborhoods where they live. They are not. They may even be looked up to by younger boys in places where toughness and violence are not only acceptable but appropriate. Indeed, groups such as the Hell's Angels may meet the needs of youngsters who are looking for a way to be important in a disorganized ghetto that offers few opportunities to gain status.

Social Disorganization Theory

Scholars associated with the University of Chicago in the 1920s became interested in socially disorganized Chicago neighborhoods where criminal values and traditions replaced conventional ones and were transmitted from one generation to the next. In their classic work *The Polish Peasant in Europe and America*, W. I. Thomas and Florian Znaniecki described the difficulties Polish peasants experienced when they left their rural Old World life to settle in an industrialized city in the New World.[39] The scholars compared the conditions the immigrants had left in Poland with those they found in Chicago. They also investigated the immigrants' assimilation.

Older immigrants, they found, were not greatly affected by the move because they managed, even within the urban slums, to continue living as they had lived in Poland. But the second generation did not grow up on Polish farms; these people were city dwellers and they were American. They had few of the Old World tradi-tions but were not yet assimilated into the new ones. The norms of the stable, homogeneous folk society were not transferable to the anonymous, materially oriented urban settings. Rates of crime and delinquency rose. Thomas and Znaniecki attributed this result to *social disorganization*—the breakdown of effective social bonds, family and neighborhood associations, and social controls in neighborhoods and communities. (See Figure 5.3.)

The Park and Burgess Model

Thomas and Znaniecki's study greatly influenced other scholars at the University of Chicago. Among them were Robert Park and Ernest Burgess, who advanced the study of social disorganization by introducing ecological analysis into the study of human society.[40] Ecology is the study of plants and animals in relation to each other and to their natural habitat, the place where they live and grow. Ecologists study these interrelationships, how the balance of nature continues and how organisms survive. Much the same approach is used by scholars who study *human ecology*, the interrelationships of people and their environment.[41]

In their study of social disorganization, Park and Burgess examined area characteristics instead of criminals for explanations of high crime rates. They developed the idea of natural urban areas, consisting of concentric zones extending out from the downtown central business district to the commuter zone at the fringes of the city. Each zone had its own structure and organization, its own cultural characteristics and unique inhabitants (Figure 5.4). Zone I, at the

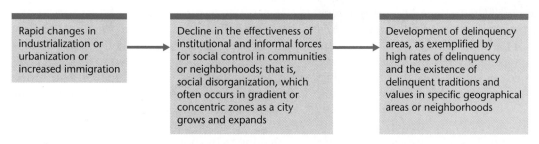

FIGURE 5.3 Social disorganization

Source: Donald J. Shoemaker, *Theories of Delinquency*, 2nd ed. (New York: Oxford University Press, 1990), p. 82.

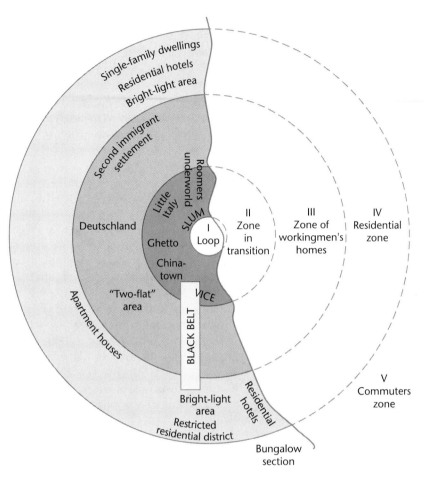

FIGURE 5.4 Park and Burgess's conception of the "natural urban areas" of Chicago

Source: Robert E. Park, Ernest W. Burgess, and R. D. McKenzie, *The City* (Chicago: University of Chicago Press, 1925), p. 55.

center, called the Loop because the downtown business district of Chicago is demarcated by a loop of the elevated train system, was occupied by commercial headquarters, law offices, retail establishments, and some commercial recreation. Zone II was the zone in transition, where the city's poor, unskilled, and disadvantaged lived in dilapidated tenements next to old factories. Zone III housed the working class, people whose jobs enabled them to enjoy some of the comforts the city had to offer at its fringes. The middle class—professionals, small-business owners, and the managerial class—lived in Zone IV. Zone V was the commuter zone of satellite towns and suburbs.

Shaw and McKay's Work

Clifford Shaw and Henry McKay, two researchers at Chicago's Institute for Juvenile Research, were particularly interested in the model Burgess had created to demonstrate how people were distributed spatially in the process of urban growth. They decided to use the model to investigate the relationship between crime rates and the various zones of Chicago. Their data, found in 55,998 juvenile court records covering a period of 33 years, from 1900 to 1933, indicated the following:

■ Crime rates were differentially distributed throughout the city, and areas of high crime rates had high rates of other community problems, such as truancy, mental disorders, and infant mortality.

■ Most delinquency occurred in the areas nearest the central business district and decreased with distance from the center.

■ Some areas consistently suffered high delinquency rates, regardless of the ethnic makeup of the population.

■ High-delinquency areas were characterized by a high percentage of immigrants, non-whites, and low-income families and a low percentage of homeownership.

■ In high-delinquency areas there was a general acceptance of nonconventional norms, but these norms competed with conventional ones held by some of the inhabitants.[42]

Shaw and McKay demonstrated that the highest rates of delinquency persisted in the same areas of Chicago over the extended period from 1900 to 1933, even though the ethnic composition changed (German, Irish, and English at the turn of the century; Polish and Italian in the 1920s; an increasing number of blacks in the 1930s). This finding led to the conclusion that the crucial factor was not ethnicity but, rather, the position of the group in terms of economic status and cultural values. Finally, through their study of three sets of Cook County juvenile court records—1900 to 1906, 1917 to 1923, and 1927 to 1933—they learned that older boys were associated with younger boys in various offenses and that the same techniques for committing delinquent acts had been passed on through the years. The evidence clearly indicated to them that delinquency was socially learned behavior, transmitted from one generation to the next in disorganized urban areas.[43] This phenomenon is called **cultural transmission.**

Tests of Social Disorganization Theory

More recent evidence supports the social disorganization and ecological approach of the Chicago school. Ongoing research since 1955 in Racine, Wisconsin, has analyzed delinquency and crime rates in relation to urban neighborhoods. The longitudinal study of 6127 persons from three birth cohorts (1942, 1949, and 1955) continues to demonstrate a decline from inner-city areas to suburban fringe areas in the amount and seriousness of delinquent and criminal careers. According to Lyle Shannon, seriousness of delinquent and criminal acts was related to area of residence, race, having delinquent friends in the area, and dropping out of school. He noted that over time there had been a "hardening of the inner city."[44]

Robert Sampson and W. Byron Groves analyzed data from two large national surveys of England and Wales in order to test Shaw and McKay's social disorganization theory. They found that communities characterized by unsupervised teenagers, low participation in organizations, and few friendship networks had high rates of reported criminal victimizations.[45]

Douglas Smith looked at police behavior and characteristics of 60 neighborhoods in 3 large U.S. cities (Rochester, New York: St. Louis, Missouri; Tampa/St. Petersburg, Florida). His major findings suggest that police officers are less likely to file reports of crime incidents in high-crime areas than in low-crime areas and that they are more likely to assist residents and initiate contacts with suspicious-looking people in low-crime neighborhoods.[46] Other researchers have compared gang delinquency in black and Hispanic communities, studied the correlation of delinquency with single-parent households, and investigated how neighborhood changes (such as urban renewal and increased homeownership) affect violence.[47]

An increasing amount of research has focused on the relationship between social disorganization of neighborhoods and the fear of crime. Researchers are asking whether the belief that crime is a serious local problem makes people lose confidence in their neighborhood and trust in their neighbors. Do they become more fearful? According to recent studies, they usually do.[48]

Evaluation: Social Disorganization Theory

Though their influence has been great, the scholars who initiated the ecological approach to crime research have not been immune to challenges. Their work has been criticized for its

AT ISSUE
Social Disorganization in Los Angeles

On April 29, 1992, Los Angeles exploded in a firestorm of riots. It was the day of the announcement of the not-guilty verdicts in the trial of the four L.A. Police Department officers accused of beating black motorist Rodney King. While the variety of crimes that were committed during the week of rioting and looting might serve as case studies for many of the explanations of criminal behavior we consider in this section, the context in which the riots occurred provides a clear example of social disorganization. We shall let excerpts from the report of a special advisory committee that assessed the event tell the story, beginning with a description of the riots:

> Crowds began to congregate in South Central Los Angeles to protest the verdicts. As these street corner protests began to grow in number and size, they first became angry and then turned violent. . . . Over the course of the next six days, the reaction escalated into a terrifying reign of violence, widespread looting, and mass destruction of property in many communities across the City. . . . The perpetrators of this violence were not confined to any single racial or ethnic classification. . . . People of all ages and gender participated in the looting. . . .

A Context for Violence

The Rodney King incident did not occur in a vacuum but within the context of the entire social, economic, and political climate of the City. In the past decade, Los Angeles has experienced rapid demographic and economic changes. The population of the City as a whole has grown by 17 percent during that period and now exceeds 3.5 million people. At the same time, the makeup of the population has shifted to 40 percent Hispanic, 37 percent Anglo, 13 percent African-American, 9 percent Asian-American, and 1 percent Native American. As the ethnic makeup of the City has changed fundamentally, so too has the economic stratification of its population. By 1990, more than 18.5 percent of Los Angeles residents were living below the poverty line.

Since its beginnings as a Spanish mission, the City has seen a steady immigration of diverse peoples. Today, the Los Angeles Unified School District consists of 700 schools with approximately 640,000 students who speak 100 different languages. This influx of people provides an enormous amount of creativity and energy . . . but the rapid growth also frustrates the development of a common civic culture. Indeed, the increasingly diverse population of Los Angeles is viewed as increasingly difficult to govern and . . . to police.

A Tinderbox Ready to Explode

The decade of the 1980s brought fewer jobs—but plenty of drugs, crime and violence—to many Los Angeles neighborhoods. Los Angeles street gangs now had crack cocaine. Like no other drug before it, crack had a devastating impact on families. . . . By early 1992, the problems of the inner city—gangs, crime, crack cocaine, poverty and homelessness, and racial and ethnic tension—had come to dominate daily life for a great many residents of Los Angeles. The struggle to preserve a sense of community in the City had begun in earnest. The City of Los Angeles had become a tinderbox ready to explode at the striking of a single match.

Source: The City in Crisis: A Report by the Special Advisor to the Board of Police Commissioners on the Civil Disorder in Los Angeles, Oct. 21, 1992, pp. 11, 13, 23, 34–35, 41–42.

Questions for Discussion

1. In Los Angeles it was an unpopular jury verdict that sparked a series of violent riots. If similar riots could be caused by natural disasters, political events, or mechanical failures like blackouts, what are the implications for policy makers?
2. The report's analysis of the social climate in Los Angeles makes it sound as if the riots were almost inevitable. Why, then, was the city apparently so unprepared for the reaction of the public to the Rodney King verdicts?

National Guardsmen keeping order in Los Angeles riots, 1992.

dependence on official data, which may primarily reflect zealous police surveillance in disadvantaged neighborhoods, and for its focus on how crime patterns are transmitted, not on how they start in the first place. The approach has also been faulted for failing to explain why delinquents stop committing crime as they grow older, why most people in socially disorganized areas do not commit criminal acts, and why some bad neighborhoods seem to be insulated from crime. Finally, critics claim that this approach does not come to grips with middle-class delinquency.

Clearly, however, modern criminology owes a debt to social disorganization theorists, particularly to Shaw and McKay, who in the 1920s began to look at the characteristics of people and places and to relate both to crime.[49] They have stimulated research not only in crime causation but also in crime prevention.

From Theory to Practice

Theorists of the Chicago school were the first social scientists to suggest that most crime is committed by normal people responding in expected ways to their immediate surroundings, rather than by abnormal individuals acting out individual pathologies. If social disorganization is at the root of the problem, crime control must involve social organization. The community, not individuals, needs treatment. Helping the community, then, should lower its crime rate.

The Chicago Area Project

Social disorganization theory was translated into practice in 1934 with the establishment of the Chicago Area Project (CAP), an experiment in neighborhood reorganization. The project was initiated by the Institute for Juvenile Research, at which Clifford Shaw and Henry McKay were working. It coordinated the existing community support groups—local schools, churches, labor unions, clubs, and merchants. Special efforts were made to control delinquency through recreational facilities, summer camps, better law enforcement, and the upgrading of neighborhood schools, sanitation, and general appearance.[50]

In 1984 this first community-based delinquency-prevention program celebrated its fiftieth anniversary.[51] South Chicago, its largest area, remains physically very much the way it was over half a century ago. The pollution from the surrounding steel mills has been cleaned up, but the urban decay has not. Boarded-up buildings, trash-littered lots, and badly deteriorated housing still characterize the area with which Shaw and McKay were originally concerned. CAP continues to work as a self-help group, committed mainly to community treatment of juvenile delinquency. Its motto is still "Concerned people striving to make South Chicago a better place to live." It has had modest success.

Boston's Mid-City Project and Others

During the 1950s, Boston initiated the Mid-City Project, which was similar in many ways to CAP. But instead of waiting for gang members to come to community centers, workers went out into the streets to meet the gangs on their own turf. Good relationships were formed. Delinquency rates, however, stayed the same.[52] Local crime-prevention programs got a bigger boost in the 1960s, with John F. Kennedy's New Frontier and Lyndon Johnson's War on Poverty (Chapter 6).

More recently another community action project has concentrated on revitalizing a Puerto Rican slum community. Sister Isolina Ferre worked for 10 years in the violent Navy Yard section of Brooklyn, New York. In 1969 she returned to Ponce Plaza, a poverty-stricken area in Ponce, Puerto Rico, infested with disease, crime, and unemployment. The area's 16,000 people had no doctors, nurses, dentists, or social agencies. The project began with a handful of missionaries, university professors, dedicated citizens, and community members who were willing to become advocates for their neighborhood. Among the programs begun were a large community health center, Big Brother/Big Sister programs for juveniles sent from the courts, volunteer tutoring, and recreational activities to take young people off the streets. Young photographers of Ponce Plaza, supplied with a few cameras donated by friends at Kodak, mounted an exhibit at the Metropolitan Museum of Art in New York. Regular fiestas have given community members a chance to celebrate their own achievements as well.[53]

Programs based on social disorganization theory attempt to bring conventional social values to disorganized communities. They provide an opportunity for young people to learn norms other than those of delinquent peer groups. Let us see how such learning takes place.

Differential Association Theory

Many years ago hunters captured a young boy living with a flock of ostriches. He had grown up with them, run with them as fast as they did, acted on their signals, and adopted their feeding habits. He could not speak like a human, but he communicated perfectly with his ostrich family, using their sounds. He had learned the ways of his group just as we learn the ways of ours. What we eat, what we say, what we believe—in fact, the way we respond to any situation—depends on the culture in which we have been reared. In other words, to a very large extent the social influences that people encounter determine their behavior. Whether a person becomes law-abiding or criminal, then, depends on contacts with criminal values, attitudes, definitions, and behavior patterns. This proposition underlies one of the most important theories of crime causation in American criminology—differential association.

Sutherland's Theory

In 1939 Edwin Sutherland introduced differential association theory in his textbook *Principles of Criminology*. Since then scholars have read, tested, reexamined, and sometimes ridiculed this theory, which claimed to explain the development of all criminal behavior. The theory states that crime is learned through social interaction. People come into constant contact with "definitions favorable to violations of law" and "definitions unfavorable to violations of law." The ratio of these definitions—criminal to noncriminal—determines whether a person will engage in criminal behavior.[54] In formulating this theory, Sutherland relied heavily on Shaw and McKay's findings that delinquent values are transmitted within a community or group from one generation to the next.

Sutherland's Nine Propositions

Nine propositions explained the process by which this transmission of values takes place:

1. Criminal behavior is learned.
2. Criminal behavior is learned in interaction with other persons in a process of communication. A person does not become a criminal simply by living in a criminal environment. Crime is learned by participation with others in verbal and nonverbal communications.
3. The principal part of the learning of criminal behavior occurs within intimate personal groups. Families and friends have the most influence on the learning of deviant behavior. Their communications far outweigh those of the mass media.
4. When criminal behavior is learned, the learning includes *(a)* techniques of committing the crime, which are sometimes very complicated, sometimes very simple, and *(b)* the specific direction of motives, drives, rationalizations, and attitudes. Young delinquents learn not only how to shoplift, crack a safe, pick a lock, or roll a joint but also how to rationalize and defend their actions. One safecracker accompanied another safecracker for 1 year before he cracked his first safe.[55] In other words, criminals, too, learn skills and gain experience.
5. The specific direction of motives and drives is learned from definitions of the legal codes as favorable or unfavorable. In some societies an individual is surrounded by persons who invariably define the legal codes as rules to be observed, while in others he or she is surrounded by persons whose definitions are favorable to the violation of the legal codes. Not everyone in our society agrees that the laws should be obeyed; some people define them as unimportant. In American society, where definitions are mixed, we have a culture conflict in relation to legal codes.
6. A person becomes delinquent because of an excess of definitions favorable to violation of law over definitions unfavorable to violation of law. This is the key principle of differential association. In other words, learning criminal behavior is not simply a matter of associating with bad companions. Rather, learning criminal behavior depends on how many defini-

tions we learn that are favorable to law violation as opposed to those that are unfavorable to law violation.

7. Differential associations may vary in frequency, duration, priority, and intensity. The extent to which associations and definitions will result in criminality is related to the frequency of contacts, their duration, and their meaning to the individual.

8. The process of learning criminal behavior by association with criminal and anticriminal patterns involves all the mechanisms that are involved in any other learning. Learning criminal behavior patterns is very much like learning conventional behavior patterns and is not simply a matter of observation and imitation.

9. While criminal behavior is an expression of general needs and values, it is not explained by those general needs and values, since noncriminal behavior is an expression of the same needs and values. Shoplifters steal to get what they want. Others work to get money to buy what they want. The motives—frustration, desire to accumulate goods or social status, low self-concept, and the like—cannot logically be the same because they explain both lawful and criminal behavior.

Tests of Differential Association Theory

Since Sutherland presented his theory, more than 50 years ago, researchers have tried to determine whether his principles lend themselves to empirical measurement. James Short tested a sample of 126 boys and 50 girls at a training school and reported a consistent relationship between delinquent behavior and frequency, duration, priority, and intensity of interactions with delinquent peers.[56] In another test, Albert Reiss and A. Lewis Rhodes found that the chance of committing a delinquent act depends on whether friends commit the same act.[57] Similarly, Travis Hirschi demonstrated that boys with delinquent friends are more likely to become delinquent.[58] Research on seventh- and eighth-grade students attending Rochester, New York, public schools in the late 1980s and early 1990s shows that gang membership is strongly associated with peer delinquency and the amount of delinquency and drug use.[59]

Mark Warr demonstrated that while the duration of delinquent friendships over a long period of time has a greater effect than exposure over a short period, it is recent friendships rather than early friendships that have the greatest effect on delinquency.[60]

Adults have also been the subjects of differential association studies. Charles Tittle asked 2000 residents of New Jersey, Oregon, and Iowa such questions as how many people they knew personally had engaged in deviant acts and how many were frequently in trouble. He also asked the residents how often they attended church (assumed to be related to definitions unfavorable to the violation of law). His differential association scale correlated significantly with such crimes as illegal gambling, income tax cheating, and theft.[61]

Evaluation: Differential Association Theory

Many researchers have attempted to validate Sutherland's differential association theory. Others have criticized it. Much of the criticism stems from errors in interpretation. Perhaps this type of error is best demonstrated by the critics who ask why it is that not everyone in heavy, prolonged contact with criminal behavior patterns becomes a criminal. Take, for argument's sake, corrections officers, who come into constant contact with more criminal associations than noncriminal ones. How do they escape from learning to be law violators themselves?

The answer, of course, is that Sutherland does not tell us that individuals become criminal by associating with criminals or even by association with criminal behavior patterns. He tells us, rather, that a person becomes delinquent because of an "excess of definitions favorable to violation of law over definitions unfavorable to violation of law." The key word is "definitions." Furthermore, unfavorable definitions may be communicated by persons who are not robbers or murderers or tax evaders. They may, for example, be law-abiding parents who, over time, define certain situations in such a way that their children get verbal or nonverbal messages to the effect that antisocial behavior is acceptable.

Several scholars have asked whether the principles of differential association really explain all types of crime. They might explain theft, but what about homicide resulting from a jealous rage?[62] Why do some people who learn criminal behavior patterns not engage in criminal acts? Why is no account taken of nonsocial variables, such as a desperate need for money? Furthermore, while the principles may explain how criminal behavior is transmitted, they do not account for the origin of criminal techniques and definitions. In other words, the theory does not tell us how the first criminal became a criminal.

Differential association theory suggests there is an inevitability about the process of becoming a criminal. Once you reach the point where your definitions favorable to law violation exceed your definitions unfavorable to law violation, have you crossed an imaginary line into the criminal world? Even if we could add up the definitions encountered in a lifetime, could scientists measure the frequency, priority, duration, and intensity of differential associations?

Despite these criticisms, the theory has had a profound influence on criminology.[63] Generations of scholars have tested it empirically, modified it to incorporate psychologically based learning theory (see Chapter 4), and used it as a foundation for their own theorizing (Chapter 6). The theory has also had many policy implications.

From Theory to Practice

If, according to differential association theory, a person can become criminal by learning definitions favorable to violating laws, it follows that programs which expose young people to definitions favorable to conventional behavior should reduce criminality. Such educational efforts as Head Start and the Perry Preschool Project have attempted to do just that. The same theory underlies many of the treatment programs for young school dropouts and pregnant teenagers.

An innovative Ohio program is trying to break the vicious cycle between poverty-welfare–school dropout–drugs-delinquency and teenage pregnancy. This program, LEAP (for Learning, Earning, and Parenting), provides financial rewards for teenage single parents to stay in, or return to, school and deductions from the welfare checks of those who do not participate in education. A 1993 evaluation found that the program, which costs the state very little, has been moderately successful. Success appears to increase with increased counseling and aid services. Several states have instituted similar "learnfare" programs (for example, Virginia, Florida, Maryland, and Oklahoma), while others are considering this option.[64]

Culture Conflict Theory

Differential association theory is based on the learning of criminal (or deviant) norms or attitudes. Culture conflict theory focuses on the source of these criminal norms and attitudes. According to Thorsten Sellin, **conduct norms**—norms that regulate our daily lives—are rules that reflect the attitudes of the groups to which each of us belongs.[65] Their purpose is to define what is considered appropriate or normal behavior and what is inappropriate or abnormal behavior.

Sellin argues that different groups have different conduct norms and that the conduct norms of one group may conflict with those of another. Individuals may commit crimes by conforming to the norms of their own group if that group's norms conflict with those of the dominant society. According to this rationale, the main difference between a criminal and a noncriminal is that each is responding to different sets of conduct norms.

Sellin distinguishes between primary and secondary conflicts. *Primary conflict* occurs when norms of two cultures clash. A clash may occur at the border between neighboring cultural areas; when the law of one cultural group is extended to cover the territory of another; or when members of one group migrate to another culture. *Secondary conflict* arises when a single culture evolves into a variety of cultures, each having its own set of conduct norms. This type of conflict occurs when the homogeneous societies of simpler cultures become complex societies, such as our own, in which the number of social groupings multiplies constantly and norms are often at odds. Your college may make dormitory living mandatory for all freshmen, for example, but to follow the informal code of your peer group, you

CRIMINOLOGICAL FOCUS
Culture Conflict in Waco, Texas

A fire swept through the headquarters of a religious cult in Waco, Texas, in April 1993, killing nearly every one of the 90 adults in the compound and all 17 children. The fire was the final event in a 3-month-long standoff between the cult and U.S. federal agents who wanted to investigate the community's stockpile of weapons. What enabled so many people to defy American law-and-order authority for so long? This was a classic case of a deviant culture clashing with the dominant one.

Different Rules

What kind of community was it that kept so many people together in the face of attempts to impose law and order from the outside—and led them all to die? The answer is simple: the cult members' rules of conduct, shaped by their religious beliefs, were different from those of the world outside the compound. David Koresh, the leader of the cult, was a key factor. Thought to be a psychopath, Koresh was described in one report as follows: "David Koresh—high school dropout, rock musician, polygamist preacher—built his church on a simple message: 'If the Bible is true, then I'm Christ.'"(1)

As Christ, Koresh ruled over more than 100 people in the compound, keeping the men separate from the women, taking as wives anyone of his choosing (some 12 of whom bore his children), preaching long sermons to cult members, strictly rationing their food, and subjecting the children to frequent and severe physical punishment in "the whipping room." Traditional family structure was disrupted; fathers never lived with families, and children were taken from their mothers by age 12.(2)

Shared Apocalypse

Clearly a departure from the society they had lived in outside, all this was accepted by the cult members, who sought religious fulfillment. Koresh often told his followers that the end of the world was coming, and the raid by the federal agents probably served to strengthen his hold on the community.

Sources

1. Richard Lacayo, "Cult of Death," *Time,* Mar. 15, 1993, p. 36.
2. Sophfronia Scott Gregory, "Children of a Lesser God," *Time,* May 17, 1993, p. 54.

Questions for Discussion

1. Among the crimes that may have been committed inside the cult's compound were arson, statutory rape, child abuse, polygamy, financial fraud, and murder. When a group has obviously different conduct norms from those of the society in which its members live, should exceptions be made under the First Amendment in imposing criminal law? Where would you draw the line?
2. Could the conflict between conduct norms of deviant cultures and the rules of middle-class society be eased? Does this possibility hold any promise for crime-prevention strategies? Explain.

(*right*) David Koresh preaching in Australia. (*below*) Armageddon at Waco, Texas, April 1993, after federal law enforcement officers assaulted the Branch Davidian compound.

may seek the freedom of off-campus housing. Or you may have to choose whether to violate work rules by leaving your job half an hour early to make a mandatory class or to violate school rules by walking into class half an hour late. Life situations are frequently controlled by conflicting norms, so no matter how people act, they may be violating some rule, often without being aware that they are doing so.

In the next chapter, which deals with the formation and operation of subcultures, we will expand the discussion of the conflict of norms. We will also examine the empirical research that seeks to discover whether there is indeed a multitude of value systems in our society and, if so, whether and how they conflict.

■ REVIEW

Contemporary criminologists tend to divide the sociological explanation of crime into three categories: strain, cultural deviance, and social control. The strain and cultural deviance perspectives focus on the social forces that cause people to engage in deviant behavior. They assume that there is a relationship between social class and criminal behavior. Strain theorists argue that all people in society share one set of cultural values and that since lower-class persons often do not have legitimate means to attain society's goals, they may turn to illegitimate means instead. Cultural deviance theorists maintain that the lower class has a distinctive set of values and that these values often conflict with those of the middle class.

Cultural deviance theories—social disorganization, differential association, and culture conflict—relate criminal behavior to the learning of criminal values and norms. Social disorganization theory focuses on the breakdown of social institutions as a precondition for the establishment of criminal norms. Differential association theory concentrates on the processes by which criminal behavior is taught and learned. Culture conflict theory focuses on the specifics of how the conduct norms of some groups may clash with those of the dominant culture.

■ NOTES

1. Ysabel Rennie, *The Search for Criminal Man* (Lexington, Mass.: Lexington Books, 1978), p. 125.
2. James T. Carey, *Sociology and Public Affairs: The Chicago School* (Beverly Hills, Calif.: Sage, 1975), pp. 19–20.
3. See the discussion of sociological theory in Frank P. Williams III and Marilyn D. McShane, *Criminological Theory* (Englewood Cliffs, N.J.: Prentice-Hall, 1988).
4. Émile Durkheim, *The Division of Labor in Society* (New York: Free Press, 1964).
5. Émile Durkheim, *Rules of Sociological Method* (New York: Free Press, 1966).
6. For a lengthy discussion of Durkheim's use of the term "anomie," see Stjepan G. Mestrovic and Helene M. Brown, "Durkheim's Concept of Anomie as Derèglement," *Social Problems,* **33** (1985): 81–99.
7. Émile Durkheim, *Suicide* (Glencoe, Ill.: Free Press, 1951), pp. 241–276. For anomie-related research on suicide, see Andrew Henry and James F. Short, *Suicide and Homicide* (Glencoe, Ill.: Free Press, 1954); Ronald W. Maris, *Social Forces in Urban Suicide* (Homewood, Ill.: Dorsey, 1969); and Jack P. Gibbs and Walter T. Martin, *Status Integration and Suicide* (Eugene: University of Oregon Press, 1964).
8. Durkheim, *Suicide*, p. 247.
9. Robert K. Merton, "Social Structure and Anomie," *American Sociological Review,* **3** (1938): 672–682. Several measures of anomie have been developed. Probably the best-known indicator of anomie at the social level was formulated by Bernard Lander in a study of 8464 cases of juvenile delinquency in Baltimore between 1939 and 1942. Lander devised a measure that included the rate of delinquency, the percentage of nonwhite population in a given area, and the percentage of owner-occupied homes. According to Lander, those factors were indicative of the amount of normlessness (anomie) in a community. See Bernard Lander, *Towards an Understanding of Juvenile Delinquency* (New York: Columbia University Press, 1954), p. 65. See also Roland J. Chilton, "Continuity in Delinquency Area Research: A Comparison of Studies of Baltimore, Detroit, and Indianapolis," *American Sociological Review,* **29** (1964): 71–83.
10. U.S. Department of Commerce, Bureau of the Census, *Statistical Abstract of the United States* 1990 (Washington, D.C.: U.S. Government Printing Office, 1991), table 731.
11. U.S. Department of Commerce, Bureau of the Census, *Statistical Abstract of the United States* 1991 (Washington, D.C.: U.S. Government Printing Office, 1993), p. 462.
12. Robert K. Merton, *Social Theory and the Social Structure* (New York: Free Press, 1957), p. 187.
13. Ibid., p. 151.
14. John P. Clark and Eugene P. Wenninger, "Socioeconomic Class and Area as Correlates of Illegal Behav-

ior among Juveniles," *American Sociological Review,* **27** (1962): 826–834; Albert J. Reiss, Jr., and Albert L. Rhodes, "The Distribution of Juvenile Delinquency in the Social Class Structure," *American Sociological Review,* **26** (1961): 720–732. For the relationship between economic changes and crime, see Pamela Irving Jackson, "Crime, Youth Gangs, and Urban Transition: The Social Dislocations of Postindustrial Economic Development," *Justice Quarterly,* **8** (1991): 380–397.

15. F. Ivan Nye, James F. Short, and Virgil J. Olson, "Socioeconomic Status and Delinquent Behavior," *American Journal of Sociology,* **63** (1958): 381–389; Robert A. Dentler and Lawrence J. Monroe, "Early Adolescent Theft," *American Sociological Review,* **26** (1961): 733–743; Martin Gold, "Undetected Delinquent Behavior," *Journal of Research in Crime and Delinquency,* **3** (1966): 27–46; Harwin L. Voss, "Socioeconomic Status and Reported Delinquent Behavior," *Social Problems,* **13** (1966): 314–324.

16. Charles R. Tittle, Wayne J. Villemez, and Douglas A. Smith, "The Myth of Social Class and Criminality: An Empirical Assessment of the Empirical Evidence," *American Sociological Review,* **43** (1978): 652; Charles R. Tittle and Robert F. Meier, "Specifying the SES/Delinquency Relationship by Social Characteristics of Contexts," *Journal of Research in Crime and Delinquency,* **28** (1991): 430–455.

17. Travis Hirschi, *Causes of Delinquency* (Berkeley: University of California Press, 1969), p. 67. See also Marvin D. Krohn, Ronald L. Akers, Marcia J. Radosevich, and Lonn Lanza-Kaduce, "Social Status and Deviance," *Criminology,* **18** (1980): 303–318; and Richard E. Johnson, "Social Class and Delinquent Behavior: A New Test," *Criminology,* **18** (1980): 86–93.

18. John Braithwaite, "The Myth of Social Class and Criminality Reconsidered," *American Sociological Review,* **46** (1981): 41. See also Delbert S. Elliott and Suzanne S. Ageton, "Reconciling Race and Class Differences in Self-Reported and Official Estimates of Delinquency," *American Sociological Review,* **45** (1980): 95–110; and Donald Clelland and Timothy J. Carter, "The New Myth of Class and Crime," *Criminology,* **18** (1980): 319–336.

19. Terence P. Thornberry and Margaret Farnworth, "Social Correlates of Criminal Involvement: Further Evidence on the Relationship between Social Status and Criminal Behavior," *American Sociological Review,* **47** (1982): 505–518; Thomas J. Bernard, "Control Criticisms of Strain Theories: An Assessment of Theoretical and Empirical Adequacy," *Journal of Research in Crime and Delinquency,* **21** (1984): 353–372; Delbert S. Elliott and David Huizinga, "Social Class and Delinquent Behavior in a National Youth Panel," *Criminology,* **21** (1983): 149–177.

20. David Brownfield, "Social Class and Violent Behavior," *Criminology,* **24** (1986): 421–438.

21. William R. Avison and Pamela L. Loring, "Population Diversity and Cross-National Homicide: The Effects of Inequality and Heterogeneity," *Criminology,* **24** (1986): 733–749; Harvey Krahn, Timothy F. Hartnagel, and John W. Gartrell, "Income Inequality and Homicide Rates: Cross-National Data and Criminological Theories," *Criminology,* **24** (1986): 269–295.

22. Krahn et al., "Income Inequality," p. 288. For a study that found no relationship between economic inequality and homicide, see Steven F. Messner and Kenneth Tardiff, "Economic Inequality and Levels of Homicide: An Analysis of Urban Neighborhoods," *Criminology,* **24** (1986): 297–317.

23. Brownfield, "Social Class and Violent Behavior."

24. David Matza, "The Disreputable Poor," in *Class, Status, and Power,* ed. Reinhard Bendix and Seymour M. Lipset (New York: Free Press, 1966). For the effects of adverse conditions (hunger, unemployment), see Bill McCarthy and John Hagan, "Mean Streets: The Theoretical Significance of Situational Delinquency among Homeless Youths," *American Journal of Sociology,* **98** (1992): 597–627. See also Chris Hale, "Unemployment and Crime: Differencing Is No Substitute for Modeling," *Journal of Research in Crime and Delinquency,* **28** (1991): 426–429.

25. Judith R. Blau and Peter M. Blau, "The Cost of Inequality: Metropolitan Structure and Violent Crime," *American Sociological Review,* **47** (1982): 114–129. See also Miles Harer and Darrell Steffensmeier, "The Differing Effects of Economic Inequality on Black and White Rates of Violence," *Social Forces,* **70** (1992): 1035–1054; and Steven F. Messner and Reid M. Golden, "Racial Inequality and Racially Disaggregated Homicide Rates: An Assessment of Alternative Theoretical Explanations," *Criminology,* **30** (1992): 421–446. For the relationship between ethnic inequality and homicide, see James W. Balkwell, "Ethnic Inequality and the Rate of Homicide," *Social Forces,* **69** (1990): 53–70.

26. Peter M. Blau and Joseph E. Schwartz, *Crosscutting Social Circles* (Orlando, Fla.: Academic Press, 1984); Kirk R. Williams, "Economic Sources of Homicide: Reestimating the Effects of Poverty and Inequality," *American Sociological Review,* **49** (1984): 283–289; Peter M. Blau and Reid M. Golden, "Metropolitan Structure and Criminal Violence," *Sociological Quarterly,* **27** (1986): 15–26.

27. John Braithwaite, *Inequality, Crime, and Public Policy* (London: Routledge & Kegan Paul, 1979), p. 219.

28. Robert J. Sampson, "Race and Criminal Violence: A Demographically Disaggregated Analysis of Urban Homicide," *Crime and Delinquency,* **31** (1985): 47–82; Reid M. Golden and Steven F. Messner, "Dimensions of Racial Inequality and Rates of Violent Crime," *Criminology,* **25** (1987): 525–541. For a discussion of the influence of black power on black violence, see Roy Austin, "Progress toward Racial Equality and Reduction of Black Criminal Violence," *Journal of Criminal Justice,* **15** (1987): 437–459.

29. Delbert Elliott and Harwin L. Voss, *Delinquency and Dropout* (Lexington, Mass.: Lexington Books, 1974);

Hirschi, *Causes of Delinquency;* William S. Laufer, "Vocational Interests of Homeless, Unemployed Men," *Journal of Vocational Behavior,* **18** (1981): 196–201.

30. For recent developments in strain theory, see *Advances in Criminological Theory: The Legacy of Anomie,* vol. 6, ed. Freda Adler and William S. Laufer (New Brunswick, N.J.: Transaction, 1994), particularly the following articles: Robert K. Merton, "Opportunity Structure: The Emergence, Diffusion and Differentiation of a Sociological Concept, 1930s–1950s"; Thomas J. Bernard, "Merton vs. Hirschi: Who Is Faithful to Durkheim's Heritage?"; Nikos Passas, "Continuities in the Anomie Tradition"; Robert Agnew, "The Contribution of Social-Psychological Strain Theory to the Explanation of Crime and Delinquency"; Gary F. Jensen, "Salvaging Structure through Strain: A Theoretical and Empirical Critique"; Richard Rosenfeld and Steven F. Messner, "Crime and the American Dream: An Institutional Analysis"; Deborah Vidaver Cohen, "Ethics and Crime in Business Firms: Organizational Culture and the Impact of Anomie"; Elin Waring and David Weisburd, "White Collar Crime and Anomie"; Ko-lin Chin and Jeffrey Fagan, "Social Order and Gang Formation in Chinatown"; John Hoffman and Timothy Ireland, "Cloward and Ohlin's Strain Theory Re-Examined: An Elaborated Theoretical Model"; Freda Adler, "Synnomie to Anomie: A Macrosociological Formulation." See also Robert Agnew and Helene Raskin White, "An Empirical Test of General Strain Theory," *Criminology,* **30** (1992): 475–499; Velmer S. Burton and Francis T. Cullen, "The Empirical Status of Strain Theory," *Journal of Crime and Justice,* **15** (1992): 1–30; and Robert Agnew, "Foundations for a General Strain Theory of Crime and Delinquency," *Criminology,* **30** (1992): 47–87.

31. Ian Taylor, Paul Walton, and Jock Young, *The New Criminology* (New York: Harper & Row, 1973), p. 107.

32. Edwin M. Lemert, *Human Deviance, Social Problems, and Social Control,* 2d ed. (Englewood Cliffs, N.J.: Prentice-Hall, 1972), pp. 26–61. See also William S. Laufer, "Vocational Interests of Criminal Offenders: A Typological and Demographic Investigation," *Psychological Reports,* **46** (1980): 315–324.

33. Freda Adler, *Nations Not Obsessed with Crime* (Littleton, Colo.: Fred B. Rothman, 1983).

34. M. Deutsch, "The Historical Context and the Challenge of Head Start," keynote presentation for the twentieth anniversary celebration of Head Start, New York University, Sept. 26, 1985; R. H. McKey, L. Condelle, H. Ganson, B. J. Barrett, C. McConkey, and M. C. Planty, Executive Summary: *The Impact of Head Start on Children, Families, and Communities: Final Report of the Head Start Evaluation, Synthesis, and Utilization Project,* for U.S. Department of Health and Human Services, Administration for Children, Youth, and Families (Washington, D.C.: U.S. Government Printing Office, 1985).

35. L. A. Meyer, "Long-Term Academic Effects of the Direct Instruction Project Follow-Through," *Elementary School Journal,* **84** (1984): 380–394.

36. Michael Kramer, "Getting Smart about Head Start," *Time,* Mar. 8, 1993, p. 43; Barbara Kantrowitz and Pat Wingert, "No Longer a Sacred Cow—Head Start Has Become a Free-Fire Zone," *Newsweek,* Apr. 12, 1993, p. 57.

37. John R. Berrueta-Clement, Lawrence J. Schweinhart, W. Steven Barnett, Ann S. Epstein, and David P. Weekart, *Changed Lives: The Effects of the Perry Preschool Program on Youths through Age 19* (Ypsilanti, Mich.: High/Scope, 1984).

38. Jane Gross, "Remnants of the War on Poverty, Job Corps Is Still a Quiet Success," *New York Times,* Feb. 17, 1992, pp. 1, 14.

39. W. I. Thomas and Florian Znaniecki, *The Polish Peasant in Europe and America* (Boston: Gorham, 1920).

40. Robert E. Park, "Human Ecology," *American Journal of Sociology,* **42** (1936): 1–15.

41. For a contemporary discussion of the human ecology approach to crime, see Rodney Stark, "Deviant Places: A Theory of the Ecology of Crime," *Criminology,* **25** (1987): 893–909.

42. Clifford R. Shaw, Frederick M. Forbaugh, Henry D. McKay, and Leonard S. Cottrell, *Delinquency Areas* (Chicago: University of Chicago Press, 1929).

43. Clifford R. Shaw and Henry D. McKay, "Social Factors in Juvenile Delinquency," in *National Commission of Law Observance and Enforcement Report on the Causes of Crime,* vol. 2 (Washington, D.C.: U.S. Government Printing Office, 1931); Clifford R. Shaw and Henry D. McKay, *Juvenile Delinquency and Urban Areas* (Chicago: University of Chicago Press, 1942); see also the revised and updated edition: Clifford R. Shaw and Henry D. McKay, *Juvenile Delinquency and Urban Areas: A Study of Delinquency in Relation to Differential Characteristics of Local Communities in American Cities* (Chicago: University of Chicago Press, 1969). Replication in other countries supports the idea of high-crime-rate areas, but not always decreasing rates from the center of the city outward. In Buenos Aires, Argentina, for example, the highest rate was found near the outskirts of the city, partly because the wealthy tend to live near the center. See Lois B. De Fleur, "Ecological Variables in the Cross-Cultural Study of Delinquency," *Social Forces,* **45** (1967): 556–570. Solomon Kobrin investigated further the process of cultural transmission and found both conventional and criminal value systems in high-crime areas; see Solomon Kobrin, "The Conflict of Values in Delinquency Areas," *American Sociological Review,* **16** (1951): 653–661. See also Clifford R. Shaw, *The Jack-Roller* (Chicago: University of Chicago Press, 1930); Clifford R. Shaw, Henry D. McKay, and James McDonald, *Brothers in Crime* (Chicago: University of Chicago Press, 1938); and Frederick M. Thrasher, *The Gang* (Chicago: University of Chicago Press, 1927).

44. Lyle W. Shannon, *Changing Patterns of Delinquency and Crime* (Boulder, Colo.: Westover Press, 1991), p. 144. See also Barbara D. Warner and Glenn L. Pierce,

"Reexamining Social Disorganization Theory Using Calls to the Police as a Measure of Crime," *Criminology*, **31** (1993): 493–517.

45. Robert J. Sampson and W. Byron Groves, "Community Structure and Crime: Testing Social Disorganization Theory," *American Journal of Sociology*, **94** (1989): 774–802. Sampson concluded from another study that in neighborhoods where fewer people "watch over" the area, there were more opportunities for criminal acts; see Robert J. Sampson, "Neighborhood and Crime: The Structural Determinants of Personal Victimization," *Journal of Research in Crime and Delinquency*, **22** (1985): 7–40. See also Robert J. Sampson and John D. Wooldredge, "Linking the Micro- and Macro-Level Dimensions of Lifestyle—Routine Activity and Opportunity Models of Predatory Victimizations," *Journal of Quantitative Criminology*, **3** (1987): 371–393.

46. Douglas A. Smith, "The Neighborhood Context of Police Behavior," in *Communities and Crime*, ed. Albert J. Reiss and Michael Tonry (Chicago: University of Chicago Press, 1986), pp. 313–341; Douglas A. Smith and C. Roger Jarjoura, "Social Structure and Criminal Victimization," *Journal of Research in Crime and Delinquency*, **25** (1988): 27–52. See also Robert J. Sampson, "Family Management and Child Development: Insights from Social Disorganization Theory," in *Advances in Criminological Theory*, vol. 3, ed. Joan McCord (New Brunswick, N.J.: Transaction, 1992); John M. Hagedorn, "Gangs, Neighborhoods, and Public Policy," *Social Problems*, **38** (1991): 529–542; Jackson, "Crime, Youth Gangs, and Urban Transition"; Terance D. Miethe, Michael Hughes, and David McDowall, "Social Change in Crime Rates: An Evaluation of Alternative Theoretical Approaches." *Social Forces*, **70** (1991): 165–185; Ronet Bachman, "An Analysis of American Indian Homicide: A Test of Social Disorganization and Economic Deprivation at the Reservation County Level," *Journal of Research in Crime and Delinquency*, **28** (1991): 456–471; E. Britt Paterson, "Poverty, Income Inequality, and Community Crime Rates," *Criminology*, **29** (1991): 755–776; Robert L. Hale, "Arrest Rates and Community Characteristics: Social Ecology Theory Applied to a Southern City," *American Journal of Criminal Justice*, **16** (1992): 17–32; Jerry Neapolitan, "Poverty, Race, and Population Concentrations: Interactive Associations to Violent Crime," *American Journal of Criminal Justice*, **16** (1992): 143–153; Josefina Figueira-McDonough, "Community Structure and Delinquency: A Typology," *Social Service Review*, **65** (1991): 65–91; and Denise C. Gottfredson, Richard J. McNeil, and Gary D. Gottfredson, "Social Area Influence on Delinquency: A Multilevel Analysis," *Journal of Research in Crime and Delinquency*, **28** (1991): 197–226.

47. G. David Curry and Irving A. Spergel, "Gang Homicide, Delinquency, and Community," *Criminology*, **26** (1988): 381–405; Ora Simcha-Fagan and Joseph E. Schwartz, "Neighborhood and Delinquency: An Assessment of Contextual Effects," *Criminology*, **24**

(1986): 667–703; Ralph B. Taylor and Jeanette Covington, "Neighborhood Changes in Ecology and Violence," *Criminology*, **26** (1988): 553–589. See also Leo A. Schuerman and Solomon Kobrin, "Community Careers in Crime," in Reiss and Tonry, *Communities and Crime*.

48. Lynn Newhart Smith and Gary D. Hill, "Victimization and Fear of Crime," *Criminal Justice and Behavior*, **18** (1991): 217–239; Carol G. Thompson, William B. Bankston, and Roberta L. St. Pierre, "Parity and Disparity among Three Measures of Fear of Crime: A Research Note," *Deviant Behavior*, **13** (1992): 373–389; Randy L. LaGrange, Kenneth F. Ferraro, and Michael Supancic, "Perceived Risk of Fear of Crime: Role of Social and Physical Incivilities," *Journal of Research in Crime and Delinquency*, **29** (1992): 311–334.; Stephanie W. Greenberg, "Fear and Its Relationship to Crime, Neighborhood Deterioration, and Informal Social Control," in *The Social Ecology of Crime*, ed. James M. Byrne and Robert J. Sampson (New York: Springer-Verlag, 1986), pp. 47–62. For research that measures safety and perceived safety resources in the context of other environmental concerns (as an alternative to measuring fear of crime), see John J. Gibbs and Kathleen J. Hanrahan, "Safety Demand and Supply: An Alternative to Fear of Crime," *Justice Quarterly*, **10** (1993): 369–394.

49. James M. Byrne, "Cities, Citizens, and Crime: The Ecological/Nonecological Debate Reconsidered," in Byrne and Sampson, *The Social Ecology of Crime*, pp. 77–101. See also Robert J. Bursik, Jr., "Social Disorganization and Theories of Crime and Delinquency: Problems and Prospects," *Criminology*, **26** (1988): 519–551. For a reformulation of social disorganization theory that emphasizes the importance of strong networks of associations among residents, see Robert J. Bursick, Jr., and Harold G. Grasmick, *Neighborhoods and Crime: The Dimensions of Effective Community Control* (New York: Lexington Books, 1993).

50. Solomon Kobrin, "The Chicago Area Project: 25 Years of Assessment," *Annals of the American Academy of Political and Social Science*, **332** (1959): 20–29.

51. Steven Schlossman, Goul Zellman, and Richard Shavelson, "Delinquency Prevention in South Chicago: A Fifty-Year Assessment of the Chicago Area Project," report prepared for the National Institute of Education by the Rand Corporation, May 1984, p. 1.

52. Walter Miller, "The Impact of a 'Total Community' Delinquency Control Project," *Social Problems*, **10** (1962): 168–191.

53. M. Isolina Ferre, "Prevention and Control of Violence through Community Revitalization, Individual Dignity, and Personal Self-Confidence," *Annals of the American Academy of Political and Social Science*, **494** (1987): 27–36.

54. Edwin H. Sutherland, *Principles of Criminology*, 3d ed. (Philadelphia: Lippincott, 1939).

55. William Chambliss, *Boxmen* (New York: Harper & Row, 1972).

56. James S. Short, "Differential Association as a Hypothesis: Problems of Empirical Testing," *Social Problems,* **8** (1960): 14–15; Mark Warr and Mark Stafford, "The Influence of Delinquent Peers: What They Think or What They Do?" *Criminology,* **29** (1991): 851–866; Shannon, *Changing Patterns of Delinquency and Crime;* Mark Warr, "Age, Peers, and Delinquency," *Criminology,* **31** (1993): 17–40. See also Charles R. Tittle, Mary Jean Burke, and Elton F. Jackson, "Modeling Sutherland's Theory of Differential Association: Toward an Empirical Clarification," *Social Forces,* **65** (1986): 405–432; and R. Matsueda and K. Heimer, "Race, Family Structure, and Delinquency: A Test of Differential Association and Social Control Theories," *American Sociological Review,* **52** (1987): 826–840.

57. Reiss and Rhodes, "The Distribution of Juvenile Delinquency." For drug abuse studies that test differential association, see Susan M. Jaquith, "Adolescent Marijuana and Alcohol Use: An Empirical Test of Differential Association Theory," *Criminology,* **19** (1981): 271–280; Brenda S. Griffin and Charles T. Griffin, "Marijuana Use among Students and Peers," *Drug Forum,* **7** (1978): 155–165; and Ross L. Matsueda, "Testing Control Modeling Approach," *American Sociological Review,* **47** (1982): 489–504.

58. Hirschi, *Causes of Delinquency,* p. 95.

59. Beth Bjerregaard and Carolyn Smith, "Patterns of Male and Female Gang Membership," working paper no. 13, Rochester Youth Development Study (Albany, N.Y.: Hindelang Criminal Justice Research Center, 1992), p. 20. For the relationship of delinquents to their delinquent siblings, see Janet L. Lauritsen, "Sibling Resemblance in Juvenile Delinquency: Findings from the National Youth Survey," *Criminology,* **31** (1993): 387–409.

60. Warr, "Age, Peers, and Delinquency."

61. Charles Tittle, *Sanctions and Social Deviance* (New York: Praeger, 1980). See also James D. Orcutt, "Differential Association and Marijuana Use: A Closer Look at Sutherland (with a Little Help from Becker)," *Criminology,* **25** (1987): 341–358; Tittle et al., "Modeling Sutherland's Theory"; and Matsueda and Heimer, "Race, Family Structure, and Delinquency."

62. Clayton A. Hartjen, *Crime and Criminalization* (New York: Praeger, 1974), p. 51.

63. Ross L. Matsueda, "The Current State of Differential Association," *Crime and Delinquency,* **34** (1988): 277–306; Gary F. Jenson, "Parents, Peers, and Delinquent Action: A Test of the Differential Association Perspective," *American Journal of Sociology,* **78** (1972): 562–575, in which he finds no support for differential association theory; Ronald L. Simons, Martin G. Miller, and Stephen M. Aigner, "Contemporary Theories of Deviance and Female Delinquency: An Empirical Test," *Journal of Research in Crime and Delinquency,* **17** (1980): 42–57, which uses differential association theory to look at the relationship between values of friends and self-reported delinquency (result: girls tended more than boys to be influenced by their friends); D. A. Andrews, "Some Experimental Investigations of the Principles of Differential Association through Deliberate Manipulations of the Structure of Service Systems," *American Sociological Review,* **45** (1980): 448–462; Ivor D. Shorts, "Delinquency by Association?" *British Journal of Criminology,* **26** (1986): 156–163; Craig Reinarman and Jeffrey Fagan, "Social Organization and Differential Association: A Research Note from a Longitudinal Study of Violent Juvenile Offenders," *Crime and Delinquency,* **34** (1988): 307–327.

64. Susan Chira, "A Program That Works for Teen-Age Mothers," *New York Times,* Apr. 28, 1993, p. A12.

65. Thorsten Sellin, *Culture Conflict and Crime,* Bulletin 41 (New York: Social Science Research Council, 1938). For an empirical test of the relation between homicide rates and conflicting norms, see Avison and Loring, "Population Diversity and Cross-National Homicide." For a test demonstrating conflict resolution among Korean Americans in disputes involving insults, disrespect, and cheating, see Mark R. Pogrebin and Eric D. Poole, "Culture Conflict and Crime in the Korean-American Community," *Criminal Justice Policy Review,* **4** (1990): 69–78.

6

The Formation of Subcultures

KEY TERMS
culture of poverty
differential opportunity theory
reaction formation
subculture
subculture of violence

Two wanna-bes of the Black N White gang had just been inducted, after proving their worth in the required fistfights with veteran gang members and downing cans of beer. But somehow the initiation rite seemed incomplete. At that moment two teenagers, Elizabeth Pena and Jennifer Ertman, happened to cross the gang's path. Their nude bodies were found a few days later. They had been raped by every gang member and strangled, one with a belt, the other with a shoelace. "To ensure that both of them were dead," a police spokesman said, "the suspects stood on the girls' necks."[1] When the six 14- to 18-year old suspects were taken into custody, they were defiant, hurling insults and trying to kick a reporter's camera. One 17-year-old proclaimed, "Hey, great! We've hit the big time."[2] Another gang member had appeared on a TV show about gangs, the night before the killings, and had announced—between slurps of beer: "Human life means nothing!" Houston, where the events occurred, is in shock. So is the nation.

Gangs like the Black N White inhabit the streets and back alleys of most cities. And their numbers continue to grow. Twenty-three cities nationwide had known street gangs in 1961. Now, in the 1990s, about 187 cities, spread across almost every state, have gang problems. Gang violence—at one time an inner-city phenomenon—has also become a concern of suburban areas with populations as small as 5000.[3] Reports about juvenile gang activities fill the files of police departments, of juvenile courts, and of adult courts as well. How did these groups get started in American society? What keeps them going?

THE FUNCTION OF SUBCULTURES

Strain theorists explain criminal behavior as a result of the frustrations suffered by lower-class individuals deprived of legitimate means to reach their goals. Cultural deviance theorists assume that individuals become criminal by learning the criminal values of the groups to which they belong. In conforming to their own group standards, these people break the laws of the dominant culture. These two perspectives are the foundation for subcultural theory, which

emerged in the mid-1950s and held criminologists' attention for over a decade.

A **subculture** is a subdivision within the dominant culture that has its own norms, beliefs, and values. Subcultures typically emerge when people in similar circumstances find themselves isolated from the mainstream and band together for mutual support. Subcultures may form among members of racial and ethnic minorities, among prisoners, among occupational groups, among ghetto dwellers. Subcultures exist within a larger society, not apart from it. They therefore share some of its values. Nevertheless, the lifestyles of their members are significantly different from those of individuals in the dominant culture.

SUBCULTURAL THEORIES OF DELINQUENCY AND CRIME

Subcultural theories in criminology have been developed to account for delinquency among lower-class males, especially for one of its most important expressions—the teenage gang. According to subcultural theorists, delinquent subcultures, like all subcultures, emerge in response to special problems that members of the dominant culture do not face. Theories developed by Albert Cohen and by Richard Cloward and Lloyd Ohlin are extensions of the strain, social disorganization, and differential association theories. They explain why delinquent subcultures emerge in the first place (strain), why they take a particular form (social disorganization), and how they are passed on from one generation to the next (differential association).

The explanations of delinquency developed by Marvin Wolfgang and Franco Ferracuti and by Walter Miller are somewhat different from those mentioned above. These theorists do not suggest that delinquency begins with failure to reach middle-class goals. Their explanations are rooted in culture conflict theory. The subculture of violence thesis argues that the value systems of some subcultures demand the use of violence in certain social situations. This norm, which affects daily behavior, conflicts with conventional middle-class norms. Along the same lines, Miller suggests that the characteristics of lower-class delinquency reflect the value system of the lower-class culture and that the lower-class values and norms conflict with those of the dominant culture.

Although Miller contends that the lower-class culture as a whole—not a subculture within it—is responsible for criminal behavior in urban slums, his theory is appropriate to our discussion because it demonstrates how the needs of young urban males are met by membership in a street gang. Miller's street gangs, like those of Cohen and of Cloward and Ohlin, condone violent criminal activitiy as one of the few means of attaining status in a slum.

The Middle-Class Measuring Rod

Albert Cohen was a student of Robert Merton and of Edwin Sutherland, both of whom had made convincing arguments about the causes of delinquency. Sutherland persuaded Cohen that differential association and the cultural transmission of criminal norms led to criminal behavior. From Merton he learned about structurally induced strain. Cohen combined and expanded these perspectives to explain how the delinquent subculture arises, where it is found within the social structure, and why it has the particular characteristics that it does.[4]

According to Cohen, delinquent subcultures emerge in the slum areas of larger American cities. They are rooted in class differentials in parental aspirations, child-rearing practices, and classroom standards. The relative position of a youngster's family in the social structure determines the problems the child will have to face throughout life.

Lower-class families who have never known a middle-class lifestyle, for example, cannot socialize their children in a way that prepares them to enter the middle class. The children grow up with poor communication skills, lack of commitment to education, and an inability to delay gratification. Schools present a particular problem. There, lower-class children are evaluated by middle-class teachers on the basis of a middle-class measuring rod. The measures are based on such middle-class values as self-reliance, good manners, respect for property, and long-range planning. By such measures, lower-class children fall far short of the standards they must meet if they are to compete successfully with middle-class children. Cohen argues that they experience status frustration and strain, to which they respond by adopting one of three roles: corner boy, college boy, or delinquent boy.

Corner Boy, College Boy, Delinquent Boy

Corner boys try to make the best of a bad situation. The corner boy hangs out in the neighborhood with his peer group, spending the day in some group activity such as gambling or athletic competition. He receives support from his peers and is very loyal to them. Most lower-class boys become corner boys. Eventually they get menial jobs and live a conventional lifestyle.

There are very few *college boys*. These boys continually strive to live up to middle-class standards, but their chances for success are limited because of academic and social handicaps.

Delinquent boys band together to form a subculture in which they can define status in ways that to them seem attainable. Cohen claims that even though these lower-class youths set up their own norms, they have internalized the norms of the dominant class and they feel anxious when they go against these norms. To deal with this conflict, they resort to **reaction formation**, a mechanism that relieves anxiety through the process of rejecting with abnormal intensity what one wants but cannot obtain. These boys turn the middle-class norms upside down, thereby making conduct right in their subculture precisely because it is wrong by the norms of the larger culture (Figure 6.1).

Consequently, their delinquent acts serve no useful purpose. They do not steal things to eat them, wear them, or sell them. In fact, they often discard or destroy what they have stolen. They appear to delight in the discomfort of others and in breaking taboos. Their acts are directed against people and property at random, unlike the goal-oriented activities of many adult criminal groups. The subculture is typically characterized by short-run hedonism, pure pleasure-seeking, with no planning or deliberation about what to do, where, or when. The delinquents hang out on the street corner until someone gets an idea; then they act impulsively, without considering the

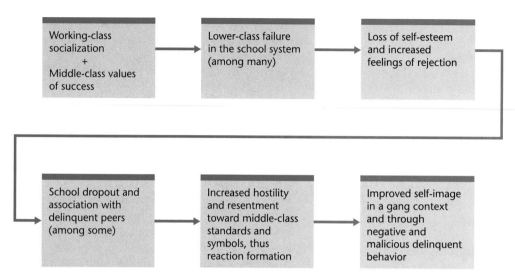

FIGURE 6.1 The process of reaction formation among delinquent boys

Source: Donald J. Shoemaker, *Theories of Delinquency: An Examination of Explanations of Delinquent Behavior*, 2nd ed. (New York: Oxford University Press, 1990), p. 119.

consequences. The group's autonomy is all-important. Its members are loyal to each other and resist any attempts on the part of family, school, or community to restrain their behavior.

Tests of Cohen's Theory

Criminological researchers generally agree that Cohen's theory is responsible for major advances in research on delinquency.[5] Among them are researchers who have found a relationship between delinquency and social status in our society (Chapter 5). Much evidence also supports Cohen's assumption that lower-class children perform more poorly in school than middle-class children.[6] Teachers often expect them to perform less ably than their middle-class students, and this expectation is one of the components of poor performance.

Researchers have demonstrated that poor performance in school is related to delinquency. When Travis Hirschi studied more than 4000 California schoolchildren, he found that youths who were academically incompetent and performed poorly in school came to dislike school. Disliking it, they rejected its authority; rejecting its authority, they committed delinquent acts (Chapter 7).[7] Delbert Elliott and Harwin Voss also investigated the relationship between school and delin-

quency. They analyzed annual school performance and delinquency records of 2000 students in California from ninth grade to 1 year after the expected graduation date. Their findings indicated that those who dropped out of school had higher rates of delinquency than those who graduated. They also found that academic achievement and alienation from school were closely related to dropping out of school.[8]

From analysis of the dropout-delinquency relationship among over 5000 persons nationwide, G. Roger Jarjoura concluded that while dropouts were more likely to engage in delinquent acts than graduates, the reason was not always simply the fact that they had dropped out. Dropping out because of a dislike for school, poor grades, or financial reasons was related to future involvement in delinquency; dropping out because of problems at home was not. Dropping out for personal reasons such as marriage or pregnancy was significantly related to subsequent violent offending.[9] All these findings support Cohen's theory. Other findings, however, do not.

In a study of 12,524 students in Davidson County, Tennessee, Albert Reiss and Albert Rhodes found only a slight relationship between delinquency and status deprivation.[10] This conclusion was supported by the research of Marvin

Krohn and his associates.[11] Furthermore, several criminologists have challenged Cohen's claim that delinquent behavior is purposeless. They contend that much delinquent behavior is serious and calculated, and often engaged in for profit.[12] John Kitsuse and David Dietrick have also questioned the consistency of the theory: Cohen argues that the behavior of delinquent boys is a deliberate response to middle-class opinion, yet he also argues that the boys do not care about the opinions of middle-class people.[13]

Evaluation of Cohen's Theory

Researchers have praised and criticized Cohen's work. Cohen's theory answers a number of questions left unresolved by the strain and cultural deviance theories. It explains the origin of delinquent behavior and why some youths raised in the same neighborhoods and attending the same schools do not become involved in delinquent subcultures. His concepts of status deprivation and the middle-class measuring rod have been useful to researchers. Yet his theory does not explain why most delinquents eventually become law-abiding even though their position in the class structure remains relatively fixed. Some criminologists also question whether youths are driven by some serious motivating force or whether they are simply out on the streets looking for fun.[14] Moreover, if delinquent subcultures result from the practice of measuring lower-class boys by a middle-class measuring rod, how do we account for the growing number of middle-class gangs?

Other questions concern the difficulty of trying to test the concepts of reaction formation, internalization of middle-class values, and status deprivation, among others. To answer some of his critics, Cohen, with his colleague James Short, expanded the idea of delinquent subcultures to include not only lower-class delinquent behavior but also such variants as middle-class delinquent subcultures and female delinquents.[15] Cohen took Merton's strain theory a step further by elaborating on the development of delinquent behavior. He described how strain actually creates frustration and status deprivation, which in turn foster the development of an alternative set of values that give lower-class boys a chance

Differential opportunity: Members of the Los Angeles Bloods gang as they appeared in a rap video made in March 1993. The Bloods and another gang, the Crips, have expanded their primary business (drug dealing) to a number of other cities.

to achieve recognition. Since the mid-1950s Cohen's theory has stimulated not only research but the formulation of new theories.

DELINQUENCY AND OPPORTUNITY

Like Cohen's theory, the theory of differential opportunity developed by Richard Cloward and Lloyd Ohlin combines strain, differential association, and social disorganization concepts.[16] Both theories begin with the assumption that conventional means to conventional success are not equally distributed among the socioeconomic classes, that lack of means causes frustration for lower-class youths, and that criminal behavior is learned and culturally transmitted. Both theories also agree that the common solution to shared problems leads to the formation of delinquent subcultures. They disagree, however, on the content of these subcultures. As we have noted, norms in Cohen's delinquent subcultures are right precisely because they are wrong in the dominant culture. Delinquent acts are negative and nonutilitarian. Cloward and Ohlin disagree; they suggest that lower-class delinquents remain goal-oriented. The kind of delinquent behavior they engage in depends on the illegitimate opportunities available to them.

According to Cloward and Ohlin's **differen-**

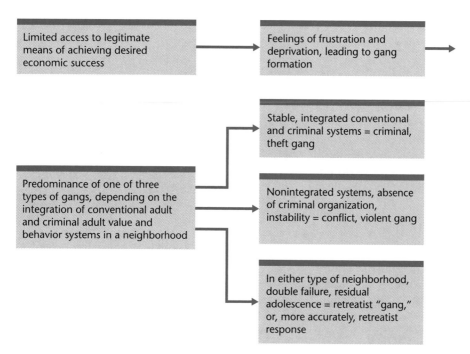

FIGURE 6.2 Factors leading to development of three types of delinquent gangs

Source: Donald J. Shoemaker, *Theories of Delinquency: An Examination of Explanations of Delinquent Behavior,* 2nd ed. (New York: Oxford University Press, 1990) p. 129.

tial opportunity theory, delinquent subcultures flourish in lower-class areas and take the particular forms they do because opportunities for illegitimate success are no more equitably distributed than those for conventional success. Just as means—opportunities—are unequally distributed in the conventional world, opportunities to reach one's goals are unequally distributed in the criminal world. A person cannot simply decide to join a theft-oriented gang or, for that matter, a violence-oriented one. Cloward and Ohlin maintain that the types of subcultures and of the juvenile gangs that flourish within them depend on the types of neighborhoods in which they develop (Figure 6.2).

In areas where conventional and illegitimate values and behavior are integrated by a close connection of illegitimate and legitimate businesses, *criminal gangs* emerge. Older criminals serve as role models. They teach youngsters whom to exploit, the necessary criminal skills, the importance of loyal relationships with criminal associates, and how to make the right conections with shady lawyers, bail bondsmen, crooked politicians, and corrupt police officers. Adolescent members of criminal gangs, like adult criminals in the neighborhood, are involved in extortion, fraud, theft, and other activities that yield illegal income.

This type of neighborhood was described by one of its members in a classic work published in 1930:

> Stealing in the neighborhood was a common practice among the children and approved by the parents. Whenever the boys got together they talked about robbing and made more plans for stealing. I hardly knew any boys who did not go robbing. The little fellows went in for petty stealing, breaking into freight cars, and stealing junk. The older guys did big jobs like stick-ups, burglary, and stealing autos. The little fellows admired the "big shots" and longed for the day when they could get into the big racket. Fellows who had "done time" were the big shots and looked up to and gave the little fellows tips on how to get by and pull off big jobs.[17]

Neighborhoods characterized by transience and instability, Cloward and Ohlin argue, offer few opportunities to get ahead in organized criminal activities. This world gives rise to *conflict gangs,* whose goal is to gain a reputation for toughness and destructive violence. Thus "one particular biker would catch a bird and then bite off its head, allowing the blood to trickle from his mouth as he yelled 'all right!'"[18] It is the world of the warrior: fight, show courage against all odds, defend and maintain the honor of the group. Above all, never show fear.

Violence is the means used to gain status in the conflict gangs. Conventional society's recognition of the "worst" gangs becomes a mark of prestige, perpetuating the high standards of their members. Conflict gangs emerge in lower-class areas where neither criminal nor conventional adult role models exercise much control over youngsters.

A third subcultural response to differential opportunities is the formation of *retreatist gangs.* Cloward and Ohlin describe members of retreatist gangs as double failures because they have not been successful in the legitimate world and have been equally unsuccessful in the illegitimate worlds of organized criminal activity and violence-oriented gangs. This subculture is characterized by a continuous search for getting high through alcohol, atypical sexual experiences, marijuana, hard drugs, or a combination of these.

The retreatist hides in a world of sensual adventure, borrowing, begging, or stealing to support his habit, whatever it may be. He may peddle drugs or work as a pimp or look for some other deviant income-producing activity. But the income is not a primary concern; he is interested only in the next high. Belonging to a retreatist gang offers a sense of superiority and well-being that is otherwise beyond the reach of these least successful dropouts.

Not all lower-class youngsters who are unable to reach society's goals become members of criminal, conflict, or retreatist gangs. Many choose to accept their situation and to live within its constraints. These law-abiding youngsters are Cohen's corner boys.

Tests of Opportunity Theory

Cloward and Ohlin's differential opportunity theory presented many new ideas, and a variety of studies emerged to test it empirically.

The first of Cloward and Ohlin's assumptions—that blocked opportunities are related to delinquency—has mixed support. Travis Hirschi, for example, demonstrated that "the greater one's acceptance of conventional (or even quasi-conventional) success goals, the less likely one is to be delinquent, regardless of the likelihood these goals will someday be attained."[19] Delbert Elliott and Harwin Voss, too, have found no relationship between actual or anticipated failure to reach occupational success and self-reported delinquency. In other words, the youngsters who stick to hard work and education to get ahead in society are the least likely to become delinquent, no matter what their real chances of reaching their goals.[20]

Judson Landis and Frank Scarpitti disagree. When they compared a group of incarcerated youths and a high school control group, they found that the delinquent boys perceived opportunities to be much more limited than the nondelinquent boys did.[21] There is also evidence that both gang and nongang boys believe the middle-class values of hard work and scholastic achievement to be important. Gang boys, however, are more ready to approve of a wide range of behaviors, including aggressive acts and drug use.[22]

The second assumption of differential opportunity theory—that the type of lower-class gang depends on the type of neighborhood in which it emerges—has also drawn the attention of criminologists. Empirical evidence suggests that gang behavior is more versatile and involves a wider range of criminal and noncriminal acts than the patterns outlined by Cloward and Ohlin. Ko-lin Chin's research on New York gangs in 1993 demonstrates that Chinese gangs are engaged in extortion, alien smuggling, heroin trafficking, and the running of gambling establishments and houses of prostitution.[23] A recent report from the Denver Youth Survey showed that while the most frequent form of illegal activity is fighting with other gangs, gang members are also involved in robberies, joyriding, assaults, stealing, and drug sales.[24] Similarly, Alan Lizotte and James Tesoriero found that among 675 students in the Rochester Youth Development Study, large numbers of boys owned illegal guns, were members of gangs, committed gun crime, and used or sold drugs.[25]

The new subculture that emerged in the 1980s combined violence, which had become much more vicious than in earlier years, with big business in cocaine and crack trafficking. Rival gangs killed for more than simply turf. In cities around the world teenagers began to drive BMWs with Uzi submachine guns concealed under the driver's seat and thousands of dollars in their pockets so that they could make bail at any moment.

Evaluation: Differential Opportunity Theory

For three decades criminologists have reviewed, examined, and revised the work of Cloward and Ohlin. One of the main criticisms is that their theory is class-oriented. If, as Cloward and Ohlin claim, delinquency is a response to blocked opportunities, how can we explain middle-class delinquency? Another question arises from contradictory statements. How can delinquent groups be nonutilitarian, negativistic, and malicious (Cohen)—and also goal-oriented and utilitarian? Despite its shortcomings, however, differential opportunity theory has identified some of the reasons why lower-class youngsters may become alienated. Cloward and Ohlin's work has also challenged researchers to study the nature of the subcultures in our society. Marvin Wolfgang

and Franco Ferracuti have concentrated on one of them—the subculture of violence.

THE SUBCULTURE OF VIOLENCE

Like Cohen, and like Cloward and Ohlin, Marvin Wolfgang and Franco Ferracuti turned to subcultural theory to explain criminal behavior among lower-class young urban males. All three theories developed by these five researchers assume the existence of subcultures made up of people who share a value system that differs from that of the dominant culture. And they assume that each subculture has its own rules or conduct norms that dictate how individuals should act under varying circumstances. The three theories also agree that these values and norms persist over time because they are learned by successive generations. The theories differ, however, in their focus.

Cohen and Cloward and Ohlin focus on the origin of the subculture, specifically culturally induced strain. The major thrust of Wolfgang and Ferracuti's work is on culture conflict. Furthermore, the earlier theories encompass all types of delinquency and crime; Wolfgang and Ferracuti concentrate on violent crime. They argue that in some subcultures behavior norms

WINDOW TO THE WORLD
The Emergence of Subcultures of Violence: The Former Yugoslavia

Yugoslavia, once a Balkan state with six major republics and ethnic groups, no longer exists. Civil war in Yugoslavia resulted in independence for Croatia and Slovenia in 1991; Macedonia and Bosnia-Herzegovina also declared their independence. But as Yugoslavia began to collapse, Serbia, the largest of the six republics that made up the old federation, began a fierce battle to acquire territory and to protect the many pockets of Serbian minority populations in Croatia and Bosnia-Herzegovina.

Among the strategies used by the Serbs was a policy called "ethnic cleansing":

Considered in the context of the conflicts in the former Yugoslovia, "ethnic cleansing" means rendering an area ethnically homogeneous by using force or intimidation to remove persons of given groups from the area. "Ethnic cleansing" is contrary to international law.

Based on the many reports describing the policy and practices conducted in the former Yugoslavia, "ethnic cleansing" has been carried out by means of murder, torture, arbitrary arrest and detention, extra-judicial executions, rape and sexual assault, confinement of civilian population in ghetto areas, forcible removal, displacement and deportation of civilian population, deliberate military attacks or threats of attacks on civilians and civilian areas, and wanton destruction of property. Those practices constitute crimes against humanity."(1)

In human terms, ethnic cleansing has meant beatings, random shootings, and extended periods of near starvation for Muslims in prison camps.(2) There have been reports of the systematic rape of thousands of women. Homes, churches, schools, and hospitals have been bombed, leaving children without educational opportunities and the wounded and sick without medical care. Enclaves of ethnic groups were surrounded and kept without food, supplies, or medical assistance for months on end.(2)

It is impossible to guess how the conflict in the former Yugoslavia will end. In 1984, Yugoslavia hosted the Winter Olympics in the beautiful city of Sarajevo. Now Bosnia-Herzegovina is being destroyed by a bloody civil war, and Sarajevo, its capital, is a ruined and besieged city. What began as an ethnic conflict over new political boundaries has become an international issue that seems incapable of resolution. The United Nations has made a number of attempts using a variety of strategies, but so far nothing has worked:

■ Negotiations to stop the fighting and set up a mechanism to resolve the issues have been unsuccessful.

■ U.N. peacekeeping forces on the ground have been unable to keep roads and channels of communication open so that relief efforts can continue. Tens of thousands of refugees are

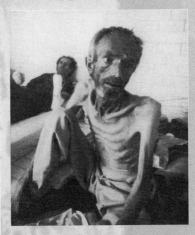

A news photo of a Muslim prisoner in a Serb detention camp near Sarajevo in Bosnia.

trapped in besieged areas whose meager resources are already exhausted.

■ The U.N. Security Council has established an International War Crimes Tribunal to try those responsible for war crimes. This tribunal held its first session on November 17, 1993. But there is as yet no way to arrest some of those who will be indicted for trial by the court at the Hague in the Netherlands. The worst offenders are still hiding behind their armies.(3)

Sources

1. *Interim Report of the Commission of Experts Established Pursuant to Security Council Resolution 780* (1992), submitted to the U.N. Security Council by the Secretary General (S/25274, of Jan. 26, 1993), p. 16.; *Second Interim Report* (S/26645, of Nov. 17, 1993).
2. Chuck Sudetic, "Released Muslims Report Abuses," *New York Times,* Sept. 7, 1993, p. A4; European Community investigation into the treatment of Muslim women in the former Yugoslavia, Annex I to letter dated Feb. 2, 1993, from the Permanent Representative of Denmark to the United Nations addressed to the Secretary General, S/25240 of Feb. 3, 1993. See "War Crimes Tribunal Opens Inquiry on Yugoslav Fighting," *New York Times,* Nov. 17, 1993, p. A8.
3. Resolution of the United Nations Security Council, S/RES/808, Feb. 22, 1993.

Questions for Discussion

1. Does the emergence of subcultures of violence on the international or cross-cultural level follow the same pattern as the emergence of such subcultures in our own society? Why or why not?
2. Does subculture theory offer any models for dealing with international subcultures of violence? If so, are the strategies adopted by the international community in the former Yugoslavia appropriate?

are dictated by a value system that demands the use of force or violence.[26] Subcultures that adhere to conduct norms conducive to violence are referred to as **subcultures of violence.**

Violence is not used in all situations, but it is frequently an expected response. The appearance of a weapon, a slight shove or push, a derogatory remark, or the opportunity to wield power undetected may very well evoke an aggressive reaction that seems uncalled for to middle-class people. Fists rather than words settle disputes. Knives or guns are readily available, so confrontations can quickly escalate. Violence is a pervasive part of everyday life. Child-rearing practices (hitting), gang activities (street wars), domestic quarrels (battering), and social events (drunken brawls) are all permeated by violence.

Violence is not considered antisocial. Members of this subculture feel no guilt about their aggression. In fact, individuals who do not resort to violence may be reprimanded. The value system is transmitted from generation to generation, long after the original reason for the violence has disappeared. The pattern is very hard to eradicate.

When Wolfgang and Ferracuti described population groups that are likely to respond violently to stress, they posed a powerful question to the criminal justice system. How does one go about changing a subcultural norm? This question becomes increasingly significant with the merging of the drug subculture and the subculture of violence.

Tests of the Subculture of Violence

Howard Erlanger, using nationwide data collected for the President's Commission on the Causes and Prevention of Violence, found no major differences in attitudes toward violence by class or race. Erlanger concluded that though members of the lower class show no greater approval of violence than middle-class persons do, they lack the sophistication necessary to settle grievances by other means.[27] The subculture of violence thesis has also generated a line of empirical research that looks at regional differences in levels of violent crime.

The South (as you will see in Chapter 10) has the highest homicide rate in the country. Some researchers have attributed this high rate to subcultural values.[28] They argue that the southern subculture of violence has its historical roots in an exaggerated defense of honor by southern gentlemen, mob violence (especially lynching), a military tradition, the acceptance of personal vengeance, and the widespread availability and use of handguns.[29]

The problem with many of these studies is that it is difficult to separate the effects of economic and social factors from those of cultural values. Several researchers have sought to solve this problem. Colin Loftin and Robert Hill, for example, using a sophisticated measure of poverty, found that economic factors, not cultural ones, explained regional variation in homicide rates.[30] Similarly, others suggest that high homicide rates and gun ownership may have a great deal to do with socioeconomic conditions, especially racial inequality in the South.[31] (See Figure 6.3)

Researchers who support the subculture of violence thesis point to statistics on characteristics of homicide offenders and victims: lower class, inner-city black males are disproportionately represented in the FBI's Uniform Crime Reports. In addition:

■ The majority of the offenders are young, most in their twenties but many in their late teens.

■ Typically the offender and the victim know each other.

■ The offender and the victim are usually in the same age group and of the same race.[32]

Furthermore, in a study of 556 males interviewed at age 26, 19 percent of the respondents, all inner-city males, reported having been shot or stabbed. These victimizations were found to be highly correlated with both self-reported offenses and official arrest statistics. In fact, the best single predictor of committing a violent act was found to be whether or not the individual had been a victim of a violent crime. Though most people in the dominant society who are shot or stabbed do not commit a criminal act in response, it appears that many inner-city males alternate the roles of victim and offender in a way that maintains the values and attitudes of a violent subculture.[33]

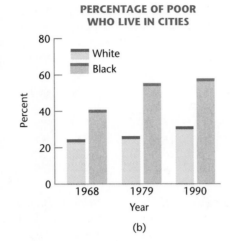

THE PRICE OF POVERTY TODAY

	Billions
Low-income assistance, including food and housing, excluding medical care	$120
Cost of police and corrections*	$50
Additional gain to GNP if poor were fully employed	$60
TOTAL	$230

*Assumes most crime is linked to poverty.

The Growing Disadvantage of the Poor

(a)

PERCENTAGE OF POOR WHO LIVE IN CITIES

(b)

PERCENTAGE OF POOR WHO LIVE IN FAMILIES HEADED BY WOMEN

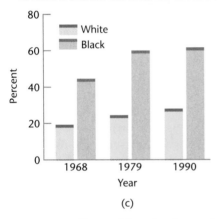

(c)

PERCENTAGE OF HEADS OF POOR FAMILIES WITHOUT JOBS

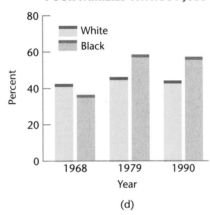

(d)

FIGURE 6.3 The social costs of poverty and crime: being poor often means living in a decaying urban center in a single-parent family whose head does not have a job.

Source: *Business Week,* May 18, 1992, pp. 40–41.

Evaluation: The Subculture of Violence Theory

Though empirical evidence remains inconclusive, the subculture of violence theory is supported by the distribution of violent crime in American society.[34] The number of gangs and the violence associated with their activities are growing.[35] Jeffrey Fagan noted that "drug use is widespread and normative" among gangs.[36] Gang warfare, which takes the lives of innocent bystanders in ghetto areas, is a part of life in most of the impoverished, densely populated neighborhoods in such major cities as Los Angeles, New York, Chicago, Miami, Washington, D.C., and Atlanta and in smaller disintegrating urban centers as well. For example, over the 3 years between 1985 and 1988, Jamaican "bosses"—gangs transplanted from Kingston, Jamaica, to the United States—have been involved in 1400 homicides.[37]

Though not all persons in these subcultures follow the norm of violence, it appears that a dismaying number of them attach less and less im-

Violence and police raids are part of everyday life in many inner city housing projects.

portance to the value of human life and turn increasingly to violence to resolve immediate problems and frustrations.

FOCAL CONCERNS: MILLER'S THEORY

All the theorists we have examined thus far explain criminal and delinquent behavior in terms of subcultural values that emerge and are perpetuated from one generation to the next in lower-class urban slums. Walter Miller reasons differently. According to Miller:

> In the case of "gang" delinquency, the cultural system which exerts the most direct influence on behavior is that of the lower-class community itself—a long-established, distinctively patterned tradition with an integrity of its own—rather than a so-called "delinquent subculture" which has arisen through conflict with middle-class culture and is oriented to the deliberate violation of middle-class norms.[38]

To Miller, juvenile delinquency is not rooted in the rejection of middle-class values; it stems from lower-class culture, which has its own value system. This value system has evolved as a response to living in slums. Gang norms are simply the adolescent expression of the lower-class culture in which the boys have grown up. This lower-class culture exists apart from the middle-class culture, and it has done so for generations. The value system, not the gang norms, generates delinquent acts.

Miller has identified six focal concerns, or areas, to which lower-class males give persistent attention: trouble, toughness, smartness, excitement, luck, and autonomy. Concern over *trouble* is a major feature of lower-class life. Staying out of trouble and getting into trouble are daily preoccupations. Trouble can get a person into the hands of the authorities or it can result in prestige among peers. Lower-class individuals are often evaluated by the extent of their involvement in activities such as fighting, drinking, and sexual misbehavior. In this case, the greater the involvement or the more extreme the performance, the greater the prestige or "respect" the person commands.

These young men are almost obsessively concerned with *toughness;* the code requires a show of masculinity, a denial of sentimentality, and a display of physical strength. Miller argues that this concern with toughness is related to the fact that a large proportion of lower-class males grow up in female-dominated households and have no male figure from whom to learn the male role. They join street gangs in order to find males with whom they can identify.

Claude Brown's classic 1965 autobiography, *Manchild in the Promised Land,* illustrates the concerns about trouble and toughness among adolescents growing up in an urban slum:

> My friends were all daring like me, tough like me, dirty like me, ragged like me, cursed like me, and had a great love for trouble like me. We took pride in being able to hitch rides on trolleys, buses, taxicabs and in knowing how to steal and fight. We knew that we were the only kids in the neighborhood who usually had more than ten dollars in their pockets. . . . Somebody was always trying to shake us down or rob us. This was usually done by the older hustlers in the neighborhood or by storekeepers or cops. . . . We accepted this as a way of life.[39]

Another focal concern is *smartness*—the ability to gain something by outsmarting, outwitting, or conning another person. In lower-class neighborhoods youngsters practice outsmarting each other in card games, exchanges of insults, and other trials. Prestige is awarded to those who demonstrate smartness.

Many aspects of lower-class life are related to another focal concern, the search for *excitement.* Youngsters alternate between hanging out with peers and looking for excitement, which can be found in fighting, getting drunk, and using drugs. Risks, danger, and thrills break up the monotony of their existence.

Fate, particularly *luck,* plays an important role in lower-class life. Many individuals believe that their lives are subject to forces over which they have little control. If they get lucky, a rather drab life could change quickly. Common discussions center on whether lucky numbers come up, cards are right, or dice are good. Brown recalls:

> After a while [Mama] settled down, and we stopped talking about her feelings, then somebody came upstairs and told her she had hit the numbers. We just forgot all about her feelings. I forgot about her feelings. Mama forgot about her feelings. Everybody did. She started concentrating on the number. This was the first time she'd had a hit in a long time. They bought some liquor. Mama and Dad started drinking: everyone started making a lot of noise and playing records.[40]

Miller's last focal concern, *autonomy,* stems from the lower-class person's resentment of external controls, whether parents, teachers, or police. This desire for personal freedom is expressed often in such terms as "No one can push me around" and "I don't need nobody."[41]

According to Miller, in every class status is associated with the possession of qualities that are valued. In the lower class the six focal concerns define status. It is apparent that by engaging in behavior that affords status by these criteria, many people will be breaking the laws of the dominant society (Figure 6.4).

Tests of Miller's Theory

An obvious question is whether in our urban, heterogeneous, secular, technologically based society any isolated pockets of culture are still to be found. The pervasiveness of mass advertising, mass transit, and mass communication makes it seem unlikely that an entire class of people could be unaware of the dominant value system. Empirical research on opportunity theory has found that lower-class boys share the conventional success goals of the dominant culture.[42] This finding suggests that the idea of isolation from the dominant system does not fit with reality. Empirical research has also found, however, that while gang boys may support middle-class values, they are willing to deviate from them. If an opportunity arises to gain prestige in a fight, gang boys are willing to take the chance that their act will not result in punishment.

Most empirical tests of values question young people on their attachment to middle-class values. Stephen Cernovich expanded this type of research by investigating attachment to lower-class focal concerns.[43] He found that toughness, excitement, trouble, and pleasure-seeking were

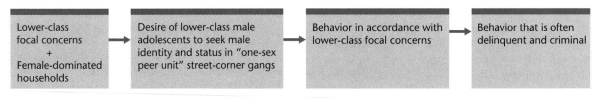

FIGURE 6.4 The relationship between delinquency and lower-class focal concerns

Source: Donald J. Shoemaker, *Theories of Delinquency: An Examination of Explanations of Delinquent Behavior,* 2nd ed. (New York: Oxford University Press, 1990) p. 137.

related to self-reported delinquency in all classes. His findings also showed that boys of all classes were committed to delayed gratification, hard work, and education. Cernovich concluded that it is values, rather than class, that are associated with delinquency.

Evaluation: Miller's Theory

Criminologists have been disturbed by Miller's assumption that the lower-class lifestyle is generally focused on illegal activity. In making such an assumption, they say, Miller disregards the fact that most people in the lower class do conform to conventional norms. Moreover, some criminologists ask, if lower-class boys are conforming to their own value system, why would they suffer guilt or shame when they commit delinquent acts?[44]

The Culture of Poverty

Angela D'Arpa-Calandra, a former probation officer who now directs a Juvenile Intensive Supervision program, says she recently walked into a New York courtroom and "saw a mother and grandmother sitting with the 14-year-old offender. 'I had the grandmother in criminal court in 1963,' D'Arpa-Calandra says. 'We didn't stop it there. The grandmother was 14 when she was arrested. The mother had this child when she was 14. It's like a cycle we must relive.'"[45]

Perhaps the best support for Miller's ideas is found in such qualitative, rather than quantitative, accounts of life in a lower-class slum. In the 1960s Oscar Lewis used the term **culture of poverty** to describe groups characterized by helplessness, cynicism, and mistrust of authority as represented by schools and the police.[46] Nearly 20 years later, Ken Auletta referred to

members of these cultures as the *underclass*.[47] They have little in the way of education or skills to enable them to keep up with the demands of a modern society. These cultures have been the subject of television documentaries, movies, plays, newspaper stories, and autobiographical accounts, such as Brown's *Manchild in the Promised Land*.

Life on the Edge, Generation to Generation

In our discussion of cultural deviance and subcultural theories we noted that the values and norms that define behavior in slums and ghettos do not change much over time or from place to place. Successive generations have to deal with the same problems. They typically share similar responses. By and large, descriptions of life in poverty-stricken areas, whether written by people who have lived in them or by people who have studied them, reveal dreary routine, boredom, constant trouble, and incessant problems with drugs, alcohol, and crime. As the father tells his son in Eugene O'Neill's autobiographical play *Long Day's Journey into Night*, "There was no damned romance in our poverty."[48] There still isn't. In 1993, *The New York Times* ran a series of profiles of youth in poverty:

> Derrick White rides through the crumbling asphalt roads of the Hurt Village housing project where he played tag among the steel clotheslines and shot baskets through bent and wobbly hoops. He passes the trash bins where men with black plastic bags mine for cans to sell to a recycling center. He passes the "dope track," where he saw a friend shot in the neck and killed.
>
> Beyond the project he passes the supermarket that refused him a job interview because, he believes, his address marks him as a project kid.[49]

In America's poverty stricken inner cities, survival often depends on associations with peers who share the same ethnic values and background.

FEMALE DELINQUENT SUBCULTURES

Traditionally, gang membership has been primarily limited to young, inner-city males. Theoretical and empirical studies in this area therefore focused on that population. Little was known about female subcultures until recently.

Early Research

In one of the few early studies, done in 1958, Albert Cohen and James Short suggested that female delinquent subcultures, like their male counterparts, were composed of members who had been frustrated in their efforts to achieve conventional goals (respectability, marriage, status). The girls had drifted into a subculture that offered them substitute status, albeit outside legitimate society. Drug use and prostitution became all but inevitable. Since the research that led to this finding was conducted among mostly lower-class black females, Cohen and Short admitted that their findings probably could not be generalized to all female delinquent subcultures.[50]

Recent Studies

Twenty-six years after these tentative findings, Anne Campbell published the first major work on the lifestyle of female gang members in New York. She spent 2 years with three gangs: one Hispanic (the Sex Girls), one black (the Five Percent Nation), and one racially mixed (the Sandman Ladies). Campbell's findings demonstrate that girls, like boys, join gangs for mutual support, protection, and a sense of belonging. They, too, gain status by living up to the value system of their gang. Campbell also noted that these youngsters will probably end up, as their mothers have, living on welfare assistance in a ghetto apartment. Men will come and go in their lives, but after their gang days the women feel they have lost their support group and are constantly threatened by feelings of isolation.[51]

About 10 percent of gang members nationwide are female. Many of the female gangs are affiliates of male gangs, often offering support for the young men they refer to as their "homeboys." They do, however, have their own initiation rites (which mimic male ceremonies but are usually much less violent) and their own gang colors, and a strong allegiance exists among each gang's members. For many of these youngsters the gang takes the place of a family. Shorty, a member of Los Angeles's Tiny Diablas, had no family except a grandmother, who had given up on trying to control her. Shorty's mother, who had been a gang member, abandoned her at an early age. Her father overdosed on heroin and was identified by a tattoo of Shorty's name. Her aunt had a teardrop tattoo next to her eye, to signify 1 year in jail; her uncle had two teardrops. Such family ties are not unusual among gang members.[52]

Not all female gangs have male affiliates. In a study of crack sales and violence among gangs in San Francisco, researchers interviewed members of an all-female group, the Potrero Hill Posse (PHP).[53] This independent group was formed in the mid-1980s when the females realized that their gang-affiliated boyfriends were not distributing the profits and labor of their crack sales fairly. The PHP young women run "rock houses" (outlets for crack sales, lent by tenants who receive a small quantity of crack in return), procure other women to provide sex to male customers, and engage in a major shoplifting business that fills orders placed by people who do not want to pay retail prices.

CRIMINOLOGICAL FOCUS
The Girls In the Gang

Psychologist Anne Campbell studied female gangs in New York City and published her findings in her 1984 book *The Girls in the Gang*. She summarizes some of her observations here:

All the girls in the gang come from families that are poor. Many have never known their fathers. Most are immigrants from Puerto Rico. As children the girls moved from apartment to apartment as they were evicted or burned out by arsonists. Unable to keep any friends they managed to make and alienated from their mothers, whose lack of English restricted their ability to control or understand their daughters' lives, the girls dropped out of school early and grew up on the streets. In the company of older kids and street-corner men, they graduated early into the adult world. They began to use drugs and by puberty had been initiated into sexual activity. By fifteen many were pregnant. Shocked, their mothers tried to pull them off the streets. Some sent their daughters back to relatives in Puerto Rico while they had their babies. Abortion was out of the question in this Catholic world.

Those who stayed had "spoiled their identity" as good girls. Their reputations were marred before they ever reached adulthood. On the streets, among the gang members, the girls found a convenient identity in the female gang. Often they had friends or distant relatives who introduced them as "prospects." After a trial period, they could undertake the initiation rite: they had to fight an established member nominated by the godmother. What was at issue was not winning or losing but demonstrating "heart," or courage. Gangs do not welcome members who join only to gain protection. The loyalty of other gang members has to be won by a clear demonstration of willingness to "get down," or fight.

Paradoxically, the female gang goes to considerable lengths to control the sexual behavior of its members. Although the neighborhood may believe they are fast women, the girls themselves do not tolerate members who sleep around. A promiscuous girl is a threat to the other members' relationships with their boyfriends. Members can take a boyfriend from among the male gang members (indeed, they are forbidden to take one from any other gang) but they are required to be monogamous. A shout of "Whore!" is the most frequent cause of fistfights among the female members.

On the positive side, the gang provides a strong sense of belonging and sisterhood. After the terrible isolation of their lives, the girls acquire a ready-made circle of friends who have shared many of their experiences and who are always willing to support them against hostile words or deeds by outsiders. Fighting together generates a strong sense of camaraderie and as a bonus earns them the reputation of being "crazy." This reputation is extremely useful in the tough neighborhoods where they live. Their reputation for carrying knives and for solidarity effectively deters outsiders from challenging them. They work hard at fostering their tough "rep" not only in their deeds but in their social talk. They spend hours recounting and embroidering stories of fights they have been in. Behind all this bravado it is easy to sense the fear they work so hard to deny. Terrified of being victims (as many of them have already been in their families and as newcomers in their schools), they make much of their own "craziness"—the violent unpredictability that frightens away anyone who might try to harm them.

Source: Written by Anne Campbell. Adapted from Anne Campbell, The Girls in the Gang (New York and Oxford: Basil Blackwell, 1984).

Questions for Discussion

1. How similar are Campbell's female gangs to the male gangs described in this chapter? Are there any significant differences?
2. Would you expect female gangs to become as involved in criminal activity as male gangs? Why or why not?

California's All-Girl Asian-American Gangs, 1993

All-girl gangs exist in major cities throughout the United States. California's all-girl gangs in 1993 included these Asian-American groups:

Sisters 4 Life
Sacramento Bad Girls
Pretty in Yellow
Best Side Posse
Lady Rascal Gangsters
National Color Girls
Koreatown Crazy Chicas
West Coast Ladies
Southside Scissors

Gang members rely on the gang for assistance ("Nobody will mess with me . . . because they know that I got back-up. I got back-up. I got my homegirls behind me. And whatever goes down with me, they are going to have to take up with them") and for status ("It [membership] means being bad, being tough, and being able to walk without . . . you know, everybody just respects me because they know I am on the Potrero Hill Posse girls").[54]

Overall, according to 1992 gang research done as part of the Rochester Youth Development Study, the extent and nature of female participation has changed considerably over the last few decades. The findings show increased participation in gangs (in this study, about equal to that of males) and in gang-related activities, including serious delinquent acts and drug abuse.[55]

MIDDLE-CLASS DELINQUENCY

Despite the various interpretations of the origins of delinquency, theorists' descriptions of the norms of delinquent inner-city subcultures are generally quite similar. Recently, researchers have demonstrated that suburbs and small towns are no longer free from violent gang activity.[56] Let us see now whether the values, norms, and behavior of middle-class delinquents in the suburbs and smaller towns differ from those of lower-class delinquents. Here is a description of gang activity in one of New York's suburbs in 1993:

A few of the middle-class teen-agers in baggy shorts and backwards baseball caps smoking cigarettes on the lawn behind Mark Twain Junior High School were quick to claim membership in a street gang.

"Ooh, ooh, I'm in one!" said George Clementi, a 14-year-old in a Looney Tunes T-shirt. Actually, he said, he belongs to two groups, the Crime Related Artists and the United Crime Kings.

His crimes? He said he paints graffiti on underpasses and drinks occasionally. Once, he said, he was arrested for trespassing. In the most serious incident he could recall, a group of Irish boys known as the Woodlawn Kidz shot up a friend's pink Geo jeep, just three days off the lot.[57]

Not all middle-class gang delinquency ends with property damage. Recently there were two fatal shootings, including one drive-by. Police are concerned that members of the Lawrence Street Posse, another suburban gang, may be responsible.

Explanations

Most explanations of middle-class delinquency are extensions of subcultural explanations of lower-class delinquency. Albert Cohen, for example, suggested that changes in the social structure have weakened the value traditionally associated with delay of gratification. Some criminologists say that a growing number of middle-class youngsters no longer believe that the way to reach their goals is through hard work and delayed pleasure. Behavior has become more hedonistic and more peer-oriented. While most of this youth subculture exhibits nondelinquent behavior, sometimes the pleasure-seeking activities have led to delinquent acts.[58] Bored and restless, these youngsters seek to break the monotony with artificial excitement and conspicuous indulgence: fast cars, trendy clothes, alcohol, drugs, and sexual activity.[59]

Contemporary Rites of Passage?

In America today there is no official point at which one passes from childhood to adulthood. Rather, there is a vague in-between stage during which young people have one foot in childhood and the other in adulthood. We have no organized rites of passage comparable to those in more primitive societies. Margaret Mead describes one such formal ritual:

The essentials of the initiation remain the same: there is a ritual segregation from the company of women, during which time the novice observes certain special food taboos, is incised, eats a sacrificial meal of the blood of the older men, and is shown various marvelous things . . . that he has never seen before, such as masks and other carvings. . . .

His childhood is ended. From one who has been grown by the daily carefulness and hard work of others, he now passes into the class of those whose care is for others' growth.[60]

AT ISSUE
The New Suburban Middle-Class Gangs

Most people think of gangs as synonymous with the inner city, with slums, with low-income housing projects, with "turf wars" and tattoos, with secret signals and violent initiation rites. But now the gang lifestyle is moving to suburbia, as this news article shows:

In suburban Hawthorne, social workers tell of the police officers who responded to a report of gang violence, only to let the instigators drive away in expensive cars, thinking they were a group of teen-agers on their way to the beach.

In Tucson, Ariz., a white middle-class teen-ager wearing gang colors died, a victim of a drive-by shooting, as he stood with black and Hispanic members of the Bloods gang.

At Antelope Valley High School in Lancaster, Calif., about 50 miles north of Los Angeles, 200 students threw stones at a policeman who had been called to help enforce a ban on the gang outfits that have become a fad on some campuses.

Around the country, a growing number of well-to-do youths have begun flirting with gangs in a dalliance that can be as innocent as a fashion statement or as deadly as hard-core drug dealing and violence.

The phenomenon is emerging in a variety of forms. Some affluent white youths are joining established black or Hispanic gangs like the Crips and Bloods; others are forming what are sometimes called copycat or mutant or yuppie gangs.

The development seems to defy the usual socioeconomic explanations for the growth of gangs in inner cities, and it appears to have caught parents, teachers and law-enforcement officers off guard.

Police experts and social workers offer an array of reasons: a misguided sense of the romance of gangs; pursuit of the easy money of drugs; self-defense against the spread of established hard-core gangs. And they note that well-to-do families in the suburbs can be as empty and loveless as poor families in the inner city, leaving young people searching for a sense of group identity.

Furthermore, "kids have always tried to shock their parents," said Marianne Diaz-Parton, a social worker who works with young gang members in the Los Angeles suburb of Lawndale, "and these days becoming a gang member is one way to do it."

A member of the South Bay Family gang in Hermosa Beach, a 21-year-old surfer called Road Dog who said his family owned a chain of pharmacies, put it this way: "This is the 90's, man. We're the type of people who don't take no for an answer. If your mom says no to a kid in the 90's, the kid's just going to laugh." He and his friends shouted in appreciation as another gang member lifted his long hair to reveal a tattoo on a bare shoulder: "Mama tried."

Separating their gang identities from their home lives, the South Bay Family members give themselves nicknames that they carry in elaborate tattoos around the backs of their necks. They consented to interviews on the condition that only these gang names be used.

The gang's leader, who said he was the son of a bank vice president, flexed a bicep so the tattooed figure of a nearly naked woman moved suggestively. Voicing his own version of the basic street philosophy of gang solidarity, the leader, who is called Thumper, said, "If you want to be able to walk the mall, you have to know you've got your boys behind you."(1)

A recent article discussed the differences between some suburban gangs and their inner-city counterparts:

In the suburban sprawl, gang members are more likely to meet at school than on the block, and when trouble breaks out it is often at malls and movie theaters. Both the police and gang members said most fights in suburbia were not about territory at all, but start when a member of one group offends a member of another group. Instead of drive-by shootings, there are drive-by beatings in which a group with baseball bats jumps out of a car and attacks a rival group. Because the disputes are often fleeting, suburban gang members are less likely to form long-term allegiances or wear gang colors that identify their affiliation. And suburban gang rosters and even gang names are constantly changing. Many groups are gangs in name only, made up of youths who mouth "gangsta" rap lyrics and wear prison-inspired fashions like pants with no belts and boxers showing—a look that began with inmates who are not allowed to wear belts.(2)

Sources
1. Excerpted from Seth Mydans, "Not Just the Inner City: Well-to-Do Join Gangs," *New York Times,* Apr. 10, 1990, p. A10.
2. Excerpted from Melinda Henneberger, "Gang Membership Grows in Middle-Class Suburbs," *New York Times,* July 24, 1993, p. 1.

Questions for Discussion
1. How do middle-class suburban gangs differ from urban gangs?
2. List several factors that make gangs attractive to suburban youths. Do you think the trend toward gang formation in the suburbs will continue? Why or why not?

Research by G. O. W. Mueller, using the classic work of Margaret Mead as a foundation, demonstrates that American boys at the age of puberty undergo initiation tests and rites whose symbolism is remarkably similar to those of the official rites of tribal societies. But the rites of young American men are considered delinquent acts, while those of the young tribal men are required and sanctioned by their societies.[61]

American middle-class youths, according to Ralph England, have been gradually removed from the economic life of the community by protective labor laws and the loss of apprenticeship roles in a high-technology society. They face conflicting demands: teenagers cannot work, but they should not loaf; they should delay marriage but are not to be sexually promiscuous; they cannot vote, but they can join the army. Conflict produces tensions; tensions are relieved by creation of a new value system in which their needs can be met: the middle-class teen culture.[62] Herbert Bloch and Arthur Niederhoffer have suggested that perhaps delinquency is a general problem of adolescence, not of a particular class, culture, or race.[63] Perhaps the tattoos, leather jackets, motorcycles, hand signals, fast cars, and drugs are all aspects of contemporary American rites of passage.

FROM THEORY TO PRACTICE

Subcultural theory assumes that individuals engage in delinquent or criminal behavior because (1) legitimate opportunities for success are blocked and (2) criminal values and norms are learned in lower-class slums. The theory was translated into action programs during the 1960s. Two presidents, John F. Kennedy and Lyndon Johnson, directed that huge sums of money be spent on programs to help move lower-class youths into the social mainstream.

MOBY

The best-known program, Mobilization for Youth (MOBY), was based on opportunity theory.[64] It provided employment, social services, teacher training, legal aid, and other crime-prevention services to an area on New York's Lower East Side. The cost was over $12 million. MOBY ultimately became highly controversial. Many people accused it of being too radical, especially when neighborhood participants became involved in rent strikes, lawsuits charging discrimination, and public demonstrations. News of the conflict between supporters and opponents, and between the staff and the neighborhood it served, reached Congress, which made it clear that the point of the project was to reduce delinquency, not to reform society.

Little was done to evaluate the program's success. The project was eventually abandoned, and the commission that had established it ceased to exist. The political climate had changed, and federal money was no longer available for sweeping social programs. However, MOBY's failure does not disprove the opportunity theory on which it was based.

Other Programs

Many other programs based on subcultural theory have attempted to change the attitudes and behavior of ghetto youngsters who have spent most of their lives learning unconventional street norms. Change is accomplished by setting up an extended family environment for high-risk youths, one that provides positive role models, academic and vocational training, strict rules for behavior, drug treatment, health care, and other services. For many youths these programs provide the first warm, caring living arrangement they have ever had. One such program is the House of Umoja (a Swahili word for "unity") in Philadelphia.

At any given time about 25 black male teenage offenders live together as "sons" of the founder, Sister Fattah. Each resident signs a contract with Umoja obligating himself to help in the household, become an active part of the family group, study, and work in one of the program's businesses (a restaurant, a moving company, a painting shop) or elsewhere. By many measures this program is successful. In 1972 a newly elected mayor threatened, "All gang members have ten days to turn their guns in to the nearest firehouse, after which time we [the police] will kick your door in and take them."[65] Umoja responded by calling a meeting of representatives of all gangs.

The House of Umoja program in Philadelphia, founded and led by Sister Fattah, shown here with some of the boys in front of the Umoja building, has been a successful change program for high-risk inner city youths for more than two decades.

More than 5000 youths from 75 gangs showed up. The result was a 60-day truce, and during those 60 days no one died in gang warfare.

Programs similar to Umoja exist throughout the country; they include Argus in New York's South Bronx; Violent Juvenile Offender Research and Development programs in Chicago, Dallas, New Orleans, Los Angeles, and San Diego; and Neighborhood Anticrime Self-Help programs in Baltimore, Newark, Cleveland, Boston, Miami, and Washington, D.C. All have the same mission: to provide a bridge from a delinquent subcultural value system to a conventional one.[66]

Other means have been used to break up delinquent subcultures. Street workers, many of them former gang members (called OGs, for "original gangsters"), serve as a "street-smart diplomatic corps" in many of the poorest ghettos in the country.[67] In Los Angeles, where some 130,000 gang members control the streets, the OGs work for the Community Youth Gang Service (a government-funded agency). Five nights a week more than 50 of these street workers cover the city, trying to settle disputes between rival gangs and to discourage nonmembers from joining them. They look for alternatives to violence, in baseball matches, fairs, and written peace

treaties. During a typical evening the street workers may try to head off a gang fight:

Parton [street worker]: Hey, you guys, Lennox is going to be rollin' by here. . . .

Ms. Diaz [street worker]: You with your back to the street, homeboy. They goin' to be lookin' for this car, some burgundy car.

Boy: If they want to find me, they know where I'm at.

Ms. Diaz: I'm tellin' you to be afraid of them. There are some girls here. You better tell them to move down the street. . . . We are goin' back over there to try to keep them there. Don't get lazy or drunk and not know what you're doin'. I know you don't think it's serious, but if one of your friends gets killed tonight, you will.

Boy: It's serious, I know.

Ms. Diaz: We're goin' to keep them in their 'hood, you just stay in yours for a while.

Boy: All right.[68]

After 2 hours of negotiation, the fight was called off. There was plenty of work left for the team. They would continue the next day to help the gang members find jobs.

Getting Out: Gang Banging or the Morgue

The most difficult problem counselors and street workers face is the power of gangs over their members. Gangs, through loyalty and terror, make it almost impossible for members to quit. Many gang members would gladly get out, but any move to leave leads to gang banging or the morgue. A Wichita, Kansas, group, the church-sponsored Project Freedom, has created an "underground railroad," a network of local contacts which leads families with gang members to anonymity and freedom out of state.[69]

Gangs, once a local problem, have become a national concern. The federal antigang budget goes primarily to police and prosecution. In 1992 the Department of Justice spent $500 million on law enforcement, while the Department of Health and Human Services spent $40 million on prevention programs over a 3-year period.[70]

Experts agree that unless we put more money into educational and socioeconomic programs, there is little likelihood that America's gang problems will lessen as we enter the twenty-first century.

■ REVIEW

In the decade between the mid-1950s and mid-1960s, criminologists began to theorize about the development and content of youth subcultures and the gangs that flourish within them. Some suggested that lower-class males, frustrated by their inability to meet middle-class standards, set up their own norms by which they could gain status. Often these norms clashed with those of the dominant culture. Other investigators have refuted the idea that delinquent behavior stems from a rejection of middle-class values. They claim that lower-class values are separate and distinct from middle-class values and that it is the lower-class value system that generates delinquent behavior.

Explanations of female delinquent subcultures and middle-class delinquency are an extension of subcultural explanations of lower-class delinquency. While the theories of reaction formation, the subculture of violence, and differential opportunity differ in some respects, they all share one basic assumption—that delinquent and criminal behaviors are linked to the values and norms of the areas where youngsters grow up.

■ NOTES

1. Michele Ingrassia with Peter Annin, Nina Archer Biddle, and Susan Miller, "Life Means Nothing," *Newsweek*, July 19, 1993, p. 16.
2. Barbara Kantrowitz, "Wild in the Streets," *Newsweek*, Aug. 2, 1993, p. 43.
3. Sylvester Monroe, "Life in the 'Hood," *Time*, June 15, 1992, p. 38. For how gangs spread, see Richard G. Zevitz and Susan R. Takata, "Metropolitan Gang Influence and the Emergence of Group Delinquency in a Regional Community," *Journal of Criminal Justice*, **20** (1992): 93–106; and Cheryl L. Maxon, "Investigating Gang Migration: Contextual Issues for Intervention," *Gang Journal*, **1** (1993): 1–8.
4. Albert K. Cohen, *Delinquent Boys: The Culture of the Gang* (Glencoe, Ill.: Free Press, 1955).
5. E. g., James F. Short, Jr., and Fred L. Strodtbeck, *Group Process and Gang Delinquency* (Chicago: University of Chicago Press, 1965).
6. Kenneth Polk and Walter B. Schafer, eds., *School and Delinquency* (Englewood Cliffs, N.J.: Prentice-Hall, 1972); Alexander Liazos, "School, Alienation, and Delinquency," *Crime and Delinquency*, **24** (1978): 355–370.
7. Travis Hirschi, *Causes of Delinquency* (Berkeley: University of California Press, 1969).
8. Delbert S. Elliott and Harwin L. Voss, *Delinquency and Dropout* (Lexington, Mass.: Lexington Books, 1974).
9. G. Roger Jarjoura, "Dropping Out of School Enhances Delinquent Involvement? Results from a Large-Scale National Probability Sample," *Criminology*, **31** (1993): 149–172. See also Randall G. Shelden, Ted Snodgrass, and Pam Snodgrass, "Comparing Gang and Non-Gang Offenders: Some Tentative Findings," *Gang Journal*, **1** (1992): 73–86.
10. Albert J. Reiss and Albert L. Rhodes, "Deprivation and Delinquent Behavior," *Sociological Quarterly*, **4** (1963): 135–149.
11. Marvin Krohn, R. L. Akers, M. J. Radosevich, and L. Lanza-Kaduce, "Social Status and Deviance," *Criminology*, **18** (1980): 303–318. For a discussion of being a have-not in a community of haves, see John W. C. Johnstone, "Social Class, Social Areas, and Delinquency," *Sociological and Social Research*, **63** (1978): 49–72.
12. David F. Greenberg, "Delinquency and the Age Structure of Society," *Contemporary Crisis*, **1** (1977): 189–223.
13. John I. Kitsuse and David C. Dietrick, "Delinquent Boys: A Critique," *American Sociological Review*, **24** (1959): 208–215.
14. David J. Bordua, "Delinquent Subcultures: Sociological Interpretations of Gang Delinquency," *Annals of the American Academy of Political and Social Science*, **338** (1961): 119–136.
15. Albert K. Cohen and James F. Short, Jr., "Research in Delinquent Subcultures," *Journal of Social Issues*, **14** (1958): 20–37.
16. Richard A. Cloward and Lloyd E. Ohlin, *Delinquency and Opportunity* (Glencoe, Ill.: Free Press, 1960).
17. Clifford R. Shaw, *The Jack-Roller* (Chicago, Ill.: University of Chicago Press, 1930), p. 54.
18. James R. David, *Street Gangs* (Dubuque, Iowa: Kendall/Hunt, 1982).
19. Hirschi, *Causes of Delinquency*, p. 227.
20. Elliott and Voss, *Delinquency and Dropout*.
21. Judson Landis and Frank Scarpitti, "Perceptions Regarding Value Orientation and Legitimate Opportunity: Delinquency and Non-Delinquents," *Social Forces*, **84** (1965): 57–61. See also Felix M. Padilla, *The Gang as an American Enterprise: Puerto Rican Youth and the American Dream* (New Brunswick, N.J.: Rutgers University Press, 1992).

22. James Short, Ramon Rivera, and Ray Tennyson, "Perceived Opportunities, Gang Membership, and Delinquency," *American Sociological Review,* **30** (1965): 56–57. For a discussion of adolescent goals, see Robert Agnew, "Goal Achievement and Delinquency," *Sociology and Social Research,* **68** (1984): 435–451.

23. Lecture by Ko-lin Chin, Rutgers University, November 22, 1993. See also K. Chin, *Chinese Subculture and Criminality: Non-Traditional Crime Groups in America,* Criminology and Penology Series, 29 (Westport, CT: Greenwood, 1990); K. Chin and J. Fagan, "Social Order and Gang Formation in Chinatown," in *Advances in Criminological Theory,* vol. 6, ed. Freda Adler and William S. Laufer (New Brunswick, N.J.: Transaction, 1994); R. Kelly, K. Chin, and J. Fagan, "The Activity, Structure, and Control of Chinese Gangs: Law Enforcement Perspectives," *Journal of Contemporary Criminal Justice,* **9** (1993); R. Kelly, K. Chin, and J. Fagan, "The Dragon Breathes Fire: Chinese Organized Crime in New York City," *Contemporary Crises: Crime, Law and Social Change,* **19** (1993): 245–269.

24. Finn-Aage Esbensen and David Huizinga, "Gangs, Drugs, and Delinquency in a Survey of Urban Youth," *Criminology,* **31** (1993): 565–587. See also Irving Spergel, *Racketville, Slumtown, and Haulberg* (Chicago: University of Chicago Press, 1964); Dean G. Rojek and Maynard L. Erickson, "Delinquent Careers: A Test of the Career Escalation Model," *Criminology,* **20** (1982): 5–28; Robert J. Bursik, Jr., "The Dynamics of Specialization in Juvenile Offenses," *Social Forces,* **58** (1980): 851–864; and Gerald D. Robin, "Gang Member Delinquency: Its Extent, Sequence, and Typology," *Journal of Criminal Law, Criminology, and Police Science,* **55** (1964): 59–69.

25. Alan J. Lizotte and James M. Tesoriero, "Patterns of Adolescent Firearms Ownership and Use," working paper no. 11 (Albany: Hindelang Criminal Justice Research Center, 1991); Terence P. Thornberry, *The Development of Delinquency and Drug Use,* UNAFEI Resource Material Series, no. 40 (Tokyo: United Nations Asia and Far East Institute, December 1992); Terence P. Thornberry, Marvin D. Krohn, Alan J. Lizotte, and Deborah Chard-Wierschem, "The Role of Juvenile Gangs in Facilitating Delinquent Behavior," *Journal of Research in Crime and Delinquency,* **30** (1993): 55–87. See J. Michael Olivero, *Honor, Violence, and Upward Mobility: A Case Study of Chicago Gangs during the 1970s and 1980s* (Edinburg: University of Texas–Pan American Press, 1991); and Malcolm Klein, Cheryl L. Maxson, and Lea C. Cunningham, "'Crack,' Street Gangs, and Violence," *Criminology,* **29** (1991): 623–650.

26. Marvin E. Wolfgang and Franco Ferracuti, *The Subculture of Violence* (London: Tavistock, 1967).

27. Howard S. Erlanger, "The Empirical Status of the Subcultures of Violence Thesis," *Social Problems,* **22** (1974): 280–292. See also Sandra Ball-Rokeach, "Values and Violence: A Test of the Subculture of Violence Thesis," *American Sociological Review,* **38** (1973): 736–749. For the relationship of the thesis to routine activities, see Leslie W. Kennedy and Stephen W. Baron, "Routine Activities and a Subculture of Violence: A Study on the Street," *Journal of Research in Crime and Delinquency,* **30** (1993): 88–112.

28. William G. Doerner, "A Regional Analysis of Homicide Rates in the United States," *Criminology,* **13** (1975): 90–101; Raymond D. Gastel, "Homicide and a Regional Culture of Violence," *American Sociological Review,* **36** (1971): 412–427. See also Sheldon Hackney, "Southern Violence," *American Historical Review,* **74** (1969): 906–925; John S. Reed, *The Enduring South: Subcultural Persistence in Mass Society* (Lexington, Mass.: Lexington Books, 1972); and John S. Reed, *One South: An Ethnic Approach to Regional Culture* (Baton Rouge: Louisiana State University Press, 1982).

29. Jo Dixon and Alan J. Lizotte, "Gun Ownership and the Southern Subculture of Violence," *American Journal of Sociology,* **93** (1987): 383–405.

30. Colin Loftin and Robert Hill, "Regional Subculture of Violence: An Examination of the Gastril-Hackney Thesis," *American Sociological Review,* **39** (1974): 714–724.

31. Judith Blau and Peter Blau, "Metropolitan Structure and Violent Crime," *American Sociological Review,* **47** (1982): 114–129. For a study that examines the subculture of violence thesis as it relates to three groups—blacks, Hispanics, and American Indians—see Donald J. Shoemaker and J. Sherwood Williams, "The Subculture of Violence and Ethnicity," *Journal of Criminal Justice,* **15** (1987): 461–472.

32. Wolfgang and Ferracuti, *The Subculture of Violence,* pp. 258–265. See also Marvin E. Wolfgang, *Patterns in Criminal Homicide* (Philadelphia: University of Pennsylvania Press, 1958); and Franco Ferracuti, "La personalità dell´omicida," *Quaderni di Criminologia Clinica,* **4** (1961): 419–456.

33. Marvin E. Wolfgang, Robert M. Figlio, and Thorsten Sellin, *Delinquency in a Birth Cohort* (Chicago: University of Chicago Press, 1972); Simon I. Singer, "Victims of Serious Violence and Their Criminal Behavior: Subcultural Theory and Beyond," *Violence and Victims,* **1** (1986): 61–70. See also Neil Alan Weiner and Marvin E. Wolfgang, "The Extent and Character of Violent Crime in America, 1969–1982," in *American Violence and Public Policy,* ed. Lynn Curtis (New Haven, Conn.: Yale University Press, 1985), pp. 17–39.

34. Steven Messner, "Regional and Racial Effects on the Urban Homicide Rate: The Subculture of Violence Revisited," *American Journal of Sociology,* **88** (1983): 997–1007.

35. Irving A. Spergel, "Youth Gangs: Continuity and Change," in *Crime and Justice: A Review of Research,* Vol. 12, ed. M. Tonry and Norval Morris (Chicago, University of Chicago Press, 1990), pp. 171–275.

36. Jeffrey Fagan, "The Social Organization of Drug Use and Drug Dealing among Urban Gangs," *Criminology,* **27** (1989): 633–666; Jeffrey Fagan, J. G. Weis, and

Y. Cheng, "Drug Use and Delinquency among Inner City Students," *Journal of Drug Issues,* **20** (1990): 349–400.

37. Joseph B. Treaster, "Jamaica's Gangs Take Root in U.S.," *New York Times,* Nov. 13, 1988, p. 15. For a comparison of the seriousness of the gang problem in Hispanic and black communities, see G. David Curry and Irving A. Spergel, "Gang Homicide, Delinquency, and Community," *Criminology,* **26** (1988): 381–405.

38. Walter B. Miller, "Lower-Class Culture as a Generating Milieu of Gang Delinquency," *Journal of Social Issues,* **14** (1958): 5–19.

39. Claude Brown, *Manchild in the Promised Land: A Modern Classic of the Black Experience* (New York: New American Library, 1965), p. 22.

40. Ibid., p. 129.

41. Miller, "Lower-Class Culture."

42. Short, Rivera, and Tennyson, "Perceived Opportunities, Gang Membership, and Delinquency."

43. Stephen A. Cernovich, "Value Orientations and Delinquency Involvement," *Criminology,* **15** (1978): 443–458.

44. Gresham Sykes and David Matza, "Techniques of Neutralization: A Theory of Delinquency," *American Sociological Review,* **22** (1957): 664–673.

45. Barbara Kantrowitz, "Wild in the Streets," *Newsweek,* Aug. 2, 1993, p. 46.

46. Oscar Lewis, *La Vida* (New York: Random House, 1965); Oscar Lewis, "The Culture of Poverty," *Scientific American,* **215** (1966): 19–25.

47. Ken Auletta, *The Under Class* (New York: Random House, 1982).

48. Eugene O'Neill, *Long Day's Journey into Night,* in *Great Scenes from the World Theater,* ed. James L. Steffenson, Jr. (New York: Avon, 1965), p. 199.

49. Peter T. Kilborn, "Finding a Way: The Quest of Derrick, 19," *New York Times,* Apr. 22, 1993, p. 1.

50. Cohen and Short, "Research in Delinquent Subcultures."

51. Anne Campbell, *The Girls in the Gang* (New York and Oxford: Basil Blackwell, 1984), p. 267.

52. Seth Mydans, "Life in Girl's Gang: Colors and Bloody Noses," *New York Times,* Jan. 29, 1990, pp. 1, 20.

53. David Lauderback, Joy Hansen, and Dan Waldorf, "'Sisters Are Doin' It for Themselves': A Black Female Gang in San Francisco," *Gang Journal,* **1** (1992): 57–72.

54. Ibid., p. 67.

55. Beth Bjerregaard and Carolyn Smith, *Rochester Youth Development Study: Patterns of Male and Female Gang Membership,* working paper no. 13 (Albany: Hindelang Criminal Justice Research Center, 1992).

56. C. Ronald Huff, ed., *Gangs in America* (Newbury Park, Calif.: Sage, 1990).

57. Melinda Henneberger, "Gang Membership Grows in Middle-Class Suburbs," *New York Times,* July 24, 1993, pp. 1, 25.

58. Albert K. Cohen, "Middle-Class Delinquency and the Social Structure," in *Middle-Class Delinquency,* ed. E. W. Vaz (New York: Harper & Row, 1967), pp. 207–221. See also Fred J. Shanley, "Middle-Class Delinquency as a Social Problem," *Sociology and Social Research,* **51** (1967): 185–198.

59. Pamela Richards, Richard A. Berk, and Brenda Forster, *Crime as Play: Delinquency in a Middle-Class Suburb* (Cambridge, Mass.: Ballinger, 1979), p. 11.

60. Margaret Mead, *Sex and Temperament in Three Primitive Societies* (1935; New York: New American Library, 1950), pp. 66, 68, 69.

61. G. O. W. Mueller, *Puberty and Delinquency: Examination of a Juvenile Delinquency Fad* (South Hackensack, N.J.: Fred B. Rothman, 1971).

62. Ralph England, "A Theory of Middle-Class Delinquency," *Journal of Criminal Law, Criminology, and Police Science,* **50** (1960): 535–540.

63. Herbert Bloch and Arthur Niederhoffer, *The Gang: A Study of Adolescent Behavior* (New York: Philosophical Library, 1958).

64. J. Robert Lilly, Francis T. Cullen, and Richard A. Ball, *Criminological Theory: Context and Consequences* (Newbury Park, Calif.: Sage, 1989), pp. 78–80.

65. Quoted in David Fattah, "The House of Umoja as a Case Study for Social Change," *Annals of the American Academy of Political and Social Science,* **494** (1987): 37–41.

66. Lynn A. Curtis, Preface to "Policies to Prevent Crime: Neighborhood, Family, and Employment Strategies," *Annals of the American Academy of Political and Social Science,* **494** (1987).

67. Robert Reinhold, "In the Middle of L.A.'s Gang Warfare," *New York Times Magazine,* May 22, 1988, p. 31.

68. Ibid., p. 70.

69. Jon D. Hull, "No Way Out," *Time,* Aug. 17, 1992, p. 40.

70. *Time,* June 15, 1992, p. 37.

7
Social Control Theory

KEY TERMS
attachment
belief
commitment
conformity
containment theory
direct control
drift
indirect control
internalized control
involvement
macrosociological studies
microsociological studies
social control theory
synnomie

In William Golding's novel *Lord of the Flies*, a group of boys is stranded on an island far from civilization. Deprived of any superior authority—all the grown-ups, their parents, their teachers, the government, that have until now determined their lives—they begin to decide on a structure of government for themselves. Ralph declares:

> "We can't have everybody talking at once. We'll have to have 'Hands up' like at school. . . . Then I'll give him the conch."
>
> "Conch?"
>
> "That's what this shell is called. I'll give the conch to the next person to speak. He can hold it when he's speaking!" . . .
>
> Jack was on his feet.
>
> "We'll have rules!" he cried excitedly. "Lots of rules!"[1]

But do rules alone guarantee the peaceful existence of the group? Who and what ensure compliance with the rules? Social control theorists study these questions.

Strain theories, as we noted, study the question of why some people violate norms, for example, by committing crimes. Social control theorists are interested in learning why people conform to norms. Control theorists take it for granted that drugs can tempt even the youngest schoolchildren; that truancy can lure otherwise good children onto a path of academic failure and lifetime unemployment; that petty fighting, petty theft, and recreational drinking are attractive features of adolescence and young adulthood. They ask why people conform in the face of so much temptation and peer pressure. The answer is that juveniles and adults conform to the law in response to certain controlling forces in their lives. They become criminals when the controlling forces are weak or absent.

WHAT IS SOCIAL CONTROL?

What are those controlling forces? Think about the time and energy you have invested in your school, your job, your extracurricular activities. Think about how your academic or vocational ambition would be jeopardized by persistent delinquency. Think about how the responsibility of homework has weighed you down, setting limits on your free time. Reflect on the quality of your relationships with your family, friends, and acquaintances and on how your attachment to them has encouraged you to do right and discouraged you from doing wrong.

Social control theory focuses on techniques and strategies that regulate human behavior and lead to conformity, or obedience to society's rules—the influences of family and school, religious beliefs, moral values, friends, and even beliefs about government. The more involved and committed a person is to conventional activities and values and the greater the attachment to parents, loved ones, and friends, the less likely that person is to violate society's rules and to jeopardize relationships and aspirations.

The concept of social control emerged around the turn of the century in a volume by E. A. Ross, one of the founders of American sociology. According to Ross, belief systems, rather than specific laws, guide what people do and universally serve to control behavior. Since that time, the concept has taken on a wide variety of meanings. Social control has been conceptualized as representing practically any phenomenon that leads to conformity. The term is found in studies of laws, customs, mores, ideologies, and folkways describing a host of controlling forces.[2]

Is there danger in defining social control so broadly? It depends on your perspective. To some sociologists, the vagueness of the term—its tendency to encompass almost the entire field of sociology—has significantly decreased its value as a concept.[3] To others, the value of social control lies in its representation of a mechanism by which society regulates its members. According to this view, social control defines what is considered deviant behavior, what is right or wrong, and what is a violation of the law.

Theorists who have adopted this orientation consider law, norms, customs, mores, ethics, and etiquette to be forms of social control. Donald Black, a sociologist of law, noted: "Social control is found whenever people hold each other to standards, explicitly or implicitly, consciously or not: on the street, in prison, at home, at a party."[4]

If an example would help, consider that as recently as 20 years ago there were no legal restrictions, norms, or customs regulating the

Lord of the Flies: Boys cast away on an uninhabited island, without the social controls of their society, search for new norms to control a new society.

smoking of cigarettes in public places. The surgeon general's declaration in 1972 that second-hand smoke poses a health hazard ushered in two decades of controls over behavior that not too long ago was considered sociable—if not sophisticated and suave.

At present 46 states have laws restricting or banning smoking in public places. Los Angeles recently became the thirty-second city in California to outlaw smoking in all its restaurants.[5] Laws, norms, customs, and etiquette relating to smoking exert strong controls over this behavior.

THEORIES OF SOCIAL CONTROL

Why is social control conceptualized in such different ways? Perhaps because social control has been examined from both a macrosociological and a microsociological perspective. **Macrosociological studies** explore formal systems for the control of groups:

■ The legal system, laws, and particularly law enforcement

■ Powerful groups in society

■ Social and economic directives of governmental or private groups

These types of control can be either positive—that is, they inhibit rule-breaking behavior by a type of social guidance—or negative—that is, they foster oppressive, restrictive, or corrupt practices by those in power.[6]

The microsociological perspective is similar to the macrosociological approach in that it, too, explains why people conform and considers the source of control to be external (outside the person). **Microsociological studies,** however, focus on informal systems. Researchers collect data from individuals (usually by self-report methods), are often guided by hypotheses that apply to individuals as well as groups, and frequently make reference to or examine a person's internal control system.

The Microsociological Perspective: Hirschi

Travis Hirschi has been the spokesperson of the microsociological perspective since the publication of his *Causes of Delinquency* in 1969. He is not, however, the first scholar to examine the extent of individual social control and its relationship to delinquency. In 1957 Jackson Toby introduced the notion of individual "commitment" as a powerful determining force in the social control of behavior.[7] Eight years later Scott Briar and Irving Piliavin extended Toby's thesis by advancing the view that the extent of individual commitment and conformity plays a role in decreasing the likelihood of deviance. They noted that the degree of an adolescent's commitment is reflected in relationships with adult authority figures and with friends and is determined in part by "belief in God, affection for conventionally behaving peers, occupational aspirations, ties to parents, desire to perform well at school, and fear of material deprivations and punishments associated with arrest."[8]

Briar and Piliavin were not entirely satisfied with control dimensions alone, however, and added another factor: individual motivation to be delinquent. This motivation may stem from a person's wish to "obtain valued goods, to portray courage in the presence of, or to belong to, peers, to strike out at someone who is disliked, or simply to get his kicks."[9]

Hirschi was less interested in the source of an individual's motivation to commit delinquent acts than in the reasons why people do *not* commit such acts. He claimed that social control theory explains conformity and adherence to rules, not deviance. It is thus not a crime-causation theory in a strict sense but a theory of prosocial behavior used by criminologists to explain deviance.

Social Bonds

Hirschi posited four social bonds that promote socialization and conformity: attachment, commitment, involvement, and belief. The stronger

FIGURE 7.1 Items from Travis Hirschi's measure of social control

1. In general, do you like or dislike school?
   A. Like it
   B. Like it and dislike it about equally
   C. Dislike it

2. How important is getting good grades to you personally?
   A. Very important
   B. Somewhat important
   C. Fairly important
   D. Completely unimportant

3. Do you care what teachers think of you?
   A. I care a lot
   B. I care some
   C. I don't care much

4. Would you like to be the kind of person your father is?
   A. In every way
   B. In most ways
   C. In some ways
   D. In just a few ways
   E. Not at all

5. Did your mother read to you when you were little?
   A. No
   B. Once or twice
   C. Several times
   D. Many times, but not regularly
   E. Many times, and regularly
   F. I don't remember

6. Do you ever feel that "there's nothing to do"?
   A. Often
   B. Sometimes
   C. Rarely
   D. Never

Source: Travis Hirschi, *Causes of Delinquency* (Berkeley: University of California Press, 1969).

these bonds, he claimed, the less likelihood of delinquency.[10] To test this hypothesis, he administered a self-report questionnaire to 4077 junior and senior high school students in California (see Figure 7.1) that measured both involvement in delinquency and the strength of the four social bonds. Hirschi found that weakness in any of the bonds was associated with delinquent behavior.

Attachment

The first bond, **attachment,** takes three forms: attachment to parents, to school (teachers), and to peers. According to Hirschi, youths who have formed a significant attachment to a parent refrain from delinquency because the consequences of such an act might jeopardize that relationship. The bond of affection between a parent and a child thus becomes a primary deterrent to criminal activities.[11] Its strength depends on the depth and quality of parent–child interaction. The parent–child bond forms a path through which conventional ideals and expectations can pass. This bond is bolstered by:

■ The amount of time the child spends with parents, particularly the presence of a parent at times when the child is tempted to engage in criminal activity

■ The intimacy of communication between parent and child

■ The affectional identification between parent and child[12]

Next Hirschi considered the importance of the school. As we saw in Chapter 6, Hirschi linked inability to function well in school to delinquency through the following chain of events: academic incompetence leads to poor school performance; poor school performance results in a dislike of school; dislike of school leads to rejection of teachers and administrators as authorities. The result is delinquency. Thus attachment to school depends on a youngster's appreciation for the institution, perception of how he or she is received by teachers and peers, and level of achievement in class.

Hirschi found that attachment to parents and school overshadows the bond formed with peers:

As was true for parents and teachers, those most closely attached to or respectful of their friends are least likely to have committed delinquent acts. The relation does not appear to be as strong as was the case for parents and teachers, but the ideas that delinquents are unusually dependent upon their peers, that loyalty and solidarity are characteristic of delinquent groups, that attachment to adolescent peers fosters nonconventional behavior, and that the delinquent is unusually likely to sacrifice his personal advantage to the "requirements of the group" are simply not supported by the data.[13]

Commitment

Hirschi's second group of bonds consists of **commitment** to or investment in conventional lines of action—that is, support of and participation in social activities that tie the individual to the society's moral or ethical code. Hirschi identified a number of stakes in conformity or commitments: vocational aspirations, educational expectations, educational aspirations.

Though Hirschi's theory is at odds with the competing theories of Albert Cohen and Richard Cloward and Lloyd Ohlin (Chapter 6), Hirschi provided empirical support for the notion that the greater the aspiration and expectation, the more unlikely delinquency becomes. Also, "students who smoke, those who drink, and those who date are more likely to commit delinquent acts; . . . the more the boy is involved in adult activities, the greater his involvement in delinquency."[14]

Involvement

Hirschi's third bond is **involvement,** or preoccupation with activities that promote the interests of society. This bond is derived from involvement in school-related activities (such as homework) rather than in working-class adult activities (such as smoking and drinking). A person who is busy doing conventional things has little time for deviant activities.

Belief

The last of the bonds, **belief,** consists of assent to the society's value system. The value system of any society entails respect for its laws and for the people and institutions that enforce them. The results of Hirschi's survey lead to the conclusion that if young people no longer believe laws are fair, their bond to society weakens, and the prob-

The more children are involved in activities that promote the interests of society, the less time and energy they have for deviant activities: Third graders in a bilingual class in a Brooklyn, New York, public school.

ability that they will commit delinquent acts increases.[15]

Empirical Tests of Hirschi's Theory

Hirschi's work has inspired a vast number of studies. We can examine only a small selection of some of the more significant research.

Michael Hindelang studied rural boys and girls in Grades 6 through 12 on the East Coast. His self-report delinquency measure and questionnaire items were very similar to those devised by Hirschi. Hindelang found few differences between his results and those of Hirschi. Two of those differences, however, were significant. First, he found no relationship between attachment to mother and attachment to peers. Hirschi had observed a positive relationship (the stronger the attachment to the mother, the stronger the attachment to peers). Second, involvement in delinquency was positively related to attachment to peers.[16] Hirschi had found an inverse relationship (the stronger the attachment to peers, the less the involvement in delinquency).

Marvin Krohn and James Massey administered a self-report questionnaire to 3056 male and female students in three midwestern states. These researchers were critical of Hirschi's con-

AT ISSUE
Respect for Authority: Carjacking

In his attempts to explain the links between respect for authority and criminal behavior, Travis Hirschi quoted developmental psychologist Jean Piaget: "Respect is the source of the law."(1) Hirschi went on to explain,

> "Insofar as the child respects (loves and fears) his parents, and adults in general, he will accept their rules. Conversely, insofar as this respect is undermined, the rules will tend to lose their obligatory character. . . . Lack of respect for the police presumably leads to lack of respect for the law."(1)

Certainly many criminals seem to lack respect for the police, for law, and for their victims. Carjackers provide a good example. The armed theft of cars from drivers, *carjacking* was defined as a violent crime in 1992, when the director of the FBI announced that carjacking was becoming such a serious problem nationwide that it warranted full attention from his bureau.(2) The

nation was appalled by a 1992 case in which a Maryland woman was killed when carjackers threw her from her car and then dragged her, tangled in a seat belt, for nearly 2 miles. The carjackers tossed her 22-month-old daughter—in her car seat—into the road, and she was rescued unharmed. But in an example of the extreme lack of respect for authority shown by carjackers, that shocking incident—far from slowing other carjackers—was followed by seven more carjackings in a single day in the Washington area.

How has carjacking become such a problem? Two scholars, Tod W. Burke and Charles E. O'Rear, offered their theories in a 1993 article.(3) The crime is an outgrowth of simple car theft, which has become less simple as car manufacturers increasingly attempt to prevent theft by providing steering-column locks, sophisticated alarm systems, and tracking devices for stolen vehicles. When the vehicle is occupied, however, such devices are

likely to be disengaged, so carjackers specialize in accosting drivers at stop signs, in gas stations, on highway entrance ramps, and in "bump and rob" simulated accidents.

The theory suggested by Burke and O'Rear, and supported by Hirschi's ideas about respect for authority, is the "brazen theory":

> The "brazen theory" is based upon the arrogance and self-confidence of the suspects, who tend to believe they are invincible and that their weapons will speak for themselves. Furthermore, with minimal chances of police apprehension and a firm belief that they will beat the system if caught, they consider the risk is worthwhile and cost-effective. . . .

Of 70,000 vehicles stolen in Los Angeles during one recent reporting period, more than 4188 were stolen "by fear or force," and assailants used handguns, knives, blunt instruments, machetes, simulated guns, and even a broken bottle.(3) Thumbing their noses at authority, carjackers continue to plague the nation.

Sources

1. Travis Hirschi, *Causes of Delinquency* (Berkeley: University of California Press, 1969), pp. 30, 202.
2. "FBI Forms Unit to Battle 'Carjacking,'" *New York Times*, Sept. 16, 1992, p. A21.
3. Tod W. Burke and Charles E. O'Rear, "Armed Carjacking: A Violent Problem in Need of a Solution," *Police Chief*, January 1993, pp. 18–24.

Questions for Discussion

1. Could the "brazen theory" be used to account for other crimes besides carjacking? Explain.
2. What approaches to preventing carjacking might serve to increase the amount of respect potential carjackers feel for the police and the law?

This 17-year-old used a crutch to drive a stolen car. He was crippled in a previous stolen car wreck.

ceptualization of both commitment and involvement, finding it difficult to understand how he separated the two. Serious involvement, they argued, is quite unlikely without commitment. They combined commitment and involvement items and ended up with only three bonds: attachment, commitment, and belief.[17]

The study related these bonds to alcohol and marijuana use, use of strong drugs, minor delinquent behavior, and serious delinquent behavior. The results suggested that strong social bonds were more highly correlated with less serious deviance than with such delinquent acts as motor vehicle theft and assault. Also, the social bonds were more predictive of deviance in girls than in boys. Moreover, Krohn and Massey noticed that the commitment bond (now joined with involvement) was more significantly correlated with delinquent behavior than were attachment and belief.

Michael Wiatrowski, David Griswold, and Mary Roberts, using the results of questionnaires administered to 2213 tenth-grade boys at 86 schools, sought to answer three questions: First, are Hirschi's four bonds distinct entities? Second, why did Hirschi name only four bonds? Third, why were some factors related to educational and occupational aspiration (such as ability and family socioeconomic status) omitted from his questionnaire? The researchers constructed new scales for measuring attachment, commitment, involvement, and belief. They used a self-report measure to assess delinquency. They found little that is independent or distinctive about any of the bonds.[18]

Robert Agnew provided the first longitudinal test of Hirschi's theory by using data on 1886 boys in the tenth and eleventh grades. Eight social control scales (parental attachment, grades, dating index, school attachment, involvement, commitment, peer attachment, and belief) were examined at two periods in relation to two self-report scales (one measuring total delinquency and the other measuring seriousness of delinquency). Agnew found the eight control scales to be strongly correlated with the self-reported delinquency, but the social control measures did little to predict the extent of future delinquency reported at the second testing. Agnew

concluded that the importance of Hirschi's control theory has probably been exaggerated.[19]

Evaluation: Hirschi's Social Control Theory

While social control theory has held a prominent position in criminology for several decades, it is not without weaknesses. For example, social control theory seeks to explain delinquency, not adult crime. It concerns attitudes, beliefs, desires, and behaviors that, though deviant, are often characteristic of adolescents. This is unfortunate because there has long been evidence that social bonds are also significant explanatory factors in postadolescent behavior.[20]

In an exceptional extension of Hirschi's theory to the life span, Robert J. Sampson and John H. Laub found that family, school, and peer attachments were most strongly associated with delinquency from childhood to adolescence (through age 17).[21] From the transition to young adulthood through the transition to middle adulthood, attachment to work (job stability) and family (marriage) appears most strongly related to crime causation. This study squarely addressed one of the most significant weaknesses of control theory—its role in postadolescent behavior.

Questions also have been raised about the bonds. Hirschi claims that antisocial acts result from a lack of affective values, beliefs, norms, and attitudes that inhibit delinquency. But these terms are never clearly defined.[22] Critics have also faulted Hirschi's work for other reasons:

- Having too few questionnaire items that measure social bonds
- Failing to describe the chain of events that results in defective or inadequate bonds
- Creating an artificial division of socialized versus unsocialized youths
- Suggesting that social control theory explains why delinquency occurs, when in fact it typically explains no more than 50 percent of delinquent behavior and only 1 to 2 percent of the variance in future delinquency.[23]

Despite the criticisms, Hirschi's work has made a major contribution to criminology. The mere fact that a quarter century of scholars have tried to validate and replicate it testifies to its importance.

Furthermore, research using and extending Hirschi's constructs has become increasingly sophisticated. Recent research coming from the Rochester Youth Development Study, for example, has considered not only the role of weakened bonds to family and school in promoting delinquency but the role of delinquent behavior in attenuating the strength of these very bonds. Criminologists have refined Hirschi's constructs so that the effects of social control on delinquency, as well as the effects of delinquency on social control, are both considered.[24]

SOCIAL CONTROL AND DRIFT

In the 1960s David Matza developed a different perspective on social control that explains why some adolescents drift in and out of delinquency. According to Matza, juveniles sense a moral obligation to be bound by the law. A "bind" between a person and the law, something that creates responsibility and control, remains in place most of the time. When it is not in place, the youth may enter into a state of **drift,** or a period when he or she exists in a limbo between convention and crime, responding in turn to the demands of each, flirting now with one, now with the other, but postponing commitment, evading decision. Thus, the person drifts between criminal and conventional actions.[25]

If adolescents are indeed bound by the social order, how do they justify their delinquent acts? The answer is that they develop techniques to rationalize their actions. These techniques are *defense mechanisms* that release the youth from the constraints of the moral order:

- Denial of responsibility ("It wasn't my fault; I was a victim of circumstances.")
- Denial of injury ("No one was hurt, and they have insurance, so what's the problem?")
- Denial of the victim ("Anybody would have done the same thing in my position—I did what I had to do given the situation.")
- Condemnation of the condemner ("I bet the

judge and everyone on the jury has done much worse than what I was arrested for.")
- Appeal to higher loyalties ("My friends were depending on me and I see them every day— what was I supposed to do"?)[26]

Empirical support for drift theory has not been clear. Some studies show that delinquents consider these rationalizations valid,[27] while other research suggests that they do not. Later investigations also demonstrate that delinquents do not share the moral code or values of nondelinquents.[28]

PERSONAL AND SOCIAL CONTROL

Over the last 40 years support has increased for the idea that both social (external) and personal (internal) control systems are important forces in keeping individuals from committing crimes. In other words, Hirschi's social bonds and Matza's drift paradigm may not be enough by themselves to explain why people do not commit crimes.

Failure of Control Mechanisms

Albert J. Reiss, a sociologist, was one of the first researchers to isolate a group of personal and social control factors. According to Reiss, delinquency is the result of (1) a failure to internalize socially accepted and prescribed norms of behavior; (2) a breakdown of internal controls; and (3) a lack of social rules that prescribe behavior in the family, the school, and other important social groups.

To test these notions, Reiss collected control-related data on 1110 juvenile delinquents placed on probation in Cook County (Chicago), Illinois. He examined three sources of information: (1) a diverse set of data on such variables as family economic status and moral ideals and/or techniques of control by parents during childhood; (2) community and institutional information bearing on control, such as residence in a delinquency area and homeownership; and (3) personal control information, such as ego or superego controls, from clinical judgments of social workers and written psychiatric reports. Reiss

CRIMINOLOGICAL FOCUS
Out of Control: School Violence

Law-enforcement and public-health officials describe a virtual "epidemic" of youth violence in the last five years, spreading from the inner cities to the suburbs. "We're talking about younger and younger kids committing more and more serious crimes," says Indianapolis Prosecuting Attorney Jeff Modisett. "Violence is becoming a way of life."(1)

Much of that violence is occurring inside the nation's schools. Consider these statistics:

- Almost 3 million crimes occur on or near school campuses every year.(2)
- One-quarter of the nation's large urban school districts use metal detectors to search for weapons on students.(2)
- One student in five reports carrying a weapon of some sort and one in twenty a gun.(2)
- Almost 60 percent of sixth-through twelfth-graders say they could get a handgun if they wanted one, and one-third of those said they could get a handgun within an hour.(1)

And consider these individual cases: In New Orleans, a third-grader recently took a .357 magnum to school. In Dartmouth, Massachusetts, three teenagers fatally stabbed another student in a social studies class. An argument over a book bag in another school led a 14-year-old to open fire with his 9-mm semiautomatic pistol, killing a student and wounding a teacher, neither of whom had been involved in the dispute.

Risk Factors

What happened to the days when throwing a spitball or an eraser got students into big trouble? Experts say that students are growing up with violence—one survey of inner-city children showed that 43 percent of 7- to 19-year-olds have seen a homicide.(2) And the decay of social support systems worsens the problem. One reporter summed up the situation this way:

> In this heightened atmosphere of violence, normal rules of behavior don't apply. As traditional social supports—home, school, community—have fallen away, new role models take their place. "It takes an entire village to raise a child, but the village isn't there for the children anymore," says Modisett.(1)

A 5-year study of 4000 students allowed criminologist Terence Thornberry to identify a number of risk factors, any of which increase the likelihood that students will become delinquent. The list includes exposure to child abuse and maltreatment, spouse abuse, violent behavior, and poverty and parents who began having children when they were teenagers or who are unemployed, on welfare, or poorly educated.(1) The availability of weapons is another essential ingredient. Law-enforcement officials say that 80 to 90 percent of the guns used by students come from their parents.(2)

Solutions

Thornberry says that the best solution to school violence is to eliminate risk factors—and that prevention programs need to begin very early. A California program that starts with third-graders trains students to resolve conflicts without violence. Other people claim the problem should be solved by limiting the availability of handguns—not just in schools but in society as a whole. One advocate expressed his concern about schools bearing the responsibility for such control: "The school setting is almost impossible to police without tyrannical dictatorship. At what point do we create such a hostile environment that these are no longer schools?"(2)

Sources

1. Barbara Kantrowitz, "Wild in the Streets," *Newsweek*, Aug. 2, 1993, pp. 40–47.
2. Tom Morganthau, "It's Not Just New York . . . ," *Newsweek*, Mar. 9, 1992, pp. 25–29.

Questions for Discussion

1. Some states have passed legislation making parents responsible for their children's crimes if the crimes are committed with the parents' guns. Do you think such laws will result in safer schools?
2. Do the problems of school violence change your position on gun control? Explain.

Two young brothers wear bulletproof clothing to school: jackets and caps are designed to stop a 9 mm slug. The school bag will stop a knife or a shotgun blast.

concluded that measures of both personal and social control seem "to yield more efficient prediction of delinquent recidivism than items which are measures of the strength of social control."[29]

Stake in Conformity

Six years after the publication of Reiss's study, Jackson Toby proposed a different personal and social control model. Toby discussed the complementary role of neighborhood social disorganization and an individual's own stake in conformity. He agreed that the social disorganization of the slums explains why some communities have high crime rates while others do not: in slums both the community and the family are powerless to control members' behavior. Thieves and hoodlums usually come from such neighborhoods. But a great many law-abiding youngsters come from slums as well. Toby questioned how a theory that explained group behavior could account for individual differences in response to a poor environment. In other words, how can the theory of social disorganization explain why only a few among so many slum youths actually commit crimes?[30]

According to Toby, the social disorganization approach can explain why one neighborhood has a much higher crime rate than another but not why one particular individual becomes a hoodlum while another does not. What accounts for the difference is a differing stake in **conformity**, or correspondence of behavior to society's patterns, norms, or standards. One person may respond to conditions in a "bad" neighborhood by becoming hostile to conventional values, perhaps because he or she knows that the chances for legitimate success are poor. Another person in the same neighborhood may maintain his or her stake in conformity and remain committed to abiding by the law. Toby reminds us that when we try to account for crime in general, we should look at both group-level explanations (social disorganization) and individual-level explanations (stake in conformity).

Multiple Control Factors

The idea that both internal and external factors are involved in controlling behavior has interested a number of scholars. Ivan Nye, for example, developed the notion that multiple control factors determine human behavior. He argued that **internalized control,** or self-regulation, was a product of guilt aroused in the conscience when norms have been internalized. **Indirect control** comes from an individual's identification with noncriminals and a desire not to embarrass parents and friends by acting against their expectations.

Nye believes that social control involves "needs satisfaction," by which he means that control depends on how well a family can prepare the child for success at school, with peers, and in the workplace. Finally, **direct control,** a purely external control, depends on rules, restrictions, and punishments.[31]

Other researchers have looked at direct controls in different ways. Parental control, for example, may depend on such factors as a broken home, the mother's employment, and number of children in the family; such factors indicate some loss of direct control. Once again we find mixed results. Some studies indicate very little relationship between a broken home and delinquency, except for minor offenses such as truancy and running away.[32] The same can be said about the consequences of a mother's employment and family size.[33] A national study of 1886 males concluded, however, that direct parental control as measured by strictness and punitiveness is indeed correlated with delinquent behavior, and the study warned us not to dismiss this fact lightly. But the question remains open.[34]

Self-Control

In a recent book entitled *A General Theory of Crime,* Michael Gottfredson and Travis Hirschi propose a new model of personal and social control—one designed to explain an individual's propensity to commit crime.[35] Gottfredson and Hirschi claim that their model, unlike earlier conceptualizations, explains the tendency to commit *all* crimes, from crimes of violence such as robbery and sexual assault to white-collar offenses such as mail fraud and federal securities violations.[36]

This "general theory" of propensity to commit crimes, shown in Figure 7.2, assumes that offend-

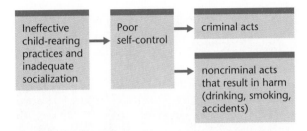

FIGURE 7.2 The Gottfredson-Hirschi self-control model
Gottfredson and Hirschi's model assumes that poor self-control is an intervening variable that explains all crime, as well as differences in crime rates, by age, gender, and race.

ers have little control over their own behavior and desires. When the need for momentary pleasure and immediate gratification outweighs long-term interests, crime occurs. In short, crime is a function of poor self-control.

What leads to poor self-control? Inadequate socialization and poor child-rearing practices, coupled with poor attachment, increase the probability of impulsive and uncontrolled acts. According to Gottfredson and Hirschi, individuals with low self-control also tend to be involved in noncriminal events that result in harm, such as drinking, smoking, and most types of accidents including auto crashes, household fires, and unwanted pregnancies.

Evidence that may support this model is still unfolding. In their analysis of interviews and breathalyzer tests, Carl Keane, Paul S. Maxim, and James J. Teevan found a definite association between self-control and DUI.[37] Equivocal results, however, were obtained by other researchers who examined interview data from a sample of adults from Oklahoma City.[38]

Additional research will be necessary to evaluate the strength of the self-control model. Earlier research on self-control and impulse control in relation to social control had some surprising results.[39] Analyses performed during the construction of a measure of control that combined self-control and social control variables showed that both these groups of items tapped the same dimension of control. In other words, the social bonds that make up the theory of social control

(attachment, commitment, involvement, and belief) appear to act as self-controls.

CONTAINMENT THEORY

A broad analysis of the relationship between personal and social controls is found in Walter Reckless's presentation of containment theory.[40] **Containment theory** assumes that for every individual there exists a containing external structure and a protective internal structure, both of which provide defense, protection, or insulation against delinquency.

According to Reckless, *outer containment*, or the structural buffer that holds the person in bounds, can be found in the following components:

■ A role that provides a guide for a person's activities

■ A set of reasonable limits and responsibilities

■ An opportunity for the individual to achieve status

■ Cohesion among members of a group, including joint activity and togetherness

■ A sense of belongingness (identification with the group)

■ Identification with one or more persons within the group

■ Provisions for supplying alternative ways and means of satisfaction (when one or more ways are closed)[41]

Inner containment, or personal control, is ensured by:

■ A good self-concept

■ Self-control

■ A strong ego

■ A well-developed conscience

■ A high frustration tolerance

■ A high sense of responsibility

Reckless suggests that the probability of deviance is directly related to the extent to which internal pushes (such as a need for immediate gratification, restlessness, and hostility), external pressures (such as poverty, unemployment, and blocked opportunities), and external pulls are controlled by one's inner and outer containment. The primary containment factor is found in self-concept, or the way one views oneself in relation to others, and to the world as well. A strong self-concept, coupled with some additional inner controls (such as a strong conscience and sense of responsibility), plus outer controls, makes delinquency highly unlikely.

Table 7.1 shows how the probability of deviance changes as an individual's inner and outer containment weakens. But why is it important to examine inner and outer controls simultaneously? Consider John, a college freshman, who had extensive community ties and strong family attachments and was valedictorian of his high school class. He also was a dealer in cocaine. All efforts to explain John's drug selling would prove disappointing if measures of social control were used alone. In other words, according to Hirschi's social control theory, John should be a conformist—he should focus his efforts on becoming a pharmacist or teacher. Containment theory, on the other hand, would be sensitive to the fact that John, while socially controlled and bonded by external forces, had a poorly developed self-concept, had an immature or undeveloped conscience, and was extremely impulsive. In short, he was driven to drugs as a result of a poor set of inner controls.

Empirical Tests of Containment Theory

To test containment theory, Reckless and his associates asked how boys living in bad neighborhoods can grow up to be good, law-abiding citizens. How are these boys protected from crime-producing influences? To answer the ques-

Ninety-eight percent of the members of the Harlem Boys Choir, known all over the world for its concerts, go on to college. In the neighborhoods from which the boys come, over 75 percent do not complete secondary school.

tion the researchers had high school teachers in a high-crime neighborhood nominate boys they believed would neither commit delinquent acts nor come into contact with police and juvenile court.

The 125 "good boys" scored high on a social responsibility test and low on a delinquency-proneness test. These boys avoided trouble, had good relations with parents and teachers, and had a good self-concept. They thought of themselves as obedient. Reckless concluded that nondelinquent boys follow conventional values even in bad neighborhoods if they maintain a positive self-image. It is this positive self-image that protects them. In a follow-up study the research team compared "good boys" with those nominated by teachers as "bad boys" (those they believed were headed for trouble). The good boys scored better on parental relation, self-

TABLE 7.1   THE PROBABILITY OF DEVIANCE AS INDICATED BY INNER AND OUTER CONTAINMENT*

Outer Containment (Social Control)	Inner Containment (Personal Control)	
	Strong	Weak
STRONG	+ +	+ −
WEAK	+ −	− −

*+ + = very low; + − = average; − − = very high.

Source: Adapted from Walter C. Reckless, "A Non-Causal Explanation: Containment Theory," *Excerpta Criminologia*, 2 (1962): 131–132.

image, and social responsibility tests. Far more of the bad boys had acquired police and juvenile court records.[42]

Evaluation: Containment Theory

Containment theory, like Hirschi's social control theory, has received significant criticism.[43] The most damaging has come from Clarence Schrag, who contends that the terminology used is vague and poorly defined, that the theory is difficult to test empirically, and that the theory fails to consider why some poorly contained youths commit violent crimes while others commit property crimes.[44] These criticisms are not easy to answer. And because little empirical research has been done to test the findings of Reckless and his colleagues over the intervening 30 years, there is little evidence of the validity of containment theory.

INTEGRATED THEORIES

Interest in social control theory stimulated a series of attempts to merge, or integrate, its premises with those of other prominent theories.[45] Some theorists believe that only by combining traditional theories will we have a better explanation of the wide range of the causes of criminal behavior. But integration presents some problems. Critics contend that difficulties arise when we try to reconcile basic differences among the theories and that we can learn more by making individual theories more precise.

But despite the problems, important attempts have been made to integrate theories. In discussing the concept of strain theory (Chapter 5), we focused on the fact that a society's institutions often fail to provide the means for attaining its goals. It may seem that social control would be a strange fit with strain theory. What does lack of opportunity have to do with attachment to parents or school? But the ways in which we are socialized, the values that are instilled in us, and the bonds that we develop are very closely related to social class. It is social class that helps form our vision of cultural goals and the means of attaining them.

Delbert Elliott and his colleagues have proposed a theory that integrates social control and strain theories. They suggest that limited or blocked opportunities and a subsequent failure to achieve cultural goals would weaken or even destroy a bond to the social order. In other words, even if someone establishes strong bonds in childhood, a series of bad experiences in school, in the community, and at home, along with blocked access to opportunity, would be likely to lead to a weakening of those social bonds. As strain weakens social bonds, the chance of delinquency increases.[46]

Another integrated theory combines control with learning theory (Chapter 4). Terence Thornberry argues that the potential for delinquency begins with the weakening of a person's bonds to the conventional world (parents, school, and accepted values). But if the potential is to become a reality, one needs a social setting in which to learn delinquent values. It is quite clear that social position is also important. The poorest youngsters are typically the least bonded and the most exposed to influences that can teach them criminal behavior.[47]

FROM THEORY TO PRACTICE

Social control theory tells us that people commit crimes when they have not developed adequate attachments, have not become involved in and committed to conventional activities, and have not internalized the rules of society (or do not care about them). Efforts to prevent crime must therefore include the teaching of conventional values. It is also necessary to find ways to strengthen individual bonds to society, commitment to the conventional order, and involvement in conventional activities. One way is to strengthen the institutions that socialize people and continue to regulate their behavior throughout life—the family, the school, and the workplace.[48]

Family

In the early 1980s an experimental school-based parent training program opened in Seattle, Washington, as part of a delinquency-prevention project. First-graders in six schools were assigned

WINDOW TO THE WORLD
Nations With Low Crime Rates

Most criminologists devote their efforts to learning why people commit crime and why there is so much crime. A few have looked at the question from the opposite perspective: In places with little crime, what accounts for the low crime rate? Using the United Nations' first World Crime Survey (1970–1975), Freda Adler studied the two countries with the lowest crime rates in each of five general cultural regions of the world(1):

Western Europe: Switzerland and the Republic of Ireland

Eastern Europe: The former German Democratic Republic (East Germany) and Bulgaria

Arab countries: Saudi Arabia and Algeria

Asia: Japan and Nepal

Latin America: Costa Rica and Peru(2)

This is an odd assortment of countries. They seem to have little in common. Some are democratic, others authoritarian. Some are republics, others monarchies. Some were ruled by dictators, others by communal councils. Some are rural, others highly urbanized. Some are remote and isolated; others are in the political mainstream. Some are highly religious, some largely atheistic. Some have a very high standard of living, others a very low one. What explains their common characteristic of low crime rates?

Investigations slowly revealed a common factor in all ten countries: each appeared to have an intact social control system, quite apart from whatever formal control system (law enforcement) it had. Here are brief descriptions of the types of social control systems identified:

Western Europe: Switzerland fostered a strong sense of belonging to and participating in the local community.(3) The family was still strong in the Republic of Ireland, and it was strengthened by shared religious values.

Eastern Europe: The German Democratic Republic involved all youths in communal activities, organized by groups and aimed at having young people excel for the glory of self and country. In Bulgaria, industrialization focused on regional industry centers so that the workers would not be dislodged from their hometowns, which served as continuing social centers.

The Arab countries: Islam continued to be strong as a way of life and exercised a powerful influence on daily activities, especially in Saudi Arabia. Algeria had, in addition, a powerful commitment to socialism in its postindependence era, involving the citizens in all kinds of commonly shared development activities.

Asia: Nepal retained its strong family and clan ties, augmented by councils of elders that oversaw the community and resolved problems. Highly industrialized Japan had lost some of the social

controls of family and kinship, but it found a substitute family in the industrial community, to which most Japanese belonged: Mitsubishi might now be the family that guided one's every step.

Latin America: Costa Rica spent all the funds that other governments devoted to the military on social services and social development, caring for and strengthening its families. Peru went through a process of urbanization in stages: village and family cohesion marked the lives of people in the countryside, and this cohesion remained with the people as they migrated from Andean villages to smaller towns and then to the big city, where they were received by and lived surrounded by others from their own hometowns.

The study concluded that **synnomie**, a term derived from the Greek *syn* meaning "with" and *nomos* meaning "norms," marked societies with low crime rates.

Sources

1. United Nations, *Report of the Secretary General on Crime Prevention and Control*, A/32/199 (popularly known as the First U.N. World Crime Survey) (New York: United Nations, 1977).
2. Freda Adler, *Nations Not Obsessed with Crime* (Littleton, Colo.: Fred B. Rothman, 1983).
3. Marshall B. Clinard, *Cities with Little Crime: The Case of Switzerland* (Cambridge, Mass.: Cambridge University Press, 1978).

Questions for Discussion

1. People in the United States work in factories, live in family groups, go to church, and join youth groups. Why do these institutions not function effectively as forms of social control to keep the crime rate low?
2. How could government or community decision makers use the information presented by this study to help solve crime problems in the United States?

Morning exercises, Japanese workers at a saké distillery.

A National Day celebration in Singapore, a multicultural nation that has hardly any crime and also has very strong formal and informal social control systems.

to an experimental classroom or a control classroom. The parents of those in the experimental group were given training and the parents of the children in the control group were not.

The major premise of the experiment was that a child's bond to a family is crucial. To develop this bond, parents learned to provide opportunities that would help the child participate and succeed in a social unit such as the school (by demonstrating good study habits, for example) and to reinforce conformity or punish violations of the group's norms. Preliminary results suggest that such a training program decreases children's aggressiveness and increases parental skills.[49]

School

A program called PATHE (Positive Action Through Holistic Education) operated in four middle schools and three high schools of Charleston County, South Carolina, between 1980 and 1983. Its object was to reduce delinquency by strengthening students' commitment to school and attachment to conforming members—in other words, by bonding young people to the conventional system.

PATHE brought together students, school staff, and community members to plan and implement a program designed to foster a better school climate (encourage more open discussion), improve academic skills, and prepare students for careers. The results of the program were higher grades, better attendance, fewer dropouts, and increased commitment to education.[50]

Neighborhood

Historically church and family have helped to protect and maintain the social order in neighborhoods, to instill a sense of pride and comfort in residents. This is no longer the case in many areas. The neighborhood as an institution of informal social control has been very much weakened. Various agencies have tried to reverse this trend: between 1981 and 1986 programs to prevent juvenile crime were implemented through neighborhood-based organizations in Chicago, Dallas, Los Angeles, New York, New Orleans, and San Diego. These federally funded programs sought to reduce crime by strengthening neighborhood cohesion. Each program assessed the needs of residents and then set up crisis intervention centers, mediation (between youngsters and school, family, or police and between warring gangs), youth training, supervision programs, and family support systems.

Within the first 3 years, serious juvenile crime decreased in three of the target areas.[51] Hundreds of such community crime-prevention projects around the country have been organized by government agencies, private persons, and religious groups.[52] They have made a local impact, but they have not been able to change the national crime rate. The most successful models, however, may offer a plan for crime prevention on a broader, perhaps even a national, scale.

As our understanding of control theory evolves, so will our appreciation of the effects of control interventions. If nothing else, it is fair to say that social control programs and interventions are proliferating and may be found in every state. Here are just a few examples:

Homebuilders (Tacoma, Washington): a family preservation program that seeks to keep at-risk children at home[53]

Families First (Michigan): a program that strengthens vulnerable families [54]

S.W.E.A.T. Team (Bridgeport, Connecticut): a project that employs teenagers to create new activities for children who may be tempted into joining gangs or selling drugs[55]

Learnfare (Ohio, Virginia, Florida, Maryland, and Oklahoma): programs that provide financial and social support for teenage welfare mothers who attend school[56]

these bonds, Hirschi claimed, the less the likelihood of delinquency.

Most investigators today believe that personal (inner) controls are as important as social (external) controls in keeping people from committing crimes. Albert Reiss found that personal controls reinforce social controls. Jackson Toby stressed the importance of a stake in conformity in keeping a person from responding to social disorganization with delinquent behavior. Ivan Nye believed that multiple control factors operate simultaneously to determine human behavior: internalized, indirect, and direct controls. Michael Gottfredson and Travis Hirschi argue that poor self-control, a result of ineffective child-rearing practices, explains a person's propensity to commit crime.

According to the containment theory of Walter Reckless, every person has a containing external structure (a role in a social group with reasonable limits and responsibilities and alternative means of attaining satisfaction). In addition, each individual has a protective internal structure that depends on a good self-concept, self-control, a well-developed conscience, a tolerance for frustration, and a strong sense of responsibility.

As an effort to reduce delinquency, a variety of programs at the local and regional levels help parents, schools, and neighborhood groups develop social controls.

■ REVIEW

The term "social control" has taken on a wide variety of meanings. In general, it describes any mechanism that leads to conformity to social norms. Mainstream studies of social control take one of two approaches. Macrosociological studies focus on formal systems of social control. Most contemporary criminological research takes the microsociological approach, which focuses on informal systems. Travis Hirschi's social control theory has had a long-lasting impact on the scholarly community. Hirschi identified four social bonds that promote adherence to society's values: attachment, commitment, involvement, and belief. The stronger

■ NOTES

1. William Golding, *Lord of the Flies* (New York: Coward-McCann, 1954), p. 31.
2. Jack P. Gibbs, "Social Control, Deterrence, and Perspectives on Social Order," *Social Forces,* **56** (1977): 408–423. See also Freda Adler, *Nations Not Obsessed with Crime* (Littleton, Colo.: Fred B. Rothman, 1983).
3. Travis Hirschi, *Causes of Delinquency* (Berkeley: University of California Press, 1969).
4. Donald J. Black, *The Behavior of Law* (New York: Academic Press, 1976), p. 105. See Allan V. Horwitz, *The Logic of Social Control* (New York: Plenum, 1990), for an exceptional evaluation of Black's work.
5. Joseph Perkins, "Smoke Signals Taxes, Harsh Rules Go Too Far in Crusade to Snuff Out Habit," *San Diego Union-Tribune,* Mar. 12, 1993, p. B7; Editorial: "Smoke Clouds the Political Air in California's City of Angels," *Washington Times,* July 17, 1993, p. C2.
6. Nanette J. Davis and Bo Anderson, *Social Control: The*

Production of Deviance in the Modern State (New York: Irvington, 1983); S. Cohen and A. Scull, eds., *Social Control and the State* (New York: St. Martin's Press, 1983).

7. Jackson Toby, "Social Disorganization and Stake in Conformity: Complementary Factors in the Predatory Behavior of Hoodlums," *Journal of Criminal Law, Criminology, and Police Science*, **48** (1957): 12–17.

8. Scott Briar and Irving Piliavin, "Delinquency, Situational Inducements, and Commitment to Conformity," *Social Problems*, **13** (1965): 41.

9. Ibid., p. 36.

10. Hirschi, *Causes of Delinquency*.

11. See John Bowlby, *Attachment and Loss*, 2 vols. (New York: Basic Books, 1969, 1973); John Bowlby, "Forty-Four Juvenile Thieves: Their Characteristics and Home Life," *International Journal of Psychoanalysis*, **25** (1944): 19–25; and John Bowlby, *The Making and Breaking of Affectional Bonds* (London: Tavistock, 1979).

12. Hirschi, *Causes of Delinquency*.

13. Ibid., p. 145.

14. Ibid., p. 169.

15. Ibid., p. 55.

16. Michael J. Hindelang, "Causes of Delinquency: A Partial Replication and Extension," *Social Problems*, **20** (1973): 471–487.

17. Marvin D. Krohn and James L. Massey, "Social Control and Delinquent Behavior: An Examination of the Elements of the Social Bond," *Sociological Quarterly*, **21** (1980): 529– 544. For a critique of this study, see Richard L. Amdur, "Testing Causal Models of Delinquency: A Methodological Critique," *Criminal Justice and Behavior*, **16** (1989): 35–62.

18. Michael D. Wiatrowski, David Griswold, and Mary K. Roberts, "Social Control Theory and Delinquency," *American Sociological Review*, **46** (1985): 525–541.

19. Robert Agnew, "Social Control Theory and Delinquency: A Longitudinal Test," *Criminology*, **23** (1985): 47–61. See also Michael D. Wiatrowski and Kristine L. Anderson, "The Dimensionality of the Bond," *Journal of Quantitative Criminology*, **3** (1987): 65–81; Jennifer Friedman and Dennis P. Rosenbaum, "Social Control Theory: The Salience of Components by Age, Gender, and Type of Crime," *Journal of Quantitative Criminology*, **4** (1988): 363–381; James R. Lasley, "Toward a Control Theory of White-Collar Offending," *Journal of Quantitative Criminology*, **4** (1988); 347–362; Josine Junger-Tas, "An Empirical Test of Social Control Theory," *Journal of Quantitative Criminology*, **8** (1992): 9–28; Scott Menard, "Demographic and Theoretical Variables in the Age-Period-Cohort Analysis of Illegal Behavior," *Journal of Research in Crime and Delinquency*, **29** (1992): 178–199; Stephen A. Cernovich and Peggy C. Giordano, "School Bonding, Age, Race, and Delinquency," *Criminology*, **30** (1992): 261–291; Kimberly L. Kempf, "The Empirical Status of Social Control Theory," in *New Directions in Criminological Theory*, ed. Freda Adler and William S.

Laufer (New Brunswick, N.J.: Transaction, 1993), pp. 143–185; Marc LeBlanc and Aaron Caplan, "Theoretical Formalization, a Necessity: The Example of Hirschi's Bonding Theory," in Adler and Laufer, *New Directions in Criminological Theory*, pp. 237–336; and Orlando Rodriguez and David Weisburd, "The Integrated Social Control Model and Ethnicity: The Case of Puerto Rican American Delinquency," *Criminal Justice and Behavior*, **18** (1991): 464–479.

20. Karen S. Rook, "Promoting Social Bonding: Strategies for Helping the Lonely and Socially Isolated," *American Psychologist*, **39** (1984): 1389–1407.

21. Robert J. Sampson and John H. Laub, *Crime in the Making: Pathways and Turning Points through Life* (Cambridge, Mass.: Harvard University Press, 1993).

22. Milton Rokeach, *The Nature of Human Values* (New York: Free Press, 1973).

23. See Donald J. Shoemaker, *Theories of Delinquency: An Examination of Explanations of Delinquent Behavior*, 2d ed. (New York: Oxford University Press, 1990), pp. 172–207, for an evaluation of social control theory.

24. Terence P. Thornberry, Alan J. Lizotte, Marvin D. Krohn, Margaret Farnsworth, and Sung Juon Jung, "Testing Interactional Theory: An Examination of Reciprocal Causal Relationships among Family, School, and Delinquency," *Journal of Criminal Law and Criminology*, **82** (1991): 3–35.

25. David Matza, *Delinquency and Drift* (New York: Wiley, 1964), p. 21.

26. Gresham Sykes and David Matza, "Techniques of Neutralization: A Theory of Delinquency," *American Sociological Review*, **22** (1957): 664–670. For a more recent look at techniques of neutralization, see John Hamlin, "The Misplaced Role of Rational Choice in Neutralization Theory," *Criminology*, **26** (1988): 425–438.

27. Richard A. Ball, "An Empirical Exploration of Neutralization Theory," *Criminologica*, **4** (1966): 103–120. See also N. William Minor, "The Neutralization of Criminal Offense," *Criminology*, **18** (1980): 103–120.

28. Robert Gordon, James F. Short, Jr., D. Cartwright, and Fred L. Strodtbeck, "Values and Gang Delinquency: A Study of Street Corner Groups," *American Journal of Sociology*, **69** (1963): 109–128.

29. Albert J. Reiss, "Delinquency as the Failure of Personal and Social Controls," *American Sociological Review*, **16** (1951): 206.

30. Toby, "Social Disorganization," p. 137.

31. Francis Ivan Nye, *Family Relationships and Delinquent Behavior* (New York: Wiley, 1958).

32. L. Edward Wells and Joseph H. Rankin, "Broken Homes and Juvenile Delinquency: An Empirical Review," *Criminal Justice Abstracts*, **17** (1985): 249–272; Lawrence Rosen and Kathleen Neilson, "Broken Homes," in *Contemporary Criminology*, ed. Leonard Savitz and Norman Johnston (New York: Wiley, 1982).

33. Mary Reige, "Parental Affection and Juvenile Delinquency in Girls," *British Journal of Criminology*, **12**

(1972): 55–73; Hirschi, *Causes of Delinquency*, p. 237; Lawrence Rosen, "Family and Delinquency: Structure or Function?" *Criminology*, **23** (1985): 553–573.

34. L. Edward Wells and Joseph H. Rankin, "Direct Parental Controls and Delinquency," *Criminology*, **26** (1988): 263–285. See also Douglas Smith and Raymond Paternoster, "The Gender Gap in Theories of Deviance: Issues and Evidence," *Journal of Research in Crime and Delinquency*, **24** (1987): 140–172; and John Hagan, A. R. Gillis, and John Simpson, "The Class Structure of Gender and Delinquency: Toward a Power-Control Theory of Common Delinquent Behavior," *American Journal of Sociology*, **90** (1985): 1151–1178. For a discussion of paternal and maternal patterns of control on male and female children, see Gary D. Hill and Maxine P. Atkinson, "Gender, Familial Control, and Delinquency," *Criminology*, **26** (1988): 127–149. In a 30-year follow-up of 250 boys treated in the Cambridge-Somerville Youth Study, Joan McCord found that poor parental supervision was the best predictor of property and personal crime later in life; see Joan McCord, "Some Child-Rearing Antecedents of Criminal Behavior in Adult Men," *Journal of Personality and Social Psychology*, **36** (1979): 1477–1486. Lee Robins reports similar results in "Sturdy Childhood Predictors of Adult Outcomes: Republications from Longitudinal Studies," in *Stress and Mental Disorders*, ed. J. E. Barrett, R. M. Rose, and G. L. Kleerman (New York: Raven, 1979), pp. 219–235. London studies by D. J. West and David P. Farrington found that cruel parents, poor supervision, passive parental attitudes, and parental conflict predicted juvenile delinquency; see their *Who Becomes Delinquent?* (London: Heinemann, 1973). For an examination of the family backgrounds of female offenders, see Jill Leslie Rosenbaum, "Family Dysfunction and Female Delinquency," *Crime and Delinquency*, **35** (1989): 31–44.

35. Michael R. Gottfredson and Travis Hirschi, *A General Theory of Crime* (Stanford, Calif.: Stanford University Press, 1990); T. Hirschi and M. Gottfredson, "Towards a General Theory of Crime," in *Explaining Criminal Behavior: Interdisciplinary Approaches*, ed. Wouter Buikhuisen and Sarnoff A. Mednick (Leiden, Netherlands: E. J. Brill, 1988); Michael Gottfredson and Travis Hirschi, "A Propensity-Event Theory of Crime," in *Advances in Criminological Theory*, Vol. 1, ed. W. Laufer and F. Adler (New Brunswick, N.J.: Transaction, 1989).

36. Travis Hirschi and Michael Gottfredson, "The Significance of White-Collar Crime for a *General Theory of Crime*," *Criminology*, **27** (1989): 359–371; Darrell Steffensmeier, "On the Causes of 'White Collar' Crime: An Assessment of Hirschi and Gottfredson's Claim," *Criminology*, **27** (1989): 345–358; Travis Hirschi and Michael Gottfredson, "Causes of White-Collar Crime," *Criminology*, **25** (1987): 949–974.

37. Carl Keane, Paul S. Maxim, and James J. Teevan, "Drinking and Driving, Self-Control, and Gender: Testing a *General Theory of Crime*," *Journal of Research in Crime and Delinquency*, **30** (1993): 30–46.

38. Harold G. Grasmick, Charles R. Tittle, and Robert J. Bursik, Jr., "Testing the Core Empirical Implications of Gottfredson and Hirschi's *General Theory of Crime*," *Journal of Research in Crime and Delinquency*, **30** (1993): 5–29; Travis Hirschi and Michael Gottfredson, "Commentary: Testing the *General Theory of Crime*," *Journal of Research in Crime and Delinquency*, **30** (1993): 47–54.

39. William S. Laufer, "The Development of a Measure of Psychosocial Control," Ph.D. dissertation, Rutgers University, School of Criminal Justice, 1987.

40. Walter C. Reckless, "A New Theory of Delinquency and Crime," *Federal Probation*, **25** (1961): 42–46; Walter C. Reckless, Simon Dinitz, and Barbara Kay, "The Self Component in Potential Delinquency and Potential Non-Delinquency," *American Sociological Review*, **22** (1957): 556–570; Walter C. Reckless, Simon Dinitz, and E. Murray, "Self-Concept as an Insulator against Delinquency," *American Sociological Review*, **21** (1956): 744–746; Frank R. Scarpitti, Ellen Murray, Simon Dinitz, and Walter C. Reckless, "The Good Boy in a High Delinquency Area: Four Years Later," *American Sociological Review*, **25** (1960): 555–558; E. P. Donald and Simon Dinitz, "Self-Concept and Delinquency Proneness," in *Interdisciplinary Problems in Criminology*, ed. Walter C. Reckless and C. Newman (Columbus: Ohio State University Press, 1964).

41. Walter C. Reckless, "A Non-Causal Explanation: Containment Theory," *Excerpta Criminologia*, **2** (1962): 131–132.

42. Reckless et al., "Self-Concept as an Insulator"; Scarpitti et al., "The Good Boy in a High Delinquency Area."

43. Gary F. Jensen, "Delinquency and Adolescent Self-Conceptions: A Study of the Personal Relevance of Infraction," *Social Problems*, **20** (1972): 84–103; S. S. Tangri and M. Schwartz, "Delinquency and the Self-Concept Variable," *Journal of Criminal Law and Criminology*, **58** (1967): 182–190.

44. Clarence Schrag, *Crime and Justice American Style* (Washington, D.C.: U.S. Government Printing Office, 1971), pp. 82–89.

45. Alan Liska, Marvin D. Krohn, Steven F. Messner, "Strategies and Requisites for Theoretical Integration in the Study of Crime and Deviance," in *Theoretical Integration in the Study of Deviance and Crime: Problems and Prospects*, ed. S. F. Lessner, M. D. Krohn, and A. Liska, (New York: SUNYA, 1989), p. 4. See also R. J. Hepburn, "Testing Alternative Models of Delinquency Causation," *Journal of Criminal Law and Criminology*, **67** (1977): 450–460; T. Ross Matsueda, "Testing Control Theory and Differential Association: A Causal Modeling Approach," *American Sociological Review*, **47** (1982): 489–497; W. E. Thompson, J. Mitchell, and R. A. Dodder, "An Empirical Test of Hirschi's Control Theory of Delinquency," *Deviant Behavior*, **5** (1984): 11–22; and Frank S. Pearson and

Neil A. Weiner, "Toward an Integration of Criminological Theories," *Journal of Criminal Law and Criminology*, **76** (1985): 116–150.

46. Delbert S. Elliott, Suzanne S. Ageton, and R. J. Canter, "An Integrated Theoretical Perspective on Delinquent Behavior," *Journal of Research in Crime and Delinquency*, **16** (1979): 3–27.

47. Terence P. Thornberry, "Toward an Interactional Theory of Delinquency," *Criminology*, **25** (1987): 863–891. See also Madeline G. Aultman and Charles F. Wellford, "Toward an Integrated Model of Delinquency Causation: An Empirical Analysis," *Sociology and Social Research*, **63** (1979): 316–317.

48. See W. Timothy Austin, "Crime and Custom in an Orderly Society: The Singapore Prototype," *Criminology*, **25** (1987): 279–294; Charles Fenwick, "Culture, Philosophy and Crime: The Japanese Experience," *International Journal of Comparative and Applied Criminal Justice*, **9** (1985): 76–81; J. M. Day and William S. Laufer, eds., *Crime, Values, and Religion* (Norwood, N.J.: Ablex, 1987); and Freda Adler and William S. Laufer, "Social Control and the Workplace," in *US-USSR Approaches to Urban Crime Prevention*, ed. James Finckenauer and Alexander Yakovlev (Moscow: Soviet Academy of State and Law, 1987).

49. J. David Hawkins, Richard F. Catalano, Gwen Jones, and David Fine, "Delinquency Prevention through Parent-Training: Results and Issues from Work in Progress," in *From Children to Citizens:* Vol. 3, *Families, Schools, and Delinquency Prevention*, ed. James Q.

Wilson and Glenn C. Loury (New York: Springer Verlag, 1987), pp. 186–204.

50. Denise C. Gottfredson, "An Empirical Test of School-Based Environmental and Individual Interventions to Reduce the Risk of Delinquent Behavior," *Criminology*, **24** (1986): 705–731.

51. Jeffrey Fagan, "Neighborhood Education, Mobilization, and Organization for Juvenile Crime Prevention," *Annals of the American Academy for the Advancement of Political and Social Sciences*, **494** (1987): 54–70.

52. For an examination of community social control, see David Weisburd, "Vigilantism as Community Social Control: Developing a Quantitative Criminological Model," *Journal of Quantitative Criminology*, **4** (1988): 137–153. For a discussion of how interventions must make sure that labeling a child or family as a problem does not affect the child's self-concept or social involvement, see Charles E. Wellford, "Delinquency Prevention and Labeling," in Wilson and Loury, *Families, Schools, and Delinquency Prevention*, pp. 257–267.

53. "Fostering the Family: An Intensive Effort to Keep Kids with Parents," *Newsweek,* June 22, 1992, p. 64.

54. Ibid.

55. George Judson, "Fighting Temptations of Summer: Bridgeport Puts Teenagers to Work Helping Other Youths," *New York Times,* Aug. 22, 1992, p. B1.

56. Susan Chirn, "A 'Learnfare' Program Offers No Easy Lessons," *New York Times,* Apr. 28, 1993, p. A12.

8

Alternative Explanations of Crime: Labeling, Conflict, and Radical Theories

KEY TERMS
conflict theory
consensus model
due process
equal protection
labeling theory
penologists
radical criminology
social interactionists

Each era of social and political turmoil has produced profound changes in people's lives. Perhaps no such era was as significant for criminology as the 1960s. A society with conservative values was shaken out of its complacency when young people, blacks, women, and other disadvantaged groups demanded a part in the shaping of national policy. They saw the gaps between philosophical political demands and reality: blacks had little opportunity to advance, women were kept in an inferior status, old politicians made wars in which the young had to die. Rebellion broke out, and some criminologists joined it.

These criminologists turned away from theories that explained crime by characteristics of the offender or of the social structure. They set out to demonstrate that individuals become criminals because of what people with power, especially those in the criminal justice system, do. Their alternative explanations largely reject the consensus model of crime, on which all earlier theories rested. The new theories not only question the traditional explanations of the creation and enforcement of criminal law but blame that law for the making of criminals. (See Table 8.1.)

It may not sound so radical to assert that unless an act is made criminal by law, no person who performs that act can be adjudicated a criminal. The exponents of contemporary alternative explanations of crime grant that much. But they also ask: Who makes these laws in the first place? And why? Is breaking such laws the most important criterion for being a criminal? Are all people

TABLE 8.1   COMPARISON OF FOUR CRIMINOLOGICAL PERSPECTIVES

Perspective	Origin of Criminal Law	Causes of Criminal Behavior	Focus of Study
Traditional/consensus	Laws reflect shared values.	Psychological, biological, or sociological factors.	Psychological and biological factors (Chap. 4); unequal opportunity (Chap. 5); learning criminal behavior in disorganized neighborhoods (Chap. 5); subculture values (Chap. 6); social control (Chap. 7).
Labeling	Those in power create the laws, decide who will be the rule breakers.	The process that defines (or labels) certain persons as criminals.	Effects of stigmatizing by the label "criminal"; sociopolitical factors behind reform legislation; origin of laws; deviant behavior (Chap. 8).
Conflict	Powerful groups use laws to support their interests.	Interests of one group do not coincide with needs of another.	Bias and discrimination in criminal justice system; differential crime rates of powerful and powerless; development of criminal laws by those in power; relationship between rulers and ruled (Chap. 8).
Critical (Marxist)	Laws serve interests of the ruling class.	Class struggle over distribution of resources in a capitalist system.	Relationship between crime and economics; ways in which state serves capitalist interests; solution to crime problem based on collapse of capitalism (Chap. 8).

who break these laws criminals? Do all members of society agree that those singled out by the criminal law to be called "criminals" are criminals and that others are not?

LABELING THEORY

The 1950s was a period of general prosperity and pride for Americans. Yet some social scientists, uneasy about the complacency they saw, turned their attention to the social order. They noted that some of the ideals the United States had fought for in World War II had not been achieved at home. Human rights existed on paper but were often lacking in practice. It was clear that blacks continued to live as second-class citizens. Even though the Fourteenth Amendment to the Constitution guaranteed blacks equal rights, neither the law of the country nor the socioeconomic system provided them with equal opportunities.

Nowhere was this fact more apparent than in the criminal justice system. Social scientists and liberal lawyers pressed for change, and the Supreme Court, under Chief Justice Earl Warren, responded. In case after case the Court found a pervasive influence of rules and customs that violated the concepts of **due process,** under which a person cannot be deprived of life, liberty, or property without lawful procedures, and **equal protection,** under which no one can be denied the safeguards of the law. The result of hundreds of Supreme Court decisions was that both black and white citizens now were guaranteed the right to counsel in all criminal cases, freedom from self-incrimination, and other rights enumerated in the first ten amendments to the Constitution. Nevertheless, a great deal of social injustice remained.

In this social climate, a small group of social scientists, known as labeling theorists, began to explore how and why certain acts were defined as criminal or, more broadly, deviant behavior and others were not and how and why certain people were defined as criminal or deviant. These theorists viewed criminals not as inherently evil persons engaged in inherently wrong acts but, rather, as individuals who had had criminal status conferred upon them by both the

criminal justice system and the community at large.

Viewed from this perspective, criminal acts themselves are not particularly significant; the social reaction to them, however, is. Deviance and its control involve a process of social definition in which the response of others to an individual's behavior is the key influence on subsequent behavior and on individuals' view of themselves. The sociologist Howard S. Becker has written:

> Deviance is not a quality of the act the person commits, but rather a consequence of the application by others of rules and sanctions to an "offender." The deviant is one to whom that label has successfully been applied; deviant behavior is behavior that people so label.[1]

In focusing on the ways in which social interactions create deviance, **labeling theory** declares that the reaction of other people and the subsequent effects of those reactions create deviance. Once it becomes known that a person has engaged in deviant acts, he or she is segregated from conventional society, and a label ("thief," "whore," "junkie") is attached to the transgressor. This process of segregation creates "outsiders" (as Becker called them), or outcasts from society, who begin to associate with others like themselves.[2]

As more people begin to think of these people as deviants and to respond to them accordingly, the deviants react to the response by continuing to engage in the behavior society now expects of them. Through this process their self-images gradually change as well. So the key factor is the label that is attached to an individual: "If men define situations as real, they are real in their consequences."[3]

The Origins of Labeling Theory

The intellectual roots of labeling theory can be traced to the post–World War I work of Charles Horton Cooley, William I. Thomas, and George Herbert Mead. These scholars, who viewed the human self as formed through a process of social interaction, were called **social interactionists.** In 1918 Mead compared the impact of social labeling to "the angel with the fiery sword at the gate who can cut one off from the world to which he belongs."[4]

Labeling separates the good from the bad, the conventional from the deviant. Mead's interest in deviance focused on the social interactions by which an individual becomes a deviant. The person is not just a fixed structure whose action is the result of certain factors acting upon it. Rather, social behavior develops in a continuous process of action and reaction.[5] The way we perceive ourselves, our self-concept, is built not only on what we think of ourselves but also on what others think of us.

Somewhat later, the historian Frank Tannenbaum (1893–1969) used the same argument in his study of the causes of criminal behavior. He described the creation of a criminal as a process: Breaking windows, climbing onto roofs, and playing truant are all normal parts of the adolescent search for excitement and adventure. Local merchants and others who experience these activities may consider them a nuisance or perhaps even evil. This conflict is the beginning of the process by which the evil act transforms the transgressor into an evil individual. From that point on, the evil individuals are separated from those in conventional society. Given a criminal label, they gradually begin to think of themselves as they have been officially defined.

Tannenbaum maintained that it is the process of labeling, or the "dramatization of evil," that locks a mischievous boy into a delinquent role ("the person becomes the thing he is described as being"). Accordingly, "the entire process of dealing with young delinquents is mischievous insofar as it identifies him to himself and to the environment as a delinquent person."[6] The system starts out with a child in trouble and ends up with a juvenile delinquent.

Basic Assumptions of Labeling Theory

In the 1940s the sociologist Edwin Lemert elaborated on Tannenbaum's discussion by formulating the basic assumptions of labeling theory.[7] He reminded us that people are constantly involved in behavior that runs the risk of being labeled delinquent or criminal. But although many run

that risk, only a few are so labeled. The reason, Lemert contended, is that there are two kinds of deviant acts: primary and secondary.[8]

Primary deviations are the initial deviant acts that bring on the first social response. These acts do not affect the individual's self-concept. It is the *secondary deviations,* the acts that follow the societal response to the primary deviation, that are of major concern. These are the acts that result from the change in self-concept brought about by the labeling process.[9] The scenario goes somewhat like this:

1. An individual commits a simple deviant act (primary deviation)—throwing a stone at a neighbor's car, for instance.
2. There is an informal social reaction: the neighbor gets angry.
3. The individual continues to break rules (primary deviations)—he lets the neighbor's dog out of the yard.
4. There is increased, but still primary, social reaction: the neighbor tells the youth's parents.
5. The individual commits a more serious deviant act—he is caught shoplifting (still primary deviation).
6. There is a formal reaction: the youth is adjudicated a "juvenile delinquent" in juvenile court.
7. The youth is now labeled "delinquent" by the court and "bad" by the neighborhood, by his conventional peers, and by others.
8. The youth begins to think of himself as "delinquent"; he joins other unconventional youths.
9. The individual commits another, yet more serious, deviant act (secondary deviation)—he robs a local grocery store with members of a gang.
10. The individual is returned to juvenile court, has more offenses added to his record, is cast out further from conventional society, and takes on a completely deviant lifestyle.

According to Lemert, secondary deviance sets in after the community has become aware of a primary deviance. Individuals experience "a continuing sense of injustice, which [is] reinforced by job rejections, police cognizance, and strained interaction with normals."[10] In short, deviant individuals have to bear the stigma of the "delinquent" label, just as English and American convicts, as late as the eighteenth century, bore stigmas, in the form of an M for murder or a T for thief, burned or cut into their bodies to designate them as persons to be shunned.[11] Once such a label is attached to a person, a deviant or criminal career has been set in motion. The full significance of labeling theory was not recognized, either in Europe or in the United States, until political events provided the opportunity.[12]

Labeling in the 1960s

The 1960s witnessed a movement among students and professors to join advocacy groups and become activists in the social causes that rapidly were gaining popularity on college campuses across the nation, such as equal rights for minorities, liberation for women, and peace for humankind. The protests took many forms—demonstrations and rallies, sit-ins and teach-ins, beards and long hair, rock music and marijuana, dropping out of school, burning draft cards.

Arrests of middle-class youths increased rapidly; crime was no longer confined to the ghettos. People asked whether arrests were being made for behavior that was not really criminal. Were the real criminals the legislators and policy makers who pursued a criminal war in Vietnam while creating the artificial crime of draft-card burning at home? Were the real criminals the National Guardsmen who shot and killed campus demonstrators at Kent State University? Labeling theorists made their appearance and

Kent State University protester grieving over body of fellow student shot by National Guardsmen, Ohio 1970.

provided answers. The sociologist Kai Erickson has put it well:

> Deviance is not a property inherent in certain forms of behavior; it is a property conferred upon these forms by audiences which directly or indirectly witness them. The critical variable in the study of deviance, then, is the social audience rather than the individual actor, since it is the audience which eventually determines whether or not any episode or behavior or any class of episodes is labeled deviant.[13]

Edwin Schur, a leading labeling theorist of the 1960s, elaborated Erickson's explanation:

> Human behavior is deviant to the extent that it comes to be viewed as involving a personally discreditable departure from a group's normative expectation, and it elicits interpersonal and collective reactions that serve to "isolate," "treat," "correct," or "punish" individuals engaged in such behavior.[14]

Schur also expanded on Lemert's secondary deviance with his own concept of "secondary elaboration," by which he meant that the effects of the labeling process become so significant that individuals who want to escape from their deviant groups and return to the conventional world find it difficult to do so. Schur points to members of the gay and drug cultures.[15] The strength of the label, once acquired, tends to exclude such people permanently from the mainstream culture.[16] Schur found that involvement in activities that are disapproved of may very well lead to more participation in deviance than one had originally planned, and so increase the social distance between the person labeled deviant and the conventional world.[17]

The labeling theorists then asked: Who makes the rules that define deviant behavior, including crime? According to Howard Becker, it is the "moral entrepreneurs"—the people whose high social position gives them the power to make and enforce the social rules by which members of society have to live. By making the rules that define the criminal, Becker argues, certain members of society create outsiders.

The whole process thus becomes a political one, pitting the rule makers against the rule breakers. Becker goes even further, suggesting

that people can be labeled simply by being falsely accused. As long as others believe that someone has participated in a given deviant behavior, that individual will experience negative social reaction. People can also suffer the effects of labeling when they have committed a deviant act that has not been discovered. Since most people know how they would be labeled if they were caught, these secret deviants may experience the same labeling effects as those who have been caught.[18]

Empirical Evidence for Labeling Theory

Empirical investigations of labeling theory have been carried out by researchers in many disciplines using a variety of methodologies. One group of investigators arranged to have eight sane volunteers apply for admission to various mental hospitals. In order to get themselves admitted, the subjects claimed to be hearing voices, a symptom of schizophrenia. Once admitted to the hospital, however, they behaved normally. The experiences of these pseudopatients clearly reveal the effects of labeling.

Doctors, nurses, and assistants treated them as schizophrenic patients. They interpreted the normal everyday behavior of the pseudopatients as manifestations of illness. An early arrival at the lunchroom, for example, was described as exhibiting "oral aggressive" behavior; a patient seen writing something was referred to as a "compulsive note-taker." Interestingly enough, none of the other patients believed the pseudopatients were insane; they assumed they were researchers or journalists. When at length the subjects were discharged from the hospital, it was as schizophrenics "in remission."

The findings support criminological labeling theory. Once the sane individuals were labeled schizophrenic, they were unable to eliminate the label by acting normally. Even when they supposedly had recovered, the label stayed with them in the form of "schizophrenia in remission," which implied that future episodes of the illness could be expected.[19]

Researchers have also looked at how labels affect people and groups with unconventional lifestyles, whether prohibited by law or not—

CRIMINOLOGICAL FOCUS
On Being Sane in Insane Places

Psychologist D. L. Rosenhan reported the results of an experiment in which sane volunteers were admitted to psychiatric hospitals after complaining that they had been hearing voices. Length of hospitalization for the volunteers, who stopped "hearing voices" and said they felt fine as soon as they were admitted, ranged from 7 to 52 days, with an average of 19 days. In this passage, Rosenhan describes how one patient was viewed:

As far as I can determine, diagnoses were in no way affected by the relative health of the circumstances of a pseudopatient's life. Rather, the reverse occurred: the perception of his circumstances was shaped entirely by the diagnosis. A clear example of such translation is found in the case of a pseudopatient who had had a close relationship with his mother but was rather remote from his father during his early childhood. During adolescence and beyond, however, his father became a close friend, while his relationship with his mother cooled. His present relationship with his wife was characteristically close and warm. Apart from occasional angry exchanges, friction was minimal. The children had rarely been spanked. Surely there is nothing especially pathological about such a history. Indeed, many readers may see a similar pattern in their own experiences, with no markedly deleterious consequences. Observe, however, how such a history was translated in the psychopathological context, this from the case summary prepared after the patient was discharged.

"This white 39-year-old male . . . manifests a long history of considerable ambivalence in close relationships, which begins in early childhood. A warm relationship with his mother cools during his adolescence. A distant relationship to his father is described as becoming very intense. Affective stability is absent. His attempts to control emotionality with his wife and children are punctuated by angry outbursts and, in the case of the children, spankings. And while he says that he has several good friends, one senses considerable ambivalence embedded in those relationships also. . . ."

The facts of the case were unintentionally distorted by the staff to achieve consistency with a popular theory of the dynamics of a schizophrenic reaction. Nothing of an ambivalent nature had been described in relations with parents, spouse, or friends. To the extent that ambivalence could be inferred, it was probably not greater than is found in all human relationships. It is true the pseudopatient's relationships with his parents changed over time, but in the ordinary context that would hardly be remarkable—indeed, it might very well be expected. Clearly, the meaning ascribed to his verbalizations (that is, ambivalence, affective instability) was determined by the diagnosis: schizophrenia. An entirely different meaning would have been ascribed if it were known that the man was "normal."

A psychiatric label has a life and an influence of its own. Once the impression has been formed that the patient is schizophrenic, the expectation is that he will continue to be schizophrenic. When a sufficient amount of time has passed, during which the patient has done nothing bizarre, he is considered to be in remission and available for discharge. But the label endures beyond discharge, with the unconfirmed expectation that he will behave as a schizophrenic again. Such labels, conferred by mental health professionals, are as influential on the patient as they are on his relatives and friends, and it should not surprise anyone that the diagnosis acts on all of them as a self-fulfilling prophecy. Eventually, the patient himself accepts the diagnosis, with all of its surplus meanings and expectations, and behaves accordingly.

Source: D. L. Rosenhan, "On Being Sane in Insane Places," Science, 179 (1973): 253–254.

Questions for Discussion
1. Hospital staff assumed the sane volunteers were schizophrenic, while 35 of 118 hospital patients in one experiment voiced their suspicions about the pseudopatients' insanity. What accounts for that difference in perception?
2. Have you ever been in a situation in which you felt you had been labeled unfairly or incorrectly and were suffering the consequences? Describe what happened.

"gays", "public drunks," "junkies," "strippers," "streetwalkers."[20] The results of research, no matter what the group, were largely in conformity: "once a _____ , always a _____." Labeling by adjudication may have lifelong consequences. Richard Schwartz and Jerome Skolnick, for example, found that employers were reluctant to hire anyone with a court record even though the person had been found not guilty.[21]

The criminologist Anthony Platt has investigated how certain individuals are singled out to receive labels. Focusing on the label "juvenile delinquent," he shows how the social reformers of the late nineteenth century helped create delinquency by establishing a special institution, the juvenile court, for the processing of troubled youths. The Chicago society women who lobbied for the establishment of juvenile courts may have had the best motives in trying to help immigrants' children who, by their standards, were out of control. But by getting the juvenile court established, they simply widened the net of state agencies empowered to label some children as deviant.

The state thus aggravated the official problem of juvenile delinquency, which until then had been a neighborhood nuisance handled by parents, neighbors, priests, the local grocer, or the police officer on the street. Juvenile delinquency, according to Platt, was invented. Through its labeling effect it contributed to its own growth.[22]

The criminologist William Chambliss also studied the question of the way labels are distributed. Consider the following description:

Eight promising young men [the Saints]—children of good, stable, white upper-middle-class families, active in school affairs, good pre-college students—were some of the most delinquent boys at Hanibal High School. . . . The Saints were constantly occupied with truancy, drinking, wild driving, petty theft and vandalism. Yet not one was officially arrested for any misdeed during the two years I observed them.

This record was particularly surprising in light of my observations during the same two years of another gang of Hanibal High School students, six lower-class white boys known as the Roughnecks. The Roughnecks were constantly in trouble with police and community even though their rate of delinquency was about equal with that of the Saints.[23]

What accounts for the different responses to these two groups of boys? According to Chambliss, the crucial factor is the social class of the boys, which determined the community's reaction to their activities. The Roughnecks were poor, outspoken, openly hostile to authority, and highly visible because they could not afford cars to get out of town. Their behavior was discovered, processed, and punished. The Saints, on the other hand, had reputations for being bright, they acted apologetic when authorities confronted them, they held school offices, they played on athletic teams, and they had cars to get them out of town so that their delinquent acts would not be noticed. Their behavior went undiscovered, unprocessed, and unpunished.

Up to this point, the contentions of labeling theorists and the evidence they present provide a persuasive argument for the validity of labeling theory. But despite supportive scientific evidence, labeling theory has been heavily criticized.

Evaluation: Labeling Theory

Critics ask: Why is it that individuals, knowing they might be labeled, get involved in socially disapproved behavior to begin with? Most labeled persons have indeed engaged in some act that is considered morally or legally wrong.[24] According to the sociologist Ronald Akers, the impression is sometimes given that people are passive actors in a process by which the bad system bestows a derogatory label, thereby declaring them unacceptable, or different, or untouchable.[25] Critics suggest that the labels may identify real behavior rather than create it. After all, many delinquents have in fact had a long history of deviant behavior, even though they have never been caught and stigmatized. These critics question the overly active role labeling theory has assigned to the community and its criminal justice system and the overly passive role it has assigned to offenders.

Some criminologists also question how labeling theory accounts for individuals who have gone through formal processing but do not continue deviant lifestyles. They suggest that punishment really does work as a deterrent.[26] The argument is that labeling theorists are so intent on the reaction to behavior that they completely neglect the fact that someone has defied the conventions of society.[27] The criminologist Charles Wellford reminds us that, by and large, offenders get into the hands of authorities because they have broken the law. Furthermore, the decisions made about them are heavily influenced by the seriousness of their offenses. He concludes:

> The assumption that labels are differentially distributed, and that differential labelling affects behavior, is not supported by the existing criminological research. In sum, one should conclude that to the degree that these assumptions can be taken to be basic to the labelling perspective, the perspective must be seriously questioned; and criminologists should be encouraged to explore other ways to conceptualize the causal process of the creation, perpetuation, and intensification of criminal and delinquent behavior.[28]

While most critics believe that labeling theorists put too much emphasis on the system, others of a more radical or Marxist persuasion believe that labeling theorists have not gone far enough. They claim that the labeling approach concentrates too heavily on "nuts, sluts, and perverts," the exotic varieties of deviants who capture public imagination, rather than on "the unethical, illegal and destructive actions of powerful individuals, groups, and institutions of our society."[29] We will look at this argument more closely in a moment.

Empirical evidence that substantiates the claims of labeling theory has been modest. All the same, the theory has been instrumental in calling attention to some important questions, particularly about the way defendants are processed through the criminal justice system. Labeling theorists have carried out important scientific investigations of that system which complement the search of mainstream criminologists for the causes of crime and delinquency.

Some of the criticism of labeling theory can best be countered by one of its own proponents. Howard Becker explains that labeling is intended not as a theory of causation but, rather, as a perspective, "a way of looking at a general area of human activity, which expands the traditional research to include the process of social control."[30] Labeling theory has provided this perspective; it has also spawned further inquiry into the causes of crime.

CONFLICT THEORY

Labeling theorists are as well aware as mainstream criminologists that some people make rules and some break them. Their primary concern is the consequences of making and enforcing rules. One group of scholars has carried this idea further by questioning the rule-making process itself. They claim that a struggle for power is a basic feature of human existence. It is by means of such power struggles that various interest groups manage to control lawmaking and law enforcement.[31] To understand the theoretical approach of these conflict theorists, we must go back to the traditional approach, which views crime and criminal justice as arising from communal consensus.

The Consensus Model

Sometimes (as we saw in Chapter 1) members of a society consider certain acts so threatening to community survival that they designate these acts as crimes. If the vast majority of a group's members share this view, the group has acted by consensus. This is the **consensus model** of criminal-law making. The model assumes that members of society by and large agree on what is right and wrong and that law is the codification of these agreed-upon social values. The law is a mechanism to settle disputes that arise when individuals stray too far from what the community considers acceptable.

In Durkheim's words, "We can . . . say that an act is criminal when it offends strong and defined states of the collective conscience."[32] Consensus theorists view society as a stable entity in which laws are created for the general good. The laws' function is to reconcile and to harmonize most of the interests that most members of a community cherish, with the least amount of sacrifice.[33]

Deviant acts not only are part of the normal functioning of society but in fact are necessary, because when the members of society unite against a deviant, they reaffirm their commitment to shared values. Durkheim captured this view:

> We have only to notice what happens, particularly in a small town, when some moral scandal has been committed. They stop each other on the street, they visit each other, they seek to come together to talk of the event and to wax indignant in common. From all the similar impressions which are exchanged, for all the temper that gets itself expressed, there emerges a unique temper, more or less determinate according to the circumstances, which is everybody's without being anybody's in particular. That is the public temper.[34]

Societies in which citizens agree on right and wrong and the occasional deviant serves a useful purpose are scarce today. It could be found among primitive peoples at the very beginning of social evolution. By and large, consensus theory recognizes that not everyone can agree on what is best for society. Yet consensus theory holds that conflicting interests can be reconciled by means of law.[35]

The Conflict Model

With this view of the consensus model, we can understand and evaluate the arguments of the conflict theorists. In the 1960s, while labeling theorists were questioning why some people were designated as criminals, another group of scholars began to ask who in society has the power to make and enforce the laws. Conflict theory, already well established in the field of sociology, thus became popular as an explanation of crime and justice as well.

Like labeling theory, **conflict theory** has its roots in rebellion and the questioning of values. But while labeling theorists and traditional criminologists focused on the crime and the criminal, including the labeling of the criminal by the system, conflict theorists questioned the system itself. The clash between traditional and labeling theorists, on the one hand, and conflict theorists, on the other, became ideological.

Conflict theorists asked: If people agree on the value system, as consensus theorists suggest, why are so many people in rebellion, why are there so many crimes, so many punitive threats, so many people in prison? Clearly conflict is found everywhere in the world, between one country and another, between gay rights and antigay groups, between people who view abortion as a right and others who view it as murder, between suspects and police, between family members, between neighbors. If the criminal law supports the collective communal interest, why do so many people deviate from it?

Conflict theorists answered that, contrary to consensus theory, laws do not exist for the collective good; they represent the interests of specific groups that have the power to get them enacted.[36] The key concept in conflict theory is power. The people who have political control in any given society are the ones who are able to make things happen. They have power. Conflict theory holds that the people who possess the power work to keep the powerless at a disadvantage. The laws thus have their origin in the interests of the few; these few shape the values, and the values, in turn, shape the laws.[37]

It follows that the person who is defined as criminal and the behavior that is defined as crime at any given time and place mirror the society's power relationships. The definitions are subject to change as other interests gain power. The changing of definitions can be seen in those acts we now designate as "victimless" crimes. Possession of marijuana, prostitution, gambling, refusing to join the armed forces—all have been legal at some times, illegal at others. We may ask, then, whether any of these acts is inherently evil. The conflict theorist would answer that all are *made* evil when they are so designated by those in power and thus defined as crimes in legal codes.

The legal status of victimless crimes is subject to change. But what about murder, a crime considered evil in all contemporary societies? Many conflict theorists would respond that the definition of murder as a criminal offense is also rooted in the effort of some groups to guard their power.

AT ISSUE
The Rights of the Poorest

The poorest and least powerful have had little influence on the making of laws and on society's reaction to the breaking of laws. Somehow, the poorest have to survive in a society on which they have no apparent impact. In recent years court cases in New York have served as the battleground over what for some is a basic question of survival: Do the poor have a constitutional right to beg?

Yes-No-Yes: Court Rulings
Yes, said New York federal district court judge Leonard Sand in January 1990,(1) they have a right to panhandle in subway cars. His ruling was overturned by the federal court of appeals in May of the same year, thus denying citizens the right to beg in the New York City subway system.(2) In 1993, when the question concerned the rights of the poor to beg in city streets and public parks, a federal court of appeals decided in favor of the poor.(3)

What did the justices consider in their efforts to decide whether

beggars are criminals? Sand's novel ruling stated that panhandling is a form of free speech protected by the First Amendment. "A true test of one's commitment to constitutional principles," he wrote, "is the extent to which recognition is given to the rights of those in our midst who are the least affluent, least powerful and least welcome."(1) The case he decided grew out of attempts by the Metropolitan Transit Authority (MTA) to crack down on panhandling in New York City subway cars and stations. The Legal Action Center for the Homeless had filed a class action against the MTA on behalf of homeless panhandlers.

The court of appeals, in reversing the decision of the district court, criticized the lower court for overlooking the concerns of the MTA's millions of riders. It said that "whether intended as so, or not, begging in the subway often amounts to nothing less than assault, creating in the passengers the apprehension of imminent danger."(2)

Critical Commentary
Judge Sand's ruling created a spate of mostly virulent comments focusing on the judiciary's right to rule on the conduct of those dispossessed of power. One critic, Jill Adler, responded to these attacks:

> Judges as the ultimate guardians and interpreters of the Constitution have been charged with the duty of insuring that its fundamental guarantees such as freedom of speech and assembly are not abridged by the government. In this capacity they may sometimes be required to make unpopular decisions.
>
> It is at least arguable that panhandling or begging is a form of symbolic speech—if only because it may be the only avenue of expression open to those society has shunned. Time, place, and manner restrictions, while undoubtedly an important protection for the community, can also be a convenient means of ignoring constitutional guarantees. They will not, however, make the homeless disappear.(4)

A decision by the U.S. Supreme Court is to be expected.

Sources
1. 729 F. Supp. 341 (S.D.N.Y. 1991).
2. 903 F. 2d 146 (2d Cir. 1990).
3. Docket No. 92-9127, United States Court of Appeals for the Second Circuit, July 29, 1993.
4. Andrea Sachs, *Time,* Feb. 12, 1990, p. 55; Jill Adler, *International Herald Tribune,* Feb. 15, 1990, p. 9.

Questions for Discussion
1. Begging has been regulated throughout history in the United States, and some 25 states currently have statutes that limit or ban begging. What do you suppose the U.S. Supreme Court will do to these statutes?
2. Do you agree that subway begging should be viewed as different from begging on the street?

Woman carrying baby, begging on the New York subway.

Three-card monte: Illegal on New York's Fifth Avenue, but legitimate if played in a licensed casino in Atlantic City or Las Vegas.

A political terrorist may very well become a national hero.

Conflict theorists emphasize the relativity of norms to time and place: capital punishment is legal in some states, outlawed in others; alcohol consumption is illegal in Saudi Arabia but not in the United States. Powerful groups maintain their interests by making illegal any behavior that might be a threat to them. Laws thus become a mechanism of control, or "a weapon in social conflict."[38]

Conflict Theory and Criminology

The sociologist George Vold (1896–1967) was the first theorist to relate conflict theory to criminology. He argued that individuals band together in groups because they are social animals with needs that are best served through collective action. If the group serves its members, it survives; if not, new groups form to take its place. Individuals constantly clash as they try to advance the interests of their particular group over those of all the others. The result is that society is in a constant state of conflict, "one of the principal and essential social processes upon which the continuing ongoing of society depends." For Vold, the entire process of lawmaking and crime control is a direct reflection of conflict between interest groups, all trying to get laws passed in their favor and to gain control of the police power.[39]

The sociologist Ralf Dahrendorf and the criminologist Austin Turk are major contemporary contributors to the application of conflict theory to criminology. To Dahrendorf, the consensus model of society is utopian. He believes that enforced constraint, rather than cooperation, binds people together. Whether society is capitalist, socialist, or feudal, some people have the authority and others are subject to it. Society is made up of a large number of interest groups. The interests of one group do not always coincide with the needs of another—unions and management, for instance.

Dahrendorf argues that social change is constant, social conflicts are ever-present, disintegration and change are ongoing, and all societies are characterized by coercion of some people by others. The most important characteristics of class, he contends, are power and authority. The inequities remain for him the lasting determinant of social conflict. Conflict can be either destructive or constructive, depending on whether it leads to a breakdown of the social structure or to positive change in the social order.[40]

Austin Turk has continued and expanded this theoretical approach. "Criminality is not a biological, psychological, or even behavioral phenomenon," he says, "but a social status defined by the way in which an individual is perceived, evaluated, and treated by legal authorities." Criminal status is defined by those he calls the "authorities," the decision makers. Criminal status is imposed on the "subjects," the subordinate class. Turk explains that this process works so that both authorities and subjects learn to interact as performers in their dominant and submissive roles. There are "social norms of dominance" and "social norms of deference." Conflict arises when some people refuse to go along and they challenge the authorities. "Law breaking, then, becomes a measure of the stability of the ruler/ruled relationship."[41] The people who make the laws struggle to hold on to their power, while those who do not make laws struggle to do so.

People with authority use several forms of power to control society's goods and services:

police or war power, economic power, political power, and ideological power (beliefs, values).[42] The laws made by the "ins" to condemn or condone various behaviors help shape all social institutions—indeed, the entire culture. Where education is mandatory, for example, the people in power are able to maintain the status quo by passing on their own value system from one generation to the next.[43]

History seems to demonstrate that primitive societies, in their earliest phases of development, tend to be homogeneous and to make laws by consensus. The more a society develops economically and politically, the more difficult it becomes to resolve conflict situations by consensus. For an early instance of criminal lawmaking by the conflict model, we can go back to 1530, when King Henry VIII of England broke away from the Roman Catholic church because the pope refused to annul his marriage to Catherine of Aragon so that he could marry Anne Boleyn. Henry confiscated church property and closed all the monasteries. Virtually overnight, tens of thousands of people who had been dependent on the monasteries for support were cast out, to roam the countryside in search of a living. Most ended up as beggars. This huge army of vagrants posed a burden on and danger to the establishment. To cope with the problem, Parliament revived the vagrancy laws of 1349, which prohibited the giving of aid to vagrants and beggars. Thus the powerful, by controlling the laws, gained control over the powerless.[44]

Empirical Evidence for the Conflict Model

Researchers have tested several conflict theory hypotheses, such as those pertaining to bias and discrimination in the criminal justice system, differential crime rates of powerful and powerless groups, and the intent behind the development of the criminal law. The findings offer mixed support for the theory.

Alan Lizotte studied 816 criminal cases in the Chicago courts over a 1-year period to test the assumption that the powerless get harsher sentences. His analysis relating legal factors (such as the offense committed) and extralegal factors (such as the race and job of the defendant) to length of prison sentence pointed to significant sentencing inequalities related to race and occupation.[45] When Freda Adler studied the importance of nonlegal factors in the decision making of juries, she found that the socioeconomic level of the defendants significantly influenced their judgment.[46]

While these and similar studies tend to support conflict theory by demonstrating class or racial bias in the administration of criminal justice, others, unexpectedly, show an opposite bias.[47] When we evaluate the contribution of conflict theory to criminological thought, we must keep in mind Austin Turk's warning that conflict theory is often misunderstood. The theory does not, he points out, suggest that most criminals are innocent or that powerful persons engage in the same amount of deviant behavior or that law enforcers typically discriminate against people without power. It does acknowledge, however, that behaviors common among society's more disadvantaged members have a greater likelihood of being called "crime" than the activities in which the more powerful typically participate.[48]

Conflict theory does not attempt to explain crime; it simply identifies social conflict as a basic fact of life and as a source of discriminatory treatment by the criminal justice system of groups and classes that lack the power and status of those who make and enforce the laws. Once we recognize this, we may find it possible to change the process of criminalizing people, to provide greater justice. Conflict theorists anticipate a guided evolution, not a revolution, to improve the existing criminal justice system.

RADICAL THEORY

While labeling and conflict theorists were developing their perspectives, social and political conditions in the United States and Europe were changing rapidly and drastically. The youth of America were deeply disillusioned about a political and social structure that had brought about the assassinations of John F. Kennedy, Robert Kennedy, and Martin Luther King, Jr., the war in Vietnam, and the Watergate debacle. Many looked for radical solutions to social problems, and a number of young criminologists searched for radical answers to the nation's questions about crime and criminal justice. They found their answers in Marxism, a philosophy born in similar social turmoil a century earlier.

The Intellectual Heritage of Marxist Criminology

The major industrial centers of Europe suffered great hardships during the nineteenth century. The mechanization of industry and of agriculture, heavy population increases, and high rates of urbanization had created a massive labor surplus, high unemployment, and a burgeoning class of young urban migrants forced into the streets by poverty. London is said to have had at least 20,000 individuals who "rose every morning without knowing how they were to be supported through the day or where they were to lodge on the succeeding night, and cases of death from starvation appeared in the coroner's lists daily."[49] In other cities conditions were even worse.

Engels and Marx

It was against this background that Friedrich Engels (1820–1895) addressed the effects of the Industrial Revolution. A partner in his father's industrial empire, Engels was himself a member of the class he attacked as "brutally selfish." After a 2-year stay in England, he documented the awful social conditions, the suffering, and the great increase in crime and arrests. All these problems he blamed on one factor—competition. In *The Condition of the Working Class in England*, published in 1845, he spelled out the association between crime and poverty as a political problem:

> The earliest, crudest, and least fruitful form of this rebellion was that of crime. The working man lived in poverty and want, and saw that others were better off than he. . . . Want conquered his inherited respect for the sacredness of property, and he stole.[50]

Though Karl Marx (1818–1883) paid little attention to crime specifically, he argued that all

Young boys working at midnight in an Indiana glassworks, 1908. At one time, children formed one-third of the industrial labor force in the United States.

aspects of social life, including laws, are determined by economic organization. His philosophy reflects the economic despair that followed the Industrial Revolution. In his *Communist Manifesto* (1848) Marx viewed the history of all societies as a documentation of class struggles: "Freeman and slave, patrician and plebeian, lord and serf, guildmaster and journeyman, in a word, oppressor and oppressed, stood in constant opposition to one another."[51]

Marx went on to describe the most important relationship in industrial society as that between the capitalist bourgeoisie, who own the means of production, and the proletariat, or workers, who labor for them. Society, according to Marx, has always been organized in such a hierarchical fashion, with the state representing not the common interest but the interests of those who own the means of production. Capitalism breeds egocentricity, greed, and predatory behavior; but the worst crime of all is the exploitation of workers. Revolution, Marx concluded, is the only means to bring about change, and for that reason it is morally justifiable.

Many philosophers before Marx had noted the link between economic conditions and social problems, including crime. Among them were Plato, Aristotle, Virgil, Horace, Sir Thomas More, Cesare Beccaria, Jeremy Bentham, André Guerry, Adolphe Quételet, and Gabriel Tarde (several of whom we met in Chapter 3). But none of them had advocated revolutionary change. And none had constructed a coherent criminological theory that conformed with economic determinism, the cornerstone of the Marxist explanation that people who are kept in a state of poverty will rebel by committing crimes. Not until 1905 can we speak of Marxist criminology.

Willem Adriaan Bonger

As a student at the University of Amsterdam, Willem Adriaan Bonger (1876–1940) entered a paper in a competition on the influence of economic factors on crime. His entry did not win; but its expanded version, *Criminality and Economic Conditions,* which appeared in French in 1905, was selected for translation by the American Institute of Criminal Law and Criminology. Bonger wrote in his preface, "[I am] convinced that my ideas about the etiology of crime will not be shared by a great many readers of the American edition."[52] He was right. Nevertheless, the book is considered a classic and is invaluable to students doing research on crime and economics.

Bonger explained that the social environment of primitive people was interwoven with the means of production. People helped each other. They used what they produced. When food was plentiful, everyone ate. When food was scarce, everyone was hungry. Whatever they had, they shared. People were subordinate to nature. In a modern capitalist society, people are much less altruistic. They concentrate on production for profit rather than for the needs of the community. Capitalism encourages criminal behavior by creating a climate that is less conducive to social responsibility. "We have a right," argued Bonger, "to say that the part played by economic conditions in criminality is predominant, even decisive."[53]

Willem Bonger died as he had lived, a fervent antagonist of the evils of the social order. An archenemy of Nazism and a prominent name on Hitler's list of people to be eliminated, he refused to emigrate even when the German army was at the border. On May 10, 1940, as the German invasion of Holland began, he wrote to his son: "I don't see any future for myself and I cannot bow to this scum which will now overmaster us."[54] He then took his own life. He left a powerful political and criminological legacy. Foremost among his followers were German socialist philosophers of the progressive school of Frankfurt.

Georg Rusche and Otto Kirchheimer

Georg Rusche and Otto Kirchheimer began to write their classic work at the University of Frankfurt. Driven out of Germany by Nazi persecution, they continued their search in exile in Paris and completed it at Columbia University in New York in 1939. In *Punishment and the Social Structure* they wrote that punishments had always been related to the modes of production and the availability of labor, rather than to the nature of the crimes themselves.

Consider galley slavery. Before the development of modern sailing techniques, oarsmen were needed to power merchant ships; as a result, galley slavery was a punishment in antiquity and in the Middle Ages. As sailing techniques were perfected, galley slavery was no longer necessary, and it lost favor as a sanction. By documenting the real purposes of punishments through the ages, Rusche and Kirchheimer made **penologists,** who study the penal system, aware that severe and cruel treatment of offenders had more to do with the value of human life and the needs of the economy than with preventing crime.

The names Marx, Engels, Bonger, and Rusche and Kirchheimer were all but forgotten by mainstream criminologists of the 1940s and 1950s, perhaps because of America's relative prosperity and conservatism during those years. But when tranquility turned to turmoil in the mid-1960s, the forgotten names provided the intellectual basis for American and European radical criminologists, who explicitly stated their commitment to Marxism.

Radical Criminology from the 1970s to the 1990s

Radical criminology (also called *critical, new,* and *Marxist criminology*) made its first public appearance in 1968, when a group of British sociologists organized the National Deviancy Conference (NDC), a group of more than 300 intellectuals, social critics, deviants, and activists of various persuasions. What the group members had in common was a basic disillusion with the criminological studies being done by the British Home Office, which they believed was system-serving and "practical." They were concerned with the way the system controlled people rather than with traditional sociological and psychological explanations of crime. They shared a respect for the interactionist and labeling theorists but believed these theorists had become too traditional. Their answer was to form a new criminology based on Marxist principles.

The conference was followed by the publication in 1973 of *The New Criminology*, the first textual formulation of the new radical criminology. According to its authors, Ian Taylor, Paul Walton, and Jock Young, it is the underclass, the "labor forces of the industrial society," that is controlled through the criminal law and its enforcement, while "the owners of labor will be bound only by a civil law which regulates their competition between each other." The economic institution, then, is the source of all conflicts. Struggles between classes always relate to the distribution of resources and power, and only when capitalism is abolished will crime disappear.[55]

About the time that Marxist criminology was being formulated in England, it was also developing in the United States, particularly at the School of Criminology of the University of California at Berkeley, where Richard Quinney, Anthony Platt, Herman and Julia Schwendinger, William Chambliss, and Paul Takagi were at the forefront of the movement. These researchers were also influenced by interactionist and labeling theorists, as well as by the conflict theories of Vold, Dahrendorf, and Turk.

Though the radical criminologists share the central tenet of conflict theory, that laws are created by the powerful to protect their own interests, they disagree on the number of forces competing in the power struggle. For Marxist criminologists, there is only one dominating segment, the capitalist ruling class, which uses the criminal law to impose its will on the rest of the

people in order to protect its property and to define as criminal any behavior that threatens the status quo.[56] The leading American spokesman for radical criminology is Richard Quinney. His earliest Marxist publications appeared in 1973: "Crime Control in Capitalist Society" and "There's a Lot of Us Folks Grateful to the Lone Ranger."[57]

The second of these essays describes how Quinney drifted away from capitalism, with its folklore myths embodied in individual heroes like the Lone Ranger. He asserts that

> [t]he state is organized to serve the interests of the dominant economic class, the capitalist ruling class; that criminal law is an instrument the state and the ruling class use to maintain and perpetuate the social and economic order; that the contradictions of advanced capitalism . . . require that the subordinate classes remain oppressed by whatever means necessary, especially by the legal system's coercion and violence; and that only with the collapse of capitalist society, based on socialist principles, will there be a solution to the crime problem.[58]

In *Class, State, and Crime*, Quinney proclaims that "the criminal justice movement is . . . a state-initiated and state-supported effort to rationalize mechanisms of social control. The larger purpose is to secure a capitalist order that is in grave crisis, likely in its final stage of development."[59] Quinney challenges criminologists to abandon traditional ways of thinking about causation, to study what could be rather than what is, to question the assumptions of the social order, and to "ultimately develop a Marxist perspective."[60]

Marxist theory also can be found in the writings of other scholars who have adopted the radical approach to criminology. William Chambliss and Robert Seidman present their version in *Law, Order, and Power*:

> Society is composed of groups that are in conflict with one another and . . . the law represents an institutionalized tool of those in power (ruling class) which functions to provide them with superior moral as well as coercive power in conflict.[61]

They comment that if, in the operation of the criminal justice system by the powerful, "justice or fairness happen to be served, it is sheer coincidence."[62]

To Barry Krisberg, crime is a function of privilege. The rich create crimes to distract attention from the injustices they inflict on the masses. Power determines which group holds the privilege, defined by Krisberg as that which is valued by a given social group in a given historical time.[63] Herman and Julia Schwendinger warn that because of

> the inherent antagonisms built into the capitalist system, all laws generally contradict their stated purpose of producing justice. Legal relations maintain patterns of individualism and selfishness and in so doing perpetuate a class system characterized by anarchy, oppression, and crime.[64]

Anthony Platt, in a forceful attack on traditional criminology, has even suggested it would not be "too farfetched to characterize many criminologists as domestic war criminals" because they have "serviced domestic repression in the same way that economics, political science, and anthropology have greased the wheels and even manufactured some of the important parts of modern imperialism."[65]

He suggests that traditional criminology serves the state through research studies that purport to "investigate" the conditions of the lower class but in reality only prove, with their probes of family life, education, jobs, and so on, that the members of the lower class are in fact less intelligent and more criminal than the rest of us. Platt claims that these inquiries, based as they are on biased and inaccurate data, are merely tools of the middle-class oppressors.

A number of other areas have come under the scrutiny of Marxist criminologists.[66] They have studied how informal means of settling disputes outside courts actually extend the control of the criminal justice system by adjudicating cases that are not serious enough for the courts; how juvenile court dispositions are unfairly based on social class; how sentencing reform has failed to benefit the lower class; how police practices during the latter half of the nineteenth century were geared to control labor rather than crime; how rape victims are made to feel guilty; how penitentiary reform has benefited the ruling class by giving it more control over the lower class; and how capitalist interests are strengthened by private policing.[67]

Evaluation: Marxist Criminological Theory

Critiques of Marxist criminology range from support for the attention the approach calls to the crimes of the powerful to accusations that it is nothing more than a revival of the Robin Hood myth, in which the poor steal from the rich in order to survive.[68] By far the most incisive criticism is that of the sociologist Carl Klockars, who points out that the division of society into social classes may have a beneficial effect, contrary to Marxist thought. Standards, he argues, are created by some people to inspire the remainder of society. In present-day America, Klockars claims, poverty has lost some of its meaning because luxuries and benefits are spread out over classes. To him, ownership and control of industry are two different things. Anyone who buys a share of stock, for example, can be an owner, while control is handled by bureaucrats who may or may not be owners.[69]

Class Interests versus Interest Groups

Klockars attacks Marxists for focusing exclusively on class interests and ignoring the fact that society is made up of many interest groups. This Marxist bias has yielded results that are untrustworthy and predictable, ignore reality, explain issues that are self-evident (some businesspeople are greedy and corrupt), and do not explain issues that are relevant (why socialist states have crime).[70]

Not without a note of sympathy, Richard Sparks summed up the criticism when he said:

> Marxist criminologists tend to be committed to praxis and the desire for radical social reform; but this commitment is not entailed by the scientific claims which Marxists make, and it has sometimes led to those claims being improperly suspect.[71]

Opposition to the new criminology follows many paths, but the most popular, in one way or another, is concerned with its oversimplification of causation by the exclusive focus on capitalism.[72] Critics also attack Marxist criminologists for their assertion that even by studying crime empirically, criminologists are supporting the status quo. That puts Marxist criminologists on the defensive, because if they are not ideologi-

WINDOW TO THE WORLD
Criminal Law in an Age of Ethnic Diversity

There is hardly a region in the world that is free from ethnic conflict. We live in an age of ethnicity and of a drive, often by force of arms, to break nation-states up into ethnic states. What does this have to do with criminal law? A great deal.

It has been the practice of nation-states to adopt a single penal code that governs everyone, regardless of ethnic group. But such a policy can lead to problems for law enforcement and criminal justice: a penal code written and imposed by a distant "central authority" that is itself of one particular ethnic group may not be effective with another group far from the seat of government. Everywhere in the world, ethnic groups are fighting for greater autonomy; they want to be governed by laws of their own making, compatible with their own customs and traditions.

The Case of the Former Soviet Union

The dissolution of the Soviet Union provides a good example of the importance of ethnicity in the formulation of criminal law. On January 1, 1992, the once-mighty Soviet Union ceased to exist as a nation. It had been the largest country in the world—two and a half times the size of the United States—with nearly 300 million people of over 100 nationalities. The three Baltic nations, Lithuania, Latvia, and Estonia, annexed by the Soviet Union in 1939, regained their independence in 1991. All the other former Soviet republics followed suit, although nine republics have joined in a loose-knit federation.

To some extent, the central authorities of the Soviet Union had made allowances for ethnic diversity. The Soviet Penal Code of 1953 imposed only its General Part on the entire U.S.S.R., with its Special Part, which defined the various crimes and punishments, reserved for variations among the republics. (1)

Vice Becomes Virtue

What happens now that the various republics are independent? The three Baltic states, whose populations are not Slavic, are in the process of resurrecting their pre-1939 national penal codes. The predominantly Islamic republics (Kazakhstan, Uzbekistan, Turkmenistan, and Kyrgyzstan) had long been unhappy with a Russian-inspired penal code and are now searching for something more compatible with their traditions. The countries with predominantly Christian traditions, including Belarus, Ukraine, Moldova, Georgia, and Armenia, also want to shed the Russian imprint. And Russia itself is rapidly discarding the Soviet features of its penal code. For example, a law of 1961 made it criminal for persons to "avoid socially useful work, derive unearned income from the exploitation of land plots, automobiles, or housing, or commit other anti-social acts which enable them to lead a parasitic way of life."(2) What was a vice and a crime has now become a virtue: today people are encouraged to exploit land plots, automobiles, or housing and to derive "unearned income" from investments.

Penal codes, to be respected, must conform to the cultural norms of a society; otherwise, the people addressed will not comply readily, and the police and courts will have a difficult time enforcing the codes.

Sources
1. Harold J. Berman and James W. Spindler, *Soviet Criminal Law and Procedure* (Cambridge, Mass.: Harvard University Press, 1966), pp. 15–16.
2. Edict of the Presidium of the Supreme Soviet of the RSFSR of May 4, 1961, as quoted in Berman and Spindler, p. 9.

Questions for Discussion
1. Some crimes, like murder, robbery, or arson, seem to be so universal that they should be included in all penal codes. Right or wrong?
2. What makes for the severity of the various crimes defined in a penal code? Is there agreement on severity within a country or between countries?

Russians toppled the statue of Felix Derzhinsky, founder of the KGB, in a Moscow square and replaced it with a monument to those tortured and killed by the KGB.

cally in a position to expose their theories to empirical research or are unwilling to do so, their assertions will remain just that—assertions with no proof.[73]

Radical Feminist Theory

One significant limitation to critical and Marxist work is an almost exclusive focus on crime committed by males. This limitation has been addressed only recently by both radical and socialist (Marxist) feminists. The former find the cause of crime in women to be male aggression, as well as men's attempts to control and subordinate women. The latter view female crime in terms of class, gender, and race oppression.[74]

Research by both radical and socialist feminists has revealed important insights into our conceptualization of law, social control, power relationships, and crime-causation theory. They include:

- Reframing the way in which rape is conceptualized (see Chapter 13)
- Acknowledging the fact that the way in which criminologists conceive of and define violence is male-centered
- Uncovering the relationship between male power, female economic dependency, and battery (for example, spouse abuse)
- Revealing the powerful effect of gender on justice processing[75]

Collapse of the Economic Order

Even sharper criticism of Marxist theory can be anticipated in the wake of the collapse of the Marxist economic order in the Soviet Union, Poland, Czechoslovakia, Hungary, the German Democratic Republic, Bulgaria, Albania, and Romania, as well as in countries in Africa and Latin America.[76] Many East European criminologists are no longer quoting Marx in their publications, which tend increasingly to focus on the classical rule-of-law concept. But Quinney has never seen the conditions in those countries as representative of Marxism. According to him, a true Marxist state has not yet been attained, but the ideal is worth pursuing.[77]

To the credit of radical criminologists, it must be said that they have encouraged their more traditional colleagues to look with a critical eye at all aspects of the criminal justice system, including the response of the system to both poor and rich offenders. Their concern is the exercise of power. They ask: Whose power? On whose behalf? For whose benefit? What is the legitimacy of that power? And who is excluded from the exercise of power, by whom, and why? Criminologists have had to address all these questions. Many may not have changed their answers, but the fact that the questions have been raised has ensured clearer answers than had been offered before.[78]

■ REVIEW

Labeling theory, conflict theory, and radical theory offer alternative explanations of crime, in the sense that they do not restrict their inquiry to individual characteristics or to social or communal processes. These three theories examine the impact of lawmaking and law enforcement processes on the creation of offenders. The labeling and conflict theories, as critical as they are of the existing system of criminal justice, envisage a system made more just and equitable by reform and democratic processes; radical theory demands revolutionary change. With long historical antecedents, all three theories gained prominence in the 1960s and early 1970s, during an era of rebellion against social, political, and economic inequities.

Labeling theory does not presume to explain all crime, but it does demonstrate that the criminal justice system is selective in determining who is to be labeled a criminal. It explains how labeling occurs, and it blames the criminal justice system for contributing to the labeling process and, therefore, to the crime problem.

Conflict theory goes a step beyond labeling theory in identifying the forces that selectively decide in the first place what conduct should be singled out for condemnation—usually, so it is claimed, to the detriment of the powerless and the benefit of the powerful.

Radical theory singles out the relationship between the owners of the means of production and the workers under capitalism as the root cause of crime and of all social inequities. Radical theory demands the overthrow of the existing order, which is said to perpetuate criminality by keeping the oppressed classes under the domination of the capitalist ruling class.

All three theories have adherents and opponents. Research to demonstrate their validity has produced mixed results. More important, all these theories have challenged conventional criminologists to rethink their approaches and to provide answers to questions that had not been asked before.

■ NOTES

1. Howard S. Becker, *Outsiders: Studies in the Sociology of Deviance* (New York: Macmillan, 1963), p. 9.
2. For an excellent discussion of how society controls deviance, see Nicholas N. Kittrie, *The Right to Be Different* (Baltimore: Johns Hopkins University Press, 1972).
3. William I. Thomas, *The Unadjusted Girl* (1923; New York: Harper & Row, 1967).
4. George Herbert Mead, "The Psychology of Punitive Justice," *American Journal of Sociology*, **23** (1918): 577–602. See also Charles Horton Cooley, "The Roots of Social Knowledge," *American Journal of Sociology*, **32** (1926): 59–79.
5. Herbert Blumer, "Sociological Implications of the Thought of George Herbert Mead," in *Symbolic Interactionism*, ed. Blumer (Englewood Cliffs, N.J.: Prentice-Hall, 1969), pp. 62, 65, 66.
6. Frank Tannenbaum, *Crime and the Community* (Boston: Ginn, 1938), p. 27.
7. Edwin M. Lemert, *Social Pathology* (New York: McGraw-Hill, 1951).
8. Edwin M. Lemert, *Human Deviance, Social Problems, and Social Control* (Englewood Cliffs, N.J.: Prentice-Hall, 1967), chap. 3.
9. Lemert, *Social Pathology*, pp. 75–76.
10. Lemert, *Human Deviance*, p. 46. See also Albert K. Cohen, *Deviance and Control* (Englewood Cliffs, N.J.: Prentice-Hall, 1966), pp. 24–25.
11. Erving Goffman, *Stigma: Notes on the Management of Spoiled Identity* (Englewood Cliffs, N.J.: Prentice-Hall, 1963).
12. Gerhard O. W. Mueller, "Resocialization of the Young Adult Offender in Switzerland," *Journal of Criminal Law and Criminology*, **43** (1953): 578–591, at p. 584. At the time that Lemert was developing the principles of labeling theory in the United States, Swiss correctional administrators already fully comprehended the significance of labeling. Convicts were "considered as being afflicted with the self conception of being criminal or wayward by either their own imagination . . . or the acceptance of the repeated judgment of others tendered on them."
13. Kai T. Erikson, "Notes on the Sociology of Deviance," in *The Other Side: Perspectives on Deviance*, ed. Howard S. Becker (New York: Free Press, 1964), p. 11.
14. Edwin Schur, *Labeling Deviant Behavior* (New York: Harper & Row, 1971), p. 21.
15. Edwin M. Schur, *Crimes without Victims* (Englewood Cliffs, N.J.: Prentice-Hall, 1965).
16. M. Ray, "The Cycle of Abstinence and Relapse among Heroin Addicts," *Social Problems*, **9** (1961): 132–140.
17. David Matza, *Becoming Deviant* (Englewood Cliffs, N.J.: Prentice-Hall, 1969), pp. 44–53.
18. Becker, *Outsiders*, pp. 18, 20.
19. D. L. Rosenhan, "On Being Sane in Insane Places," *Science*, **179** (1973): 250–258. See also Bruce G. Link, "Understanding Labeling Effects in the Area of Mental Disorders: An Assessment of the Effects of Expectations of Rejection," *American Sociological Review*, **52** (1987): 96–112; and Anthony Walsh, "Twice Labeled: The Effect of Psychiatric Labeling on the Sentencing of Sex Offenders," *Social Problems*, **37** (1990): 375–389.
20. Carol Warren and John Johnson, "A Critique of Labeling Theory from the Phenomenological Perspective," in *Theoretical Perspectives on Deviance*, ed. J. D. Douglas and R. Scott (New York: Basic Books, 1973), p. 77; James P. Spradley, *You Owe Yourself a Drunk: An Ethnography of Urban Nomads* (Boston: Little, Brown, 1979), p. 254; M. Ray, "The Cycle of Abstinence"; M. Salutin, "Stripper Morality," *Transaction*, **9** (June 1971): 12–27; Bernard Cohen, *Deviant Street Networks: Prostitution in New York City* (Lexington, Mass.: Lexington Books, 1980). For a recent extension of labeling theory to white-collar criminality, see Doreen McBarnet, "Whiter than White Collar Crime: Tax, Fraud Insurance and the Management of Stigma," *British Journal of Sociology*, **42** (1991): 323–344.
21. Richard D. Schwartz and Jerome H. Skolnick, "Two Studies of Legal Stigma," *Social Problems*, **10** (1962): 133–138.
22. Anthony Platt, *The Child Savers* (Chicago: University of Chicago Press, 1969). For a further discussion of the effects of stigmatization by the criminal justice system, see Charles W. Thomas and Donna M. Bishop, "The Effect of Formal and Informal Sanctions on Delinquency: A Longitudinal Comparison of Labeling and Deterrence Theories," *Journal of Criminal Law and Criminology*, **75** (1984): 1222–1245. See also Anne Rankin Maloney, "The Effect of Labeling upon Youths in the Juvenile Justice System: A Review of the Evidence," *Law and Society Review*, **8** (1974): 583–614; Dennis B. Anderson and Donald F. Schoen, "Diversion Programs: Effects of Stigmatization on Juvenile/Status Offenders," *Juvenile and Family Court Journal*, **36** (Summer 1985): 13–25; Gordon Bazemore, "Delinquent Reform and the Labeling Perspective," *Criminal Justice and Behavior*, **12** (1985): 131–169; and Douglas A. Smith and Raymond Paternoster, "Formal Processing and Future Delinquency: Deviance Amplification as Selection Artifact," *Law and Society Review*, **24** (1990): 1109–1132.
23. William J. Chambliss, "The Saints and the Roughnecks," *Society*, **11** (1973): 24–31.

24. Walter R. Gove, "Deviant Behavior, Social Intervention, and Labeling Theory," in *The Uses of Controversy in Sociology*, ed. Lewis A. Coser and Otto N. Larsen (New York: Free Press, 1976), pp. 219–227; Ross L. Matsueda, "Reflected Appraisals, Parental Labeling, and Delinquency: Specifying a Symbolic Interactionist Theory," *American Journal of Sociology*, **97** (1992): 1577–1611.

25. Ronald L. Akers, "Problems in the Sociology of Deviance," *Social Forces*, **46** (1968): 455–465.

26. Ronald L. Akers, *Deviant Behavior: A Social Learning Approach*, 2d ed. (Belmont, Calif.: Wadsworth, 1977); David Ward and Charles R. Tittle, "Deterrence or Labeling: The Effects of Informal Sanctions," *Deviant Behavior*, **14** (1993): 43–64.

27. Jack P. Gibbs, "Conceptions of Deviant Behavior: The Old and the New," *Pacific Sociological Review*, **9** (Spring 1966): 9–14.

28. Charles Wellford, "Labelling Theory and Criminology: An Assessment," *Social Problems*, **22** (1975): 343; Charles F. Wellford and Ruth A. Triplett, "The Future of Labeling Theory: Foundations and Promises," in *Advances in Criminological Theory*, vol. 4, eds. Freda Adler and William S. Laufer (New Brunswick, N.J.: Transaction, 1993).

29. Alexander Liazos, "The Poverty of the Sociology of Deviance: Nuts, Sluts, and Perverts," *Social Problems*, **20** (1972): 103–120.

30. Howard S. Becker, "Labelling Theory Reconsidered," in *Outsiders: Studies in the Sociology of Deviance*, rev. ed., ed. Becker (New York: Free Press, 1973), pp. 177–208. See also Schur, *Labeling Deviant Behavior*, for an excellent review of labeling theory.

31. Compare this perspective with the emerging notion of criminology as peacemaking; see Harold E. Pepinsky and Richard Quinney, eds., *Criminology as Peace-Making* (Bloomington: University of Indiana Press, 1991).

32. Émile Durkheim, *The Division of Labor in Society* (New York: Free Press, 1947), p. 80.

33. Roscoe Pound, "A Survey of Social Interests," *Harvard Law Review*, **57** (1943): 1–39, at p. 39.

34. Durkheim, *The Division of Labor in Society*, p. 102.

35. Roscoe Pound, *An Introduction to the Philosophy of Law* (Boston: Little, Brown, 1922), p. 98.

36. Richard Quinney, *Crime and Justice in Society* (Boston: Little, Brown, 1969), pp. 26–30.

37. William Chambliss, "The State, the Law, and the Definition of Behavior as Criminal or Delinquent," in *Handbook of Criminology*, ed. Daniel Glaser (Chicago: Rand McNally, 1974), pp. 7–44.

38. Austin Turk, "Law as a Weapon in Social Conflict," *Social Problems*, **23** (1976): 276–291.

39. George Vold, *Theoretical Criminology* (New York: Oxford University Press, 1958), pp. 204, 209.

40. Ralf Dahrendorf, *Class and Class Conflict in Industrial Society* (Stanford, Calif.: Stanford University Press, 1959). See also Ralf Dahrendorf, "Out of Utopia: Toward a Reorientation of Sociological Analysis," *American Journal of Sociology*, **64** (1958): 127.

41. Austin Turk, *Criminality and Legal Order* (Chicago: Rand McNally, 1969), pp. 25, 33, 41–42, 48. See also Thomas O'Reilly-Fleming et al., "Issues in Social Order and Social Control," *Journal of Human Justice*, **2** (1990): 55–74.

42. Austin Turk, *Political Criminality: The Defiance and Defense of Authority* (Beverly Hills, Calif.: Sage, 1982), p. 15.

43. Turk, "Law as a Weapon."

44. William J. Chambliss, "A Sociological Analysis of the Law of Vagrancy," *Social Problems*, **12** (1966): 67–77. For an opposing view on the historical development of criminal law, see Jeffrey S. Adler, "A Historical Analysis of the Law of Vagrancy," *Criminology*, **27** (1989): 209–229; and a rejoinder to Adler: William J. Chambliss, "On Trashing Criminology," ibid., pp. 231–238.

45. Alan Lizotte, "Extra-Legal Factors in Chicago's Criminal Courts: Testing the Conflict Model of Criminal Justice," *Social Problems*, **25** (1978): 564–580. See also Kathleen Daly, "Neither Conflict nor Labeling nor Paternalism Will Suffice: Intersections of Race, Ethnicity, Gender, and Family in Criminal Court Decisions," *Crime and Delinquency*, **35** (1989): 136–168; and Elizabeth Comack, ed., "Race, Class, Gender and Justice," *Journal of Human Justice*, **2** (1990): 1–124.

46. Freda Adler, "Socioeconomic Variables Influencing Jury Verdicts," *New York University Review of Law on Social Change*, **3** (1973): 16–36. See also Martha A. Myers, "Social Background and the Sentencing Behavior of Judges," *Criminology*, **26** (1988): 649–675.

47. Celesta A. Albonetti, Robert M. Hauser, John Hagan, and Ilene H. Nagel, "Criminal Justice Decision-Making as a Stratification Process: The Role of Race and Stratification Resources in Pretrial Release," *Journal of Quantitative Criminology*, **5** (1989): 57–82. See also Theodore Chiricos and Gordon Waldo, "Socioeconomic Status and Criminal Sentencing: An Empirical Assessment of a Conflict Proposition," *American Sociological Review*, **40** (1975): 753–772. For a compilation of recent tests of the conflict model, see John Hagan, *Structural Criminology* (New Brunswick, N.J.: Rutgers University Press, 1989).

48. Austin Turk, "Law, Conflict, and Order: From Theorizing toward Theories," *Canadian Review of Sociology and Anthropology*, **13** (1976): 282–294.

49. Georg Rusche and Otto Kirchheimer, *Punishment and Social Structure* (New York: Columbia University Press, 1939), p. 93.

50. Friedrich Engels, "To the Working Class of Great Britain," Introduction to *The Condition of the Working Class in England* (1845), in Karl Marx and Friedrich Engels, *Collected Works*, vol. 4 (New York: International Publishers, 1974), pp. 213–214, 298.

51. Karl Marx and Friedrich Engels, *The Communist Manifesto* (1848; New York: International Publishers, 1979), p. 9.

52. Willem Adriaan Bonger, *Criminality and Economic Conditions*, trans. Henry P. Horton (Boston: Little, Brown, 1916).

53. Ibid., p. 669.

54. J. M. Van Bemmelen, "Willem Adriaan Bonger," in

Pioneers in Criminology, ed. Hermann Mannheim (London: Stevens, 1960), p. 361.

55. Ian Taylor, Paul Walton, and Jock Young, *The New Criminology: For a Social Theory of Deviance* (London: Routledge & Kegan Paul, 1973), pp. 264, 281. See also Jock Young, "Radical Criminology in Britain: The Emergence of a Competing Paradigm," *British Journal of Criminology,* **28** (1988): 159–183.

56. Gresham Sykes, "The Rise of Critical Criminology," *Journal of Criminal Law and Criminology,* **65** (1974): 206–213.

57. Richard Quinney, "Crime Control in Capitalist Society: A Critical Philosophy of Legal Order," *Issues in Criminology,* **8** (1973): 75–95; Richard Quinney, "There's a Lot of Us Folks Grateful to the Lone Ranger: Some Notes on the Rise and Fall of American Criminology," *Insurgent Sociologist,* **4** (1973): 56–64.

58. Richard Quinney, "Crime Control in Capitalist Society," in *Critical Criminology,* ed. Ian Taylor, Paul Walton, and Jock Young (London: Routledge & Kegan Paul, 1975), p. 199.

59. Richard Quinney, *Class, State, and Crime: On the Theory and Practice of Criminal Justice,* 2d ed. (New York: David McKay, 1977), p. 10.

60. Richard Quinney, *Critique of Legal Order: Crime Control in a Capitalist Society* (Boston: Little, Brown, 1974), pp. 11–13.

61. William Chambliss and Robert Seidman, *Law, Order, and Power* (Reading, Mass.: Addison-Wesley, 1971), p. 503.

62. Ibid., p. 504.

63. Barry Krisberg, *Crime and Privilege: Toward a New Criminology* (Englewood Cliffs, N.J.: Prentice-Hall, 1975).

64. Herman Schwendinger and Julia Schwendinger, "Delinquency and Social Reform: A Radical Perspective," in *Juvenile Justice,* ed. Lamar Empey (Charlottesville: University of Virginia Press, 1979), pp. 246–290.

65. Elliot Currie, "A Dialogue with Anthony M. Platt," *Issues in Criminology,* **8** (1973): 28.

66. Steven F. Messner and Marvin D. Krohn, "Class, Compliance Structures, and Delinquency: Assessing Integrated Structural-Marxist Theory," *American Journal of Sociology,* **96** (1990): 300–328.

67. Lance H. Selva and Robert M. Bohm, "A Critical Examination of the Informalism Experiment in the Administration of Justice," *Crime and Social Justice,* **29** (1987): 43–57; Timothy Carter and Donald Clelland, "A Neo-Marxian Critique, Formulation, and Test of Juvenile Dispositions as a Function of Social Class," *Social Problems,* **27** (1979): 96–108; David Greenberg and Drew Humphries, "The Co-optation of Fixed Sentencing Reform," *Crime and Delinquency,* **26** (1980): 216–225; Sidney L. Harring and Lorraine M. McMullen, "The Buffalo Police, 1897–1900: Labor Unrest, Political Power, and the Creation of the Police Institution," *Crime and Social Justice,* **4** (1975): 5–14; Herman Schwendinger and Julia Schwendinger, "Rape Victims and the False Sense of Guilt," *Crime and Social Justice,* **13** (1980): 4–17; Paul

Takagi, "The Walnut Street Jail: A Penal Reform to Centralize the Powers of the State," *Federal Probation,* **39** (1975): 18–26; Steven Spitzer and Andrew T. Scull, "Privatization and Capitalist Development: The Case of the Private Police," *Social Problems,* **25** (1977): 18–29. See, e.g., ed. Ezzat A. Fattah *Towards a Critical Victimology* (New York: St. Martin's Press, 1992).

68. Jackson Toby, "The New Criminology Is the Old Sentimentality," *Criminology,* **16** (1979): 516–526; Jim Thomas and Aogan O'Maolchatha, "Reassessing the Critical Metaphor: An Optimistic Revisionist View," *Justice Quarterly,* **6** (1989): 143–171; David Brown and Russell Hogg, "Essentialism, Radical Criminology and Left Realism," *Australian and New Zealand Journal of Criminology,* **25** (1992): 195–230; Stuart Henry and Dragan Milovanovic, "Constitutive Criminology: The Maturation of Critical Theory," *Criminology,* **29** (1991): 293–315; Brian MacLean et al., "Critical Criminology in Canada," *Journal of Human Justice,* **1** (1989): 1–112.

69. Carl B. Klockars, "The Contemporary Crises of Marxist Criminology," *Criminology,* **16** (1979): 477–515.

70. Ibid.

71. Richard F. Sparks, "A Critique of Marxist Criminology," in *Crime and Justice: An Annual Review of Research,* ed. Norval Morris and Michael Tonry (Chicago: University of Chicago Press, 1980), p. 159.

72. Milton Mankoff, "On the Responsibility of Marxist Criminology: A Reply to Quinney," *Contemporary Crisis,* **2** (1978): 293–301.

73. Austin T. Turk, "Analyzing Official Deviance: For Nonpartisan Conflict Analysis in Criminology," in *Radical Criminology: The Coming Crisis,* ed. James A. Inciardi (Beverly Hills, Calif.: Sage, 1980), pp. 78–91. See also Sykes, "Rise of Critical Criminology," p. 212.

74. Meda Chesney-Lind, "Feminism and Criminology," *Justice Quarterly,* **5** (1988): 497–538; Pat Carlen, "Women, Crime, Feminism, and Realism," *Social Justice,* **17** (1990): 106–123.

75. Sally Simpson, "Feminist Theory, Crime and Justice," *Criminology,* **27** (1989): 605–632; Meda Chesney-Lind, "Judicial Enforcement of the Female Sex Role: The Family Court and the Female Delinquent," *Issues in Criminology,* **8** (1973): 51–69.

76. Philip L. Reichel and Andrzej Rzeplinski, "Student Views of Crime and Criminal Justice in Poland and the United States," *International Journal of Comparative and Applied Criminal Justice,* **13** (1989): 65–81.

77. Quinney, *Class, State, and Crime,* p. 40.

78. Compare the emergence of "left realism" with the development of critical theory in the 1960s. See John Lowman and Brian D. MacLean, eds., *Realist Criminology: Crime Control and Policing in the 1990s* (Ontario: University of Toronto Press, 1990); Martin D. Schwartz and Walter S. DeKeseredy, "Left Realist Criminology: Strengths, Weaknesses and the Feminist Critique," *Crime, Law and Social Change,* **15** (1991): 51–72; Walter S. DeKeseredy and Martin D. Schwartz, "British and U.S. Left Realism: A Critical Comparison," *International Journal of Offender Therapy and Comparative Criminology,* **35** (1991): 248–262.

PART III

Types of Crimes

The word "crime" conjures up many images: mugging and murder, cheating on taxes, and selling crack. Penal codes define thousands of different crimes. But all crimes have certain elements in common. All are human acts in violation of law, committed by an actor who acted with a criminal intent to cause a specified harm. The various legal defenses to crime are based on the defendant's alleging that one of the required elements was missing.

After analyzing the common ingredients of all crimes, we examine criminal events from two criminological perspectives (Chapter 9). The rational-choice perspective explains the criminal event in terms of the criminal, the motivation, and the situation surrounding the crime. The routine-activities perspective explains the criminal event in terms of motivated offenders, suitable targets, and the absence of guardians. Violent crime (Chapter 10); a broad range of crimes against property (Chapter 11); white-collar, corporate, and organized crime (Chapter 12); and a variety of crimes related to drug and alcohol trafficking and consumption and to sexual mores (Chapter 13) are explained in terms of legal and criminological perspectives. Their occurrence, frequency, and pervasiveness are also discussed in comparison with the occurrence of crime in other parts of the world. Chapter 14, which is concerned with comparative criminology, includes a discussion of transnational crimes.

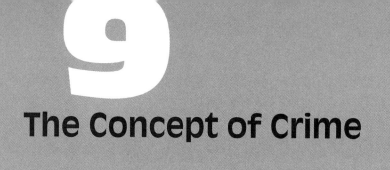

9

The Concept of Crime

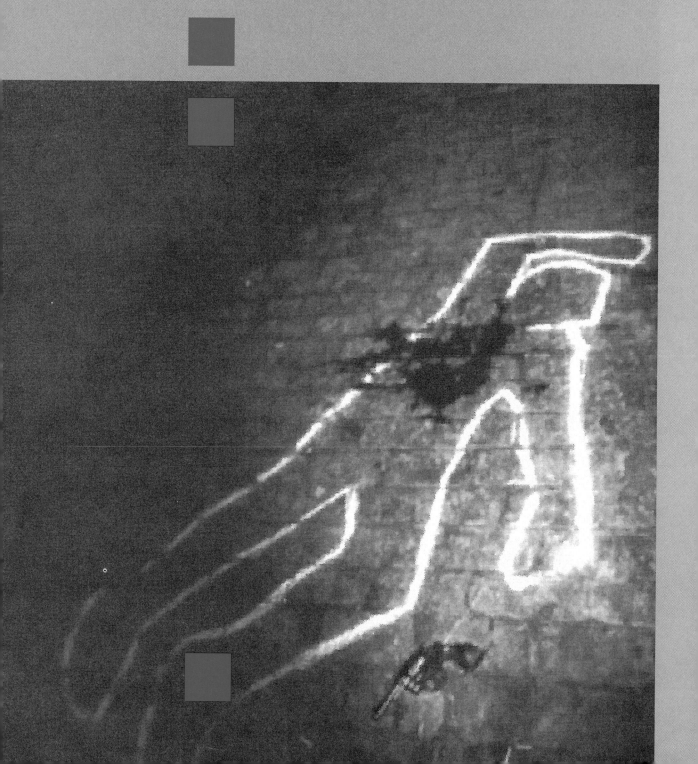

KEY TERMS
accomplices
criminal attempt
felonies
mens rea
misdemeanors
principals
rational-choice perspective
routine-activities perspective
strict liability
target hardening
torts
violations

There is hardly a subject on which the public holds stronger views than that of crime. Perhaps this is as it should be, since crime concerns the entire community. Yet crime is not just an emotional issue capable of being discussed by everybody. It is also a technical subject, a legal construct developed over the centuries by monarchs, courts, and legal scholars. In addition, it is a concept (or concepts) developed and still being refined by social and behavioral scientists.

In this chapter we explore crime as a legal construct, and we discuss the theoretical and practical implications affecting criminal liability. We place our discussion (in this and the following chapters in this part) in the context of the situational aspects of crime's occurrence: opportunity for a crime to be committed, motivation of the perpetrator, role the victim plays, a socioeconomic environment that favors the event, and any other factors that may relate to a crime's occurrence.

TYPOLOGIES OF CRIME

All crimes have something in common, a set of characteristics, or elements, that distinguish them from all noncrimes. The general term "crimes" covers a wide variety of different types of crimes with their own distinct features. Murder and arson, for example, both are crimes. They have the same seven general elements, including a criminal intent (mens rea), and a harm element. But these elements take different forms in different crimes. In murder the criminal intent takes the form of intending to kill another human being wrongfully, while in arson the intent is that of burning the property of another. Lawyers and criminologists have searched for a system of grouping the many types of crimes into coherent, rational categories, for ease of understanding, of learning, and of finding them in the law books and for purposes of studying them from both a legal and a criminological perspective. Such categorizations are called *typologies*.

Here are some examples: The ancient Romans classified their crimes as those against the gods and those against other human beings. As late as the eighteenth century, some English lawyers simply listed crimes alphabetically. The French of the early nineteenth century created a typology with three categories: serious crimes (which we would call felonies), medium serious crimes (which we would call misdemeanors), and crimes of a petty character (which we would call violations). The more serious crimes were grouped into categories based on the harm those crimes entailed, such as harm against life, against physical integrity, against honor, against property, and so on.

Nowadays the French categorization is generally accepted, worldwide, although lawyers and criminologists may differ on the desirability of lumping various crime types together into categories. Lawyers, after all, may be much more interested in the procedural consequences that flow from the categorizations, while criminologists may be much more concerned with criminological implications for studying different types of perpetrators and devising schemes of crime prevention.

There are also political considerations in devising a typology. For example, the criminal codes of the former communist countries have large categories of political crimes, which are given the most prominent place in those codes. They include many crimes which in Western democracies are grouped in other categories, such as property crimes or crimes against the person, or which may have no counterpart at all.

The typology we have chosen for this book seeks to accommodate both the established legal typology—for example, that used in the Model Penal Code—and the criminological objectives that are so important for the study of crime from a sociological and behavioral perspective. These categories are:

- Violent crimes
- Crimes against property
- Organizational criminality
- Drug-, alcohol-, and sex-related crimes

Since criminologists want to know much more about crime than prosecutors, judges, and jurors need to know to establish the guilt or innocence of an individual offender, we have chosen the perspectives of two criminological theories of crime to explain crime types within the four categories. These are the rational-choice and the routine-activities theories.

THEORIES OF CRIME

In recent years, some criminologists have focused on why offenders choose to commit one offense rather than another at a given time and place. They stress the important distinction between theories of crime and theories of criminality. Theories of criminality, Michael Gottfredson and Travis Hirschi point out, explain why some people are more likely than others to commit crimes; theories of crime identify conditions under which those who are prone to commit crime will in fact do so.[1]

Crimes are events. They take place at a specific time in a specific place. The presence of an offender is only one of the necessary components; crimes require many conditions that are independent of the offender, such as the availability of goods to be stolen or persons to be assaulted. Some experts have argued that if crimes are to be prevented and effective crime-control policies developed, the study of criminal behavior must be closely tied to the decision-making process of offenders and to the criminal acts themselves.

Rational Choice

The **rational-choice perspective,** developed by Derek Cornish and Ronald Clarke, takes into account the entire criminal event, which includes the criminal, the motivation, and the situation.[2] "Rational" refers to the fact that criminals process information and evaluate alternatives. "Choice" suggests that they make decisions.

According to Cornish and Clarke, an individual commits a crime after he or she has made a rational decision to do so—that is, has weighed the risks and benefits of the act and selected a particular offense according to various criteria.[3] Before committing a theft, for example, an offender may consider:

The number of targets and their accessibility
His or her familiarity with the chosen method
    (for example, fraud by credit card)
The monetary yield per crime

The expertise needed
The time required to commit the act
The physical danger involved
The risk of apprehension

Consider the following scenario: A young man is unemployed. He has no savings. Most of the money he makes doing odd jobs goes into his car, which the bank is about to repossess. He feels desperate. He needs money just to tide him over. Some of his peers have suggested that he work in the local crack house. He knows that though the rewards are good, the risks are high. Instead, he decides to commit a robbery. Where can he find the best target? The local bank? No, it's too well protected. The gasoline station? No, it has guard dogs—and besides, he knows some of the guys who work there. The Burger Queen in the next town is perfect. Only two people work behind the counter after midnight, a side street offers a quick getaway, police seldom put in an appearance, and no one over there knows him.

Let us analyze this scenario in terms of the rational-choice approach. The young man is desperate for money and needs it fast (the motive). He weighs the risks. The probability of a raid on the crack house is too high. He looks for suitable targets that are not well protected and are likely to have quite a bit of cash on hand. Two distinct sets of characteristics, then, are involved in law-violating behavior: those of the offender and those of the offense. The offender's characteristics include specific needs, values, learning experiences, and so on. The characteristics of the offense include the location of the target and the potential yield. According to rational-choice theory, involvement in crime depends on a personal decision made after one has weighed available information.

What will happen if the young man is frustrated in his holdup attempt? Suppose he arrives at the Burger Queen only to find police officers having dinner there. Will he then automatically look for another place to rob? Cornish and Clarke argue that *displacement*—the commission of a qualitatively similar crime at a different time or place—does not always follow. Of course, some offenders will try again, but the rational-choice approach suggests that others will quit for some time—or, indeed, forever. We consider the

Cabs jam Manhattan streets to protest escalating violence against cabbies: In 1994 cabs were again being fitted with partitions between driver and passenger plus metal shields embedded in back of the driver's seat after 43 cabbies were killed in robberies in 1993, 38 of whom were driving cabs without partitions.

choices made by offenders further when we discuss specific types of crimes in later chapters.

Routine Activities

Another new approach, the **routine-activities perspective,** is closely linked to rational-choice theory. It, too, focuses on the characteristics of the crime rather than on those of the offender. According to Lawrence Cohen and Marcus Felson, there will always be a good supply of motivated offenders.[4] What we need to understand is the range of options among which offenders choose when they decide to commit a crime. "Just as lions look for deer near their watering hole," Felson says, "criminal offenders disproportionately find victims in certain settings."[5] This approach focuses on the circumstances in which crimes are committed.

Each criminal act requires the convergence of three elements:

- Likely and motivated offenders (for example, unemployed teenagers)
- Suitable targets (for example, easily transportable goods)

- An absence of capable guardians to prevent the would-be offender from committing the crime (for example, friends or neighbors)

Cohen and Felson point out that crime rates rise along with the number of suitable targets and the absence of people to protect those targets. Over the last few decades, the number and variety of suitable targets—goods easily transported and sold, such as videocassette recorders and compact disc players—have increased steadily. At the same time, changes in the routine activities of everyday life have left most of those targets unguarded a good part of the day.

In the past, American neighborhoods were smaller than they are now; when people left home, they walked. They shopped at neighborhood stores and visited movie houses, restaurants, clubs, and friends close to home. Few places they went to regularly were more than a couple of blocks away. Since World War II, the territory of routine activities has expanded outward. The development of suburbs and expressways, the ease of air travel, the proliferation of day-care centers and nursery schools, and the increasing participation of women in the labor force have left homes empty and unguarded.

The logic of the argument is straightforward: routine patterns of work, play, and leisure time affect the convergence in time and place of motivated offenders, suitable targets, and the absence of guardians. Cohen and Felson argue that if one component is missing, crime is not likely to be committed. And if all components are in place and one of them is strengthened, crime is likely to increase. Even if the proportions of motivated offenders and targets stay the same, for example, changes in routine activities of the sort we have experienced since World War II will alone raise the crime rate by multiplying the opportunities for crime. This approach has helped explain, among other things, rates of victimization for specific crimes, rates of urban homicide, and "hot spots"—areas that produce a disproportionate number of calls to police.[6] We will return to the routine-activities approach in the following chapters.

Situational Crime Prevention

Both the rational-choice and the routine-activities perspectives demonstrate that the commission of crime does not depend just on the biological and psychological characteristics of individuals or on social and economic factors. Accordingly, rather than focusing only on the people who commit crimes, we should also concentrate on the situational factors that influence the commission of crimes. This approach is particularly important for the development of crime-control policy and "situational" crime prevention, which consists of changing the conditions and circumstances under which crime is committed.

Situational crime prevention includes such measures as **target hardening** (taking steps that make it more difficult for offenders to carry out crimes against specific targets—for instance, installing better locks); organizing Neighborhood Watch groups, whose members are alert to any nonroutine activity at neighboring homes; and changing environmental designs of buildings and streets to afford more protection (for example, installing more streetlights). Theories of crime, according to Gottfredson and Hirschi,

"acknowledge the ability of society to control crime without fundamental reconstruction of itself or the individuals within it."[7]

THE INGREDIENTS OF CRIME  ESSAY

In the remaining chapters of Part III we will examine what criminologists have discovered about the characteristics of violent crimes, property crimes, organizational crimes, and crimes related to drugs, alcohol, and sex. Before we do so, it is important to review that part of criminal law which deals with the common legal ingredients, or elements, found in all crimes. With few exceptions, if any one of these elements is not present, no crime has been committed. All the defenses available to a person charged with a crime allege that at least one of these elements is not present.

The Seven Basic Requirements

The American criminal law scholar Jerome Hall has developed the theory that a human event, in order to qualify as a crime, must meet seven basic requirements[8]:

1. The act requirement
2. The legality requirement
3. The harm requirement
4. The causation requirement
5. The mens rea requirement
6. The concurrence requirement
7. The punishment requirement[9]

The Act Requirement

Law scholars have long agreed that one fundamental ingredient of every crime is a human act. In this context, what is an "act"? Suppose a sleepwalker, in a trance, grabs a stone and hurls it at a passerby, with lethal consequences. The law does not consider this event to be an act; before any human behavior can qualify as an act, there must be a conscious interaction between mind and body, a physical movement that results from the determination or effort of the actor. Thus the Model Penal Code (MPC), which the American Law Institute proposed to legislatures in 1962, says that the following behaviors are *not* voluntary acts:

- A reflex or convulsion
- A bodily movement that occurs during unconsciousness or sleep
- Conduct that occurs during hypnosis or results from hypnotic suggestion
- A bodily movement that is not determined by the actor, as when somebody is pushed by another person[10]

Free Will?

This formula gives the impression that the law is based on "free will," the idea that people are accountable only if they freely choose to do a thing and then consciously do it. But scientists and lawyers have yet to discover an individual who is completely free to make choices. All of us have been molded by factors beyond our control, and our choices are to some extent conditioned by external factors and forces. It is only when choices are overpoweringly influenced by forces beyond our control, such as the case of the sleepwalking stone thrower, that the law will consider behavior irrational and beyond its reach.

Determinists, however, argue that all human behavior is determined by forces beyond the control of human actors (see Chapter 3). Rational-choice and routine-activities scholars take no position in this debate. Rational-choice theory neither demands nor presupposes the existence of free will. To choose one moment rather than another, or one target rather than another, does not require free will. Even a mouse learns quickly that it cannot get at the cheese by gnawing at the refrigerator door. But cheese on an open tray is fair game. Obviously the mouse prefers the tray to be in the room without the cat. Rational-choice theorists are interested in preventing a crime (once something is recognized to be a crime). They would recommend putting a glass dome over the cheese tray.

Act vs. Status

The criminal law, in principle, does not penalize anyone for a status or condition. Suppose the law made it a crime to be more than 6 feet tall or to have red hair. Or suppose the law made it a crime to be a member of the family of an army deserter or to be of a given religion or ethnic background. That was exactly the situation in the Soviet Union under Stalin's penal code, which made it a crime to be related to a deserter from the Red Army. It was also the situation in Hitler's Germany, where the crime was to be Jewish, and it was punishable by death.

There is more to the act requirement than the issue of a behavior's being voluntary and rational: there is the problem of distinguishing between act and status. A California law made it a criminal offense, subject to a jail term, to be a drug addict. In *Robinson v. California* the U.S. Supreme Court held that statute to be unconstitutional. By making a status or condition a crime, the statute violated the Eighth Amendment to the U.S. Constitution, which prohibits "cruel and unusual punishments." Addiction, the Court noted, is a condition, an illness, much like leprosy or venereal disease. Even babies born of addict mothers are addicts. Said the Court: "Even one day in prison would be cruel and unusual punishment for the 'crime' of having a common cold."[11]

In a subsequent case, *Powell v. Texas*, the Supreme Court backed away from its recognition of the act requirement.[12] A Texas statute had made it a crime to be drunk in public. Powell was a chronic alcoholic, prosecuted for being in a public place while drunk. It was contended in his behalf that chronic alcoholics cannot refrain from drinking. If they are homeless, they cannot help being in public places. The Supreme Court, however, upheld Powell's conviction, in essence saying that he had not been punished for being a chronic alcoholic but for doing something—for going to a public place in an intoxicated state. This ruling is considered by many to be inconsistent with the *Robinson* decision.

Failure to Act

The act requirement has yet another aspect. An act requires the interaction of mind and body. If only the mind is active and the body does not move, we do not have an act: just thinking about punching someone in the nose is not a crime (Figure 9.1). We are free to think. But if we carry a thought into physical action, we commit an act, which may be a crime.

Then there is the problem of omission, or fail-

© 1962 The Saturday Evening Post

FIGURE 9.1

Has a crime been committed? Is walking on the grass prohibited by law, subject to punishment? Did the actor commit the act by actually walking on the grass, or did he merely have a criminal intent to do so? Perhaps the actor is incapable of forming a legally relevant intent because he is too young to do so!

ure to act. If the law requires that young men register for the draft, and if you are a young man and you decide not to fill out the registration form, you are guilty of a crime by omission. But haven't you really acted? You told your hand not to pick up that pen, not to fill out the form. Inaction may be action when the law clearly spells out what you have to do and you decide not to do it.

The law in most U.S. states imposes no duty to be a good Samaritan, to offer help to another person in distress. The Kitty Genovese case is a well-known example. Not one of her 38 neighbors was a good Samaritan. The law requires action only if one has a legal duty to act. Lifeguards, for example, are contractually obligated to save bathers from drowning; parents are obligated by law to protect their children; law enforcement officers and firefighters are required to rescue people in distress; baby-sitters must protect babies in their care from harm. In addition, the law imposes a

duty to continue rescue operations on anybody who, though not required to do so, has voluntarily come to the aid of a person in need.

The Legality Requirement

Marion Palendrano was charged with, among other things, being a "common scold" because she disturbed "the peace of the neighborhood and of all good and quiet people of this State." Mrs. Palendrano moved that the charge be dismissed, and the Superior Court of New Jersey agreed with her, reasoning:

1. Such a crime cannot be found anywhere in the New Jersey statute books. Hence there is no such crime, although, long ago, the common law of England may have recognized such a crime.
2. "Being a common scold" is so vague a concept that to punish somebody for it would violate constitutional due process: "We insist that laws give the person of ordinary intelligence a reasonable opportunity to know what is prohibited, so that he may act accordingly," ruled the court.[13]

If we want a person to adhere to a standard, the person has to know what that standard is. Thus we have the ancient proposition that only conduct which has been made criminal by law before an act is committed can be a crime; in Latin, *nullum crimen sine lege* ("no crime without law"). Police, prosecutors, and courts are not interested in the billions of acts human beings engage in unless such acts have previously been defined by law as criminal. The law is interested only in an act (*actus*) that is *reus*, in the sense of guilty, evil, and prohibited. Additionally, as Marion Palendrano's case demonstrates, when the law has made some behavior a crime, the language defining it must be clear enough to be understood.

The Harm Requirement

Every crime has been created to prevent something bad (a given harm) from happening. Murder is prohibited because we don't want people to be killed. Arson and theft are prohibited

CRIMINOLOGICAL FOCUS
Thirty-Eight Witnesses

On March 27, 1964, *The New York Times* printed the following story:

For more than half an hour thirty-eight respectable, law-abiding citizens in Queens watched a killer stalk and stab a woman in three separate attacks in Kew Gardens.

Twice the sound of their voices and the sudden glow of their bedroom lights interrupted him and frightened him off. Each time he returned, sought her out and stabbed her again. Not one person telephoned the police during the assault; one witness called after the woman was dead.

That was two weeks ago today. But Assistant Chief Inspector Frederick M. Lussen, in charge of the borough's detectives and a veteran of twenty-five years of homicide investigations, is still shocked.

He can give a matter-of-fact recitation of many murders. But the Kew Gardens slaying baffles him—not because it is a murder, but because the "good people" failed to call the police.

"As we have reconstructed the crime," he said, "the assailant had three chances to kill this woman during a thirty-five-minute period. He returned twice to complete the job. If we had been called when he first attacked, the woman might not be dead now."

This is what the police say happened beginning at 3:30 A.M. in the staid, middle-class, tree-lined Austin Street area:

Twenty-eight-year-old Catherine Genovese, who was called Kitty by almost everyone in the neighborhood, was returning home from her job as manager of a bar in Hollis. She parked her red Fiat . . . turned off the lights of her car, locked the door and started to walk the 100 feet to the entrance of her apartment. . . . Miss Genovese noticed a man at the far end of the lot. . . . She halted. Then, nervously, she headed up Austin Street . . . where there is a call box to the 102d Police Precinct in nearby Richmond Hill.

She got as far as a street light in front of a bookstore before the man grabbed her. She screamed. Lights went on in the ten-story apartment house . . . which faces the bookstore. Windows slid open and voices punctured the early-morning stillness.

Miss Genovese screamed: "Oh, my God, he stabbed me! Please help me! Please help me!"

From one of the upper windows in the apartment house, a man called down: "Let that girl alone!"

The assailant looked up at him, shrugged and walked down Austin Street. . . . Miss Genovese struggled to her feet.

Lights went out. The killer returned to Miss Genovese [and] stabbed her again.

"I'm dying!" she shrieked. "I'm dying!"

Windows were opened again, and lights went on in many apartments. The assailant got into his car and drove away. Miss Genovese staggered to her feet. It was 3:35 A.M.

The assailant returned. By then, Miss Genovese had crawled to the back of the building. . . . The killer . . . saw her slumped on the floor at the foot of the stairs. He stabbed her a third time—fatally.

It was 3:50 by the time the police received their first call from a man who was a neighbor of Miss Genovese. In two minutes they were at the scene.

It was 4:25 A.M. when the ambulance arrived for the body of Miss Genovese. It drove off. "Then," a solemn police detective said, "the people came out."

Source: Excerpted from A. M. Rosenthal, Thirty-Eight Witnesses (New York: McGraw-Hill, 1964).

Questions for Discussion
1. Could the Kitty Genovese case have happened in the 1990s? Why or why not?
2. Excuses offered by the witnesses for not calling the police when they first heard screams included "I was tired," "We were afraid," "I didn't want my husband to get involved," and "I don't know." Would you have called the police?

(1) Where she parked her car.

(2) Place of initial attack.

(3) Place of second attack.

(4) Place of third attack.

because we don't want people to be deprived of their property. This detrimental consequence that we are trying to avoid is called *harm*. If the specified harm has not been created by the defendant's act, the crime is not complete. Just think of would-be assassin John W. Hinckley, Jr., who tried to kill President Reagan. He shot Reagan, but the president did not die. The harm envisioned by the law against murder had not been accomplished. (Hinckley could have been found guilty of attempted murder—but he was acquitted by reason of insanity.)

Sometimes the harm is less drastic than a dead person or a burned house. Pooper-scooper laws (you must clean up after your dog) are designed to prevent the harm of dirty streets and sidewalks. In the case of drunk-driving statutes, the harm is not of a physical nature. It consists of the grave danger to the public which driving while intoxicated constitutes. (If the drunk driver kills someone, a more serious charge is brought.)

From a criminological perspective, most crimes are grouped by the harm that each entails. Offenses against the person involve harm to an individual, and offenses against property involve damage to property or loss of its possession. The notion of harm is of particular importance to the rational-choice and routine-activities theories. After all, criminal law is meant to prevent the harm envisaged by penal statutes. The interests threatened by criminal harm, the values of life and property, need protection from people who have a motivation and an opportunity to inflict such harm.

The Causation Requirement

What is the act of hitting a home run? Of course it is a hit that allows a batter to run to first, second, and third base and then back to home plate. Actually it is much more complicated than that. It starts with the decision to swing a bat, at a certain angle, with a particular intensity, in a specific direction, in order to cause a home run. Suppose that at a San Diego Padres home game, the batter hits a ball unusually high into the air. A passing pelican picks it up, flies off with it, and then drops it into the bleachers. Has the batter hit a home run? We doubt it.

It's the same in crime. Causation requires that

the actor achieve the result (the harm) through his or her own effort. Suppose that A, in an effort to kill B, wounds him and that B actually dies when the ambulance carrying him to the hospital collides with another vehicle. Despite B's death, A did not succeed in her personal attempt to kill B. Thus the act of murder is incomplete, although A may be guilty of an attempt to kill. The causation requirement, then, holds that a crime is not complete unless the actor's conduct necessarily caused the harm without interference by somebody else, and that it is the proximate cause of the act.[14]

Mens Rea: The "Guilty Mind" Requirement

Every crime, according to tradition, requires **mens rea,** a "guilty mind." Let us examine the case of Ms. Lambert. She was convicted in Los Angeles of an offense created by city ordinance: having lived in the city without registering with the police as a person previously convicted of a crime. Ms. Lambert had no idea that Los Angeles had such a registration requirement. Nor could she possibly have known that she was required to register. She appealed all the way to the U.S. Supreme Court, and she won. Said the Court: "Where a person did not know [of the prohibition] (s)he may not be convicted consistent with due process."[15]

Of course, to blame Ms. Lambert for violating the Los Angeles city ordinance would make no sense. Ms. Lambert had no notion that she was doing something wrong by living in Los Angeles and not registering herself as a convicted person. The potential of blame that follows a choice to commit a crime is meant to be a powerful incentive to do the right thing and avoid doing the wrong thing. That is the function of mens rea. (We will return to Ms. Lambert later on.)

With Ms. Lambert's case we have reached a fundamental point: No one can be guilty of a crime unless he or she acted with the knowledge of doing something wrong. This principle always has existed. It is implicit in the concept of crime that the perpetrator know the wrongfulness of the act. It is not required that the perpetrator know the penal code or have personal feelings of guilt. It is enough that the perpetrator knows that he or she had no right to do what he or she did and decided to do it anyway.[16]

Anyone who violently attacks another person, takes another's property, invades another's home, forces intercourse, or forges a signature on someone else's check knows rather well that he or she is doing something wrong. All these examples of mens rea entail an intention to achieve harm or a knowledge that the prohibited harm will result. For some crimes, however, less than a definite intention suffices: reckless actions by which the actors consciously risk producing a prohibited harm (for example, the driver who races down a rain-slicked highway or the employer who sends his employees to work without safety equipment, knowing full well that lives are thereby being endangered).

Strict liability is an exception to the mens rea requirement. There is a class of offenses for which legislatures or courts require no showing of criminal intent or mens rea. For these offenses, the fact that the actor makes an innocent mistake and proceeds in good faith does not affect criminal liability. Such offenses are called strict-liability offenses, and they crept into our law with the Industrial Revolution. Most of them involve conduct subject to regulation, conduct that threatens the public welfare as a whole. Strict-liability offenses range all the way from distributing adulterated food to passing a red light. Typically these offenses are subject to small penalties only, but in a few cases substantial punishments can be and have been imposed.[17]

The Concurrence Requirement

The concurrence requirement states that the criminal act must be accompanied by an equally criminal mind. Suppose a striker throws a stone at an office window in order to shatter it, and a broken piece of glass pierces the throat of a secretary, who bleeds to death. Wanting to damage property deserves condemnation, but of a far lesser degree than wanting to kill. Act and intent did not concur in this case, and the striker should not be found guilty of murder. The law has created many exceptions to the concurrence requirement, one of which, the felony murder rule, we discuss in Chapter 10.

The Punishment Requirement

The last ingredient needed to constitute a crime is that of punishment. An illegal act coupled with an evil mind (criminal intent or mens rea) still does not constitute a crime unless the law subjects it to a punishment. If a sign posted in the park states "Do not step on the grass" and you do it anyway, have you committed a criminal offense? Not unless there is a law that subjects that act to punishment. Otherwise it is simply an improper or inconsiderate act.

The punishment requirement, more than any of the others, helps us differentiate between crimes (which are subject to punishments) and **torts,** civil wrongs for which the law does not prescribe punishment but merely grants the injured party the right to recover damages.

The nature and severity of punishments also help us differentiate between grades of crime. Most penal codes recognize three degrees of severity: **Felonies** are severe crimes, subject to punishments of a year or more in prison or to capital punishment. **Misdemeanors** are less severe crimes, subject to a maximum of 1 year in jail. (For crimes of both grades, fines can also be imposed as punishments.) **Violations** are minor offenses, normally subject only to fines.

THE DEFENSES: EXCUSES

When we turn to the various defenses recognized by law, we discover that each defense simply claims that one or more of the seven basic constituent elements of the crime does not exist. In other words, what at first glance may indicate that a crime was committed—a dead body or a burned building—may turn out not to be a crime after all because, for example, the perpetrator lacked criminal intent or the law granted the actor the right to do what he or she did so that the "illegality" is absent.

The Insanity Defense

On March 30, 1981, a young man stood in front of the Hilton Hotel in Washington, D.C., and mixed with the crowd that had assembled to greet Pres-

external condition, his or her mind did not participate in the behavior, so he or she did not commit the required act or form the guilty mind. In the next group of defenses the defendant fulfills all the act and intent requirements, and still the law does not impose criminal liability: the act is no longer prohibited by law, since the law itself gives the actor permission to act.

Duress

A robber approaches a bank teller with the following demand: "Your money or your life!" A simple choice. The teller probably reaches into the drawer and hands over the cash. Is the teller guilty of larceny or embezzlement? It is not her money. Her job as a teller does not give her the right to steal, to give away, or to embezzle funds entrusted to her.

To deal with such situations, the law has established the defense of duress:

> It is . . . [a] defense that the actor engaged in the conduct charged to constitute an offense because he was coerced to do so by the use of, or a threat to use, unlawful force against his person or the person of another, which a person of reasonable firmness in his situation would have been unable to resist.[30]

This defense applies when the actor has done something the law prohibits. The bank teller took money entrusted to her and gave it to someone else. She was not authorized to do so. All the elements of a crime are there. But the teller had no choice. And that is precisely the point. The law recognizes that we cannot be expected to yield our lives, our limbs, the safety of our relatives, our houses, or our property when we are confronted by a criminal threat that forces us to violate a law. But there is a general requirement that the evil which threatens the actor ("Your money or your life!") and the evil created by the actor (handing over the bank's cash) be commensurate, that is, not out of proportion.

Necessity

As a general rule, necessity is a defense to a criminal charge when one has violated a law in the reasonable belief that the act was necessary to avoid an imminent and greater harm. Suppose two hikers are surprised by a snowstorm. They stumble upon a vacation cottage. Under the rule of necessity, they may break into and enter the cottage and use its provisions to stay alive.

If the necessity defense is to apply, the paramount threat must emanate from a force other than a human aggressor. The cause is, as it has been called, an "act of God"—a storm, a fire, a shipwreck. (If the source of the threat is a human aggressor, the defense is duress.)[31]

The question that has caused the most trouble is whether the defense of necessity ever permits the taking of an innocent life. Courts in England and the United States have reached contrasting solutions. English law does not permit the taking of an innocent life, even under dire necessity. American law permits the taking of innocent lives under certain conditions. A person who has fulfilled all legal obligations may sacrifice innocent human life, by random lot selection, in order to save more lives.

Public Duty

Jus is the Latin word for law. Thus *justifications* are instances in which the law itself has created a counterlaw. The law prohibits an act; the counterlaw commands or authorizes it (see Table 9.1).

By far the most frequent justification defense is use of force in law enforcement. Law enforcement officers may use as much force as necessary, for example, to effect an arrest, but no more. The use of deadly force is subject to severe restrictions. Law enforcement officers who use more force than necessary are likely to be committing a criminal offense, such as assault and battery, or a civil rights violation under federal law, as was demonstrated by the federal conviction of the officers who beat Rodney King in Los Angeles.

Self-Defense, Defense of Others, Defense of Property

On the Saturday before Christmas in 1984, Bernhard H. Goetz entered a subway car at the IRT station at Seventh Avenue and 14th Street in Manhattan. He sat down close to four young men in their late teens. One of them offered a "How are ya"; then he approached Goetz and asked for

WINDOW TO THE WORLD
Necessity at Sea

Two cases of lives sacrificed to save others after a shipwreck show the difference between the American and English approaches to necessity as a defense. The descriptions below are from *Outlaws of the Ocean*.

The American Case

The American packet [passenger vessel] *William Brown* was en route from Liverpool to Philadelphia with a shipload of 65 Scottish and Irish immigrants when she struck an iceberg on April 19, 1841, 250 miles southeast of Race, Newfoundland. She sank rapidly in a howling nor'easter. . . . The first mate and eight sailors manned the longboat, filling it with thirty-two passengers. Even while the longboat was shoving off, they saw the *William Brown* go down, with the remaining passengers screaming, praying, and disappearing in the waves. . . . The first mate managed to keep the longboat afloat, but the seas and wind grew worse. The sea cock plug was lost, and the boat took on more and more water. The crew bailed as much as they could. The first mate shouted to his fellow sailors, "This work won't do. Help me, God. Men, go to work." Finally, the sailors obeyed, throwing a number of passengers overboard, being careful not to separate husband from wife, or mother from child. By such action the longboat was saved, and all still aboard were rescued by a passing vessel.

Holmes, one of the sailors, was tried on a murder charge and found guilty of manslaughter, but only because, as the court said, he had failed to exercise his duties toward passengers by throwing some of them overboard indiscriminately rather than by casting lots . . . . Unlike English law, American law recognizes the defense of necessity in taking of innocent lives on the high seas under extreme conditions.*

The English Case

[T]hree shipwrecked sailors had been adrift in an open boat in the doldrums of the equatorial Atlantic. Their predicament had lasted for weeks. They had neither food nor water. They were delirious and the end appeared near, especially for the cabin boy, who was about to expire. In phantasmagoric exasperation, Dudley and Stephens killed the cabin boy and ate his flesh. This enabled them to survive for another few days until they were rescued by a passing vessel. The Court of Kings Bench convicted them of murder. Innocent human life must never be taken even to save one's own life, and even under the most dire necessity . . . . As Chief Justice Lord Coleridge stated: "We are often compelled to set up standards we cannot reach ourselves, and to lay down rules which we could not ourselves satisfy."†

Dudley and Stephens' [capital] sentences were commuted to the misdemeanor range, six months imprisonment.

* *United States v. Holmes,* I Wall Jr. I, 26 Fed. Cas. 360 (U.S. Cir. Ct., E.D. Pa., 1842).

† *Regina v. Dudley and Stephens,* 14 Q.B.D. 273 (1884).

Source: G. O. W. Mueller and Freda Adler, *Outlaws of the Ocean: The Complete Book of Contemporary Crime on the High Seas* [New York: Hearst Marine Books (William Morrow), 1985], pp. 217–218.

Questions for Discussion

1. What other defenses might have applied in these cases? Self-defense? Public duty? Duress? Why or why not?
2. Which view of necessity as a defense do you support, the American or the British? Explain your position.

The crew of the yacht *Mignonette* in an open boat at sea, from sketches by Mr. Stephens, mate of the *Mignonette,* who survived by killing and eating the cabin boy.

TABLE 9.1   LAW PROHIBITIONS AND COUNTERLAW JUSTIFICATIONS

Law Prohibitions	Counterlaw Justifications
The law prohibits the taking of life (criminal homicide).	The counterlaw requires execution of a convict sentenced to capital punishment.
	The counterlaw permits the shooting of a fleeing felon who is armed and constitutes a threat to life.
The law prohibits the taking of property (as in larceny).	The counterlaw allows impoundment of an illegally parked car.
The law prohibits the seizure of a person (as in false imprisonment or kidnapping).	The counterlaw requires the arrest of a suspect on probable cause.

$5. At that point Goetz pulled out a .38-caliber revolver and shot all four youths (one in the back).[32]

Few cases have ignited as much controversy as the Goetz case. Some people saw Goetz as an avenging angel, the city dweller who constantly suffers from crime and the fear of crime. Others labeled him a vigilante. Or was he simply the meek underdog, as his appearance suggested, trying to defend himself against yet another attack on the subway? He could have been any one of those. Goetz was charged with attempted murder, assault, and illegal possession of a

Bernhard Goetz, riding the New York subway on his way to court to face charges of having shot four young men he thought were going to rob him on an earlier subway ride.

weapon. In legal terms, the case simply raised the question of the right to use force, even deadly force, in self-defense, as well as the extent to which the defense still exists if the actor is mistaken about the actual threat that confronts him.

It is safe to say that in most states a person can use as much force as is reasonably necessary to defend himself or herself against what appears to be an immediate threat of violence by another, as long as the following four elements are present:

- The person must have an "honest and reasonable belief" that the force is necessary.
- The person must believe that the harm threatened will be immediately forthcoming.
- The harm threatened must be unlawful.
- The force used must be reasonable—only as much as appears necessary under the circumstances.

Let us return to the Goetz case. Did Goetz find himself in a life-threatening situation? We will never know. As it turned out, some of his victims had criminal records. They carried no firearms, only screwdrivers, which they said they used to pilfer vending machines. Objectively, it appears that Goetz was in no immediate physical danger. What, then, went on in his mind? He had earlier been the victim of a brutal mugging in similar circumstances. Like many other subway riders, he feared the predators who seemed to be ever present beneath the streets.

The defense made a strong case that Goetz was in fear of his life. The legal question was whether he should be judged by a subjective standard (whether *he* felt in fear of his life) or by an objective standard (whether *a reasonable person*

TABLE 9.2   JUSTIFIABLE USE OF DEADLY FORCE EVEN IF LIFE IS NOT THREATENED*

State	Deadly Force May Be Justified		
	To Protect Dwelling	To Protect Property	Against Specific Crime
Alabama	Yes	No	Arson, burglary, rape, kidnapping, robbery
Alaska	Yes	No	Actual commission of felony
Arizona	Yes	No	Arson, burglary, kidnapping, aggr. assaults
Arkansas	Yes	No	Felonies (defined by statute)
California	Yes	No	Unlawful or forcible entry
Colorado	Yes	No	Felonies
Connecticut	Yes	No	Any violent crime
Delaware	Yes	No	Felonious activity
District of Columbia	Yes	No	Felony
Florida	Yes	No	Forcible felony
Georgia	Yes	Yes	Actual commission of a forcible felony
Hawaii	Yes	Yes	Felonious property damage, burglary, robbery, etc.
Idaho	Yes	Yes	Felonious breaking and entering
Illinois	Yes	Yes	Forcible felony
Indiana	Yes	No	Unlawful entry
Iowa	Yes	Yes	Breaking and entering
Kansas	Yes	No	Breaking and entering, incl. attempts
Kentucky	No	No	—
Louisiana	Yes	No	Unlawful entry, incl. attempts
Maine	Yes	No	Criminal trespass, kidnapping, rape, arson
Maryland	No	No	—
Massachusetts	No	No	—
Michigan	Yes	No	Case-by-case basis
Minnesota	Yes	No	Felony
Mississippi	Yes	—	Felony, including attempts
Missouri	No	No	—
Montana	Yes	Yes	Any forcible felony
Nebraska	Yes	No	Unlawful entry, kidnapping, rape
Nevada	Yes	—	Actual commission of felony
New Hampshire	Yes	—	Felony
New Jersey	Yes	No	Burglary, arson, robbery
New Mexico	Yes	Yes	Any felony
New York	Yes	No	Burglary, arson, kidnapping, robbery, incl. attempts
North Carolina	Yes	No	Intending to commit a felony
North Dakota	Yes	No	Any violent felony
Ohio	—	—	—
Oklahoma	Yes	No	Felony within a dwelling
Oregon	Yes	—	Burglary in a dwelling, incl. attempts
Pennsylvania	Yes	—	Burglary or criminal trespass
Rhode Island	Yes	—	Breaking or entering
South Carolina	No	No	—
South Dakota	Yes	—	Burglary, incl. attempts
Tennessee	Yes	No	Felony
Texas	Yes	No	Burglary, robbery, or theft at night
Utah	Yes	—	Felony

TABLE 9.2 JUSTIFIABLE USE OF DEADLY FORCE EVEN IF LIFE IS NOT THREATENED* (Continued)

| State | Deadly Force May Be Justified | | |
	To Protect Dwelling	To Protect Property	Against Specific Crime
Vermont	Yes	—	Forcible felony
Virginia	No	No	—
Washington	No	No	—
West Virginia	Yes	No	Any felony
Wisconsin	No	No	—
Wyoming	No	No	—

* All states allow ultimate recourse to deadly force when life is in immediate danger.

Source: U.S. Department of Justice, *Report to the Nation on Crime and Justice,* 2d ed. (Washington, D.C.: U.S. Government Printing Office, 1988).

in the same situation would have been in fear of his or her life). The jury resolved this issue by acquitting him of all charges except one: illegal possession of a handgun.

The right to use reasonable force, and if necessary deadly force, extends to the defense of others. In most jurisdictions, a defender can use as much force on behalf of another as he or she could have used in self-defense. Of course, such defenders must reasonably believe that if they were in the other person's position, they would have the right to defend themselves, and the amount of force used must be necessary. Some states require, in addition, that the person being assisted must also have the right to use force, regardless of the defender's perception.

The law views the protection of property and human life differently (Table 9.2). With few exceptions, the right of self-defense is far more extensive than the right of defense of property. The general rule in this area is that nondeadly force may be used, typically after some request has been made to desist, when it is necessary to stop an intrusion. When there is some indication that the intruder intends to commit a felony on the premises, and a warning to desist has been issued and ignored, deadly force may be used.

ATTEMPT AND ACCESSORYSHIP

The doctrines pertaining to defenses are not the only doctrines of criminal law used to determine

criminal charges. Foremost among the remaining doctrines is the one pertaining to attempted crimes. What should the law do to someone who tries to commit a crime but does not succeed? Under early common law, attempts to commit crimes were not considered crimes, because the *actus reus* was not completed. But a person who tries to complete a crime surely has the same mens rea and thus the same culpability as one who succeeds. Should the would-be perpetrator be treated differently just because he or she did not succeed? In 1784, it was decided in England that an attempt to commit a felony was indeed a crime.[33] That case laid the foundation for our present conceptualization of **criminal attempt:** "an act or omission constituting a substantial step in a course of conduct planned to culminate in the commission of a crime."[34]

The common law also created a sophisticated system for determining the liability of all persons involved in the commission of a crime. When, where, and how the various parties could be prosecuted, and the use of evidence at trial, depended on the type of participation.

Today most states recognize only **principals** (all persons who commit an offense by their own conduct) and **accomplices** (all those who aid the perpetrator). That system has not solved all the problems, because the line between committing a crime and aiding in its commission is a fine one. Though principals and accomplices are usually considered equally culpable, in practice judges often impose lighter sentences on accomplices.

AT ISSUE
The Battered Woman—Self-Defense and the Penal Codes

The law is very strict when it comes to the application of force in self-defense. The Model Penal Code decrees:

> The use of force upon or toward another person is justifiable when the actor believes that such force is immediately necessary for the purpose of *protecting himself* against the use of unlawful force by such other person on the present occasion.(1)

In recent years an increasing number of women abused by their mates have resorted to deadly force. The law has treated such women leniently in some respects, harshly in others. To begin with, the standard of law is phrased in terms of "protecting himself." How will courts translate the "protecting himself" standard, based on centuries of experience with male self-defense, into a "protecting herself" standard? Lenore E. Walker's study of the battered woman syndrome permitted her to conclude:

> Occasionally (less than 15 percent of all homicides) a woman will kill her abuser while trying to defend herself or her children. Sometimes, she strikes back during a calm period, knowing that the tension is building towards another acute battering incident, where this time she may die. When examining the statistics, we find that more women than men are charged with first or second degree murder. There seems to be a sexist bias operating in which the courts find it more difficult to see justifiable or mitigating circumstances for women who kill. The now classic Broverman et al. (1970) studies demonstrated that the kinds of behaviors and emotions expressed when committing an aggressive act will be viewed as normal for men but not for women. On the other hand, a woman's violence is more likely to be found excusable, if her insanity under the law can be demonstrated. Any changes in the insanity laws will probably have the greatest impact on women and other assault victims who reach a breaking point and no longer know the difference between right and wrong and/or can no longer refrain from an irresistible impulse to survive.
>
> In most states' criminal codes, self-defense is defined as the justifiable commission of a criminal act by using the least amount of force necessary to prevent imminent bodily harm which needs only to be reasonably perceived as about to happen. The perception of how much force is necessary must also be reasonable. Such a definition works against women because they are not socialized to use physical force, are rarely equal to a man in size, strength, or physical training, and may have learned to expect more injury with inadequate attempts to repel a man's attack. Thus, some courts have ruled it would be reasonable for a woman to defend herself with a deadly weapon against a man armed only with the parts of his body he learned to use as a deadly weapon. Courts also have been allowing evidence to account for the cumulative effects of repeated violence in self-defense and diminished-capacity assertions. Expert witness testimony has been admitted in many states to help explain the reasonableness of such perceptions.(2)

It would be rash to conclude that the penal codes need immediate reform to protect women who kill in perceived self-defense. But it is reasonable to expect that penal code reformers review the entirety of penal codes to see that men and women are covered and protected equally, with particular consideration of contemporary life situations.

Sources
1. American Law Institute, Model Penal Code, sec. 3.04.
2. Lenore E. Walker, *The Battered Woman Syndrome* (New York: Springer Verlag, 1984), pp. 142–143.

Questions for Discussion
1. Should the difference between men and women in the way threats of violence are perceived be taken into account in self-defense cases?
2. How should the constant threat of violence a battered woman experiences be interpreted in terms of the law's "present occasion" requirement for self-defense?

■ REVIEW

Unlike theories of criminality, which explain why people commit crimes, recent approaches, such as the theories of rational choice and routine activities, try to explain why specific crimes are committed. The emphasis of these new, crime-specific theories is on the crime rather than on the perpetrator, so it becomes necessary to focus on the meaning of crime. In terms of the *legal* meaning of crime, in order for a crime to exist, seven basic elements must be present: (1) an act (*actus*) that (2) is in violation of law (*reus*), that (3) causes (4) the harm identified by the law, and that is committed with (5) criminal intent (mens rea, or a guilty mind). In addition, (6) the criminal act must concur with the guilty mind, and (7) the act must be subject to punishment.

Defenses to crime simply negate the existence of one of the seven basic elements, usually the mens rea (as in mistake of fact and insanity), sometimes even the act itself (as in some insanity defenses), and sometimes the unlawfulness of the act (as in justification defenses).

■ NOTES

1. Michael Gottfredson and Travis Hirschi, "A Propensity-Event Theory of Crime," in *Advances in Criminological Theory*, vol. 1, ed. William S. Laufer and Freda Adler (New Brunswick, N.J.: Transaction, 1989), pp. 57–67.
2. Derek B. Cornish and Ronald V. Clarke, eds., *The Reasoning Criminal* (New York: Springer Verlag, 1986), p. vi; Ronald V. Clarke and Marcus Felson, "Introduction: Criminology, Routine Activity, and Rational Choice," in *Routine Activity and Rational Choice, Advances in Criminological Theory*, vol. 5, ed. Ronald V. Clarke and Marcus Felson (New Brunswick, N.J.: Transaction, 1993), pp. 1–14; Ezzat A. Fattah, "The Rational Choice/Opportunity Perspectives as a Vehicle for Integrating Criminological and Victimological Theories," in Clarke and Felson, *Routine Activity and Rational Choice*, pp. 225–258; Derek Cornish, "Theories of Action in Criminology: Learning Theory and Rational Choice Approaches," in Clarke and Felson, *Routine Activity and Rational Choice*, pp. 351–382. For critique of rational choice, see Ronald L. Akers, "Rational Choice, Deterrence, and Social Learning Theory in Criminology: The Path Not Taken," *Journal of Criminal Law and Criminology*, **81** (1990): 653–676.
3. Derek B. Cornish and Ronald V. Clarke, "Understanding Crime Displacement: An Application of Rational Choice Theory," *Criminology*, **25** (1987): 933–947, at p. 940; Pierre Tremblay, "Searching for Suitable Co-Offenders," in Clarke and Felson, *Routine Activity and Rational Choice*, pp. 17–36.
4. Lawrence E. Cohen and Marcus Felson, "Social Changes and Crime Rate Trends: A Routine Activity Approach," *American Sociological Review*, **44** (1979): 588–608.
5. Marcus Felson, "Routine Activities and Crime Prevention in the Developing Metropolis," *Criminology*, **25** (1987): 911–931, at p. 914; John D. Wooldredge, Francis T. Cullen, and Edward J. Latessa, "Victimization in the Workplace: A Test of Routine Activities Theory," *Justice Quarterly*, **9** (1992): 325–335; Leslie W. Kennedy and Stephen W. Baron, "Routine Activities and a Subculture of Violence: A Study of Violence on the Street," *Journal of Research in Crime and Delinquency*, **30** (1993): 88–112; Patricia L. Brantingham and Paul J. Brantingham, "Environment, Routine, and Situation: Toward a Pattern Theory of Crime," in Clarke and Felson, *Routine Activity and Rational Choice*, pp. 259–294; Maurice Cusson, "A Strategic Analysis of Crime: Criminal Tactics as Responses to Precriminal Situations," in Clarke and Felson, *Routine Activity and Rational Choice*, pp. 295–304; Gordon Trasler, "Conscience, Opportunity, Rational Choice, and Crime," in Clarke and Felson, *Routine Activity and Rational Choice*, pp. 305–322.
6. Lawrence W. Sherman, Patrick R. Gartin, and Michael E. Buerger, "Hot Spots of Predatory Crime: Routine Activities and the Criminology of Place," *Criminology*, **27** (1989): 27–55; Ronald V. Clarke and Patricia M. Harris, "A Rational Choice Perspective on the Targets of Automobile Theft," *Criminal Behaviour and Mental Health*, **2** (1992): 25–42.

   See also the following articles, in Clarke and Felson, *Routine Activity and Rational Choice*: Raymond Paternoster and Sally Simpson, "A Rational Choice Theory of Corporate Crime," pp. 37–58; Richard W. Harding, "Gun Use in Crime, Rational Choice, and Social Learning Theory," pp. 85–102; Richard B. Felson, "Predatory and Dispute-Related Violence: A Social Interactionist Approach," pp. 103–125; Nathaniel J. Pallone and James J. Hennessy, "Tinderbox Criminal Violence: Neurogenic Impulsivity, Risk-Taking, and the Phenomenology of Rational Choice," pp. 127–157; Max Taylor, "Rational Choice, Behavior Analysis, and Political Violence," pp. 159–178; Pietro Marongiu and Ronald V. Clarke, "Ransom Kidnapping in Sardinia, Subcultural Theory and Rational Choice," pp. 179–199; Bruce D. Johnson, Mangai Natarajan, and Harry Sanabria, "'Successful.' Criminal Careers: Toward an Ethnography within the Rational Choice Perspective," pp. 201–221.
7. Gottfredson and Hirschi, "A Propensity-Event Theory," p. 58; Ronald V. Clarke, ed., *Situational Crime Prevention: Successful Case Studies* (Albany: Harrow and Heston, 1992); Ross Homel, "Drivers Who Drink

and Rational Choice: Random Breath Testing and the Process of Deterrence," in Clarke and Felson, *Routine Activity and Rational Choice*, pp. 59–84; C. Ray Jeffery and Diane L. Zahm, "Crime Prevention through Environmental Design, Opportunity Theory, and Rational Choice Models," in Clarke and Felson, *Routine Activity and Rational Choice*, pp. 323–350.

See also the following articles, in Clarke, *Situational Crime Prevention:* John F. Decker, "Curbside Deterrence?" pp. 39–51; Pat Mayhew, Ronald V. Clarke, and Mike Hough, "Steering Column Locks and Car Theft," pp. 52–65; Paul Ekblom, "Preventing Post Office Robberies in London: Effects and Side Effects," pp. 66–74; Dennis Challinger, "Less Telephone Vandalism: How Did It Happen?" pp. 75–88; Roger Matthews, "Developing More Effective Strategies for Curbing Prostitution," pp. 89–98; Barry Poyner and Barry Webb, "Reducing Theft from Shopping Bags in City Center Markets," pp. 99–107; John Bell and Barbara Burke, "Cruising Cooper Street," pp. 108–112; Johannes Knutsson and Eckart Kuhlhorn, "Macro Measures against Crime: The Example of Check Forgeries," pp. 113–123; Ronald V. Clarke, "Deterring Obscene Phone Callers: The New Jersey Experience," pp. 124–132; Mary Jane Scherdin, "The Halo Effect: Psychological Deterrence of Electronic Security Systems," pp. 133–138; Scott DesChamps, Patricia L. Brantingham, and Paul J. Brantingham, "The British Columbia Transit Fare Evasion Audit," pp. 139–150; Henk Van Andel, "The Care of Public Transport in the Netherlands," pp. 151–163; John Eck and William Spelman, "Thefts from Vehicles in Shipyard Parking Lots," pp. 164–173; Barry Poyner, "Situational Crime Prevention in Two Parking Facilities," pp. 174–184; Barry Poyner, "Video Cameras and Bus Vandalism," pp. 185–193; Ronald D. Hunter and C. Ray Jeffery, "Preventing Convenience Store Robbery through Environmental Design," pp. 194–204; David B. Griswold, "Crime Prevention and Commercial Burglary," pp. 205–215; Jan M. Chaiken, Michael W. Lawless, and Keith A. Stevenson, "Exact Fare on Buses," pp. 216–222; Ken Pease, "Preventing Burglary on a British Public Housing Estate," pp. 223–229; Gloria Laycock, "Operation Identification, or the Power of Publicity?" pp. 230–238; Maryalice Sloan-Howitt and George L. Kelling, "Subway Graffiti in New York City: 'Gettin Up' vs. 'Meanin It and Cleanin It,'" pp. 239–248; Clifford D. Shearing and Phillip C. Stenning, "From the Panopticon to Disney World: The Development of Discipline," pp. 249–255.

8. The Anglo-American concept of crime was developed by a long line of distinguished legal scholars. Works that have contributed to this concept include Sir James Fitzjames Stephen, *A Digest of the Criminal Law of England* (London: Macmillan, 1877); Sir James Fitzjames Stephen, *History of the Criminal Law of England*, 3 vols. (London: Macmillan, 1883) (a revision of *A General View of the Criminal Law.*, 1869); Glanville L. Williams, *Criminal Law—The General Part*, 2d ed.

(London: Stevens, 1961); Joel Prentice Bishop, *Commentaries on the Criminal Law*, 2 vols. (Boston: Little, Brown, 1856, 1858); Francis W. Wharton, *A Treatise on the Criminal Law of the United States* (Philadelphia: J. Key, 1852); George Fletcher, *Rethinking Criminal Law* (Boston: Little, Brown, 1978); Paul H. Robinson, *Fundamentals of Criminal Law* (Boston: Little, Brown, 1988); and Paul H. Robinson, *Criminal Law Defenses* (St. Paul, Minn.: West, 1984). For a general assessment of criminal law scholarship, see G. O. W. Mueller, *Crime, Law, and the Scholars* (London: Heinemann; Seattle: University of Washington Press, 1969).

9. Jerome Hall, *General Principles of Criminal Law*, 2d ed. (Indianapolis: Bobbs-Merrill, 1960).

10. American Law Institute, Model Penal Code, sec. 2.01(1). The American Law Institute, dedicated to law reform, is an association of some of the most prestigious American lawyers. Between 1954 and 1962 this group sought to codify the best features of the penal codes of the various states. The resultant Model Penal Code (MPC) has had considerable influence on law reform in many states, and has been adopted nearly in full by New Jersey and Pennsylvania. We shall have frequent occasion to refer to the MPC as "typical" American criminal law.

11. *Robinson v. California*, 370 U.S. 660 (1962).

12. *Powell v. Texas*, 392 U.S. 514 (1968).

13. *State v. Palendrano*, 120 N.J. Super. 336, 293 A. 2d 747 (1972).

14. G. O. W. Mueller, "Causing Criminal Harm," in *Essays in Criminal Science*, ed. Mueller (South Hackensack, N.J.: Fred B. Rothman; London: Sweet & Maxwell, Ltd., 1961), pp. 167–214.

15. *Lambert v. California*, 355 U.S. 225 (1957). This decision must be approached with care: it does not stand for the proposition that ignorance of the law is an excuse. The Supreme Court was very careful to limit the scope of its decision to offenses by omission of adherence to regulations not commonly known, when the defendant in fact did not know—and had no means of knowing—of the prohibition.

16. G. O. W. Mueller, "On Common Law Mens Rea," *Minnesota Law Review*, **42** (1958): 1043–1104, at p. 1060.

17. Wayne R. LaFave and Austin W. Scott, Jr., *Criminal Law* (St. Paul, Minn.: West, 1983), p. 222.

18. Peter W. Low, John Calvin Jeffries, Jr., and Richard J. Bonnie, *The Trial of John W. Hinckley, Jr.* (Mineola, N.Y.: Foundation Press, 1986).

19. Richard Moran, *Knowing Right from Wrong: The Insanity Defense of Daniel McNaughten* (New York: Free Press, 1981), is a fascinating discussion of the M'Naghten case. See also Bernard L. Diamond, "Isaac Ray and the Trial of Daniel M'Naghten," *American Journal of Psychiatry*, **112** (1956): 651–656.

20. *Daniel M'Naughten's Case*, 10 C.F. 200, 210–211, 8 Eng. Rep. 718, 722–723 (1843).

21. G. O. W. Mueller, "M'Naghten Remains Irreplaceable: Recent Events in the Law of Incapacity," *Georgetown Law Journal*, **50** (1961): 105–119. The literature on

the law of insanity is extensive. Among more recent works are Abraham S. Goldstein, *The Insanity Defense* (New Haven, Conn.: Yale University Press, 1967); Joel Feinberg, *Doing and Deserving: Essays in the Theory of Responsibility* (Princeton, N.J.: Princeton University Press, 1970); Herbert Fingarette and Ann Fingarette Hasse, *Mental Disabilities and Criminal Responsibility* (Berkeley: University of California Press, 1979); Norval Morris, *Madness and the Criminal Law* (Chicago: University of Chicago Press, 1982); Donald H. J. Herfmann, *The Insanity Defense: Philosophical, Historical, and Legal Perspectives* (Springfield, Ill.: Charles C. Thomas, 1983); and Michael S. Moore, *Law and Psychiatry: Rethinking the Relationship* (New York: Cambridge University Press, 1984).

22. See *Parsons v. State,* 81 Ala. 577, 2 So. 854 (1887).
23. *Durham v. United States,* 214 F. 2d 862 (D.C. Cir. 1954); *States v. Pike,* 49 N.H. 399 (1869).
24. *United States v. Brawner,* 471 F. 2d 696 (D.C. Cir. 1972).
25. Model Penal Code, sec. 4.01.
26. 18 U.S. Code, sec. 17.
27. Richard A. Pasewark, Richard Jeffrey, and Stephen Bieber, "Differentiating Successful and Unsuccessful Insanity Plea Defendants in Colorado," *Journal of Psychiatry and Law,* **15** (1987): 55–82, at p. 65, covering the period July 1, 1980, to June 30, 1983.
28. Robert J. Michaels, "The Market for Heroin before and after Legalization," in *Dealing with Drugs,* ed. Ronald Hamowy (Lexington, Mass.: Lexington Books, 1987), pp. 311–318.
29. Paul H. Robinson, *Fundamentals of Criminal Law* (Boston: Little, Brown, 1988), pp. 287 ff.
30. Basically, the defense is not available if the actor was at fault by placing himself in the situation: Model Penal Code, sec. 2.09(1).
31. American Law Institute, Model Penal Code, Tentative Draft No. 8 (Philadelphia, 1958), pp. 5–10.
32. For a fascinating legal and factual analysis of the case, see George P. Fletcher, *A Crime of Self-Defense: Bernhard Goetz and the Law on Trial* (New York: Free Press, 1988).
33. *Rex v. Scofield* (1784 Cald. 402).
34. Model Penal Code, sec. 5.01(1) (c).

10
Violent Crimes

KEY TERMS
aggravated assault
assault
battery
felony murder
homicide
involuntary manslaughter
justifiable homicide
kidnapping
malice aforethought
manslaughter
mass murder
murder
rape
robbery
serial murder
simple assault
sociopath
stranger homicide
terrorism
victim precipitation
voluntary manslaughter

To millions of Americans few things are more pervasive, more frightening, more real today than violent crime and the fear of being assaulted, mugged, robbed, or raped. The fear of being victimized by criminal attack has touched us all in some way. People are fleeing their residences in cities to the expected safety of suburban living. Residents of many areas will not go out on the street at night. Others have added bars and extra locks to windows and doors in their homes. Bus drivers in major cities do not carry cash because incidents of robbery have been so frequent. In some areas local citizens patrol the streets at night to attain the safety they feel has not been provided. . . .

There are numerous conflicting definitions of criminal violence as a class of behavior. Police, prosecutors, jurists, federal agents, local detention officials, and behavioral scientists all hold somewhat different viewpoints as to what constitute acts of violence. All would probably agree, however, as the police reports make abundantly clear, that criminal violence involves the use of or the threat of force on a victim by an offender.[1]

The penal law defines types of violent crime, and each is distinguished by a particular set of elements. We concentrate on criminological characteristics: the frequency with which each type of violent crime is committed, the methods used in its commission, and its distribution through time and place. We also examine the people who commit the offense and those who are its victims. If we can determine when, where, and how a specific type of crime is likely to be committed, we will be in a better position to reduce the incidence of that crime by devising appropriate strategies to prevent it.

We begin with homicide, since the taking of life is the most serious harm one human being can inflict on another. Serious attacks that fall short of homicide are assaults of various kinds, including serious sexual assault (rape) and the forceful taking of property from another person (robbery). Other patterns of violence are not defined as such in the penal codes but are so important in practice as to require separate discussion. Family-related violence and terrorism, both of which encompass a variety of crimes, fall into this category.

HOMICIDE

Homicide is the killing of one human being by another. Some homicides are sanctioned by law. In this category of **justifiable homicide,** we find homicides committed by law enforcement officers in the course of carrying out their duties (see Chapter 9) and homicides committed by soldiers in combat, or when a homeowner has no recourse other than to kill an intruder who threatens the lives of family members. Criminologists are most interested in *criminal homicides—* unlawful killings, without justification or excuse. Criminal homicides are subdivided into three categories: murder, manslaughter, and negligent homicide.

Murder

At common law, **murder** was defined as the intentional killing of another person with **malice aforethought.** Courts have struggled with an exact definition of "malice." To describe it, they have used such terms as "evil mind" and "abandoned and malignant heart." Actually, malice is a very simple concept. It is the defendant's awareness that he or she had no right to kill but intended to kill anyway.[2]

Originally the malice had to be "aforethought": the person had to have killed after some contemplation, rather than on the spur of the moment. The concept eventually became meaningless because some courts considered even a few seconds sufficient to establish forethought. The dividing line between planned and spur-of-the-moment killings disappeared. But many legislators believed contemplation was an appropriate concept, because it allowed us to distinguish the various types of murder. They reintroduced it, calling it "premeditation and deliberation." A premeditated, deliberate, intentional killing became murder in the first degree; an intentional killing without premeditation and deliberation became murder in the second degree.

States that had the death penalty reserved it for murder in the first degree. Some state statutes listed particular means of committing murder as

WINDOW TO THE WORLD
Assassinations around the Globe

Since earliest times the fate of nations and world history have been affected by assassinations. Assassinations were so common in ancient Rome that it became forbidden to carry daggers into the Senate. That did not keep Gaius Julius Caesar's assassins from stabbing him to death in 44 B.C.; their weapons were stilichos, pencil-like tools used to write on wax tablets.

Assassinations are just as likely to occur in politically stable countries as in countries with turmoil, in both developed and developing countries. Is there an effective deterrent? Our penal codes treat the assassination of a head of state or government as a category of homicide distinct from, or higher than, ordinary murder. The Federal Criminal Code, Title 18 U.S. Code 1751, imposes the death penalty for the assassination of the president of the United States, the president-elect, other potential successors, and specially appointed executive staff members. The United States has had more than its share of assassinations. Abraham Lincoln was killed in 1865, and American presidents and political leaders have remained favorite targets: James A. Garfield, 1881; William McKinley, 1901; John F. Kennedy, 1963; Senator Robert F. Kennedy, 1968; Dr. Martin Luther King, Jr., 1968. Presidents Theodore Roosevelt, Franklin Delano Roosevelt, Harry S. Truman, Richard Nixon, Gerald Ford, and Ronald Reagan and Governor George C. Wallace of Alabama have all been the targets of attempted assassinations.

In the last 20 years the number of assassinations around the world appears to have increased. In 1975 President Richard Ratsimandraua of Madagascar, King Faisal of Saudi Arabia, and President Sheik Mujibur Rahman of Bangladesh were assassinated; in 1976 the Nigerian head of state, General Murtala Ramat Mohammed, and Chilean foreign minister Orlando Letelier; in 1977 President Marien Ngouabi of the Congo; in 1978 former Iraqi premier Abdul Razak Al-Naif and former Italian premier Aldo Moro; in 1979 Lord Mountbatten and South Korean president Park Chung Hee; in 1980 Liberian president William R. Tolbert and former Nicaraguan president Anastasio Somoza Debayle; in 1981 Egyptian president Anwar El-Sadat; in 1982 Lebanese president-elect Bishir Gemayel; in 1983 Philippine opposition leader Benigno Acquino; in 1984 Indian prime minister Indira Gandhi; in 1986 Swedish prime minister Olof Palme; in 1988 Lebanese premier Rashid Karami; and in 1992 Indian prime minister Rajiv Gandhi. In the first four months of 1993, Sri Lanka's former minister Lalith Athulathmudali, African National Congress leader Chris Hani, Palestinian official Hussein Salem, and Bosnia-Herzegovina's deputy prime minister Hakija Turajlik were assassinated. Many more assassinations of political leaders have occurred around the world, and hundreds more have been attempted but did not succeed.

What prompts people to kill a national leader? Obviously some assassins are psychologically disturbed. Several recent American assassins fall into this category: Lee Harvey Oswald, who has been identified as the killer of President Kennedy; President Ford's two would-be assassins; and John Hinckley, who tried to kill President Reagan. But some assassins act for political, idealistic reasons, such as the Puerto Rican nationalists Oscar Collazo and Griselio Torresola, who tried to kill President Truman.

Are all political assassins bad? The citizens of the former Federal Republic of Germany commemorate July 20, the day on which Colonel Count Klaus von Stauffenberg in 1944 detonated a bomb in Adolf Hitler's bunker. That was to be the last of 43 attempted assassinations of Hitler, who committed suicide less than a year later—but not before Colonel von Stauffenberg and more than 200 coconspirators had been summarily tried by Nazi courts and hanged.

Questions for Discussion

1. Do you think assassination should be considered such a serious crime that insanity not be allowed as a defense?
2. Can you think of anything that might serve (or currently serves) as an effective deterrent to would-be assassins?

Source: James F. Kirkham, Sheldon G. Levy, and William J. Crotty, Assassinations and Political Violence (Washington, D.C.: U.S. Government Printing Office, 1969).

. . . "There are at least three separate elements woven into the concept of 'assassination' which identify it as a particular kind of murder: (1) a target that is a prominent political figure; (2) a political motive for the killing; (3) the potential political impact of the death or escape from death, as the case may be. . . . All three elements, however, do not necessarily coexist."

indicative of premeditation and deliberation, such as killing by poison or by lying in wait. More recently the charge of murder in the first degree has been reserved for the killing of a law enforcement officer or of a corrections officer and for the killing of any person by a prisoner serving a life sentence. Among the most serious forms of murder is *assassination*, the killing of a head of state or government or of an otherwise highly visible figure.

A special form of murder, **felony murder,** requires no intention to kill. It requires, instead, the intention to commit some other felony, such as robbery or rape, and the death of a person during the commission of, or flight from, that felony. Even accomplices are guilty of felony murder when one of their associates has caused a death. For example, while A and B are holding up a gas station attendant, A fires a warning shot, and the bullet ricochets and kills a passerby. Both A and B are guilty of felony murder. The rule originated in England centuries ago, when death sentences were imposed for all felonies, so it made no difference whether a perpetrator actually intended to kill or merely to rob. Most states today apply the felony murder rule only when the underlying felony is a life-endangering one, such as arson, rape, or robbery.

Manslaughter

Manslaughter is the unlawful killing of another person without malice. Manslaughter may be either voluntary or involuntary.

Voluntary Manslaughter

Voluntary manslaughter is a killing committed intentionally but without malice—for example, in the heat of passion or in response to strong provocation. Persons who kill under extreme provocation cannot make rational decisions as to whether they have a right to kill or not. They therefore act without the necessary malice.[3]

Just as passion, fright, fear, or consternation may affect a person's capacity to act rationally, so may drugs or alcohol. In some states a charge of murder may be reduced to voluntary manslaughter when the defendant was so grossly intoxicated as not to be fully aware of the implications of his or her actions. All voluntary-

Body bags contain the five passengers killed when a Manhattan subway train derailed as it came around the curve into the station on August 28, 1991. An additional 171 passengers were injured. In October 1992 a jury concluded that the motorman, Robert E. Ray, was guilty of second-degree manslaughter as a result of recklessness.

manslaughter cases have one thing in common: the defendant's awareness of the unlawfulness of the act was dulled or grossly reduced by shock, fright, consternation, or intoxication.

Involuntary Manslaughter

A crime is designated as **involuntary manslaughter** when a person has caused the death of another unintentionally but recklessly by consciously disregarding a substantial and unjustifiable risk that endangered another person's life. Many states have created an additional category, *negligent homicide,* to establish criminal liability for grossly negligent killing in situations where the offender assumed a lesser risk.

Manslaughter plays an increasingly prominent role in our society, with its high concentrations of population, high-tech risks, and chemical and even nuclear dangers. The reach of the crime of involuntary manslaughter was clearly demonstrated in the 1942 Coconut Grove disaster in Boston, in which 491 people perished because of a nightclub owner's negligence in creating fire hazards. The nightclub was overcrowded, it was furnished and decorated with highly flammable materials, and exits were blocked. The court ruled that a reasonable person would have recognized the risk. If the defendant is so "stupid" as not to have recognized the risk, he is nevertheless guilty of manslaughter.[4]

The Extent of Homicide

Social scientists who look at homicide have a different perspective from that of the legislators who define such crimes. Social scientists are concerned with rates and patterns of criminal activities.

Homicide Rates in the United States Today

The American murder rate always has been high. It reached a peak in 1980 and has been declining erratically since then. In 1992, our population of close to 250 million experienced 23,760 murders and nonnegligent homicides (as reported to the police), or 9.3 per 100,000 of the population. This rate is not equally distributed over the whole country: murder rates are higher in the southern and western states (11 and 10 per 100,000, respectively) than in the northeastern and midwestern states (both 8 per 100,000).

Your chance of becoming a murder victim is much higher if you are male than if you are female: of all murder victims, 78 percent are male, 22 percent female. Age plays a role—nearly half of all murder victims are between the ages of 20 and 34; and so does race—47 percent of all murder victims are white, 50 percent are black, and the remaining 3 percent are of other ethnic origins.[5]

Ninety-four percent of the black murder victims were slain by black offenders, and 83 percent of the white murder victims were killed by white offenders. Intentional criminal homicide apparently is an intraracial crime. But it is not an intragender crime. The data show that males were most often killed by males (87 percent); nine out of ten female victims were murdered by males. The population at the highest risk consists of black men between 25 and 35 years of age.[6]

Homicide Rates over Time

Researchers have asked what happens to homicide rates over time when the composition of the population changes. What is the effect, for example, of a change in the racial composition of a city? Roland Chilton, using data on offenses committed in Chicago between 1960 and 1980 and census data for those years, found that about 20 percent of the total increase in homicide rates could be explained by increases in the nonwhite male population. The same correlation is found in most major cities in the United States. Chilton argues that the problem will remain because of the poverty and demoralization of the groups involved. We can even expect that it will get worse if municipal governments are unable to improve the schools, reduce unemployment, and extend social services.[7]

Until conditions change, what has been poignantly referred to as "the subculture of exasperation" will continue to produce a high homicide rate among nonwhite inner-city males.[8] Coramae Mann has found that although black women make up about 11 percent of the female population in the United States, they are arrested for three-fourths of all homicides committed by females. She argues that given such a disproportionate involvement in violent crime, one has to question whether the subculture of exasperation alone is entirely responsible.[9] But so few studies have been done on the subject that we cannot reach any definitive conclusion. Other investigators agree that homicide rates cannot be explained solely by such factors as poverty; the rates are also significantly associated with cultural approval of a resort to violence.[10]

The Nature of Homicide

Let us take a closer look at killers and their victims and see how they are related to each other. In the 1950s Marvin Wolfgang studied homicide situations, perpetrators, and victims in the Philadelphia area. Victims and offenders were predominantly young black adults of low socioeconomic status. The offenses were committed in the inner city; they occurred primarily in the home of the victim or offender, on weekends, in the evening hours, and among friends or acquaintances.

Building on the pioneering work of Hans von Hentig,[11] Wolfgang found that many of the victims had actually initiated the social interaction that led to the homicidal response, in a direct or subliminal way. He coined the term **victim precipitation** for such instances, which may account for as many as a quarter to a half of all intentional homicides. In such cases it is the victim who, by insinuation, bodily movement, verbal incitement, or the actual use of physical force, initiates a series of events that results in his or her own death. For example:

> During an argument in which a male called a female many vile names, she tried to telephone the police. He grabbed the phone from her hands, knocked her down, kicked her, and hit her with a tire gauge. She ran to the kitchen, grabbed a butcher knife, and stabbed him in the stomach.[12]

Recent studies have provided additional insight into the patterns of homicide. Robert Silverman and Leslie Kennedy demonstrated that gender relationships, age, means of commission of the act, and location vary with relational distance, from closest relatives (lovers, spouses) to total strangers.[13]

Margaret Zahn and Philip Sagi have developed a model that distinguishes among homicides on the basis of characteristics of victims, offenders, location, method of attack, and presence of witnesses. They conclude that all these characteristics and variables serve to differentiate four categories of homicides: (1) those within the family, (2) those among friends and acquaintances, (3) stranger homicides associated with felonies, and (4) stranger homicides not associated with felonies.[14]

Stranger Homicides

The rate of **stranger homicide**—a killing in which killer and victim have had no known previous contact—has not varied between 1977 (13.4 percent) and 1992 (14 percent).[15] Marc Riedel, however, found these stranger homicide rates to be considerably understated. The true figures, according to Riedel, ranged from 14 to 29 percent. Furthermore, the impact of stranger homicides on the quality of urban life—especially the fear of crime they engender—is far greater than their relatively small numbers would suggest.[16]

Relatives and Acquaintances

Almost half of all homicides occur among relatives and acquaintances (39 percent of the relationships are unknown.)[17] Of these homicides, those in which women killed their mates have received particular attention. Researchers take special interest in the factors behind such crimes. Angela Browne found a high incidence of long-term abuse suffered by women who subsequently killed their mates.[18] And a recent study by two psychologists suggests that mate homicides are the result of a husband's efforts to control his wife and the wife's efforts to retain her independence.[19]

Some recent trends are also noteworthy: an increase in women who kill in domestic encounters, more planned killings, and less acceptance of self-defense as a motive in such cases.[20] Children are also at risk of death at the hands of family members. One investigator found that in the 5- to 9-year age group, black boys had the highest homicide fatality rate: 25 per 100,000 (3.7 times higher than the rate for white boys). High rates of child homicide persist in low-income areas.[21] Once again, many observers blame the subculture of exasperation.[22]

Young and Old Perpetrators

Not surprisingly, the very young and the elderly have low homicide rates. In 1992, 304 homicide charges were placed against youngsters under 15,[23] but this figure does not include the number of homicides in which the young killers were dealt with by juvenile courts or welfare agencies. Of the 19,491 persons of all ages arrested for homicide in 1992, 2829 were under 18. The elderly, too, are underrepresented among killers. People age 55 and older accounted for only 2.4 percent of all murders in 1992.[24]

Homicide without Apparent Motive

In most homicides, the killer has a motive or a reason for killing the victim; the vast majority of homicides are committed for a reason. Popular fiction tells us that detectives tend to consider a case solved if they can establish the motive. But research shows that in a substantial number of murders, the motive remains unclear. The "unmotivated" murderers are a puzzle—and they constitute 25 percent of all homicide offenders.

Though in most respects the killers without motive are similar to those who kill for a reason, they are more likely to have "(1) no history of alcohol abuse; (2) a recent release from prison; (3) claims of amnesia for the crime; (4) denial of the crime; and (5) a tendency to exhibit psychotic behavior following the crime and to be assessed not guilty of the crime due to mental illness."[25]

Mass and Serial Murders

Criminological researchers have paid special attention to two types of murders that are particularly disturbing to the community: **serial murders,** killings of several victims over a period of time, and **mass murders,** killings of multiple victims in one event or in very quick succession. Between 1970 and 1993 U.S. police knew of approximately 125 cases of multiple homicides. The literature on the subject is enormous.[26] Some recent serial murderers have become infamous.

Theodore "Ted" Bundy, law student and former crime commission staff member, killed between 19 and 36 young women in the northwestern states and Florida. David Berkowitz, the "Son of Sam," killed 6 young women in New York. Douglas Clark, the "Sunset Strip killer,"

The serial murders of five college students in Gainesville, Florida, in August 1990, which had terrified the university community, were finally solved in February 1994 when Danny H. Rolling pleaded guilty to five murder charges.

killed between 7 and 50 prostitutes in Hollywood. The "Green River killer" of Seattle may have killed more than 45 victims. In the Midwest, Jeffrey Dahmer preserved, and took Polaroid photographs of, the mutilated body parts of his 11 to 17 victims; and on Long Island, Joel Rifkin collected souvenirs—a shoe, an earring, a driver's license—from the more than 13 streetwalkers he claimed as his victims.

In 1991, the worst mass murder in U.S. history took place in a Texas café. An unemployed young man drove his pickup through the restaurant's glass window and opened fire with a semiautomatic pistol, leaving 22 dead. James Huberty walked into a McDonald's in California and killed 20 people. Colin Ferguson boarded a train where he killed six and wounded seventeen in the Long Island massacre of 1993. Recently, there has been an increase in mass murders in the workplace. San Franciscan failed businessman Gian Luigi Ferri, who blamed lawyers for his problems, burst into the thirty-fourth-floor law office where he had been a client and, with two pistols, killed eight persons working in the firm. Disgruntled employee Paul Calder returned 8 months after being fired to kill three and wound two at a Tampa insurance company. The U.S. Postal Service, where 38 employees died violently between 1986 and 1993, is now looking into ways to reduce employer-employee tension, especially when layoffs are imminent.

It is popularly believed that multiple murderers are mentally ill; their offenses, after all, are often quite bizarre. In many such cases psychiatrists have indeed found severe pathology.[27] Yet juries are reluctant to find these offenders not guilty by reason of insanity. Albert Fish, who cooked and ate the children he murdered, died in the electric chair.[28] Edmund Kemper, who killed hitchhikers as well as his own mother (he used her head as a dartboard), received a life term.[29]

The criminologists Jack Levin and James Fox do not agree with the hypothesis that all mass and serial murderers are mentally diseased (for example, psychotic) and therefore legally insane or incompetent. On the contrary, they say, serial killers are **sociopaths,** persons who lack internal controls, disregard common values, and have an intense desire to dominate others. But psychological characteristics alone cannot explain the actions of these people. They are also influenced by the social environment in which they function: the openness of our society, the ease of travel, the availability of firearms, the lack of external controls and supervision, and the general friendliness and trust of Americans in dealing with each other and with strangers.[30]

Levin and Fox suggest that the recent increase in mass and serial murders, despite a general decline in the murder rate, is to some extent attributable to the publicity given to mass murders and the resulting copy-cat phenomenon, the repetition of a crime as a result of the publicity it receives. When one person killed at random by poisoning Tylenol capsules with cyanide, others copied the idea. This phenomenon has prompted Ronald Holmes and James de Burger to recommend that the media cooperate with the criminal justice system when the circumstances demand discretion.[31] Yet cooperation may be hard to achieve when media help is needed to alert the public to a health hazard (as in the Tylenol cases). In any event, the First Amendment's guarantee of freedom of the press does not permit controls.

Gang Murder

Up to this point we have dealt largely with homicides committed by single offenders. But what about homicides by gangs of offenders?

Are there any differences between the two types? On the basis of an analysis of data contained in 700 homicide investigation files, researchers found that "gang homicides differ both qualitatively and quantitatively from nongang homicides. Most distinctly, they differ with respect to ethnicity [more likely to be intraethnic, age [gang killers are 5 years younger], number of participants [two and a half times as many participants], and relationship between the participants [gang killers are twice as likely not to know their victims]."[32] But similarities can also be seen. The causes of gang homicides are attributable to social disorganization, economic inequality, and deprivation.[33]

Since the 1950s the nature of gang murder has changed dramatically. In Los Angeles, for example, gang membership tripled and gang-related homicides increased from 271 to 771 annually between 1985 and 1991. An estimated 40 percent of the 22,000 inmates in the Los Angeles county jail belong to gangs.[34]

Compare those 771 murders with the number of gang killings in the 1950s and 1960s, when such cities as Philadelphia and Los Angeles reported 30 or 40 a year. Gang homicides have also gotten more brutal. Drive-by and cross-fire shootings of intended victims and innocent bystanders are no longer uncommon. In Brooklyn, New York, all three brothers in one family fell victim to street violence. Motives also have changed through the years. Once, gang wars, with a few related homicides, took place over "turf," territory that members protected, with knives, rocks, or metal chains as weapons. Now the wars are over drugs, and the weapons are assault rifles or semiautomatic guns.[35]

A Cross-National Comparison of Homicide Rates

The criminal homicides we have been discussing are those committed in the United States. By comparing homicide rates in this country with those of other countries, we can gain a broader understanding of that crime. In 1985 the United Nations World Crime Survey revealed that the average rate of intentional homicide for developed (industrialized Western) countries was 2.3 per 100,000.[36]

The survey figures demonstrated that by comparison with the other developed countries, the United States was not doing well: its homicide rate was 10 per 100,000 population, the highest among industrialized Western countries. Figure 10.1 shows that the United States is the leader in homicide rates.

One cross-national study found a moderate association between inequality of income and rate of homicide. It likewise revealed a relationship between a youthful population and the homicide rate. The analysis, the study concluded, "suggests that homicide rates are higher in poorer countries, more culturally diverse countries, in countries which spend less on defense, in less democratic societies, and in countries where fewer young people are enrolled in school."[37] Another researcher who compared the homicide rates in 76 countries with the rate in the United States found that when he took into consideration the differences in the age and sex distributions of the various populations, the United States had a higher rate than all but 15 countries,[38] most of which were experiencing civil war or internal strife.

Dane Archer and Rosemary Gartner collected their own crime statistics—the Comparative Crime Data File (CCDF)—from 110 nations over a 5-year period. A comparison of their homicide rates with historical and socioeconomic data led the researchers to the following conclusions:

- Combatant nations experience an increase in homicides following cessation of hostilities (violence has come to be seen as a legitimate means of settling disputes).
- The largest cities have the highest homicide rates; the smallest have the lowest homicide rates; but, paradoxically, as a city grows, its homicide rate per capita does not.
- The availability of capital punishment does not result in fewer homicides and in fact often results in more; abolition of capital punishment decreases the homicide rate.[39]

Most international comparative studies find some link between economic development and the homicide rate.[40] These, then, are the characteristics of criminal homicide on which social scientists focus: the extent of homicide in the society under consideration, its spatial and temporal features, the demographic characteristics of killers and of their victims, and the relationship between killers and victims.

We have seen that murder rates are not distributed equally among countries or within a single country. They are not even distributed equally within neighborhoods (Figure 10.2). In the United States a greater proportion of males, young people, and blacks are perpetrators and victims of homicide, which tends to be committed against someone the killer knows, at or near the home of at least one of the persons involved, in the evening or on a weekend. These patterns of homicide have recently been interpreted in accordance with the rational-choice and routine-activities framework discussed in Chapter 9. Advocates of this approach hold that when the wide variety of findings concerning homicide are related to the normal, everyday patterns of interactions, the information can help in the development of various preventive measures.[41]

ASSAULT

The crimes of homicide and serious assault share many characteristics. Both are typically committed by young males, and a disproportionate number of arrestees are members of minority groups. Assault victims, too, often know their attackers. Spatial and temporal distributions are also quite comparable. Assault rates, like those of homicide, are highest in urban areas, during the summer months, in the evening hours, and in the South.

Though the patterns are the same, the legal definitions are not. A murder is an act that causes the death of another person and that is intended to cause death. An **assault** is an attack on another person that is made with apparent ability to inflict injury and that is intended to frighten or to cause physical harm. (An attack that results in touching or striking the victim is called a **battery.**) Modern statutes usually recognize two types of assault: a **simple assault** is one that inflicts little or no physical hurt; a felonious assault, or **aggravated assault,** is one in which the perpetrator inflicts serious harm on the victim or uses a deadly weapon.

Population	City	Number of homicides

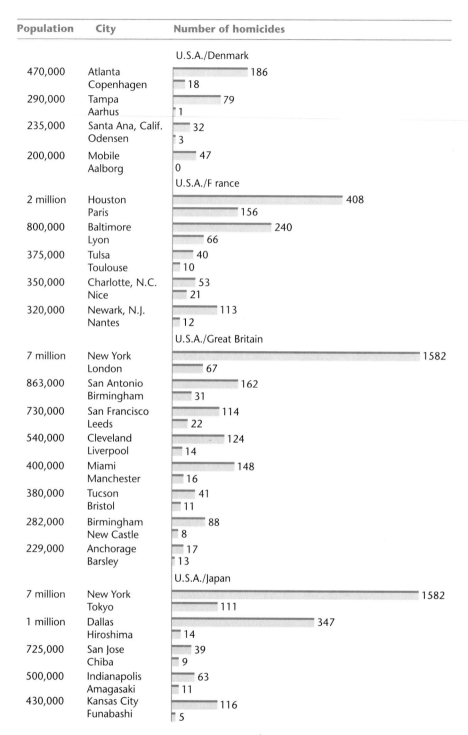

U.S.A./Denmark

470,000	Atlanta	186
	Copenhagen	18
290,000	Tampa	79
	Aarhus	1
235,000	Santa Ana, Calif.	32
	Odensen	3
200,000	Mobile	47
	Aalborg	0

U.S.A./France

2 million	Houston	408
	Paris	156
800,000	Baltimore	240
	Lyon	66
375,000	Tulsa	40
	Toulouse	10
350,000	Charlotte, N.C.	53
	Nice	21
320,000	Newark, N.J.	113
	Nantes	12

U.S.A./Great Britain

7 million	New York	1582
	London	67
863,000	San Antonio	162
	Birmingham	31
730,000	San Francisco	114
	Leeds	22
540,000	Cleveland	124
	Liverpool	14
400,000	Miami	148
	Manchester	16
380,000	Tucson	41
	Bristol	11
282,000	Birmingham	88
	New Castle	8
229,000	Anchorage	17
	Barsley	13

U.S.A./Japan

7 million	New York	1582
	Tokyo	111
1 million	Dallas	347
	Hiroshima	14
725,000	San Jose	39
	Chiba	9
500,000	Indianapolis	63
	Amagasaki	11
430,000	Kansas City	116
	Funabashi	5

FIGURE 10.1 Number of homicides in U.S. cities and in cities of comparable size in four other industrialized nations, 1988

Source: *The Police Chief*, March 1988, pp. 36–37.

Since last last December,* 10 people have been killed on or near Beekman Avenue, a short but extraordinary violent street in the Mott Haven section of the Bronx. The police say drugs were involved in all of the cases except the shooting on Jan. 3, for which they have no suspected motive.

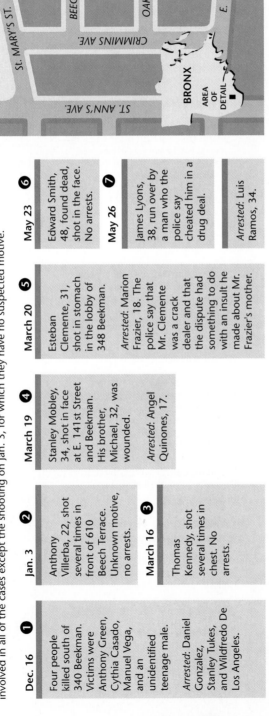

Dec. 16 ❶

Four people killed south of 340 Beekman. Victims were Anthony Green, Cythia Casado, Manuel Vega, and an unidentified teenage male.

Arrested: Daniel Gonzalez, Stanley Tukes, and Wildfredo De Los Angeles.

Jan. 3 ❷

Anthony Villerba, 22, shot several times in front of 610 Beech Terrace. Unknown motive, no arrests.

March 16 ❸

Thomas Kennedy, shot several times in chest. No arrests.

March 19 ❹

Stanley Mobley, 34, shot in face at E. 141st Street and Beekman. His brother, Michael, 32, was wounded.

Arrested: Angel Quinones, 17.

March 20 ❺

Esteban Clemente, 31, shot in stomach in the lobby of 348 Beekman.

Arrested: Marion Frazier, 18. The police say that Mr. Clemente was a crack dealer and that the dispute had something to do with an insult he made about Mr. Frazier's mother.

May 23 ❻

Edward Smith, 48, found dead, shot in the face. No arrests.

May 26 ❼

James Lyons, 38, run over by a man who the police say cheated him in a drug deal.

Arrested: Luis Ramos, 34.

*December 1991 to October 1992.

FIGURE 10.2 A deadly neighborhood

Source: New York Times, Oct. 13, 1992. p. 85.

237

AT ISSUE
Date Rape, Stranger Rape

"From the beginning I had this feeling that I was the one who was on trial rather than the guy they picked up and charged," said a [27-year-old] woman, raped by an intruder who entered her apartment through a window from an adjacent rooftop.

"If I had it to do again, I would never have gone through with the prosecution. I wouldn't even have reported it," said the woman. Despite extensive body bruises and a wound in her forehead that took six stitches to close, the defense attorney argued that "vigorous love play" did not necessarily indicate nonconsent and, in fact, could even indicate enthusiastic approval and passionate involvement in the act.

"Right after it happened . . . I mean here I was lying on the floor, I was damned near hysterical when I called the police. They arrived and the very first question this one guy asked me was, 'Did you enjoy it? Did you *really* try to resist the guy?'

"Later at the police station. They caught the guy from my description. He was sitting there and one of the cops went out to get him a cup of coffee and gave him a cigarette. They told me, 'Sit over there, lady, we'll get to you in a minute.'

"Over and over again, the police, the district attorney, the defense attorneys, even my own goddamned private lawyer asked me the same thing: 'Are you sure you really resisted? Did you *really* want to get raped subconsciously?'

"In the end the guy who did it got off."(1)

In a society in which rape victims such as the woman quoted above often wonder who's on trial, it is not surprising that the idea of rape by someone the victim knows may not be taken seriously. Called *date rape* or *acquaintance rape,* the crime recently has been the focus of workshops, counseling sessions, and codes of conduct on college campuses across the country.

Some people feel that "date rape" is a misleading term:

> In the courts, "date rape" is treated no differently than rape by a stranger. But some dislike the term. Robert S. Hudd, police chief at the University of Connecticut, argues that you wouldn't call it "date burglary" if a friend broke into your house. "It demeans the crime and makes people more comfortable with it," Hudd said. "In an ideal world, we would look at it as a serious felony like any other sexual assault."(2)

Others feel that the attention paid to acquaintance rape endangers the progress that has been made in society's attitude toward stranger rape.

> [A]uthor Katie Roiphe says that colleges and feminists belittle violent rape by calling too many incidents sexual assault. "The vocabulary is being used in the broadest possible way," she said. "We should be able to separate rape from bad sexual experience."(2)

A 1992 federal law requires colleges to have sexual-assault policies and to conduct disciplinary hearings. But campus approaches to and attitudes about date rape vary enormously. Students at Wesleyan University use a bathroom stall in the student center to record the names of young men accused of date rape "because women are

FBI's Uniform Crime Reports 1992 Statistics (most recent available)

102,555	rapes reported
39,160	reports resulted in arrest
18,024	convictions

"An assessment of 18 states showed that 21% of those convicted of forcible rape receive probation."
—Alice Vachss, "Rape and Denial," *New Republic,* November 22, 1993, pp. 14–15.

frustrated with how sexual assault is handled," according to one student.(2) At the other extreme, Antioch College has a 13-page sexual-offense policy that requires "willing and verbal consent" for each individual sexual act; failure to comply with the rules can result in punishments ranging from a reprimand from the dean to expulsion from the college.(3)

Violent rape, stranger rape, date rape, acquaintance rape—do these qualifiers add anything meaningful to the definition of rape? How society approaches rape in the future depends, at least in part, on an answer to that question.

Sources
1. Freda Adler, *Sisters in Crime* (New York: McGraw-Hill, 1975), pp. 214–215.
2. Kathryn Kranhold and Katherine Farrish, "Anxiety about Sex, Dating, Rape Transforms College Life," *Hartford Courant,* Oct. 10, 1993, p. A1.
3. Jane Gross, "Combating Rape on Campus in a Class on Sexual Consent," *New York Times,* Sept. 25, 1993, p. 1.

Questions for Discussion
1. How would you answer the question posed in the last paragraph?
2. What approaches to preventing date rape do you think have the best chance of success on college campuses

Rape Prevention Workshop on a California campus.

Criminologists have looked closely at situations in which assaults are committed. David Luckenbill has identified six stages of a confrontational situation that leads to an assault:

1. One person insults another.
2. The insulted person perceives the significance of the insult, often by noting the reactions of others present, and becomes angry.
3. The insulted person contemplates a response: fight, flight, or conciliation. If the response chosen is a fight, the insultee assaults the insulter then and there. If another response is chosen, the situation advances to stage 4.
4. The original insulter, now reprimanded, shamed, or embarrassed, makes a counter-move: fight or flight.
5. If the choice is a fight, the insulter assaults (and possibly kills) the insultee.
6. The "triumphant" party either flees or awaits the consequences (for example, police response).[42]

We can see that crucial decisions are made at all stages, and that the nature of the decisions depends on the context in which they are made.

Tonya Harding (left) and Nancy Kerrigan (right) practice at Lillehammer. The 1994 Winter Olympics were nearly upstaged by the January 6, 1994, assault on Kerrigan, allegedly by persons close to Harding, a rival skater on the U.S. team.

At stage 1, nobody is likely to offer an insult in a peaceful group or situation. At stage 2, the witnesses to the scene could respond in a conciliatory manner. (Let us call this a conflict-resolution situation.) At stage 3, the insulted person could leave the scene with dignity. (A confrontational person would call it flight; a conflict-resolution-minded person would call it a dignified end to a confrontational situation.) Stage 4 is a critical stage, since it calls for a counterresponse. The original aggressor could see this as the last chance to avoid violence and withdraw with apologies. That would be the end of the matter. In a confrontational situation, however, the blows will be delivered now, if none have been dealt already.

The National Crime Victimization Survey estimates that 3,975,000 simple assaults were committed in 1992.[43] Assault is the most common of all violent crimes reported to the police. The number of aggravated assaults has risen in recent years, reaching 1,436,000 in 1992. These figures, however, grossly underestimate the real incidence. Many people involved in an assault consider the event a private matter, particularly if the assault took place within the family or household. Consequently, until quite recently little was known about family-related violence. But the focus of recent research is changing that situation rapidly.

FAMILY-RELATED CRIMES

In 1962 five physicians exposed the gravity of the "battered-child syndrome" in the *Journal of the American Medical Association*.[44] When they reviewed X-ray photographs of patients in the emergency rooms of 71 hospitals across the country over the course of a year, they found 300 cases of child abuse, of which 11 percent resulted in death and over 28 percent in permanent brain damage. Shortly thereafter, the women's movement rallied to the plight of the battered wife and, somewhat later, to the personal and legal problems of wives who were raped by their husbands.[45]

In the 1960s and 1970s various organizations, fighting for the rights of women and children, exposed the harm that results from physical and psychological abuse in the home. They demanded public action. They created public awareness of the extent of the problem. Psychologists, physicians, anthropologists, and social scientists, among others, increasingly focused attention on the various factors that enter into episodes of domestic violence. Such factors include the sources of conflict, arguments, physical attacks, injuries, and temporal and spatial elements.

Within three decades family violence, the "well-kept secret," has come to be recognized as a major social problem. Family violence shares some of the characteristics of other forms of violence, yet the intimacy of marital, cohabitational, or parent–child relationships sets family violence apart. The physical and emotional harm inflicted in such violent episodes tends to be spread over longer periods of time and to have a more lasting impact on all members of the living unit. Moreover, such events tend to be self-perpetuating.

Spouse Abuse

Tracey Thurman had repeatedly requested police assistance because she feared her estranged husband. Even after he threatened to shoot her and her son, the police merely told her to get a restraining order. Eventually, the husband attacked Thurman, inflicting multiple stab wounds that caused paralysis from the neck down and permanent disfigurement. The police had delayed in responding to her call on that occasion, and the city of Torrington, Connecticut, was held liable for having failed to provide her with equal protection of the laws. In the suit that followed, Ms. Thurman was awarded $2.3 million in damages.[46]

The Thurman case is rare. The majority of assault incidents within the family either are unreported to the police or, if reported, are classified as simple assaults.

The Extent of Spouse Abuse

In a national sample of 6002 households, Murray A. Strauss and Richard J. Gelles found the following:

■ One of every six couples experienced a physical assault. This indicates that 8.7 million of

the 54 million couples who then lived in the United States experienced at least one physical assault during the year.[47]

■ Both husbands and wives perpetrated acts of violence, but the consequences of their acts differed. Men, who more often used guns, knives, or fists, inflicted more pain and injury.[48]

■ About 60 percent of the assaults consisted of minor shoving, slapping, pushing; the other 40 percent were considered severe violence: punching, kicking, stabbing, choking.[49]

Researchers agree that assaultive behavior within the family is a highly underreported crime.[50] Data from the National Crime Victimization Survey indicate:

■ One-half of the incidents of domestic assault are not reported.

■ The most common reason given for failure to report a domestic assault to the police was that the victim considered the incident a private matter.

■ Victims who reported such incidents to the police did so to prevent future assaults.

■ Though the police classified two-thirds of the reported incidents of domestic violence as simple assaults, half of them inflicted bodily injury as serious as or more serious than the injuries inflicted during rapes, robberies, and aggravated assaults.[51]

The Nature of Spouse Abuse

Before we can understand spouse abuse, we need information about abusers. Some experts have found that interpersonal violence is learned at home and transmitted from one generation to the next.[52] Studies demonstrate that children who are raised by aggressive parents tend to grow up to be aggressive adults.[53] Other researchers have demonstrated how stress, frustration, and severe psychopathology take their toll on family relationships.[54] A few researchers have also explored the role of body chemistry; one investigation ties abuse to the tendency of males to secrete adrenaline when they feel sexually threatened.[55]

The relationship between domestic violence and the use of alcohol and drugs has also been explored. Abusive men with severe drug and alcohol problems are more likely to abuse their wives or girlfriends when they are drunk or high and to inflict more injury.[56]

Several studies of other societies demonstrate cultural support for the abuse of women. Moroccan researcher Mohammed Ayat reported that, of 160 battered women, about 25 percent believed that a man who does *not* beat his wife must be under some magic spell; 8 percent believed that such a man has a weak personality and is afraid of his wife; 2 percent believed that he must be abnormal; and another 2 percent believed that he doesn't love her or has little interest in her.[57] Wife beating, then, appears to be accepted as a norm by over one-third of the women studied—women who are themselves beaten. It even appears to be an expected behavior. In fact, in only 15 of 90 cultures studied by David Levinson was spouse beating rare or nonexistent.[58]

Spouse abuse has often been attributed to the imbalance of power between male and female partners. According to some researchers, the historical view of wives as possessions of their husbands persists even today.[59] Until recently spousal abuse was perceived as a problem more of social service than of criminal justice.[60] Police responding to domestic disturbance calls typically do not make an arrest unless the assailant is drunk, has caused serious injury, or has assaulted the officers.[61] By and large, the victims of family violence—those who are willing to look for help—have turned to crisis telephone lines and to shelters for battered women (safe havens that first appeared in the early 1970s to provide legal, social, and psychological services).[62]

Whether informal interventions are as effective as the criminal justice system, however, is a matter of controversy.[63] In a study conducted some years ago, the Minneapolis Domestic Violence Experiment, three types of action were taken: (1) the batterer was arrested, (2) the partners were required to separate for a designated period of time, and (3) a mediator intervened between the partners. Over a 6-month period the offenders who were arrested had the lowest recidivism rate (10 percent), those who were required to separate had the highest (24 percent), and those who submitted to mediation fell in between (19 percent).[64] More recently, a 1991 study revealed that neither short-custody arrests for domestic violence in inner-city areas nor longer-term arrests are effective in curbing domestic violence, especially in the long run.[65] Questions on the subject of spouse abuse still far outnumber answers. Personal, ethical, and moral concerns make the issue highly sensitive.[66] Researchers, however, are seeking answers.

Child Abuse

Spouse abuse is closely related to child abuse. One-half to three-quarters of men who batter women also beat their children, and many sexually abuse them as well. Children are also injured as a result of reckless behavior on the part of their fathers while the latter are abusing their mothers. In fact, the majority of abused sons over 14 suffer injuries trying to protect their mothers.[67]

The Extent of Child Abuse

It is very difficult to measure the extent of child abuse. Battering usually takes place in the home, and the child victims rarely notify the police. Edna Erez and Pamela Tontodonato found that the parental abuse that is reported often involves serious physical encounters.[68] Most of the available data on the extent of child abuse come from the National Incidence Study (NIS), sponsored by the National Center on Child Abuse and Neglect, and from official reports compiled by the American Humane Association (AHA).

The NIS collected information on child maltreatment (abuse and neglect) from hospitals, police, courts, schools, and child protection agencies in a randomly selected sample of 26 counties in 10 states during 1979 and 1980. These data—which covered reported cases only—yielded the following nationwide estimates:

- 5.7 children per 1000 under age 18 are physically, sexually, or emotionally abused annually (physically abused children make up the largest category: 3.4 per 1000).
- 5.3 children per 1000 under age 18 are neglected annually.[69]

The mid-1980 AHA National Study of Child Abuse and Neglect Reporting estimated, from

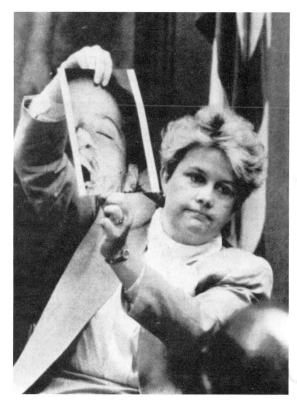

An expert witness holds a photo of Lisa Steinberg during the trial of her foster father Joel Steinberg, a disbarred lawyer, for second-degree murder. The evidence showed that Steinberg had severely beaten Lisa and then simply left her.

cases reported to official child protection agencies across the country, that 30.6 children per 1000 are maltreated (physically abused, emotionally abused, sexually abused, or neglected) annually.[70]

The estimates yielded by these two large surveys are obviously far apart. Part of the increase that occurred in the 5-year period may be due to better reporting, part to greater public awareness, and part to differences in the surveys themselves. Nevertheless, even the figure of 30.6 per 1000 is considered a low estimate of the actual number of battered children in our society.[71] Moreover, we know very little about these children, except that most of them are between 12 and 17 years old, that girls are more likely to be abused than boys, and that low-income families are disproportionately represented in the official statistics.[72]

The Nature of Child Abuse

When child abuse first began to be investigated in the early 1960s, the investigators were predominantly physicians, who looked at the psychopathology of the abusers. They discovered that a high proportion of abusers suffered from alcoholism, drug abuse, mental retardation, poor attachment, low self-esteem, or sadistic psychosis. Later the search for causes moved in other directions. Some researchers pointed out that abusive parents did not know how to discipline children or, for that matter, even how to provide for basic needs, such as nutrition and medical attention. Claims have been made that abusers have themselves been abused; to date, however, the evidence in regard to this hypothesis is mixed.[73]

The list of factors related to child abuse is long. We know, for example, that the rate of child abuse in lower-class families is high. This finding is probably related to the fact that low-income parents have few resources for dealing with the stress to which they are subjected, such as poor housing and financial problems. When they cannot cope with their responsibilities, they may become overwhelmed. The rate of child abuse may also be related to the acceptance of physical responses to conflict situations in what has been termed the "subculture of violence" (Chapter 6). Moreover, since child abuse among poor families is likely to be handled by a public agency, these cases tend to appear in official statistics.

Some researchers have found that formal action—arrest and prosecution—is the most effective means for limiting repeat offenses in the case of battered wives. The situation seems to be different when children are involved. Several advocates for children oppose any involvement of the criminal justice system. They believe that the parent-child attachment remains crucial to the child's development, and they fear that punishment of parents can only be detrimental to the child's need for a stable family environment. Only in the most extreme cases would they separate children from parents and place them in shelters or in foster homes. The preference is to prevent child abuse by other means, such as self-help groups (Parents Anonymous), baby-sitting assistance, and crisis phone lines.

The results of various types of intervention are characterized by the title of a 1986 report on child maltreatment: "Half Full and Half Empty."[74] Rates of repeated abuse are high, yet some families have had positive results, and advances have been made in identifying the best treatment for various types of problems. But though our understanding of the problem has indeed increased, we need to know a great deal more about the offense before we can reduce its occurrence.[75]

Abuse of the Elderly

Abuse of the elderly has become an area of special concern to social scientists. The population group that is considered to be elderly is variously defined. The majority of researchers consider 65 the age at which an individual falls into the category "elderly." As health care in the United States has improved, longevity has increased. The population of elderly people has grown larger over the decades: from 4 percent of the total population in 1900 to 11 percent in the 1980s. Every day 1000 more people join the ranks. It is estimated that by the year 2020, 20 percent of the population will be elderly.[76]

Elderly persons who are being cared for by their adult children are at a certain risk of abuse. The extent of the problem, however, is still largely unknown. The abused elderly frequently do not talk about their abuse for fear of the embarrassment of public exposure and possible retaliation by the abuser. Congressional hearings on domestic abuse estimate that between 500,000 and 2.5 million elderly people are abused annually.[77] Among the causes of such abuse are caregivers who themselves grew up in homes where violence was a way of life, the stress of caregiving in a private home rather than an institution, generational conflicts, and frustration with gerontological (old-age) problems of the care receiver, such as illness and senility.[78]

We can see that criminologists share a growing concern about family-related violence. Child abuse has received the attention of scholars for three decades. Spousal abuse has been studied for two decades. The abuse of the elderly has begun to receive attention much more recently.

Family abuse is not new; our awareness of the size and seriousness of the problem is. The same could be said about yet another offense. It was not until the 1960s that women's advocates launched a national campaign on behalf of victims of rape. Since then rape has become a major topic in criminological literature and research.

RAPE AND SEXUAL ASSAULT

The common law defined **rape** as an act of enforced intercourse by a man of a woman (other than the attacker's wife) without her consent. Intercourse includes any sexual penetration, however slight. The exclusion of wives from the crime of rape rested on several outdated legal fictions, among them the propositions that the marriage vows grant implicit permanent rights of sexual access and that spouses cannot testify against each other. Older laws universally classify rape as a sex crime. But rape has always been much more than that. It is inherently a crime of violence, an exercise of power.

Oddly, as Susan Brownmiller forcefully argues, it really started as a property crime. Men as archetypal aggressors (the penis as a weapon) subjugated women by the persistent threat of rape. That threat forced each woman to submit to a man for protection and thus to become a wife, the property of a man. Rape then was made a crime to protect one man's property—his wife—from the sexual aggressions of other men.[79] But even that view regards rape as a violent crime against the person, one that destroys the freedom of a woman (and nowadays of a man as well) to decide whether, when, and with whom to enter a sexual relationship.

Well over a thousand books, scholarly articles, and papers have been produced on the topic of rape and sexual assault since the 1960s. Much that was obscure and poorly understood has now been clarified by research generated largely by the initiatives of the feminist movement, the National Center for the Prevention and Control of Rape (NCPCR), and other governmental and private funding agencies. While most of the crimes in our penal codes have more or less retained their original form, the law on rape has changed rapidly and drastically. The name of the crime, its definition, the rules of evidence and procedure, society's reaction to it—all have changed.[80]

Americans regard rape as one of the most serious crimes. Respondents to the 1985 National Survey of Crime Severity rated the severity of forcible rape that resulted in injury requiring hospitalization as the fourteenth most serious of 204 offenses. Among the crimes considered more serious were stabbing that results in death, planting bombs in public places when life is lost, and armed robbery that results in death.[81]

Characteristics of the Rape Event

According to the Uniform Crime Reports, there were 109,062 forcible rapes in 1992. This figure represents 6 percent of the total number of violent crimes.[82] The incidence of rape rose 15 percent between 1988 and 1992. Of all the men arrested for forcible rape, 16 percent were under age 18; 44 percent were between 18 and 25 years old; and over half were white. Most rapes are committed in the summer, particularly in July. Several decades ago, Menachem Amir demonstrated that close to half of all rapes in Philadelphia from 1958 to 1965 were committed by a person known to or even friendly with the victim.[83] Recent victimization data show that the situation has not changed: 48 percent of rapes are committed by men who know their victims.[84] The offender may even be the husband, who in some states can now qualify as a rapist.

Research in this area thus far has not been extensive. One report estimates that 12 percent of wives are raped by their husbands.[85] Recent studies have focused attention on yet another form of rape in relational situations: *date rape*.[86] One study indicated that as many as 25 percent of all female college students may have experienced rape.[87] Criminologists have difficulty estimating the frequency of date rape, but in all likelihood such rape has increased significantly.[88] It is estimated that only one-tenth of date rapes committed are reported to the police. A recent study demonstrated that prosecutions for date rape are particularly susceptible to long-held prejudices against victims.[89]

There is an arrest made for all types of forcible rape in about 52 percent of the cases. James L.

LeBeau, who studied rapes in San Diego, made the point that many "stranger rapists" remain at large because they commit their acts in ways that produce little tangible evidence as to their identities. They maintain a distance from the victim by not interacting with her before the attack. The serial rapist also attacks strangers, but because he finds his victims repeatedly in the same places, his behavior is more predictable and so leads to a better arrest rate.[90]

Who Are the Rapists?

Explanations of rape fall into two categories, psychological and sociocultural. While research in these areas has expanded over the last two decades, the causes of rape remain speculative.[91]

Psychological Factors

Several experts view rapists as suffering from mental illness or personality disorders. Richard Rada argues that some rapists are psychotic, sociopathic, or sadistic or feel deficient in masculinity.[92] Paul Gebhard and his associates have found that most rapists show hostile feelings toward women, have histories of violence, and tend to attack strangers.[93] Some rapists view women as sex objects whose role is to satisfy them. Nicholas Groth claims that all forcible rapes are committed because of anger, a drive for power (expressed as sexual conquest), or the enjoyment of maltreating a victim (sadism).[94]

Sociocultural Factors

Psychological explanations assume that men who rape are maladjusted in some way. But several studies done in the 1980s demonstrate that rapists are indistinguishable from other groups of offenders.[95] These studies generally conclude that rape is culturally related to societal norms that approve of aggression as a demonstration of masculinity[96] (as we saw in Chapter 6) or that rape is the mechanism by which men maintain their power over women.

The social significance of rape has long been a part of anthropological literature. A cross-cultural study of 95 tribal societies found that 47 percent were rape-free, 35 percent intermediate, and 18 percent rape-prone. In the rape-prone societies women had low status and little decision-

CRIMINOLOGICAL FOCUS
Hate Crimes

- In July 1991, a real estate office in Canarsie, Brooklyn, was fire-bombed for showing properties to blacks.(1)

- In March 1992, a small school in North Hollywood was "decorated" by vandals with swastikas and slurs against Jews.(2)

- In January 1993, in Hillsborough County, Florida, a black man was covered with gasoline and set on fire. A note found nearby, signed "KKK," said, "one les nigger more to go."(3)

Destruction of property, arson, vandalism, assault, attempted homicide—what do these crimes have in common? They all fit into the definition of "hate crime," or "bias crime": crimes that are committed against a person or property "because of the race, religion, color, disability, sexual orientation, national origin or ancestry of that person or the owner or occupant of that property."(4) No such crime existed under common law, which assumed that civilized society would resolve its problems of prejudice by civil, rather than criminal, means. But hate crimes recently have become the focus of public concern.

Whether these acts actually have increased in number (see the accompanying figure) is a difficult question; law enforcement agencies have categorized such acts as hate crimes only recently, thereby allowing assessment of the problem. The National Hate Crime Statistics Act of 1990 mandates comprehensive reports on bias crimes, and in early 1993 the first such report was issued by the FBI.(3) Although fewer than a fifth of the nation's law enforcement agencies contributed data for the report, 4558 hate-crime incidents reported in 1991 were included in the study. The FBI found that blacks are the targets of most hate crimes (36 percent), followed by whites (19 percent) and Jews (17 percent). Religious bias motivated two of every ten incidents reported, with ethnic and sexual-orientation bias accounting for one of every ten incidents. Racial bias was responsible for the greatest number of incidents by far—six of every ten.

With only one report issued so far, the FBI cannot conclude that hate crimes are on the rise. But concern about such acts definitely has increased, and half the states in the country have sentence-enhancement laws, which allow states to impose harsher sentences on criminals who choose victims on the basis of personal characteristics.(4) Federal legislation for hate-crime sentence enhancement passed the House of Representatives in 1992 and was under consideration again in 1993.

In a 1993 Supreme Court ruling on one state's sentence-enhancement statute, Chief Justice William H. Rehnquist wrote:

[T]he . . . statute singles out for enhancement bias-inspired conduct because this conduct is thought to inflict greater individual and societal harm. . . . [B]ias-motivated crimes are more likely to provoke retaliatory crimes, inflict distinct emotional harms on their victims, and incite community unrest.(4)

Sources
1. N. R. Kleinfield, "Bias Crimes Hold Steady, but Leave Many Scars," *New York Times*, Jan. 27, 1992, p. 1. See also Jack Levin and Jack McDevitt, *Hate Crimes: The Rising Tide of Bigotry and Bloodshed* (New York: Plenum, 1993).
2. Sally Ann Stewart, "Hate Crimes: 'Litany of Shame,'" *USA Today*, Mar. 13, 1992, p. 3A.
3. "Hatred Turns Out Not to Be Color-Blind," *Time*, Jan. 18, 1993, p. 22.
4. Linda Greenhouse, "Justices Uphold Stiffer Sentences for Hate Crimes," *New York Times*, June 12, 1993, p. 1.

Questions for Discussion
1. Wisconsin's sentence-enhancement law was challenged by a defendant who claimed that his First Amendment (freedom of speech) rights were violated because the statute punishes offenders' bigoted beliefs and not just their acts. Do you agree with the U.S. Supreme Court decision to uphold the Wisconsin statute?
2. The FBI study found that intimidation was the most common type of hate crime, followed by vandalism and assault. Do you think these crimes are serious enough to warrant the extra attention they receive?

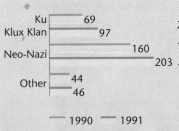

Growth in the Number of Hate Groups

Ku Klux Klan 69 (1990), 97 (1991)
Neo-Nazi 160 (1990), 203 (1991)
Other 44 (1990), 46 (1991)

Number of Anti-Semitic Incidents

Reports of vandalism, harassment, threats, and assaults

489 ('80) ... 1879 ('91)

Hate Groups, Crimes Increase

(*Source:* Figures from Southern Poverty Law Center and Anti-Defamation League, B'nai B'rith; in *USA Today*, Mar. 13, 1992, p. 3.)

making power, and they lived apart from men. The author of this study concluded: "Violence is socially, not biologically, programmed."[97]

Despite anthropologists' traditional interest in gender relationships, it was not until the feminist movement and radical criminology focused on the subject that the relationship of rape, gender inequality, and socioeconomic status was fully articulated.[98] Writing from the Marxist perspective, which we explored in Chapter 8, Julia and Herman Schwendinger posited that "the impoverishment of the working class and the widening gap between rich and poor" create conditions for the prevalence of sexual violence.[99] A test of this hypothesis showed that while the incidence of sexual violence was not related to ethnic inequality, it was significantly related to general income inequality.[100]

A more recent study analyzed these findings and concluded that economic inequality was not the sole determinant of violent crime in our society. Forcible rape was found to be an added "cost" of many factors, including social disorganization.[101] In sum, many factors have been associated with the crime of rape: psychological problems, social factors, and even sociopolitical factors. Some experts suggest that boys are socialized to be aggressive and dominating, that the innate male sex drive leads to rape, and that pornography encourages men to rape by making sex objects of women, degrading women, and glamorizing violence against them. Rape has been explained in such a wide variety of ways that it is extremely difficult to plan preventive strategies and to formulate crime-control policy. Moreover, it has created major difficulties in the criminal justice system.

Rape and the Legal System

The difficulties of rape prosecutions have their roots in the English common law. Sir Matthew Hale, a seventeenth-century jurist, explained in *Pleas of the Crown* (1685, 1736) how a jury was to be cautious in viewing evidence of rape: "[It] must be remembered . . . that it is an accusation easily to be made and hard to be proved, and harder to be defended by the party accused, tho never so innocent."[102] This instruction, which so definitively protects the defendant, has until recently been a mandatory instruction to juries in the United States. Along with many other legal and policy changes, many jurisdictions have now cast it aside. The requirement of particularly stringent proof in rape cases had always been justified by the seriousness of the offense and the heavy penalties associated with it, plus the stigma attached to such a conviction.

Difficulties of Prosecution

Victims of rape have often been regarded with suspicion by the criminal justice system. The victim's testimony has not sufficed to convict the defendant, no matter how unimpeachable that testimony may have been. There had to be "corroborating evidence," such as semen, torn clothes, bruises, or eyewitness testimony.

Another major issue has been that of consent. Did the victim encourage, entice, or maybe even agree to the act? Was the attack forced? Did the victim resist? Martin Schwartz and Todd Clear sum up the reasons for such questions: "There is a widespread belief in our culture that women 'ask for it,' either individually or as a group." They compared rape victims to victims of other offenses: "Curiously, society does not censure the robbery victim for walking around with $10, or the burglary victim for keeping all of those nice things in his house, or the car theft victim for showing off his flashy new machine, just asking for someone to covet it."[103]

Because defendants in rape cases so often claim that the victim was in some way responsible for the attack, rape victims in the courtroom tend to become the "accused," required to defend their good reputations, their propriety, and their mental soundness. In sum, so many burdens are placed on the victim that no one seriously wonders why only a fraction of rapes are reported and why so few men accused of rape are convicted.

Legislative Changes

The feminist movement has had a considerable impact on laws and attitudes concerning rape in our country. The state of Michigan was a leader in the movement to reform such laws by creating, in 1975, the new crime of "criminal sexual conduct" to replace the traditional rape laws. It distinguishes four degrees of assaultive sexual acts, differentiated by the amount of force used, the infliction of injury, and the age and mental condition of the victim.[104]

The new law is gender-neutral, in that it makes illegal any type of forcible sex, including homosexual rape. Other states have followed Michigan's lead. Schwartz and Clear have suggested that reform should go one step further. They argue that if rape were covered by the general assault laws rather than by a separate sex-crime statute, the emphasis would be on the assault (the action of the offender) and not on the resistance (the action of the victim).[105]

Recent legislation has also removed many of the barriers women encountered as witnesses in the courtroom. Thus in states with rape shield laws women are no longer required to disclose their prior sexual activity, and corroboration requirements have been reduced or eliminated; as noted earlier, some states have reversed two centuries of legal tradition by striking down the "marital rape exemption" so that a wife may now charge her husband with rape.[106] But law reform has limits. Unfortunately, prejudices die hard. One study concludes that "forcible rape cases are more likely to be dropped than other kinds of cases and that the reasons for this pattern do not necessarily conform to prior expectations that reluctant victims are responsible for much of the case attrition."[107]

Community Response

Women's advocates have taken an interest not only in legislative reform but also in the community's response to the victims of rape. In 1970 the first rape-specific support project, the Bay Area Women Against Rape—a volunteer-staffed emergency phone information service—was established in Berkeley, California.[108] By 1973, similar projects had spread throughout the country. Run by small, unaffiliated groups, they handled crises, monitored agencies (hospitals, police, courts) that came in contact with victims, educated the public about the problems of victims, and even provided lessons in self-defense.

By the late 1970s the number of these centers and their activities had increased dramatically. The mass media reported on their successes. Federal and, later, state and local support for such services rose. As the centers become more professional, they formed boards of directors, prepared detailed budgets to comply with the requirements of funding agencies, hired social workers and mental-health personnel, and developed their political action component. But even with increased support, the demand for the services of rape crisis centers far outweighs the available resources.

ROBBERY

The very concept of rape has undergone rapid change. But legal and public response to another crime of violence that also involves a temporary and complete domination of the victim has not changed at all. It is defined as it always has been: **robbery** is the taking of property from a victim by force and violence or by the threat of violence.[109]

The MPC (Model Penal Code) (sec. 222.1) grades robbery as a felony of the second degree, commanding a prison term of up to 10 years. If the robber has intentionally inflicted serious physical injury or attempted to kill, the sentence may be as long as life. In reality, however, the average sentence upon conviction for one charge of robbery is 6.4 years. It increases to 17.6 years if the charges number four or more.[110] In 1992, the number of robbery offenses, 672,478, was 24 percent higher than in 1988.

Offenders display weapons, mostly guns and knives, in almost half of all robberies. Since 44 percent of all robberies net the perpetrator less than $50, the overall reporting rate for robbery is only slightly higher than 50 percent. Robberies of individuals occur most frequently on the street (61.3 percent). The remaining robberies take place in parking lots and garages (14 percent), in residences (9.3 percent), in commercial buildings (5.2 percent), in transit stations or on public transportation (3.8 percent), in nightclubs, bars or restaurants (2.7 percent), and in miscellaneous establishments (3.7 percent).[111]

Characteristics of Robberies and Robbers

Criminologists have classified the characteristics of robberies as well as the characteristics of robbers. According to Frederick McClintock and Evelyn Gibson, there are five distinct varieties of robbery, each with a different frequency of commission. In their sample of London robberies, robberies of commercial establishments and street robberies seem to have been most prevalent.[112] André Normandeau found a similar distribution in Philadelphia, but with a disproportionate number of street robberies.[113]

Robbery attracts a variety of perpetrators. John Conklin detected four types:

■ The *professional robber* carefully plans and executes a robbery, often with many accomplices; steals large sums of money; and has a long-term, deep commitment to robbery as a means of supporting a hedonistic lifestyle.

■ The *opportunistic robber* (the most common) has no long-term commitment to robbery; targets victims for small amounts of money ($20 or less); victimizes elderly women, drunks, cab drivers, and other people who seem to be in no position to resist; and is young and generally inexperienced.

■ The *addict robber* is addicted to drugs, has a low level of commitment to robbery but a high level of commitment to theft, plans less than professional robbers but more than opportunistic robbers, wants just enough money for a fix, and may or may not carry a weapon.

■ The *alcoholic robber* has no commitment to robbery as a way of life, has no commitment to theft, does not plan his or her robberies, usually robs people after first assaulting them, takes few precautions, and is apprehended more often than other robbers.[114]

In a classification system restricted to bank robbers, Terry Baumer and Michael Carrington identified three types. First is the *unarmed lone bandit*, who passes a note to the teller demanding money and often leaves without ever raising the suspicions of patrons or other employees. The second type is the *armed lone bandit*, who usually shows a handgun and makes an oral demand. Two-thirds of Baumer and Carrington's sample fell into this category. Third, *armed teams* present themselves as robbers, order employees and customers to "get down on the floor," and proceed with a well-formulated plan. They usually take large sums of money. Of all bank robbers, tellers most fear the armed teams.[115]

The Consequences of Robbery

Robbery is a property crime as well as a violent crime. It is the combination of the motive for economic gain and the violent nature of robbery that makes it so serious. An estimated $562 million was lost as a result of robbery in 1991 alone. The value of stolen property per incident averaged $817, and the average amount of money stolen ranged from $387 (from convenience stores) to $3177 (from banks).[116] Loss of money, however, is certainly not the only consequence of robbery. The million-odd robberies that take place each year leave psychological and physical trauma in their wake, not to mention the pervasive fear and anxiety that have contributed to the decay of inner cities.

Not all criminologists agree, however, that the high level of fear is warranted. After examining trends in robbery-homicide data from 52 of the largest cities in the United States, Philip Cook found "little support for the fears that there is a new breed of street criminals who cause more serious injuries and deaths in robberies. Very recent trends point in the other direction. Killing a robbery victim appears to be going out of fashion."[117] Franklin E. Zimring and James Zuehl agree. They found that injuries were inflicted in a moderate number of Chicago robberies (28 percent) and that about 11 percent of robberies ended in death.[118]

Opportunities for Robbery

What determines the attractiveness of an opportunity for robbery? Cook's research on commercial robbery suggests that some offenders carefully examine the location of the potential robbery, the potential gain, the capability of security personnel, the possibility of intervention by bystanders, and the presence of guards, cameras, and alarms.[119] Criminologists have found that potential victims and establishments can do quite a bit to decrease the likelihood of being robbed. Following a series of convenience-store robberies in Gainseville, Florida, in 1985, a city ordinance required store owners to clear their windows of signs that obstructed the view of the interior, to position cash registers where they would be visible from the street, and to install approved electronic cameras. Within little over a year, convenience-store robberies had decreased 64 percent.[120] This is a perfect example of crime control through target hardening (see Chapter 9).

Individual victims of robbery also play a role in the success or failure of a robbery in progress. Some criminologists have suggested that forceful resistance decreases the chance of the robbery's success but increases the risk of physical injury to the victim. Nonforceful resistance also decreases the risk of losing one's property and tends to reduce the risk of injury.[121] But such preliminary findings should not be taken as a guide for future robbery victims. Robberies, for the most part, are potentially lethal events.

KIDNAPPING AND TERRORISM

Seizing and holding a person for ransom or reward is like robbery, in that it involves the use or threat of violence for the purpose of acquiring property illegally. Kidnapping in the form of hostage taking is frequently an element of a larger scheme that encompasses several distinct crimes of violence. The totality of such violence is called terrorism.

Kidnapping

Kidnapping as such was not recognized as a felony under English common law; it was a misdemeanor. Some forms of kidnapping were later criminalized by statute. In the eighteenth century, the most frequent form of kidnapping, according to the great legal scholar Sir William Blackstone, was stealing children and sending them to servitude in the American colonies. Other forms of kidnapping were the "crimping," or shanghaiing, of persons for involuntary service aboard ships and the abduction of women for purposes of prostitution abroad.

All these offenses have elements in common and together they define the crime of **kidnapping:** abduction and detention by force or frau...

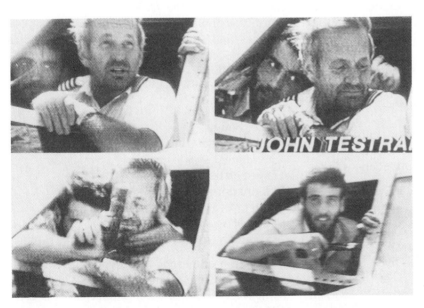

An armed terrorist holds a gun on Trans World Airlines pilot John Testrake during an interview from the hijacked plane as it sat on the ground at the Beirut airport. Top left, gunman is behind the pilot; top right, gunman moves to end the interview; bottom left, gunman waves gun in front of the pilot as he grabs him around the neck; bottom right, gunman tells the ABC news crew to leave.

and transportation beyond the authority of the place where the crime was committed. It was not until the kidnapping of the infant son of Charles Lindbergh in 1932 that comprehensive kidnapping legislation was enacted in the United States. In passing the federal kidnapping statute—the so-called Lindbergh Act [now 18 U.S. Code (sec.) 1201]—Congress made it a felony to kidnap and transport a victim across a state or national border. The crime was subject to the death penalty, unless the victim was released unharmed; the death penalty has since been dropped.

Terrorism

Terrorism is a resort to violence or a threat of violence on the part of a group seeking to accomplish a purpose against the opposition of constituted authority. Crucial to the terrorists' scheme is the exploitation of the media to attract attention to the cause. Many clandestine organizations around the world have sought to draw attention to their causes—the Irish Republican Army (IRA), committed to the cause of uniting the British counties of Northern Ireland with the Republic of Ireland; Islamic fundamentalists committed to the protection of Islam in its purist form against any Western influence; various Palestinian factions opposed to Israeli occupation or to any Mideast peace settlement; radical groups all over the world seeking an end to capitalism or colonialism or the imposition of one or another form of totalitarian rule.

From the outset the member states of the United Nations have been concerned about international terrorism because it endangers or takes innocent lives and jeopardizes fundamental freedoms, such as the freedom to travel and to congregate for public events. The U.N. effort to control international terrorism concentrates on removal of the underlying grievances that provoke people to sacrifice human lives, including their own, in an attempt to effect radical changes.[122] This approach to control of terrorism is not concerned with the individual motivations of terrorists. Some of them may be highly motivated idealists; others are recruited for substantial rewards. The control effort is directed rather at the conditions that give rise to terrorism and at the removal of such conditions.

To the extent that some grievances have been reduced by political action, such as the granting of independence to colonies, terrorism has declined. But other problems remain, especially in Northern Ireland, India, Central America, Africa, and the West Bank and Gaza Strip occupied by Israel. Crimes of a terrorist nature occur virtually every day and are likely to continue wherever the underlying problems are not resolved. Terrorist activities include but are not restricted to assassinations, hostage taking, and interference with or destruction of ships, aircraft, or means of land transport (see Table 10.1). When funding by clandestine supporters is not forthcoming, terrorists have carried out robberies to finance their operations.

The Extent of Terrorism

The incidence of terrorism may seem slight in the light of overall national crime statistics, especially those of the United States. But the worldwide destructive impact of such acts is considerable. So too are the costs of increased security to combat terrorism. The airline industry alone is spending $500 million a year for security.[123] After the bombing of the U.S. embassy complex in Beirut, Lebanon, with the loss of the lives of 241 marines and sailors, the strengthening of U.S. embassy security all over the world cost well over $3 billion.

In one year alone (1985) terrorists were responsible for:

4 letter bombs
5 barricade–hostage incidents
9 hijackings
17 specific threats
54 kidnappings
70 attempted attacks
84 armed assaults
165 bombings and arsons

Of these crimes, 12 were committed in Belgium, 14 in Chile, 29 in Colombia, 12 in Cyprus, 35 in West Germany, 12 in France, 29 in Greece, 17 in Italy, 47 in Lebanon, 10 in Peru, 18 in Portugal, 15 in Spain, 10 in the United Kingdom, and 148 in other countries that experienced fewer than 10 incidents each. Regionally, Western Europe was hardest hit (182), followed by the Middle East (70) and South America (62).

TABLE 10.1 TERRORIST EVENTS AGAINST AMERICANS, 1983–1993

- On October 23, 1983, a suicide terrorist in a TNT-laden truck blew up U.S. Marine Corps headquarters in Beirut, Lebanon, killing 241 marines and sailors. A second truck blew up a French paratrooper barracks 2 miles away, killing 58.

- On October 7, 1985, five hijackers seized the Italian cruiseliner *Achille Lauro*. They held some 400 persons for ransom and killed a wheelchair-bound American passenger.

- On April 2, 1986, a bomb exploded aboard TWA flight 840 at Athens airport, killing four Americans.

- On April 5, 1986, terrorists exploded a bomb in a West Berlin disco frequented by American service person- nel, killing 2 and injuring 200. The incident prompted an American air strike against Libya in retaliation.

- On September 5, 1986, four Pakistani gunmen, members of Abu Nidal, attempted to hijack a Pan Am 747 in Karachi, Pakistan. After keeping the plane on the runway overnight, the gunmen were overpowered by secu- rity; 21 passengers died.

- On December 21, 1988, terrorists exploded Pan Am flight 103, en route from Frankfurt, Germany, to New York, killing 270 passengers, crew, and people on the ground at Lockerby, Scotland.

- On February 26, 1993, a terrorist bomb in the basement garage of the World Trade Center in New York City killed 6 people, injured over 1000 people, and caused extensive damage to the building.

Source: National Center for Health Statistics, World Health Organization, and country reports.

The remaining incidents were spread all over the other regions, with Asia and the Far East suffer- ing the fewest incidents. Of the targets, 151 were political, 80 were diplomatic, 79 were economic, and 54 were random public places, specific per- sons, and various facilities.[124] It is noteworthy that 31 of the 408 terrorist acts were committed on behalf of governments.

Among the most active terrorist groups were the Islamic Jihad (35 acts), the Fatah Revolution- ary Council (24), the West German Red Army Faction (19), the Portuguese Popular Forces of 25 April (15), and the Chilean Manuel Rodríguez Popular Front (14). In the course of these acts of terrorism, 265 persons were killed, among them 46 Americans, 16 French, 15 British, 11 Germans, 11 Italians, 10 Israelis, and 9 staff members of international organizations. The terrorists suf- fered fewer deaths.

International Efforts to Control Terrorism

Many years ago the world community agreed on three international conventions to combat ter- rorism:

- Convention on Offenses and Certain Other Acts Committed on Board Aircraft, signed at Tokyo on September 14, 1963

- Convention for the Suppression of Unlawful Seizure of Aircraft, signed at The Hague on December 16, 1970

- Convention for the Suppression of Unlawful Acts against the Safety of Civil Aviation, signed at Montreal on September 23, 1971

These conventions, which provide for wide- spread international cooperation in the preven- tion of airplane hijacking and the pursuit and extradition (surrender to a requesting country) of offenders, produced a dramatic drop in the num- ber of such incidents. Subsequently, the interna- tional community agreed on two further conven- tions to protect diplomats, their families, and their installations:

- Convention on the Prevention and Punish- ment of Crimes against Internationally Pro- tected Persons, Including Diplomatic Agents, adopted by the General Assembly of the United Nations on December 14, 1973

- International Convention against the Taking of Hostages, adopted by the General Assem- bly of the United Nations on December 17, 1979[125]

It appears that by 1989 several governments that had been supporting certain "freedom fighters" (elsewhere called terrorist groups) had grown disenchanted with the groups' exercise of arbitrary violence against uninvolved civilian targets, such as airplane passengers, and had ceased to support such groups.[126] Nevertheless, terrorist groups proliferate. Several international directories list well over a thousand groups, many of them well financed. Until all grievances are removed—and some of them have been built up over centuries—such groups will continue to resort to violent crime in order to use the world media as leverage to advance their causes.

VIOLENCE AND GUN CONTROL

Clearly, violence is a massive problem throughout the world. Researchers have suggested a variety of causes. Violence in the United States is frequently attributed to historical conditioning (the need of frontier people to survive in a hostile environment), social factors (poverty, inequities, and other inner-city problems), and the laxity of the criminal justice system (failure to apprehend and convict enough criminals and to imprison long enough those who are convicted). Some researchers have focused on one common element in a large proportion of violent crime: the availability of firearms in the United States.

One of the hottest and longest political and scholarly debates in our history centers on this point: Should and can Americans drastically restrict the availability of firearms, and would such controls substantially reduce the rate and severity of violent crime?

The Extent of Firearm-Related Offenses

Though exact figures are not known, it is estimated that over 100 million firearms are privately owned in the United States: 37 percent rifles, 33 percent shotguns, and 30 percent handguns.[127] Half of the handguns are so-called Saturday-night specials (defined by the Bureau of Alcohol, Tobacco, and Firearms as a small weapon of .32 caliber or less with a barrel length of less than 3 inches and costing $50 or less). The supply of handguns increases by about 1.5 million each year.[128]

"IF THERE WAS A TOUGH GUN CONTROL LAW, WE PROBABLY WOULDN'T HAVE GOTTEN OURSELVES INTO THIS MESS."

Approximately 13,500 of every 100,000 Americans own handguns. Compare this figure with the rates of other Western industrialized nations: Canada, 3000 in every 100,000; Austria, 3000; the Netherlands, under 500; and Great Britain, also under 500.[129] *Time* magazine devoted its issue of July 17, 1989, to "Death by Gun." Reporting on "America's toll in one typical week," a 28-page portfolio described the deaths and provided photographs of most of the victims: 464 Americans who died violently by gun during the first week of May 1989. Of these, 216 (47 percent) had shot themselves to death. Nine of the suicides killed someone else before taking their own lives. Twenty-two deaths were preventable accidents. Only 14 people were killed in self-defense. The rest of the deaths were criminal homicides.

The Federal Bureau of Investigation has reported that a handgun is used in about half of all murders and one-third of the rapes and robberies. Two-thirds of police deaths in the line of duty are attributed to the use of handguns.[130] Rates of crime involving guns are far lower in most other developed Western nations than in the United States.[131] According to the Task Force on Firearms of the National Commission on the Causes and Prevention of Violence, the rate of homicide by gun is 40 times higher in the United States than in England and Wales, and our rate of robbery by gun is 60 times higher.

Youth and Guns

Three young thugs boarded a city bus in Queens yesterday, brandished guns like Wild West bandits and staged a frontier-style holdup. They strode up and down the aisle, fired shots into the roof, terrorized and robbed 22 passengers, struck a girl in the face with a gun butt and escaped with $300 in cash and fistfulls of jewelry.

The outlaws—one armed with a silver revolver and another with a pair of guns, while a third carried a book bag—made no effort to conceal their faces as they boarded the Q-85 bus at 8:30 A.M. at 140th Avenue and Edgewood Avenue in Springfield Gardens, a residential neighborhood just northeast of Kennedy International Airport.[132]

The "bandits" were three youths age 15 to 19. In a growing number of incidents across the United States, young people are using guns for robberies, gang warfare, initiation rites (drive-by shootings by wanna-be gang members), random shootings (not too long ago James Jordan, father of basketball star Michael Jordan, fell victim)—and for protection from their peers.

Concern is mounting over the increase in adolescent illegal gun ownership and use. A self-report study of 11,361 high school students in the United States found that 1 in every 20 high school students carries a firearm, usually a handgun. Black and Hispanic males were most likely to carry the weapons and were at the highest risk for homicide victimization.[133]

In the decade of the 1980s, over 7150 homicides were committed by high school youths using illegal guns.[134] Research done in Seattle, Washington, found that among eleventh-grade students, 34 percent reported having access to handguns, while 6.4 percent reported owning a firearm. Moreover, students indicated a high rate of handgun use: 33 percent had shot someone.[135] In many cities the problem has reached a stage where high schools deploy metal detectors and use teams of security guards who make random searches of purses, backpacks, and book bags.[136]

Why have youths turned to guns? When asked, many of them respond the way three teenagers did: "You fire a gun and you can just *hear* the power. It's like *yeah!*" or "It became cool to say you could get a gun," or "Nobody messes with you if they think you may have a gun."[137] While there are many studies on adolescent violent behavior, there are few on adolescent illegal gun use. One of the few, a recent study of ninth- and tenth-grade boys, 14- and 15-year-olds, in Rochester, New York, found that most boys who owned illegal guns had friends who owned guns; over half of the illegal gun owners were gang members; and selling drugs was a prime motivation for carrying a gun. Moreover, illegal gun ownership, friends' gun ownership, gang membership, and drug use were closely related to gun crime, street crime, and minor delinquency.[138] Illegal firearms have traditionally been used by youths in low-income urban neighborhoods. Now, the problem is spreading to the suburbs.

Controlling Handgun Use

While most people agree that gun-related crime is a particularly serious part of our crime problem, there is little agreement as to what to do about it. Civic organizations and police associations call for more laws prescribing mandatory sentences for the illegal purchase, possession, or use of firearms. Close to 20,000 laws that regulate firearms already exist in the United States.

A variety of methods of controlling handgun use have been tried:

A *prohibition against carrying guns* in public seemed to be related to a drop in gun crimes in Boston[139] and a leveling off of handgun violence in Detroit.[140]

Some states have passed what are referred to as *sentence-enhancement statutes:* the punishment for an offense is more severe if a person commits it under certain conditions, such as by using a gun. The Massachusetts law (1975) mandates a minimum sentence of 1 year's incarceration upon conviction for the illegal carrying of a firearm.[141] Michigan created a new offense—commission of a felony while possessing a firearm—and added a mandatory 2-year prison sentence to the sentence received for the commission of the felony itself. The state mounted a widespread publicity campaign: "One with a gun gets you two," read the billboards and bumper stickers.[142]

Sentence enhancement has been studied in six U.S. cities. Homicides committed with firearms decreased in all six after sentence-enhancement laws took effect, although the decline in homi-

Fernando Mateo, a Manhattan businessman, and his son. In the Christmas 1993 season, Mateo initiated a program called Toys for Guns to get guns off the streets and out of the wrong hands. Similar programs have been created nationwide to exchange guns for food, lottery tickets, and vouchers for other goods.

cides was large in some cities and small in others. Researchers studying sentence enhancement point out that its effectiveness is related to how closely judges follow the law. An additional 3 years in prison may deter criminals from using guns, while an additional month may not.[143]

A *total ban on handguns* was tried in Washington, D.C., beginning in 1976. Both gun homicides and gun suicides dropped visibly after the ban took effect, while no change occurred in homicides and suicides not committed with guns.[144]

Some communities have tried *buy-back programs.* St. Louis, San Francisco, Philadelphia, New York, and several other cities have embarked on such programs to reduce the number of handguns in circulation in the community.

Police departments buy guns, no questions asked, for $50. In October 1991, the St. Louis Police Department bought 5371 guns from citizens in 10 days. The Philadelphia police received 1044 guns within a 2-week period.

All these methods resulted in some decrease in handgun-related deaths, but none caused drastic reductions. As two gun-control researchers point out, the important question to be answered with regard to gun control is this: How many deaths must be prevented by a gun-control method to justify its use? Very few of the millions of people who own guns commit crimes with them, and control policies will affect legitimate owners as well as criminals. David McDowall and Alan Lizotte ask:

> Is the legitimate happiness of 10 million gun owners worth the lives of 10,000 murder victims? One murder victim? In another context, is a highly restrictive measure that would save 200 lives better than a less restrictive measure that would save 100? There is no obvious answer to these questions, and different people will draw the line in different places.[145]

Perhaps we can learn from the countries with low gun-related homicide rates. Many citizens of Switzerland and Israel, for example, have army-issue firearms at their constant disposal by virtue of citizen-army requirements, yet these weapons are rarely used for homicides. What factors control the use of handguns in these countries? Even if comparative studies come up with useful findings, some researchers believe the political problems surrounding gun control in the United States will probably continue to hinder the development of nationwide, or even statewide, gun-control policies for some time to come.[146]

The Gun-Control Debate

The battle line on gun control appears to be clearly drawn between the opponents of regulation (including the 3 million members of the National Rifle Association, or NRA, and their supporters), on the one hand, and the advocates of control (including the 12 major law enforcement groups, the private organization Handgun Control, and three-quarters of the American public), on the other. The gun lobby likes to say that it is people who kill, not guns, so it is the people who use guns illegally who should be punished. To deter these people, gun enthusiasts say, we need to have stiffer penalties, including mandatory sentences that take these offenders off the streets.

Gun-control opponents often have bumper stickers that read, "When guns are outlawed, only outlaws will have guns." Moreover, most gun owners claim that it is their right to own firearms to protect their homes, especially when they lose confidence in the police and courts.[147] And by controlling guns, they say, the government intrudes in their private affairs. They interpret the Second Amendment to the Constitution as giving them an individual right "to keep and bear arms." Furthermore, the gun lobby maintains, people may wish to enjoy their guns as collectors or for sport and hunting.

Another argument concerns what is called the displacement effect: people who are deterred by gun-control legislation from using guns to commit offenses will use some other weapon to achieve their goals. Or perhaps even more violent offenses will be committed if offenders can rely on the fact that the consequences of a non-firearm offense are less serious.[148]

Gun-control advocates compare our extremely high homicide rate to the much lower rates of other countries with tighter gun-control laws, including our neighbor Canada. They also argue that the availability of a gun makes homicide and suicide much more probable, because it is easier to produce death with a gun than with any other weapon. Moreover, they claim, better regulation or prohibition of gun ownership is a much faster way to lessen gun-related criminality than such long-term approaches as finding remedies for social problems. Researchers are testing the claims, but thus far no definitive conclusions have been reached.

The gun-control controversy is a prime example of the difference between the offender-specific and crime-specific approaches to crime. The offender-specific approach ("Guns don't kill people, people do") suggests that we look into the reasons why people kill. The offense-specific approach focuses on changing the situation by subjecting firearms to strict control in the expectation that fewer firearms will result in fewer deaths. The offense-specific approach received a major boost when Congress, in November 1993, passed the "Brady Bill," which imposes a five-day waiting period for gun purchases, allowing police to check the backgrounds of purchasers.

■ REVIEW

Murder, assaults of various kinds, rape, robbery, kidnapping—all share the common element of violence, though they differ in many ways: in the harm they cause, the intention of the perpetrator, the punishment they warrant, and other legal criteria. Social scientists have been exploring the frequency with which these crimes are committed in our society and elsewhere, their distribution through time and place, and the role played by circumstances, including the environment and behavior patterns (routine activities), in facilitating or preventing them.

Such categories as mass murder, serial murder, gang murder, and date rape are shorthand designations for frequently occurring crime patterns that have not been specifically identified in penal codes. Two other patterns of crime that also are not defined as such in the penal codes have become so important that they may be considered in conjunction with the other crimes of violence: family-related crime and terrorism. Both patterns encompass a variety of violent crimes.

The gun-control controversy demonstrates that both the definitions of crimes and the social and environmental characteristics associated with them must be studied in order to develop control and prevention strategies. Our violence-prone society will have to make serious choices if it is to reach that level of peaceful living achieved by many other modern societies.

■ NOTES

1. *Crimes of Violence: A Staff Report Submitted to the National Commission on the Causes and Prevention of Violence* (Washington, D.C.: U.S. Government Printing Office, December 1969), vol. 12, p. xxvii; vol. 11, p. 4.
2. G. O. W. Mueller, "Where Murder Begins," *New Hampshire Bar Journal,* **2** (1960): 214–224; G. O. W.

Mueller, "On Common Law Mens Rea," *Minnesota Law Review,* **42** (1958): 1043–1104.

3. Wayne R. LaFave and Austin W. Scott, *Handbook on Criminal Law* (St. Paul, Minn.: West, 1972), pp. 572–577. The provocation is judged by an objective standard; in other words, the provocation must be the kind that would have prompted a reasonable person to act similarly in that situation.

4. *Commonwealth v. Welansky,* 316 Mass. 383, N.E. 2d 902 (1944), at pp. 906–907. See G. O. W. Mueller, "The Devil May Care—Or Should We? A Reexamination of Criminal Negligence," *Kentucky Law Journal,* **55** (1966–1967): 29–49.

5. U.S. Department of Justice, Federal Bureau of Investigation, *Crime in the United States, 1992* (Washington, D.C.: U.S. Government Printing Office, 1993), pp. 16–17; hereafter cited as Uniform Crime Reports. For a discussion of homicide rates in the workplace, see Catherine A. Bell, "Female Homicides in United States Workplaces, 1980–1985," *American Journal of Public Health,* **81** (1991): 729–732.

6. Uniform Crime Reports, 1991, p. 17. See also Ann Goetting, "Female Victims of Homicide: A Portrait of Their Killers and the Circumstances of Their Deaths," *Violence and Victims,* **6** (1991): 159–168.

7. Roland Chilton, "Twenty Years of Homicide and Robbery in Chicago: The Impact of the City's Changing Racial and Age Composition," *Journal of Quantitative Criminology,* **3** (1987): 195–213. See also Carolyn Rebecca Block, *Homicide in Chicago* (Chicago: Loyola University of Chicago, 1986), p. 7; and William Wilbanks, *Murder in Miami* (Lanham, Md.: University Press of America, 1984).

8. William B. Harvey, "Homicide among Young Black Adults: Life in the Subculture of Exasperation," in *Homicide among Black Americans,* ed. Darnell F. Hawkins (Lanham, Md.: University Press of America, 1986), pp. 153–171. On this issue, all the articles in Hawkins's volume are worthy of attention. See also Robert L. Hampton, "Family Violence and Homicide in the Black Community: Are They Linked?" in *Violence in the Black Family,* ed. Hampton (Lexington, Mass.: Lexington Books, 1987), pp. 135–156.

9. Coramae Richey Mann, "Black Women Who Kill," in Hawkins, *Homicide among Black Americans,* pp. 157–186.

10. Larry Baron and Murray A. Straus, "Cultural and Economic Sources of Homicide in the United States," *Sociological Quarterly,* **29** (1988): 371–390.

11. Hans von Hentig, *The Criminal and His Victim* (New Haven, Conn.: Yale University Press, 1948).

12. Marvin E. Wolfgang, *Patterns in Criminal Homicide* (Philadelphia: University of Pennsylvania Press, 1958), p. 253. See also Marvin E. Wolfgang, "A Sociological Analysis of Criminal Homicide," in *Studies in Homicide,* ed. Wolfgang (New York: Harper & Row, 1967), pp. 15–28.

13. Robert A. Silverman and Leslie W. Kennedy, "Relational Distance and Homicide: The Role of the Stranger," *Journal of Criminal Law and Criminology,* **78** (1987): 272–308. See also Nanci Koser Wilson, "Gendered Interaction in Criminal Homicide," in *Homicide: The Victim/Offender Connection,* ed. Anna Victoria Wilson (Cincinnati, Ohio: Anderson, 1993), pp. 43–62.

14. Margaret A. Zahn and Philip C. Sagi, "Stranger Homicides in Nine American Cities," *Journal of Criminal Law and Criminology,* **78** (1987): 377–397.

15. Uniform Crime Reports, 1991, p. 17; Supplementary Homicide Reports. For a discussion of the Supplementary Homicide Report (SHR), see Colin Loftin, "The Validity of Robbery-Murder Classifications in Baltimore," *Violence and Victims,* **1** (1986): 191–204.

16. Marc Riedel, "Stranger Violence: Perspectives, Issues, and Problems," *Journal of Criminal Law and Criminology,* **78** (1987): 223–258.

17. See, e.g., Colin Loftin, Karen Kindley, Sandra L. Norris, and Brian Wiersema, "An Attribute Approach to Relationships between Offenders and Victims in Homicide," *Journal of Criminal Law and Criminology,* **78** (1987): 259–271.

18. Angela Browne, "Assault and Homicide at Home: When Battered Women Kill," *Advances in Applied Social Psychology,* **3** (1986): 57–79.

19. Martin Daly and Margo Wilson, *Homicide* (New York: Aldine–De Gruyter, 1988), pp. 294–295.

20. Coramae Richey Mann, "Getting Even?: Women Who Kill in Domestic Encounters," *Justice Quarterly,* **5** (1988): 33–51.

21. Joshua E. Muscat, "Characteristics of Childhood Homicide in Ohio, 1974–1984," *American Journal of Public Health,* **78** (1988): 822–824.

22. This theory is not necessarily inconsistent with the sociobiological explanation offered by Martin Daly and Margo Wilson, "Children as Homicide Victims," in *Child Abuse and Neglect: Biosocial Dimension,* ed. Richard J. Gelles and Jane B. Lancaster (New York: Aldine–De Gruyter, 1987), pp. 201–214.

23. For one of the first efforts to deal with juvenile homicide from clinical and theoretical perspectives, see Elissa P. Benedek and Dewey G. Cornell, eds., *Juvenile Homicide* (Washington, D.C.: American Psychiatric Press, 1989).

24. Uniform Crime Reports, 1992, pp. 227–228.

25. William R. Holcomb and Anasseril E. Daniel, "Homicide without an Apparent Motive," *Behavioral Sciences and the Law,* **6** (1988): 429–439.

26. See, especially, Michael Newton, *Mass Murder: An Annotated Bibliography* (New York: Garland, 1988).

27. Psychoanalysts are more likely to find such murderers to be psychotic. See, e.g., three works by David Abrahamsen: *The Murdering Mind* (New York: Harper & Row, 1973), *The Psychology of Crime* (New York: Columbia University Press, 1960), and *Crime and the Human Mind* (New York: Columbia University Press, 1944).

28. Mel Heimer, *The Cannibal: The Case of Albert Fish* (New York: Lyle Stuart, 1971).

29. Margaret Cheney, *The Co-ed Killer* (New York: Walker, 1976).

30. Jack Levin and James Alan Fox, *Mass Murder: Amer-*

ica's Growing Menace (New York: Plenum, 1985). See also Ronald M. Holmes and Stephen T. Holmes, "Understanding Mass Murder: A Starting Point," *Federal Probation,* **56** (1992): 53–61.

31. Ronald M. Holmes and James de Burger, *Serial Murder* (Newbury Park, Calif.: Sage, 1988), p. 155. For a criminal justice response to serial murder, see Pierce R. Brooks, Michael J. Devine, Terence J. Green, Barbara L. Hart, and Merlyn D. Moore, "Serial Murder: A Criminal Justice Response," *Police Chief,* **54** (1987): 37–43.

32. Cheryl L. Maxson, Margaret A. Gordon, and Malcolm W. Klein, "Differences between Gang and Nongang Homicides," *Criminology,* **23** (1985): 209–222.

33. G. David Curry and Irving A. Spergel, "Gang Homicide, Delinquency, and Community," *Criminology,* **26** (1988): 381–405.

34. *Newsweek,* Mar. 25, 1988, p. 20.

35. Sam Howe Verhovek, "Houston Knows Murder, But This . . . ," *New York Times,* July 9, 1993, p. A8.

36. "Third United Nations Survey of Crime Trends, Operation of Criminal Justice Systems and Crime Prevention Strategies," A CONF. 144/6, of July 27, 1990. These data are unadjusted for such factors as the age structures of the populations. For a more sophisticated method of comparing international homicide statistics, see Glenn D. Deane, "Cross-National Comparison of Homicide: Age/Sex-Adjusted Rates Using the 1980 U.S. Homicide Experience as a Standard," *Journal of Quantitative Criminology,* **3** (1987): 215–227. In 1988, the National Academy of Sciences assessed the understanding of violence in the United States; see Albert J. Reiss, Jr., and Jeffrey A. Roth, eds., *Understanding and Preventing Violence* (Washington, D.C.: National Academy Press, 1993).

37. Harvey Krahn, Timothy F. Hartnagel, and John W. Gartrell, "Income Inequality and Homicide Rates: Cross-National Data and Criminological Theories," *Criminology,* **24** (1986): 269–295.

38. Deane, "Cross-National Comparison of Homicide." This study was conducted on the basis of the statistics of the International Criminal Police Organization (Interpol).

39. Dane Archer and Rosemary Gartner, *Violence and Crime in Cross-National Perspective* (New Haven, Conn.: Yale University Press, 1984).

40. M. Harvey Brenner, "Time-Series Analysis: Effects of the Economy on Criminal Behavior and the Administration of Criminal Justice in the United States, Canada, England and Wales, and Scotland," in *Economic Crises and Crime: Correlations between the State of the Economy, Deviance, and the Control of Deviance,* publication no. 15, United Nations Social Defense Research Institute (Rome 1976), pp. 25–65. See also Philip J. Cook and Gary A. Zarkin, "Homicide and Economic Conditions: A Replication and Critique of M. Harvey Brenner's New Report to the U.S. Congress," *Journal of Quantitative Criminology,* **2** (1986): 69–103.

41. Steven F. Messner and Kenneth Tardiff, "The Social Ecology of Urban Homicide: An Application of the Routine Activities Approach," *Criminology,* **23** (1985): 241–267.

42. David F. Luckenbill, "Criminal Homicide as a Situated Transaction," *Social Problems,* **25** (1977): 176–186. Although Luckenbill focused on homicides, the stages he identified are identical in assaults.

43. U.S. Department of Justice, Bureau of Justice Statistics, *Crime and the Nation's Households, 1992* (Washington, D.C.: U.S. Government Printing Office, 1993), p. 2.

44. C. H. Kempe, F. N. Silverman, B. F. Steele, W. Droegemueller, and H. K. Silver, "The Battered-Child Syndrome," *Journal of the American Medical Association,* **181** (1962): 17–24.

45. Elizabeth Pleck, "Criminal Approaches to Family Violence, 1640–1980," in *Family Violence,* ed. Lloyd Ohlin and Michael Tonry, vol. 2 (Chicago: University of Chicago Press, 1989), pp. 19–57.

46. *Thurman v. Torrington,* 596 F. Supp. 1521 (1985).

47. Murray A. Straus and Richard J. Gelles, "How Violent Are American Families?: Estimates from the National Family Violence Resurvey and Other Studies," in *Family Abuse and Its Consequences,* ed. Gerald T. Hotaling, David Finkelhor, John T. Kirkpatrick, and Murray A. Straus (Newbury Park, Calif.: Sage, 1988). The Conflict Tactics Scales used to measure violence are described in Murray A. Straus, *Measuring Physical and Emotional Abuse of Children with the Conflict Tactics Scales* (Durham: Family Research Laboratory, University of New Hampshire, 1988). For a discussion comparing the U.S.A. with other Western nations, see Margo I. Wilson and Martin Daly, "Who Kills Whom in Spouse Killings: On the Exceptional Sex Ratio of Spousal Homicides in the United States," *Criminology,* **30** (1992): 189–215; and Pamela Haag, "The 'Ill-Use of a Wife': Patterns of Working-Class Violence in Domestic and Public New York City, 1860–1880," *Journal of Social History,* **25** (1992): 447–477. See also Elizabeth Kandel-Englander, "Wife Battering and Violence outside the Family," *Journal of Interpersonal Violence,* **7** (1992): 462–470; and Emilio C. Viano, ed., *Intimate Violence: Interdisciplinary Perspectives* (Washington, D.C.: Hemisphere, 1992).

48. Murray A. Straus, Richard J. Gelles, and S. K. Steinmetz, *Behind Closed Doors: Violence in the American Family* (Garden City, N.Y.: Doubleday, 1980); Murray A. Straus, "Victims and Aggressors in Marital Violence," *American Behavioral Scientists,* **23** (1980): 681–704. See also M. D. Pagelow, *Family Violence* (New York: Praeger, 1984), p. 274; and S. F. Berk and D. R. Loseke, "'Handling' Family Violence: Situational Determinants of Police Arrest in Domestic Disturbances," *Law and Society Review,* **15** (1981): 317–346.

49. Straus and Gelles, "How Violent Are American Families?" p. 17. See also Scott L. Feld and Murray A. Straus, "Escalation and Desistance of Wife

Assault in Marriage," *Criminology,* **27** (1989): 141–161.

50. R. E. Dobash and R. P. Dobash, "Wives: The 'Appropriate' Victims of Marital Violence," *Victimology,* **2** (1977–1978): 426–442; J. P. Deschner, *The Hitting Habit* (New York: Free Press, 1984); D. J. Sonkin, *Learning to Live without Violence: A Handbook for Men,* 2d ed. (San Francisco: Volcano, 1985); P. A. Klaus and M. R. Rand, *Family Violence,* U.S. Department of Justice (Washington, D.C.: U.S. Government Printing Office, 1984); D. E. H. Russell, *Rape in Marriage* (New York: Macmillan, 1982); L. W. Kennedy and D. G. Dutton, *The Incidence of Wife Assault in Alberta,* Edmonton Area Series report no. 53 (Edmonton: University of Alberta, Population Research Laboratory, 1987); W. H. Meredith, D. A. Abbott, and S. L. Adams, "Family Violence: Its Relation to Marital and Parental Satisfaction and Family Strengths," *Journal of Family Violence,* **1** (1986): 299–305.

51. Patrick A. Langan and Christopher A. Innes, *Preventing Domestic Violence against Women,* for U.S. Department of Justice, Bureau of Justice Statistics (Washington, D.C.: U.S. Government Printing Office, 1986).

52. Ibid., pp. 14–20; Marvin E. Wolfgang and Franco Ferracuti, *The Subculture of Violence: Toward an Integrated Theory in Criminology* (London: Tavistock, 1967).

53. Joan McCord, "Parental Aggressiveness and Physical Punishment in Long-Term Perspective," in Hotaling et al., *Family Abuse,* pp. 91–98; see also D. J. Sonkin, D. Martin, and L. E. Walker, eds., *The Male Batterer: A Treatment Approach* (New York: Springer, 1985).

54. See Robert L. Burgess and Patricia Draper, "The Explanation of Family Violence: The Role of Biological, Behavioral, and Cultural Selection," in Ohlin and Tonry, *Family Violence,* pp. 59–116. See also Phyllis D. Coontz and Judith A. Martin, "Understanding Violent Mothers and Fathers: Assessing Explanations Offered by Mothers and Fathers for Their Use of Control Punishment," in Hotaling et al., *Family Abuse,* pp. 77–90; and Nancy Hutchings, ed., *The Violent Family* (New York: Human Sciences Press, 1988).

55. Donald G. Dutton, *The Domestic Assault of Women* (Boston: Allyn and Bacon, 1988), p. 15.

56. Lenore E. Walker, *The Battered Woman Syndrome* (New York: Springer Verlag, 1984); Angela Browne, *When Battered Women Kill* (New York: Free Press, 1987); G. T. Hotaling and D. B. Sugarman, "An Analysis of Risk Markers in Husband to Wife Violence: The Current State of Knowledge," *Violence and Victims,* **1** (1986): 101–124; Brenda A. Miller, Thomas H. Nochajski, Kenneth E. Leonard, Howard T. Blane, Dawn M. Gondoli, and Patricia M. Bowers, "Spousal Violence and Alcohol/Drug Problems among Parolees and Their Spouses," *Women and Criminal Justice,* **1** (1990): 55–72.

57. Study conducted by Mohammed Ayat, Atiqui Abdelaziz, Najat Kfita, and El Khazouni Zineb, at the request of UNESCO and the Union of Arab Lawyers, Fez, Morocco, 1989.

58. David Levinson, *Family Violence in Cross-Cultural Perspective* (Newbury Park, Calif.: Sage, 1989).

59. Carolyn F. Swift, "Surviving: Women's Strength through Connections," in *Abuse and Victimization across the Life Span,* ed. Martha Straus (Baltimore: Johns Hopkins University Press, 1988), pp. 153–169. See also Dobash and Dobash, "Wives."

60. For an account of public policy and family privacy, see Frank E. Zimring, "Toward a Jurisprudence of Family Violence, in Ohlin and Tonry, *Family Violence,* pp. 547–569. For a review of early literature on women and domestic homicide, see Christine Rasche, "Early Models for Contemporary Thought on Domestic Violence and Women Who Kill Their Mates: A Review of the Literature from 1895 to 1970," *Women and Criminal Justice,* **1** (1990): 31–53.

61. R. A. Berk, S. F. Berk, and P. J. Newton, "An Empirical Analysis of Police Responses to Incidents of Wife Battery," paper presented at the Second National Conference of Family Violence Researchers, University of New Hampshire, Durham, July 1984; R. E. Worden and A. A. Pollitz, "Police Arrests in Domestic Disturbances: A Further Look," *Law and Society Review,* **18** (1984): 105–119; R. Tong, *Women, Sex, and the Law* (Totowa, N.J.: Rowman & Allanheld, 1984). On prosecution of cases, see Lisa G. Lerman, "Prosecution of Wife Beaters: Institutional Obstacles and Innovations," in *Violence in the Home: Interdisciplinary Perspectives,* ed. Mary Lystad (New York: Brunner/Mazel, 1986).

62. Lee H. Bowker, *Ending the Violence* (Holmes Beach, Fla.: Learning Publications, 1986); Daniel G. Saunders and Sandra T. Azar, "Treatment Programs for Family Violence," in Ohlin and Tonry, *Family Violence,* pp. 481–546; Anna F. Kuhl and Linda E. Saltzman, "Battered Women and the Criminal Justice System," in *The Changing Roles of Women in the Criminal Justice System,* ed. Imogene L. Moyer (Prospect Heights, Ill.: Waveland, 1985).

63. Jeffrey Fagan and Sandra Wexler, "Crime at Home and in the Streets: The Relationship between Family and Stranger Violence," *Violence and Victims,* **2** (1987): 5–23; Jeffrey Fagan, Douglas K. Stewart, and Karen V. Hansen, "Violent Men or Violent Husbands?: Background Factors and Situational Correlates," in *The Dark Side of Families,* ed. David Finkelhor, Murray A. Straus, Gerald T. Hotaling, and Richard J. Gelles (Beverly Hills, Calif.: Sage, 1983), pp. 49–67. See also N. M. Shields and C. R. Hanneke, "Battered Wives' Reactions to Marital Rape," in Finkelhor et al., *The Dark Side of Families;* and Jeffrey Fagan, "Cessation of Family Violence: Deterrence and Dissuasion," in Ohlin and Tonry, *Family Violence,* pp. 377–425.

64. Lawrence W. Sherman and Richard A. Berk, "The Minneapolis Domestic Violence Experiment," *Police Foundation Reports,* **1** (1984): 1–8; Lawrence W. Sher-

man and Richard A. Berk, "The Specific Deterrent Effects of Arrest for Domestic Assault," *American Sociological Review*, **49** (1984): 261–272. See also *Strategies for Confronting Domestic Violence*, New York: United Nations (ST/CSDHA/20, 1993); Delbert S. Elliott, "Criminal Justice Procedures in Family Violence Cases," in Ohlin and Tonry, *Family Violence*, pp. 427–480; and Eve S. Buzawa and Carl G. Buzawa, *Domestic Violence: The Criminal Justice Response* (Newbury Park, Calif.: Sage, 1990). For an overview, see J. David Hirschel, Ira W. Hutchinson, Charles W. Dean, and Anne-Marie Mills, "Review Essay on the Law Enforcement Response to Spouse Abuse: Past, Present and Future," *Justice Quarterly*, **9** (1992): 247–283; Edward W. Gondolf and J. Richard McFerron, "Handling Battering Men: Police Action in Wife Abuse Cases," *Criminal Justice and Behavior*, **16** (1989): 429–439; and Cynthia Grant Bowman, "The Arrest Experiments: A Feminist Critique," *Journal of Criminal Law and Criminology*, **83** (1992): 201–208. For a discussion of batterers, see Albert R. Roberts, "Psychosocial Characteristics of Batterers: A Study of 234 Men Charged with Domestic Violence Offenses," *Journal of Family Violence*, **2** (1987): 81–93.

See also Elizabeth A. Stanko, "Missing the Mark? Police Battering," in *Women, Policing, and Male Violence: International Perspectives*, ed. Jalna Hanmer, Jill Radford, and Elizabeth A. Stanko (New York: Routledge, 1989), pp. 46–69; Rose Mary Stanford and Bonney Lee Mowry, "Domestic Disturbance Danger Rate," *Journal of Police Science and Administration*, **17** (1990): 244–249; and Kathleen J. Ferraro, "Policing Woman Battering," *Social Problems*, **36** (1989): 61–74. For a discussion of possible unintended consequences of policies favoring arrests in domestic violence cases, see Susan L. Miller, "Unintended Side Effects of Pro-Arrest Policies and Their Race and Class Implications for Battered Women: A Cautionary Note," *Criminal Justice Policy Review*, **3** (1989): 299–317. For a discussion of restraining orders in domestic violence cases, see Judy Hails Kaci, "A Study of Protective Orders Issued under California's Domestic Violence Prevention Act," *Criminal Justice Review*, **17** (1992): 61–76. See also literature on child abuse and policing: Susan E. Martin and Edwin E. Hamilton, "Police Handling of Child Abuse Cases: Policies, Procedures, and Issues," *American Journal of Police*, **9** (1990): 1–24; Cecil L. Willis and Richard H. Wells, "The Police and Child Abuse: An Analysis of Police Decisions to Report Illegal Behavior," *Criminology*, **26** (1988): 695–716; Lisa A. Frisch, "Research That Succeeds, Policies That Fail," *Journal of Criminal Law and Criminology*, **83** (1992): 209–216; David B. Mitchell, "Contemporary Police Practices in Domestic Violence Cases: Arresting the Abuser: Is It Enough?" *Journal of Criminal Law and Criminology*, **83** (1992): 241–249; Lisa G. Lerman, "The Decontextualization of Domestic Violence," *Journal of Criminal*

Law and Criminology, **83** (1992): 217–240; Lawrence W. Sherman, Janell D. Schmidt, Dennis P. Rogan, Patrick R. Gartlin, Ellen G. Cohn, Dean J. Collins, and Anthony R. Bacich, "From Initial Deterrence to Long-Term Escalation: Short Custody Arrest for Poverty Ghetto Domestic Violence," *Criminology*, **29** (1991): 821–850.

65. Lawrence W. Sherman, Janell D. Schmidt, Dennis P. Rogan, Douglas A. Smith, Patrick R. Gartlin, Ellen G. Cohn, Dean J. Collins, and Anthony R. Bacich, "The Variable Effects of Arrest on Criminal Careers: The Milwaukee Domestic Violence Experiment," *Journal of Criminal Law and Criminology*, **83** (1992): 137–169. See also James Meeker and Arnold Binder, "Experiments as Reforms: The Impact of the 'Minneapolis Experiment' on Police Policy," *Journal of Police Science and Administration*, **17** (1990): 147–153; Michael Steinman, "Lowering Recidivism among Men Who Batter Women," *Journal of Police Science and Administration*, **17** (1990): 124–132; and Lawrence W. Sherman and Douglas A. Smith, "Crime, Punishment, and Stake in Conformity: Legal and Informal Control of Domestic Violence," *American Sociological Review*, **57** (1992): 680–690. See also J. David Hirschel and Ira W. Hutchinson III, "Female Spouse Abuse and the Police Response: The Charlotte, North Carolina Experiment," *Journal of Criminal Law and Criminology*, **83** (1992): 73–119; and Richard A. Beck, Alec Campbell, Ruth Klap, and Bruce Western, "A Baysian Analysis of the Colorado Springs Spouse Abuse Experiment," *Journal of Criminal Law and Criminology*, **83** (1992): 170–200. For an integrated approach to control, see Jeffrey Fagan, "The Social Control of Spouse Assault," in *Advances in Criminological Theory*, vol. 4, eds. Freda Adler and William S. Laufer (New Brunswick, N.J.: Transaction, 1993), pp. 187–235.

66. For evidence that many people are unsympathetic to battered women, see C. S. Greenblat, "Don't Hit Your Wife . . . Unless . . . ": Preliminary Findings on Normative Support for the Use of Physical Force by Husbands," *Victimology*, **10** (1985): 221–241; D. G. Saunders, A. B. Lynch, M. Grayson, and D. Linz, "The Inventory of Beliefs about Wife Beating: The Construction and Initial Validation of a Measure of Beliefs and Attitudes," *Violence and Victims*, **2** (1986): 39–57; and D. G. Saunders, "When Battered Women Use Violence: Husband-Abuse or Self-Defense?" *Victims and Violence*, **1** (1986): 47–60. For an article on methodological problems in family violence research, see Joseph G. Weis, "Family Violence Research Methodology and Design," in Ohlin and Tonry, *Family Violence*, pp. 117–162. For a general survey and critique of the literature, see Irene Hanson Frieze and Angela Browne, "Violence in Marriage," in Ohlin and Tonry, *Family Violence*, 163–218.

67. Joan Zorza, "The Criminal Law of Misdemeanor Domestic Violence, 1970–1990," *Journal of Criminal Law and Criminology*, **83** (1992): 46–72. See also Kathleen M. Heide, *Why Kids Kill Parents: Child Abuse and*

Adolescent Homicide (Columbus: Ohio State University Press, 1992); and Candace Kruttschnitt and Maude Dornfeld, "Will They Tell? Assessing Preadolescents' Reports of Family Violence," *Journal of Research in Crime and Delinquency,* **29** (1992): 136–147.

68. Edna Erez and Pamela Tontodonato, "Patterns of Reported Parent-Child Abuse and Police Response," *Journal of Family Violence,* **4** (1989): 143–159; Edna Erez, "Intimacy, Violence, and the Police," *Human Relations,* **39** (1986): 265–281.

69. K. Burgdorf, "Recognition and Reporting of Child Maltreatment," in *Findings from the National Study of the Incidence and Severity of Child Abuse and Neglect* (Washington, D.C.: National Center on Child Abuse and Neglect, 1980), p. 370. For a discussion of the underestimates of the NIS, see S. D. Petgers, G. E. Wyatt, and D. Finkelhor, "Prevalence," in *A Sourcebook on Child Sexual Abuse,* ed. D. Finkelhor, S. Araji, L. Baron, A. Browne, S. D. Peters, and G. E. Wyatt (Newbury Park, Calif.: Sage, 1986).

70. American Association for Protecting Children, *Highlights of Official Child Neglect and Abuse Reporting, 1984* (Denver: American Humane Association, 1986).

71. For a comprehensive discussion of the estimates of child maltreatment, see James Garbarino, "The Incidence and Prevalence of Child Maltreatment," in Ohlin and Tonry, *Family Violence,* pp. 219–261.

72. Mildred Daley Pagelow, "The Incidence and Prevalence of Criminal Abuse of Other Family Members," in Ohlin and Tonry, *Family Violence,* pp. 263–311.

73. Cathy Spatz Widom, "The Cycle of Violence," *Science,* **244** (1989): 160–166; E. C. Herrenkohl, R. C. Herrenkohl, and L. J. Toedter, "Perspectives on the Intergenerational Transmission of Abuse," in Finkelhor et al., *The Dark Side of Families;* Joan McCord, "A Forty Year Perspective on the Effects of Child Abuse and Neglect," *Child Abuse and Neglect,* **7** (1983): 265–270. For a discussion of the higher arrest rates of adults who were abused or neglected as children, see Cathy Spatz Widom, "Child Abuse, Neglect, and Violent Criminal Behavior," *Criminology,* **27** (1989): 251–271.

74. Deborah Daro, "Half Full and Half Empty: The Evaluation of Results of Nineteen Clinical Research and Demonstration Projects," *Summary of Nineteen Clinical Demonstration Projects Funded by the National Center on Child Abuse and Neglect, 1978–81* (Berekely: University of California, School of Social Welfare, 1986).

75. Richard J. Gelles, "What to Learn from Cross-Cultural and Historical Research on Child Abuse and Neglect: An Overview," in *Child Abuse and Neglect,* ed. Richard J. Gelles and Jane B. Lancaster (New York: Aldine–De Gruyter, 1987), pp. 15–30. On child sex abuse, see Thomas H. Roane, "Male Victims of Sexual Abuse: A Case Review within a Child Protective Team," *Child Welfare,* **71** (1992): 231–239; and Craig M. Allen, *Women and Men Who Sexually Abuse*

Children: A Comparative Analysis (Orwell, Vt.: Safer Society Press, 1991). For a special issue on child sexual abuse, see *Criminal Justice and Behavior,* **19** (1992): 1–792. For the impact of child victimization, see Candace Kruttschnitt and Maude Dornfeld, "Childhood Victimization, Race, and Violent Crime," *Criminal Justice and Behavior,* **18** (1991): 448–463.

76. Craig J. Forsyth and Robert Gramling, "Elderly Crime: Fact and Artifact," in *Older Offenders,* ed. Belinda McCarthy and Robert Langworthy (New York: Praeger, 1988), pp. 3–13; Terry Fulmer, "Elder Abuse," in Straus, *Abuse and Victimization,* pp. 188–199.

77. Pagelow, "Incidence and Prevalence of Criminal Abuse," p. 267.

78. Mary Joy Quinn and Susan K. Tomita, *Elder Abuse and Neglect* (New York: Springer, 1986), chap. 4. See also Rachel Filinson and Stanley R. Ingman, eds. *Elder Abuse: Practice and Policy* (New York: Human Sciences Press, 1989); Alan A. Malinchak, *Crime and Gerontology* (Englewood Cliffs, N.J.: Prentice-Hall, 1980).

79. Susan Brownmiller, *Against Our Will: Men, Women, and Rape* (New York: Simon & Schuster, 1975), pp. 1–9.

80. Duncan Chappell, "Sexual Criminal Violence," in *Pathways to Criminal Violence,* ed. Neil Alan Weiner and Marvin E. Wolfgang (Newbury Park, Calif.: Sage, 1989), pp. 68–108.

81. Marvin E. Wolfgang, Robert M. Figlio, Paul E. Tracy, and Simon I. Singer, *The National Survey of Crime Severity* (Washington, D.C.: U.S. Government Printing Office, 1985).

82. Uniform Crime Reports, 1992, p. 58. For a special issue devoted to an overview of adult sexual assault, see *Journal of Social Issues,* **48** (1992): 1–195, with an Introduction by Susan B. Sorenson and Jacqueline W. White.

83. Menachem Amir, *Patterns in Forcible Rape* (Chicago: University of Chicago Press, 1977), pp. 233–234.

84. U.S. Dept. of Justice, Bureau of Justice Statistics, *Highlights from 20 Years of Surveying Crime Victims* (Washington, D.C.: U.S. Government Printing Office, 1993) p. 24.

85. David Finkelhor and Kersti Yllo, "Forced Sex in Marriage: A Preliminary Research Report," *Crime and Delinquency,* **28** (1982): 459–478. See also the report presented by Diana Russel to the American Sociological Association and quoted in the *New York Times,* Nov. 29, 1982, p. 20.

86. Andrea Parrot, *Coping with Date Rape and Acquaintance Rape* (New York: Rosen, 1988). See also John E. Murphy, "Date Abuse and Forced Intercourse among College Students," in Hotaling et al., *Family Abuse,* pp. 285–296.

87. M. P. Koss, C. A. Gidycz, and N. Wisniewski, "The Scope of Rape: Incidence and Prevalence of Sexual Aggression and Victimization in a National Sample of Higher Education Students," *Journal of Consulting and Clinical Psychology,* **55** (1987): 162–170.

88. On this subject, see R. Thomas Dull and David J. Giacopassi, "Demographic Correlates of Sexual and Dating Attitudes: A Study of Date Rape," *Criminal Justice and Behavior,* **14** (1987): 175–193.

89. Joanne Belknap and Sandra Evans Skovron, "Public Perceptions of Date Rape" (1988), report on file with National Council on Crime and Delinquency—School of Criminal Justice Library, Rutgers University; John P. Smith and Janice G. Williams, "From Abusive Household to Dating Violence," *Journal of Family Violence,* **7** (1992): 153–165.

90. James L. LeBeau, "Patterns of Stranger and Serial Rape Offending: Factors Distinguishing Apprehended and At Large Offenders," *Journal of Criminal Law and Criminology,* **78** (1987): 309–326.

91. See Lynne Goodstein and Faith Lutze, "Rape and Criminal Justice System Responses," *The Changing Roles of Women in the Criminal Justice System,* 2d ed., ed. Imogene L. Moyer (Prospect Heights, Ill.: Waveland, 1992), pp. 153–179.

92. Richard Rada, *Clinical Aspects of the Report* (New York: Grune & Stratton, 1978), pp. 123–130.

93. Paul H. Gebhard, John H. Gagman, Wardell B. Pomeroy, and Cornelia V. Christenson, *Sex Offenders: An Analysis of Types* (New York: Harper & Row, 1965), pp. 198–204.

94. Nicholas A. Groth, *Men Who Rape: The Psychology of the Offender* (New York: Plenum, 1979), pp. 14–58.

95. J. Marolla and D. Scully, *Attitudes toward Women, Violence, and Rape: A Comparison of Convicted Rapists and Other Felons* (Rockville, Md.: National Institute of Mental Health, 1982); M. P. Koss and K. E. Leonard, "Sexually Aggressive Men: Empirical Findings and Theoretical Implications," in *Pornography and Sexual Aggression,* ed. N. Malamuth and E. Donnerstein (New York: Academic Press, 1984), pp. 213–232; Ilsa L. Lottes, "Sexual Socialization and Attitudes toward Rape," in *Rape and Sexual Assault,* ed. Ann Wolbert Burgess (New York: Garland, 1988), pp. 193–220.

96. Christine Alder, "An Exploration of Self-Reported Sexually Aggressive Behavior," *Crime and Delinquency,* **31** (1985): 306–331.

97. P. R. Sanday, "The Socio-Cultural Context of Rape: A Cross-Cultural Study," *Journal of Social Issues,* **37** (1981): 5–27.

98. Susan Estrich, *Real Rape* (Cambridge, Mass.: Harvard University Press, 1987); S. Griffin, "Rape: The All-American Crime," *Ramparts,* **10** (1971): 26–35.

99. Julia R. Schwendinger and Herman Schwendinger, *Rape and Inequality* (Beverly Hills, Calif.: Sage, 1983), p. 220.

100. M. Dwayne Smith and Nathan Bennett, "Poverty, Inequality, and Theories of Forcible Rape," *Crime and Delinquency,* **31** (1985): 295–305.

101. Ruth D. Peterson and William C. Bailey, "Forcible Rape, Poverty, and Economic Inequality in U.S. Metropolitan Communities," *Journal of Quantitative Criminology,* **4** (1988): 99–119.

102. Matthew Hale, *History of the Pleas of the Crown,* vol. 1 (London, 1736), p. 635.

103. Martin D. Schwartz and Todd R. Clear, "Toward a New Law on Rape," *Crime and Delinquency,* **26** (1980): 129–151.

104. Chappell, "Sexual Criminal Violence," p. 76.

105. Schwartz and Clear, "Toward a New Law."

106. Andrew Z. Soshnick, Comment: "The Rape Shield Paradox: Complainant Protection amidst Oscillating Trends of State Judicial Interpretation," *Journal of Criminal Law and Criminology,* **78** (1987): 644–698; Ken Polk, "Rape Reform and Criminal Justice Processing," *Crime and Delinquency,* **31** (1985): 191–205; Gilbert Geis, "Rape-in-Marriage: Law and Law Reform in England, the United States, and Sweden," *Adelaide Law Review,* **6** (1978): 284–303.

107. Kristen M. Williams, *The Prosecution of Sexual Assaults* (Washington, D.C.: Institute of Law and Social Research, 1978), p. 30. See also Gary LaFree, *Rape and Criminal Justice: The Social Construction of Sexual Assault* (Belmont, Calif.: Wadsworth, 1989).

108. Janet Gornick, Martha R. Burt, and Karen J. Pittman, "Structures and Activities of Rape Crisis Centers in the Early 1980's," *Crime and Delinquency,* **31** (1985): 247–268.

109. Philip J. Cook, "Robbery Violence," *Journal of Criminal Law and Criminology,* **78** (1987): 357–376; Colin Loftin, "The Validity of Robber-Murder Classifications in Baltimore," *Violence and Victims,* **1** (1986): 191–204.

110. U.S. Department of Justice, *Report to the Nation on Crime and Justice,* 2d ed. (Washington, D.C.: U.S. Government Printing Office, 1988), p. 97.

111. U.S. Department of Justice, Bureau of Justice Statistics, *Criminal Victimization in the United States, 1991* (Washington, D.C.: U.S. Government Printing Office, 1992), p. 76.

112. Frederick H. McClintock and Evelyn Gibson, *Robbery in London* (London: Macmillan, 1961).

113. André Normandeau, "Trends and Patterns in Crimes of Robbery," Ph.D. dissertation, University of Pennsylvania, 1968.

114. John Conklin, *Robbery and the Criminal Justice System* (Philadelphia: Lippincott, 1972), pp. 59–78.

115. Terry L. Baumer and Michael D. Carrington, *The Robbery of Financial Institutions,* for U.S. Department of Justice (Washington, D.C.: U.S. Government Printing Office, 1986).

116. Uniform Crime Reports, 1991, p. 27.

117. Philip J. Cook, "Is Robbery Becoming More Violent?: An Analysis of Robbery Murder Trends since 1968," *Journal of Criminal Law and Criminology,* **76** (1985): 480–489. According to Bureau of Justice Statistics, *Highlights from 20 Years of Surveying Crime Victims,* p. 10, the victim suffered a serious injury and lost property in 1 in 20 robberies.

118. Franklin E. Zimring and James Zuehl, "Victim Injury and Death in Urban Robbery: A Chicago Study," *Journal of Legal Studies,* **15** (1986): 1–40.

119. Philip J. Cook, *Robbery in the United States: An Analy-*

sis of Recent Trends and Patterns, for U.S. Department of Justice (Washington, D.C.: U.S. Government Printing Office, 1983).

120. Wayland Clifton, Jr., *Convenience Store Robberies in Gainesville, Florida* (Gainesville, Fla.: Gainesville Police Department, 1987), p. 15; Ronald D. Hunter, "Convenience Store Robbery in Tallahassee: A Reassessment," *Journal of Security Administration*, **13** (1990): 3–18; James D. Calder and John R. Bauer, "Convenience Store Robberies: Security Measures and Store Robbery Incidents," *Journal of Criminal Justice*, **20** (1992): 553–566.

121. Richard Block and Wesley G. Skogan, "Resistance and Non-Fatal Outcomes in Stranger-to-Stranger Predatory Crime," *Violence and Victims*, **1** (1986): 241–253.

122. United Nations General Assembly Resolution 40/61, Dec. 9, 1985. For a discussion of violence and terrorism, see Paul Wilkinson, *Terrorism and the Liberal State*, 2d ed. (New York: New York University Press, 1986), pp. 23–68; Beau Grosscup, *The Explosion of Terrorism* (Far Hills, N.J.: New Horizon, 1987); and Robert J. Kelly and Rufus Schatzberg, "Galvanizing Indiscriminate Political Violence: Mind-Sets and Some Ideological Constructs in Terrorism," *International Journal of Comparative and Applied Criminal Justice*, **16** (1992): 15–41.

123. Harvey J. Iglarsh, "Terrorism and Corporate Costs," *Terrorism*, **10** (1987): 227–230.

124. Ariel Merari, Tamar Prat, Sophia Kotzer, Anat Kurz, and Yoram Schweitzer, *Inter 85: A Review of International Terrorism in 1985* (Boulder, Colo.: Westview, 1986), p. 106.

125. Noemi Gal-Or, *International Cooperation to Suppress Terrorism* (New York: St. Martin's Press, 1985), pp. 90–96.

126. United Nations General Assembly Resolution 40/61.

127. James D. Wright, Peter H. Rossi, and Kathleen Daly, *Under the Gun: Weapons, Crime, and Violence in America* (New York: Aldine, 1983), p. 42.

128. Samuel Walker, *Sense and Nonsense about Crime* (Monterey, Calif.: Brooks/Cole, 1985), pp. 149–150.

129. George D. Newton, Jr., and Frank E. Zimring, *Firearms and Violence in American Life: A Staff Report Submitted to the National Commission on the Causes and Prevention of Violence* (Washington, D.C.: National Commission on the Causes and Prevention of Violence, 1969), p. 121.

130. Walker, *Sense and Nonsense about Crime*, pp. 149–150.

131. Franklin E. Zimring and Gordon Hawkins, *The Citizen's Guide to Gun Control* (New York: Macmillan, 1987), p. 5.

132. Robert D. McFadden, "On a Bus in Queens, Three Bandits Stage a Frontier Robbery," *New York Times*, July 31, 1993, p. 1.

133. U.S. Public Health Service, "Weapon-Carrying among High School Students—United States, 1990," *Morbidity and Mortality Report*, **40** (1991): 681–696.

134. Ibid.

135. Charles M. Callahan and Frederick P. Rivara, "Urban High School Youth and Handguns: A School-Based Survey," *Journal of the American Medical Association*, **267** (1992): 3038–3042. See also Derral Cheatwood and Kathleen J. Block, "Youth and Homicide: An Investigation of the Age Factor in Criminal Homicide," *Justice Quarterly*, **7** (1990): 265–292.

136. Juan Keen, "Students' Searches Yield Fear," *USA Today*, Nov. 12, 1991, pp. A1–A2.

137. Jon D. Hull, "A Boy and His Gun," *Time*, Aug. 2, 1993.

138. Alan J. Lizotte and James M. Tesoriero, "Patterns of Adolescent Firearms Ownership and Use," working paper no. 11, Rochester Youth Development Study (Albany, N.Y.: Hindelang Criminal Justice Research Center, 1991).

139. Glenn L. Pierce and William J. Bowers, "The Bartley-Fox Gun Law's Short-Term Impact on Crime in Boston," *Annals of the American Academy of Political and Social Science*, **455** (1981): 120–137.

140. Patrick W. O'Carroll, Colin Loftin, John B. Waller, Jr., David McDowall, Allen Bukoff, Richard O. Scott, James A. Mercy, and Brian Wiersema, "Preventing Homicide: An Evaluation of the Efficacy of a Detroit Gun Ordinance," *American Journal of Public Health*, **81** (1991): 576–581.

141. James A. Beha II, "And Nobody Can Get You Out: The Impact of a Mandatory Prison Sentence for the Illegal Carrying of a Firearm on the Administration of Criminal Justice in Boston," *Boston University Law Review*, **57** (1977): 96–146, 289–333.

142. Colin Loftin, Milton Heumann, and David McDowall, "Mandatory Sentencing and Firearms Violence: Evaluating an Alternative to Gun Control," *Law and Society Review*, **17** (1983): 288–318.

143. David McDowall, Colin Loftin, and Brian Wiersema, "A Comparative Study of the Preventive Effects of Mandatory Sentencing Laws for Gun Crimes," discussion paper 6 (College Park, Md.: Violence Research Group, Institute of Criminal Justice and Criminology, University of Maryland, 1991).

144. Colin Loftin, David McDowall, Brian Wiersema, and Talbert J. Cottey, "Effects of Restrictive Licensing of Handguns on Homicide and Suicide in the District of Columbia," *New England Journal of Medicine*, **325** (1991): 1615–1620.

145. David McDowall and Alan Lizotte, "Gun Control," in *Introduction to Social Problems*, ed. Craig Calhoun and George Ritzer (New York: Primis Database, McGraw-Hill, 1993).

146. James D. Wright, Peter H. Rossi, and Kathleen Daly, with the assistance of Eleanor Weber-Burdin, *Under the Gun: Weapons, Crime and Violence in America* (New York: Aldine, 1983), p. 244.

147. Robert L. Young, David McDowall, and Colin Loftin, "Collective Security and the Ownership of Firearms for Protection," *Criminology*, **25** (1987):

47–62; John A. Arthur, "Criminal Victimization, Fear of Crime, and Handgun Ownership among Blacks: Evidence from National Survey Data," *American Journal of Criminal Justice,* **16** (1992): 121–141; Carol Y. Thompson, William B. Bankston, and Roberta L. St. Pierre, "Single Female-Headed Households, Handgun Possession, and the Fear of Rape," *Sociological Spectrum,* **11** (1991): 231–244.

148. Glenn L. Pierce and William J. Bowers, *The Impact of the Massachusetts Gun Law on Gun and Non-Gun-Related Crime* (Boston: Northeastern University Press, 1979). For a discussion of the deterrent effect of gun ownership by citizens, see Gary S. Green, "Citizen Gun Ownership and Criminal Deterrence: Theory, Research, and Policy," *Criminology,* **25** (1987): 63–81.

11

Crimes Against Property

KEY TERMS

arson
burglary
check forging
confidence game
false pretenses, obtaining property by
fence
fraud
larceny
shoplifting

The motion picture *The Gods Must Be Crazy* introduces us to a society of happy aborigines, remote from the hustle and bustle of modern life. Such tools as they have are shared and can easily be replaced from an abundance of sticks and stones.

High up, a "noisy bird" passes over the camp of these happy people. The pilot of the noisy bird casually throws an empty Coke bottle out of the cockpit. It lands in the middle of the camp. The aborigines stare at this foreign object. They handle it delicately and then discover what a useful object it is: it holds water; it can be used for rolling dough, for hammering, for many things. Everybody needs it and wants it. Fights ensue over who can have it. The peace and tranquility of this little society are shattered. These people have discovered the concept of property, and they are experiencing all the troubles that go with the possession of property, including property crime.

The film has a happy ending. The aborigines finally get rid of the bottle, and life returns to normal.

We have explored some of the patterns of social interaction and the routine activities of daily life that set the stage for offenders to commit violent crimes and for other people—family members, acquaintances, strangers, airplane passengers—to become victims. We know that if we are to develop effective policies to prevent and control violent crime, we must have a thorough understanding of the characteristics of specific offenses; we need to know where, when, and how they are committed, and which individuals are most likely to commit them. The same is true for property offenses. To develop crime-prevention strategies, we need to study the characteristics that differentiate the various types of offenses which deprive people of their property.

Do such offenses as pocket-picking, shoplifting, check forgery, theft by use of stolen credit cards, car theft, and burglary have different pay-offs and risks? What kinds of resources are needed (weapons, places to sell stolen property)? Are any specific skills needed to carry out these offenses? The opportunities to commit property crime are all but unlimited. Studies demonstrate that if these opportunities are reduced, the incidence of crime is reduced as well.

The traditional property crimes are larceny (theft, stealing); obtaining property by fraud of various sorts, including false pretenses, confidence games, forgery, and unauthorized use of credit cards; burglary, which does not necessarily involve theft; and arson, which not only deprives the owner of property but also endangers lives. We shall defer until Chapter 12 discussion of the crimes by which criminals deprive people of their property through organizational manipulations—individual white-collar crimes, corporate crimes, and activities related to organized crime.

LARCENY

Larceny (theft, stealing) is the prototype of all property offenses. It is also the most prevalent crime in our society; it includes such contemporary forms as purse-snatching, pickpocketing, shoplifting, art theft, and vehicle theft. In the thirteenth century, when Henry de Bracton set out to collect from all parts of England what was common in law—and thus common law—he learned to his surprise that there was no agreement on a concept of larceny. He found a confusing variety of ancient Germanic laws. So he did what he always did in such circumstances: he remembered what he had learned about Roman law from Professor Azo in Bologna, and simply inserted it into his new text of English law. Thus our common law definition of larceny is virtually identical with the concept in Roman law.[1]

The Elements of Larceny

Here are the elements of **larceny** (or theft, or stealing):

A trespassory

Taking and

Carrying away of

Personal property

Belonging to another

With the intent to deprive the owner
   of the property permanently

Each of these elements has a long history that gives it its meaning. The first element is perhaps the easiest. There must be a trespass. "Trespass," a Norman-French term, has a variety of meanings. In the law of larceny, however, it simply means any absence of authority or permission for the taking. Second, the property must be taken: the perpetrator must exert authority over the property, as by putting a hand on a piece of merchandise or getting into the driver's seat of the targeted car.

Third, the property must be carried away. The slightest removal suffices to fulfill this element: moving merchandise from a counter, however slightly; loosening the brakes of a car so that it starts rolling, even an inch. Fourth, the property in question, at common law, has to be personal property. (Real estate is not subject to larceny.) Fifth, the property has to belong to another, in the sense that the person has the right to possess that property. Sixth, the taker must intend to deprive the rightful owner permanently of the property. This element is present when the taker (thief) intends to deprive the rightful owner of the property forever. In many states, however, the law no longer requires proof that the thief intended to deprive the owner "permanently" of the property.

The Extent of Larceny

Larceny, except for the most petty varieties, was a capital offense in medieval England.[2] Courts interpreted all its elements quite strictly—that is, in favor of defendants—so as to limit the use of capital punishment. Only once did the courts expand the reach of larceny, when they ruled that a transporter who opens a box entrusted to him and takes out some items has committed larceny by "breaking bulk." For the other forms of deceptive acquisition of property, such as embezzlement and obtaining property by false pretenses, Parliament had to enact separate legislation.

In the United States the rate of larceny is extraordinarily high. Figure 11.1 shows the percentage change over a recent 5-year period. The UCR reported 7.9 million thefts in 1992, or a rate of 3103 for each 100,000 of the population. The NCVS figure, 20 million, is more than double the

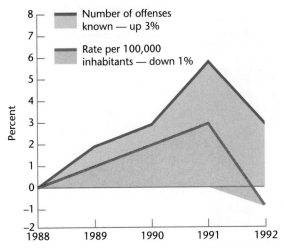

FIGURE 11.1 Percentage increase in larcenies and in rate per 100,000, 1988–1992

Source: Uniform Crime Reports, 1993.

UCR number, and both figures do not include automobile thefts.[3] The vast majority of thefts are, and always have been, committed furtively *(secreting)* and without personal contact with the victims. Thefts involving personal contact—pocket-picking, purse-snatching, and other varieties of larceny—lag behind. Figure 11.2 shows the distribution of all larcenies known to the police in 1992. The estimated dollar value of stolen goods to victims nationally was $3.8 billion.[4]

Who Are the Thieves?

Nobody knows exactly how many of the total number of thefts are committed by amateurs who lead rather conventional lives and how many are the work of professionals. According to some criminologists, the two types differ considerably.[5]

The Amateur Thief

Amateur thieves are occasional offenders who tend to be opportunists. They take advantage of a chance to steal when little risk is involved. Typically their acts are carried out with little skill, are unplanned, and result from some pressing situation, such as the need to pay the rent or a gambling debt.[6] In other words, amateurs resolve

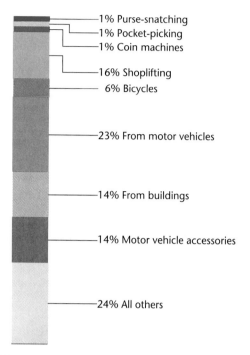

1% Purse-snatching
1% Pocket-picking
1% Coin machines
16% Shoplifting
6% Bicycles
23% From motor vehicles
14% From buildings
14% Motor vehicle accessories
24% All others

FIGURE 11.2 Distribution of larcenies known to police, 1992

Source: Uniform Crime Reports, 1993.

some immediate crisis by stealing. Most occasional offenders commit few crimes; some commit only one crime. Many are juveniles who do not go on to commit crimes in adulthood.

Amateur thieves do not think of themselves as professional criminals, nor are they recognized as such by those who do think of themselves as professionals. The lives of amateur thieves are quite conventional: amateurs work, go to school, have conventional friends, and find little support or approval for their criminal behavior.

The Professional Thief

Professional thieves make a career of stealing. They take pride in their profession. They are imaginative and creative in their work and accept its risks. The most common crimes committed by professional thieves are pickpocketing, shoplifting, forgery, confidence swindling, and burglary. Professional thieves also are involved in art theft, auto vehicle theft, and fraud or theft by use of stolen or forged credit cards, among other crimes.

Thomas Bartholomew Moran, a professional thief who died in a Miami rescue mission in 1971, has been considered the best of American pickpockets. His career began in 1906, when, as a teenager, he started to pick women's purses. Under the careful guidance of Mary Kelly, a well-known pickpocket, he soon sharpened his skills until he could take wallets from pants, jeweled pins from clothing, and watches from vests without alerting the victims. He devoted his life to shoplifting, forgery, and other forms of theft. In 1912 he boarded the *Titanic,* with the intention of profiting handsomely from proximity to

the more than 300 first-class passengers whose collective wealth exceeded $250 million. His immediate ambitions were dimmed, however, when the *Titanic* brushed an iceberg in the North Atlantic [and sank] only two hours and forty minutes later. But Moran was among the 705 passengers who managed to find space in one of the ship's twenty lifeboats, and his career in crime continued to flourish for the better part of the 59 remaining years of his life.[7]

The most influential study of professional thieves was conducted by Edwin Sutherland in 1937. Sutherland found that professional thieves share five characteristics:

1. They have well-developed technical skills for their particular mode of operation.
2. They enjoy status, accorded to them by their own subculture and by law enforcement.
3. They are bound by consensus, a sharing of values with their own peers.
4. Not only do they learn from each other, but they also protect each other.
5. They are organized, however loosely.[8]

Subsequent studies have tended to confirm Sutherland's findings.

Shoplifting

Shoplifting, the stealing of goods from retail merchants, is a very common crime; it constitutes about 16 percent of all larcenies. A recent survey in Spokane, Washington, revealed that every twelfth shopper is a shoplifter, and that men and women are equally likely to be offenders.[9] Perhaps shoplifting is so frequent because it is a low-risk offense, with a detection rate of perhaps less than 1 percent.[10] Shoppers are extremely reluctant to report shoplifters to the store management.[11] Interviews with 740 shoplifters in 50 Minneapolis stores revealed that almost half of those who expressed motivation for stealing said that they stole the merchandise because they liked it and did not have enough money to pay for it.[12]

Mary Owen Cameron found that professional shoplifters largely conform to Sutherland's five characteristics but that amateurs do not. She estimates that of all shoplifters, only 10 percent are professionals—people who derive most of their income from the sale of stolen goods.[13] A broad range of motivations may lead to shoplifting. Among amateurs, need and greed as well as opportunity may precipitate the event.[14] Some researchers point to depression and other emotional disturbances and to the use of various prescription drugs.[15]

To most people, shoplifting is a rather insignificant offense. After all, how much can be stolen? On an individual basis, usually not very much: each shoplifter in a store takes only one item, with an average value of $11.19. All those thefts in all those stores, however, may add up to billions a year.[16] As shoplifters decrease store profits, the price of goods goes up; stepped-up security adds more to costs. Stores typically hire more and more security personnel, although it has been demonstrated that physical or electronic methods of securing merchandise are more cost-effective than the deployment of guards.[17] It is only the amateur shoplifter who is deterred by the presence of guards or store personnel, not the professional.[18]

Art Theft

At the high end of the larceny scale we find art theft. The public knows and seems to care little about art theft, yet it is as old as art itself. Looters have stolen priceless treasures from Egyptian tombs ever since they were built. As prices for antiques and for modern art soar, the demand for stolen art soars. Mexico and other countries with a precious cultural heritage are in danger of losing their treasures to gangs of thieves who destroy what they cannot take with them from historic and archeological sites.

Edward Munch's *The Scream,* stolen from the Oslo Museum in February 1994 (but recovered later).

The International Foundation for Art Research in New York began reporting art thefts in 1976. In 1979 it had a record of 1300 stolen works. By May 1989 the number of cases on file stood at 30,000, most of them thefts of priceless and irreplaceable works by great masters. One of the most grandiose art thefts occurred on May 21, 1986, when a gang of Irish thieves invaded an estate in Ireland with commando precision and made off with 11 paintings, among them a Goya, two Rubenses, a Gainsborough, and a Vermeer.

Italy has produced some of the greatest art of Western culture. It therefore has offered the greatest opportunity for art thieves. The Italian government established an art theft office within the Carabinieri (the national police force) to deal with the problem. Every day this office receives reports on 20 to 30 art thefts, most committed by professionals. Most works stolen by professionals are not recovered. Many wind up in private collections. Works stolen for ransom are recovered more frequently, and the thieves are likely to be arrested.

Nobody knows the overall cost of art theft. Some paintings are worth $50, others $5000, others $50 million. Tens of thousands of paintings and other art objects are missing.[19]

People who commit larceny aim for places and objects that seem to offer the highest and most secure rewards. Our open, mercantile society affords an abundance of opportunities. While shoplifters need little expertise and a low level of professional connection, art thieves must have sophisticated knowledge of art and its value and good connections in the art world if they are to dispose of the items they steal. Other types of larceny, such as theft of automobiles and boats, require a moderate degree of skill—but more and more members of the general public are acquiring such skills.

Motor Vehicle Theft

Over 1.6 million motor vehicles were stolen in the United States in 1992, according to the UCR, for a total loss of over $7.6 billion. Between 1973 and 1985, the overall loss from motor vehicle theft was $52 billion to owners, before insurance compensation and recovery of vehicles. After insurance and recovery, the loss was $16.1 billion, but even the difference ($35.9 billion) ultimately is paid by the public, largely in high insurance rates.

Motor vehicle thefts have increased steadily from 440.1 per 100,000 population in 1973 to 631 in 1992.[20] In 1992, 80 percent of the vehicles stolen were passenger cars. The clearance rate (by arrest), as distinguished from the recovery rate of vehicles, is low—about 14 percent. Many cars are stolen during July and August, when schools are not in session. Forty-four percent of car thieves are youngsters under 18. Most of their acts amount to *joyriding*, a type of larceny that lacks the element of "intent to deprive the owner of the property permanently." The thieves simply take the vehicle for momentary pleasure or transportation.

More recently young car thieves have used stolen vehicles for racing, a show of status among peers, or the "kick" of destroying them. At the other end of the spectrum are older, professional auto thieves who steal designated cars on consignment for resale in an altered condition (with identifying numbers changed) or for disposition in "chop shops," which strip the cars for the resale value of their parts.[21]

Manufacturers of automobiles have tried to make cars more theftproof. The invention of the ignition key made it harder to steal cars. In recent years, steering-shaft locks, better door locks, and alarm systems have increased the security of protected cars. Such efforts (as we saw in Chapter 9) are examples of target hardening—that is, designing the target (the car) in such a way that it is harder to steal. Other means of providing for greater car protection include safer parking facilities. Ronald Clarke has demonstrated that parking lots with attendants experience far fewer motor vehicle thefts than unattended lots.[22]

Vehicle theft protection can also come as an unforeseen by-product of a totally unrelated development. When German legislation in 1980 mandated that motorcyclists wear crash helmets, motorcycle thefts dropped 60 percent. Perhaps most motorcycle thefts had been spur-of-the-moment affairs. Obviously, spur-of-the-moment thieves do not carry crash helmets on the off chance that they may see an unattended motorcycle and feel like taking it. Surprisingly, researchers noted no displacement effect: frustrated motorcycle thieves did not switch to stealing bikes or cars.[23]

Boat Theft

It is not our purpose to classify all larceny by the type of property stolen. We have singled out automobile theft and art theft to demonstrate the socioeconomic significance of these types of larceny, their dependence on the economic situation, and the challenge of changing the situational conditions that encourage people to commit them. Another type of larceny, the theft of working and pleasure boats, of little fishing skiffs and rowboats, is similarly tied to socioeconomic conditions.

No statistics were kept on boat theft in the United States before 1970. Obviously boat thefts have occurred ever since there have been boats, but such thefts attained high proportions only in the 1970s and 1980s. The FBI's National Crime Information Center started a stolen-boat file in 1969. During the first few years this service was little known, and the number of boats listed as stolen was initially small. But by the mid-1970s, law enforcement agencies all over the country had become familiar with this service and had

AT ISSUE
"Follow This Car! I'm Being Stolen!"

Over one and a half million vehicles are stolen each year in the United States, and untold numbers of car radios, tape decks, CD players, and now even car computers are removed from autos. Car owners who want to protect their vehicles can spend $40 for a steering-wheel lock or several thousand dollars for a highly sophisticated antitheft system. Fears about auto theft and carjacking have driven annual sales in the auto security business to $473 million.(1)

While most antitheft devices are sold to customers for cars they already own, nearly 8 percent of 1992 cars had alarms installed before they were shipped to dealers. Strategies available for deterring car thieves include chip-encoded ignition keys, alarm systems, steering-column locks, owner-operated ignition-kill and fuel-cutoff switches, pagers that alert owners when their cars are tampered with, and remote-control headlights and interior lights to illuminate the carjacker or thief as he or she makes a getaway.(1)

Lo-Jack
One of the most successful of the high-tech options for car protection may be electronic tracking systems. One such system is "Lo-Jack." A small electronic transmitter, installed in the car, is activated by police transmitters once theft of the car is reported, and a "homing signal" allows tracking computers in police cruisers to find the stolen car. A direction finder and a signal strength meter let the police know how close they are to the stolen car, thereby facilitating the search.(2)

The vice president of Lo-jack claims that the speediest recovery of a protected car was 3 minutes; the benefit of quick recovery is that thieves do not have time to damage the car and remove valuable components. Lo-Jack began operating in New England in 1986, and car theft in Boston has declined 35 percent since then. The system now is in use in 200,000 cars in southern Florida, New Jersey, Michigan, most of Illinois, Los Angeles County, and northern Virginia. Nearly 5000 stolen cars have been recovered. Car owners pay $595 for the installation of the transmitter.(2)

Anticarjacking Devices
Concern that the increased sophistication of antitheft devices has increased the popularity of carjacking has led to development of anticarjacking systems. One of the "lowest-tech" approaches—but not necessarily the least effective—is the use of an inflatable dummy as a passenger in a single-occupant car. High-tech options include a setup that makes the car "die" if it is driven by someone unfamiliar with the system and remote-control alarm systems that draw attention to the escaping carjacker.

Do all the new systems and alarms significantly reduce car theft and carjacking? Probably not in cases involving professional thieves. "If he has to have that car," says an auto theft expert at an insurance company, "he'll find a way."(1) But effective deterrence may not show up in car theft statistical summaries. "The fundamental purpose of a car alarm—a vehicle security device—isn't that it prevents the car from being stolen," notes an industry official. "It's that it convinces the car thief to go steal somebody else's car."(1)

Sources
1. Tom Incantalupo, "Car Buyers Adding Some Heavy Artillery as Car Thieves Get More Aggressive," *Newsday,* Sept. 26, 1993, p. 91.
2. Eric Peters, "Anti-Car-Theft System Lo-Jack Starts in Va.; D.C., Md. Next," *Washington Times,* Aug. 13, 1993, p. G2.

Questions for Discussion
1. One criticism of Lo-Jack and similar systems is that police will focus on recovery of Lo-Jack-equipped cars and neglect other thefts, thus discriminating against those who can't afford to have the transmitter installed. Do you think this is a valid concern?
2. Should auto manufacturers be required by state or federal law to install alarm or security systems in new cars?

The Club is a popular and well-publicized device for protecting an automobile from theft.

begun reporting the number of stolen boats in their jurisdictions. Between 1975 and 1990 the number of boats stolen and not recovered more than doubled, from 11,000 to 26,000, and that number did not include boats eliminated from the file after a given expiration period (of from 1 to 5 years).

Most boat thefts, both in the water and on land, are linked to the vast increase in the number of boats in the United States. Increased boat ownership among all population groups goes hand in hand with a proliferation of skills in handling boats and outboard motors. The number of automobile thefts rose during the days when automobile ownership and driving skills increased rapidly. Now we are witnessing the same phenomenon with boats. Some of the same crime-specific approaches developed to render cars more theftproof are currently being tried to protect boats and boating equipment—registration, secret and indelible identification numbers, locking devices, alarm systems, marina guards, protection campaigns for boat owners. Already we have some indication that the choices for boat thieves are becoming more limited and that the thieves are choosing their targets with increasing care.

With the exception of some brazen pickpockets, people who commit larcenies tend to avoid personal contact with their victims. Other criminals seek such contact in order to deprive victims of their property by deception.

FRAUD

Fraud is the acquisition of the property of another person through cheating or deception. In England such crimes owed their existence to the interaction of five circumstances: the advancement of trade and commerce, the inventiveness of swindlers in exploiting these economic advances, the demand of merchants for better protection, the unwillingness of the royal courts to expand the old concept of larceny, and the willingness of Parliament to designate new crimes in order to protect mercantile interests. In brief, medieval England developed a market economy that required the transport of goods by

wagon trains across the country, from producer or importer to consumer. Later on, when the Crown sought to encourage settlement of colonies overseas, stock companies were created to raise money for such ventures. People with money to invest acquired part ownership in these companies in the expectation of profit.

Just as some dishonest transporters withheld some of the property entrusted to them for transport, some dishonest investment clerks used funds entrusted to them for their own purposes. Merchants suffered greatly from such losses, yet the royal courts refused to extend the definition of larceny to cover this new means of depriving owners of their property. But merchants demanded protection, and from time to time, as need arose, Parliament designated new, noncapital offenses so that the swindlers could be punished.

Obtaining Property by False Pretenses

The essence of the crime of **obtaining property by false pretenses** is that the victim is made to part with property voluntarily, as a result of the perpetrator's untrue statements regarding a supposed fact. Say the doorbell rings. A gentleman greets you politely and identifies himself as a representative of a charitable organization, collecting money for disaster victims. On a typed list are the names of all the households in your building, with a dollar amount next to each name. Each household has supposedly contributed an average of $20. Not wanting to be considered cheap, you hand the gentleman a $20 bill. He promptly writes "$20" next to your name and thanks you.

Of course, the gentleman does not represent the charitable organization, there may not even be such a charity, there may not have been a disaster, and you may have been the first victim on his list. The man has obtained property from you by false pretenses. He has not committed a common law larceny because he did not engage in any "trespassory taking" of property.

Cheating was made a crime relatively late in history (in 1757 in England). Until that time the attitude was that people should look out for their own interests. Today obtaining property by false pretenses is a crime in all 50 states, and some states have included it in their general larceny statutes.

Confidence Games and Frauds

In an attempt to protect people from their own greed, a few fraud statutes have included a statutory offense called **confidence game.** In an effort to cover the enormous variety of confidence swindles, legislators have worded the statutory definitions somewhat vaguely. The essence of the offense is that the offender gains the confidence of the victim, induces in the victim the expectation of a future gain, and—by abusing the trust thus created—makes the victim part with some property. In a sense, confidence games are an aggravated form of obtaining property by false pretenses.

To illustrate: A woman (A) sees a shiny object lying on the sidewalk. As she stoops to pick it up, a man (B) grabs it. A dispute ensues over who should have the "lost diamond ring." A third person (C) comes by and offers to mediate. He happens to be a jeweler, he says. C takes a jeweler's loupe out of his pocket, examines the diamond ring, and pronounces it worth $500. At this point, B generously offers his share in the ring to A for a mere $100. A pays—and gets what turns out to be a worthless object. By the time she discovers this fact, B and C are long gone.

Frauds of this sort have been with us for centuries. But frauds change with commercial developments. Some of the more prevalent fraud schemes of today would have been unimaginable a few decades ago, simply because the commercial opportunities for their occurrence had not yet been invented.

Check Forgery

Those motivated to deprive others of their property have always exploited new opportunities to do so. The invention of "instant cash," or credit, by means of a check issued by a creditable, trustworthy person provided just such new opportunities. Ever since checks were invented, they have been abused. All jurisdictions make it a criminal offense to use a counterfeit or stolen check or to pass a check on a nonexisting account, or even on one with insufficient funds, with intent to defraud. The intent may be demonstrated by the defendant's inability or unwillingness to reimburse the payee within a specified time period.

Another fraud, called **check forging,** consists of altering a check with intent to defraud. The criminologist Edwin Lemert found that most check forgers—or "hot-check artists," as they are frequently called—are amateurs who act in times of financial need or stress, do not consider themselves criminals, and often believe that nobody really gets hurt.[24]

Credit Card Crimes

Just as the introduction of checks for payment for goods and services opened up opportunities for thieves to gain illegitimate financial advantage, so did the introduction of "plastic money." There were 7 billion credit card transactions worldwide in 1991; of these, 3 billion took place in the United States. Visa and MasterCard reported losses from credit card fraud of half a billion dollars in the United States in 1991. This type of crime increases as the volume of cards in circulation goes up. Losses from credit card crime are expected to surpass all other retailer-reported losses, such as those from bad checks, counterfeit currency, and shoplifting.

Credit card fraud during the 1980s was associated primarily with counterfeiting and lost or stolen cards. Recently, the major problem involves cards stolen from the mails.[25] Traffickers in stolen cards sell them for cash, with the amount based on the credit limit of the account—a $2000 credit line might bring $250.[26]

The economic rewards of credit card fraud are quick and relatively easy. The risks are low. Usually merchants do not ask for personal identification; cards are issued in banks that are often in other states or countries; and authorization procedures are weak. Originally the users of stolen credit cards had the inconvenience of selling the merchandise they obtained with the cards. But when banks introduced the practice of cashing the checks of strangers as long as the transactions were guaranteed by a credit card, perpetrators gained direct access to cash and no longer had to resort to dealers in stolen goods.[27]

The banking industry has studied credit card schemes and has improved the electronic system with target-hardening responses. In 1971 Congress enacted legislation that limited the financial liability of owners of stolen credit cards to $50. Many states have enacted legislation making it a distinct offense to obtain property or services by means of a stolen or forged credit card, while others include this type of fraud under their larceny statutes.

Insurance Fraud

Insurance fraud is a major problem in the United States. Auto insurance, in particular, has been the target of many dishonest schemes. About $60 billion is paid in auto insurance claims annually. It is estimated that 10 percent of these claims are fraudulent.[28] The National Automobile Theft Bureau houses manufacturers' records on 188 million vehicles (about 95 percent of U.S. cars); its theft and loss data indicate that 15 percent of all reported thefts are fraudulent.[29] Auto insurance schemes include:

- *Staged claims:* Parts of a car are removed, reported stolen, and later replaced by the owner.
- *Owner dumping:* The car is reported stolen; it is stripped by the owner, and the parts are sold.
- *Abandoned vehicles:* The car is left in a vulnerable spot for theft; then it is reported stolen.[30]
- *Staged accidents:* No collision occurs, but an "accident scene" is prepared with glass, blood, and so forth.
- *Intended accidents:* All parties to the "accident" are part of the scheme.
- *Caused accidents:* The perpetrator deliberately causes an innocent victim in a targeted car to crash into his or her car (often in the presence of "friendly" witnesses).[31]

There are many types of insurance fraud besides that involving automobiles. One rapidly growing type involves filing fraudulent health insurance claims. Recently the Fraud Division of the New Jersey Department of Insurance staged a sting operation to catch "ghost riders," a term used to describe those who file insurance claims for injuries sustained in rides on public trans-portation they never took (see Figure 11.3). At some of the staged bus accidents, people falsely claiming to have been riding the bus outnumbered the undercover investigators who actually were aboard. In other cases, healthy investigators were enticed to see doctors who then treated them and billed the insurance company for the unnecessary treatments, plus others that were never provided.

Credit card crimes and insurance schemes are comparatively recent types of fraud, but they are not the last opportunities for swindlers to deprive others of their property. Computer crime, for example, is a growing concern, and technological advances continue to offer new possibilities for theft. Opportunities will always challenge the imagination of entrepreneurs—illegitimate as well as legitimate. In regard to the illegitimate entrepreneurs, the problem invariably is whether they are in violation of existing criminal laws or whether new legislation will have to be drawn up to cover their schemes.

BURGLARY

A "burg," in Anglo-Saxon terminology, was a secure place for the protection of oneself, one's family, and one's property. If the burg protects a person from larceny and assault, what protects the burg? The burghers, perhaps. But there had to be a law behind the burghers. And that was the law of burglary, which made it a crime to break and enter the dwelling of another person at night with the intention of committing a crime therein. (Of course it had to be at night, for during the day the inhabitants could defend themselves, or so it was thought.) The common law defined **burglary** as:

The breaking
And entering
Of the dwelling house
Of another person
At night
With the intention to commit a felony or larceny inside

By "breaking," the law meant any trespass (unauthorized entry), but usually one accompa-

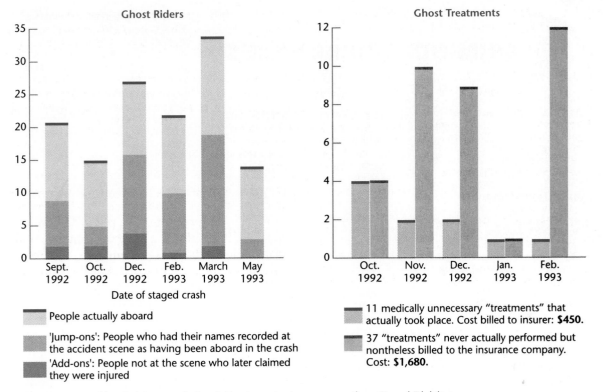

FIGURE 11.3 Ghost riders and ghost treatments: insurance sting, Fraud Division, New Jersey Department of Insurance

Source: Peter Kerr, "'Ghost Riders' Are Target of an Insurance Sting," *New York Times,* Aug. 18, 1993, pp. A1, D2.

nied by a forceful act, such as cracking the lock, breaking a windowpane, or scaling the roof and entering through the chimney. The "entering" was complete as soon as the perpetrator extended any part of his or her body into the house in pursuit of the objective of committing a crime in the house. The house had to be a "dwelling," but that definition was extended to cover the "curtilage," the attached servants' quarters, carriage houses, and barns. The dwelling also had to be that of "another." And, as we mentioned, the event had to occur at night, between sundown and sunup.

The most troublesome element has always been the "intention to commit a felony or larceny" (even a petty or misdemeanor larceny) inside the premises. How can we know what a burglar intends to do? The best evidence of intent is what the burglar actually does inside the premises: steal jewelry? rape someone? set the house afire? Any crime the burglar commits

inside is considered evidence of criminal intention at the moment the burglar broke and entered the dwelling.[32]

Today burglary is no longer limited to night attacks, although by statute the crime may be usually considered more serious if it is committed at night. Statutes have also added buildings other than dwellings to the definition. The UCR define burglary simply as the unlawful entry into a structure (criminal trespass) to commit a felony or theft. The use of force to gain entry is not a required element of burglary under the UCR.

Burglary rates have declined 13 percent since 1983. Even so, in 1992, almost 3 million burglaries were reported to the police, with an overall loss of $3.8 billion. These crimes account for nearly a quarter of all Index offenses. Most burglaries (87 percent) are not cleared by arrests.[33]

Criminologists ask questions about the characteristics of offenders who commit burglaries and of the places that are burglarized. Neal

CRIMINOLOGICAL FOCUS
High-Tech Crime

HARTFORD, Conn., May 12, 1993—This is a tale of audacity, high-tech thievery and, to no small degree, loss of innocence. For it seems that even the lowly automated teller machine, so common as to be almost invisible in malls and marketplaces everywhere, is not always to be trusted.

For two weeks, an ATM machine—ordinary-looking in just about every way, but completely bogus—operated in a shopping mall near here, giving nothing but apologetic receipts that said no transactions were possible. Meanwhile, police investigators and bank officials say, the machine was recording the card numbers and the personal identification numbers that hundreds of customers entered in their vain attempts to make the machine dispense cash.

Starting late last Friday in Manhattan, while the machine was still running at the Buckland Hills Mall in Manchester, the first withdrawals began. Using counterfeit bank cards encoded with the numbers stolen from Connecticut customers, the thieves strolled through midtown Manhattan, tapping into the 24-hour automated teller network, and netting, by today, at least $50,000.(1)

As our lives have become increasingly dependent on sophisticated electronic equipment, criminals have learned to use such equipment to their advantage. In 1992 a nationwide network of computer hackers was cracked—but not before they had broken into the electronic files of a credit-rating company, created credit card accounts for themselves, and used other people's card numbers to make millions of dollars worth of purchases. Credit card fraud reportedly cost MasterCard International $381 million in 1991, and 1989 losses for Visa International were $259 million.(2) Estimates of total annual losses attributed to high-tech criminals in the United States have reached $3 to $5 billion.(3)

Defining Computer Crime

Computer crime is defined as "any illegal act for which knowledge of computer technology is used to commit the offense," and there are several different categories.(3) Internal computer crimes are committed when programs are altered to perform unauthorized functions, such as the deletion of records from the files of an insurance company. Telecommunications crimes include "phone phreaking" (making long distance calls without an account), illegal bulletin boards, hacking, and misuse of telephone systems. Embezzlement and fraud can be carried out with the use of computers, and criminals also are using computers to support their enterprises, entering data on drug distribution, "client transactions," the daily availability of prostitutes, and other useful information.

Fighting High-Tech Crime

Fighting high-tech crime is difficult. Many victims are reluctant to report the crime, not wanting customers to know that computer security systems have been broken into. Even when the crimes are reported and charges pressed, investigations may take anywhere from 4 months to a year or longer, and few people in the criminal justice system are trained to carry them out.(3) The feelings of investigators dealing with the phony ATM machine in the Buckland Hills Mall probably are typical. Shortly after the scam was discovered, one officer commented: "We're not hot on the heels of anything at this point. This is a really complicated thing. Where it's going to take us, I don't know."(1)

Sources

1. Kirk Johnson, "One Less Thing to Believe In: High-Tech Fraud at an ATM," *New York Times,* May 13, 1993, p. 1.
2. "A Nationwide Computer-Fraud Ring Is Broken Up," *New York Times,* Apr. 19, 1992, p. 25.
3. Catherine H. Conly and J. Thomas McEwen, "Computer Crime," *NIJ Reports,* January–February 1990, pp. 2–7.

Questions for Discussion

1. Some high-tech criminals obtain the information they need to commit credit card fraud in a very low-tech way: they call people and ask for their personal identification numbers. What steps might be taken to prevent such tactics?
2. Do high-tech crimes represent a whole new category of crime or just a new way of committing crimes already defined by society?

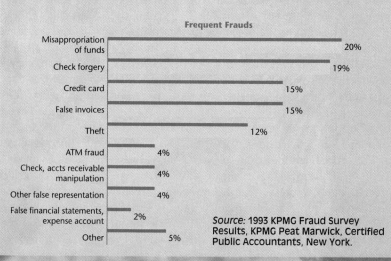

Frequent Frauds

Category	Percentage
Misappropriation of funds	20%
Check forgery	19%
Credit card	15%
False invoices	15%
Theft	12%
ATM fraud	4%
Check, accts receivable manipulation	4%
Other false representation	4%
False financial statements, expense account	2%
Other	5%

Source: 1993 KPMG Fraud Survey Results, KPMG Peat Marwick, Certified Public Accountants, New York.

Shover described the "good burglar" as one having competence, personal integrity, a specialty in burglary, financial success, and an ability to avoid prison.[34] Another study demonstrated that burglars are versatile, committing a wide range of offenses, but that they do specialize in burglary for short periods of time. Compared with male burglars, female burglars begin offending at a later age, more often commit burglaries with others, and have fewer contacts with the criminal justice system.[35]

Recent research on burglary asks questions not only about who is likely to commit a burglary or what distinguishes one burglar from another. Criminologists are asking:

What is the process that leads to the burglary of a particular house in a specific neighborhood?

How does a burglar discriminate between individual areas and targets when there are so many alternatives?

How can we make the process of burglary more difficult for any burglar?

In short, criminologists are increasingly interested in the factors that go into a decision to burglarize: the location or setting of a building, the presence of guards or dogs, the type of burglar alarms and external lighting, and so forth.[36] Does a car in the driveway or a radio playing music in

Householder in Flint, Michigan, hardens a potential burglary target by locking her iron gates.

a house have a significant impact on the choice of home to burglarize? Such questions are being asked and studied today.

The criminologist–geographer George Rengert has conducted extensive interviews with burglars in an effort to understand their techniques. He found significant differences with respect to several factors:

■ *The amount of planning* that precedes a burglary: Professional burglars plan more than do amateur criminals.

■ The extent to which a burglar engages in *systematic selection of a home:* Some burglars examine the obvious clues, such as presence of a burglar alarm, a watchdog, mail piled up in a mailbox, newspapers on a doorstep. More experienced burglars look for subtle clues, for example, closed windows coupled with air conditioners that are turned off.

■ The extent to which a burglar pays *attention to situational cues:* Some burglars routinely choose a corner property because it offers more avenues of escape, has fewer adjoining properties, and offers better visibility.[37]

Rengert and his colleagues have also examined the use of time and place in burglaries. Time is a critical factor to burglars, for three reasons:

■ They must minimize the time spent in targeted places so as not to reveal their intention to burglarize.

■ Opportunities for burglary occur only when a dwelling is unguarded.

■ Burglars have "working hours"; that is, they have time available only during a limited number of hours (if they have a legitimate job, for example).

Place is another significant factor. Burglars commit their offenses in certain areas for important reasons: familiarity with the area, fear of recognition, concern over "standing out" as someone who does not belong, or the perception (following some successful burglaries) that a particular area is no longer cost-beneficial.

Researchers have also compared burglary target choices of experienced burglars (ages 18 to 33) with those of a control group of students and householders. As one might expect, the burglars' responses were far more alike in their assessment of the vulnerability of a house (for example, a corner location, lack of security devices).[38] Similarly, young English burglars (ages 15 to 17) largely agreed on their target selections (for example, presence of bushes or other cover, absence of the family car, no dog, no alarm).[39] Perceived risks and anticipated penalties are calculated.[40]

Burglaries tend to be concentrated in certain "hot spots." In a study of 323,979 calls to the Minneapolis police from December 1985 to December 1986, Lawrence Sherman, Patrick Garten, and Michael Buerger found that these calls came from 155,000 addresses and intersections but that the 15,901 burglary calls among them came from only 11 percent of those addresses and intersections.[41] It thus becomes possible to target the hot spots for special prevention strategies and substantially reduce opportunities for burglary.

Irvin Waller and Norman Okihiro suggest that householders can make their homes less attractive to burglars by being careful to keep doors locked, by increasing surveillance, and by ensuring that someone is in the house much of the time.[42] Burglars to not want contact with occupants; they depend on stealth for success.

"FENCING": RECEIVING STOLEN PROPERTY

We are treating burglary as a property crime. An occasional burglar enters with the intention of committing rape, arson, or some other felony inside the building. But most burglars are thieves; they are looking for cash and for other property that can be turned into cash. Burglars and thieves depend on a network of "fences" to turn stolen property into cash.

Jonathan Wild controlled the London underworld from about 1714 until his hanging in 1725. For over two and half centuries he has captured the imagination of historians, social scientists, and writers. Henry Fielding wrote *The Life of Mr. Jonathan Wild, the Great*, and Mack the Knife in John Gay's *Beggar's Opera* was modeled on Wild. Wild was known as a "thief-taker." Thief-takers made an occupation of capturing thieves and claiming the rewards offered for their arrest. By

law, thief-takers were allowed to keep the possessions of the thieves they caught, except objects that had been stolen, which were returned to their owners.

Wild added a devious twist to his trade: he bought stolen goods from thieves and sold them back to their rightful owners. The owners paid much more than the thief could get from the usual fences, so both Wild and the thief made a considerable profit. To thieves, he was a fellow thief; to honest people, he was a legitimate citizen helping to get back their property. Playing both roles well, he ran competing fencing operations out of business, employed about 7000 thieves, and became the most famous fence of all time.[43]

A **fence** is a person who buys stolen property on a regular basis, for resale. Fences, or dealers in stolen property, operate much like legitimate businesses: they buy and sell for profit. Their activity thrives on an understanding of the law governing the receiving of stolen property, on cooperation with the law when necessary, and on networking. The difference between a legitimate business and a fencing operation is that the channeling of stolen goods takes place in a clandestine environment (created by law enforcement and deviant associates) with high risks and with a need to justify one's activities in the eyes of conventional society.

Carl Klockars's *Professional Fence* and Darrell Steffensmeier's *Fence*, each focusing on the life of a particular fence, present us with fascinating accounts of this criminal business. The proprietors of such businesses deal in almost any commodity. "Oh, I done lots of business with him," said Klockars's fence, Vincent Swazzi. "One time I got teeth, maybe five thousand teeth in one action. You know, the kind they use for making false teeth—you see, you never know what a thief's gonna come up with." And many fences are quite proud of their positions in the community. Said Swazzi, "The way I look at it, this is actually my street. I mean I am the mayor. I walk down the street an' people come out the doors to say hello."[44]

Until recently it was believed that professional thieves and fences were totally interdependent and that their respective illegal activities were mutually reinforcing. Recent research, however, demonstrates a change in the market for stolen goods. D'Aunn Webster Avery, Paul F. Cromwell, and James N. Olson conducted extensive interviews with 38 active burglars, shoplifters, and their fences and concluded that it is no longer the professional fence who takes care of stolen goods but, rather, occasional receivers—otherwise honest citizens—who buy from thieves directly or at flea markets.[45] This willingness to buy merchandise that the buyers must at least suspect has been stolen may indicate that the general public is more tolerant of stealing than previous generations were.

ARSON

The crimes against property that we have discussed so far involve the illegitimate transfer of possession. The property in question is "personal property" rather than real property, or real estate. Only two types of property crime are concerned with real property. Burglary is one; the other is arson.

The common law defined **arson** as the malicious burning of or setting fire to the dwelling of another person. Modern statutes have distinguished degrees of severity of the offense and have increased its scope to include other structures and even personal property, such as automobiles. The most severe punishments are reserved for arson of dwellings, because of the likelihood that persons in the building may be injured or die.

Arson always has been viewed as a more violent crime than burglary. In comparison with burglary, however, arson is a fairly infrequent offense. A total of 102,009 arson offenses were reported in 1992. A national survey of fire departments, however, indicates that the actual number of arson incidents is likely to be far higher than the reported figure.[46]

Buildings were the most frequent targets (54 percent); 27 percent of the targets were mobile property (motor vehicles, trailers, and the like).[47] The National Fire Protection Association estimates the national property loss at close to $6 billion. In 1986, 4985 lives were lost due to arson.[48]

The seriousness of this crime is demonstrated by a series of spectacular fires set in resort hotels in such cities as San Juan, Puerto Rico (in con-

Police and fire officials outside the Happyland Social Club in the Bronx following a fire set by someone angry over a personal matter that killed 87 people.

junction with a labor dispute), and Las Vegas, Nevada. Although these fires were not set with the intent to kill any of the people in the buildings, many lives were lost. The inferno created by arsonists in the Du Pont Plaza Hotel in San Juan in 1987 killed 97 people. The arson at the Las Vegas Hilton caused no deaths but $14 million in damages, not including the loss of business.

While insurance fraudsters and organized-crime figures may be responsible for some of the more spectacular arsons, it is juveniles who account for the single most significant share. Consider the following statistics:

■ In 1992 juveniles under age 18 accounted for about 49 percent of the arson arrests nationwide.

■ Nationwide arson arrests of juveniles rose 8

percent between 1991 and 1992, while adult arrests showed a 3 percent decrease.[49]

■ One of every sixteen persons arrested for arson is under age 10, and one of every four is under age 15.

■ Juveniles were responsible for approximately 50 percent of the arson fires in Seattle.

■ Thirty-eight percent of children in Grades 1 to 8 in Rochester, New York, admitted playing with fire.[50]

Why do children set fires?[51] Recent research suggests that the motive may be psychological pain, anger, revenge, need for attention, malicious mischief, or excitement.[52] Juvenile firesetters have been classified in three groups: the playing-with-matches firesetter, the crying-for-help firesetter, and the severely disturbed firesetter.[53] Many juvenile firesetters are in urgent need of help. In response to their needs, juvenile arson intervention programs have been established in recent years.[54]

An interesting English study found that while arsonists were in many respects comparable to offenders classified as violent, they had a lower incidence of interpersonal aggression and rated themselves as less assertive than did violent offenders—perhaps because, as the study showed, arsonists were taken into care at an earlier age.[55] The motives of adult arsonists are somewhat different from those of juveniles. Though here, too, we find disturbed offenders (pyromaniacs) and people who set fires out of spite, we are much more likely to encounter insurance fraudsters and organized-crime figures who force compliance or impose revenge by burning establishments (the "torches").[56]

John M. Macdonald, a psychiatrist, classifies all firesetters by motive:

■ Revenge, jealousy, and hatred
■ Financial gain (mostly insurance fraud)
■ Intimidation and/or extortion (often involving organized crime)
■ Need for attention
■ Social protest
■ Arson to conceal other crimes
■ Arson to facilitate other crimes
■ Vandalism and accidental firesetting[57]

As arson continues to be a serious national problem, policy makers have been developing two distinct approaches for dealing with it. The offender-specific approach focuses on educational outreach in schools and the early identification of troubled children, for purposes of counseling and other assistance.[58] The offense-specific (geographic) approach focuses on places. It seeks to identify areas with a record of or a high potential for arson. The aim, then, is to deploy arson specialists to correct problems and to stabilize endangered buildings and neighborhoods.[59]

REARRANGING LIVES: THEORIES OF CRIME AND CRIME PREVENTION

Throughout this chapter we have looked at research about who commits property crimes. We have also used the theories of crime to identify conditions under which those persons who are prone to commit crime will in fact do so. The practical value of this theoretical approach is implicit in people's reactions to crime. Over the last two decades people have been rearranging their lives because of crime—or sometimes just the fear of crime. The new theories of crime can be used to determine the effectiveness of those "rearrangements." Here are some:

■ Airports, schools, movie houses, nightclubs, convention centers, libraries, and even department stores have installed electronic detection gates for improved security.

■ Security fences patrolled by guards have spread from businesses in high-crime areas to wealthy, private residential neighborhoods to low-income housing projects.

■ Because tough "vandal-proof" pay phones are vandalized frequently (175,000 times a year in New York City alone), phone companies all over the world are converting to call-on-a-card, coinless telephones.

■ Hackers and thieves who charge their calls to others' phones cost cellular-telephone companies an estimated $1 million a day, forcing the development of new digital technology to guard against criminal abuse.

■ The convenience of cash machines has brought with it a rash of robbers forcing cus-

Because many teenagers now have access to lethal weapons and will use them, these students must be searched with a metal detector as they enter school each day.

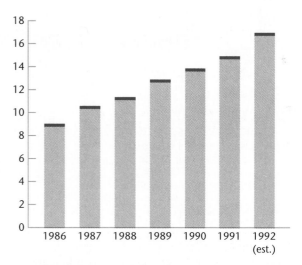

FIGURE 11.4 Residential security systems in use in the United States, 1986–1992 (in millions)

Source: New York Times, Feb. 9, 1992, pp. E1, E4.

tomers to make withdrawals or to hand over the cash just withdrawn. The New York City Council passed a measure requiring tough new security measures for the protection of cash machines and their customers.

■ Over 16 million electronic security systems protect American homes, and individual actions aimed at evading criminals also are on the increase (see Figure 11.4). People don't visit certain neighborhoods, they don't go out at night, they don't park their cars at certain locations, they don't wear jewelry in public, they don't jog where they used to, they go to self-defense training classes, and they buy and carry handguns.

■ Some public places—shops, transportation terminals—are piping in classical music to stop troublemaking youngsters from congregating. Some speakers have been stolen, but otherwise the technique has had modest crime-fighting success.

Appropriate Prevention Measures

Are all these crime-evasion techniques worth the cost involved? As the body of research by crime theorists grows, we are learning more and more about appropriate and cost-beneficial crime-prevention strategies. When is it necessary to intervene in order to minimize which criminal danger? What targets of criminals need what type of protection (target hardening)? When is the right time, if ever, to build a fence, buy a gun, install an alarm system, change an industrial product, deploy more police or private security, install a new lighting system?

Sometimes a change made by only a few people protects many, as researchers found in a study of obscene phone calls in New Jersey. Requests to trace annoyance calls decreased by 25 percent in areas where Caller-ID—a service that provides the phone number of incoming calls—was available, even though only a small number of people had actually subscribed to the service. Apparently just the possibility that they would be identified easily was enough to deter some would-be obscene-call makers. As crime theorists develop more ideas and publish more case studies about the factors that contribute to the commission of a crime, they help build a solid foundation for effective crime-prevention strategies.[60]

Comparative Crime Rates

The rates of property crime are much higher than those of the violent crime we discussed in Chap-

WINDOW TO THE WORLD
Crime on the Oceans: Whose Problem?

While no accurate estimates of worldwide losses from modern-day piracy are possible, knowledgeable experts think the total is probably near $250 million a year. The thieves make off with tons of cement, coffee, sugar, tomato paste, ladies' undergarments, steel, and whatever other cargo they think they can fence on shore. Even more common is the direct attack on the safe in the captain's cabin—pirates may be able to collect $50,000 in cash during a 15-minute job. In 1991 more than 120 pirate attacks were reported worldwide, and it is likely that only 40 percent of the total are reported to authorities.(1)

The Lack of Policing

Unhappily, the world does not yet have an international marine enforcement agency to police the oceans. There is no one to spot a vessel dumping nuclear waste into the high seas or into an exclusive economic zone. Who can intercept arms or narcotics smugglers? Even powerful nations, like the United States, have trouble policing their own zones. The problems are much worse for small nations that cannot afford to maintain marine police forces of any size.(2) A look at the Law of the Sea Treaty map indicates that most regions affected by piracy and terrorism are in areas of notoriously underpoliced territorial waters.

The Scope of Crime on the Oceans

All these problems are magnified when we realize that piracy is only one of many crimes committed on the oceans. For example:

- Frauds in the marine shipping industry have caused severe damage to international trade and threatened the collapse of entire national economies in Africa and Latin America.
- The international drug trade uses the oceans for about half its shipments from the points of origin or manufacture to the points of distribution.
- Currently about 30,000 American boats are listed in the FBI's Stolen Boat File as having been stolen and not recovered.

Sources

1. G. O. W. Mueller and Freda Adler, *Outlaws of the Ocean* (New York: Hearst Marine Books, 1985, p. 150); Alan Farnham, "Pirates," *Fortune*, July 15, 1991, pp. 113–118.
2. Roger Villar, *Piracy Today* (London: Conway Maritime Press, 1985), p. 59.

Questions for Discussion

1. What crimes against property are committed by those who engage in maritime fraud?
2. Propose a mechanism to control property crime on the high seas. Defend your proposal.

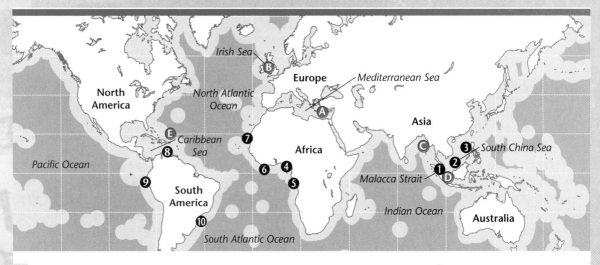

200-mile exclusive economic zones

Piracy
1. Malacca Strait
2. South China Sea
3. Philippines
4. Nigerian coast (Lagos)
5. Congo coast
6. Coasts of Liberia, Ivory Coast
7. Coast of Senegal (Dakar)
8. Coast of Venezuela
9. Coast of Ecuador
10. Coast of Brazil

Terrorism
A. Eastern Mediterranean
B. Irish Sea
C. Coastal waters of Myanmar
D. Singapore
E. Puerto Rico

ter 10. It is interesting to compare these rates for various regions of the world. If we compare the property-owning, consumer-oriented countries of the industrialized Western world with the still largely agricultural but rapidly urbanizing countries of the Third World, we note a significant discrepancy: the rate of theft per 100,000 in the developed countries was 4200, while the rate in developing countries was 600.[61]

Recall the Coca-Cola bottle that disrupted the lives of the aborigines in *The Gods Must Be Crazy*. We just may have discovered the secret of that bottle: if there is no Coke bottle, no one is going to steal it. The more property people have, especially portable property, the more opportunity other people have to make off with it. Europeans have an old saying: "Opportunity makes thieves." The foremost opportunity for theft may simply be an abundance of property.

■ REVIEW

Not all crimes against property are aimed at acquiring such property. A burglar invades a dwelling or other structure usually—but not necessarily—to commit a larceny inside. An arsonist endangers the existence of the structure and its occupants. Both amateurs and professionals commit property crimes of all sorts. Each new form of legitimate trade, such as the development of credit cards, offers criminals new opportunities to exploit the situation for gain. In this perpetual struggle between the developers of legitimate pursuits and the exploiters, scientists have begun—but just begun—to play a positive new role. By studying opportunities for crime and by analyzing the way criminals choose their targets, social scientists are helping to reduce crime by devising strategies that make crimes harder to commit.

Some property-oriented crimes, as we shall see in Chapter 12, depend not only on the cunning and daring of the perpetrator who targets a lone victim but on the normal business operations of legitimate enterprises—and of illegitimate ones as well.

■ NOTES

1. J. W. Cecil Turner, *Kenny's Outlines of Criminal Law*, 2d ed. (Cambridge, Mass.: Cambridge University Press, 1958), p. 238.
2. Jerome Hall, *Theft, Law, and Society* (Indianapolis: Bobbs-Merrill, 1935).
3. U.S. Department of Justice, Bureau of Justice Statistics, *Highlights from 20 Years of Surveying Crime Victims: The National Crime Victimization Survey, 1973–92* (Washington, D.C.: U.S. Government Printing Office, 1993), p. 13.
4. Uniform Crime Reports, 1992, p. 44.
5. See Abraham S. Blumberg, "Typologies of Criminal Behavior," in *Current Perspectives on Criminal Behavior*, 2d ed., ed. Abraham S. Blumberg (New York: Knopf, 1981).
6. See John Hepburn, "Occasional Criminals," in *Major Forms of Crime*, ed. Robert Meier (Beverly Hills, Calif.: Sage, 1984), pp. 73–94; and John Gibbs and Peggy Shelly, "Life in the Fast Lane: A Retrospective View by Commercial Thieves," *Journal of Research in Crime and Delinquency*, **19** (1982): 299–330, at p. 327.
7. James Inciardi, "Professional Thief," in Meier, *Major Forms of Crime*, p. 224. See also Harry King and William Chambliss, *Box Man—A Professional Thief's Journal* (New York: Harper & Row, 1972).
8. *The Professional Thief*, annotated and interpreted by Edwin H. Sutherland (Chicago: University of Chicago Press, 1937).
9. Jo-Ann Ray, "Every Twelfth Shopper: Who Shoplifts and Why?" *Social Casework*, **68** (1987): 234–239.
10. Abigail Buckle and David P. Farrington, "An Observational Study of Shoplifting," *British Journal of Criminology*, **24** (1984): 63–73.
11. Donald Hartmann, Donna Gelfand, Brent Page, and Patrice Walder, "Rates of Bystander Observation and Reporting of Contrived Shoplifting Incidents," *Criminology*, **10** (1972): 247–267.
12. P. James Carolin, Jr., "Survey of Shoplifters," *Security Management*, **36** (1992): 11–12.
13. Mary Owen Cameron, *The Booster and the Snitch* (New York: Free Press, 1964). See also John Rosecrance, "The Stooper: A Professional Thief in the Sutherland Manner," *Criminology*, **24** (1986): 29–40.
14. Richard Moore, "Shoplifting in Middle America: Patterns and Motivational Correlates," *International Journal of Offender Therapy and Comparative Criminology*, **28** (1984): 53–64; Hepburn, "Occasional Criminals." See also Charles A. Sennewald and John H. Christman, *Shoplifting* (Boston: Butterworth-Heinemann, 1992).
15. Trevor N. Gibbens, C. Palmer, and Joyce Prince, "Mental Health Aspects of Shoplifting," *British Medical Journal*, **3** (1971): 612–615; Richard Williams and J. Thomas Dalby, "Benzodiazepines and Shoplifting," *International Journal of Offender Therapy and Comparative Criminology*, **30** (1986): 35–39.

16. Roger Griffin, *Shoplifting in Supermarkets* (San Diego, Calif.: Commercial Service Systems, 1988).

17. Barry Poyner and Ruth Woodall, *Preventing Shoplifting: A Study in Oxford Street* (London: Police Foundation, 1987). For a general "ethnography" of English shoplifting, see Daniel J. I. Murphy, *Customers and Thieves* (Brookfield, Vt.: Gower, 1986).

18. John Carroll and Frances Weaver, "Shoplifters' Perceptions of Crime Opportunities: A Process-Tracing Study," in *The Reasoning Criminal,* ed. Derek Cornish and Ronald V. Clarke (New York: Springer-Verlag, 1986), pp. 19–38.

19. See Truc-Nhu Ho, *Art Theft in New York City: An Exploratory Study in Crime Specifity.* Ph.D. dissertation, Rutgers University, 1992; Christopher Dickey, "Missing Masterpieces," *Newsweek,* May 29, 1989, pp. 65–68; and Milton Esterow, "Confessions of an Art Cop," *Art News,* May 1988, pp. 134–137. The journal *Art and Antiques,* which reaches most dealers, publishes a " Most Wanted" column, with pictures of recently stolen art objects. See *Art and Antiques,* January 1994: 13.

20. Uniform Crime Reports, 1973, p. 50, and 1992, p. 49.

21. See Charles McCaghy, Peggy Giordano, and Trudy Knicely Henson, "Auto Theft," *Criminology,* **15** (1977): 367–385.

22. Ronald V. Clarke, "Situational Crime Prevention: Theoretical Basis and Practical Scope," in *Crime and Justice: An Annual Review of Research,* vol. 4, ed. Michael Tonry and Norval Morris (Chicago: University of Chicago Press, 1983). See also Gloria Laycock and Claire Austin, "Crime Prevention in Parking Facilities," *Security Journal,* **3** (1992): 154–160; Ronald V. Clarke and Patricia M. Harris, "Auto Theft and Its Prevention," in *Crime and Justice: A Review of Research,* vol. 16, ed. Michael Tonry (Chicago and London: University of Chicago Press, 1992), pp. 1–54.

23. Pat Mayhew, Ronald V. Clarke, and David Elliott, "Motorcycle Theft, Helmet Legislation and Displacement," *Howard Journal of Criminal Justice,* **28** (1989): 1–8.

24. Edwin Lemert, "An Isolation and Closure Theory of Naive Check Forgery," *Journal of Criminal Law, Criminology, and Police Science* **44** (1953–1954): 296–307.

25. Barry Masuda, "Card Fraud: Discover the Possibilities," *Security Management,* **36** (1992): 71–74.

26. Ibid.

27. Pierre Tremblay, "Designing Crime," *British Journal of Criminology,* **26** (1986): 234–253.

28. Leonard Sloane, "Rising Fraud Worrying Car Insurers," *New York Times,* Nov. 16, 1991, p. 48.

29. Michael Clarke, "The Control of Insurance Fraud," *British Journal of Criminology,* **30** (1990): 1–23.

30. Sloane, "Rising Fraud Worrying Car Insurers."

31. Edmund J. Pankan and Frank E. Krzeszowski, "Putting a Claim on Insurance Fraud," *Security Management* **37,** (1993): 91–94.

32. Kenneth C. Sears and Henry Weihofen, *May's Law of Crimes,* 4th ed. (Boston: Little, Brown, 1948), pp. 307–317.

33. Uniform Crime Reports, 1992, p. 39.

34. Neal Shover, "Structures and Careers in Burglary," *Journal of Criminal Law and Criminology,* **63** (1972): 540–549.

35. Scott Decker, Richard Wright, Allison Redfern, and Dietrich Smith, "A Woman's Place Is in the Home: Females and Residential Burglary," *Justice Quarterly,* **10** (1993): 143–162.

36. James Garofalo and David Clark, "Guardianship and Residential Burglary," *Justice Quarterly,* **9** (1992): 443–463; Daniel B. Kennedy, "Probability, Vulnerability, and Criticality as Architectural Security Considerations," *Security Journal,* **3** (1992): 199–209; Paul F. Cromwell, James N. Olson, and D'Aunn Webster Avery, *Breaking and Entering: An Ethnographic Analysis of Burglary* (Newbury Park, Calif.: Sage, 1991); John D. Wooldredge, Francis T. Cullen, and Edward J. Latessa, "Victimization in the Workplace: A Test of Routine Activities Theory," *Justice Quarterly,* **9** (1992): 326–335.

37. George Rengert and John Wasilchick, *Suburban Burglary: A Time and a Place for Everything* (Springfield, Ill.: Charles C. Thomas, 1985).

38. M. Taylor and C. Nee, "The Role and Cues in Simulated Residential Burglary," *British Journal of Criminology,* **28** (1988): 396–401.

39. Richard Wright and Robert H. Logie, "How Young House Burglars Choose Targets," *Howard Journal of Criminal Justice,* **27** (1988): 92–104.

40. Scott Decker, Richard Wright, and Robert Logie, "Perceptual Deterrence among Active Residential Burglars: A Research Note," *Criminology,* **31** (1993): 135–147.

41. Lawrence W. Sherman, Patrick R. Garten, and Michael E. Buerger, "Hot Spots of Predatory Crime: Routine Activities and the Criminology of Place," *Criminology,* **27** (1989): 27–55. On hot spots and routine activities, see also Dennis Roncek and Pamela A. Maier, "Bars, Blocks and Crimes Revisited: Linking the Theory of Routine Activities to the Empiricism of Hots Spots," *Criminology,* **29** (1991): 725–753.

42. Irvin Waller and Norman Okihiro, *Burglary: The Victim and the Public* (Toronto: University of Toronto Press, 1978). See also Ronald Clarke and Tim Hope, eds., *Cope with Burglary* (Boston: Kluwer-Nijhoff, 1984).

43. Darrell Steffensmeier, *The Fence: In the Shadow of Two Worlds* (Totowa, N.J.: Rowman & Littlefield, 1986), p. 7.

44. Carl Klockars, *The Professional Fence* (New York: Free Press, 1976), pp. 110, 113.

45. D'Aunn Webster Avery, Paul F. Cromwell, and James N. Olson, "Marketing Stolen Property: Burglars and Their Fences," paper presented at the 1988 Annual Meeting of the American Society of Criminology, Reno, Nev.

46. Patrick G. Jackson, "Assessing the Validity of Official Data on Arson," *Criminology,* **26** (1988): 181–195. See also Frederick Mercilliott, "The Effectiveness of Alternative Approaches to Investigating Arson: A

Study of 155 Cities," Ph.D. dissertation, City University of New York, 1988.

47. Uniform Crime Reports, 1992, p. 54.

48. Michael J. Kartes, Jr., "A Look at Fire Loss during 1986," *Fire Journal*, September–October 1987, p. 40.

49. Uniform Crime Reports, 1992, p. 56.

50. See Rebecca K. Hersch, *A Look at Juvenile Firesetter Programs*, for U.S. Department of Justice, Office of Justice Programs, Office of Juvenile Justice and Delinquency Prevention (Washington, D.C.: U.S. Government Printing Office, May 1989), p. 1.

51. Irving Kaufman and Lora W. Heims, "A Re-Evaluation of the Dynamics of Firesetting," *American Journal of Orthopsychiatry*, **31** (1961): 123–136.

52. Hersch, *A Look at Juvenile Firesetter Programs*.

53. Wayne S. Wooden and Martha Lou Berkey, *Children and Arson* (New York: Plenum, 1984), p. 3.

54. See Jessica Gaynor and Chris Hatcher, *The Psychology of Child Firesetting* (New York: Brunner/Mazel, 1987).

55. Howard F. Jackson, Susan Hope, and Clive Glass, "Why Are Arsonists Not Violent Offenders?" *International Journal of Offender Therapy and Comparative Criminology*, **31** (1987): 143–151.

56. See Wayne W. Bennett and Karen Matison Hess, *Investigating Arson* (Springfield, Ill.: Charles C. Thomas, 1984), pp. 34–38.

57. John M. Macdonald, *Bombers and Firesetters* (Springfield, Ill.: Charles C. Thomas, 1977), pp. 198–204.

58. See Federal Emergency Management Agency, U.S. Fire Administration, *Interviewing and Counselling Juvenile Firesetters* (Washington, D.C.: U.S. Government Printing Office, 1979).

59. Clifford L. Karchmer, *Preventing Arson Epidemics: The Role of Early Warning Strategies*, Aetna Arson Prevention Series (Hartford, Conn.: Aetna Life & Casualty, 1981).

60. Ronald V. Clarke, ed. *Situational Crime Prevention: Successful Case Studies* (New York: Harrow and Henton, 1992).

61. "Third United Nations Survey of Crime Trends, Operations of Criminal Justice Systems and Crime Prevention Strategies," A/CONF. 144/6, July 27, 1990.

Organizational Criminality

KEY TERMS
bankruptcy fraud
boiler rooms
churning
computer espionage
computer fraud
computer hacking
computer sabotage
consumer fraud
corporate crime
embezzlement
Federal Witness Protection Program
insider trading
Mafia
occupational crimes
Racketeer Influenced and Corrupt
  Organizations (RICO) Act
Sherman Antitrust Act
stock manipulation
theft of computer time, software, and
  hardware
white-collar crime

■ Del Webb Corp. subsidiary paid a $1 million fine Wednesday—the largest ever in Arizona for an environmental crime—for the systematic dumping of as many as 100 truckloads of batteries and other debris into Lake Powell.

In addition, ARA Leisure Services, which took over the marina boat-renting concessions from Del Webb's Marina Operation Corp. in 1988, agreed to pay a $225,000 fine.

Both companies agreed to pay a total of $100,000 to cover investigative costs, bringing the total to more than $1.3 million.

During a press conference, Arizona Attorney General Grant Woods described the case as "one of

the biggest environmental outrages in this state," "the worst form of environmental stewardship" and "an embarrassment."

Also, Woods accused National Park Service employees of "lying" in the course of a three-year investigation that found boat-related debris at five marinas on Lake Powell—one in Arizona and four in Utah. The marinas are run by concessionaires under Park Service supervision.

State investigators displayed photographs of a marina storm drain that was used to dump liquid hazardous wastes directly into the lake.

They also showed a videotape displaying all manner of debris from boats, including batteries,

steering cables, flashlights, refrigerators, coolers, chairs, propellers, anchors, toilets and barbecue grills.

"This shows a pattern of abuse and neglect of a natural Arizona jewel that went on for years," said Woods, who described the dumping from 1980 to 1990 as part of "standard operating procedure" at the marinas.[1]

* * *

General Electric has been charged with price fixing and other monopolistic practices not only for its light bulbs, but for turbines, generators, transformers, motors, relays, radio tubes, heavy metals, and lightning arresters. At least 67 suits have been brought against General Electric by the Antitrust Division of the Justice Department since 1911, and 180 antitrust suits were brought against General Electric by private companies in the early 1960's alone. General Electric's many trips to court hardly seem to have "reformed" the company: In 1962, after 50 years' experience with General Electric, even the Justice Department was moved to comment on General Electric's proclivity for frequent and persistent involvement in antitrust violations.[2]

* * *

A Mafia boss found dead last week was involved in the 1992 murder of Cosa Nostra's enemy number one, Judge Giovanni Falcone, Italian state television channels said Sunday.

The reports said Antonino Gioe, who hanged himself with his shoelaces from the bars of his cell Thursday, was at Palermo airport when Falcone arrived there and he had apparently tipped off the Mafia commando which killed the judge minutes later.

Falcone, his wife and three bodyguards died May 23, 1992, when their armor-plated cars were blown up by a huge bomb buried under the highway between Palermo and the airport.

Falcone's murder, followed by that of his colleague Paolo Borsellino two months later, proved a major turning point in Italian politics and provoked a strong state reaction. Leading members of the Mafia were arrested after years on the run.

The reports said Gioe had killed himself because he knew the Mafia had condemned him to death for making too many mistakes. He was apparently hoping his suicide would spare his family any bloody reprisals by his former associates.

According to the reports, investigators traced a call made by Gioe on his mobile phone at Palermo airport two minutes after Falcone and his wife had landed.

The call, to a member of the Madonia clan on whose "territory" the judge was killed, ended only seconds before the killers detonated the bomb. The man Gioe was calling is also under arrest but his name has not been disclosed.

Investigators still do not know who told the Mafia Falcone was making the unannounced trip from Rome to Palermo aboard a secret service plane. The inquiry has centered around a former senior member of the intelligence service and a Sicilian MP.

Gioe, a 37-year-old Mafioso from Corleone, was being kept in solitary confinement in the same wing of Rome's maximum security jail as Salvatore "Toto" Riina, the Mafia godfather arrested last January after 23 years on the run.[3]

What do the crimes of the Del Webb Corporation, General Electric, and the Cosa Nostra, or Mafia, have in common? According to the criminologist Dwight Smith, white-collar, corporate, and organized crimes all involve business enterprises.[4] An offender—whether a corporation employee, the corporation itself, or a lieutenant in a Mafia family—uses a business enterprise (perhaps an insurance company, a garbage collection company, or a prostitution ring) to profit illegally. It is the use of a legitimate or illegitimate business enterprise for illegal profit that distinguishes organizational crimes from other types of offenses. Organizational offenses are also different in another important respect. Unlike violent crimes and property offenses, which the Model Penal Code classifies quite neatly, organizational offenses are a heterogeneous mix of crimes, from homicide, fraud, and conspiracy to racketeering, gambling, and the violation of a host of federal environmental statutes.

How much white-collar crime is committed each year? What are the attributes of organized crimes? How much crime is committed by major U.S. corporations? Answers to such questions, no matter how preliminary, may provide valuable information to guide efforts to control and prevent white-collar, corporate, and organized crime.

DEFINING WHITE-COLLAR CRIME

Initial reports of a crisis in the U.S. savings and loan industry appeared on front pages of newspapers across the country in 1989. They alleged that some savings and loan officers had ruined their institutions financially for personal profit, thereby causing the greatest amount of white-collar crime ever uncovered. Bailing out the insolvent banks may cost an estimated $300 to $500 billion by the year 2021.[5]

But white-collar crime is not a new phenomenon. In ancient Greece public officials reportedly violated the law by purchasing land slated for government acquisition.[6] Much of what we today define as white-collar crime, however, is the result of laws passed within the last century. For example, the Sherman Antitrust Act, passed by Congress in 1890, authorized the criminal prosecution of corporations engaged in monopolistic practices.[7] Federal laws regulating the issuance and sale of stocks and other securities were passed in 1933 and 1934. In 1940 Edwin H. Sutherland provided criminologists with the first scholarly account of white-collar crime. He defined it as crime "committed by a person of respectability and high social status in the course of his occupation."[8]

The Del Webb Corporation and General Electric cases demonstrate that Sutherland's definition is not entirely satisfactory: white-collar crime can be committed by a corporation as well as by an individual. As Gilbert Geis has noted, Sutherland's work is limited by his own definition. He has a "striking inability to differentiate between the corporations themselves and their executive management personnel."[9] Other criminologists have suggested that the term "white-collar crime" not be used at all; we should speak instead of "corporate crime" and "occupational crime."[10] Comprehensively, however, **white-collar crime** is defined as a violation of the law committed by a person or group of persons in the course of an otherwise respected and legitimate occupation or business enterprise.[11]

Just as white-collar and corporate offenses include a heterogeneous mix of corporate and individual crimes, from fraud, deception, and corruption (as in the S&L case) to pollution of the environment, victims of white-collar crime range from the savvy investor to the unsuspecting consumer. No one person or group is immune.[12] The Vatican lost millions of dollars in a fraudulent stock scheme; fraudulent charities have swindled fortunes from unsuspecting investors; and many banks have been forced into bankruptcy by losses due to deception and fraud.[13]

Crimes Committed by Individuals

As we have noted, white-collar crime occurs during the course of a legitimate occupation or business enterprise. Over time socioeconomic developments have increasingly changed the dimensions of such crimes.[14] Once, people needed only a few business relationships to make their way through life. They dealt with an employer or with employees. They dealt on a basis of trust and confidence with the local shoemaker and grocer. They had virtually no dealings with government.

This way of life has changed significantly and very rapidly during the last few decades. People have become dependent on large bureaucratic structures; they are manipulated by agents and officials with whom they have no personal relationship. This situation creates a basis for potential abuses in four sets of relations:

■ Employees of large entities may abuse their authority for private gain by making their services to members of the public contingent on a bribe, a kickback, or some other favor. A corrupt employee of an insurance company, for example, may write a favorable claim assessment in exchange for half of the insurance payment.

■ Taking advantage of the complexity and anonymity of a large organization, such as a corporation, employees may abuse the systems available to them or the power they hold within the structure for purposes of unlawful gain, as by embezzlement.

■ Members of the public who have to deal with a large organization do not have the faith and trust they had when they dealt with individual merchants. If they see an opportunity to defraud a large organization, they may seize it in the belief that the organization can easily absorb the loss and nobody will be hurt.

■ Since the relation of buyer to seller (or of service provider to client) has become increasingly less personal in an age of medical group practice, large law firms, and drugstore chains, opportunities for **occupational crimes**—crimes committed by individuals for themselves in the course of rendering a service—have correspondingly increased.

CRIMINOLOGICAL FOCUS
Corporate Crime—Who Are the Victims?

By most estimates corporate crime costs us more in human lives and in dollars than the more highly publicized, more severely punished, and far more familiar street crime. For example, it is estimated that in the United States 100,000 to 200,000 people die each year from unquestionably job-related illnesses and injuries. That is a rate five times higher than the number of people murdered by street criminals each year.(1) If you add to this the number of people who die each year from causes related to corporate "oversight," marketing, or profiteering, the rate is far higher. "All things considered," concludes sociologist Sandra Walklate, "this evidence strongly suggests that we are at far more physical risk of being victimized as a result of the activities and inactivities of business and industry than by street crime or burglary."(2)

Victims of corporate crime rarely, it seems, make their victimization known to authorities—sometimes because they don't even realize they *are* victims.(3, p. 73) In general, corporate crime not only goes unpunished; it goes unreported and even undetected. "The majority of those suffering from corporate crime remain unaware of their victimization—either not knowing it has happened to them or viewing their 'misfortune' as an accident or 'no one's fault,'" one researcher explained.(4, p. 17) "Clearly a major problem in controlling corporate crime is raising victim and public consciousness to a level where the community desires and supports a policy of more active and effective state control and regulation.(4, p. 66)

"Raising victim and public consciousness" is a problem. When victims are the public-at-large or another corporation, they do not fit our traditional picture of a victim—they are not individuals. Even when the victim is an individual, as in a case of death caused by occupational safety violations, we may not think of him or her as a victim of *crime*. Since we do not know

whom in particular to blame (the offender is "depersonalized"), we tend not to blame anyone and to say it was an accident.

According to criminologist David Shichor, several scholars have suggested that social control of corporations will not occur until public opinion toward "big business" has been changed. A better understanding of corporate victimization could improve efforts to educate the public about corporate crime through publicity, "personalization of the harm," 'individualization of the victim," and "personalization of the offender." The goal, says Shichor, is "to demonstrate to the public and to corporate executives that many corporate actions and business practices are often more harmful than street crimes, victimize a large number of people, undermine public trust in social institutions and deviate from social and legal norms."(3, p. 82).

Sources
1. David R. Simon and D. Stanley Eitzen, *Elite Deviance* (Boston: Allyn and Bacon, 1993), p. 40.
2. Sandra Walklate, *Victimology: The Victim and the Criminal Justice Process* (London: Unwin Hyman, 1989), p. 91.
3. David Shichor, "Corporate Deviance and Corporate Victimization: A Review and Some Elaborations," *International Review of Victimology*, **1** (1989): 67–88, at pp. 73, 82.
4. S. Box, *Power, Crime and Mystification* (London: Tavistock, 1983), pp. 17, 66.

Questions for Discussion
1. Those injured by corporations may sue the corporation for damages. When an individual is pitted against a giant corporate entity, is the likelihood of a lawsuit an incentive for the corporation to change its practices?
2. Few victims report being victimized. What strategies might induce a larger number of victims of corporate crime to report their victimization to the authorities?

Woman watches as workers fence off her property from an alley where the highest concentrations of PCB ever recorded near a home in Michigan were found.

Medicare fraud, misuse of clients' funds by lawyers and brokers, substitution of inferior goods—all such offenses are occupational crimes.[15]

Types of White-Collar Crimes

White-collar crimes are as difficult to detect as they are easy to induce.[16] The detection mechanisms on which police and government traditionally rely seem singularly inadequate for this vast new body of crimes. Moreover, though people have learned through the ages to be wary of strangers on the street, they have not yet learned to protect themselves against vast enterprises. Much more scientific study has to be undertaken on the causes, extent, and characteristics of white-collar crimes before we can develop workable prevention strategies.[17]

Nine categories of white-collar offenses committed by individuals may be identified:

- Securities-related crimes
- Bankruptcy fraud
- Fraud against the government
- Consumer fraud
- Computer crimes
- Insurance fraud
- Tax fraud
- Bribery, corruption, and political fraud
- Insider-related fraud[18]

Let us briefly examine each type of crime.

Securities-Related Crimes

State and federal securities laws seek to regulate both the registration and issuance of a security and the employment practices of personnel in the securities industries. After the stock market crash on October 26, 1929, the federal government enacted a series of regulatory laws, including the Securities Act of 1933 and the Securities Exchange Act of 1934, aimed at prohibiting manipulation and deceptive practices. The 1934 act provided for the establishment of the Securities and Exchange Commission (SEC), an organization with broad regulatory and enforcement powers. The SEC is empowered to initiate civil suits and administrative actions and to refer criminal cases to the U.S. Department of Justice.

Ivan Boesky, having pleaded guilty to conspiracy to violate securities laws, was fined $100 million, barred from security trading for life, and sentenced to three years in prison.

Even so, crime in the securities field remains common. Four kinds of offenses are prevalent: churning, trading on insider information, stock manipulation, and boiler-room operations.

Churning is the practice of trading a client's shares of stock frequently in order to generate large commissions. A broker earns a commission on every trade, so whether or not the stock traded increases or decreases in value, the broker makes money. Churning is difficult to prove, because brokers typically are allowed some discretion. Therefore, unless the client has given the broker specific instructions in writing, a claim of churning often amounts to no more than the client's word against the broker's.

Insider trading is the use of material, nonpublic, financial information to obtain an unfair advantage in trading securities.[19] A person who has access to confidential corporate information may make significant profits by buying or selling stock on the strength of that information. Dennis Levine, a 34-year-old managing director of the securities firm Drexel Burnham Lambert, used insider information to purchase stock for himself and others in such corporations as International Telephone and Telegraph (ITT), Sperry Corporation, Coastal Corporation, American National Resources, and McGraw Edison. After the SEC found out, Levine implicated other Wall Street executives—including Ivan Boesky, who had made millions of dollars in illegal profits.

Stock manipulation is common in the over-the-counter market, in which some stocks are traded at very low prices, but it is by no means limited to such stocks. Brokers who have a stake in a particular security may make misleading or even false statements to clients to give the impression that the price of the stock is about to rise and thus to create an artificial demand for it.

Boiler rooms are operations run by stock manipulators who, through deception and misleading sales techniques, seduce unsuspecting and uninformed individuals into buying stocks in obscure and often poorly financed corporations. Significant federal legislation has been passed (Penny Stock Reform Act of 1990), but the manipulation continues.

Bankruptcy Fraud

The filing of a bankruptcy petition results in proceedings in which the property and financial obligations of an insolvent person or corporation are disposed of. Bankruptcy proceedings are governed by laws enacted to protect insolvent debtors. Unscrupulous persons have devised numerous means to commit **bankruptcy fraud**—any scam designed to take advantage of loopholes in the bankruptcy laws. The most common are the "similar-name" scam, the "old-company" scam, the "new-company" technique, and the "successful-business" scam.

The *similar-name scam* involves the creation of a corporation that has a name similar to that of an established firm. The objective is to create the impression that this new company is actually the older one. If the trick is successful, the swindlers place large orders with established suppliers and quickly resell any merchandise they receive, often to fences. At the same time the swindlers remove all money and assets of the corporation and either file for bankruptcy or wait until creditors sue. Then they leave the jurisdiction or adeptly erase their tracks.

The *old-company scam* involves employees of an already established firm who, motivated by a desire for quick profits, bilk the company of its money and assets and file for bankruptcy. Such a scam is typically used when the company is losing money or has lost its hold on a market.

The *new-company scam* is much like the similar-name scam: a new corporation is formed, credit is obtained, and orders are placed. Once merchandise is received, it is converted into cash with the assistance of a fence. By the time the company is forced into bankruptcy, the architects of this scheme have liquidated the corporation's assets.

The *successful-business scam* involves a profitable corporation that is well positioned in a market but experiences a change in ownership. After the new owners have bilked the corporation of all its money and assets, the firm is forced into bankruptcy.

Fraud against the Government

Governments at all levels are victims of a vast amount of fraud, which includes collusion in bidding, payoffs and kickbacks to government officials, expenditures by a government official that exceed the budget, the filing of false claims, the hiring of friends or associates formerly employed by the government, and offers of inducements to government officials.

Consider, for example, the fall of Wedtech—a military contractor with annual sales in excess of $100 million. At one time the Wedtech Corporation was hailed as the first major employer of blacks and Hispanics in New York City's blighted South Bronx. Before its fall from grace, Wedtech was a high flier on the New York Stock Exchange. What fueled the company? As a minority-controlled business, it won defense contracts without the need to bid. But in early 1986 Wedtech lost its status as a minority business, and by the end of that year the company was in ruins.

Wedtech officials had used fraudulent accounting methods, issued false financial reports, and counted profits before they were received. Caught in the cross-fire of charges was Congressman Mario Biaggi, who was later convicted of soliciting bribes in order to obtain special government support for Wedtech. Other company and government officials either pleaded guilty or were convicted.[20]

Is the Wedtech scandal an isolated case? Clearly not. In fiscal 1987 alone, the Department

Major Fraud Act, signed by President Ronald Reagan in November 1988, which creates a separate offense of government contract fraud in excess of $1 million. What kinds of activities does this act cover? Federal prosecutors can seek indictments against contractors who engage in deceptive pricing or overcharging by submitting inaccurate cost and pricing data; mischarging by billing the government for improper or nonallowable charges; collusion in bidding (a conspiracy between presumed competitors to inflate bids); product substitution or the delivery of inferior, nonconforming, or untested goods; or the use of bribes, gratuities, conflicts of interest, and a whole range of techniques designed to influence procurement officials.

Clearly there is more to government-related fraud than the manipulation of contractors and consultants.[22] The Inspector General's Office in the Department of Health and Human Services reported that about $2 billion may by lost annually to fraud in the Medicare program alone.[23] Welfare fraud may amount to as much as 9 percent of the total welfare budget. Fortunately, recent studies suggest that computer programs matching welfare benefits with other information (motor vehicle licenses, voter registrations, income tax returns) may significantly reduce such fraud.

Ex-Congressman Mario Biaggi of New York on his way to prison in 1989.

of Defense reported fraud amounting to $53.8 million. And this may be a conservative estimate. In response to a tip from a former navy employee in 1987, the Federal Bureau of Investigation and the Naval Intelligence Service began a secret 2-year investigation of bribery, fraud, illegal exchanges of information, and collusion at the Pentagon. This investigation has already resulted in the issuance of 200 grand-jury subpoenas, as well as the execution of 38 search warrants in 12 states and Washington, D.C.[21] It is hoped that this investigation will produce an accurate estimate of government contract fraud.

An important step to curb government contract fraud was taken with the passage of the

Consumer Fraud

Consumer fraud is the act of causing a consumer to surrender money through deceit or a misrepresentation of a material fact. Consumer frauds often appear as confidence games and may take some of the following forms:

- *Home-improvement fraud:* Consumers have been defrauded through the promise of low-cost home renovation. The homeowners give sizable down payments to the contractors, who have no plans to complete the job. In fact, contractors often leave the jurisdiction or declare bankruptcy.
- *Deceptive advertising:* Consumers are often lured into a store by an announcement that a product is priced low for a limited period of time. Once in the store, the customer is told that the product is sold out, and he or she is offered a substitute, typically of inferior qual-

ity or at a much higher price. Such schemes are known as "bait-and-switch advertising."

■ *Land fraud:* Consumers are easy prey for land-fraud swindlers. Here the pitch is that a certain piece of vacation or retirement property is a worthy investment, many improvements to the property will be made, and many facilities will be made available in the area. Consumers often make purchases of worthless or overvalued land.

■ *Business opportunity fraud:* The objective of business opportunity fraud is to persuade a consumer to invest money in a business concern through misrepresentation of its actual worth. Work-at-home frauds are common: victims are told they can make big money by addressing envelopes at home or performing some other simple task. Consumers lose large sums of money investing in such ventures.

Computer Crimes

Computer crime has increased considerably since the mid-1960s, but its true extent remains unknown. Quite apart from the difficulty of defining computer criminality, and apart from the absence of clearly applicable legislation in many jurisdictions, computer crime shares with other forms of economic crime the difficulty of detecting it.

Most such crimes—some investigators claim as many as 99 percent—are not reported because publicity about a company's economic problems may undermine public confidence in that institution. Claims filed with insurance companies for losses through computer fraud indicate that such claims are filed in less than 20 percent of known cases.[24] In 1976 the General Accounting Office found 69 cases of computer criminality known to federal law enforcement agencies; in 1984 the Federal Bureau of Investigation had fewer than 50 such cases pending.[25]

Research in a number of Western countries indicates that computer criminality has not yet become the menace it was predicted to become in the early 1970s. A survey of 2000 institutional computer users in Australia indicated that 53 cases of computer crime had become known there by 1980. A similar survey among 648 computer users in Canada revealed 13 cases. In Fin-land, 17 cases were known to the police. The government of Japan reported that 30 computer crimes had been committed by 1982. There were 22 cases in Sweden and 22 in Austria by 1983. Research conducted by the Max Planck Institute at Freiburg revealed 38 prosecutions for computer crimes in the Federal Republic of Germany, and that country's Federal Criminal Police Office reported 53 such cases by the mid-1980s.[26]

The number of reported computer crimes may seem to be insignificant, but many of those that have been successful have netted huge profits. Even as early as 1974, it was estimated that the "average" loss in computer fraud cases amounted to $450,000.[27] The Equity Funding Corporation acquired $1.8 million through computer manipulation; the employees involved netted another $144,000.[28] Some investigators have estimated the total annual losses through computer fraud to be as high as $5 billion.[29]

Let us look at the various types of computer crimes to see what they have in common and how they differ. The rebellious students who briefly held New York University's Argonne National Laboratory computer for $100,000 ransom in the turbulent 1960s obviously committed a computer crime, but investigators generally focus on activities that entail access to the computer's hardware and software. Most such acts have in common a loss to the rightful owner of data, and often the perpetrator gains financially. But this need not be the case. Some computer crimes may pose a threat to the national security, as happened when the data base of the Los Alamos National Laboratory was entered.

Computer crimes show little uniformity in motive or harm. But these crimes can be viewed in the context of existing crime categories. We therefore propose the following five basic categories as a framework:

■ **Computer fraud** involves falsification of stored data or deception in legitimate transactions by manipulation of data or programming, including the unlawful acquisition of data or programs for purposes of financial gain of the perpetrator or of a third party.

■ **Computer espionage** consists of activities by which unauthorized computer access yields information for purposes of exploitation from data bases belonging to government or private parties.

■ **Computer sabotage** consists of the tampering with, destruction of, or scrambling of data or software by means of gaining surreptitious access to data banks.

■ **Computer hacking** is the act of gaining unlawful access to data banks for malicious, though not necessarily destructive, purposes and for neither financial gain nor purposes of espionage.

■ **Theft of computer time, software, and hardware** includes the unauthorized use of computer time and software services as well as the unauthorized copying of software programs and the outright theft of computer equipment.

These categories could well serve federal and state legislators in their efforts to develop legislation encompassing a comprehensive set of prohibitions to protect society against computer abuses. During the 1980s the federal government and 47 states passed computer crime legislation of various sorts and of various degrees of effectiveness.[30] For example, Congress passed two acts (the Counterfeit Access Device and Computer Fraud and Abuse Act of 1984 *and* the Computer Fraud and Abuse Act of 1986) defining offenses and prescribing corresponding penalties. So far, most known computer crimes seem to involve manipulations for purposes of fraud or industrial espionage. But the number of computer nuisance crimes, including sabotage and hacking, has been increasing, and thefts of computer time and software are predicted to rise rapidly.[31]

Insurance Fraud

There are many varieties of insurance fraud: policyholders defraud insurers, insurers defraud the public, management defrauds the public, and third parties defraud insurers. Policyholder fraud is most often accomplished by the filing of false claims for life, fire, marine, or casualty insurance. Sometimes an employee of the insurance company is part of the fraud and assists in the preparation of the claim. The fraud may be simple—a false death claim—or it may become complex when multiple policies are involved.

A different type of insurance fraud is committed when a small group of people create a "shell" insurance firm without true assets. Policies are sold with no intent to pay legitimate claims. In fact, when large claims are presented to shell insurance companies, the firms disband, leaving a trail of policyholder victims. In yet another form of insurance fraud, mid- and upper-level managers of an insurance company loot the firm's assets by removing funds and debiting them as payments of claims to legitimate or bogus policyholders.[32]

Criminologists Paul Tracy and James Fox conducted a field experiment to find out how many auto-body repair shops in Massachusetts inflate repair estimates to insurance companies, and by how much. These researchers rented two Buick Skylarks with moderate damage, a Volvo 740 GLE with superficial damage, and a Ford Tempo with substantial damage. They then obtained 191 repair estimates, some with a clear understanding that the car was insured, others with the understanding that there was no insurance coverage. The results were unequivocal: repair estimates for insured vehicles were significantly higher than those for noncovered cars. This finding is highly suggestive of fraud.[33]

Tax Fraud

The Internal Revenue Code makes willful failure to file a tax return a misdemeanor. An attempt to evade or defeat a tax, nonpayment of a tax, or willful filing of a fraudulent tax return is a felony. What must the government prove? In order to sustain a conviction, the government must present evidence of income tax due and owing, willful avoidance of payment, and an affirmative act toward tax evasion.[34] How are tax frauds accomplished? Consider the following techniques:

■ *Keeping two sets of books:* A person may keep one set of books reflecting actual profits and losses and another set for the purpose of misleading the Internal Revenue Service.

■ *Shifting funds:* In order to avoid detection, tax evaders often shift funds continually from account to account, from bank to bank.

■ *Faking forms:* Tax evaders often use faked

invoices, create fictitious expenses, conceal assets, and destroy books and records.

The IRS lacks the resources to investigate all suspicious tax forms. When the difficulty of distinguishing between careless mistakes and willful evasion is taken into account, the taxes that go uncollected each year are estimated to exceed $100 billion.[35]

Bribery, Corruption, and Political Fraud

Judges who fix traffic tickets in exchange for political favors, municipal employees who speculate with city funds, businesspeople who bribe local politicians to obtain favorable treatment—all are part of the corruption in our municipal, state, and federal governments. The objectives of such offenses vary—favors, special privileges, services, business. The actors include officers of corporations as well as of government; indeed, they may belong to the police or the courts.

Bribery and other forms of corruption are ingrained in the political machinery of local and state governments. Examples abound: mayors of large cities attempt to obtain favors through bribes, manufacturers pay off political figures for favors, municipal officials demand kickbacks from contractors.[36] In response to the seriousness of political corruption and bribery, Congress established two crimes: it is now a felony to accept a bribe or to provide a bribe.[37] Of course, political bribery and other forms of corruption do not stop at the nation's borders. Kickbacks to foreign officials are common practice.[38]

Corruption can be found in private industry as well. One firm pays another to induce it to use a product or service; a firm pays its own board of directors or officers to dispense special favors; two or more firms, presumably competitors, secretly agree to charge the same prices for their products or services.

Insider-Related Fraud

Insider-related fraud involves the use and misuse of one's position for pecuniary gain or privilege. This category of offenses includes embezzlement, employee-related thefts, and sale of confidential information.

Embezzlement is the conversion (misappropriation) of property or money with which one is entrusted or for which one has a fiduciary responsibility. Yearly losses attributable to embezzlement are estimated at over $1 billion.[39]

Employee-related thefts of company property are responsible for a significant share of industry losses. Estimates place such losses between $4 billion and $13 billion each year. Criminologists John Clark and Richard Hollinger have estimated that the 35 percent rate of employee pilferage in some corporations results primarily from vocational dissatisfaction and a perception of exploitation.[40] And not only goods and services are taken; time and money are at risk as well. Phony payrolls, fictitious overtime charges, false claims for business-related travel, and the like are common.

Finally, in a free marketplace where a premium is placed on competition, corporations must guard against the *sale of confidential information* and trade secrets. The best insurance policy is employee loyalty. Where there is no loyalty, or where loyalty is compromised, abuse of confidential information is possible. The purchase of confidential information from employees willing to commit industrial espionage is estimated to be a multimillion-dollar business.[41]

CORPORATE CRIME

Corporate crime is a criminal act committed by one or more employees of a corporation that is attributed to the organization itself. Between 1984 and 1990, 2000 corporations were convicted in federal courts for offenses ranging from tax law violations to environmental crimes (see Table 12.1). The vast majority of these companies were small- to medium-size privately held corporations.

One problem with corporate crime is defining it. In 1989 the supertanker *Exxon Valdez* ran aground in Prince William Sound, Alaska, spilling 250,000 barrels of oil. The spill became North America's largest ecological disaster. Prosecutors were interested in determining the liability of the captain, his officers, and his crew. But there were additional and far-reaching questions. Was the Exxon Corporation liable? If so, was this a corporate crime?

During the Great Depression thousands of

TABLE 12.1 NUMBER OF CORPORATIONS SENTENCED IN FEDERAL COURTS, 1984–1990

Type of Offense	Year of Sentencing (Number of Offenses)							
	1984	1985	1986	1987	1988	1989	1990	Total
Against persons	1	0	0	0	0	0	0	1
Property	5	8	15	9	12	12	11	72
Public officials	5	4	6	4	—	6	4	29
Drugs	1	4	2	2	—	3	0	12
Racketeering	12	4	5	2	10	4	3	40
Fraud and deceit	116	94	128	105	109	82	55	689
Obscenity	0	4	1	1	—	15	8	29
Civil rights	2	1	3	2	—	0	0	8
Administration of justice	7	0	2	2	—	2	0	13
Public safety	5	3	1	0	—	2	2	13
Immigration	0	1	1	0	—	4	0	6
National defense	11	6	4	4	18	6	4	53
Food and drug laws	38	37	32	23	9	14	14	167
Environmental	10	24	17	8	28	28	21	136
Antitrust	93	70	47	68	98	58	23	457
Monetary transactions	0	0	0	0	8	5	3	16
Taxation	21	35	16	26	14	26	16	154
Other offenses	17	16	22	13	21	6	2	97
Total	344	311	302	269	328	273	173	2000

Source: United States Sentencing Committee Guidelines for Organizations, Supplementary Report, 1991, p. D10.

unemployed people heard that there was work to be had in the little West Virginia town of Hawk's Nest, where a huge tunnel was to be dug. Thousands of people came to work for a pittance. The company set the men up in crude camps and put them to work drilling rock for the tunnel project—without masks or other safety equipment. The workers breathed in the silicon dust that filled the air. Many contracted silicosis, a chronic lung disease that leads to certain death. They died by the dozens. Security guards dragged the bodies away and buried them secretly. No one was to know. The work went on. The deaths multiplied. Who was to blame? The corporation?[42]

Theories of Corporate Liability

A *corporation* is an artificial person created by state charter. The charter provides such an entity with the right to engage in certain activities—to buy and sell certain goods or to run a railroad, for instance. The charter limits the liability of the persons who own the corporation (the shareholders) to the extent of the value of their investment (their shares). The corporation thus is an entity separate from the people who own or man-

age it. This convenient form of pooling resources for commercial purposes, with a view toward profiting from one's investment, has had a significant impact on the development of the United States as a commercial and industrial power. Moreover, millions of wage earners whose savings or union funds are invested in corporate stocks and bonds reap dividends from such investments in the form of income or retirement benefits.

But what if a senior official of a corporation engages in unlawful activity? Can we say that the corporation committed the crime? If so, what can be done about it?[43] Initially corporations were considered incapable of committing crimes. After all, crimes require *mens rea*, an awareness of wrongdoing. Since corporations are bodies without souls, they were deemed to be incapable of forming the requisite sense of wrongdoing. Nor could a corporation be imprisoned for its crimes. Further, corporations were not authorized to commit crimes; they were authorized only to engage in the business for which they had been chartered.

A different theory of corporate criminal liability eventually emerged when courts and legisla-

Coal miners' protest: Should a company in an industry that allegedly kills eleven persons a day be charged with criminal homicide?

tors began to ask why, if a corporation is chartered to run a railroad, it should not be held accountable for manslaughter if the negligent action of its operatives causes the death of a human being. After all, the actions of its employees are part of running a railroad. And so it was decided in 1917.[44] Thereafter, the theory that a corporation can be held accountable for criminal acts was widened, until the Model Penal Code broadly subjected corporations to liability for most criminal offenses, especially those that were "authorized, requested, commanded, performed or recklessly tolerated by the board of directors or by a high managerial agent acting in behalf of

the corporation within the scope of his office or employment."[45]

Governmental Control of Corporations

Corporate misconduct is covered by a broad range of federal and state statutes, including the federal conspiracy laws; the Racketeer Influenced and Corrupt Organizations (RICO) Act; federal securities laws; mail-fraud statutes; the Federal Corrupt Practices Act; the Federal Election Campaign Act; legislation on lobbying, bribery, and corruption; the Internal Revenue Code (especially as regards major tax crimes, slush funds, and improper payments); the Bank Secrecy Act; and federal provisions on obstruction of justice, perjury, and false statements.

The underlying theory is that if the brain of the artificial person (usually the board of directors of the corporation) authorizes or condones the act in question, the body (the corporation) must suffer criminal penalty. That seems fair enough, except for the fact that if the corporation gets punished—usually by a substantial fine—the penalty falls on the shareholders, most of whom had no say in the corporate decision. And the financial loss resulting from the fine may be passed on to the consumer.

Reliance on Civil Penalties

Beginning in the nineteenth century, corporations were suspected of wielding monopolistic power to the detriment of consumers. The theory behind monopoly is simple: if you buy out all your competitors or drive them out of business, then you are the only one from whom people can buy the product you sell. So you can set the price, and you set it very high, for your profit and to the detriment of the consumers. The Sugar Trust was one such monopoly. A few powerful businessmen eliminated all competitors and then drove the price of sugar up, to the detriment of the public. Theodore Roosevelt fought and broke up the Sugar Trust.

In 1890 Congress passed the **Sherman Antitrust Act,** which effectively limited the exercise of monopolies.[46] The act prohibited any contract, conspiracy, or combination of business interests in restraint of foreign or interstate trade. This legislation was followed by the Clayton Antitrust Act (1914), which further curbed the ability of corporations to enrich their shareholders at the expense of the public by prohibiting such acts as price-fixing.[47] But the remedies this act provided consisted largely of splitting up monopolistic enterprises or imposing damages, sometimes triple damages, for the harm caused. In a strict sense, this was not a use of the criminal law to govern corporate misconduct.

Criminal Liability

A movement away from exclusive reliance on civil remedies was apparent in the 1960s, when it was discovered that corporate mismanagement or negligence on the part of officers or employees could inflict vast harm on identifiable groups of victims. Negligent management at a nuclear power plant can result in the release of radiation and injury to thousands or millions of people. The marketing of an unsafe drug can cause crippling deformities in tens of thousands of bodies.[48] Violation of environmental standards can cause injury and suffering to generations of people who will be exposed to unsafe drinking water, harmful air, or eroded soil. The manufacture of hazardous products can result in multiple deaths.[49]

The problem of corporate criminal liability since the 1960s, then, goes far beyond an individual death or injury. Ultimately it concerns the health and even the survival of humankind. Nor is the problem confined to the United States. It is a global problem. It thus becomes necessary to look at the variety of activities attributable to corporations which in recent years have been recognized as particularly harmful to society.

When it comes to proving corporate criminal liability, prosecutors face formidable problems: Day-to-day corporate activity has a low level of visibility. Regulatory agencies that monitor corporate conduct have different and uncoordinated recording systems. Offending corporations operate in a multitude of jurisdictions, some of which regard a given activity as criminal, while others do not. Frequently the facts of a case are not adjudicated at a trial; the parties may simply agree on a settlement approved by the court. The accused corporation may be permitted to plead *nolo con-*

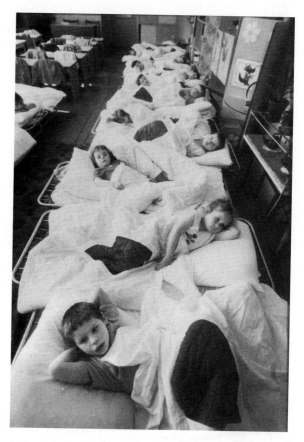

Scientists expect the casualties of the April 1986 Chernobyl nuclear meltdown to reach into the thousands. These children lie in a hospital ward near the disaster site, still suffering intestinal problems four years after the explosion and fire. Causes of this accident: human error, criminal negligence, and management fraud.

tendere ("no contest") in return for an agreed-upon fine or settlement.

Investigating Corporate Crime

We know very little about the extent of economic criminality in the United States. There is no national data base for the assessment of corporate criminality, and corporations are not likely to release information about their own wrongdoing. The situation is worse in other countries, and worst in the developing countries of Africa south of the Sahara, where few national crime statistics are kept and where corporations are least subject to governmental control. Yet the evidence in regard to corporate crime is gradually coming in.[50]

As we noted earlier, the first American criminologist who was alert to the potential for harm in corporate conduct was Edwin Sutherland, who described the criminal behavior of 70 of the 200 largest production corporations in his 1946 book *White Collar Crime*.[51] An even more ambitious study was completed by Marshall B. Clinard and Peter C. Yeager, who investigated corporations within the jurisdiction of 25 federal agencies during 1975 and 1976. Of 477 major American corporations whose conduct was regulated by these agencies, 60 percent had violated the law. Of the 300 violating corporations, 38 (or 13 percent) accounted for 52 percent of all violations charged in 1975 and 1976, an average of 23.5 violations per firm.[52] Large corporations were found to be the chief violators, and a few particular industries (pharmaceutical, automotive) were the most likely to violate the law.

According to Clinard and Yeager, what makes it so difficult to curb corporate crime is the enormous political power corporations wield in the shaping and administration of the laws that govern their conduct. This is particularly the case in regard to multinational corporations that wish to operate in developing countries. The promise of jobs and development by a giant corporation is a temptation too great for the governments of many such countries to resist. They would rather have employment opportunities that pollute air and water than unemployment in a clean environment. Government officials in some Third World countries can be bribed to create or maintain a legal climate favorable to the business interests of the corporation, even though it may be detrimental to the people of the host country.

The work of Sutherland, Clinard and Yeager, and other traditional scholars, as well as that of a group of radical criminologists;[53] hearings on white-collar and corporate crime held by the Subcommittee on Crime of the House Judiciary Committee, under the leadership of Congressman John Conyers, Jr., in 1978; the consumer protection movement, spearheaded by Ralph Nader; and recent investigative reporting by the press have all contributed to public awareness of large corporations' power to inflict harm on large population groups.

In 1975 James Q. Wilson still considered such crime to be insignificant,[54] but more recent studies show that the public considers corporate criminality more serious than street crime. Marvin Wolfgang and his associates found in a national survey that Americans regard illegal retail price-fixing (the artificial setting of prices at a high level, without regard for the demand for the product) as a more serious crime than robbery committed with a lead pipe.[55] Within the sphere of corporate criminality perhaps no other group of offenses has had so great an impact on public consciousness as crimes against the environment. As we shall see, however, enforcement of major environmental statutes has been weak.

Environmental Crimes

Warren D. Mooney makes life sweet—sodas, candies. His company, Liquid Sugars Inc., is the confection in Jelly Belly, the gourmet bean that everyone chewed after presidential candidate Ronald Reagan said they were his favorite.

On Friday, Mooney was indicted by the federal grand jury in Sacramento on nine felony counts, including conspiracy to pollute. Prosecutors say they are strictly enforcing the law; the defense calls it "justice run amok."

If found guilty of violating the Clean Water Act, Mooney could be sentenced to 29 years in jail and be fined $2.25 million. The company faces a fine of $4.5 million.

The indictments concluded a two-year investigation into Liquid Sugars, a company headquartered in Emeryville, managed by Mooney and accused of violating water-pollution laws at its Port of Stockton facility. The company blends sweeteners for manufacturers—its most notable client being Jelly Belly maker Herman Goelitz Candy Co. of Fairfield.

Mooney and Liquid Sugars are charged with dumping into the Stockton sewer waste water trucked from Goelitz's Fairfield facility. The waste was water contaminated with sweetener from washing down the equipment that produces exotically flavored beans—buttered popcorn, toasted marshmallow, pina colada.

Similarly, the indictment said the company

trucked in waste water from a second customer, pickle-maker G. L. Mezzetta of Sonoma.

In addition to conspiracy, Liquid Sugars is charged with violating regulations imposed on industries that dump waste into sewers: four counts of dumping into the sewer waste hauled in from elsewhere, and four counts of dumping into the system waste with a pH below 5.[56]

The world's legal systems include few effective laws and mechanisms to curb destruction of the environment. The emission of noxious fumes into the air and the discharge of pollutants into the water have until recently been regarded as common law nuisances at the level of misdemeanors, commanding usually no more than a small fine. Industrial polluters could easily absorb such a fine and regard it as a kind of business tax. Only in 1969 did Congress pass the National Environmental Policy Act (NEPA). Among other things, the act created the Environmental Protection Agency (EPA). It requires environmental impact studies so that any new development that would significantly affect the environment can be prevented or controlled.

The EPA is charged with enforcing federal statutes and assisting in the enforcement of state laws enacted to protect the environment. The agency monitors plant discharges all over the country and may take action against private industry or municipal governments. Yet during the first 5 years of its existence the EPA referred only 130 cases to the U.S. Department of Justice for criminal prosecution, and only 6 of these involved major corporate offenders.[57] The government actually charged only one of the corporations, Allied Chemical, which admitted responsibility for 940 misdemeanor counts of discharging toxic chemicals into the Charles River in Virginia, thereby causing 80 people to become ill.[58]

A 1979 report of the General Accounting Office stated that the EPA inadequately monitored, inaccurately reported, and ineffectively enforced the nation's basic law on air pollution, although the agency's then chief contended that corrective action had been taken during the previous year.[59] The situation improved during the 1980s, but the environment is far from safe. Catastrophic releases of toxic and even nuclear substances, usually attributable to inadequate safeguards and human negligence, pose a particularly grave hazard, as the disasters at

A catastrophic explosion at a Union Carbide plant spewed toxic chemicals over Bhopal, India, and its environs, killing at least 4,000 and injuring 200,000 people. It also killed animals, like these sacred cows lying in a field near the plant.

Bhopal in India and at Chernobyl in the former Soviet Union have demonstrated.

Enforcing Legislation

The difficulties of enforcing legislation designed to protect the environment are enormous. Consider the 250,000 barrels of oil spilled by the *Exxon Valdez* in 1989. What legislation could have prevented the disaster? Developing effective laws to protect the environment is a complex problem. It is far easier to define the crimes of murder and theft than to define acts of pollution, which are infinitely varied. A particular challenge is the separation of harmful activities from socially useful ones. Moreover, pollution is hard to quantify. How much of a chemical must be discharged into water before the discharge is considered noxious and subjects the polluter to punishment? Discharge of a gallon by one polluter may not warrant punishment, and a small quantity may not even be detectable. But what do we do with a hundred polluters, each of whom discharges a gallon?

Many other issues must be addressed as well. For instance, should accidental pollution warrant the same punishment as intentional or negligent pollution? Since many polluters are corporations, what are the implications of penalties that force a company to install costly antipollution devices? To cover the costs, the corporation may have to increase the price of its product, and so the consumer pays. Should the company be allowed to lower plant workers' wages instead? Should the plant be forced or permitted to shut down, thereby increasing unemployment in the community? The company may choose to move its plant to another state or country that is more hospitable.

Addressing Sensitive Issues

Fines imposed on intentional polluters have been increased so that they can no longer be shrugged off as an ordinary cost of doing business. The General Electric Company was fined $7 million and the Allied Chemical Corporation $13.2 million for pollution offenses. Fines of such magnitude are powerful incentives to corporations to limit pollution. But since many of the enterprises that are likely to pollute are in the public sector, or produce for the public sector, the public ultimately will have to pay the fine in the form of increased gas or electricity bills.[60]

In the Third World, problems of punishing and preventing pollution are enormous. Industries preparing to locate there have the power to influence governments and officials, surreptiously and officially, into passing legislation favorable to the industry. The desire to industrialize outweighs the desire to preserve the environment. Some countries find ways to address the problem, only to relinquish controls when they prove irksome. While Japan was trying to establish its industrial dominance, for example, it observed a constitutional provision stating: "The conservation of life environment shall be balanced against the needs of economic development."[61] This provision was deleted in 1970, when Japan had achieved economic strength.

Developing Effective Legislation

U.S. legislators have several options in developing legislation to protect the environment:

■ *The independent use of the criminal sanction:* direct prohibition of polluting activities. This is the way American legislators have typically tried to cope with the problem in the past. They simply made it a criminal offense to maintain a "nuisance," that is, an ongoing activity that pollutes the water, the soil, or the air.

■ *The dependent-direct use of the criminal sanction:* prohibition of certain polluting activities that exceed specified limits. This is a more sophisticated legislative method. If pollution is to be kept at a low level, no one person or company can be allowed to emit more than an insignificant amount of noxious waste into the environment. This amount is fixed by administrative regulation. Anyone who exceeds the limit commits a criminal offense.

■ *The dependent-indirect approach:* criminal sanction reserved for firms that fail to comply with specific rulings rendered by administrative organs against violators of standards. Under this option, polluters have already been identified by regulatory agencies, and they are now under order to comply with the agencies' requirements. If they violate these

AT ISSUE
Dangerous Ground: The World of Hazardous Waste Crime

What kind of person would illegally dump hazardous waste into the waterways and landscapes of America? Many would guess it might be a sinister organized crime operator. Some past published works on hazardous waste crime have, in fact, described this area of crime as being synonymous with syndicate crime.

This is the introduction to criminologist Donald J. Rebovich's controversial book *Dangerous Ground: The World of Hazardous Waste Crime*, in which he reports the results of an empirical study of hazardous waste offenders in four states. He continues:

Surprisingly enough, the study has found that, most commonly, the criminal dumper is an ordinary, profit-motivated businessman who operates in a business where syndicate crime activity may be present but by not means pervasive. The research uncovers a criminal world of the hazardous waste offender unlike any theorized in the past. It is a world where the intensity, duration, and methods of the criminal act will be more likely determined by the criminal opportunities available in the legitimate marketplace than by the orders of a controlling criminal syndicate.

Rebovich's portrait of hazardous waste crime replaces our ideas about midnight dumping and masked dumpers with straightforward descriptions of hazardous waste treatment/storage/disposal (TSD) facilities failing to comply with state and federal regulations:

The mark of a successful hazardous waste criminal—one who can maintain his criminal lifestyle for a lengthy duration—is his skill in effectively analyzing the potential threats to his livelihood and his versatility in adapting to those threats. For many TSD-facility operators, the serious game of working the system was played out by eluding the regulatory inspectors by capitalizing on either the inspectors' unfamiliarity with treatment apparatus or their lack of diligence in inspecting thoroughly.

TSD-facility offenders did have to contend with monitoring devices, installed by regulators, that were used to gauge volume and properties of effluents released into local sewer systems to determine compliance with existing discharge standards. The mechanisms were intended to sample effluents randomly but, in reality, offenders found the system seriously flawed and did not hesitate to seize their opportunities to work the system in a new way. . . . The tests were simply rigged to elicit a false impression of the toxicity of the substances discharged into the sewer.

Rebovich makes this prediction:

The characteristics of future hazardous waste offenders, and the crimes that they commit, will more than likely be determined by developments in several areas external to the criminal act: (1) pressure from the general public and public interest groups for stricter enforcement, (2) legislative expansion of the scope of legal coverage, (3) redesigned enforcement, and (4) future availability of affordable disposal outlets. These areas can be seen as the components of an equation that could lead to a reduction in hazardous waste crime.

Source: Donald J. Rebovich, Dangerous Ground: The World of Hazardous Waste Crime (New Brunswick, N.J.: Transaction, 1992).

Questions for Discussion

1. Illegal hazardous waste practices may be punished by fining the company or industry. Should individuals be punished as well?
2. Some TSD-facility operators have claimed that they were forced to use illegal practices because it is economically impossible to take care of hazardous wastes under current regulations. What is your reaction to such a defense?

EPA Superfund site in New York State: Once hazardous waste left from some long-ago business activity has made a place unlivable, it is often difficult to trace those criminally responsible.

orders, a criminal punishment can be imposed.

■ *The preventive use of the criminal sanction:* penalties imposed for failure to install or maintain prescribed antipollution equipment. This is the newest and most sophisticated means of regulating polluting industries. The law determines what preventive and protective measures must be taken (to filter industrial waste water, to put chemical screens on smokestacks, and so on). Any firm that fails to take the prescribed measures is guilty of a violation.[62]

In the past, legal systems relied primarily on the independent use of the criminal sanction. More recent legislation has concentrated on administrative orders and technological prevention.

Curbing Corporate Crime

Laws and regulations prescribing criminal sanctions have been passed and continue to be passed to guard the public against the dangers rooted in the power of corporate enterprise. Recently, for example, Congress passed new guidelines for sentencing corporations in federal courts. These guidelines significantly increased corporate sanctions.[63] While such laws and regulations may help to curb the propensity of corporations to inflict harm on the general public, many governments recognize that criminal justice systems are not yet prepared to deal with economic crimes.[64] They also recognize the importance of attacking this problem at the international level, perhaps by designing strategies, standards, and guidelines that may be helpful to all governments.[65]

A disturbing thought remains: Is the imposition of criminal liability for the conduct of corporations on the corporations themselves really the best way to curb corporate misconduct? If corporations act on the decisions of their principal officers or agents, might it not be appropriate to restrict the reach of the law to these corporate actors rather than to subject the innocent and uninformed shareholders to financial loss? The idea of penalizing corporate officials, together with their corporations, has been gaining in pop-

ularity since business crimes began to proliferate in the 1980s.

ORGANIZED CRIME

Earlier we noted that all forms of organizational criminality have in common the use of business enterprises for illegal profit. We have recognized some significant problems not only with existing definitions and conceptualizations of white-collar and corporate crime but with the criminal justice response to such offenses. Similar problems arise in efforts to deal with organized crime. It, too, depends on business enterprises. And like corporate crime, organized crime comes in so many varieties that attempts to define it precisely lead to frustration.

The difficulty of gaining access to information on organized crime has also hindered attempts to conceptualize the problems posed by this kind of law violation. Finally, law enforcement efforts have been inadequate to control the influence of organized crime. As will be evident, a greater effort must be made to uncover the nature, pattern, and extent of organized crime.

The History of Organized Crime

Organized crime had its origin in the great wave of immigrants from southern Italy (especially from Sicily) to the United States between 1875 and 1920. These immigrants came from an environment that historically had been hostile to them. Suppressed by successive waves of invaders and alien rulers (Roman, Byzantine, Arab, Norman, Spanish) and exploited by mostly absentee landlords with their armies, Sicilians had learned to survive by relying on the strength of their own families. Indeed, these families had undergone little change since Greco-Roman times, two millennia earlier.

A traditional Sicilian family has been described as an extended family, or clan; it includes lineal relations (grandparents, parents, children, grandchildren) and lateral relations through the paternal line—uncles, aunts, and cousins as far as the bloodline can be traced. This *famiglia* is hierarchically organized and administered by the head of the family, the *capo di famiglia* (the Romans called him *pater familias*), to whom all members owe obedience and loyalty. Strangers, especially those in positions of power in state or church, are not to be trusted. All problems are resolved within the family, which must be kept strong. Its prestige, honor, wealth, and power have to be defended and strengthened, sometimes through alliances with more distant kin.[66]

Throughout history these strong families have served each other and Sicily. Upon migration to the United States, members of Sicilian families soon found that the social environment in their new country was as hostile as that of the old. Aspirations were encouraged, yet legitimate means to realize them were often not available. And the new country seemed already to have an established pattern for achieving wealth and power by unethical means. Many of America's great fortunes—those of the Astors, the Vanderbilts, the Goulds, the Sages, the Stanfords, the Rockefellers, the Carnegies, the Lords, the Harrimans—had been made by cunning, greed, and exploitation.

As time passed, new laws were enacted to address conspiracies in restraint of trade and other economic offenses. Yet by the time the last wave of Sicilian immigrants reached the United States, the names of the great robber barons were connected with major universities, foundations, and charitable institutions.[67] At the local level, the Sicilian immigrants found themselves involved in a system of politics in which patronage and protection were dispensed by corrupt politicians and petty hoodlums from earlier immigrant groups—German, Irish, and Jewish. The Sicilian family structure helped its members to survive in this hostile environment. It also created the organizational basis that permitted them to respond to the opportunity created when, on January 16, 1920, the Eighteenth Amendment to the Constitution outlawed the manufacture, sale, and transportation of alcoholic beverages.

Howard Abadinsky explains what happened:

Prohibition acted as a catalyst for the mobilization of criminal elements in an unprecedented manner. Pre-prohibition crime, insofar as it was organized, centered around corrupt political machines, vice entrepreneurs, and, at the bottom, gangs. Prohibition unleashed an unparalleled level of competitive criminal violence and changed the order—the gang leaders emerged on top.[68]

During the early years of Prohibition, the names of the most notorious bootleggers, mobsters, and gangsters sounded German, Irish, and Jewish: Arthur Fiegenheimer (better known as "Dutch Schultz"), Otto Gass, Bo and George Weinberg, Arnold Rothstein, John T. Nolen ("Legs Diamond"), Vincent "Mad Dog" Coll, Joe Rock. By the time Prohibition was repealed, Al Capone, Lucky Luciano, Frank Costello, Johnny Torrio, and many other Sicilians were preeminent in the underworld. They had become folk heroes and role models for the kids in the Italian ghettos, many of whom were to seek their own places in this new society.

Sicilian families were every bit as ruthless in establishing their crime empires as the earlier immigrant groups had been. They were so successful in their domination of organized crime that, especially after World War II, organized crime became virtually synonymous with the Sicilian Mafia.

The term "Mafia" appears to derive from an Arabic word denoting "place of refuge." The concept, which was adopted in Sicily during the era of Arab rule, gradually came to describe a mode of life and survival. The Mafia provided "protection against the arrogance of the powerful, remedy to any damage, sturdiness of body, strength and security of spirit, and the best and most exquisite part of life."[69] Ultimately, the **Mafia** became the entirety of those Sicilian families that were loosely associated with one another in operating organized crime, both in America and in Sicily.[70] Ever since the testimony of the mafioso Joseph Valachi before the Senate's McClellan Committee in 1963, the Mafia has also been referred to as *La Cosa Nostra*, "our thing."[71]

Despite Valachi's testimony and later revelations, some scholars still doubt the existence of a Sicilian-based American crime syndicate. To the criminologist Jay Albanese, for instance:

[I]t is clear . . . that despite popular opinion which has for many years insisted on the existence of a secret criminal society called "the Mafia," which somehow evolved from Italy, many separate historical investigations have found no evidence to support such a belief.[72]

WINDOW TO THE WORLD
Sicilian Mafiosi: A Dying Breed

In January 1993 Salvatore (Toto) Riina, the undisputed boss of the Sicilian Mafia, was arrested. It was one of a series of events marking what many saw as the disintegration of the Mafia's influence in Italy. *The New Yorker* writer Alexander Stille traced the collapse of Mafia power to the 1992 assassinations of Giovanni Falcone, the head of Italy's national anti-Mafia task force, and his designated successor, Paolo Borsellino. Part of Stille's 1993 article is excerpted here:

The capture of Toto Riina is the culmination of a remarkable reversal for the Mafia, which began last summer after the devastating murders of Giovanni Falcone and Paolo Borsellino. . . . [A]ll the elements that led to the capture of Toto Riina can be tied directly to specific political decisions that were made after the murders of Falcone and Borsellino, decisions that the two prosecutors themselves had been pushing for years. It was only three months ago that

a special squad of police was assigned to work exclusively on the capture of Riina, even though the government had known for a dozen years that he was at the pinnacle of Cosa Nostra. Only last summer was a law finally passed to protect Mafia witnesses and their families—the most basic tool of organized-crime investigations. Not until June were convicted Mafia bosses moved to "hard" prisons, far from their base of power in Sicily, where they had frequently enjoyed long stays in hotel-like prison infirmaries.

To the outside world, the elimination of Falcone and Borsellino seemed to demonstrate the Mafia's total invincibility; those familiar with the inner workings of Cosa Nostra saw something different. "The Mafia is on its last legs," Tommaso Buscetta said last July, from his hideaway in the United States, where he is in the witness-protection program. "The Mafia is not used to these kind of large-scale public killings. It is used to silence. I think it is fighting for its

survival." At the time, Buscetta's statement seemed wildly improbable, but once again he has proved a subtle interpreter of the world of Cosa Nostra.

The Minister of Justice, Claudio Martelli, vowed that the murder of Falcone would "prove the Mafia's worst mistake." And the Italian parliament not only quickly passed many of the tough anti-Mafia measures that Falcone and Borsellino had been pushing but also made the extraordinary decision to send seven thousand Army troops to Sicily to set up roadblocks, guard judges and politicians, and free up the police to concentrate on investigative work.

Besides stimulating new legislation, the Falcone-Borsellino killings set off a kind of moral revolt in Palermo. A city that had been criticized in the past for its cautious silences and passive complicity erupted in a series of protests that did not, as in the past, peter out almost as soon as the dead were buried. Since last spring, the city has been in a nearly constant state of ferment.

Ultimately, however, the question of Cosa Nostra's future is political. "I think the collusion between the Mafia and politics—at least on a national level—is finished," Francesco Renda, a professor emeritus of history at the University of Palermo, says. "If you can break that bond and isolate the Mafia, you have solved half the problem."

Source: Alexander Stille, "Letter from Palermo: The Mafia's Biggest Mistake," The New Yorker, Mar. 1, 1993, pp. 60–73.

Questions for Discussion

1. How might the disintegration of the power of the Sicilian Mafia affect organized crime in the United States?
2. Why has the Mafia not become as woven into the fabric of life in the United States as it has in Sicily?

Salvatore Riina at his conviction in Palermo on organized crime charges. Italy at last had the legendary Mafioso behind bars.

The Structure and Impact of Organized Crime

Americans have felt the impact of organized crime, and they have followed the media coverage of the mob wars and their victims with fascination. But little was known about the Mafia's actual structure in the United States until a succession of government investigations began to unravel its mysteries. The major investigations were conducted by the Committee on Mercenary Crimes, in 1932; the Special Senate Committee to Investigate Organized Crime in Interstate Commerce (the Kefauver Crime Committee), from 1950 to 1951; the Senate Permanent Subcommittee on Investigations (the McClellan Committee), from 1956 to 1963; President Lyndon Johnson's Commission on Law Enforcement and Administration of Justice (the Task Force on Organized Crime), from 1964 to 1967; and the President's Commission on Organized Crime, which reported to President Reagan in 1986 and 1987.[73]

The findings of these investigations established the magnitude of organized crime in the United States. It had become an empire almost beyond the reach of government, with vast resources derived from a virtual monopoly on gambling and loan-sharking, drug trafficking, pornography and prostitution, labor racketeering, murder for hire, the control of local crime activities, and the theft and fencing of securities, cars, jewels, and consumer goods of all sorts.[74] Above all, it was found that organized crime had infiltrated a vast variety of legitimate types of business, such as stevedoring (the loading and unloading of ships), the fish and meat industries, the wholesale and retail liquor industry (including bars and taverns), the vending machine business, the securities and investment business, the waste disposal business, and the construction industry.[75]

Specific legislation and law enforcement programs have allowed governmental agencies to assert some measure of control over organized crime. Cases have been successfully prosecuted under the **Racketeer Influenced and Corrupt Organizations (RICO) Act** of 1970. This statute attacks racketeering activities by prohibiting the investment of any funds derived from racketeering in any enterprise that is engaged in interstate commerce. In addition, the **Federal Witness Protection Program,** established under the Organized Crime Control Act of 1970, has made it easier for witnesses to testify in court by guaranteeing them a new identity, thus protecting them against revenge. There are currently 14,000 witnesses in the program.[76]

The information provided by the governmental commissions, in combination with scholarly research, has established that the structure of an organized crime group is similar to that of a Sicilian family. Family members are joined by "adopted" members; the family is then aided at the functional level by nonmember auxiliaries.[77] The use of military designations such as *caporegima* ("lieutenant") and "soldier" does not alter the fact that a criminal organization is rather more like a closely knit family business enterprise than like an army.[78] On the basis of testimony presented by Joseph Valachi in 1963, the commission's Task Force on Organized Crime was able to construct an organization chart of the typical Mafia, or Cosa Nostra, family (Figure 12.1).

Relations among the various families which

"I TAKE IT YOU'RE ALSO IN THE FEDERAL WITNESS-PROTECTION PROGRAM."

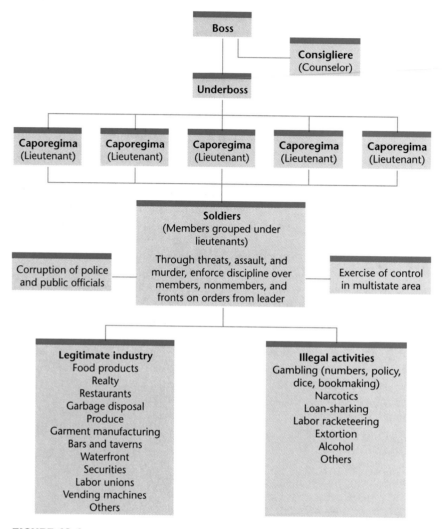

FIGURE 12.1 Organization chart of the typical Mafia family

Source: President's Commission on Law Enforcement and Administration of Justice, Task Force Report: Organized Crime (Washington, D.C.: U.S. Government Printing Office, 1967), p. 9.

were formerly determined in ruthlessly fought gang wars have more recently been facilitated by a loosely formed coordinating body called "the Commission." By agreement, the country has been divided into territorial areas of jurisdiction, influence, and operation. These arrangements are subject to revision from time to time, by mutual agreement. Likewise, rules of conduct have become subject to control or regulation by the heads of the various crime families. They consider, for example, to what extent each family should enter the hard-drug market, how much

violence should be used, and how each will deal with public officials and the police.[79]

Informants at the "convention" of the so-called Apalachin conspirators provided a rare opportunity to learn about the way crime families reach agreement on their operations. On November 14, 1957, 63 of the country's most notorious underworld figures were arrested in Apalachin, New York, at or near the home of Joseph M. Barbara, a well-known organized-crime figure. Apparently they had congregated at Barbara's home to settle a dispute among the families, which had earlier resulted in the assassination of mobster Albert Anastasio and the attempted murder of Frank Costello. None of the conspirators, however, publicly revealed the true nature of their meeting. Some suggested that, quite by coincidence, all had simply come to visit their sick friend Joe Barbara. All were indicted and convicted for refusing to answer the grand jury's questions about the true purpose of the meeting. The convictions were subsequently reversed.[80]

The activities of the Mafia appear to have shifted from the once extremely violent bootlegging and street crime operations to a far more sophisticated level of criminal activity.[81] Modern organized crime has assumed international dimensions.[82] It extends not only to international drug traffic but also to such legitimate enterprises as real estate and trade in securities, as well as to many other lucrative business enterprises. This transition has been accomplished both by extortion and by entry with laundered money derived from illegitimate activity. It is tempting to wonder whether we may be witnessing the same kind of metamorphosis that occurred a century ago, when the robber barons became legitimate business tycoons and, ultimately, philanthropists.

The New Ethnic Diversity in Organized Crime

Organized crime is not necessarily synonymous with the Mafia. Other organized-crime groups also operate in the United States. Foremost among them are the Colombian, Bolivian, Peruvian, and Jamaican crime families, which since the 1970s have organized the production, transportation, and distribution within the United States of cocaine and marijuana.

Another form of organized crime, initiated by disillusioned veterans of the Korean War and

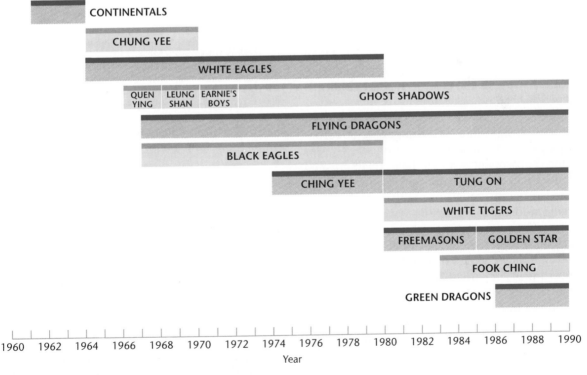

FIGURE 12.2   Time line of New York City's Chinese gangs: 1960–1990

Source: Ko-lin Chin, *Chinese Subculture and Criminality* (New York: Greenwood Press, 1990), p. 76.

reinforced by veterans of Vietnam, appears in the outlaw motorcycle gangs. Among them are the Hell's Angels, the Pagans, the Outlaws, and the Bandidos. All are organized along military lines; all are devoted to violence; all are involved in the production and distribution of narcotics and other drugs. Many members are also involved in other criminal activities, including extortion and prostitution, trafficking in stolen motorcycles and parts, and dealing in automatic weapons and explosives.

Among other organized groups engaged in various criminal activities are Chinese gangs (see Figure 12.2), the so-called Israeli Mafia, the recently emerging Russian-Jewish Mafia, and the Japanese Yakuza. All these groups have demonstrated potential for great social disruption.[83]

■ REVIEW

Organizational crimes are characterized by the use of a legitimate or illegitimate business enterprise for illegal profit. As American corporations grew in the nineteenth and twentieth centuries, they amassed much of the nation's wealth. Many corporations abused their economic power. Government stepped in to curb such abuses by legislation.

Edwin Sutherland, who provided the first scholarly insight into the wrongdoing of corporations, originated the concept of white-collar crime. Subsequent scholars have distinguished white-collar crime, committed by individuals, from corporate crime, committed by business organizations. Corporate or individual white-collar offenses include securities-related crimes, such as misrepresentation and churning; bankruptcy fraud of various kinds; fraud against the government, in particular contract and procurement fraud; consumer fraud; computer fraud; insurance fraud; tax fraud; bribery and political fraud; and insider-related fraud. In the twentieth century, corporations have been subjected to criminal liability for an increasing number of offenses, including common law crimes and environmental as well as other statutory offenses.

Organized crime got its start in this country

when Sicilian immigrants replicated their traditional family structure in organizing criminal activities in their new home. These families and their associates were so successful in controlling bootlegging, gambling, prostitution, loan-sharking, labor racketeering, drug trafficking, and other illegal enterprises that they were able to assume control of many legitimate businesses. In recent years members of other ethnic groups— Latin Americans, Jamaicans, Israelis, Russian Jews, Japanese, Chinese—have challenged the Sicilian Mafia for supremacy in organized crime.

■ NOTES

1. Steve Yozwiak, "Big Fines for Lake Powell Dumping Exceed $1.3 Million," *Arizona Republic*, May 13, 1993, p. A1.
2. Marshall B. Clinard and Peter C. Yeager, *Corporate Crime* (New York: Free Press, 1980), pp. 59–60.
3. "Mafia Chief Tied to Crime-Busting Judge's Murder," *Reuters*, Aug. 1, 1993.
4. Dwight Smith, "White-Collar Crime, Organized Crime, and the Business Establishment: Resolving a Crisis in Criminological Theory," in *White Collar and Economic Crime*, ed. Peter Whickman and Timothy Dailey (Lexington, Mass.: Lexington Books, 1982).
5. Kitty Calavita and Henry N. Pontell, "'Other People's Money' Revisited: Collective Embezzlement in the Savings and Loan and Insurance Industries," *Social Problems*, 38 (1991): 94–112; Kitty Calavita and Henry N. Pontell, "'Heads I Win, Tails You Lost': Deregulation, Crime, and Crisis in the Savings and Loan Industry," *Crime and Delinquency*, 36 (1990): 309–341.
6. P. Renfrew, "Introduction to Symposium on White Collar Crime," *Memphis State University Law Review*, 10 (1980): 416.
7. Sally S. Simpson, "Strategy, Structure, and Corporate Crime: The Historical Context of Anticompetitive Behavior," in *Advances in Criminological Theory*, vol. 4, eds. Freda Adler and William S. Laufer (New Brunswick, N.J.: Transaction, 1993), pp. 71–93.
8. Edwin H. Sutherland, "White Collar Criminality," *American Sociological Review*, 5 (1940): 1–20.
9. Gilbert Geis, *On White Collar Crime* (Lexington, Mass.: Lexington Books, 1982), p. 9.
10. Marshall B. Clinard and Richard Quinney, *Criminal Behavior Systems*, 2d ed. (New York: Holt, Rinehart & Winston, 1982); Marshall B. Clinard, *Corporate Corruption: The Abuse of Power* (Westport, Conn.: Praeger, 1990); Gilbert Geis and Paul Jesilow, eds. "White-Collar Crime," *Annals of the American Academy of Political and Social Science*, 525 (1993): 8–169; David Weisburd, Stanton Wheeler, and Elin Waring, *Crimes*

of the Middle Classes: White-Collar Offenders in the Federal Courts (New Haven, Conn.: Yale University Press, 1991); John Braithwaite, "Poverty, Power, White-Collar Crime and the Paradoxes of Criminological Theory," *Australian and New Zealand Journal of Criminology*, **24** (1991): 40–48; Frank Pearce and Laureen Snider, eds. "Crimes of the Powerful," *Journal of Human Justice*, **3** (1992): 1–124; Hazel Croall, *White Collar Crime: Criminal Justice and Criminology* (Buckingham, England, and Philadelphia, Pa.: Open University Press, 1991); Stephen J. Rackmill, "Understanding and Sanctioning the White Collar Offender," *Federal Probation* **56** (1992): 26–33; Brent Fisse, Michael Bersten, and Peter Grabosky, "White Collar and Corporate Crime," *University of New South Wales Law Journal*, **13** (1990): 1–171; Susan P. Shapiro, "Collaring the Crime Not the Criminal: Reconsidering the Concept of White-Collar Crime," *American Sociological Review*, **55** (1990): 346–365; Kip Schlegel and David Weisburd, eds. *White-Collar Crime Reconsidered* (Boston: Northeastern University Press, 1992); David Weisburd, Stanton Wheeler, Elin Waring, et al., *Crimes of the Middle Classes: White-Collar Offenders in the Federal Courts* (New Haven, Conn.: Yale University Press, 1991); David Weisburd, Ellen F. Chayet, and Elin J. Waring, "White-Collar Crime and Criminal Careers: Some Preliminary Findings," *Crime and Delinquency*, **36** (1990): 342–355; David Weisburd, Elin Waring, and Stanton Wheeler, "Class, Status, and the Punishment of White-Collar Criminals," *Law and Social Inquiry*, **15** (1990): 223–243; Lisa Maher and Elin J. Waring, "Beyond Simple Differences: White Collar Crime, Gender and Workforce Position," *Phoebe*, **2** (1990): 44–54; John Hagan and Fiona Kay, "Gender and Delinquency in White-Collar Families: A Power-Control Perspective," *Crime and Delinquency*, **36** (1990): 391–407.

11. See James W. Coleman, *The Criminal Elite: The Sociological White-Collar Crime*, 2d ed. (New York: St. Martin's Press, 1989); and Michael L. Benson and Elizabeth Moore, "Are White-Collar and Common Offenders the Same? An Empirical and Theoretical Critique of a Recently Proposed General Theory of Crime," *Journal of Research in Crime and Delinquency*, **29** (1992): 251–272.

12. Jurg Gerber and Susan L. Weeks, "Women as Victims of Corporate Crime: A Call for Research on a Neglected Topic," *Deviant Behavior*, **13** (1992): 325–347; Elizabeth Moore and Michael Mills, "The Neglected Victims and Unexamined Costs of White-Collar Crime," *Crime and Delinquency*, **36** (1990): 408–418.

13. August Bequai, *White Collar Crime: A 20th-Century Crisis* (Lexington: Mass.: Lexington Books, 1978), p. 3; Linda Ganzini, Bentson McFarland, and Joseph Bloom, "Victims of Fraud: Comparing Victims of White Collar and Violent Crime," *Bulletin of the American Academy of Psychiatry and the Law*, **18** (1990): 55–63.

14. For the relationship between patterns of crimes in the savings and loan industry and those in organized crime, see Kitty Calavita and Henry N. Pontell, "Savings and Loan Fraud as Organized Crime: Toward a Conceptual Typology of Corporate Illegality," *Criminology*, **31** (1993): 519–548.

15. Gilbert Geis, Henry N. Pontell, and Paul Jesilow, "Medicaid Fraud," in *Controversial Issues in Criminology and Criminal Justice*, eds. Joseph E. Scott and Travis Hirschi (Beverly Hills, Calif.: Sage, 1987); Maria S. Boss and Barbara Crutchfield George, "Challenging Conventional Views of White Collar Crime: Should the Criminal Justice System Be Refocused?" *Criminal Law Bulletin*, **28** (1992): 32–58.

16. For an outline of a general theory of crime causation applicable to both street crime and white-collar crime, see Travis Hirschi and Michael Gottfredson, "Causes of White-Collar Crime," *Criminology*, **25** (1987): 949–974; James W. Coleman, "Toward an Integrated Theory of White Collar Crime," *American Journal of Sociology*, **93** (1987): 406–439; and James R. Lasley, "Toward a Control Theory of White Collar Offending," *Journal of Quantitative Criminology*, **4** (1988): 347–362.

17. Donald R. Cressey, "The Poverty of Theory in Corporate Crime Research," in *Advances in Criminological Theory*, vol. 1, eds. William Laufer and Freda Adler (New Brunswick, N.J.: Transaction, 1988); for a response, see John Braithwaite and Brent Fisse, "On the Plausibility of Corporate Crime Theory," in *Advances in Criminological Theory*, vol. 2, eds. William Laufer and Freda Adler (New Brunswick, N.J.: Transaction, 1990). See also Travis Hirschi and Michael Gottfredson, "The Significance of White-Collar Crime for a General Theory of Crime," *Criminology*, **27** (1989): 359–371; and Darrell Steffensmeier, "On the Causes of 'White Collar' Crime: An Assessment of Hirschi and Gottfredson's Claims," *Criminology*, **27** (1989): 345–358.

18. Bequai, *White Collar Crime*. Bequai also includes antitrust and environmental offenses, which are corporate crimes, discussed in the next section.

19. Kenneth Polk and William Weston, "Insider Trading as an Aspect of White Collar Crime," *Australian and New Zealand Journal of Criminology*, **23** (1990): 24–38.

20. William Power, "New York Rep. Biaggi and Six Others Indicted as WedTech Scandal Greatly Expands," *Wall Street Journal*, June 4, 1987, p. 9.

21. "Annual Survey of White Collar Crime," *American Criminal Law Review*, **25** (1988): 560.

22. Robert Tillman and Henry N. Pontell, "Is Justice 'Collar-Blind'? Punishing Medicaid Provider Fraud," *Criminology*, **30** (1992): 547–574.

23. Bequai, *White Collar Crime*, pp. 70–71.

24. Peter Poerting and Ernst G. Pott, *Computer Kriminalität* (Wiesbaden: Bundeskriminalamt, 1986), p. 44.

25. General Accounting Office, *Computer-Related Crime in Federal Programs* (Washington, D.C.: U.S. Government Printing Office, 1976).

26. Poerting and Pott, *Computer Kriminalität*, pp. 24–25.

27. W. Thomas Porter, Jr., "Computer Raped by Telephone," *New York Times Magazine,* Sept. 8, 1974, p. 40.
28. Raymond L. Dirks and Leonard Gross, *The Great Wall Street Scandal* (New York: McGraw-Hill, 1974).
29. Gina Kolata, "When Criminals Turn to Computers: Is Anything Safe?" *Smithsonian,* **13** (1982): 1176–1206.
30. Richard C. Hollinger and Lonn Lanza Kaduce, "The Process of Criminalization: The Case of Computer Crime Laws," *Criminology,* **26** (1988): 101–127.
31. Poerting and Pott, *Computer Kriminalität.*
32. Andrew Tobias, *The Invisible Banker* (New York: Washington Square Press, 1982).
33. Paul E. Tracy and James A. Fox, "A Field Experiment on Insurance Fraud in Auto Body Repair," *Criminology,* **27** (1989): 589–603.
34. Kathleen F. Brickey, *Corporate Criminal Liability,* 2 vols. (Wilmette, Ill.: Callaghan, 1984).
35. Alan Murray, "IRS Is Losing Battle against Tax Evaders Despite Its New Gain," *Wall Street Journal,* Apr. 10, 1984, p. 1.
36. Ralph Salerno and John S. Tompkins, "Protecting Organized Crime," in *Theft of the City,* eds. John A. Gardiner and David Olson (Bloomington: Indiana University Press, 1984); Edwin Sutherland, *The Professional Thief* (Chicago: University of Chicago Press, 1937).
37. 18 U.S.C. [sec] 166(b) and (c).
38. Bequai, *White Collar Crime,* p. 45.
39. Ibid., p. 87.
40. John Clark and Richard Hollinger, *Theft by Employees in Work Organization* (Washington, D.C.: U.S. Government Printing Office, 1983).
41. Bequai, *White Collar Crime,* p. 89.
42. Gerhard O. W. Mueller, "Mens Rea and the Corporation: A Study of the Model Penal Code Position on Corporate Criminal Liability," *University of Pittsburgh Law Review,* **19** (1957): 21–50.
43. For a general overview of the corporate crime problem, see Francis T. Cullen, William J. Maakestad, and Gray Cavender, *Corporate Crime under Attack: The Ford Pinto Case and Beyond* (Cincinnati, Ohio: Anderson, 1987), pp. 37–99.
44. *State v. Lehigh Valley R. Co.,* 90 N.J. Law 372, 103 A. 685 (1917).
45. Model Penal Code, sec. 2.07(1) (c).
46. Sherman Antitrust Act, Act of July 2, 1890, c. 647, 26 Stat. 209, 15 U.S.C. [sec] 1–7 (1976).
47. Clayton Antitrust Act, Act of October 15, 1914, c. 322, 38 Stat. 730, 15 U.S.C. [sec] 12–27 (1976); Robinson-Patman Act, Act of June 19, 1936, c. 592, [sec] 1, 49 Stat. 1526, 15 U.S.C. [sec] 13(a) (1973). See also Kathleen F. Brickey, *Corporate Criminal Liability* 2 vols. (Wilmette, Ill.: Callaghan, 1984).
48. Phillip Knightly, Harold Evans, Elaine Potter, and Marjorie Wallace, *Suffer the Children: The Story of Thalidomide* (New York: Viking, 1979).
49. The Ford Pinto case is fully described in Cullen et al., *Corporate Crime under Attack.* For more information on crimes against consumer safety, see Raymond J. Michalowski, *Order, Law, and Crime* (New York: Random House, 1985), pp. 334–340.
50. See Russell Mokhiber, *Corporate Crime and Violence: Big Business Power and the Abuse of the Public Trust* (San Francisco: Sierra Club, 1988); Susan P. Shapiro, *Wayward Capitalists: Target of the Securities and Exchange Commission* (New Haven, Conn.: Yale University Press, 1984); M. David Ermen and Richard J. Lundman, *Corporate and Governmental Deviance: Problems of Organizational Behavior in Contemporary Society,* 2d ed. (New York: Oxford University Press, 1982); Cullen et al., *Corporate Crime under Attack;* Knightly et al., *Suffer the Children;* and W. Byron Groves and Graeme Newman, *Punishment and Privilege* (New York: Harrow & Heston, 1986).
51. Sutherland had earlier published articles on the topic, including "White Collar Criminality," *American Sociological Review,* **5** (1940): 1–12, and "Is White Collar Crime 'Crime'?" *American Sociological Review,* **10** (1945): 132–139.
52. Clinard and Yeager, *Corporate Crime,* p. 116. See also Peter C. Yeager, "Analysing Corporate Offences: Progress and Prospects," *Research in Corporate Social Performance and Policy,* **8** (1986): 93–120. For similar findings in Canada, see Colin H. Goff and Charles E. Reasons, *Corporate Crime in Canada* (Scarborough, Ontario: Prentice-Hall, 1978).
53. Richard Quinney, *Critique of Legal Order: Crime Control in Capitalist Society* (Boston: Little, Brown, 1974); Richard Quinney, *Class, State, and Crime: On the Theory and Practice of Criminal Justice* (New York: David McKay, 1977); Ian Taylor, Paul Walton, and Jock Young, *The New Criminology: For a Social Theory of Deviance* (London:: Routledge & Kegan Paul, 1973); William Chambliss and Robert Seidman, *Law, Order, and Power,* 2d ed. (Reading, Mass.: Addison-Wesley, 1982).
54. James Q. Wilson, *Thinking about Crime* (New York: Basic Books, 1975).
55. Patsy Klaus and Carol Kalish, *The Severity of Crime,* Bureau of Justice Statistics Bulletin NCJ-92326 (Washington, D.C.: U.S. Government Printing Office, 1984). See also L. Schrager and James Short, "How Serious a Crime? Perceptions of Organizational and Common Crimes," in Gilbert Geis and E. Stotland, eds. *White Collar Crime: Theory and Research* (Beverly Hills, Calif.: Sage, 1980); Francis Cullen, B. Link, and C. Polanzi, "The Seriousness of Crime Revisited," *Criminology,* **20** (1982): 83–102; Francis Cullen, R. Mathers, G. Clark, and J. Cullen, "Public Support for Punishing White Collar Crime: Blaming the Victim Revisited," *Journal of Criminal Justice,* **11** (1983): 481–493; Richard Sparks, Hazel G. Genn, and David Dodd, *Surveying Victims* (New York: Wiley, 1977).
56. Jim Mayer, "Confection Maker Indicted in Dumping," *Sacramento Bee,* July 10, 1993.
57. Mark A. Cohen, "Environmental Crime and Punishment: Legal/Economic Theory and Empirical Evidence on Enforcement of Federal Environmental Statutes," *Journal of Criminal Law and Criminology,* **82** (1992): 1054–1108.
58. Clinard and Yeager, *Corporate Crime,* p. 92, citing *New York Times* survey of July 15, 1979.

59. Gerhard O. W. Mueller, "Offenses against the Environment and Their Prevention: An International Appraisal," *Annals of the American Academy of Political and Social Science,* **444** (1979): 56–66.

60. Ibid., p. 60.

61. Ryuichi Hirano, "The Criminal Law Protection of Environment: General Report," Tenth International Congress of Comparative Law, Budapest, 1978. For a discussion of the problems of multinational corporations operating in developing countries, see Richard Schaffer, Beverly Earle, and Filiberto Agusti, *International Business Law and Its Environment* (St. Paul, Minn.: West, 2d ed., 1993). For a discussion of corporate crime in Japan, see Harold R. Kerbo and Mariko Inoue, "Japanese Social Structure and White Collar Crime: Recruit Cosmos and Beyond," *Deviant Behavior,* **11** (1990): 139–154.

62. Ibid.

63. John Braithwaite, "Challenging Just Deserts: Punishing White-Collar Criminals," *Journal of Criminal Law and Criminology,* **73** (1982): 723–763; Stanton Wheeler, David Weisburd, and Nancy Boden, "Sentencing the White-Collar Offender," *American Sociological Review,* **47** (1982): 641–659. For a thoughtful analysis of corporate illegality, see Nancy Frank and Michael Lombness, *Corporate Illegality and Regulatory Justice* (Cincinnati, Ohio: Anderson, 1988). See also William S. Laufer, "Culpability and the Sentencing of Corporations," *Nebraska Law Review,* **71** (1992): 1049–1094; Kip Schlegel, *Just Deserts for Corporate Criminals* (Boston: Northeastern University Press, 1990); and John C. Coffee, Jr., Mark A. Cohen, Jonathan R. Macey, et al., "A National Conference on Sentencing of the Corporation," *Boston University Law Review,* **71** (1991): 189–453.

64. Susan Shapiro, "Detecting Illegalities: A Perspective on the Control of Securities Violations," Ph.D. dissertation, Yale University (University Microfilms), 1980; Albert J. Reiss and Albert D. Biderman, *Data Sources on White-Collar Law-Breaking* (Washington, D.C.: National Institute of Justice, 1980); Genevra Richardson, *Policing Pollution: A Study of Regulation and Enforcement* (Oxford: Clarendon, 1982). See also Frank and Lombness, *Corporate Illegality;* Laureen Snider, "The Regulatory Dance: Understanding Reform Processes in Corporate Crime," *International Journal of the Sociology of Law,* **19** (1991): 209–236; and Sally S. Simpson and Christopher S. Koper, "Deterring Corporate Crime," *Criminology,* **30** (1992): 347–375.

65. See, e.g., Dan Magnuson, ed. *Economic Crime: Programs for Future Research* (Stockholm: National Council for Crime Prevention, 1985); Michael L. Benson, Francis T. Cullen, and William A. Maakestad, *Local Prosecutors and Corporate Crime: Final Report* (Washington, D.C.: National Institute of Justice, 1991); and Michael L. Benson, Francis T. Cullen, and William J. Maakestad, "Local Prosecutors and Corporate Crime," *Crime and Delinquency,* **36** (1990): 356–372.

66. Richard Gambino, *Blood of My Blood: The Dilemma of the Italian American* (Garden City, N.Y.: Doubleday, 1974), p. 3: Luigi Barzini, "Italians in New York: The Way We Were in 1929," *New York Magazine,* Apr. 4, 1977, p. 36; Howard Abadinsky, *Organized Crime,* 2d ed. (Chicago: Nelson Hall, 1985).

67. Abadinsky, *Organized Crime,* pp. 43–53.

68. Ibid., p. 91.

69. James Inciardi, *Careers in Crime* (Chicago: Rand McNally, 1975), p. 113; Norman Lewis, *The Honored Society: A Searching Look at the Mafia* (New York: Putnam, 1964), p. 25.

70. Abadinsky, *Organized Crime,* pp. 56–62.

71. Annelise Graebner Anderson, *The Business of Organized Crime: A Cosa Nostra Family* (Stanford, Calif.: Hoover Institution Press, 1979); Peter Maas, *The Valachi Papers* (New York: Putnam, 1968); U.S. Senate Committee on Governmental Affairs, Subcommittee on Investigations, *Organized Crime: 25 Years after Valachi* (Washington, D.C.: U.S. Government Printing Office, 1990).

72. Jay Albanese, *Organized Crime in America* (Cincinnati, Ohio: Anderson, 1985), p. 25. See also Francis A. J. Ianni, *A Family Business: Kinship and Social Control in Organized Crime* (New York: Russell Sage, 1972); Joseph Albini, *The American Mafia: Genesis of a Legend* (New York: Irvington, 1971); Merry Morash, "Organized Crime," in *Major Forms of Crime,* ed. Robert F. Meier, (Beverly Hills, Calif.: Sage, 1984), pp. 191–220.

73. For a perceptive analysis of the changing focus of the two most recent commission reports, see Jay S. Albanese, "Government Perceptions of Organized Crime: The Presidential Commissions, 1967 and 1987," *Federal Probation,* **52** (1988): 58–63.

74. Abadinsky, *Organized Crime.* See also Dwight Smith, *The Mafia Mystique* (New York: Basic Books, 1975).

75. For a discussion of predicting which legitimate businesses will be infiltrated by organized crime, see Jay S. Albanese, "Predicting the Incidence of Organized Crime: A Preliminary Model," in *Organized Crime in America: Concepts and Controversies,* ed. Timothy S. Bynum (Monsey, N.Y.: Willow Tree Press, 1987) pp. 103–114. See especially President's Commission on Law Enforcement and Administration of Justice, *Task Force Report: Organized Crime* (Washington, D.C.: U.S. Government Printing Office, 1967), p. 9.

76. Fred Montanino, "Protecting the Federal Witness," *American Behavioral Scientist,* **27** (4): 501–529; Fred Montanino, "Protecting Organized Crime Witnesses in the United States," *International Journal of Comparative and Applied Criminal Justice,* **14** (1990): 123–131.

77. Donald Cressey, *Theft of the Nation* (New York: Harper & Row, 1969).

78. Abadinsky, *Organized Crime,* pp. 8–23; Donald Cressey, in President's Commission, *Task Force Report,* pp. 7–8; Gay Talese, *Honor Thy Father* (New York: World, 1971).

79. For a discussion of violence in organized crime, see Kip Schlegel, "Violence in Organized Crime: A Content Analysis of the DeCavalcante and DeCarlo Transcripts," in Bynum, *Organized Crime in America,* pp. 55–70.

80. *United States v. Bonanno*, 180 F. Supp. 71 (S.D.N.Y. 1960), upholding the Apalachin roundup as constitutional; *United States v. Bonanno*, 177 F. Supp. 106 (S.D.N.Y. 1959), sustaining the validity of the conspiracy indictment; *United States v. Bufalino*, 285 F. 2d 408 (2d Cir. 1960), reversing the conspiracy conviction.

81. James Walston, "Mafia in the Eighties," *Violence, Aggression, and Terrorism*, **1** (1987): 13–39.

82. "New Dimensions of Criminality and Crime Prevention in the Context of Development," working paper prepared by the United Nations Secretariat, A/CONF. 121, 1985, p. 20. For a global perspective, see Robert J. Kelley, ed., *Organized Crime: A Global Perspective* (Totowa, N.J.: Rowman & Littlefield, 1986).

83. Mark Galeotti, "Organized Crime in Moscow and Russian National Security," *Low Intensity Conflict and Law Enforcement*, **1** (1992): 237–252; Joseph Serio, "Organized Crime in the Soviet Union and Beyond," *Low Intensity Conflict and Law Enforcement*, **1** (1992): 127–151; Arkady Vaksberg, *The Soviet Mafia: A Shocking Exposé of Organized Crime in the USSR* (New York: St. Martin's Press, 1991); Cyrille Fijnaut and James Jacobs, eds. *Organized Crime and Its Containment: A Transatlantic Initiative* (Deventer, Netherlands, and Boston: Kluwer Law and Taxation, 1991); Susan Flood, ed. *Illicit Drugs and Organized Crime: Issues for a Unified Europe* (Chicago: Office of International Criminal Justice, University of Illinois, 1991); Vincenzo Ruggiero and Antony A. Vass, "Heroin Use and the Formal Economy: Illicit Drugs and Licit Economies in Italy," *British Journal of Criminology*, **32** (1992): 273–291; David L. Carter, "A Forecast of Growth in Organized Crime in Europe: New Challenges for Law Enforcement," *Police Studies*, **15** (1992): 62–74; Giovanni Falcone, Edwin Kube, and G. O. W. Mueller, "Organized Crime: A World Problem . . . ," *Revue Internationale de Criminologie et de Police Technique*, **45** (1992): 389–491; James Dubro, *Dragons of Crime: Inside the Asian Underworld* (Markham, Ontario: Octopus, 1992); Michael Bersten, "Defining Organised Crime in Australia and the USA," *Australian and New Zealand Journal of Criminology*, **23** (1990): 39–59; Cyrille Fijnaut, "Organized Crime: A Comparison between the United States of America and Western Europe," *British Journal of Criminology*, **30** (1990): 321–340; Carol P. Florez and Bernadette Boyce, "Colombian Organized Crime," *Police Studies*, **13** (1990): 81–88; Frederick T. Martens, "African-American Organized Crime, an Ignored Phenomenon," *Federal Probation*, **54** (1990): 43–50; Chuen-Jim Sheu, "Nonsyndicated Organized Crime in Taipei, Taiwan," *Police Studies*, **13** (1990): 145–150; Jane Rae Buckwalter, ed., *International Perspectives on Organized Crime* (Chicago: Office of International Criminal Justice, University of Illinois, 1990); Femi Odekunle, *Towards Compensation for Victims of Organised Crime in Developing African Countries*, U.N. Asia and Far East Institute for the Prevention of Crime and the Treatment of Offenders, Resource Material Series no. 38 (Tokyo: Hiroyasu Sugihara, 1990); Hans Joachim Schneider, "Crime and Its Control in Japan and in the Federal Republic of Germany," *International Journal of Offender Therapy and Comparative Criminology*, **36** (1992): 307–321; Petrus C. van Duyne, "Organized Crime and Business Crime-Enterprises in the Netherlands," *Crime, Law and Social Change*, **19** (1993): 103–142; Gerald L. Posner, *Warlords of Crime: Chinese Secret Societies: The New Mafia* (New York: McGraw-Hill, 1988); Richard W. Slatta, *Bandidos: The Varieties of Latin American Banditry* (New York: Greenwood, 1987); Francis A. J. Ianni, "New Mafia: Black, Hispanic, and Italian Styles," *Society*, **11** (1974): 26–39; Francis A. J. Ianni, *Black Mafia: Ethnic Succession in Organized Crime* (New York: Simon & Schuster, 1974); David Gurevich, "The Mob-Today's K.G.B.," *The New York Times*, Feb. 19, 1994, p.19.

13

Drug-, Alcohol-, and Sex-Related Crime

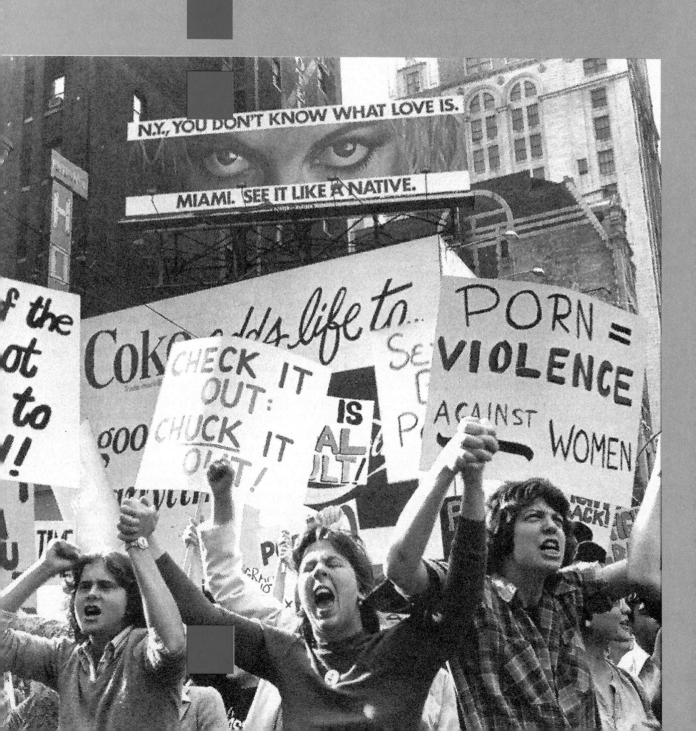

KEY TERMS
money laundering
pimp
pornography
prostitution
sodomy
statutory rape

In cities across the country and around the world, people buying and selling illicit goods and services congregate in certain areas—Times Square in New York, The Ramblas district in Barcelona, St. Pauli in Hamburg—that are easily identifiable by theater marquees advertising live sex shows. Shops feature everything from child pornography to sadomasochistic slide shows; prostitutes openly solicit clients; drunks propped up in doorways clutch brown bags; drug addicts deal small amounts of whatever they can get to sell to support their habits. The friendly locals will deliver virtually any service to visitors, for a price.

The activities involved—prostitution, drunkenness, sex acts between consenting adults for money, drug use—were commonly called "victimless" crimes. Perhaps that is because it was assumed that people who engage in them rationally choose to do so and do not view themselves as victims. Often no one complains to the police about being victimized by such consensual activity. But contemporary forms of such activities and their ramifications may entail massive victimizations: How many murders are committed during drug gang wars? How many thefts are committed by addicts seeking to support their habits? How much damage is done to persons and property by drunken drivers? Does pornography encourage physical abuse? And what of the future of children sold for prostitution?

DRUG ABUSE AND CRIME

A woman arrives at the airport in Los Angeles with very few belongings, no hotel reservations, no family or friends in the United States, and a passport showing eight recent trips from Bogotá, Colombia. A patdown and strip search reveal a firm, distended abdomen, which is discovered to hold 88 balloons filled with cocaine.[1] In New York City a heroin addict admits that "the only livin' thing that counts is the fix . . . : Like I would steal off anybody—anybody, at all, my own mother gladly included."[2] In Chicago, crack cocaine has transformed some of the country's toughest gangs into ghetto-based drug-trafficking organizations that guard their turf with automatic weapons and assault rifles.[3]

On a college campus in the Northeast a crowd sits in the basement of a fraternity house drinking beer and smoking pot through the night. At a beachfront house in Miami three young professional couples gather for a barbecue. After dinner they sit down at a card table in the playroom. On a mirror, someone lines up a white powdery substance into rows about ⅛-inch wide and an inch long. Through rolled-up paper they breathe the powder into their nostrils and await the "rush" of the coke.

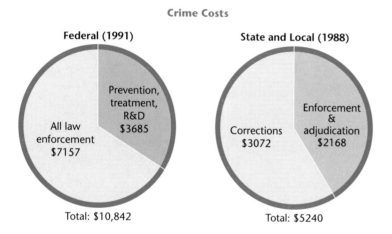

Crime Costs

Federal (1991)

Prevention, treatment, R&D $3685

All law enforcement $7157

Total: $10,842

State and Local (1988)

Enforcement & adjudication $2168

Corrections $3072

Total: $5240

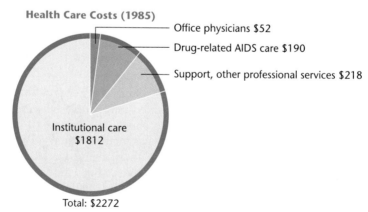

Health Care Costs (1985)

Office physicians $52
Drug-related AIDS care $190
Support, other professional services $218

Institutional care $1812

Total: $2272

FIGURE 13.1   Costs of illegal drug use (in millions)*

* Detail may not add to total due to rounding. Costs should not be summed because the methodologies and years differ.

Source: The federal drug expenditure data are from The White House. ONDCP, *National Drug Control Strategy,* budget summary, January 1992, pp. 212–214. The state and local justice expenditure estimates are from BJS, Justice Expenditure and Employment Survey, 1988, unpublished data. All other estimates are from ADAMHA. Dorothy P. Rice, Sander Kelman, Leonard S. Miller, and Sarah Dunmeyer, *The Economic Costs of Alcohol and Drug Abuse and Mental Illness: 1985,* 1990. From U.S. Department of Justice, *Drugs, Crime and the Justice System* (Washington, D.C.: U.S. Government Printing Office, 1992), p. 126.

TABLE 13.1 ROLES AND FUNCTIONS IN THE DRUG DISTRIBUTION BUSINESS COMPARED WITH THOSE IN LEGITIMATE INDUSTRY

Approximate Role Equivalents in Legal Markets	Roles by Common Names at Various Stages of the Drug Distribution Business	Major Functions Accomplished at This Level
Grower producer	Coca farmer, opium farmer, marijuana grower	Grow coca, opium, marijuana; the raw materials
Manufacturer	Collector, transporter, elaborator, chemist, drug lord	All stages for preparation of heroin, cocaine, marijuana as commonly sold
Traffickers		
Importer	Multikilo importer, mule, airplane pilot, smuggler, trafficker, money launderer	Smuggling of large quantities of substances into the U.S.
Wholesale distributor	Major distributor, investor, "kilo connection"	Transportation and redistribution of multikilograms and single kilograms
Dealers		
Regional distributor	Pound and ounce men, weight dealers	Adulteration and sale of moderately expensive products
Retail store owner	House connections, suppliers, crack-house supplier	Adulteration and production of retail-level dosage units (bags, vials, grams) in very large numbers
Assistant manager, security chief, or accountant	"Lieutenant," "muscle men," transporter, crew boss, crack-house manager/proprietor	Supervises three or more sellers, enforces informal contracts, collects money, distributes multiple dosage units to actual sellers
Sellers		
Store clerk, salesmen (door-to-door and phone)	Street drug seller, runner, juggler	Makes actual direct sales to consumer; private seller responsible for both money and drugs
Low-level distributors		
Advertiser, security guards, leaflet distributor	Steerer, tout, cop man, look-out, holder runner, help friend, guard, go-between	Assists in making sales, advertises, protects seller from police and criminals, solicits customers; handles drugs or money but not both
Servant, temporary employee	Run shooting gallery, injector (of drugs), freebaser, taster, apartment cleaner, drug bagger, fence, launder money	Provides short-term services to drug users or sellers for money or drugs; not responsible for money or drugs

Source: Bruce D. Johnson, Terry Williams, Kojo A. Dir, and Harry Sanabria, "Drug Abuse in the Inner City: Inpact on Hard-Drug Users and the Community," in Drugs and Crime, vol. 13: Crime and Justice, ed. Michael Tonry and James Q. Wilson. (Chicago: University of Chicago Press, 1990), p. 19. © 1990 by the University of Chicago Press. All rights reserved. From U.S. Department of Justice, Drugs, Crime and the Justice System (Washington, D.C.: U.S. Government Printing Office, 1992).

These incidents demonstrate that when we speak of the "drug problem," we are talking about a wide variety of conditions that stretch beyond our borders, that involve all social classes, that in one way or another touch most people's lives, and that cost society significant sums of money (Figure 13.1). The drug scene includes manufacturers, importers, primary distributors (for large geographical areas), smugglers (who transport large quantities of drugs from their place of origin), dealers (who sell drugs on the street and in crack houses), corrupt criminal justice officials, users who endanger other people's lives through negligence (train engineers, pilots, physicians), and even unborn children (see Table 13.1). The drug problem is

An opium den in New York City's Chinatown, April 12, 1926.

further complicated by the wide diversity of substances abused, their varying effects on the mind and body, and the kinds of dependencies users develop. There is also the much-debated issue of the connection between drug use and crime—an issue infinitely more complex than the stereotype of a maddened addict committing heinous acts under the influence of drugs or to get the money to support a habit. Many of the crimes we have discussed in earlier chapters are part of what has been called the nation's (or the world's) drug problem. Let us examine this problem in detail.

The History of Drug Abuse

The use of chemical substances that alter physiological and psychological functioning dates back to the Old Stone Age.[4] Egyptian relics from 3500 B.C. depict the use of opium in religious rituals. By 1600 B.C. an Egyptian reference work listed opium as an analgesic, or painkiller. The Incas of South America are known to have used cocaine at least 5000 years ago. Cannabis, the hemp plant from which marijuana and hashish are derived, also has a 5000-year history.[5]

Since antiquity, people have cultivated a variety of drugs for religious, medicinal, and social purposes. The modern era of drug abuse in th United States began with the use of drugs fo medicinal purposes. By the nineteenth century the two components of opium, which is derived from the sap of the opium poppy, were identified and given the names "morphine" and "codeine." Ignorant of the addictive properties of these drugs, physicians used them to treat a wide variety of human illnesses. So great was their popularity that they found their way into almost all patent medicines used for pain relief and were even incorporated in soothing syrups for babies (Mother Barley's Quieting Syrup and Mumm's Elixir were very popular).

During the Civil War the use of injectable morphine to ease the pain of battle casualties was so extensive that morphine addiction among veterans came to be known as "the soldier's disease."[6] By the time the medical profession and the public recognized just how addictive morphine was, its use had reached epidemic proportions. Then in 1898 the Bayer company in Germany introduced a new opiate, supposedly a nonaddictive substitute for morphine and codeine. It came out under the trade name Heroin, yet it proved to be even more addictive than morphine.[7]

When cocaine, which was isolated from the

coca leaf in 1860, appeared on the national drug scene, it too was used for medicinal purposes. (Its use to unblock the sinuses initiated the "snorting" of cocaine into the nostrils.) Its popularity spread, and soon it was used in other products: Peruvian Wine of Coca ($1 a bottle in the Sears, Roebuck catalog), a variety of tonics, and, the most famous of all, Coca-Cola, which was made with coca until 1903.[8]

As the consumption of opium products (narcotics) and cocaine spread, states passed a variety of laws to restrict the sale of these substances. Federal authorities estimated that there were 200,000 addicts in the early 1900s. Growing concern over the increase in addiction led in 1914 to the passage of the Harrison Act, designed to regulate the domestic use, sale, and transfer of opium and coca products. Though this legislation decreased the number of addicts, it was a double-edged sword: by restricting the importation and distribution of drugs, it paved the way for the drug smuggling and black-market operations that are so deeply entrenched today.

It was not until the 1930s that the abuse of marijuana began to arouse public concern. Because marijuana use was associated with groups outside the social mainstream—petty criminals, jazz musicians, bohemians, and, in the Southwest, Mexicans—a public outcry for its regulation arose.[9] Congress responded with the Marijuana Tax Act of 1937, which placed a prohibitive tax of $100 an ounce on the drug. With the passage of the Boggs Act in 1951, penalties for possession of and trafficking in marijuana (and other controlled substances) increased. Despite all the legislation, the popularity of marijuana continued.

As the drugs being used proliferated to include glue, tranquilizers (such as Valium and Librium), LSD, and many others, the public became increasingly aware of the dangers of drug abuse. In 1970 another major drug law, the Comprehensive Drug Abuse Prevention and Control Act (the Controlled Substances Act), updated all federal drug laws since the Harrison Act.[10] This act placed marijuana in the category of the most serious substances. The 1970 federal legislation made it necessary to bring state legislation into conformity with federal law. The Uniform Controlled Substances Act was drafted and

now is the law in 48 states, the District of Columbia, Puerto Rico, the Virgin Islands, and Guam.

Most of the basic federal antidrug legislation has been drawn together in Title 21 of the United States Code, the collection of all federal laws. It includes many amendments passed since 1970, especially the Anti-Drug Abuse Act of 1988, which states: "It is the declared policy of the United States Government to create a drug-free America by 1995."[11]

Title 21, as amended, has elaborate provisions for the funding of national and international drug programs; establishes the Office of National Drug Control Policy, headed by a so-called drug czar; and provides stiff penalties for drug offenses. The manufacture, distribution, and dispensing of listed substances in stated (large) quantities are each subject to a prison sentence of from 10 years to life and a fine (for individuals) of from $4 to $10 million. Even simple possession now carries a punishment of up to 1 year in prison and a $100,000 fine. Title 21, along with other recent crime-control legislation, defines many other drug crimes as well and provides for the forfeiture of any property constituting or derived from the proceeds of drug trading. (See Table 13.2.)

The Extent of Drug Abuse

Historically, the substance (other than alcohol) most frequently abused in the United States has been marijuana. In annual surveys, high school seniors were asked whether they ever used marijuana. Between 1975 and 1991, the percentage answering yes ranged from a high of 51 percent in 1979 to a low of 37 percent in 1991. The survey also found that in 1991 24 percent had used marijuana in the past year, and 14 percent in the past month.[12]

A national household survey that measured drug use among the American population ages 18 to 25 in 1991 estimated that 13 percent had used marijuana, 1 percent hallucinogens, and 2 percent cocaine.[13] Among other frequently used psychoactive drugs are amphetamines, barbiturates, LSD, cocaine, hashish, tranquilizers, codeine, methadone, and heroin.

In the 1980s cocaine constituted the country's major drug problem. An estimated 22 million

TABLE 13.2   FOUR MAJOR ANTIDRUG BILLS, 1980–1990

The 1984 Crime Control Act

- Expanded criminal and civil asset forfeiture laws
- Amended the Bail Reform Act to target pretrial detention of defendants accused of serious drug offenses
- Established a determinate sentencing system
- Increased federal criminal penalties for drug offenses

The 1986 Anti-Drug Abuse Act

- Budgeted money for prevention and treatment programs, giving the programs a larger share of federal drug-control funds than previous laws
- Restored mandatory prison sentences for large-scale distribution of marijuana
- Imposed new sanctions on money laundering
- Added controlled substances' analogs (designer drugs) to the drug schedule
- Created a drug law enforcement grant program to assist state and local efforts
- Contained various provisions designed to strengthen international drug-control efforts

The 1988 Anti-Drug Abuse Act

- Increased penalties for offenses related to drug trafficking, created new federal offenses and regulatory requirements, and changed criminal procedures
- Altered the organization and coordination of federal antidrug efforts
- Increased treatment and prevention efforts aimed at reduction of drug demand
- Endorsed the use of sanctions aimed at drug users to reduce the demand for drugs
- Targeted for reduction of drug production abroad and international trafficking in drugs

The Crime Control Act of 1990

- Doubled the appropriations authorized for drug law enforcement grants to states and localities
- Expanded drug-control and education programs aimed at the nation's schools
- Expanded specific drug enforcement assistance to rural states
- Expanded regulation of precursor chemicals used in the manufacture of illegal drugs
- Provided additional measures aimed at seizure and forfeiture of drug-trafficker assets
- Sanctioned anabolic steroids under the Controlled Substances Act
- Included provisions on international money laundering, rural drug enforcement, drug-free school zones, drug paraphernalia, and drug enforcement grants

Source: U.S. Department of Justice, Drugs, Crime and the Justice System (Washington, D.C.: U.S. Government Printing Office, 1992).

people had tried the substance, and another 4 million were using it regularly.[14] The use of heroin is much less pervasive; the number of users is estimated to be about 250,000.[15] Newer drugs on the market are crack (a derivative of cocaine) and the so-called *designer drugs*—substances that have been chemically altered in such a way that they no longer fall within the legal definition of controlled substances.[16] It is difficult to measure how many people abuse drugs in any given period. The national household survey has shown a decline in the use of illicit drugs between 1974 and 1991 of those persons between 18 and 25 years old (Figure 13.2). The most recent data, monitoring the future, however, demonstrate that once again drug abuse among high school students is increasing.[17]

Patterns of Drug Abuse

New and more potent varieties of illicit substances, as well as increasing levels of violent crime associated with drug abuse, have led researchers to ask many questions about the phenomenon. Is drug abuse a symptom of an underlying mental or psychological disorder that makes some people more vulnerable than others? Some investigators argue that the addict is characterized by strong dependency needs, feelings of inadequacy, a need for immediate gratification, and lack of internal controls.[18] Or is it possible that addicts lack certain body chemicals and that drugs make them feel better by compensating for this deficit?

Perhaps the causes are environmental. Is drug

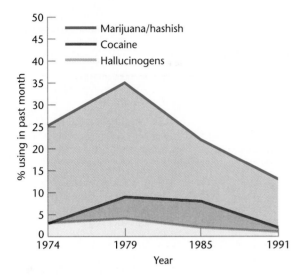

FIGURE 13.2 Declining use of illicit drugs and alcohol, ages 18–25, 1974–1991

Source: National Institute on Drug Abuse, *National Household Survey on Drug Abuse: Main Findings, 1990*, 1991, table 2.11, and *National Household Survey on Drug Abuse: Population Estimates, 1991*, 1991. From U.S. Department of Justice, *Drugs, Crime and the Justice System* (Washington, D.C.: U.S. Government Printing Office, 1992), p. 31.

abuse a norm in deteriorated inner cities, where youngsters are learning how to behave from older addicted role models? Do people escape from the realities of slum life by retreating into drug abuse?[19] If so, how do we explain drug abuse among the upper classes?

Just as there are many causes of drug abuse, there are many addict lifestyles—and the lifestyles may be linked to the use of particular substances. During the 1950s, heroin abuse began to increase markedly in the inner cities, particularly among young black and Hispanic males.[20] In fact, it was their drug of choice throughout the 1960s and early 1970s. Heroin addicts spend their days buying heroin, finding a safe place to "shoot" the substance into a vein with a needle attached to a hypodermic syringe, waiting for the euphoric feeling, or "rush," that follows the injection, and ultimately reaching a feeling of overall well-being known as a "high," which lasts about 4 hours.[21] The heroin abuser's lifestyle is typically characterized by poor health, crime, arrest, imprisonment, and temporary stays in drug treatment programs.[22] Today AIDS, which is spread, among other ways, by the shared use of needles, has become the most serious health problem among heroin addicts.

During the 1960s marijuana became one of the major drugs of choice in the United States, particularly among white, middle-class young people who identified themselves as antiestablishment. Their lifestyles were distinct from those of the inner-city heroin addicts. What began as a hippie drug culture in the Haight-Ashbury area of San Francisco spread quickly through the country's college campuses.[23] In fact, a Harvard psychologist, Timothy Leary, traveled across the country in the 1960s telling students to "turn on, tune in, and drop out." Young marijuana users tended to live for the moment. Disillusioned by what they perceived as a rigid and hypocritical society, they challenged its norms through deviant behavior. Drugs—first marijuana, then hallucinogens (principally LSD), amphetamines, and barbiturates—came to symbolize the counterculture.[24]

In the 1960s and 1970s, attitudes toward recreational drug use became quite lax, perhaps as a result of the wide acceptance of marijuana.[25] By the 1980s, cocaine, once associated only with deviants, had become the drug of choice among the privileged, who watched (and copied) the well-publicized drug-oriented lifestyles of some celebrities and athletes. Typical cocaine users were well-educated, prosperous, upwardly mobile professionals in their twenties and thirties. They were lawyers and architects, editors and stockbrokers. They earned enough money to spend at least $100 an evening on their illegal recreational activities. By and large they were otherwise law-abiding, even though they knew their behavior was against the law.

The popularity of cocaine waned toward the end of the 1980s. The same is not true for crack, however, which spread to the inner-city population that had abused heroin in the latter part of the 1980s.[26] Crack is cheaper than powdered cocaine, fast-acting, and powerful. Though individual doses are inexpensive, once a person is hooked on crack a daily supply can run between $100 and $250.

Drug addicts continually search for a new way to extend their high. In 1989 a mixture of crack and heroin, called "crank," began to be used. Crank is smoked in a pipe.[27] It is potentially very dangerous, first, because it prolongs the brief high of crack alone and, second, because it appeals to younger drug addicts who are con-

CRIMINOLOGICAL FOCUS
The Small World of Crack Users

Interviews with crack users and dealers in Detroit in the late 1980s gave investigators "insider information" on the crack culture. The researchers' report is excerpted here:

In Detroit, distribution of crack ordinarily takes place indoors; very few sales occur on the street. . . . [T]he "dope house" or "crack house" is, by a wide margin, the primary retailing mechanism.

Anecdotal information from [our] interviews showed contrasting descriptions of sale places. Some were of the "buy, get high, and party" variety, but others were strictly (and literally) "holes in the wall." A house would have a small aperture into which the customer puts his money. A few moments pass, and then a hand materializes and deposits the crack.

"Touters" are circulating salespeople who generally are also users. The "other" category . . . generally meant, to survey respondents, users who gratuitously shared their drugs with friends. "Street" sales are generally made by "runners," "rollers," or "beeper-men"—low-level retail dealers who may or may not also use the drugs they sell.

We asked the 30 respondents who admitted to dealing to characterize their own "style" of selling. Did they sell to support their own use, or mostly for profit? Were they largely "go-betweens" (touters), often accepting drugs as payment, or a combination of touter and profit-dealer? Two-thirds of those who had sold crack most frequently chose the "user-dealer" description. Twenty percent said they sold mainly for profit, and the remainder acted as touters. Of the 116 respondents who admitted they were crack users, 89 denied *any* crack-dealing activity.

Ten of the informants discussed in some detail the process of preparing crack from granular cocaine. Some said they processed as much as 1 or 2 ounces, or as little as half a gram; those who processed larger quantities tended to work toward selling enough "rock" to cover their own use costs. Some entertained ideas of profitable returns on their investment. A popular unit of transaction reported was the "eightball," which is equivalent to between 2.5 and 3.5 grams of powder cocaine. It retailed from $125 to $250 and was expected to yield 45 to 55 "rocks," which could be retailed at prices from $10 to $15.

Currently we have compiled, from the interviews, a list of more than 100 street terms for crack. These terms reflect both generic names (rock, boulder) and brand names ("Schoolcraft," "Troop," etc.). In addition to these descriptive terms, a series of number designations is also used to characterize certain methods of crack consumption. Crack crushed and sprinkled into a tobacco cigarette is referred to as a "51" or "501" or sometimes a "151."

The popularization of certain terms tells us something of the world view of the drug users and sellers themselves. For instance, the terms may reflect technologies used or believed to be used in processing. Informants have used the terms "ether-based," "synthetic," and "chemical" in describing crack types. A small number of "brand name" designations have been developed and used by particular distribution organizations. Examples of such terms include "eye-opener," "swell up," "speed," "Pony," "Eastside Player," and "Wrecking Crew."

Source: Tom Miecykowski, "Understanding Life in the Crack Culture: The Investigative Utility of the Drug Use Forecasting System," NIJ Reports, December 1989, pp. 7–9.

Questions for Discussion

1. How can information such as that presented above help police officers and other investigators work to solve the drug problem?
2. How quickly do you think the kinds of data collected for the above report become out of date and useless? Would you expect the crack culture to be relatively stable or in a constant state of flux?

A crack house in the South Bronx.

cerned about the link between AIDS and the sharing of hypodermic needles. The history of drug abuse suggests that crank, too, will be replaced by yet another substance that promises a better and faster high.

Crime-Related Activities

Many researchers have examined the criminal implications of addiction to heroin and, more recently, cocaine. James Inciardi found that 356 addicts in Miami, according to self-reports, committed 118,134 offenses (27,464 Index crimes) over a 1-year period.[28] A national program, Drug Use Forecasting, found that in 1992 47 to 78 percent of arrestees in 24 major U.S. cities had used drugs. Cocaine is the most prevalent drug used.[29] Official statistics on "drug-related offenses" make it quite clear that street crime is significantly related to drug abuse.

The nature of the drug–crime relationship, however, is less clear. Is the addict typically an adolescent who never committed a crime before he or she became hooked but who thereafter was forced to commit crimes to get money to support the drug habit? In other words, does drug abuse lead to crime?[30] Or does criminal behavior precede drug abuse? Another possibility is that both drug abuse and criminal behavior stem from the same factors (biological, psychological, or sociological).[31] The debate continues, and many questions are still unanswered. But on one point most researchers agree: whatever the temporal or causal sequence of drug abuse and crime, the frequency and seriousness of criminality increase as addiction increases. Drug abuse may not "cause" criminal behavior, but it does enhance it.[32]

Until the late 1970s most investigators of the drug–crime relationship reported that drug abusers were arrested primarily for property offenses. Recent scholarly literature, however, presents a different perspective. There appears to be an increasing amount of violence associated with drugs, and it may be attributable largely to the appearance of crack. Drug wars, for example, are becoming more frequent. Cities across the country have been divided into distinct turfs. Rival drug dealers settle disputes with guns, power struggles within a single drug enterprise lead to assaults and homicides, one dealer robs another, informers are killed, their associates

retaliate, and bystanders, some of them children, get caught in the cross-fire.[33]

The International Drug Economy

The drug problem is a worldwide phenomenon, beyond the power of any one government to deal with.[34] Nor are drugs simply a concern of law enforcement agencies. Drugs influence politics, international relations, peace and war, and the economies of individual countries and of the entire world. Let us take a brief look at the political and economic impact of the international drug trade, specifically as it concerns cocaine, heroin, and marijuana. Figure 13.3 shows the sources of these drugs and some shipping routes.

Cocaine

Today the largest cocaine producer is Peru. In 1990 a harvest of 226,000 to 282,000 metric tons of coca leaves yielded from 412 to 524 tons of pure cocaine. Bolivia is not far behind, with a yield of 111 to 153 tons.[35] Colombia, which produces only 25 tons of pure cocaine, exports more than any other country—over half of the world's supply— because it is in Colombia that much of the raw coca of Peru and Bolivia is refined into cocaine. The "cocaine cartel," which controls production and distribution, is said to be composed of no more than 12 families, located principally in Colombia and Bolivia. However, organized-crime interests in other South American countries are establishing themselves in the market.

Each year nearly half of all cocaine seized was being shipped to the United States on private planes. Small planes evade controls and land on little-used airstrips or drop their cargos offshore to waiting speedboats.[36] Boats carrying drugs then mingle with local pleasure craft and bring the cargo to shore. Wholesalers who work for the Colombian cartels take care of the nationwide distribution. Some of the estimated 100,000 Colombians living illegally in the United States are thought to belong to the distribution apparatus.

Heroin

According to intelligence estimates, nearly half of all heroin available on American streets comes from southwest Asian countries, the so-called Golden Crescent of Iran, Afghanistan, and

FIGURE 13.3   Drug pipelines to the United States

Pakistan. In 1990 Afghanistan produced between 800 and 1000 metric tons of opium; Iran, 200 to 400 tons; and Pakistan, 125 to 200 tons. More heroin comes from the so-called Golden Triangle countries of Southeast Asia—Myanmar (formerly Burma) (2000 to 2250 tons), Thailand (40 to 50), Laos (315 to 400), Cambodia, and Vietnam.

Production in these countries is organized by local warlords, illegitimate traders, and corrupt administrators; it is tending to come increasingly under the control of *triads*—organized-crime families of Chinese origin based in Hong Kong

and Taiwan. More and more, heroin in the United States comes from Mexico. Most of the heroin from the Golden Crescent and Golden Triangle enters the United States on commercial aircraft, whereas Mexican heroin comes overland. In Europe and in the United States the traditional Sicilian Mafia families have assumed significant roles in the refining and distribution of heroin.

Marijuana

Because marijuana is bulky, smugglers initially transported it on oceangoing vessels. From January through October 1986, 87 percent of the total volume of marijuana seized was taken from privately owned pleasure craft or charter vessels not engaged in commercial trade. Today, most of the Colombian marijuana—about one-third of all marijuana imported into the United States—is shipped by sea. Mexican marijuana, trucked overland, makes up another third, and the remainder comes in by private plane from such countries as Belize and Jamaica. Hashish, a concentrated form of marijuana that comes predominantly from Pakistan (60 to 65 percent) and Lebanon (25 to 30 percent), is brought in by noncommercial ships.

Money Laundering

The illegal drug economy is vast. Annual sales are estimated to be between $300 and $500 billion. The American drug economy alone generates $40 to $50 billion in sales. Profits are enormous, and no taxes are paid on them. Because the profits are "dirty money," they must undergo a **money laundering** process. Typically, the cash obtained from drug sales in the United States is physically smuggled out of the country because it cannot be legally exported without disclosure. (See Table 13.3.)

Smuggling cash is not easy—$1 million in $20 bills weighs 100 pounds—yet billions of dollars are exported, in false-bottomed suitcases and smugglers' vests, to countries that allow numbered bank accounts without identification of names (the Cayman Islands, Panama, Switzerland, Austria, and Liechtenstein, among others).

New methods of "laundering" drug profits, not involving physical transfer of cash, have recently been invented, such as bogus real estate transactions and purchases of gold, antiques, and art. Such transactions permit electronic transfer of drug funds worldwide with minimum chance of detection. Once deposited in foreign accounts, the funds are "clean" and can be returned to legitimate businesses and investments. They may also be used for illegal purposes, such as the purchase of arms for export to terrorist groups.

The Political Impact

The political impact of the drug trade on producer countries is devastating. In the late 1970s

A U.S. Coast Guard law enforcement detachment removing four tons of smuggled marijuana from a vessel.

TABLE 13.3

La Mina, The Mine, reportedly laundered $1.2 billion for the Colombian cartels over a 2-year period.

Currency from selling cocaine was packed in boxes labeled jewelry and sent by armored car to Ropex, a jewelry maker in Los Angeles.

↓

The cash was counted and deposited in banks that filed the CTRs, but few suspicions were raised because the gold business is based on cash.

↓

Ropex then wire-transferred the money to New York banks in payment for fictitious gold purchased from Ronel, allegedly a gold bullion business.

↓

Ronel shipped Ropex bars of lead painted gold to complete the fake transaction. Ropex used the alleged sale of this gold to other jewelry businesses to cover further currency conversions.

↓

Ronel then transferred the funds from American banks to South American banks where the Colombian cartel could gain access to them.

Source: "Getting Banks to Just Say 'No,'" Business Week, Apr. 17, 1989, p. 17, and Maggie Mahar, "Dirty Money: it Triggers a Bold New Attack in the War on Drugs," Barron's, 69 (June 1989): 6–38, at p.7. From the U.S. Department of Justice, Drugs, Crime and the Justice System (Washington, D.C.: U.S. Government Printing Office, 1992).

and early 1980s, the government of Bolivia became completely corrupt. The minister of justice was referred to as the "minister of cocaine." In Colombia, drug lords and terrorists combined their resources to wrest power from the democratically elected government. Thirteen Supreme Court judges and 167 police officers were killed; the minister of justice and the ambassador to Hungary were assassinated.

The message was that death was the price for refusal to succumb to drug corruption. In 1989 a highly respected Colombian presidential candidate who had come out against the cocaine cartel was assassinated. The government remained fragile and the situation precarious. But in December 1993 the Colombian government scored a major success when its security forces killed the preeminent drug exporter, Pablo Escobar, in a shootout in Medellín, Colombia. Colombia's problems have eased but are not over; it has the powerful Cali cartel to deal with. Nor is Colombia alone in its efforts to cope with the drug problem. Before General Manuel Noriega was arrested in a U.S. invasion of Panama to face charges of drug smuggling, he had made himself military dictator of Panama.

Corruption and crime rule in all drug-producing countries. Government instability is the necessary consequence. Coups replace elections. The populations of these countries are not immune to addiction themselves. Several South American countries, including Colombia, Bolivia, and Peru, are now experiencing major addiction problems; Peru alone has some 60,000 addicts. The Asian narcotics-producing countries, which thought themselves immune to the addiction problem, also became victims of their own production. Pakistan now counts about 200,000 addicts.[37]

One of the more remarkable aspects of the expansion of the drug trade has been the spread of addiction and the drug economy to the Third World and to the newly democratic, formerly socialist countries. Of all political problems, however, the most vicious is the alliance that drug dealers have forged with terrorist groups in the Near East, in Latin America, and in Europe.[38]

Drug Control

In September 1989 President George Bush unveiled his antidrug strategy. On the international level, the president sought modest funding for the United Nations effort to combat the international narcotic drug traffic. He also called for far greater expenditures for bilateral cooperation with other countries to deal with producers and traffickers. This effort extends to crop eradication programs.[39] He singled out Colombia, Bolivia, and Peru for such efforts and immediately sent U.S. Army assistance, including helicopters and crews, to Colombia for use in that country's very difficult battle with the Medellín cartel.

On the national level, the strategy focused on federal aid to state and local police for street-level attacks on drug users and small dealers, for whom alternative punishments such as house arrest (confinement in one's home rather in a jail cell) and boot camps (short but harsh incarceration with military drill) were started. It also called for rigorous enforcement of forfeiture laws, under which money is confiscated from offenders if it can be established that it came from the drug trade; property purchased with such money is also forfeited.[40] The Bush war on drugs followed a host of federal drug-control initiatives. All of them, like the Bush administration initiatives, have been at best only slightly effective.[41]

The Bush plan continued the American emphasis on law enforcement options for drug control. Treatment and prevention received only a fraction of the money allocated to traditional law enforcement efforts throughout the 1980s and early 1990s. The Clinton administration's approach, unveiled on Feburary 9, 1994, earmarks $13 billion for a national strategy that emphasizes anti-drug education as well as treatment programs. Yet most of the budget remains allocated to drug law enforcement.

A nurse at the Interim Clinic in Harlem watches as an addict takes methadone as treatment for heroin addiction.

Treatment

The treatment approach to drug control is not new. During the late 1960s and into the 1970s, hope for the country's drug problem centered on treatment programs. These programs took a variety of forms, depending on the setting and modality, for example, self-help groups (Narcotics Anonymous, Cocaine Anonymous), psychotherapy, detoxification ("drying out" in a hospital), "rap" houses (neighborhood centers where addicts can come for group therapy sessions), various community social-action efforts (addicts clean up neighborhoods, plant trees, and so on), and—the two most popular—residential therapeutic communities and methadone maintenance programs.[42]

The *therapeutic community* is a 24-hour, total-care facility where former addicts and professionals work together to help addicts become drug-free. In *methadone maintenance* programs, addicts are given a synthetic narcotic, methadone, which prevents withdrawal symptoms (physical and psychological pain associated with giving up drugs), while addicts reduce their drug intake slowly over a period of time. Throughout the program addicts receive counseling designed to help them return to a normal life.

It is difficult to assess the success of most treatment programs. Even if individuals appear to be drug-free within a program, it is hard to find out what happens to them once they leave it (or even during a week when they do not show up). In addition, it may well be that the addicts who succeed in drug treatment programs are those who have already resolved to stop abusing drugs before they voluntarily come in for treatment; the real hard-core users may not even make an effort to become drug-free.

The latest effort to divert drug offenders (users and purchasers) from criminal careers is a Dade County, Florida, "Drug Court" program. The drug court judge has the option to divert nonviolent drug offenders to a counseling program in lieu of incarceration. Of the 4,500 drug users diverted into the program since 1989, only 11 percent have been rearrested for the commission of any criminal offense in the year following dismissal of the original charges.[43]

Education

While drug treatment deals with the problem of addiction after the fact, education tries to prevent people from taking illegal drugs in the first place. The idea behind educational programs is straightforward: People who have information about the harmful effects of illegal drugs are likely to stay away from them. Sometimes the presentation of the facts has been coupled with scare techniques. Some well-known athletes and entertainers have joined the crusade with public service messages ("a questionable approach," says Howard Abadinsky, "given the level of substance abuse reported in these groups").[44]

The educational approach has several drawbacks. Critics maintain that most addicts are quite knowledgeable about the potential consequences of taking drugs but think of them as just a part of the "game."[45] Most people who begin to use drugs believe they will never become addicted, even when they have information about addiction.[46] Inner-city youngsters do not lack information about the harmful effects of drugs. They learn about the dangers from daily exposure to addicts desperately searching for drugs, sleeping on the streets, going through withdrawal, and stealing family belongings to get money.[47]

Legalization

Despite earlier increases in government funding for an expanded war on drugs, the goal of a drug-free society in the 1990s is hardly likely to be achieved. There is much evidence that all the approaches, even the "new" ones, have been tried before with little or no effect. Some experts are beginning to advocate a very different approach—legalization. Their reasoning is that since the drug problem seems to elude all control efforts, why not deal with heroin and cocaine the same way we deal with alcohol and tobacco? In other words, why not subject these drugs to some government control and restrictions, but make them freely available to all adults?[48]

They argue that current drug-control policies impose tremendous costs on taxpayers without demonstrating effective results. In addition to spending less money on crime control, the government would make money on tax revenue from the sale of legalized drugs. This is, of course, a hotly debated issue. Given the dangers of drug abuse and the moral issues at stake, legalization surely offers no easy solution and has had little public support. However, the Surgeon General of the United States, in 1994, mentioned the option of legalization—only to be rebuffed by the President. Figure 13.4 shows the history of public opinion on legalizing marijuana over the past two decades.

ALCOHOL AND CRIME

Alcohol is another substance that contributes to social problems. One of the major differences between alcohol and the other drugs we have been discussing is that the sale and purchase of alcohol are legal in most jurisdictions of the United States. The average annual consumption of alcoholic beverages by each individual 14 years of age and over is equivalent to 591 cans of beer, or 115 bottles of wine, or 35 fifths of liquor; this is more than the average individual consumption of coffee and milk.[49] Alcohol is consumed at recreational events, business meetings, lunches and dinners at home, and celebrations; in short, drinking alcohol has become the expected behavior in many social situations.

Drinking is widespread among young people. Lloyd D. Johnston, Patrick M. O'Malley, and Jerald G. Bachman asked students at 75 high schools in 7 states how many times during the last month (excluding religious services) they had consumed any beer, wine, or liquor. The responses showed that by age 15 the majority of boys and

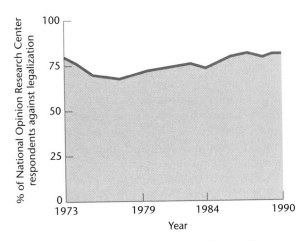

FIGURE 13.4 Opposition to legalizing marijuana, 1973–1990

* This line was constructed from interpolated data. Between 2% and 5% responded "don't know," depending on the year.

Source: Graphic: Data from the National Opinion Research Center are made available through the Roper Public Opinion Research Center as presented in BJS, *Sourcebook of Criminal Justice Statistics, 1990*, NCJ-130580, 1991, p. 228, table 2.87. From U.S. Department of Justice, *Drugs, Crime and the Justice System* (Washington, D.C.: U.S. Government Printing Office, 1992), p. 96.

girls drank on at least one occasion in any given month. Of the male students age 17 or older, one-quarter drank ten or more times a month. And a significant proportion reported that intoxication was a necessary part of their lives. Yet the authors also reported that alcohol consumption declined during recent years.[50]

The History of Legalization

Alcohol consumption is not new to our culture; in colonial days alcohol was considered safer and healthier than water. Still, the history of alcohol consumption is filled with controversy. Many people through the centuries have viewed it as wicked and degenerate. By the turn of the twentieth century, social reformers linked liquor to prostitution, poverty, the immigrant culture, and corrupt politics.

Various lobbying groups, such as the Women's Christian Temperance Union and the American Anti-Saloon League, bombarded politicians with demands for the prohibition of alcohol.[51] On January 16, 1920, the Eighteenth Amendment to the Constitution went into force, prohibiting the manufacture, sale, and transportation of alcoholic beverages. The Volstead Act of 1919 had already defined as "intoxicating liquor" any beverage that contained more than one-half of 1 percent alcohol.

Historians generally agree that no law in America has ever been more widely violated or more unpopular. Vast numbers of people continued to consume alcohol. It was easy to manufacture and to import. The illegal business brought tremendous profits to suppliers, and it could not be controlled by enforcement officers, who were too inefficient, too few, or too corrupt. The unlawful sale of alcohol was called "bootlegging." The term originated in the early practice of concealing liquor in one's boot to avoid payment of liquor taxes.

Bootlegging created empires for such gangsters as Al Capone and Dutch Schultz, as we saw in Chapter 12. Private saloons, or "speakeasies," prospered. Unpopular and unenforceable, the Eighteenth Amendment was repealed 13 years after its birth—on December 5, 1933. Except for a few places, the manufacture and sale of alcohol have been legal in the United States since that time.

Crime-Related Activities

The alcohol-related activities that have become serious social problems are violent crime, drunken driving, and public intoxication.

Violence
National surveys of inmates in jails and prisons show the following:

- Almost half of the convicted offenders incarcerated for violent crimes (particularly assaults) used alcohol immediately before the crimes.
- Almost 50 percent of the inmates drank an average of 1 ounce or more of alcohol each day (compared with 10 percent of all persons age 18 and older in the general population).
- Over one-third of the inmates drank alcoholic beverages every day during the year before they committed their crimes.
- Thirty-four to 45 percent of inmates convicted of homicide, assault, rape, and robbery described themselves as heavy drinkers.[52]

For many decades criminologists have probed the relationship between alcohol and violence. Marvin Wolfgang, in a study of 588 homicides in Philadelphia, found that alcohol was present in two-thirds of all homicide cases (both victim and offender, 44 percent; victim only, 9 percent; offender only, 11 percent).[53] Similar findings were reported from northern Sweden: two-thirds of the offenders who committed homicide between 1970 and 1981 and almost half of their victims were intoxicated when the crime was committed.[54]

Many other offenses show a significant relationship between alcohol and violence. In the United States, 58 percent of those convicted for assault and 64 percent of offenders who assaulted police officers had been drinking.[55] In about one-third of rapes, the offender, the victim, or both had been drinking immediately before the attack.[56] The role of alcohol in violent family disputes has been increasingly recognized. Among 2413 American couples, the rate of severe

AT ISSUE
Gambling: "Injurious to the Morals"

Since civilization began—and maybe before—people have risked their fortunes on all kinds of chances. They still do in the stock market and in commerce generally. That kind of chance taking has been legal in most parts of the world. But other kinds of risk taking—what we call "games of chance"—have long been considered immoral and prohibited by law.

In England in the early days of the common law, gambling was not illegal. Later statutes made "gaming," including playing billiards or tennis, illegal. In the eighteenth century, the keeping of a gaming house became a "criminal nuisance." But in the American colonies, lotteries, another form of gambling, were perfectly legal. They were used to fund Columbia University (then King's College), Harvard, Yale, Dartmouth, and Williams College. In the nineteenth century, gambling became less and less acceptable, until finally it was prohibited in almost every state.(1)

What is the situation in the United States today? All American states except Nevada prohibit gambling in general, but there are many legal exceptions. Some states have legalized certain forms—for example, dog racing, horse racing, or (in Nevada, New Jersey, and Puerto Rico) casino gambling—and state lottery programs and church-sponsored bingo also are defined as legal gambling in many jurisdictions.

Why is gambling sometimes legal and sometimes not? The great English jurist Sir James Fitzjames Stephen wrote in 1877: "Unlawful gaming means gaming carried on in such a manner, or for such a length of time or for such stakes (regard being had to the circumstances of the players) that it is likely to be injurious to the morals of those who game."(2) It appears, then, that the harm in gambling is the threat to players' morals—the idea that the gambler who wins receives an undeserved, unearned reward.

One of the problems in the question of the legality of gambling seems to have economic roots: gambling is extremely profitable for the operators of games. The 1976 Federal Commission on Gambling reported a turnover of $75 billion per year for American gambling activities; organized crime netted an estimated $7 billion. By now the figures are certainly much higher. So it is possible that states and localities hungry for money and facing budget cuts and the end of subsidies want some of the vast sums that now are siphoned off into illegal channels. Government, in other words, wants a piece of the action. Antigambling laws may seek less to protect the morals of gamblers, then, than to keep organized crime out of an extremely lucrative business.

Sources

1. Gresham M. Sykes, *Criminology* (New York: Harcourt Brace Jovanovich, 1978), pp. 192–193.
2. Sir James Fitzjames Stephen, *A Digest of the Criminal Law,* ed. 5 (London: Macmillan, 1894), p. 143.

Questions for Discussion

1. Why is the gamble you take when you place your money with a Wall Street futures trader a legal investment, while the off-track bet on the outcome of a horse race may not be legal? Is one less "injurious to the morals" than the other?
2. Do you think gambling should be legal throughout the United States, illegal throughout the United States, or decided on a state-by-state basis? Defend your position.

A state lottery: legal gambling.

violence by the husband was 2.10 per 100 couples in homes where the husbands were never drunk and 30.89 per 100 couples in homes where the husbands were drunk "very often."[57]

Many explanations have been offered for the relationship between alcohol and violence.[58] Some studies focus on the individual. When people are provoked, for example, alcohol can reduce restraints on aggression.[59] Alcohol also escalates aggression by reducing awareness of consequences.[60] Other studies analyze the social situation in which drinking takes place. Experts argue that in some situations aggressive behavior is considered appropriate or is even expected when people drink together.[61]

Drunk Driving

The effect of alcohol on driving is causing continuing concern. The incidence of drunk driving, referred to in statutes as "driving under the influence" and "driving while intoxicated" (depending on the level of alcohol found in the blood), has been steadily rising. Statistics indicate the extent of the problem:

■ Driving under the influence (DUI) arrests increased nearly 223 percent between 1970 and 1986, while the number of licensed drivers increased only 42 percent.

■ Before arrest for driving while intoxicated (DWI), convicted offenders drink at least 6 ounces of pure alcohol within 4 hours.

■ A recent national survey showed that about 7 percent of all persons confined in jails were charged with or convicted of DWI; 13 percent had a current charge or prior conviction for DWI; and almost half of those in jail for DWI had a previous sentence of probation, jail, or prison for the same offense.

■ In 1991, 398,000 persons were injured in alcohol-related crashes.

■ In 1989 there were 68,000 alcohol-related traffic accidents resulting in serious injury or deaths.

■ The annual cost of drunk driving (property damage, medical bills, and so on) is estimated at $24 billion.

■ There were 933,166 arrests for driving under the influence in 1992.[62]

Cari Lightner, age 13, was killed in May 1980 by a drunken driver while she was walking on a sidewalk.[63] The driver had been arrested only a few days before on a DUI charge. The victim's mother, Candy, took action almost immediately to push for new legislation that would mandate much stiffer penalties for drunk driving. It was difficult at first to get government to respond, but she did get the attention of journalists. By the end of the year in which Cari died, Mrs. Lightner had organized the Governor's Task Force on Drinking and Driving in California.

And her own advocacy group, Mothers Against Drunk Driving (MADD), was in the national spotlight. MADD's members were people who themselves had been injured or whose family members had been injured or killed in an accident involving an intoxicated driver. The organization has grown to more than 300 chapters.[64] Remove Intoxicated Drivers (RID) and Students Against Drunk Drivers (SADD) have joined the campaign.

The citizens' groups called public attention to a major health and social problem, demanded action, and got it. Congress proclaimed one week each December to be Drunk and Drugged Awareness Week, and the Presidential Commission on Drunk Driving was formed. Candy Lightner was appointed a commissioner. The federal government attached the distribution of state highway funds to various anti-drunk-driving measures, thereby pressuring the states into putting recommendations into action. Old laws have been changed and new laws have been passed.

After the ratification in 1971 of the Twenty-Sixth Amendment to the U.S. Constitution, which lowered the voting age to 18 years, many states lowered their minimum-age requirement for the purchase and sale of alcoholic beverages. By 1983, 33 states had done so; but by 1987, all but one state had raised the minimum drinking age back to 21. Under New York's Civil Forfeiture Law, the government can take any car involved in a felony drunk-driving case, sell it, and give the money to the victims. Texas has a similar law.[65] Tuscarawas County in Ohio places brightly colored orange plates on cars of drivers whose licenses have been suspended for drunk driving.[66]

A Students Against Drunk Driving (SADD) display of an actual wrecked car whose driver was drunk.

Other objectives of legislation have been to limit the "happy hours" during which bars serve drinks at reduced prices, to shorten hours when alcoholic beverages can be sold, to make hosts and bartenders liable for damages if their guests or patrons drink too much and become involved in an accident, to limit advertisements, and to put health warnings on bottles. Most states have increased their penalties for drunk driving to include automatic license suspension, higher minimum fines, and even mandatory jail sentences.

Thus far the results of such legislation are mixed. A study carried out in Seattle, Minneapolis, and Cincinnati found that such measures did indeed lower the number of traffic deaths, while other investigations did not show positive results.[67] Nevertheless, drunk driving has achieved national attention, and even modern technology is being used in the effort to find solutions: Japanese and American technicians have come up with a device that locks the ignition system and can be unlocked only when the attached breathalyzer (which registers alcohol in the blood) indicates that the driver is sober.[68] California, Washington, Texas, Michigan, and Oregon have passed legislation authorizing its use.

SEXUAL MORALITY OFFENSES

All societies endeavor to regulate sexual behavior, although what specifically is considered not permissible has varied from society to society and from time to time. The legal regulation of sexual conduct in Anglo-American law has been greatly influenced by both the Old and the New Testament. In the Middle Ages the enforcement of laws pertaining to sexual morality was the province of church courts. Today, to the extent that immorality is still illegal, it is the regular criminal courts that enforce such laws.

Morality laws have always been controversial, whether they seek to prevent alcohol abuse or to prohibit certain forms of sexual behavior or its public display or depiction. Sexual activity other than intercourse between spouses for the purpose of procreation has been severely penalized in many societies and until only recently in the United States. Sexual intercourse between unmarried persons ("lewd cohabitation"), seduction of a female by promise of marriage, and all forms of "unnatural" sexual relations were serious crimes, some carrying capital sentences, as late as the nineteenth century. In 1962 the Model Penal Code proposed some important changes.

Fornication and lewd cohabitation were dropped from the list of offenses, as was homosexual intercourse between consenting adults.

The idea between these changes is that the sexual relations of consenting adults should be beyond the control of the law, not only because throughout history such legal efforts have proved ineffective but also because the harm to society, if any, is too slight to warrant the condemnation of law. "The state's power to regulate sexual conduct ought to stop at the bedroom door or at the barn door," said sex researcher Alfred Kinsey four decades ago.[69]

Although the Model Penal Code (MPC) has removed or limited sanctions for conduct among consenting adults, the code retains strong prohibitions against sexual activities involving children. Penalties are severe for **statutory rape** (intercourse by an adult male with an underage female regardless of consent), deviate sexual intercourse with a child, corruption of a minor, sexual assault, and endangering the welfare of a child. Of course the recommendations of the American Law Institute are not always accepted by state legislatures.

Let us take a close look at three existing offenses involving sexual morality: "deviate sexual intercourse by force or imposition," prostitution, and pornography.

"Deviate Sexual Intercourse by Force or Imposition"

The Model Penal Code defines "deviate sexual intercourse" as "sexual intercourse per os or per anum [by mouth or by anus] between human beings who are not husband and wife, and any form of sexual intercourse with an animal" [sec. 213.2(1)]. The common law called such sexual acts **sodomy,** after the biblical city of Sodom, which the Lord destroyed for its wickedness, presumably because its citizens had engaged in such acts. The common law dealt harshly with sodomy, making it a capital offense and referring to it as *crimen innominatum*—a crime not to be mentioned by name.

Yet other cultures, including ancient Greece, did not frown on homosexual activities. And Alfred Kinsey reminded us that homosexual (from the Greek "same") relations are common among all mammals, of which humans are but one species.[70] The MPC subjects "deviate sexual intercourse" between two human beings to punishment only if it is accomplished by severe compulsion or if the other person is incapable of granting consent or is a child less than 10 years old. To conservative lawmakers, this model legislation is far too liberal; to liberals, it does not go far enough. Generally, liberal thinkers prefer the law not to interfere with the sexual practices of consenting adults at all.

The gay and lesbian rights movements have done much to destigmatize consensual, private adult sexual relationships. Yet legislatures have been slow to respond, and the U.S. Supreme Court has taken a conservative stance as well. In 1986 the Court sustained a Georgia statute that criminalizes consensual sexual acts between adults of the same gender, even if they are performed in the privacy of one's home.[71]

Prostitution

Not so long ago it was a crime to be a prostitute.[72] The law punished women for a status acquired on the basis of sexual intercourse with more than one man. Under some statutes it was not even necessary to prove that money was paid for the sexual act. The Supreme Court ruled in 1962—in a case involving the status of being a drug addict—that criminal liability can be based only on conduct, that is, on doing something in violation of law.[73] This decision would seem to apply to prostitution as well. Therefore, one can no longer be penalized for being a prostitute. But soliciting for sex is an act, not a status, and nearly all states make solicitation of sex for money the misdemeanor of **prostitution.**

The Uniform Crime Reports recorded 86,988 arrests for prostitution and commercialized vice during 1992.[74] A quarter of the arrested prostitutes were between 25 and 29 years old. Yet prostitution and commercialized vice reach into all age brackets, from under 15 to over 65 years of age. The number of recorded arrests for prostitution bears no relation to the actual number of prostitution events.

The number would be extremely high if we were to include all acts of sexual favor granted in return for some gratuity. Even if the number were limited to straightforward cash transactions (including, nowadays, credit card transactions), there is no way of arriving at a figure. Many persons may act as prostitutes for a while and then return to legitimate lifestyles. There are part-time and full-time prostitutes, male and female prostitutes, itinerant and resident prostitutes, street hookers and high-priced escorts who do not consider themselves to be prostitutes.[75]

Many law enforcement agencies do not relish the task of suppressing prostitution. In some jurisdictions the police have little time to spend on vice control, given the extent of violent and property crimes. Thus, when prostitutes are arrested, it is likely to be in response to demands by community groups, business establishments, or church leaders to "clean up the neighborhood." Occasionally the police find it expedient to arrest prostitutes because they may divulge information about unsolved crimes, such as narcotics distribution, theft, receiving stolen property, or organized crime.

Prostitution encompasses a variety of both acts and actors. The prostitute, female or male, is not alone in the business of prostitution. A **pimp** provides access to prostitutes and protects and exploits them, living off their proceeds. There are still madams who maintain houses of prostitution. And finally, there are the patrons of prostitutes, popularly called "johns." Ordinarily it is not a criminal offense to patronize a prostitute, yet the framers of the MPC proposed to criminalize this act. The section was hotly debated before the American Law Institute. A final vote of the members favored retention of the prohibition.

Researchers have found that many prostitutes come from broken homes and poor neighborhoods and are school dropouts. Yet all social classes contribute to the prostitution hierarchy. High-priced call girls, many of them well-educated women, may operate singly or out of agencies. The television "blue channels" that broadcast after midnight in most metropolitan areas carry commercials advertising the availability of call girls, their phone numbers, and sometimes their specialties. At the next-lower level of the prostitution hierarchy are the massage parlor prostitutes. When Shirley, a masseuse, was asked, "Do you consider yourself a prostitute?" she answered: "Yes, as well as a masseuse, and a healer, and a couple of other things."[76] One rung lower on the prostitution ladder are the "inmates" (a term used by the MPC) of the houses of prostitution, locally called bordellos, whorehouses, cathouses, or red-light houses.

According to people "in the life" (prostitution), the streetwalkers are the least respected class in the hierarchy. They are the "working girls" or "hookers." They are found clustered on their accustomed street corners, on thoroughfares, or in truck and bus depots, dressed in bright attire, ready to negotiate a price with any passerby. Sexual services are performed in vehicles or in nearby "hot-sheet" hotel rooms. Life for these prostitutes—some of whom are transvestite males—is dangerous and grim. Self-reports suggest that many are drug addicts and have been exposed to HIV.[77] Other varieties of prostitution range from the legal houses that a few counties permit to operate in Nevada to troupes of prostitutes who travel from one place of opportunity to another (work projects, farm labor camps, construction sites) and bar ("B") girls who entertain customers in cocktail lounges and make themselves available for sexual activities for a price.

Popular, political, and scientific opinions on prostitution have changed, no doubt largely because prostitution has changed. Around the turn of the century it probably was true that a large number of prostitutes had been forced into the occupation by unscrupulous men. Indeed, it was this pattern that led to the enactment of the "White Slave Traffic Act" (called the Mann Act, after the senator who proposed the bill), prohibiting the interstate transportation of females for purposes of prostitution. There is some evidence that today the need for money, together with few legitimate opportunities to obtain it, prompts many young women and men to become prostitutes.

Sex researcher Paul Gebhard found in 1969 that only 4 percent of U.S. prostitutes were forced into prostitution. More recently Jennifer James found that the majority entered "the life" because of its financial rewards.[78] Whatever view we take of adult prostitutes as victims of a supposedly victimless criminal activity, one subgroup clearly is a victimized class: children, female and male, who are enticed and sometimes forced into prostitution, especially in large cities. Some are runaways, picked up by procurers at bus depots;

WINDOW TO THE WORLD
Global Sexual Slavery: Women and Children

"I thought I was going to work as a waitress," a young Dominican, transported to Greece, told BBC television, her eyes welling with tears. "Then they said if I didn't have sex, I'd be sent back to Santo Domingo without a penny. I was beaten, burned with cigarettes. I knew nobody. I was a virgin. I held out for five days, crying, with no food. [Eventually] I lost my honor and my virginity for $25."(1)

This woman's story is a common one. While some women become prostitutes by choice, many are forced into it. The growing sex trade around the world needs a constant supply of bodies, and it is getting them however it can. The statistics are horrifying: For the brothels of Bombay, some 7000 adolescents from Nepal's Himalayan hill villages are sold to slave traders each year. In Brazil the number of girls forced into prostitution in mining camps is estimated at 25,000. Japan's bars feature approximately 70,000 Thai "hostesses" working as sex slaves. Some 200,000 Bangladeshi women have been kidnapped into prostitution in Pakistan.(1)

The numbers of underage prostitutes are equally shocking, whether the children were sold into slavery or are trying to survive in a harsh world by selling their bodies: 800,000 in Thailand, 400,000 in India, 250,000 in Brazil, and 60,000 in the Philippines. Child prostitution recently has increased in Russian and East European cities, with an estimated 1000 youngsters working in Moscow alone.(2) In Vietnam, fathers may act as pimps for their daughters to get money for the family to survive:

> Dr. Hoa, [a] pediatrician from Vietnam, said she asked the fathers of her young patients why they sold their daughters' services. "One father came with his 12-year-old daughter," Dr. Hoa recalled. "She was bleeding from her wounds and as torn as if she had given birth. He told me, 'We've earned $300, so it's enough. She can stop now.'"(3)

The physical wounds suffered by underage prostitutes are part of the terrible irony of the growing market for sex with children. Customers request children under the mistaken belief that they are less likely to be infected with the virus that causes AIDS. In fact, because children are so likely to incur injuries in intercourse, they are more vulnerable to infection.(2)

Experts at a 1993 conference on the sex trade and human rights cited the global AIDS epidemic, pornography, peep shows, and "sex tours" as factors responsible for the increasing demand for child prostitutes.(3) Organized sex tours form a large part of the market for bodies of any age; Taiwan, South Korea, the Philippines, and Thailand have been favorite destinations for sex tourists, and many other places are gaining in popularity.

Sources

1. Margot Hornblower, "The Skin Trade," *Time*, June 21, 1993, pp. 45–51.
2. Michael S. Serrill, "Defiling the Children," *Time*, June 21, 1993, pp. 53–55.
3. Marlise Simons, "The Sex Market: Scourge on the World's Children," *New York Times*, Apr. 9, 1993, p. A3.

Questions for Discussion

1. How would you begin to fight the exploitation of women and children in the sex market?
2. What are some of the forces at work that would make such a fight difficult?

A very young prostitute in a red light district in Dhaka, Bangladesh.

some are simply "street children"; and others have been abused and molested by the adults in their lives.[79]

Pornography

Physical sexual contact is a basic component of both sodomy and prostitution. **Pornography** requires no contact at all; it simply portrays sexually explicit material. Statutes in all states make it a criminal offense to produce, offer for sale, sell, distribute, or exhibit pornographic (sometimes called obscene, lewd, or lascivious) material. Federal law prohibits the transportation of such material in interstate commerce and outlaws the use of the mails, the telephone, radio, and television for the dissemination of pornographic material.[80]

The Problem of Definition

The term "pornographic" is derived from the Greek *pornographos* ("writing of harlots," or descriptions of the acts of harlots). The term "obscene" comes from the Latin *ob* ("against," "before") plus *caenum* ("filth"), or possibly from *obscena* ("offstage"). In Roman theatrical performances, disgusting and offensive parts of plays took place offstage, out of sight but not out of hearing of the audience.[81] Courts and legislators have used the two terms interchangeably, but nearly all statutes and decisions deal with pornography (with the implication of sexual arousal) rather than with obscenity (with its implication of filth).[82]

Scholars generally agree that the statutes in existence appear to be addressed primarily to pornographic materials.[83] What, then, is the contemporary meaning of "pornography"? The Model Penal Code (1962) says that a publication is pornographic (obscene or indecent) "if, considered as a whole, its predominant appeal is to prurient interests," and if, "in addition, it goes substantially beyond customary limits in describing or representing such matters" (sec. 251.4). This definition, which is full of ambiguities, was to play a major role in several Supreme Court decisions.

Two presidential commissions were no more successful in defining the term. The Commission on Obscenity and Pornography (1970) avoided a definition and used instead the term "explicit

sexual material."[84] The Attorney General's Commission on Pornography (1986) gave no definition.[85] The definition created by a British parliamentary committee in 1979 seems to describe pornography best:

> A pornographic representation combines two features: It has a certain function or intention, to arouse its audience sexually, and also a certain content, explicit representation of sexual materials (organs, postures, activity, etc.).[86]

This definition indicates nothing about any danger inherent in pornography. The law will step in only when pornography is exhibited or distributed in a manner calculated to produce harm.

Historically, that harm has been seen as a negative effect on public morals, especially those of children. That was the stance taken by many national and local societies devoted to the preservation of public morality in the nineteenth century. More recently, the emphasis has shifted to the question of whether the availability and use of pornography produce actual, especially violent, victimization of women, children, or, for that matter, men.

Pornography and Violence

The National Commission on Obscenity and Pornography in 1970 and the Attorney General's Commission on Pornography in 1986 reviewed the evidence of an association between pornography, on the one hand, and violence and crime, on the other. The National Commission provided funding for more than 80 studies to examine public attitudes toward pornography, experiences with pornography, the association between the availability of pornography and crime rates, the experience of sex offenders with pornography, and the relation between pornography and behavior. The commission concluded:

> [E]mpirical research designed to clarify the question has found no evidence to date that exposure to explicit sexual materials plays a significant role in the causations of delinquent or criminal behavior among youth or adults. The Commission cannot conclude that exposure to erotic materials is a factor in the causation of sex crimes or sex delinquency.[87]

Between 1970 (when the National Commission reported its findings) and 1986 (when the Attorney General's Commission issued its report) hundreds of studies have been conducted on this question. For example:

■ Researchers reported in 1977 that when male students were exposed to erotic stimuli, those stimuli neither inhibited nor had any effect on levels of aggression. When the same research team worked with female students, they found that mild erotic stimuli inhibited aggression and that stronger erotic stimuli increased it.[88]

■ Researchers who exposed students to sexually explicit films during six consecutive weekly sessions in 1984 concluded that exposure to increasingly explicit erotic stimuli led to a decrease in both arousal responses and aggressive behavior. In short, these subjects became habituated to the pornography.[89]

After analyzing such studies, the Attorney General's Commission concluded that nonviolent and nondegrading pornography is not significantly associated with crime and aggression. It did conclude, however, that exposure to pornographic materials:

> (1) leads to a greater acceptance of rape myths and violence against women; (2) results in pronounced effects when the victim is shown enjoying the use of force or violence; (3) is arousing for rapists and for some males in the general population; and (4) has resulted in sexual aggression against women in the laboratory.[90]

The Feminist View: Victimization

To feminists, these conclusions supported the call for greater restrictions on the manufacture and dissemination of pornographic material. The historian Joan Hoff has coined the term "pornerotic," meaning:

> any representation of persons that sexually objectifies them and is accompanied by actual or implied violence in ways designed to encourage readers or viewers that such sexual subordination of women (or children or men) is acceptable behavior or an innocuous form of sex education.[91]

Hoff's definition also suggests that pornography, obscenity, and erotica may do far more than offend sensitivities. Such material may victimize not only the people who are depicted but all women (or men or children, if they are the people shown). Pornographers have been accused of promoting the exploitation, objectification, and degradation of women. Many people who call for the abolition of violent pornography argue that it also promotes violence toward women. Future state and federal legislation is likely to focus on violent and violence-producing pornography, not on pornography in general.

The Legal View: Supreme Court Rulings

Ultimately, defining pornographic acts subject to legal prohibition is a task for the U.S. Supreme Court. The First Amendment to the Constitution guarantees freedom of the press. In a series of decisions culminating in *Miller v. California* (1973), however, the Supreme Court articulated the view that obscenity, really meaning pornography, is outside the protection of the Constitution. Following the lead of the Model Penal Code and reinterpreting its own earlier decisions, the Court announced the following standard for judging a representation as obscene or pornographic:

■ The average person, applying contemporary community standards, would find that the work, taken as a whole, appeals to prurient interests.

■ The work depicts or describes, in a patently offensive way, sexual conduct specifically defined by the applicable state law.

■ The work, taken as a whole, lacks serious literary, artistic, political, or scientific value.[92]

While this proposed standard is flexible enough to be expanded or contracted as standards change over time and from place to place, its terms are so vague that they give little guidance to local law enforcement officers or to federal and state courts. In 1987 the Supreme Court addressed this problem and modified the Miller decision. In *Pope v. Illinois* the Court ruled that the third aspect of Miller (that the work has "no value") may be judged by an objective test rather than by local community standards. Justice Byron White wrote for the majority:

> The proper inquiry is not whether an ordinary person of any given community will find serious literary, artistic, political, or scientific value in the allegedly obscene material, but whether a reasonable person would find such value in the material, taken as a whole.[93]

Whether this test will make juries' tasks easier when they must decide whether a film or magazine is pornographic or obscene is still not clear.

The Gap between Behavior and Law

When we examine sexual morality offenses, we note an enormous gap between the goals of law and actual behavior. As long ago as the late 1940s and early 1950s the pioneering Kinsey reports brought us evidence about this gap. According to these studies, of the total white male population in the United States:

■ Sixty-nine percent had had some experience with prostitutes.

■ Between 23 and 37 percent had had extramarital intercourse.

■ Thirty-seven percent had had at least one homosexual experience.[94]

Among women:

■ Twenty-six percent could be expected to have extramarital intercourse by age 40.

■ Nineteen percent had had some physical contact with other females which was deliberately and consciously, at least on the part of one of the partners, intended to be sexual.[95]

Morton Hunt noted that the frequency with which Americans were breaking legally imposed moral standards had increased significantly by the 1970s, yet far fewer American men were buying sex from prostitutes than had done so in the 1940s.[96] This finding raised the question of whether the sexual revolution of the 1960s and 1970s made access to sexual partners more freely available.

■ REVIEW

Intoxicating substances have been used for religious, medicinal, and recreational purposes throughout history. Lifestyles of people who use them are as varied as the drugs they favor.

Governments have repeatedly tried to prevent the abuse of these substances. The drug problem today is massive, and it grows more serious every year. Heroin and cocaine in particular are associated with many crimes. A vast international criminal empire has been organized to promote the production and distribution of drugs. Efforts of law enforcement and health agencies to control the drug problem take the forms of international cooperation in stemming drug trafficking, treatment of addicts, education of the public, and arrest and incarceration of offenders. Some observers, comparing the drug problem with the wide evasion of the Prohibition amendment and the consequent rise in crime, believe that drugs should be legalized.

Legalization of alcoholic beverages, however, has not solved all problems related to alcohol. The abuse of alcohol has been reliably linked to violence, and the incidence of drunk driving has increased so alarmingly that citizen groups have formed to combat the problem.

The legal regulation of sexual conduct has undergone striking changes in recent decades. Many sexual "offenses" once categorized as capital crimes no longer concern society or government. In this sphere, research has done much to influence public opinion and consequently legislation. Pornography, however, remains a hotly debated issue.

■ NOTES

1. *United States v. Montoya de Hernandez,* 473 U.S. 531 (1985).
2. Richard P. Retting, Manuel J. Torres, and Gerald R. Garrett, *Manny: A Criminal-Addict's Story* (Boston: Houghton Mifflin, 1977).
3. "The Drug Gangs," *Newsweek,* Mar. 28, 1988, p. 20.
4. Mark D. Merlin, *On the Trail of the Ancient Opium Poppy* (Rutherford, N.J.: Fairleigh Dickinson University Press, 1984).
5. Howard Abadinsky, *Drug Abuse: An Introduction* (Chicago: Nelson Hall, 1989), pp. 30–31, 54.
6. Michael D. Lyman, *Narcotics and Crime Control* (Springfield, Ill.: Charles C. Thomas, 1987), p. 8.
7. W. Z. Guggenheim, "Heroin: History and Pharmacology," *International Journal of the Addictions,* **2** (1967): 328.
8. Abadinsky, *Drug Abuse,* p. 52.
9. Ibid., p. 56.
10. Lyman, *Narcotics and Crime Control,* p. 10.
11. Public Law 100-690, of Nov. 18, 1988; 102 Stat. 4187.
12. Lloyd D. Johnston, Patrick M. O'Malley, and Jerald G. Bachman, *Drug Use among American High School Seniors, College Students, and Young Adults, 1975–1990,* vol. 1–2, for U.S. Department of Health and Human Services, National Institute on Drug Abuse (Washington, D.C.: U.S. Government Printing Office, 1991).
13. U.S. Department of Justice, *Drugs, Crime, and the Justice System* (Washington, D.C., U.S. Government Printing Office, 1992), p. 31.

14. Lyman, *Narcotics and Crime Control*, p. 21.
15. National Institute on Drug Abuse, *National Household Survey*, p. 9; *see* Robert J. Michaels, "The Market for Heroin before and after Legalization," in *Dealing with Drugs*, ed. Ronald Hamowy (Lexington, Mass.: Lexington Books, 1987), pp. 311–318.
16. Abadinsky, *Drug Abuse*, p. 107; Lyman, *Narcotics and Crime Control*, pp. 33–34.
17. Lloyd D. Johnston, Patrick M. O'Malley, and Jerald G. Bachman, *The National Survey Results on Drug Use from the Monitoring the Future Study, 1975–1993*, vol. 1, National Institute of Health (Washington, D.C., U.S. Government Printing Office, 1994).
18. For a summary of psychiatric approaches, see Marie Nyswander, *The Drug Addict as a Patient* (New York: Grune & Stratton, 1956), chap. 4.
19. Richard Cloward and Lloyd Ohlin, *Delinquency and Opportunity* (New York: Free Press, 1960), pp. 178–186. See also Jeffrey A. Fagan, "The Social Organization of Drug Use and Drug Dealing among Urban Gangs," *Criminology*, **27** (1989): 633–669.
20. D. F. Musto, "The History of Legislative Control over Opium, Cocaine, and Their Derivatives," in Hamowy, *Dealing with Drugs*.
21. Marsha Rosenbaum, *Women on Heroin* (New Brunswick, N.J.: Rutgers University Press, 1981), pp. 14–15; Jeannette Covington, "Theoretical Explanations of Race Differences in Heroin Use," in *Advances in Criminological Theory*, vol. 2, ed. William S. Laufer and Freda Adler (New Brunswick, N.J.: Transaction).
22. Freda Adler, Arthur D. Moffett, Frederick G. Glaser, John C. Ball, and Diana Horwitz, *A Systems Approach to Drug Treatment* (Philadelphia: Dorrance, 1974).
23. Erich Goode, *Drugs in American Society* (New York: Basic Books, 1972); also Ned Polsky, *Hustlers, Beats, and Others* (Chicago: Aldine, 1967).
24. Norman E. Zinberg, "The Use and Misuse of Intoxicants: Factors in the Development of Controlled Abuse," in Hamowy, *Dealing with Drugs*, p. 262.
25. Abadinsky, *Drug Abuse*, p. 53,
26. Ibid., p. 83. See also Jeffrey A. Fagan, "Initiation into Crack and Powdered Cocaine: A Tale of Two Epidemics," *Contemporary Drug Problems*, **16** (1989): 579–618; Jeffrey A. Fagan, Joseph G. Weis, and Y. T. Cheng, "Drug Use and Delinquency among Inner City Youth," *Journal of Drug Issues*, **20** (1990): 349–400; and James A. Inciardi et al., "The Crack Epidemic Revisited," *Journal of Psychoactive Drugs*, **24** (1992): 305–416. See also B. D. Johnson, M. Natarajan, E. Dunlap, and E. Elmoghazy, "Crack Abusers and Noncrack Abusers: A Comparison of Drug Use, Drug Sales, and Nondrug Criminality," *Journal of Drug Issues*, **24** (1994): 117–141.
27. *New York Times*, July 13, 1989, pp. A1, B3.
28. James Inciardi, "Heroin Use and Street Crime," *Crime and Delinquency*, **25** (1979): 335–346; Bruce D. Johnson, Paul J. Goldstein, Edward Preble, James Schmeidler, Douglas S. Lyston, Barry Spunt, and Thomas Miller, *Taking Care of Business: The Economics of Crime by Heroin Abusers* (Lexington, Mass.: Heath, 1985); James Inciardi, *The War on Drugs: Heroin, Cocaine,*

Crime, and Public Policy (Palo Alto, Calif.: Mayfield, 1986); Eric Wish and Bruce Johnson, "The Impact of Substance Abuse on Criminal Careers," in *Criminal Careers and Career Criminals*, ed. Alfred Blumstein, Jacqueline Cohen, Jeffrey A. Roth, and Christy A. Visher (Washington, D.C.: National Academy Press, 1986), pp. 52–58.
29. U.S. Department of Justice, *National Institute of Justice Journal* (Washington, D.C.: U.S. Government Printing Office, 1993), p. 32.
30. Stephanie Greenberg and Freda Adler, "Crime and Addiction: An Empirical Analysis of the Literature, 1920–1973," *Contemporary Drug Problems*, **3** (1974): 221–270.
31. George Speckart and M. Douglas Anglin found that criminal records preceded drug use; see their "Narcotics Use and Crime: An Overview of Recent Research Advances," *Contemporary Drug Problems*, **13** (1986): 741–769, and "Narcotics and Crime: A Causal Modeling Approach," *Journal of Quantitative Criminology*, **2** (1986): 3–28. See also Cheryl Carpenter, Barry Glassner, Bruce D. Johnson, and Julia Loughlin, *Kids, Drugs, and Crime* (Lexington, Mass.: Heath, 1988).
32. David N. Nurco, Thomas E. Hanlon, Timothy W. Kinlock, and Karen R. Duszynski, "Differential Criminal Patterns of Narcotics Addicts over an Addiction Career," *Criminology*, **26** (1988): 407–423; M. Douglas Anglin and George Speckart, "Narcotics Use and Crime: A Multisample, Multimethod Analysis," *Criminology*, **26** (1988): 197–233; M. Douglas Anglin and Yin-ing Hser, "Addicted Women and Crime," *Criminology*, **25** (1987): 359–397.
33. Paul Goldstein, "Drugs and Violent Crime," in *Pathways to Criminal Violence*, ed. Neil Alan Weiner and Marvin E. Wolfgang (Newbury Park, Calif.: Sage, 1989), pp. 16–48; *Ebony*, August 1989, p. 99.
34. This section is based on Inciardi, *The War on Drugs*.
35. Royal Canadian Mounted Police, *National Drug Intelligence Estimate* (Ottawa: 1991), p. 24.
36. Royal Canadian Mounted Police, *The Illicit Drug Situation in the United States and Canada* (Ottawa: 1984–1986), p. 19.
37. United Nations, "Commission on Narcotic Drugs, Comprehensive Review of the Activities of the United Nations Fund for Drug Abuse Control in 1985," E/CN.7/1986/ CRP.4, Feb. 4, 1986. See also Elaine Sciolino, "U.N. Report Links Drugs, Arms, and Terror," *New York Times*, Jan. 12, 1987.
38. John Warner, "Terrorism and Drug Trafficking: A Lethal Partnership," *Security Management*, **28** (1984): 44–46.
39. See Mark Moore, *Drug Trafficking* (Washington, D.C.: National Institute of Justice, 1988); and Franklin E. Zimring and Gordon Hawkins, *The Search for Rational Drug Control* (Cambridge, England, and New York: Cambridge University Press, 1992).
40. James A. Inciardi, *The War on Drugs II: The Continuing Epidemic of Heroin, Cocaine, Crack, Crime, AIDS, and Public Policy* (Mountain View, Calif.: Mayfield, 1992).
41. Alfred W. McCoy and Alan A. Block, *War on Drugs:*

Studies in the Failure of U.S. Narcotics Policy (Boulder, Colo.: Westview, 1992); Drug Policy Foundation, *The Bush Drug War Record: The Real Story of a $45 Billion Domestic War* (Washington, D.C.: Drug Policy Foundation, 1992); Marc B. Stahl, "Asset Forfeiture, Burdens of Proof and the War on Drugs," *Journal of Criminal Law and Criminology*, **83** (1992): 274–337; Diane-Michele Krasnow, "To Stop the Scourge: The Supreme Court's Approach to the War on Drugs," *American Journal of Criminal Law*, **19** (1992): 219–266.

42. Adler et al., *A Systems Approach to Drug Treatment;* George Pratsinak and Robert Alexander, eds., *Understanding Substance Abuse & Treatment* (Laurel, Md.: American Correctional Association, 1992); Geoffrey R. Sholl, *Walk the Walk and Talk the Talk: An Ethnography of a Drug Abuse Treatment Facility* (Philadelphia: Temple University Press, 1992).

43. Peter Finn and Andrea K. Newlyn, *Miami's "Drug Court,"* National Institute of Justice (Washington, D.C.: U.S. Government Printing Office, 1993).

44. Abadinsky, p. 171.

45. Harold I. Hendler and Richard C. Stephens, "The Addict Odyssey: From Experimentation to Addiction," *International Journal of the Addictions*, **12** (1977): 25–42.

46. Troy Duster, *The Legislation of Morality: Law, Drugs, and Moral Judgment* (New York: Free Press, 1970), p. 192.

47. Dan Waldorf, "Natural Recovery from Opiate Addiction," *Journal of Drug Issues*, **13** (1983): 237–280.

48. James B. Bakalar and Lester Grinspoon, *Drug Control in a Free Society* (New York: Cambridge University Press, 1984); Lyman, *Narcotics and Crime Control;* Thomas Szasz, *Our Right to Drugs: The Case for a Free Market* (Westport, Conn.: Praeger, 1992).

49. James B. Jacobs, *Drunk Driving: An American Dilemma* (Chicago: University of Chicago Press, 1989), p. xiii.

50. Johnston et al., *National Trends in Drug Use.*

51. James Inciardi, *Reflections on Crime* (New York: Holt, Rinehart & Winston, 1978), pp. 8–10.

52. U.S. Department of Justice, *Report to the Nation on Crime and Justice*, 2d ed. (Washington, D.C.: U.S. Government Printing Office, 1988), p. 50.

53. Marvin E. Wolfgang, *Patterns in Criminal Homicide* (New York: Wiley, 1966).

54. P. Linquist, "Criminal Homicides in Northern Sweden, 1970–81: Alcohol Intoxication, Alcohol Abuse, and Mental Disease," *International Journal of Law and Psychiatry*, **8** (1986): 19–37.

55. D. Mayfield, "Alcoholism, Alcohol Intoxification, and Assaultive Behavior," *Diseases of the Nervous System*, **37** (1976): 288–291; C. K. Meyer, T. Magendanz, B. C. Kieselhorst, and S. G. Chapman, *A Social-Psychological Analysis of Police Assaults* (Norman: Bureau of Government Research, University of Oklahoma, April 1978).

56. S. D. Johnson, L. Gibson, and R. Linden, "Alcohol and Rape in Winnipeg, 1966–1975," *Journal of Studies on Alcohol*, **39** (1987): 1877–1894; Menachem Amir,

Patterns of Forcible Rape (Chicago: University of Chicago Press, 1971), p. 99.

57. D. H. Coleman and M. A. Straus, "Alcohol Abuse and Family Violence," in *Alcohol, Drug Abuse, and Aggression*, ed. E. Gottheil, K. A. Druley, T. E. Skoloda, and H. M. Waxman (Springfield, Ill.: Charles C Thomas, 1983). See also C. J. Hamilton and J. J. Collins, "The Role of Alcohol in Wife-Beating and Child Abuse: A Review of the Literature," in *Drinking and Crime: Perspectives on the Relationship between Alcohol Consumption and Criminal Behavior* (New York: Guilford, 1981). For discussion of the presence of alcohol in victims of homicide, see R. A. Goodman, J. A. Mercy, R. Loya, M. L. Rosenberg, J. C. Smith, M. H. Allen, L. Vargas, and R. Kotts, "Alcohol Use and Interpersonal Violence—Alcohol Detected in Homicide Victims," *American Journal of Public Health*, **76** (1986): 144–149.

58. See James J. Collins, "Alcohol and Interpersonal Violence," in Weiner and Wolfgang, *Pathways to Criminal Violence*. For a comprehensive review of aggression and drug abuse, see Jeffrey A. Fagan, "Intoxication and Aggression," in *Crime and Justice: An Annual Review of Research:* vol. 13, *Drugs and Crime*, eds. James Q. Wilson and Michael Tonry (Chicago: University of Chicago Press, 1990).

59. K. E. Leonard, "Alcohol and Human Physical Aggression," *Aggression*, **2** (1983): 77–101.

60. C. M. Steele and L. Southwick, "Alcohol and Social Behavior: I. The Psychology of Drunken Excess," *Journal of Personality and Social Psychology*, **48** (1985): 18–34.

61. S. Ahlstrom-Laakso, "European Drinking Habits: A Review of Research and Time Suggestions for Conceptual Integration of Findings," in *Cross-Cultural Approaches to the Study of Alcohol*, eds. M. W. Everett, J. O. Waddell, and D. Heath (The Hague: Mouton, 1976).

62. Uniform Crime Reports, 1992, p. 168 and 1989, p. 224; Lawrence A. Greenfeld, *Drunk Driving*, for Bureau of Justice Statistics (Washington, D.C.: U.S. Government Printing Office, February 1988), p. 1; William K. Stevens, "Deaths from Drunken Driving Increase," *New York Times*, Oct. 29, 1987, p. 12.

63. Joseph R. Gusfield, "The Control of Drinking-Driving in the United States: A Period of Transition," in *Social Control of the Drinking Driver*, eds. Michael D. Lawrence, John R. Snortum, and Franklin E. Zimring (Chicago: University of Chicago Press, 1988).

64. Jacobs, *Drunk Driving*, p. xvi.

65. Faye Silas, "Gimme the Keys," *American Bar Association Journal*, **71** (1985): 36.

66. *Newsweek*, Dec. 21, 1987.

67. Fred Heinzelmann, *Jailing Drunk Drivers* (Washington, D.C.: National Institute of Justice, 1984); Gerald Wheeler and Rodney Hissong, "Effects of Criminal Sanctions on Drunk Drivers: Beyond Incarceration," *Crime and Delinquency*, **34** (1988): 29–42; Richard Speezlman, "Issues in the Rise of Compulsion in California's Drinking Drive Treatment System," in *Pun-*

ishment and Treatment for Driving under the Influence of Alcohol and Other Drugs, ed. M. Valverius (Stockholm: International Committee on Alcohol, Drugs, and Traffic Safety, 1985), pp. 151–180; Dale E. Bergen and John R. Snortum, "A Structural Model of Drinking and Driving: Alcohol Consumption, Social Norms, and Moral Commitments," *Criminology*, **24** (1986): 139–152.

68. *The Effectiveness of the Ignition Interlock Device in Reducing Recidivism among Driving under the Influence Cases* (Honolulu: Criminal Justice Commission, 1987).

69. Personal communication, 1951.

70. Alfred C. Kinsey, Wardel B. Pomeroy, and Clyde E. Martin, *Sexual Behavior in the Human Male* (Philadelphia: Saunders, 1948), p. 613.

71. *Bowers v. Hardwick*, 478 U.S. 186; reh. denied, 478 U.S. 1039 (1986).

72. Nickie Roberts, *Whores in History: Prostitution in Western Society* (London: Harper Collins, 1992).

73. *Robinson v. California*, 370 U.S. 660 (1962).

74. Uniform Crime Reports, 1992, p. 227.

75. Sari van der Poel, "Professional Male Prostitution: A Neglected Phenomenon," *Crime, Law, and Social Change*, **18** (1992): 259–275.

76. Jeremiah Lowney, Robert W. Winslow, and Virginia Winslow, *Deviant Reality—Alternative World Views*, 2d ed. (Boston: Allyn and Bacon, 1981), p. 156.

77. James A. Inciardi, Anne E. Pottieger, Mary Ann Forney, et al., "Prostitution, IV Drug Use, and Sex-for-Crack Exchanges among Serious Delinquents: Risks for HIV Infection," *Criminology*, **29** (1991): 221–236; Joseph B. Kuhns III and Kathleen M. Heide, "AIDS-Related Issues among Female Prostitutes and Female Arrestees," *International Journal of Offender Therapy and Comparative Criminology*, **36** (1992): 231–245; David J. Bellis, "Reduction of AIDS Risk among 41 Heroin Addicted Female Street Prostitutes: Effects of Free Methadone Maintenance," *Journal of Addictive Diseases*, **12** (1993): 7–23; L. Maher and R. Curtis, "Women on the Edge of Crime: Crack Cocaine and the Changing Contexts of Street-Level Sex Work in New York City," *Crime, Law, and Social Change*, **18** (1992): 221–258; Edward V. Morse, Patricia M. Simon, Stephanie A. Baus, et al., "Cofactors of Substance Use among Male Street Prostitutes," *Journal of Drug Issues*, **22** (1992): 977–994.

78. Paul Gebhard, "Misconceptions about Female Prostitution," *Medical Aspects of Human Sexuality*, **3** (1969): 28–30; Jennifer James, "Prostitutes and Prostitution," in *Deviants: Voluntary Action in a Hostile World*, eds. Edward Sagarin and F. Montamino (Glenview, Ill.: Scott, Foresman, 1977), p. 384.

79. Daniel S. Campagna and Donald L. Poffenberger, *The Sexual Trafficking in Children* (Dover, Mass.: Auburn House, 1988); Jeffrey J. Haugard and N. Dickon Reppucci, *The Sexual Abuse of Children* (San Francisco: Jossey-Bass, 1988); Edward Donnerstein, Daniel Linz, and Steven Penrod, *The Question of Pornography* (New York: Free Press, 1987).

80. See Gerhard O. W. Mueller, *Legal Regulation of Sexual Conduct* (New York: Oceana, 1961), pp. 139–147, tables 9A, 9B. Note, however, that some states have amended their statutes since these data were collected.

81. Donnerstein et al., *The Question of Pornography*, p. 147.

82. Joel Feinberg, "Pornography and Criminal Law," in *Pornography and Censorship*, eds. D. Copp and S. Wendell (New York: Prometheus, 1979).

83. See Donnerstein et al., *The Question of Pornography*, chap. 7; and Gordon Hawkins and Franklin E. Zimring, *Pornography in a Free Society* (Cambridge, Mass.: Cambridge University Press, 1988), p. 26.

84. *The Report of the Commission on Obscenity and Pornography* (Washington, D.C.: U.S. Government Printing Office, 1970).

85. U.S. Department of Justice, *Attorney General's Commission on Pornography, Final Report*, vols. 1 and 2 (Washington, D.C.: U.S. Government Printing Office, 1986).

86. Home Office, *Report of the Committee on Obscenity and Film Censorship* (London: Her Majesty's Stationery Office, 1979), p. 103. See also Dennis Howitt and Guy Cumberbatch, *Pornography: Impacts and Influences: A Review of Available Research Evidence on the Effects of Pornography* (London: Research and Planning Unit, U.K. Home Office, 1990).

87. *The Report of the Commission on Obscenity and Pornography*.

88. R. A. Barron and P. A. Bell, "Sexual Arousal and Aggression by Males: Effects of Type of Erotic Stimuli and Prior Provocation," *Journal of Personality and Social Psychology*, **35** (1977): 79–87.

89. Dolf Zillman and Jennings Bryant, "Pornography, Sexual Callousness, and the Trivialization of Rape," *Journal of Communication*, **32** (1984): 10–21. See also Cynthia S. Gentry, "Pornography and Rape: An Empirical Analysis," *Deviant Behavior*, **12** (1991): 277–288; and Berl Kutchinsky, "Pornography and Rape: Theory and Practice? Evidence from Crime Data in Four Countries Where Pornography Is Easily Available," *International Journal of Law and Psychiatry*, **14** (1991): 47–64.

90. Donnerstein et al., *The Question of Pornography; Final Report of the Attorney General's Commission on Pornography* (Nashville: Rutledge Hill Press, 1986), esp. pp. 38–47.

91. Joan Hoff, "Why Is There No History of Pornography?" in *For Adult Users Only: The Dilemma of Violent Pornography*, eds. Susan Gubar and Joan Hoff (Bloomington: Indiana University Press, 1989), p. 18.

92. *Miller v. California*, 413 U.S. 15 (1973).

93. *Pope v. Illinois*, 481 U.S. 497 (1987).

94. Kinsey et al., *Sexual Behavior in the Human Male*.

95. Alfred C. Kinsey, Wardel B. Pomeroy, Clyde E. Martin, and Paul H. Gebhard, *Sexual Behavior in the Human Female* (Philadelphia: Saunders, 1953), p. 453.

96. Morton Hunt, *Sexual Behavior in the 1970s* (New York: Dell, 1974).

14
Comparative Criminology

KEY TERMS
comparative criminology
international crimes
transnational crime

In June 1993 the FBI arrested eight "skinheads" who had been plotting to bomb the First African Methodist Episcopal Church in Los Angeles and shoot worshippers. American skinheads have become notorious for their random assaults on blacks, Jews, gays, immigrants, minority groups—anybody they perceive as different and whom they therefore dislike. They revere Hitler and his terror, delight in overt racist music, display swastikas and Nazi flags, and serve as shock troops for more established racist organizations. Between 3300 and 3500 skinheads are scattered in 160 or so groups, in 40 states. They have become so dangerous that the FBI had to withdraw some undercover agents who had infiltrated their ranks.[1]

Few people had heard of skinheads prior to May 1985, when groups from Britain, Belgium, Denmark, and France staged a riot at a soccer game in Belgium which left 38 people of color dead and another 200 wounded. Since then, skinheads have become a daily news item in many countries. During the Persian Gulf War, 1990 to 1991, skinheads burned 20 mosques to the ground in the London area.

Hardest hit has been Germany, the birthplace of Nazism, where the homes of Jewish families have been firebombed and hundreds of foreign workers and asylum seekers have been attacked or killed. The skinheads attack with screams of "Heil Hitler," waving their favorite symbol, the old German imperial flag.

> Their ideology, if that is the word, is primitive . . . they know nothing about Hitler, or the war, beyond the fact that Hitler exterminated people who were "different" which is what they like to do themselves. They do not even know about the "ethnic cleansing" going on . . . in Bosnia now. They do not read newspapers. They read killer comic books and listen to Oi music, which is a kind of heavy-metal rock about the pleasures of "genocide." [2]

What has caused the rise of neo-Nazism and the formation of skinhead groups, almost simultaneously, in so many different countries? Who defined this bizarre and primitive ideology? Do the groups know one another? Do they exchange information other than through heavy-metal rock? What causes them to dress alike, shave their heads, adopt identical symbols, resort to identical weapons and violent tactics? How different are these groups from the many street gangs found in American cities?

To answer these questions, criminologists must do comparative research. Criminologist Mark Hamm has begun this process with his work *American Skinheads—The Criminology and Control of Hate Crime,* which presents the phenomenon in an international perspective. He traces American developments to earlier occurrences in England and to the ideological background of Nazism in Germany.[3] Yet much more comparative research remains to be done to explain the almost simultaneous occurrence of identical crime problems in many parts of the world.

We begin this chapter on comparative criminology with an attempt to define it. That can best be done by explaining what it is not. We look next at the history of comparative criminology in order to identify its purpose and goals. Later in the chapter we focus on the prerequisites for comparative criminological research, the process itself, and the variety of research efforts in this growing field.

WHAT IS COMPARATIVE CRIMINOLOGY?

Comparison is something all human beings do every day. In choosing a home, for example, you compare such elements as number of rooms and price, location, access to transportation, shopping and recreation, age of the structure, beauty of the surroundings, and so on. This comparison can become a science if it is done in a systematic manner. And so it is with comparative criminology.

The Definition of Comparative Criminology

What is comparative criminology? Simply put, it is the application of the comparative method in the science of criminology.[4]

Many criminologists use comparisons. Just think of a study comparing one group with another group, a control group. But this is not

Neo-Nazi skinheads in Berlin displaying the old imperial German battle flag which, oddly enough, the Nazis had banned.

what we mean by comparative criminology; it requires comparison across cultures or nations. A comparative study of victimization rates between Montana and Mississippi is not comparative criminology, because the two states are part of one nation and of one basic culture. But if we were to compare the role of alcohol in the escalation of violence among the Cheyenne nation, in Montana or Wyoming, with that among the people of the rest of the state, we might well have a cross-cultural comparison, because the Cheyenne have a distinct legal system, they have a culture of their own, and they are related to the U.S. government by a treaty.

Typical of comparative criminology is research on "transnational crime and comparisons of crime and criminal justice systems across nations," as it is stated in the mission statement of the International Division of the American Society of Criminology. We would like to elaborate this definition by calling **comparative criminology** the cross-cultural or cross-national study of crime and crime control. As we will see, this kind of study is not new (Table 14.1).

The History of Comparative Criminology

When the Romans had a crime problem in the fifth century B.C., they sent a delegation to the more advanced nation of Greece to learn better techniques for dealing with crime, such as the codification and publication of laws. A thousand years later, the still relatively backward Germanic tribes—among them our legal ancestors, the Angles and the Saxons—learned how to draft legal codes from the Romans. In the late Middle Ages and during the Renaissance (fourteenth to sixteenth centuries), all of continental Europe became a vast comparative laboratory as laws that had developed in the various principalities and cities were compared against the rediscovered laws of the old Roman Empire.

Unhappily, it was also during this era that crime-control methods became ever more brutal. The situation was not to change until the eighteenth century, when—again through comparison, cooperation, and transfer—the work of the classical school (see Chapter 3) began to intro-

TABLE 14.1 EXAMPLES OF COMPARATIVE RESEARCH

Perceptions of Crime

Evans, Sandra S., and Joseph E. Scott (1984). "The Seriousness of Crime Cross-Culturally: The Impact of Religiosity," *Criminology,* **22**(1): 39–59.

Uses survey data from the U.S. and the Middle East to assess the perceptual seriousness of various crimes and sanctions in a comparative context. Also employs religious sentiments to examine perceived seriousness of crimes.

Newman, Graeme R. (1976). *Comparative Deviance:* Perception and Law in Six Cultures. New York: Elsevier. 332 pp.

Uses questionnaire data to examine public responses in six countries to legal perceptions of robbery, incest, homosexuality, abortion, factory pollution, public protest vs. govt. policy, misuse of govt. funds, drug use: India, Indonesia, Iran, Italy (Sardinia), Yugoslavia, U.S.

Violent Crime

Feirabend, I. K., and R. L. Feirabend (1966). "Aggressive Behaviors within Politics, 1948–1962: A Cross-National Study," *Journal of Conflict Resolution,* **10**: 249–271.

Uses three theoretical propositions to compare aspects of political aggression in numerous countries. Tests for (1) levels of frustration and conflict, (2) relationship between modernity and political stability, and (3) prediction of political instability over time.

Piala, Robert, and Gary LaFree (1988). "Cross-National Determinants of Child Homicide," *American Sociological Review,* **53**: 432–445.

Examines the causes of child homicide in 18 countries. Derives hypothesis from theories of social organization, social structure, culture of violence, and social isolation. Data include World Health Organization child homicide rates, World Bank unemployment rates, professional status of women (ILO), and female students (UNESCO).

Crimes against Property

Abbott, Daniel J. (1980). "Liberation Movements and Robbery: A Comparative Analysis of Uganda and the United States," *International Journal of Comparative and Applied Criminal Justice,* **4**(2): 165–178.

Compares the causes of rising robbery rates in Uganda and the U.S. during the 1960s. Reviews various theories of political changes in both countries. Findings suggest the influence in both countries of social forces on increased robbery rates.

Bacon, Margaret K., Irvin L. Child, and Herbert Barry III (1981). "A Cross-Cultural Study of Correlates of Crime," in Louise I. Shelly (ed.), *Readings in Comparative Criminology* (pp. 174–188). Carbondale, Ill.: Southern Illinois University Press.

Examines crime correlations in a sample of 48 preliterate societies, selected on the basis of geographical diversity and adequate data on aboriginal child-training practices. Focuses on the psychological and sociological determinants of crime.

Economic and Political Crime

Los, Maria (1983). "Economic Crimes in Communist Countries," in Israel L. Barak-Glantz and Elmer H. Johnson (eds.), *Comparative Criminology* (pp. 39–57). Beverly Hills, Calif.: Sage.

Discusses types of economic crimes which threaten communist processes of production and distribution of goods in the U.S.S.R. and Poland. Describes the relationship between economic crimes and the organizational forces of communist economies.

Ingraham, Barton L. (1979). *Political Crime in Europe: A Comparative Study of France, Germany, and England.* Berkeley, Calif.: University of California Press. 380 pp.

A comparative historical analysis of the characteristics of political crime and control mechanisms and their links with other forms of criminality from 1789 to 1970: France, Germany, Britain.

TABLE 14.1 EXAMPLES OF COMPARATIVE RESEARCH

Transnational Corporate Crime

Braithwaite, John (1979). "Transnational Corporations and Corruption: Towards Some International Solutions," *International Journal of the Sociology of Law*, **7**(2): 125–142.

Outlines various strategic maneuvers, such as bribery, corruption, and rule bending, which are used by transnational corporations to evade international laws and regulations. Discusses the problems of controlling corporate illegalities.

Baker, James C. (1985). "The International Infant Formula Controversy: A Dilemma in Corporate Social Responsibility," *Journal of Business Ethics*, **4**: 181–190.

Analyzes corporate and noncorporate reactions to this controversy and strategic marketing changes. Addresses legal, social, and health aspects, as well as research findings, with special reference to Third World nations such as India.

Correlates of Crime—Age, Class, Gender, Race

Friday, Paul C. (1980). "International Review of Youth Crime and Delinquency," in Graeme R. Newman (ed.), *Crime and Deviance: A Comparative Perspective* (pp. 100–129). Beverly Hills, Calif.: Sage.

Utilizes cross-cultural studies to identify structural, institutional, social, and familial conditions which contribute to youth crime.

French, Laurence (1977). "A Cultural Perspective toward Juvenile Delinquency," *International Journal of Comparative and Applied Criminal Justice*, **1**(2): 111–121.

Investigates the influence of cultural factors on juvenile delinquency. Compares the etiology of juvenile delinquency in the U.S. with traditional folk cultures of the Muer, the Hopi, the Keraki Indians of New Guinea, and the Arunta of central Australia.

Underdevelopment and Modernization

Neuman, W. Lawrence, and Ronald J. Berger (1988). "Competing Perspectives on Cross-National Crime: An Evaluation of Theory and Evidence," *Sociological Quarterly*, **29**(2): 281–313.

A comprehensive literature review that compares the Durkheimian modernization, Marxian world system, and ecological opportunity perspectives on cross-national crime rates. Recommends that comparative criminology be integrated with research on economic development and crime in general.

Social Control and Dispute Resolution

Soothill, K. L., et al. (1981). "Social Control of Deviants in Six Countries," *Medicine, Science and Law*, **21**(1): 31–40.

Part of a World Health organization research project: Compares networks of social control in Brazil, Denmark, Egypt, Swaziland, Switzerland, and Thailand. Discusses differences between the formal social control systems of health and criminal justice.

Source: Adapted from Piers Beirne and Joan Hill, Comparative Criminology-An Annotated Bibliography (New York and Westport, Conn.: Greenwood, 1991).

duce rationality and humanitarian principles into crime control in Europe and America. In the nineteenth century, as communications improved, policy makers and scholars of criminology compared approaches and introduced into one another's systems what seemed to work. Such ideas as the penitentiary, the reformatory, probation, and parole gained worldwide acceptance as a result of comparison. Yet the comparisons of the nineteenth and early twentieth centuries lacked scientific rigor; they were impressionistic and often emotional. For example, the juvenile court, first established in Chicago in 1899, seemed such a good idea that it gained acceptance in many parts of the world. But as later experience showed, it did not necessarily work everywhere.

The founders of criminology, including those of American criminology, were, for the most part, comparatists. They would gather at international meetings and trade ideas; they would visit each other and stimulate criminological thought. But truly comparative studies, measuring up to scholarly standards, could not be done until criminology itself became a science. Throughout the first half of the twentieth century internationalism met resistance from isolationism. Comparatists were regarded as dreamers, and the comparative approach was seen as not very practical.

The Global Village: Advantages

Now circumstances have changed drastically. Comparative criminologists have become a necessity, simply because the world has become a "global village." Consider these figures from the U.S. Department of Commerce: In 1960 the United States exported $30 billion worth of goods; in 1992 it exported $448 billion. In 1960 imports were $23 billion; in 1992 they were $533 billion. In 1992 Americans invested $420 billion abroad, and foreigners just as much in the United States (up from $13 billion only 20 years earlier).

World economies have become totally integrated and interdependent. The Japanese car you own was probably manufactured in the United States, and your American car may have parts made in more than 30 countries. Your shirt may come from Hong Kong, your shoes from Italy, and your Swiss watch from the American Virgin Islands. The situation is no different abroad, where Coke and Pepsi and American fast-food chains are only the most visible aspects of economic globalization.

Communications likewise have become global. Sitting in your living room before a TV, you participate in world events as they happen. Phone and fax and computer networking have made instant personal and business communications possible. Transportation advances, especially since the introduction of jumbo jets, together with the easing of frontiers, have made it possible for millions of people to move across oceans within hours.

The Global Village: Disadvantages

All these developments have been greatly beneficial. Yet they have also brought great problems. Instant communication promotes not only the spread of benefits, in goods, lifestyles, and useful knowledge, but also the dissemination of dysfunctional ideas and values—like the skinhead phenomenon. Economic globalization, as much as it promotes useful commerce, also aids organized crime and fosters the global spread of frauds that were once confined to smaller localities or single countries.

Jet planes transport not just legitimate travelers but also illegal aliens, criminal entrepreneurs, drug dealers, money launderers, and terrorists. Airlines themselves have become the targets of international criminals. Moreover, the industrialization of the world brings not just economic benefits but threats to the world ecology so severe that, unless they are checked, they could compromise the food, water, and clean air supply for all people. It is little wonder, then, that criminologists too must look across borders to study crime and crime-control efforts, and to search for internationally acceptable solutions to common problems.

The Goals of Comparative Research

Prior to the 1970s there was very little literature on comparative research in criminology. Since then, however, it has been growing rapidly. An annotated bibliography by Piers Beirne and Joan

Hill, published in 1991, listed 500 publications in the field. This increase in the literature, according to Beirne and Hill, is attributable to two facts: (1) a realization "that the explanatory power of theories can be enhanced considerably if they are tested under as diverse temporal and cultural conditions as possible"; and (2) the breaking of the American monopoly on criminological research, which "has led to renewed interest in the cultural specificity of one's own theories, in the criminology of other countries, and in trying to discover if, how, and what one can learn from the other."[5]

We may regard these two explanatory factors as goals, or purposes, for comparative criminological studies. The former is a more theoretically oriented purpose, the latter a more practical one. If we were to add to the 500 scholarly books and journal articles listed by Beirne and Hill the many studies produced under the auspices of international organizations, we might come to the conclusion that the practical goal is gaining the upper hand in comparative criminology, in a double sense. There is, first of all, a justified interest in learning from the experience of others, so that no nation need repeat costly mistakes made elsewhere. Second, there is a vastly increased need for establishing international measures to deal with dangers that threaten all human beings. (See Table 14.2.)

Thus, there now seem to be two purposes for engaging in comparative criminological research:

1. The theoretical goal of testing criminological theories in a broader cross-cultural setting.
2. The very practical goal of learning from programs, policies, and experiences in crime control around the world.

Research may be done simply to create improvements in one's own crime-control policy. It also may be done on a larger scale: to construct international crime-control and criminal justice policies that deal with internationally induced local crime problems and the various forms of transnational and international crime.

Before we can address the implementation of any of these goals, we must look at the methods used by comparative criminologists.

ENGAGING IN COMPARATIVE CRIMINOLOGICAL RESEARCH

Comparative research requires special preparatory work to ensure that research data and information are in fact comparable. Empirical research presents additional obstacles.

Preparatory Work

Studying Foreign Law

Before beginning a comparative study, the researcher must become familiar with the laws of the country or culture to which the comparison extends. Every country belongs to one or more of the world's three great families of law, or legal systems (Table 14.3):

■ The *common law system:* Common law originated in England and then spread to the various English colonies. Today it is the legal system of the United States, Canada (except Quebec), Australia, New Zealand, India, many of the Caribbean islands, and African countries that were once English colonies. Although common law is now to be found in written form, it originated from case law, and case precedents still play a determining role.

■ The *civil law system:* This system grew out of the Roman legal tradition, was refined by scholars, and was codified under Napoleon in the early nineteenth century. Today it is found in systematic codes of law. The countries of continental Europe belong to this family of law, as do their former colonies in Africa, Latin America, and Asia, including Japan and China, which chose the civil law system when they modernized.

■ *Indigenous or customary legal systems:* Among these is the largely written and highly developed Islamic law of countries in the Middle East, which is also found in a few African and Asian countries. Other societies govern themselves largely by tribal law, tradition, and custom. This customary law is generally unwritten.

Having identified the legal system to which the country under study belongs, the comparatist

TABLE 14.2 UNITED NATIONS ORGANIZATIONS AND AFFILIATES: SOLVING WORLDWIDE CRIME PROBLEMS

Crime Prevention and Criminal Justice Branch (of the U.N. Secretariat at Vienna, Austria): Reports to the U.N. Commission on Crime Prevention and Criminal Justice and conducts the quinquennial U.N. Congress on the Prevention of Crime and the Treatment of Offenders; provides extensive reports, research, documentation, and technical assistance; responsible for U.N. standards and guidelines in criminal justice; conducts worldwide statistical surveys.

UNICRI—United Nations Interregional Crime and Justice Research Institute (heretofore located in Rome, Italy): Research arm of the U.N. Secretariat in crime prevention and criminal justice; responsible for extensive research and publications.

UNAFEI—United Nations Asia and Far East Institute for the Prevention of Crime and the Treatment of Offenders (Tokyo, Japan): Services the region with training, technical assistance, research, and publications.

ILANUD—United Nations Latin American Institute for the Prevention of Crime and the Treatment of Offenders (San José, Costa Rica): Services the region with training, technical assistance, research, and publications.

UNAFRI—United Nations African Regional Institute for the Prevention of Crime and the Treatment of Offenders (Kampala, Uganda): Services the region with training and technical assistance.

HEUNI—Helsinki Eurpoean Institute for Crime Prevention and Control. Affiliated with the United Nations (Helsinki, Finland); provides extensive research, training, publications, and technical assistance services on behalf of European countries for both developed and developing countries.

AIC—Australian Institute of Criminology (Canberra, Australia): Under agreement with the U.N., provides research, publication, training, and technical assistance services for Oceania, including Australia and New Zealand.

Arab Security Studies and Training Centre (Riyadh, Saudi Arabia): In close cooperation with the U.N., provides extensive educational and training services, research, publications, and development and technical assistance to Arab countries.

International Centre for Criminal Law Reform and Criminal Justice Policy (Vancouver, B.C., Canada): Newly established, by agreement with the U.N., to provide services within its sphere of expertise.

ISPAC—International Scientific and Professional Advisory Council of United Nations Crime Prevention and Criminal Justice Programs (Milan, Italy): By agreement with the U.N., provides advisory services to the U.N. with respect to data and information, both in general and on specific subjects falling within the mandate of the U.N..

UNCJIN—United Nations Crime and Justice Information Network (Albany, N.Y.): In close cooperation with *WCJLN*—World Criminal Justice Library Network (Newark, N.J.)—assembles, integrates, and disseminates criminal justice information and data worldwide, with a view to complete electronic accessibility.

NGOs—Non governmental organizations in consultative status with the United Nations Economic and Social Council: International organizations whose expertise is made available to the U.N. They include many major scientific, professional, and advocacy groups, such as:

- International Association of Penal Law
- International Penal and Penitentiary Foundation (special status)
- International Society of Criminology
- International Society of Social Defense
- Institute of Higher Studies in Criminal Sciences
- Centro Nazionale di Prevenzione e Difesa Sociale
- International Association of Chiefs of Police
- International Prisoners Aid Association
- Amnesty International

NGO Alliances in Crime Prevention and Criminal Justice (New York, N.Y., and Vienna, Austria): Comprised of the headquarters representatives of NGOs; provide coordination and research services to the U.N.

U.N. agencies: Concerned with various aspects of crime and justice. The agencies include

- Centre for Human Rights (Geneva, Switzerland)
- *UNICEF*, United Nations Children's Fund (New York, N.Y.)

The United Nations International Drug Control Programme: Concerned with various aspects of international drug control and drug abuse prevention. The programs include:

- Division on Narcotic Drugs
- International Narcotics Control Board
- U.N. Fund for Drug Abuse Control

Regional intergovernmental organizations: Have organizational units and/or conduct programs concerned with crime prevention and criminal justice. Examples include:

- Council of Europe
- European Economic Community (EEC)
- Organization of American States
- Organization of African Unity
- North Atlantic Treaty Organization

TABLE 14.3 DOMINANT CRIMINAL JUSTICE SYSTEMS

Roman (Civil) Law	Common Law	Customary Law
Law and procedure governed by separate, comprehensive, systematized codes, which are forward-looking, wishing to anticipate all new problems.	Law and procedure governed by laws and precedents, which, if codified at all, simply organize past experiences.	Resembles common law more than civil law, largely relying on precedents transmitted orally or in writing.
Codes based on scholarly analysis and conceptualizations.	Laws reflect experience of practitioners, on a case-by-case basis.	
Supreme Courts interpret nuances of law.	Supreme Courts develop law.	
Legal proceedings must establish entire truth.	Truth finding strictly limited by pleadings and rules of evidence.	Popular justice, often without trained lawyers.
Judges free to find and interpret facts.	Rules of evidence limit fact-finding process. Parties produce evidence.	
Very little lay participation.	Grand and petit juries play strong role.	
No presumption of guilt or innocence.	Presumption of innocence.	

studies the applicable law and its precise interpretation. Foreign legal systems, just like that of the United States, contain penal codes, codes of criminal procedure, constitutions, and case reports. But they also include special legislation on such topics as environmental protection and money laundering. In federal countries both federal and state legislation may have to be studied.

Then there is the problem of finding the country's laws. For the English-speaking researcher this need not be an insurmountable task. The laws, court decisions, and textbooks of English-speaking countries, for the most part, are accessible in libraries. The constitutions,[6] criminal codes,[7] and codes of criminal procedure[8] of many other countries are available in English. For a number of non-English-speaking countries there are English-language texts about their criminal law or procedure.[9] But since there is always a gap between the law on the books and the law in action, the comparatist must also consult the criminal justice research literature.

Understanding Foreign Criminal Justice Systems

Laws function within a country's criminal justice system. It is the practitioners of the system who make the laws function. There is a considerable amount of periodical literature in English describing the functioning of criminal justice systems in a variety of countries (Table 14.4).

For example, the *Resource Material Series* produced by UNAFEI (United Nations Asia and Far East Institute for the Prevention of Crime and the Treatment of Offenders) is a rich source of information about various aspects of criminal justice in all the Asian countries. These reports are based on the experience of practitioners.[10] The Helsinki Institute for Crime Prevention and Control, affiliated with the United Nations, has published a systematic overview of the criminal justice systems of Europe and North America, including statistical information.[11]

Contemporary cross-cultural texts and treatises contain descriptions of the developments in criminology and criminal justice for over 50 countries.[12] In addition to the descriptions of entire criminal justice systems, there are accounts of the functioning of subsystems. For example, a five-volume series, edited by Canadian juvenile justice specialist V. Lorne Stewart, examines the area of delinquency and juvenile justice in more than two dozen countries and regions throughout the world.[13] Other aspects of criminal justice

TABLE 14.4 ENGLISH-LANGUAGE PERIODICAL LITERATURE FOR COMPARATIVE CRIMINOLOGY

Abstracting Services

*Criminal Justice Abstracts**
Criminology, Penology and Police Science Abstracts

Periodicals

Crime Prevention and Criminal Justice Newsletter
  (U.N.)
Criminal Justice International
Criminal Law Forum: An International Journal
Dutch Penal Law and Policy
EuroCriminology
European Journal on Criminal Policy and Research
Forensic Science International
Home Office Research and Planning Unit Research
  Bulletin
International Annals of Criminology
International Criminal Justice Review
International Criminal Police Review
International Journal of Comparative and Applied
  Criminal Justice
International Journal of Law and Psychiatry
International Journal of Offender Therapy and
  Comparative Criminology
International Journal of the Addictions
International Journal on Drug Policy
International Review of Criminal Policy (U.N.)
International Review of Victimology
Japanese Journal of Sociological Criminology
Revue de Science Criminelle et de Droit Penal
  Comparée†
Revue Internationale de Criminologie et de Police
  Technique†
Revue Internationale de Droit Penal†
Studies in Conflict and Terrorism
Studies on Crime and Crime Prevention (Norway)
Terrorism
UNAFEI Resource Material Series
Violence, Aggression and Terrorism
Violence and Victims

* Also electronically accessible.
† Some coverage in English.

have been investigated by specialists in such areas as policing,[14] corrections,[15] and the incidence of female criminality.[16]

Learning about a Foreign Culture

Comparatists may have an understanding of their own culture. To do comparative work, they must study a foreign culture: they must become familiar with its history, politics, economy, and social structure. Scholars of comparative criminology—such as Marshall B. Clinard, working in Switzerland as well as India and other developing countries;[17] Louise I. Shelley, working in Eastern European socialist countries and elsewhere;[18] and William Clifford, working in several African countries as well as Japan[19]—have successfully demonstrated that the immersion in the cultures under study that comparative research requires can be accomplished without losing the objectivity of the detached scientific researcher.

Collecting Data

Research, as we emphasized in Chapter 2, requires factual information. Although some countries do not yet have the resources for systematically collecting information on their crime problems,[20] the great majority send statistics to the International Criminal Police Organization (Interpol), which publishes the data biannually,[21] or participate in the United Nations Surveys of Crime Trends, Operation of Criminal Justice Systems and Crime Prevention Strategies. The U.N. surveys, published in five-year cycles, began with data for the year 1970 and by now include statistics from well over 100 countries on prevalence of crime and the operation of criminal systems.[22]

Several other international data bases are available to the researcher, including the homicide statistics of the World Health Organization;[23] the private-initiative Comparative Crime Data File, which covers 110 sovereignties (published 1984);[24] and the Correlates of Crime (published 1989).[25]

International (or nation-by-nation) crime statistics suffer from the same problems as American UCR statistics, only magnified several times.[26] For this reason, several scholars have recently conducted international victimization surveys. The first major survey, conducted by a team of Dutch, English, and Swiss scholars, covers 17 countries, both developed and developing.[27] Not surprisingly, this survey exposed the international "dark figure of crime"—the differences between crime reported to the police and crime as experienced by victims. Consequently, the same caution must be applied to the official

CRIMINOLOGICAL FOCUS
Cross-Cultural Research: Smoking One's Way into Cheyenne Culture

Source: As told in class, ca. 1950, by Karl N. Llewellyn, University of Chicago; Calf Woman's story is excerpted from K. N. Llewellyn and E. Adamson Hoebel, The Cheyenne Way (Norman: University of Oklahoma Press, 1941), pp. 12–13.

It was in the summer of 1935 that Karl N. Llewellyn, renowned legal philosopher, and his friend E. Adamson Hoebel, noted anthropologist, visited the northern Cheyennes on the Tongue River Reservation at Lame Deer, Montana. High Forehead of the Cheyennes served as their interpreter. Sitting in a circle with several Cheyennes, a chief filled the pipe and held it to the five directions. After the pipe had been passed around, he asked why the two white men had come.

"To learn of your laws," answered the visitors. There was silence and more pipe puffing. Obviously the term "laws" meant nothing. Llewellyn went on, "For example, your rules on homicide . . . ?" More silence, more puffing. "Well," said Llewellyn, making another attempt, "what happens when there is trouble because one of your warriors has killed another man of the tribe?"

At this there was a smile of recognition, and Calf Woman spoke:

Cries Yia Eya had been gone from the camp for three years because he had killed Chief Eagle in a whiskey brawl. The chiefs had ordered him away for his murder, so we did not see anything of him for that time. Then one day he came back, leading a horse packed with bundles of old-time tobacco. He stopped outside the camp and sent a messenger in with the horse and tobacco who was to say to the chiefs for him, "I am begging to come home."

The chiefs all got together for a meeting, and the soldier societies were told to convene. The tobacco was divided up and chiefs' messengers were sent out to invite the soldier chiefs to come to the lodge of the tribal council. "Here is the tobacco that that man sent in," [the big chiefs] told the soldier chiefs. "Now we want you soldiers to decide if you think we should accept his request. If you decide that we should let him return, then it is up to you to convince his family that it is all right." (The relatives of Chief Eagle had told everybody that they would kill Cries Yia Eya on sight if they ever found him.) The soldier chiefs took the tobacco and went out to gather their troops. Each society met in its own separate lodge to talk among themselves.

At last one man said, "I think it is all right. I believe the stink has blown from him. Let him return!" This view was passed around, and this is the view that won out among the soldiers. Then the father of Chief Eagle was sent for and asked whether he would accept the decision. "Soldiers," he replied, "I shall listen to you. Let him return! But if that man comes back, I want never to hear his voice raised against another person. If he does, we come together."

Cries Yia Eya had always been a mean man, disliked by everyone, but he had been a fierce fighter against the enemies. After he came back to the camp, however, he was always good to the people.

Llewellyn and Hoebel went on to collect hundreds of anecdotes of Cheyenne "conflict and case law." While they knew that the Cheyennes had structured institutions, they were surprised at the "juristic beauty" that the research revealed. In the introduction to their work on the subject, *The Cheyenne Way*, the authors comment:

Three years of puzzlement went into the analysis of the material before order emerged; and this happened (as it does in modern case law) when the data of sixty or eighty years were arranged not on a flat time-plane, but against the moving time-perspective of the culture and the individual life.

Questions for Discussion

1. What are some of the problems of doing criminological research in other cultures?
2. What are the best ways of ensuring that those problems are overcome?

Interpol's new headquarters in Lyon, France.

crime statistics of foreign countries as we apply to official U.S. statistics.

Comparative Research

Up to this point we have reviewed the general approach to doing comparative criminological research: studying foreign law, criminal justice systems, cultures, and available data. Comparative criminological research begins only after these requirements have been met. It is at this point that the comparatist sets sail for uncharted seas. The comparatist meets two problems right at the outset: the interdependence of all crime and criminal justice phenomena, and culture specificity.

Interdependent Phenomena

Think of an elaborately assembled mobile hanging from the ceiling. All the parts are in per-

fect balance. If you remove a single part, the whole mobile will completely shift out of balance. It is the same with problems of crime and justice in any society: the existence of each is related to all the others and is explainable by reference to the others. Bicycle thefts may exist in countries like China, Denmark, and the Netherlands—all of which rely heavily on bicycle transportation—as well as in the United States or Mexico. But such theft plays a different role in the various countries, generates different responses, and leads to different consequences.

Is the bicycle theft problem comparable around the world? What could be learned from a comparison, and what factors must be considered? Would it be more useful to compare the Chinese bicycle theft problem with the Italian automobile theft problem? How do these problems fit in their countries' respective crime and justice mobiles?

Culture-Specific Phenomena

The task of a comparative criminologist is like that of a surgeon about to transplant a heart or a liver. The surgeon studies a great variety of factors to be sure the donor's organ is compatible with the recipient's body. If we want to compare Japan's low crime rates with the high crime rates in the United States, we must consider many factors, such as the role of shame in Japanese society. Misconduct brings shame not only on individual Japanese wrongdoers, but also on their families, schools, and companies: could shaming, as a sanction, play a role in American criminal justice, or is it too culture-specific?

It is easier to ask such questions than it is to answer them, since research experience in comparative criminology is still limited. In fact, the first book entitled *"Comparative" Criminology* appeared as recently as 1965. Its author, the late German-English scholar Hermann Mannheim, relied on his vast cross-cultural experience in criminology but offered no guide to the comparative method.[28] More in the nature of a true comparative exercise—yet also without much guidance regarding the comparative method—is the Polish scholar Brunon Holyst's *Comparative Criminology* (1979), which systematically compares the incidence and causes of crime and the features of criminal justice around the world.[29]

If a comparative criminologist does research in India, he or she must first understand the culture of the subcontinent, including the fact that cows are sacred and can never be harmed or even disturbed.

The Special Problems of Empirical Research

Criminologists who cannot find or rely upon comparative data must generate their own, usually by parallel field investigations proceeding more or less simultaneously. They confront three problems: first, the identification of comparable problems; second, the identification of sources of information; and third, the selection of a research method compatible in the countries under comparison.

Identification of Comparable Problems

Researchers of New York University's Comparative Criminal Law Project, in the 1960s, compared the prevalence of delinquency in several cultures. To their surprise, they learned that Egypt had a high rate of delinquency for railroad offenses. Only local assistance could provide a plausible answer: the long railroad line running parallel to the Nile River is a favored haunt for local youths. Their delinquent acts were recorded as railroad offenses, rather than as delinquency.[30]

These "railroad offenses" had to be made comparable to nonrailroad delinquencies in both Egypt and the other countries under comparison.

Identification of Sources of Information

The social groups of one society may not be comparable to those of another. American junior high school students may represent American youngsters of that age range as a whole, but Haitian junior high school students would not. What groups are comparable to such favorite research subjects as American college students, blue-collar workers, and self-employed small-business people? What is a fair cross section of any country's population?

Police records may be highly reliable in Belgium, but are they in Mali and Malawi or in Armenia? And if they are not, what comparable substitutes can the comparatist find? Such problems challenge the researcher's ingenuity.

Selection of Compatible Research Methods

Criminologist James Finckenauer, studying attitudes toward legal and other values among American and Russian youngsters, was at first confronted with the reluctance of Russian administrators to ask youngsters to report (even anonymously) their own delinquencies. The Soviet culture had blocked any such initiative. The problem was overcome only by indirect questions to the youngsters, such as: "How wrong would it be (to do this, that, or the other)?" This was followed by further semidirect questions, such as: "Do your peers (parents, and so on) view you as a good kid, bad kid, or something in between?" It was only after the end of communism in 1992 that Finckenauer could administer a self-report delinquency questionnaire.

Certain research methods simply are unknown in many other countries or, if known, are frowned upon. In a study of perceptions of police power in four cultures, for example, the commanding officer of a foreign police department was asked to have some questionnaires distributed to his officers. At first the officer responded: "You don't seem to understand our police! It is we who ask the questions!" Finally he agreed and distributed the questionnaires. After the results were analyzed, the researchers were astonished to find that all the answers were identical. Apparently, all the questionnaires had been reviewed and "corrected" by an attorney to make sure they were accurate.[31]

THEORY TESTING

As we noted earlier, the cross-cultural testing of criminological theories has become one of the major goals of comparative criminology. Recent studies have extended to several of the crime-causation theories discussed in this book; recent research has also explored the development of crime worldwide.

Validation of Major Theories

After Sheldon and Eleanor Glueck had completed *Unraveling Juvenile Delinquency* (1960),[32] their work was criticized as too culture-specific because it was based on a sample of American children. In response, scholars replicated the Glueck research in different cultural settings—Puerto Rico, Germany, and Japan. As the Gluecks themselves put it. "All these [studies] . . . have

provided the most definite of all proofs, that of applicability to other samples by other researchers."[33] These cross-cultural validations of the Gluecks' delinquency-prediction system are some of the earliest empirical, comparative criminological studies.

More recently, criminologist Obi Ebbe has reviewed the Gluecks' studies and found their theories applicable to juvenile delinquents in Nigeria.[34] He has also examined the cross-cultural validity of other American theories, such as differential association, urban conditions, economic conditions, social control, and culture conflict theories.

During the last few years American and foreign criminologists have engaged in a number of cross-cultural validations of prominent criminological theories. Studies have tested opportunity theory,[35] situational characteristics of crime,[36] routine-activities theory,[37] differential opportunity theory,[38] social control and strain theory,[39] the synnomie explanation of low crime rates,[40] and Durkheim's anomie theory.[41] Somewhat surprisingly, most of these studies have shown the theories to have moderate to significant validity.[42]

The Socioeconomic Development Perspective

Cross-cultural researchers have devoted particular attention to the recently developed hypothesis that modernization and urbanization lead to increases in crime[43] as well as to the general question of whether socioeconomic development necessarily brings an increase in crime. Various United Nations documents, research papers, and resolutions have noted a connection between rapid and unguided economic development and an increase in certain types of crime, especially property crime.[44] Several cross-cultural studies also found moderate support for the modernization hypothesis, with results showing a strong association between level of development (or modernization) and a rise in theft rates.[45]

The complexity of the relation between development and crime has prompted some comparative criminologists to warn that, as yet, there is no universal theoretical framework linking crime and development.[46] Cross-cultural research has demonstrated that sudden urbanization and industrialization have not led to increased crime in some countries[47] but that unguided socioeconomic and political changes, such as the current transformation from a socialist to a market economy in Central and Eastern Europe, do produce an increase in crime.[48]

PRACTICAL GOALS

Learning from Others' Experiences

With increasing globalization, the similarity of crime problems increases as well. It is natural that criminologists would look at the experiences of other countries in their search for solutions, especially the experiences of countries that seem to have found workable solutions.[49] For the worldwide drunk-driving problem, for example, comparative research has been done in Australia, Norway, and the United States.[50] One gun-control study investigated the situation in 7 nations;[51] another, in 26.[52] Insurance fraud researchers have looked at the situation in eight countries;[53] insider-trading researchers, in three.[54]

A recent symposium compared differential methods of dealing with ecological crime in the

Kobans are mini-police stations that can be found in every Japanese neighborhood. This one is in the busy Ginza district of Tokyo.

United States, Germany, Austria, Japan, and Taiwan.[55] Comparative criminological research has also been done on violent crime, such as homicides of children,[56] spousal homicides,[57] homicides among young males,[58] and urban violence.[59] For the past 25 years, much attention has been devoted to the comparative study of the problem of juvenile delinquency.[60]

By now there is also a considerable body of cross-cultural research on various aspects of crime-control policy. One of the earliest studies in this area examined the perception of police power among divergent population groups in four countries.[61] The perception of law was studied in six cultures by Graeme Newman,[62] and teenagers' perception of crime and criminal justice was the subject of a more recent two-country study.[63]

Issues in policing[64] as well as sanctions[65] occupy the attention of comparatists in their search for "what works." Victimologists have been particularly active in cross-cultural study.[66]

Developing International Policies

Internationally Induced Local Crime Problems

The skinhead phenomenon is a prime example of the simultaneous appearance of a similar type of crime in various parts of the world.[67] As yet little is known about what causes such simultaneous appearances, although instantaneous reporting in the mass media may aid the process[68] and some international organizational connections also may play a role. Yet neither of these factors was present in the simultaneous reoccurrence of piracy in several widely separated waterways of the world in the mid-1970s, perpetrated in large part by rootless young offenders.[69] The skinheads are part of the broader problem of crimes of discrimination against minorities and of the worldwide spread of violence.

Transnational Crime

When criminologists speak of **transnational crime,** they are referring to crimes, criminal transactions, or criminal schemes that break the laws of more than one country or have an impact on a foreign country. It may be hypothesized that

WINDOW TO THE WORLD
Transnational Criminality: And Now They Deal in Human Body Parts!

True to his conviction that the measurement of body and brain is the key to distinguishing between criminals and noncriminals, Cesare Lombroso, the founder of positivist criminology, willed his body to science. Today, many people donate their organs to other human beings who need them to live. The first kidney transplant occurred in 1954, the first lung transplant in 1963, and the first heart transplant in 1967. By now 350,000 kidneys have been transplanted worldwide. Yet the demand for donated organs far outstrips the supply. Where do the donated organs come from? Who are the donors?

In 1988 a German physician attended a medical congress in Rio de Janeiro, Brazil. Unknown perpetrators attacked him from behind and knocked him unconscious. Several days later he found himself on a park bench, awakening from obvious anesthesia. He noticed that he had been professionally bandaged. A medical examination revealed that he was missing a kidney.

The Scope of the Problem

In Barranquilla, Colombia, the chief of the University Security Force confessed to 50 murders, committed to obtain organs for transplants. In many parts of Latin America, hospital patients, upon discharge, find out that organs have been needlessly removed; the organs are sold for transplants at exorbitant prices! It has been reported that childrens' homes in Brazil have been established as "organ farms."(1) President Rafeal Callejas of Honduras has appointed a commission to investigate charges that Honduran children had been sold abroad for illegal adoptions and organ transplants.(2) A member of the European Parliament asked for international police action to stop "barbaric practices" that included "the murder of children whose bodies are butchered for their organs," which are used for transplants in American and European clinics.(3) The Russian parliament (Supreme Soviet) passed legislation in the face of allegations "that organs for transplants are being illegally harvested on a massive scale and that criminal forces are at work in this."(4) The Mexico City weekly *Proceso* revealed the existence of "baby farms" in several Mexican states; the children are used for adoptions abroad and for organ transplants in 17 clinics in Mexican border cities.(5)

The trade in body parts is now worldwide, criminal, organized, and extremely lucrative. An advertisement in a German newspaper offered kidney transplants for $80,000, including cost of the operation and airfare for two persons to an undisclosed clinic in Asia. The "donor" of the kidney will receive little if anything for his or her organ. The risks for recipients are high: of 130 patients who had traveled to India for a kidney transplant, 8 died on the operating table and another 17 died within a year, mostly of viral and bacterial infections contracted under the unsanitary conditions of the transplant clinics. Less is known about the fate of donors. Yet the poorest inhabitants of the Third World continue to offer skin, an eye, or one or more of their other body parts to transplant clinics catering to foreign recipients.

Sources

1. Britta Buse and Katja Donges, "Illegaler Organhandel," *Magazin fur die Polizai*, **203** (1993): 4–7.
2. "Honduran Official Charges Children's Organs Sold," *Orlando Sentinel Tribune*, Apr. 17, 1993, p. A12.
3. "Euro MPs Seek Transplant Laws," *Press Association Limited, Press Association News File*, Sept. 14, 1993.
4. Svetlana Tutorskaya, "Henceforth, Donated Organs Cannot Be Bought and Sold," *Current Digest of the Post Soviet Press*, **45** (1993): 25.
5. "Latin Children Sold in the United States, Study Claims," *Inter Press Service*, Feb. 16, 1993.

Questions for Discussion

1. Based on the examples given above, what laws are violated by those who deal in human body parts or transplant illegally obtained organs?
2. What type of laws or international conventions are needed to stop "barbaric practices" in organ transplants, without hurting those who desperately need a transplant?

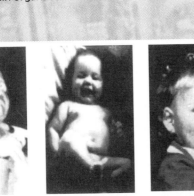

Babies for sale found by police in a trailer in Berlin. The international baby-selling ring was allegedly operated by a 42-year-old Dutch citizen.

the number of transnational crimes increases in direct proportion to the number of legitimate international transactions and activities.[70] Contemporary transnational crimes fall into the following basic categories:

■ Drug crimes
■ Terrorism
■ Economic crimes
■ Organized crime
■ Ecological crime

What these categories of crime have in common is an international complexity that makes it virtually impossible for any one government to deal with them, especially inasmuch as governments, under international law, do not have the right or power (the jurisdiction) to take law enforcement measures in any other country's territory. It therefore becomes necessary for concerned countries to perfect a system of cooperation or even to create an international criminal justice system.

Equally difficult is the problem of researching transnational crime. Data are difficult to obtain, research has to take place in many countries, and the nature of transnational crime makes it almost impossible for one researcher, or even a team, to cover it adequately. Much of the literature on transnational crime is "gray"—hard-to-find agency-generated information—or can only be found, if at all, in the internal archives of national or international agencies. Little empirical cross-cultural research is available.

■ **Drug crimes.** Three United Nations agencies—the Division on Narcotic Drugs, the International Narcotic Control Board, and the Fund for Drug Abuse Control—constitute the United Nations International Drug Programme. Located in Vienna, Austria, the Programme has worldwide responsibility for coordinating policy to deal with the problem of international traffic in narcotics. The legislative network for drug control was recently enlarged by the adoption, in December 1988, of a U.N. drug-trafficking convention. Some drug-control strategies are carried out on a regional level. For example, a recent U.S. General Accounting Office report has compared U.S. drug policies with those of Germany, the

Passengers leavng the cruise ship *Achille Lauro* after a terrorist hijacking in 1985.

United Kingdom, and Italy.[71] The successful unification of Europe will undoubtedly increase opportunities for international drug traffickers.[72]

■ **Terrorism.** Over the years the close connection between the drug trade and terrorism has become clear. Terrorist groups have financed their activities through funds obtained in drug dealing, a connection referred to as "narco-terrorism." Several studies have documented the extent of narco-terrorism.[73]

Terrorism also has an existence quite apart from the narcotics trade. Comparatists have done considerable cross-cultural research on terrorism, most of which can be found in the journals *Terrorism* (New York), *Studies in Conflict and Terrorism* (London), and *Violence, Aggression, Terrorism* (Danbury, Connecticut).

There is enough information to conclude that terrorism is a worldwide problem, that even governments have engaged in terrorism,[74] and that the international machinery to combat terrorism is fragmented and incomplete. The bombing of the World Trade Center by a group of international terrorists on February 26, 1993, brought home the message of our vulnerability and underscored the need for cross-cultural research.

■ **Economic crimes.** According to some cross-cultural researchers, an estimated $85 billion is available for investment each year from narcotics trafficking. On a daily basis, $233 million in drug money flows around the world, seeking secret investment opportunities. The process is called money laundering, meaning that "dirty" money is transferred out of the country of origin and into the banks of countries with lax banking laws. There, accounts may be opened (by number only) with no questions asked.

The governments of major drug-consuming countries (primarily the United States and Western European countries), gravely concerned about the drug–crime connection, have formed the Financial Action Task Force (FATF) to study the problem and find solutions.[75] Yet much transnational research remains to be done before the world can adopt a unified stand on money laundering. Legislative gaps among the laws of the various countries permit money laundering to flourish, and some countries openly invite "dirty" money investments in order to strengthen their economies.

Money laundering is but one of many types of transnational economic crimes. As border controls and customs barriers vanish, "transnational enterprise crimes" are on the increase.[76] They resemble the economic crime that previously was limited to one nation. These crimes include many types of fraud, corruption, and business crimes in violation of local laws.[77] Again, the reach of these crimes can be vast: the BCCI banking fraud affected 73 countries. Research into the operations of transnational economic criminals is in its infancy and can be done successfully only by international teams of researchers with access to government and business documents.

■ **Organized crime.** In our discussion in Chapter 12, we noted that organized crime, once a regional or national phenomenon, has become globalized. Comparatists have barely begun to scratch the surface in transnational organized-crime research. It is, of course, a form of economic crime (although often involving violence), but it differs from the economic crimes just discussed in that economic criminals operate with a mantle of legitimacy whereas organized criminals, on the whole, do not.[78]

Research indicates that intra-European organized crime, Italy excepted, has not been as successful in infiltrating business and government as has American organized crime, although connections are clearly emerging. Russian organized crime, on the other hand, is developing rapidly along American lines.[79] With the collapse of Russia's central market economy and the switch to capitalism, a change in the forms of economic crime and the development of organized crime were predictable, as some researchers have noted.[80]

■ **Ecological crime.** Worldwide advances in technology, especially in nuclear technology, have vastly increased risks to the environment. Criminally negligent construction and maintenance of industrial facilities are causing disasters for people all over the world. Tighter controls in some countries have led industries to relocate to countries where they can operate at greater risk to the environment.

The dangers, however, are not exclusively local. All water ultimately seeps into the same oceans, and polluted air can spread around the globe. A unified global policy to prevent ecological crime is emerging only now, in the wake of the U.N. World Congress on the Environment (Rio de Janeiro, Brazil, 1993). Some criminologists have begun to study the approaches used by various countries in search of worldwide solutions.[81]

As we noted, the cross-cultural study of transnational crime and criminal justice policies has as one of its purposes devising transnational responses to such crimes. Increasingly, this task has fallen on intergovernmental bodies like the United Nations, the Council of Europe, and the European Community. These bodies may agree on strategies and programs aimed at assisting individual countries with their problems and devising common approaches. Usually their conclusions do not have the force of law; they are simply regarded as guides for national legislation and policy. But if agreed upon as a convention, they are binding on the signatories.

AT ISSUE
BCCI: International Fraud

"Massive fraud." "World's biggest banking crash." "Financial deception of 'epic proportions.'" Journalists had a field day characterizing the magnitude of the collapse of the Bank of Credit & Commerce International (BCCI), which failed in July 1991. But let's talk numbers instead of adjectives:

- Founded in Pakistan, the international financial institution owed some $2 billion when it folded.
- A senior official admitted to playing a major role in frauds totaling $1.242 billion.
- Thousands of creditors, both businesses and individuals, lost every penny of the money they had deposited.
- In 1991, BCCI agreed to forfeit $550 million to begin compensating depositors worldwide and to salvage institutions the corporation owned secretly in the United States.
- The U.S. investigation that preceded the prosecution of a single person accused of participating in the scandal cost a whopping $20 million.
- In England alone, BCCI had a staff of 1200 and 45,000 customers—personnel who lost their jobs and customers who lost their life savings when the bank failed.

Big numbers. What are the crimes that led to this scandal of "epic proportions"? In the United States, BCCI has pleaded guilty to federal and state charges of racketeering, fraud, and money laundering. Individuals have been charged with withholding information in a scheme to defraud federal and state bank regulators and depositors. In Britain, charges against bank officials include false accounting, furnishing false information, and conspiracy to defraud.

How it Worked

A picture of the corporation's operations has unfolded since the crash:

BCCI's reported profits had been "falsely inflated" by $614 million between January 1983 and December 1985. The misuse of clients' funds by the bank amounted to another $627 million by the end of 1985. . . . By the early 1980s the bank needed to demonstrate its profitability and a healthy balance sheet to maintain the confidence of banking regulators and current and potential investors. In desperation, the bank's founder and his senior officers turned to the trading of commodities as a likely source of funds and began a series of high-risk speculations trading in futures. Most of these were in options on large-scale purchases of silver, which went badly wrong when the price of the metal turned sharply downwards. As money was lost upon money, the frauds became more widespread. The methods involved to maintain the pretense of solidity included filing accounts in which commissions on silver-trading deals that had never taken place were recorded as profits. . . . Accounts were falsified and large sums of customers' money diverted using a financial labyrinth to fool auditors into thinking the bank was solvent when it was actually hugely in deficit.[1]

A Hard Lesson

While the settlement in the United States provided funds for the compensation of some depositors, many more will never see their money again. Some consider this a "school of hard knocks" lesson about the inability of the criminal justice system to deal effectively with international fraud. Gathering the documents needed to provide evidence ranges from difficult to impossible. After one trial in the United States, a *Chicago Tribune* editorial commented: "International financial transactions can be made so complex as to effectively conceal what is really going on; key officials can always flee the jurisdiction and take vital evidence with them."[2] One lawyer summed up his observation of the outcomes of big international cases very succinctly: "No one gets caught but huge sums of money disappear."[3]

Sources

1. Ben Fenton and Sonia Purnell, "Bank Official Admits $750m Fraud, 'Financial Juggler' Was at the Heart of BCCI Scandal," *Daily Telegraph*, Sept. 28, 1993, p. 1.
2. "BCCI Still a Mystery," *Chicago Tribune,* Aug. 27, 1993, p. 23.
3. Peter Blackman, "The BCCI Problem; System's Flaws Stymie Probes of Foreign Banks," *New York Law Journal*, Aug. 26, 1993, p. 5.

Questions for Discussion

1. How could depositors be protected from losing their money in international scams like BCCI?
2. Would an international criminal court be better able to deal with massive international fraud?

Of particular significance are the United Nations guidelines, which, in the sphere of transnational crime, include the following:

- Guiding Principles for Crime Prevention and Criminal Justice in the Context of Development and a New International Economic Order (1985)
- International Co-operation for Crime Prevention and Criminal Justice in the Context of Development (General Assembly resolution 45/107, Annex. Recommendations, 1990)
- Prevention and Control of Organized Crime (Annex. Guidelines, 1990)
- Terrorist Criminal Activities (Annex. Measures against international terrorism, 1990)
- Model Treaty on Extradition (General Assembly Resolution 45/116, 1990)
- Model Treaty on Mutual Assistance in Criminal Matters (General Assembly Resolution 45/117, 1990)
- Model Treaty on the Transfer of Proceedings in Criminal Matters (General Assembly Resolution 45/118, 1990
- Model Treaty for the Prevention of Crimes That Infringe on the Cultural Heritage of Peoples in the Form of Movable Property (1990)[82]

International Crime

International crimes are the major criminal offenses so designated by the community of nations for the protection of interests common to all humankind. They may be found in precedent (much like the Anglo-American common law of crimes) or in written form in international conventions. They can be tried in the courts of countries which recognize them, or they can be tried by international courts. The war crimes tribunals that tried German and Japanese war criminals after World War II were such courts. In 1993, the U.N. Security Council ordered the establishment of an international tribunal for war crimes committed on the territory of the former Yugoslavia. This court now holds regular sessions in the Hague in the Netherlands and receives evidence that may eventually lead to indictments.

Which crimes are listed as international crimes? The Draft Code of crimes lists the following as crimes against the peace and security of mankind:

- Aggression (by one state against another)
- Threat of aggression
- Intervention (in the internal or external affairs of another state)
- Colonial domination and other forms of alien domination
- Genocide (destroying a national, ethnic, racial, or religious group)
- Apartheid (suppression of a racial or ethnic group)
- Systematic or mass violations of human rights
- Exceptionally serious war crimes
- Recruitment, use, financing, and training of mercenaries (soldiers of fortune)
- International terrorism
- Illicit traffic in narcotic drugs
- Willful and severe damage to the environment[83]

These crimes occur in many forms. For example, "systematic or mass violations of human rights" may be organized, large-scale rapes of women in occupied territories, as in Bosnia in 1992 and 1993.[84]

In addition to the listed international crimes, many others are recognized by convention; these include the cutting of undersea cables, the transportation of women for purposes of prostitution ("white slavery"), and fisheries offenses. There is now a considerable body of research and scholarship on international crimes.[85]

Writing specifically on comparative research in the area of drug use, statistician Lane Harrison has stated:

> There is much that could be learned from internationally comparative research on the interface of drug use and criminal behavior. . . . In this time of increasing homogenization of societies, we need to engage in research that helps to determine the factors that contribute to both drug use and crime. This insight could be used to construct strategies to deal with these problem behaviors.[86]

The Serb "ethnic cleansing" policy in Bosnia aimed at creating exclusively Muslim territories by killing or driving out the Muslim population.

Her comments are applicable to all the forms of crime that are currently spreading across borders, particularly those in violation of international law.

Globalization vs. Ethnic Fragmentation

Very soon, we will enter the twenty-first century. Comparative criminologists view the new millennium with some trepidation. Globalization raises great hopes for a better future for all human beings. Yet it brings with it grave dangers in terms of the internationalization of crime. Comparative criminology has a significant role to play in the investigation of new forms of transnational crime. Researchers can apply the methods used when such crimes were strictly local or national, but using the sophistication of the science of comparative criminology.

The new millennium presents additional hazards arising from the trend toward "balkanization." *Balkanization,* the opposite of globalization, is the breakup of nation-states into ethnic enti-

ties. Many ethnic groups are striving for independence and sovereignty denied to them when they were incorporated in larger nation-states, as in the former Soviet Union or Yugoslavia; or when they were joined arbitrarily with other groups in colonial times, as in Africa; or when other accidents of history included them within empires, as in Western Europe. Frequently such ethnic groups had to abide by laws and customs that were not of their own choosing and had to suppress their own languages and cultures. Now they are searching for identities, territories, and criminal justice systems of their own. Unhappily, the struggle has brought with it human rights violations, war crimes, and genocide on a massive scale. This is The latest challenge for criminologists and criminal justice specialists working on the international level.

■ REVIEW

Comparative criminology, despite its historical antecedents, is a young science, a subspecialty of criminology. In view of the globalization of the world—brought about by recent technological advances and the enormous increase in international commerce, both legal and illegal—comparative studies in criminology have become a necessity. Comparatists are called upon to assist governments in devising strategies to deal with a wide variety of international and transnational crimes.

In this chapter we have traced the history of comparative criminology, sought to define it, and attempted to identify its goals. These goals may be theoretical, like the cross-cultural testing of prominent theories of crime. They can also be very practical, like the search for transplantable crime-fighting strategies or for techniques to deal with specific transnational and international crimes.

There are a number of requirements for successful comparative research: studying foreign law, understanding foreign criminal justice systems, learning about a foreign culture, collecting reliable data, engaging in comparative research, and, when needed, doing cross-cultural empirical research.

The accomplishments of criminologists who have engaged in comparative studies form the foundation for further research. The tools of comparative criminology should prove useful in helping both individual nations and the United Nations solve some of their common crime problems. The United Nations and its agencies continue to do very practical work to help nations deal with crime on a worldwide basis.

■ NOTES

1. Peter Applebome, "Skinhead Violence Grows, Experts Say," *New York Times*, July 18, 1993, p. 25.
2. Jane Kramer, "Neo-Nazis: A Chaos in the Head," *New Yorker*, July 14, 1993, pp. 52–70, at p. 53. See also Marie C. Douglas, "Ausländer Raus! Nazi Raus! An Observation of German Skins and Jugendgangen," *International Journal of Comparative and Applied Criminal Justice*, **16** (1992): 129–134.
3. Mark S. Hamm, *American Skinheads—The Criminology and Control of Hate Crime* (Westport, Conn.: Praeger, 1993).
4. The term "comparative criminology" appears to have been coined by Sheldon Glueck. See Sheldon Glueck, "Wanted: A Comparative Criminology," in *Ventures in Criminology*, ed. Sheldon Glueck and Eleanor Glueck (London: Tavistock, 1964), pp. 304–322, based on a lecture delivered at the Fourth International Congress on Criminology, The Hague, Netherlands, Sept. 8, 1960.
5. Piers Beirne and Joan Hill, *Comparative Criminology—An Annotated Bibliography* (New York and Westport, Conn.: Greenwood, 1991), pp. vii–viii.
6. See especially Albert P. Blaustein and G. H. Flenz, *Constitutions of the Countries of the World*, 21 vols. (updated) (Dobbs Ferry, N.Y.: Oceana, 1971 and continuing).
7. The Comparative Criminal Law Project at Wayne State University Law School (formerly at New York University School of Law) has published 21 criminal codes in *The American Series of Foreign Penal Codes*, ed. G. O. W. Mueller, cont. by Edward M. Wise (Littleton, Colo.: Fred B. Rothman, since 1960). Several other foreign penal codes have been published in English by their respective governments, e.g., Denmark, Japan, Hungary, and the former U.S.S.R. The interested reader also should consult such works as J. A. Coutts, ed., *The Accused: A Comparative Study* (London: Stevens & Sons, 1966); Claude R. Sowle, ed., *Police Power and Individual Freedom* (Chicago: Aldine, 1962); G. O. W. Mueller and Fré Le Poole Griffiths, *Comparative Criminal Procedure* (New York: New York University Press, 1969); Albin Eser and George Fletcher, *Justification and Excuse—Comparative Perspectives*, 2 vols. (Freiburg, Germany: Max Planck Institut, 1987); Edward M. Wise and G. O. W. Mueller, eds., *Studies in Comparative Criminal Law*, Comparative Criminal Law Project Publications Series, vol. 9 (Littleton, Colo.: Fred B. Rothman, 1975); and Apirat Petchsiri, *Eastern Importation of Western Criminal Law: Thailand as a Case Study*, Comparative Criminal Law Project Publications Series, vol. 17 (Littleton, Colo.: Fred B. Rothman, 1987). See also Marc Ancel, *Social Defense: The Future of Penal Reform*, Comparative Criminal Law Project Publications Series, vol. 16 (Littleton, Colo.: Fred B. Rothman, 1987). For a historical survey, see G. O. W. Mueller, *Comparative Criminal Law in the United States*, Comparative Criminal Law Project Monograph Series, vol. 4 (South Hackensack, N.J.: Fred B. Rothman, 1970).
8. Seven codes of criminal procedure have appeared in Mueller and Wise, *The American Series of Foreign Penal Codes*.
9. E.g., Johannes Andenaes, *The General Part of the Criminal Law of Norway*, Comparative Criminal Law Project Publications Series, vol. 3 (Littleton, Colo.: Fred B. Rothman, 1965); Shigemitsu Dando, *Japanese Criminal Procedure*, Comparative Criminal Law Project Publications Series, vol. 4 (Littleton, Colo.: Fred B. Rothman, 1965); and Alvar Nelson, *Responses to Crime: An Introduction to Swedish Criminal Law and Procedure*, Comparative Criminal Law Project Monograph Series, vol. 6 (South Hackensack, N.J.: Fred B. Rothman, 1972).

10. UNAFEI, 1-26 Harumicho, Fuchu, Tokyo, Japan. There are 43 volumes as of 1994.

11. Ken Pease and Kristiina Hukkila, eds., *Criminal Justice Systems in Europe and North America* (Helsinki: HEUNI, 1990). A monograph on Albania appeared in 1991.

12. Elmer H. Johnson, *International Handbook of Contemporary Developments in Criminology,* 2 vols. (Westport, Conn.: Greenwood, 1983); Dae H. Chang, *Criminology: A Cross-Cultural Perspective,* 2 vols. (Durham, N.C.: Carolina Academic Press, 1976); George F. Cole, Stanislaw J. Frankowski, and Marc G. Gertz, *Major Criminal Justice Systems—A Comparative Survey,* 2d ed. (Newbury Park, Calif.: Sage, 1987), covering the United States, England, Nigeria, Federal Republic of Germany, Sweden, Japan, U.S.S.R., and Poland; Richard J. Terrill, *World Criminal Justice Systems* (Cincinnati, Ohio: Anderson, 1984), covering England, France, Sweden, Japan, and the U.S.S.R.

13. V. Lorne Stewart, *Justice and Troubled Children around the World,* vols. 1–5 (New York: New York University Press, 1980–1983).

14. David H. Bayley, *Patterns of Policing—A Comparative International Analysis* (New Brunswick, N.J.: Rutgers University Press, 1985); Dilig K. Das, *Policing in Six Countries around the World* (Chicago: University of Illinois Press, 1993).

15. E.g., Robert J. Wicks and H. H. A. Cooper, *International Corrections* (Lexington, Mass.: Lexington Books, 1979).

16. Freda Adler, ed., *The Incidence of Female Criminality in the Contemporary World* (New York: New York University Press, 1984).

17. E.g., Marshall B. Clinard and Daniel J. Abbot, *Crime in Developing Countries: A Comparative Perspective* (New York: Wiley, 1973); and Marshall B. Clinard, *Cities with Little Crime: The Case of Switzerland* (London: Cambridge University Press, 1978).

18. E.g., Louise I. Shelley, *Crime and Modernization: The Impact of Industrialization and Urbanization on Crime* (Carbondale: Southern Illinois University Press, 1981).

19. William Clifford, *Crime Control in Japan* (Lexington, Mass.: Lexington Books, 1976); William Clifford, *An Introduction to African Criminology* (Nairobi: Oxford University Press, 1974).

20. G. O. W. Mueller, *World Survey on the Availability of Criminal Justice Statistics* (Washington, D.C.: Bureau of Justice Statistics, and Newark, N.J.: Rutgers University School of Criminal Justice, 1993).

21. INTERPOL, located in Lyons, France, has published the crime statistics supplied to it by member states since 1951.

22. First survey: 1970–1975, A/32/199; second survey: 1975–1980, A/Conf. 121/18; third survey: 1980–1986, A/Conf. 144/6; fourth survey: 1986–1992, in press. See the Window to the World box in Chapter 2.

23. World Health Organization, "Homicide Statistics," in *World Health Statistics* (Geneva: World Health Organization, annually).

24. See Dane Archer and Rosemary Gartner, *Violence and Crime in Cross-National Perspective* (New Haven, Conn.: Yale University Press, 1984).

25. Richard R. Bennett, *Correlates of Crime: A Study of Nations, 1960–1984* (Ann Arbor, Mich.: Inter-University Consortium for Political and Social Research, 1989).

26. See, e.g., Richard R. Bennett and James P. Lynch, "Does a Difference Make a Difference?" *Criminology,* **28** (1990): 155–182; and Carol B. Kalish, *International Crime Rates* (Washington, D.C.: Bureau of Justice Statistics, 1988).

27. Jan J. M. Van Dijk, Pat Mayhew, and Martin Killias, *Experiences of Crime across the World: Key Findings from the 1989 International Crime Survey* (Deventer, Netherlands, and Boston: Kluwer, 1990). For a German replication, see Helmut Kury, "Crime and Victimization in East and West: Results of the First Comparative Victimological Study," *Studies on Crime and Crime Prevention* (Oslo, Norway), **1** (1992): 127–145; see also Richard R. Bennett and R. Bruce Wiegand, "Observations on Crime Reporting in a Developing Nation," *Criminology,* 32 (1994): 135–148.

28. Hermann Mannheim, *Comparative Criminology* (Boston: Houghton Mifflin, 1965).

29. Brunon Holyst, *Comparative Criminology* (Lexington, Mass.: Lexington Books, 1979). See also Louise I. Shelley, ed., *Readings in Comparative Criminology* (Carbondale: Southern Illinois University Press, 1981).

30. G. O. W. Mueller, Michael Gage, and Lenore R. Kupperstein, *The Legal Norms of Delinquency: A Comparative Study,* Criminal Law Education and Research Center Monograph Series, vol. 1 (South Hackensack, N.J.: Fred B. Rothman, 1969).

31. Anastassios Mylonas, *Perception of Police Power: A Study in Four Cities,* Comparative Criminal Law Project Monograph Series, vol. 8 (South Hackensack, N.J.: Fred B. Rothman, 1973).

32. Sheldon Glueck and Eleanor Glueck, *Unraveling Juvenile Delinquency* (New York: The Commonwealth Fund, and Cambridge, Mass.: Harvard University Press, 1950).

33. Sheldon Glueck and Eleanor Glueck, *Of Delinquency and Crime—A Panorama of Years of Search and Research,* Publications of the Criminal Law Education and Research Center, vol. 8 (Springfield, Ill.: Charles C. Thomas, 1974), p. 332; for references to cross-cultural validation studies, see pp. 313, 331–332.

34. Obi N. I. Ebbe, "Juvenile Delinquency in Nigeria: The Problem of Application of Western Theories," *International Journal of Comparative and Applied Criminal Justice,* **16** (1992): 353–370.

35. Rosemary Gartner, "The Victims of Homicide: A Temporal and Cross-National Comparison," *American Sociological Review,* **55** (1990): 92–106, testing opportunity theory and other clusters of factors; similarly, David Lester, "Crime as Opportunity: A Test of the Hypothesis with European Homicide Rates," *British Journal of Criminology,* **31** (1991): 186–191.

36. Gary LaFree and Christopher Birkbeck, "The

Neglected Situation: A Cross-National Study of the Situational Characteristics of Crime," *Criminology*, **29** (1991): 73–98.

37. Richard R. Bennett, "Routine Activities: A Cross-National Assessment of a Criminological Perspective," *Social Forces*, **70** (1991): 147–163.

38. Richard R. Bennett and P. Peter Basiotis, "Structural Correlates of Juvenile Property Crime: A Cross-National, Time-Series Analysis," *Journal of Research in Crime and Delinquency*, **28** (1991): 262–287.

39. Sam S. Souryal, "Juvenile Delinquency in the Cross-Cultural Context: The Egyptian Experience," *International Journal of Comparative and Applied Criminal Justice*, **16** (1992): 329–352, also testing the relative deprivation hypothesis.

40. Adel Helal and Charisse T. M. Coston, "Low Crime Rates in Bahrain: Islamic Social Control—Testing the Theory of Synnomie," *International Journal of Comparative and Applied Criminal Justice*, **15** (1991): 125–144.

41. Gregory C. Leavitt, "General Evaluation and Durkheim's Hypothesis of Crime Frequency: A Cross-Cultural Test," *Sociological Quarterly*, **33** (1992): 241–263; Suzanne T. Ortega, Jay Corzine, and Cathleen Burnett, "Modernization, Age Structure, and Regional Context: A Cross-National Study of Crime," *Sociological Spectrum*, **12** (1992): 257–277. See Christopher Birkbeck, "Against Ethnocentrism: A Cross-Cultural Perspective on Criminal Justice Theories and Policies," *Journal of Criminal Justice Education*, **4** (1993): 307–323.

42. The "well-established" temporal relationship between age structure and homicide was found not to be well-established at all; see Rosemary Gartner and Robert Nash Parker, "Cross-National Evidence on Homicide and the Age Structure of the Population," *Social Forces*, **69** (1990): 351–371.

43. Shelley, *Crime and Modernization.*

44. E.g., "Changes in Terms and Dimensions of Criminality—Transnational and National," working paper prepared by the Secretariat, United Nations, 1975, A/Conf. 56/3; and "New Perspectives in Crime Prevention and Criminal Justice and Development: The Role of International Co-operation," working paper prepared by the Secretariat, United Nations, 1980, A/Conf. 87/10. In general, see Hans Joachim Schneider, "The Impact of Economic and Societal Development on Crime Causation and Control," *UNAFEI Resource Material Series* (Tokyo), **37** (199): 65–86.

45. Richard R. Bennett, "Development and Crime: A Cross-National, Time-Series Analysis of Competing Models," *Sociological Quarterly*, **32** (1991): 343–363; David Shichor, "Crime Patterns and Socio-Economic Development: A Cross-National Analysis," *Criminal Justice Review*, **15** (1990): 64–78; Per-Olof H. Wikstrom, *Urban Crime, Criminals, and Victims: The Swedish Experience in an Anglo-American Comparative Perspective* (New York: Springer Verlag, 1991); John Arthur, "Development and Crime in Africa: A Test of Modernization Theory," *Journal of Criminal Justice*, **19**

(1991): 499–513. See also Hans-Gunther Heiland, Louise I. Shelley, and Hisao Katoh, eds., *Crime and Control in Comparative Perspectives* (Boston and New York: De Gruyter, 1992).

46. See Ugljesa Zvekic, ed., *Essays on Crime and Development* (Rome: United Nations Interregional Crime and Justice Research Institute, 1990).

47. Freda Adler, *Nations Not Obsessed with Crime*, Comparative Criminal Law Project Publications Series, vol. 15 (Littleton, Colo.: Fred B. Rothman, 1983).

48. See Harold S. Orenstein, "Crime and Punishment: Old Problems and New Dilemmas for an Emerging Eastern and Central Europe," *Low Intensity Conflict and Law Enforcement* (London), **1** (1992): 14–41.

49. Japan ranks high on the list of countries to which comparatists turn. See William Clifford, *Crime and Control in Japan* (Lexington, Mass.: Heath, 1976); V. Lee Hamilton and Joseph Sanders, *Everyday Justice: Responsibility and the Individual in Japan and the United States* (New Haven, Conn.: Yale University Press, 1992); Hans Joachim Schneider, "Crime and Its Control in Japan and in the Federal Republic of Germany, a Comparative Study," *International Journal of Offender Therapy and Comparative Criminology*, **36** (1992): 47–63; and Robert Y. Thornton and Ketsuya Endo, *Preventing Crime in America and Japan* (Armonk, N.Y., and London: Sharpe, 1992).

50. Dale E. Berger et al., "Deterrence and Prevention of Alcohol-Impaired Driving in Australia, the United States, and Norway," *Justice Quarterly*, **7** (1990): 453–465.

51. David B. Kopel, *The Samurai, the Mountie, and the Cowboy: Should America Adopt the Gun Controls of Other Democracies?* (Buffalo, N.Y.: Prometheus, 1992).

52. Robert L. Nay, *Firearms Regulations in Various Foreign Countries* (Washington, D.C.: Law Library of Congress, 1990).

53. Michael Clarke, "The Control of Insurance Fraud: A Comparative View," *British Journal of Criminology*, **30** (1990): 1–23.

54. Kenneth Polk and William Weston, "Insider Trading as an Aspect of White Collar Crime," *Australian and New Zealand Journal of Criminology*, **23** (1990): 24–38.

55. Yü-Hsiu Hsü, ed., *International Conference on Environmental Criminal Law* (Taipei: Taiwan/ROC Chapter of the International Association of Penal Law, 1992).

56. Rosemary Gartner, "Family Structure, Welfare Spending, and Child Homicide in Developed Democracies," *Journal of Marriage and the Family*, **53** (1991): 231–240.

57. Margo I. Wilson and Martin Daly, "Who Kills Whom in Spouse Killings? On the Exceptional Sex Ratio of Spousal Homicides in the United States," *Criminology*, **30** (1992): 189–215.

58. Lois A. Fingerhut and Joel C. Kleinman, "International and Interstate Comparisons of Homicide among Young Males," *Journal of the American Medical Association*, **263** (1990): 3292–3295.

59. F. H. McClintock and Per-Olof H. Wikstrom, "The

Comparative Study of Urban Violence—Criminal Violence in Edinburgh and Stockholm," *British Journal of Criminology*, **32** (1992): 505–520.

60. Mueller et al., *The Legal Norms of Delinquency*, was one of the first international comparative studies. More recent research includes United Nations Social Defense Research Institute, *Juvenile Justice: An International Survey* (Rome: UNSDRI, 1976); Josine Junger-Tas, Leonieke Boendermaker, and Peter H. van der Laan, eds., *The Future of the Juvenile Justice System* (Leuven, Belgium: Acco, 1991); and especially Dae H. Chang and Galan M. Janeksela, eds., "Special Issue on Comparative Juvenile Delinquency," *International Journal of Comparative and Applied Criminal Justice*, **16** (1992): 135–370, with contributions by Gaban M. Janeksela, David P. Farrington, Alison Hatch and Curt T. Griffiths, Günther Kaiser, Josine Junger-Tas, Paul C. Friday, James O. Finckenauer and Linda Kelly, Hualing Fu, Michael S. Vaughn and Frank F. Y. Huang, Byung In Cho and Richard J. Chang, Clayton A. Hartjen and Sesharajani Kethineni, Sam S. Souryhal, and Obi N. I. Ebbe.

61. Mylonas, *Perception of Police Power*.

62. Graeme Newman, *Comparative Deviance: Perception and Law in Six Cultures* (New York, Oxford, and Amsterdam: Elsevier Scientific, 1976).

63. Russel P. Dobash, R. Emerson Dobash, Scott Balliofyne, Karl Schuman, Reiner Kaulitzki, and Hans-Werner Guth, "Ignorance and Suspicion: Young People and Criminal Justice in Scotland and Germany," *British Journal of Criminology*, **30** (1990): 306–320.

64. Ronald D. Hunter, "Three Models of Policing," *Police Studies*, **13** (1990): 118–124; R. I. Mawby, *Comparable Policing Issues: The British and American Experience in International Perspective* (London: Unwin Hyman, 1990).

65. Leslie T. Wilkins, *Punishment, Crime and Market Forces* (Aldershot, England, and Brookfield, Vt.: Dartmouth, 1991); John Graham, "Decarceration in the Federal Republic of Germany: How Practitioners Are Succeeding Where Policy-Makers Have Failed," *British Journal of Criminology*, **30** (1990): 150–170; Dennis Wiechman, Jerry Kendall, and Ronald Bae, "International Use of the Death Penalty," *International Journal of Comparative and Applied Criminal Justice*, **14** (1990): 239–259.

66. See Gunther Kaiser, Helmut Kury, and Hans-Jorg Albrecht, eds., *Victims and Criminal Justice*, 3 vols. (Freiburg, Germany: Max Planck Institut, 1991); Emilio C. Viano, ed., *Critical Issues in Victimology—International Perspectives* (New York: Springer Verlag, 1992); and Hans Joachim Schneider, ed., *The Victim in International Perspective* (Berlin and New York: De Gruyter, 1982).

67. See especially Jack Levin and Jack McDevitt, *Hate Crimes—The Rising Tide of Bigotry and Bloodshed* (New York and London: Plenum, 1993).

68. See Hans-Dieter Schwind et al., "Causes, Prevention and Control of Violence," *Revue Internationale de Criminologie et de Police Technique*, **43** (1990): 395–520.

69. Gerhard O. W. Mueller and Freda Adler, *Outlaws of the Ocean: The Complete Book of Contemporary Crime on the High Seas* (New York: Hearst Marine Books, 1985); Gerhard O. W. Mueller and Freda Adler, "A New Wave of Crime at Sea," *The World and I* (February 1986): 96–103.

70. See David L. Carter, "A Forecast of Growth in Organized Crime in Europe: New Challenges for Law Enforcement," *Police Studies*, **15** (1992): 62–74.

71. U.S. General Accounting Office, *Drug Control: How Drug-Consuming Nations Are Organized for the War on Drugs* (Washington, D.C.: U.S. Government Printing Office, 1990).

72. Richard Clutterbuck, *Terrorism, Drugs and Crime in Europe after 1992* (London: Routledge, 1990).

73. Rachael Ehrenfeld, *Narco Terrorism* (New York: Basic Books, 1990); Michael Woodiwiss, "Crime's Global Reach," in *Global Crime Connections*, ed. Frank Pearce and Michael Woodiwiss (Houndmills and London: Macmillan, 1993), pp. 1–31; Bruce Bullington, "All about Eve: The Many Faces of United States Drug Policy," in Pearce and Woodiwiss, *Global Crime Connections*, pp. 32–71; Nicholas Dorn and Nigel South, "After Mr. Bennett and Mr. Bush—U.S. Foreign Policy and the Prospects for Drug Control," in Pearce and Woodiwiss, *Global Crime Connections*, pp. 72–90.

74. George Alexander, ed., *Western State Terrorism* (New York: Routledge, 1991).

75. Charles A. Intriago, *International Money Laundering* (London: Eurostudy, 1991); W. C. Gilmore, *International Efforts to Combat Money Laundering* (Cambridge, England: Grotius, 1992).

76. Frederick T. Martens, "Transnational Enterprise Crime and the Elimination of Frontiers," *International Journal of Comparative and Applied Criminal Justice*, **15** (1991): 99–107; Susan Flood, ed., *Illicit Drugs and Organized Crime: Issues for a United Europe* (Chicago: Office of International Criminal Justice, 1991); Wojciech Cebulak, "The Antitrust Doctrine: How It Was Internationalized," *International Journal of Comparative and Applied Criminal Justice*, **14** (1990): 261–267.

77. Michael Clarke et al., "Selected Papers Presented at the Second Liverpool Conference on Fraud, Corruption and Business Crime," *Corruption and Reform*, **6** (1991): 207–303; Frank Pearce and Michael Woodiwiss, eds. *Global Crime Connections: Dynamics and Control* (Toronto: University of Toronto Press, 1993).

78. See Cyrille Fijnaut, "Organized Crime: A Comparison between the United States of America and Western Europe," *British Journal of Criminology*, **30** (1990): 321–340; Jane Rae Buckwalter, *International Perspectives on Organized Crime* (Chicago: Office of International Criminal Justice, 1990).

79. U.S.S.R. Ministry of Justice, "Organized Crime Survey Response," *International Criminal Police Review*, **434** (January–February, 1992): 29–35.

80. Nanci Adler, "Planned Economy and Unplanned

Criminality: The Soviet Experience," *International Journal of Comparative and Applied Criminal Justice*, **17** (1993): 189–201; Wojciech Cebulak, "White-Collar Crime in Socialism: Myth or Reality?" *International Journal of Comparative and Applied Criminal Justice*, **15** (1991): 109–120. For the comparable situation in the reunited Germany, see Hans Joachim Schneider, "Crime, Criminological Research, and Criminal Policy in West and East Germany before and after Their Unification," *International Journal of Offender Therapy and Comparative Criminology*, **35** (1991): 283–295; Klaus Sessar, "Crime Rate Trends Before and After the End of the German Democratic Republic-Impressions and First Analyses"; Wolfgang Bilsky, Christian Pfeiffer, and Peter Wetzels, eds., *Fear of Crime and Criminal Victimization* (Stuttgart, Germany: Ferdinand Enke Verlag, 1993): 231-244.

81. See Yü-Hsiu Hsü, *International Conference on Environmental Criminal Law*, and references therein.

82. These and others may be found in United Nations, *Compendium of the United Nations Standards and Norms in Crime Prevention and Criminal Justice* (New York: United Nations, 1992), sales no. E.92.IV.1, and *The United Nations and Crime Prevention* (New York: United Nations, 1991).

83. Draft Articles of the Draft Code of Crimes against the Peace and Security of Mankind, adopted by the International Law Commission on First Reading, United Nations, New York, 1991. For a complete listing, see M. Cherif Bassiouni, *International Criminal Law—A Draft International Criminal Code* (Alphen an den Rijn, Netherlands: Sijthoff & Noordhoff, 1980).

84. Shana Swiss and Joan E. Giller, "Rape as a Crime of War," *Journal of the American Medical Association*, **270** (1993): 612–615.

85. For an analysis of all international crimes, see M. Cherif Bassiouni, ed., *International Criminal Law:* vol. 1, *Crimes* (Dobbs Ferry, N.Y.: Transnational, 1986); M. Cherif Bassiouni, *A Draft International Criminal Code and Draft Statute for an International Criminal Tribunal* (Dordrecht, Netherlands: Martinus Nijhoff, 1987); Farhad Malekian, *International Criminal Law*, 2 vols. (Motala, Sweden: Borgstroms Trycker, 1991); Gerhard O. W. Mueller and Edward M. Wise, *International Criminal Law*, Comparative Criminal Law Project, Publications Series, vol. 2 (South Hackensack, N.J.: Fred B. Rothman, 1965).

86. Lane D. Harrison, Editor's Introduction: "International Perspectives on the Interface of Drug Use and Criminal Behavior," *Contemporary Drug Problems*, **19** (1992): 181–201.

PART IV

A Criminological Approach to the Criminal Justice System

When a crime appears to have been committed and authorities have been notified, a legal apparatus is set in motion. This apparatus is called the criminal justice system, and its processes have been studied closely. Extensive research has made it possible to understand the system and its component parts. This research provides the basis for efforts to make the system more rational, more cost-beneficial, and more humane (Chapter 15). The law enforcement component of the criminal justice system is by far the most visible and costly one, because it employs the most personnel. The operations and tactics of the police, the images and perceptions of law enforcement, and its successes and failures are explained in terms of contemporary criminological research (Chapter 16).

The functions and tasks of the judiciary—the second component of the criminal justice system—are examined in light of criminological studies (Chapter 17). Much blame for America's high crime rate is bestowed, justly as well as unjustly, on the third component of the criminal justice system: corrections (Chapter 18). Corrections include institutional corrections (prisons and jails), juvenile institutions, and community-based facilities, as well as noninstitutional responses, such as fines, community service sentences, probation, and parole. The functioning, success, and failure of all the correctional responses are examined on the basis of research findings.

15

Processes and Decisions

KEY TERMS
exclusionary rule
Miranda warnings
parens patriae
plea bargaining
preliminary hearing
prima facie case
probable cause
reasonable suspicion
victimology

The great novelist Franz Kafka, in one of his most famous works, *The Trial,* portrayed the criminal justice process with a profound understanding of the frustrations and despair experienced by a person caught in its machinery. Escape doors seem blocked; a step ahead is prevented by a step that one should not have taken earlier. No one has a map to chart the way. One can only submit without hope to a fate that seems arbitrary.

Are today's criminal defendants in America as bewildered and frustrated as Kafka's defendant three-quarters of a century ago? As we explore the criminal justice system in the United States, Kafka will be much on our minds because many aspects of the U.S. criminal justice process seem bewildering and pointless to the uninitiated. Criminological research has revealed a logical structure, but one that can accommodate bias, arbitrariness, mistakes, and caprice. Moreover, in many large and congested urban areas, this system of criminal justice suffers from delay, overcrowding, indifference, and lack of funding.[1]

ENTRY INTO THE SYSTEM   PROSECUTION AND PRETRIAL SERVICES

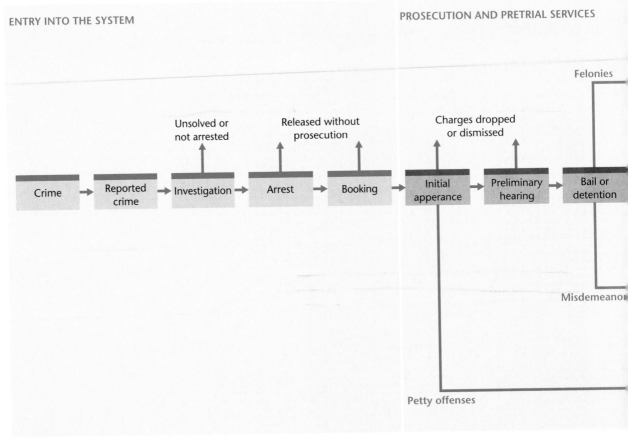

FIGURE 15.1   The paths of the criminal justice system

Source: Adapted from the President's Commission on Law Enforcement and Administration of Justice, *The Challenge of Crime in a Free Society* (Washington D.C. : U.S. Government Printing Office, 1967), pp. 8–9; in U.S. Department of Justice, Bureau of Justice Statistics, *Report to the Nation on Crime and Justice,* 2d ed. (Washington, D.C.: U.S. Government Printing Office, 1988).

THE STAGES OF THE CRIMINAL JUSTICE PROCESS

Until the 1960s criminal justice procedures from arrest to conviction were generally not seen as an orderly process. The various sectors of the system seemed to exist in isolation. In the 1960s, criminal justice came to be seen as a process similar to the production system in industry. In 1967 the President's Commission on Law Enforcement and the Administration of Justice first depicted the criminal justice system as an apparatus by which a product is produced in an orderly process (Figure 15.1).[2] Some people regard that product as justice, others as the reduction of crime; still others recognize both as the system's outputs.

Some scholars characterize criminal justice systems in terms of their predominant features, rather than their goals. For example, Herbert Packer distinguished between the *crime-control model* for criminal justice systems, in which effectiveness and efficiency are emphasized, and the *due process model,* which is oriented more to the rights of defendants.[3] Most criminologists would agree that the ideal criminal justice system should embody both these concepts.

The President's Commission depicts the crim-

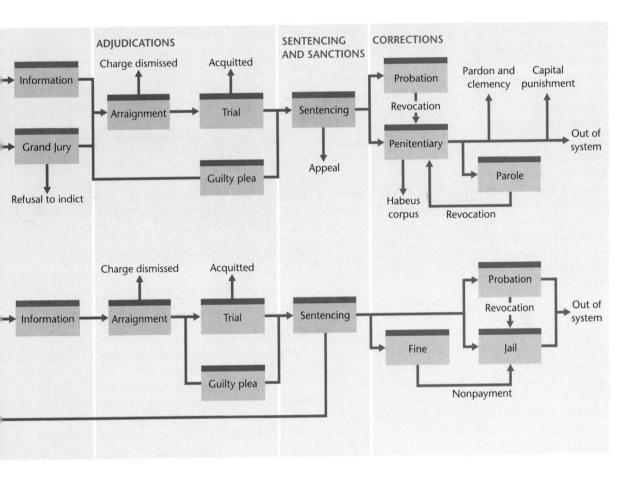

* ESSAy + FINAL

inal justice system as composed of five phases. Every criminal case may potentially flow through all five phases, though most do not, as we shall see.

In the first phase, called _entry into the system_, citizens bring criminal events to the attention of the police. The police, by investigating the case and identifying a suspect, play a crucial role. The judiciary participates by issuing search and arrest warrants.

The second phase, _prosecution and pretrial services_, is dominated by government lawyers called prosecutors, who prepare the charges; grand juries, which indict defendants; and judges, who

conduct a series of hearings, including the initial appearance of an arrested person at court and a preliminary hearing.

The third phase, _adjudication_, begins with the arraignment, at which the officially accused person pleads to (answers) the indictment or information (formal charges) against him or her, and ends with a judgment of guilty or not guilty. This phase is conducted by a judge, with or without a jury. The prosecutor, representing the state and the people, and the defense lawyer play the most active roles in this phase.

The fourth phase consists of _sentencing and sanctions_. In most cases, in most states, jurors do not participate in sentencing. The judge imposes the sentence, usually after hearing a presentence investigation (PSI) report prepared by a probation officer. Prosecutors, defense lawyers, and defendants have their say, and in some states victims as well.

The fifth and final phase, *corrections*, is in the hands of the executive branch of government, whose department of corrections executes the sentence imposed by the court. When called upon to do so, however, courts play a considerable role in ensuring compliance with law in the correctional phase.

The system flowchart devised by the President's Commission indicates four different paths through the system; we have included three of these in Figure 15.1. The first path is that for major crimes, or felonies; the second is for minor crimes, or misdemeanors. These differ in some respects: misdemeanors normally require no grand-jury indictment and no trial by jury, and the sanctions imposed are jail sentences of 1 year or less or fines rather than imprisonment for more than a year. The third path is for petty offenses, with summary proceedings resulting in minor sanctions, usually fines. The fourth path is that for juveniles (see Figure 15.5). It resembles the paths for adults in many respects, except that the proceedings are less formal and rarely include juries. We have added a sixth path through the criminal justice system, namely, a path for crime victims (see Figure 15.6). There may well be additional distinct paths, such as those for international criminals or for violators of regulatory, economic, and environmental laws.

As the flowcharts indicate, the various paths through the criminal justice system and the juvenile justice system do not end at a single exit; they lead to many exits at various points. An offender's path through the system is not inexorable or predestined. The direction that path takes depends on individual decisions all along the way, including decisions by the offender. Michael R. Gottfredson and Don M. Gottfredson point out that decision making throughout the system results in a very large attrition rate. Many more crimes are reported than are adjudicated; many more offenders are arrested than are ulti-

mately sent to prison.[4] In this chapter we examine the consequences of decision making at the various stages of the process.

Entry into the System

In the entry stage, three kinds of decisions are made. Citizens decide to bring suspected criminal events to the attention of the police. The police decide whether or not to investigate the allegation and seek an arrest warrant. The judiciary participates by granting or refusing to grant search and arrest warrants.

Decisions by Victims and Witnesses

Intake into the criminal justice system begins when a crime becomes known to the police (see Figure 15.1). As we noted in Chapter 2, the number of crimes reported does not correspond with the actual number of crimes committed. First, many events reported as crimes are not crimes— some wallets reported as stolen have actually been lost; some automobiles reported as stolen have in fact been abandoned for purposes of collecting insurance benefits. Such reports tend to inflate crime statistics. Second, many crimes are not reported to the police by the victims (see Chapter 2). Victims' decisions to invoke the criminal justice process by a report to the police are related to the seriousness of the crime, the victim's attitude toward the police, the gender of the victim, and other assorted factors.[5]

Decisions by the Police

Once information about a possible crime has come to the attention of the police, a decision has to be made about whether or not to investigate the case to determine if a crime has been committed and who committed it. The police cannot possibly investigate every complaint. Under the pressure of heavy caseloads, the police give priority to the investigation of major crimes.

Other factors also affect police decisions to make an arrest or to seek an arrest warrant. Police will consider, for example, public ambivalence about the significance of a given statute, the probability that a witness will or will not cooperate, and whether arrest may be too harsh a response. There are alternatives to arrest, ranging from outright release to release with a citation to release of a youngster into the custody of parents or guardians.[6]

✓Legal Criteria

What legal criteria determine when and whether a suspect can be taken into the criminal justice system? When may the system do something to or about a suspect? There are legal criteria for processing a suspect from one phase to the next in the criminal justice process. The Constitution, as interpreted by the Supreme Court, provides some of these criteria.

The Constitution states that nobody may be "seized" (taken into the criminal justice process) except on a warrant issued on the basis of probable cause of having committed a crime. For almost two centuries the **probable cause** requirement has been deemed to establish the point at which potential guilt is likely enough to justify taking a person into custody. Ideally the determination is made by a judge or magistrate on the basis of the testimony of witnesses (including the police), delivered under oath, that a given suspect has committed a given crime. In practice, the decision more frequently is made by a law enforcement officer at the scene of the crime.

Neither magistrates who issue warrants of arrest nor police officers who make an arrest without a warrant are guided by any precise standard of probable cause. The Supreme Court has ruled that the police have probable cause to take a suspect into custody when

> the facts and circumstances within their knowledge and of which they [have] reasonable trustworthy information [are] sufficient to warrant a prudent man in believing that the [suspect] had committed or was committing an offense.[7]

This definition, relying as it does on such vague terms as "reasonable trustworthy information" and "prudent man," lacks precision. Nevertheless, arrests made without probable cause, or not resting on a warrant issued on sworn testimony before a judge and based on a determination of probable cause, are considered to be unreasonable seizures of the person, and so in violation of the Fourth Amendment.

Evidence seized in the course of such an illegal arrest can be barred from trial. This is called the **exclusionary rule.** Its intent is to deter the police from engaging in illegal practices and to keep the courts from condoning such conduct. The Supreme Court ruled in 1961, in *Mapp v. Ohio*, that all courts in the country must apply the exclusionary rule.[8]

Civil libertarians view this ruling as a necessary safeguard against police misconduct. Conservatives argue that the rule is an arbitrary measure which "handcuffs" the police. These two positions exemplify the fundamental issues that are balanced in a Fourth Amendment analysis—that is, the need for effective law enforcement versus individual rights and liberties. Conservatives call for unhampered law enforcement, and liberals ask for the assurance of rights. Research, on the whole, establishes that law enforcement has not been seriously hindered by the exclusionary rule. On the contrary, the result has been improved legal training for law enforcement officers and consequently, some argue, improved police behavior.[9]

Recent Supreme Court decisions have strengthened police powers—unduly so, some critics say. Faced with mounting public concern over street crime in the 1960s, the Supreme Court was under pressure to legitimize prudent police action for the purpose of preventing a specific crime about to be committed, even when an officer had no probable cause to make an arrest. In 1968 the Supreme Court acknowledged the propriety of police intervention when evidence against a suspect fell short of probable cause. If a police officer has **reasonable suspicion** that a person might be engaged in the commission of a crime, the officer is authorized to stop such a person, to ask questions, and to frisk him or her to make sure that the suspect is not armed and dangerous to the officer.[10] This is called the *stop-and-frisk rule.*

In some circumstances law enforcement officers can intervene even short of reasonable suspicion. The highest court of New York, the New York Court of Appeals, stated in the case of *People v. de Bour* that police officers have the right and duty to approach a person for purposes of making an inquiry on the basis of "articulable facts" that "crime is afoot."[11]

MIRANDA WARNING

1. You have the right to remain silent.
2. Anything you say can and will be used against you in a court of law.
3. You have the right to talk to a lawyer and have him present with you while you are being questioned.
4. If you cannot afford to hire a lawyer, one will be appointed to represent you before any questioning, if you wish one.
5. You may stop answering questions at any time.
6. Do you understand each of these rights I have explained to you?
7. Having these rights in mind, do you wish to talk to us now?

FIGURE 15.2   The *Miranda* warning

The *Miranda* Warning

Assume that a police officer or a magistrate has made the decision to arrest a suspect and that a suspect has in fact been arrested. What happens now?

Immediately after the arrest, when the arrestee is in custody, the arresting officer will recite the **Miranda warnings** (Figure 15.2). The term derives from one of the Supreme Court's most important rulings, which laid down the standards of procedural fairness mandated by the Fourth, Fifth, and Sixth Amendments to the Constitution.[12] If the warning is not given, the courts may exclude from evidence at trial any statement the arrestee may have made and any evidence that has resulted from it.[13]

Once a suspect has been taken into custody, the processing of the event and of the offender begins—booking, fingerprints and mug shots (identifying photographs), filling out of forms—and the suspect waits in a holding pen for the next step.

The Right to Counsel and Counsel's Decisions

In *Gideon v. Wainwright* (1963) the Supreme Court laid down the rule that every person charged with a crime that may lead to incarceration has the right to an attorney and that the state must pay for that service if the defendant cannot

afford to do so.[14] The *Gideon* case, involving an indigent Florida defendant, established the universal right to free defense counsel for the poor. It subsequently was reflected in the *Miranda* warnings. The Supreme Court requirement has been implemented nationwide by the provision of assigned counsel, public defenders, contract counsel, or legal aid. As we shall see, however, these defense lawyers, working on tremendous caseloads, may sometimes be inclined to pressure their clients into unfavorable plea bargains.[15] Thus their decisions, too, have a considerable impact on the flow of the process.

Prosecution and Pretrial Services

During the prosecution and pretrial services phase, prosecutors and judges make the decisions. Far fewer persons are processed through this phase than are entered into the system. Many arrested persons have already been diverted out of the system; others will be diverted at this stage, when charges are dropped or cases dismissed. Charges may be dismissed for many reasons: Perhaps the evidence is not strong enough to support probable cause. Perhaps the arrested person is a juvenile who should be dealt with by the juvenile justice system or a mentally disturbed person who requires hospitalization. Perhaps the judge believes that justice is best served by compassion.

The Judicial Decision to Release

After an arrest, the arrested person must be taken before a *magistrate*, a local judge, who makes a determination that probable cause exists. As a judge, the magistrate will use a standard of probable cause that is likely to be a bit tougher than the police officer's. The magistrate must also repeat the *Miranda* warnings and then decide whether:

■ To permit the defendant to be released on bail or on percentage bail (With the latter, the defendant deposits with the court only a stipulated percentage of the bail set.)

■ To release on recognizance, or ROR (No bail is required, on condition that the defendant appear for trial and behave in the meantime.)

AT ISSUE
Exposé on Police Lockups

Criminal justice specialists generally consider conditions in *jails*, where we lock up those who are not yet convicted, far worse than those in *prisons*, where we lock up convicted felons. But the description of most jails as overcrowded, underfunded, and unsanitary, and as throwing together dangerous and nondangerous offenders (1), does not prepare us for what investigative reporter William Glaberson found in New York City's police lockups and holding pens. In an exposé written for the *New York Times* in 1990, Glaberson wrote:

> There are no mattresses, no bedding, no clean clothing and no showers. The toilets, where there are toilets at all, are open bowls along the walls and often encrusted and overflowing. Meals usually consist of a single slice of baloney and a single slice of American cheese on white bread....
>
> People who have been through the system say it is not easy to forget. Some were threatened by other prisoners. Others were chained to people who were vomiting and stinking of the streets.

With few phone privileges, many felt as if they were lost in a hellish labyrinth far from the lives they had been plucked from.(2)

Pretrial Punishment

Lockups and holding pens were designed to hold arrested persons for a few hours. They are detention facilities meant to house, not to punish, those accused or convicted of crimes. They are meant to be temporary facilities for persons in transit from one part or stage of the criminal justice system to another. Nowadays the clients of the criminal justice system are confined there often for at least several days before they are taken to court. Rather than the few hundred persons originally envisaged, thousands are occupying the dingy, dark cells in the basements of police stations and courthouses. There are no national statistics on the flow through the lockups, but it is estimated that only one-third of those who receive this "pretrial punishment" are ultimately sentenced to prison.

The situation is virtually out of control. Officials alerted to the chaos in the lockups and pens have promised to look into the situation, and a consultant has been engaged to suggest solutions to the problem. Meanwhile hell on earth continues for thousands trapped underneath New York City's police stations and courthouses.

Nationwide Chaos

Things may not be much better in the nation's thousands of county jails. *County jails*, which are in fact correctional facilities designed to house persons serving sentences for misdemeanors, are also intended for the temporary detention of prisoners. A Bureau of Statistics survey estimates that 51 percent of the adults being held in jails were not convicted—they were on trial, awaiting trial, or awaiting arraignment. Yet these individuals were being kept in filthy, overcrowded facilities. We have a long way to go before lockups and jails are places where people are cared for rather than abandoned.(3)

Sources
1. Michael T. Charles, Sesha Kethineni, and Jeffrey L. Thompson, "The State of Jails in America," *Federal Probation,* **56** (1992): 56–62.
2. William Glaberson, "Trapped in the Terror of New York's Holding Pens," *New York Times,* Mar. 23, 1990, pp. A1, B4.
3. Criminal Law Education and Research Center, *Identification and Classification: A Service Approach to Non-Punitive Detention* (New York: Criminal Law Education and Research Center, 1971).

Questions for Discussion
1. Some think the problems encountered by inmates in detention facilities are the result just of inadequate funding, while others see conditions as reflecting a societal attitude that those arrested are probably guilty and don't deserve better treatment. What is your position?
2. How could the system of police lockups and holding pens be reformed?

Lockup at a New York City station house.

A public defender counsels three of the more than 14,000 people arrested in the aftermath of the 1992 Los Angeles riots.

- To release the defendant into someone's custody
- To detain the defendant in jail pending further proceedings

In making the decision to release, judges or magistrates are strongly influenced by prosecutors' views as to whether a given defendant is a safe risk for release. In some states, release criteria have been enacted into law (see Chapter 17, Table 17.1). Historically, however, the only criterion for release on bail has been whether the defendant can be relied on to appear for the next court appearance. In practice, judges tend to rely on such factors as the gravity of the charge and the probability that the defendant may commit a crime or harass victims if he or she is released.

The District of Columbia and a few other jurisdictions permit preventive detention when there is a high probability that the defendant may commit a crime if he or she is released. Despite the difficulty of predicting anyone's behavior, the Supreme Court has ruled it to be constitutionally proper to deny bail to a person who is considered dangerous.[16] A large number of studies have been conducted to assess factors related to release decisions. The seriousness of the charge was found to be the single most important factor in the decision. Both rearrest rates and rates of failure to appear are quite low, especially if trial follows within a short time after pretrial release.[17] This finding might indicate that judges have done well in assessing the risk of releasing defendants. It could also mean that judges might want to liberalize their risk assessments. The issue requires further research.

The Preliminary Hearing

In many states, the next step in the process is the **preliminary hearing,** a preview of the trial in court before a judge, in which the prosecution must produce enough evidence to convince the judge that the case should proceed to trial or to the grand jury. In many jurisdictions the preliminary hearing is officially considered to be another probable-cause hearing. But what emerges is more than probable cause: in this proceeding, conducted with some of the rights afforded at trials, cross-examination of witnesses, and the introduction of evidence under stringent rules, enough evidence must be produced to "bind the defendant over" to the grand jury. In

Preliminary hearing in January 1992 for Jeffrey Dahmer, accused serial murderer, at which the prosecution presented sufficient evidence to bind him over to the grand jury (reasonable grounds to believe the person is guilty).

other words, the evidence must constitute a reasonable inference of guilt or reasonable grounds to believe that the defendant is guilty.

In the preliminary hearing, in which the defense need not present any evidence, the defendant gains the advantage of finding out how the prosecution's case is being developed. The defense attorney's decision to enter a plea or to engage in plea negotiations depends very much on what happens during the preliminary hearing.

The Decision to Charge

No matter what the result of the preliminary hearing, the decision to charge the defendant with a crime rests with the prosecutor. Even in states where a grand jury must determine whether a defendant is to be indicted for a felony, it is the prosecutor who decides in the first place whether to place a case before the grand jury. The prosecutor also decides what evidence to present to the grand jury and how to present it.

In a major study based on data from the Prosecutor's Management Information System (PROMIS), researchers found that prosecutors' reasons for not proceeding after an arrest vary by offense. Of all reasons given for not proceeding

with robbery cases, 43 percent were "witness problem(s)"; 35 percent, "insufficiency of evidence"; and 22 percent, "other." For nonviolent property offenses, 25 percent of the reasons were "witness problems"; 37 percent, "insufficiency of evidence"; and 36 percent, "other."[18]

As soon as the prosecutor has made a decision to charge the defendant and has informed the defense counsel accordingly, the stage is set for plea bargaining. This process is inherent in the Anglo-American system, under which a trial always proceeds in accordance with the prosecution's charge and the defendant's agreement (guilty plea) or disagreement (not-guilty plea) with that charge.

The Plea-Bargaining Process

Every criminal defendant exercises some power over the way the case is to be conducted. A defendant who pleads guilty admits all the facts alleged in the accusation, whether it is an indictment or an information, and all their legal implications: he or she admits to being guilty as charged. No trial has to be conducted. A defendant who pleads not guilty denies all the facts and their legal implications and puts the government—the prosecutor—to great expense to prove guilt in an elaborate criminal trial.

The idea arose centuries ago that both sides, prosecution and defense, could benefit if they were to agree on a plea that would save the government the expense of a trial and the defendant the risk of a very severe punishment if he or she were found guilty. By the mid-twentieth century it had become common practice in the United States for prosecutors and defense attorneys to engage in **plea bargaining,** that is, to discuss the charges against defendants and to agree on a reduced or modified plea that would spare the state the cost of a trial and guarantee the defendant a sentence more lenient than the original charge warranted.

At first, such plea negotiations were secret and officially denied. In fact, when accepting a plea, the judge would always inquire whether the plea was freely made, and the defendant always answered yes, when in fact the plea was the result of a bargain in which defendant and prosecutor manipulated each other into a deal. Contemporary legislation, federal and state, recognizes the plea-bargaining process, and simply requires guarantees that no one be coerced and that all pleas are voluntarily entered, with full awareness of the consequences.

Nevertheless, plea bargaining invites injustices of many sorts. Defendants who are morally or legally not guilty, for example, may feel inclined to accept a plea bargain in the face of strong evidence. Other defendants may plead guilty to a lesser charge even though the evidence was obtained in violation of constitutional guarantees. In some cases, by "overcharging" (charging murder instead of manslaughter, for example), a prosecutor may influence a defendant to plead guilty to the lower charge, in effect forcing him or her to relinquish the right to a jury trial.

The practice of plea bargaining is widespread. A Bureau of Justice Statistics report has estimated that in urban areas guilty pleas outnumbered trials by about 17 to 1, and nearly all of those guilty pleas were negotiated.[19] Research on why defendants accept plea bargains and on the factors that affect the decisions is inconclusive. Nevertheless, there appears to be agreement that plea bargains:

- Are necessary devices to keep the courts from getting hopelessly clogged with criminal cases
- Are desirable means of compensating for the harshness of the sanctions provided by the penal codes
- Allow for adjustment of inadequately developed legal rules regarding defenses, such as mistake, insanity, or self-defense
- Reduce the negative effects of "net widening"—that is, the tendency to include more and more offenders within the sweep of the criminal justice system
- Allow for consideration of legally irrelevant but factually important factors, ranging from poverty and despair to intense emotional distress

Abolishing plea bargaining would require broad changes in criminal law and procedure and thus in the entire criminal justice system. Until such reforms are achieved, the system will continue to rely on the decisions of prosecutors and defense counsels to agree on a plea.

If prosecutor and defense counsel have agreed on a plea bargain—for example, by reducing the charge from murder to manslaughter or by reducing the number of charges from four counts of larceny to one—the judge will have to decide whether that bargain is in the interest of justice. In considering the defendant's bargained plea, the judge must do the following:

1. Inform the defendant of the implications of the plea (that the defendant can now be sentenced).
2. Ascertain that the facts support the plea.
3. Accept the plea.[20]
4. Impose sentence.

The second requirement is particularly important, as it requires the judge to adjudicate the facts of the case in order to determine whether the plea of guilty is warranted. This determination of fact may amount to a miniature trial.

If no plea bargain is agreed upon, the case will be set for submission to the grand jury whenever a defendant has the right to trial on indictment by a grand jury. Normally this right is restricted to felony cases.

The Grand Jury's Decision to Indict

The grand jury is one of the oldest institutions of our criminal justice system. It dates to Magna Carta in A.D. 1215. It has been abolished in England, but in most American states it continues, in serious (felony) cases, to screen the prosecution's evidence in secret hearings and decide whether the defendant should be formally charged with crime.

Federal grand juries are composed of 16 to 23 citizens, and indictment requires the concurrence of at least 12 grand jurors.[21] State rules are similar. The indictment must rest on evidence indicating a *prima facie* case against the defendant.

A **prima facie case** exists when there seems to be sufficient evidence to convict the defendant. The prima facie case may be defeated by evidence at trial that raises reasonable doubt or constitutes a legal excuse. Since that is a strong evidentiary requirement, most indicted defendants are inclined to make a plea bargain at this point. Indeed, the conviction rate of those who stand trial is high. Of every sixteen persons indicted, ten plead guilty (usually in a plea bargain) and four go to trial. Three of the four are convicted; only one is acquitted, dismissed by the judge, or dismissed by the prosecutor.[22] If, after the indictment has been presented in open court, the defendant pleads not guilty, the stage is set for trial.

Adjudication Decisions

Defendants may choose to be tried by a judge (a *bench trial*) or by a jury (consisting usually of 12 citizens but as few as 6 in some states for lesser offenses).[23] In a jury trial the judge rules on matters of law, instructs the jurors about relevant legal questions and definitions, and tells them how to apply the law to the facts of the case.

A defendant may prefer a jury trial or a bench trial for any number of reasons. When the defense is based largely on the application and interpretation of technical legal propositions, a judge is likely to be the choice. If the defense appeals more to sympathy and emotion, a jury is likely to be the better choice.

Considerable research has been done on the functions and functioning of judges and juries, beginning with the University of Chicago Jury Project in the 1950s.[24] Much of the research has focused on whether jurors differ widely in their decisions. Apparently they do not. Most juries come to a unanimous verdict. That was believed to be the general requirement under American law. In a surprise decision in 1972, however, the Supreme Court ruled that a conviction decided upon by fewer than all 12 jurors is constitutionally acceptable.[25]

Sentencing Decisions

If a defendant has not been diverted out of the system, has pleaded not guilty, and has been tried and convicted, the next step in the process is the imposition of a sentence. In some states, with respect to some crimes, the statute leaves the sentencing judge no choice: a fixed sentence is imposed by law. But in most states judges still have some choice. The judge must decide whether to place the defendant on probation and, if so, what type of probation; whether to impose a sentence of incarceration and, if so, for what length of time; whether to impose a minimum or maximum term (or both) or to leave the sentence open-ended (indeterminate) within statutory limits; whether to impose a fine and, if so, how much; whether to order compensation for the victims; whether to impose court costs; and so on.

In making their sentencing decisions, judges are guided by presentence reports prepared by the court's probation department. After evaluating the probation officer's presentence investigation report, the judge may decide to place the person on probation, usually with specified conditions—that the person not commit another offense, not leave the county without permission, make payments to the victim, attend meetings of Alcoholics Anonymous, or whatever. In deciding on sentences, judges are supposed to consider what the presentence reports reveal about offenders' personal characteristics, their past and possibly their potential future, their problems, and their needs. What do judges actually consider when they decide on sentences? The National Academy of Sciences, having reviewed most of the research on sentencing, has found that two criteria predominate:

> [O]ffense seriousness and offender's prior record emerge consistently as the key determinants of sentences. The more serious the offense and the worse the offender's prior record, the more severe the sentence. The strength of this conclusion persists despite the potentially severe problems of pervasive biases arising from the difficulty of measuring—or even precisely defining—either of these complex variables. This finding is supported by a wide variety of studies using data of varying quality in different jurisdictions and with a diversity of measures of offense seriousness and prior record.[26]

To avoid bias that results in dissimilar sentences for more or less similar offenders, several researchers have developed, and several legislatures have adopted, sentencing guidelines. These guidelines assign specific values to the important sentencing criteria—principally the seriousness of the offenses and possibly prior record and other factors (Chapter 17). These guidelines are meant to help judges select the length and type of punishment.

Don Gottfredson and Bridget Stecher conducted research on what factors judges actually take into consideration when they select an "appropriate" sentence. In studying 17 judges who sentenced 982 adult offenders, they found that the main objective was rehabilitation (in 36 percent of the cases), followed by "other purposes including general deterrence" (34 percent), retribution (17 percent), special deterrence (9 percent), and incapacitation (4 percent).[27]

Corrections Decisions

The two traditional corrections choices are incarceration (the institutional choice) and routine probation (the community choice). Today there are a number of community alternatives, as well as different types of incarceration and release/parole decisions.

Decisions in the Community

The court's sentence may transfer an offender to the executive part of government, the correctional authorities. This happens when the sentence is one of incarceration. Yet far more offenders are sentenced to serve their time in the community, on probation. In that case the person remains subject to the control of the court, and the sentence is supervised by the court's probation department.

More recently many states have experimented with a variety of alternatives to the two traditional choices of incarceration and routine probation. Among these alternatives are placement in restitution programs, intensive supervision programs (ISPs), shock incarceration, and regimented discipline programs (RDPs, also called "boot camps"). Such programs are usually operated by the correctional service, rather than the probation department.

A good deal of research has been done on the success or failure of traditional probation with various types of offenders. The newer programs have not been in existence long enough to permit reliable evaluation. Initial research (discussed in Chapter 18) indicates that some types may be cost-beneficial and somewhat successful in lowering recidivism (repeat-offense) rates.[28]

Decisions in Institutions

The correctional sector of the criminal justice system is composed of institutions of varying degrees of security, with varying programs, and of quasi-institutional as well as community-based programs. Within the limitations of law, the correctional staff decides where to place sentenced offenders in view of security requirements, the availability of treatment and rehabilitation programs, and organizational needs.

All inmates must be classified in accordance with the placements that are available.[29] Such decisions are not easy. It is difficult to predict the types of security precautions an inmate will require. Nor is it possible to accurately predict the success of education, vocational training, or any other treatment program.

It is perhaps easier to decide where to assign inmates in terms of the institutional jobs that keep the institution running. Inmates do clerical and classification work, provide legal aid, and perform maintenance work; they work in the library, the infirmary, the laundry, the kitchen. But even these decisions require consideration of other factors, especially safety. All such decisions

WINDOW TO THE WORLD
Should We Abolish the Criminal Justice System?

One group of criminal justice scholars in Europe proposes to abolish the criminal justice system. Rather than helping to resolve social problems, they argue, the criminal justice system itself is a social problem. They contend that the system "can never provide for a humane and sensible way" of dealing with crime.(1) This view is termed the *abolitionist perspective.*

The System Is the Problem

According to this perspective, there are four major reasons for considering the criminal justice system itself as a social problem:

- The system inflicts suffering and furthers the existing inequality and hardship in society.
- The system does not work in terms of its own declared aims.
- The system is comprised of a number of organizations that have their own aims to achieve, making it difficult to control.
- The criminal justice approach is fundamentally flawed because there is no longer any consensus in society about how social problems should be solved.(1)

The abolitionists explain that they have "replaced the Holy Trinity of 'crime,' 'criminal,' and 'punishment' by the concepts of 'problematic situation,' 'directly involved,' and 'styles of social control/structural change.' "(1) From the abolitionist perspective, a mugging or an insurance fraud would be a "problematic situation" (not a crime) in which the perpetrators are those "directly involved" (not criminals), and there should be no punishment but varying "styles of social control/structural change." These might include social changes that would make it unnecessary for people to commit muggings or to engage in insurance fraud or structural changes that would provide for the compensation of victims. There could be therapy or, if necessary, restraint for those "directly involved."

Alternatives to Punishment

Above all, abolitionists argue, it is essential to get rid of punishment altogether, especially imprisonment. Abolitionists claim that we are well on the way to this goal already:

- The cruel punishments of the eighteenth century have been abolished.
- Capital punishment has been abolished in all but three major industrialized nations (the United States, Japan, and South Africa).
- Imprisonment for life has been abolished in many countries.
- Long-term prison sentences have been virtually abolished in Scandinavia, where a "lifer" serves 10 years.
- Short-term prison sentences have been virtually abolished in some countries.

The heart of the abolitionist perspective is the argument that prisons cannot control the crime rate but that socioeconomic and cultural reforms can. Abolitionists propose that we try such reforms, and they predict that crime rates will drop and prison will become unnecessary. The complaint of a Japanese prison official supports their view: "The situation is getting to be very serious. With the drop in crime and imprisonment in Japan, our jobs are seriously in jeopardy."(2)

Source

1. John Blad, Hans van Mastrijt, and Niels Uildriks, "Hulsman's Abolitionist Perspective: The Criminal Justice System as a Social Problem," in *The Criminal Justice System as a Social Problem: An Abolitionist Perspective*, ed. Blad, van Mastrijt, and Uildriks (Rotterdam: Erasmus University, 1987), pp. 5–17.
2. Personal communication to the authors.

Questions for Discussion

1. Unlike other industrialized nations, the United States is moving toward more capital punishment and more and longer prison sentences. What accounts for its different approach?
2. Can nations and their peoples solve crime problems through socioeconomic and cultural reform? Defend your position.

have to be reviewed on the basis of the information gathered, and new decisions have to be made from time to time.

✓ Release and Parole Decisions

To the extent that the system permits any leeway, the most important decision is whether to release an individual from the institution. There are two types of release from the correctional system. In the first, at the expiration of his or her sentence, the inmate must be released. Although correctional administrators have little choice in this type of release, the expiration point depends to some degree on their decisions. In the course of disciplinary proceedings, correctional administrators must decide whether an inmate will lose "good-time" benefits because of violations of the institution's rules. An inmate who violates the rules loses the benefit of the early release that comes with good behavior. Today release decisions are further complicated by policy decisions made at higher governmental levels. They are also made by judges, who frequently order prisoners released to make space for new ones in order to relieve prison overcrowding.

The second way an inmate may be released is through parole. In its original and ideal form, parole was a benefit bestowed on a prisoner for good behavior in prison and a promise of good conduct after discharge. Success was to be achieved with the aid of a parole officer. As parole officers' caseloads increased, however, that ideal faded; today parole is simply an early release from prison based on the decision of a parole board. Parole boards have little information to rely on in making their decisions. Conduct in the institution, however, has been demonstrated to relate to behavior outside it.[30]

Some progress has been made in the development of devices to predict success on parole; these devices are called base expectancy scales.[31] Nevertheless, parole decisions remain difficult. Statistics show that arrest rates of released inmates are very high, as are rates of reconviction and reincarceration (Chapter 18).[32] Variations in these rates depend on the number of previous incarcerations, the types of crimes committed, ethnic background, education, length of the prison term served, time elapsed since release, and other factors. Some states have abolished parole, and others are using it with steadily declining frequency. (Several special forms of parole, such as intensive-supervision parole with and without electronic monitoring, are discussed in Chapter 18.)

Diversion Out of the System

Throughout the criminal justice process, the number of persons within the system steadily decreases. This phenomenon is called the *attrition rate,* or the "mortality rate." The President's Commission on Law Enforcement and the Administration of Justice depicted the criminal justice system as a funnel. In the mid-1960s 727,000 defendants entered the wide opening at the top of the funnel—roughly one for every four of the 2.78 million Index crimes reported. Slightly more than one in five of the arrestees were convicted.[33] Two decades later, by the mid-1980s, the 1965 numbers had quadrupled or quintupled, yet the proportion remained essentially the same (Figure 15.3).

As we have seen, there are two reasons for the enormous amount of diversion from the system at various stages. First, decision makers may, for a variety of reasons, consider a case inappropriate for further processing within the normal flow of the criminal justice system. If they did not do so, the system would come to a halt. Moreover, this exercise of discretion keeps an already punitive system from being overly punitive. Thus compassion is added to the mix. Second, if a legal standard of proof is not met, the case automatically leaves the criminal justice process. In such situations decision makers have no choice. At each stage of the process the authorities must meet a legal standard of proof. These standards become progressively tighter as the case proceeds through the various stages of the process (Figure 15.4).

A very broad standard of proof—reasonable suspicion—permits a large intake into the criminal justice system. A very tight standard of proof—guilt beyond a reasonable doubt—permits persons ultimately to be convicted and retained in the system. Various intermediate standards determine whether a person should be processed to the next stage.

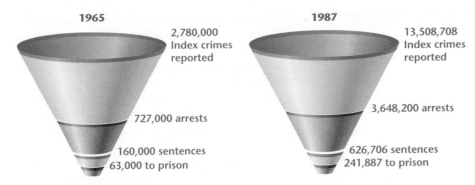

FIGURE 15.3 The funnel effect: Reported crimes through prison sentence, 1965 and 1987

Source: Presidents Commission on Law Enforcement and Administration of Justie, *Task Force Report on Science and Technology* (Washington D.C.: U.S. Government Printing Office, 1967), p. 61; compiled from the U.S. Department of Justice, *Sourcebook of Criminal Justice Statistics, 1988* (Wahington, D.C.: U.S. Government Printing Office, 1989).

JUVENILE JUSTICE

The juvenile justice system today is very large and must cope with a very sizable number of juvenile offenders.[34] Table 15.1 indicates the proportion of arrests for Index crimes committed by juveniles in 1988. Among the eight UCR Index crimes, the percentage ranges from a low of 9.0 percent for murder and nonnegligent manslaughter to a high of 42.1 percent for arson. The juveniles under 18 arrested for all Index crimes represented 18.1 percent of all persons arrested for such crimes. If we take the traditional age of majority, 21 years, as our standard, it turns out that one-third of all crimes of violence are committed by juveniles.[35]

The Development of the Juvenile Justice System

The roots of our system of juvenile justice can be traced to classical Roman law. There are two

DECISIONS TO BE MADE, AND BY WHOM

1. Decision to approach a person: police
2. Stop and frisk: police
3. Arrest: police, magistrates
4. First appearance: magistrate
5. Preliminary hearing: judge
6. Indictment: grand jury
7. Conviction: court and/or jury, defendant's guilty plea
8. Sentence to prison: judge

LEGAL STANDARD OF PROOF

Articulable facts that crime is afoot (New York)

Reasonable suspicion

Probable cause

Judicial affirmation of probable cause

Reasonable grounds to believe guilty (jacked-up probable cause)

Prima facie case

Guilt beyond a reasonable doubt

Judicial discretion within limits of statute

FIGURE 15.4 The funnel effect of the standard of proof

TABLE 15.1 INDEX CRIMES CLEARED BY ARREST OF JUVENILES, 1992

Index Crimes	Percent of Total Arrests
Murder, nonnegligent manslaughter	9.0
Forcible rape	14.3
Robbery	15.9
Aggravated assault	12.0
Burglary	19.7
Larceny-theft	23.1
Motor vehicle theft	23.9
Arson	42.1
All violent crime	12.8
All property crime	22.6
All Index crimes	20.0

Source: U.S. Department of Justice, Bureau of Justice Statistics, Crime in the United States, 1992 (Washington, D.C.: U.S. Government Printing Office, 1993), pp. 214–215.

roots, one clearly punitive, the other supportive and caring. The punitive root brought the imposition of adult criminal liability on children. In the Middle Ages, under the law of the church, the Roman law classification of children with respect to criminal liability took definite shape and was taken over by the common law.

This classification scheme subjected children between ages 7 and 14 to the rigors of adult criminal liability, proceedings, and punishments. It still affects our thinking, and its impact can be seen in the laws of many states. Theoretically, today a 10-year-old can be tried as an adult in Vermont, a 12-year-old in Montana, and a 13-year-old in Georgia, Illinois, and Mississippi (see Table 15.2).

The second root, also originating in Roman law, is that of concern for troubled children. We find its traces in the concepts used today in juvenile court proceedings. It was very much present in the concept of **parens patriae,** which to the Romans meant that the emperor, and in medieval times the king or queen, could exercise "parental power" *in loco parentis* ("in the place of a parent" deemed incapable or unworthy) over children in trouble or in danger of becoming wayward. The power of the monarch was eventually transferred to the people of the state, as represented by the juvenile court judge.

These doctrines guided American practice for dealing with troubled children after 1838 and the case *Ex parte Crouse.* On the petition of her mother, a young girl, Mary Ann Crouse, had been committed by the court to the Philadelphia House of Refuge as wayward and incorrigible. When Mary Ann's father, who was estranged from his wife, learned what had happened, he sought a writ of habeas corpus to secure the release of his daughter, who, so he alleged, had been imprisoned without a jury trial. The Pennsylvania Supreme Court rejected this argument,

TABLE 15.2 YOUNGEST AGE OF POSSIBLE CRIMINAL LIABILITY*

Age (years)	Jurisdiction†
No specific age	Alaska, Arizona, Arkansas, Delaware, Florida, Indiana, Kentucky, Maine, Maryland, New Hampshire, New Jersey, Oklahoma, South Dakota, West Virginia, Wyoming, federal districts
10	Vermont
12	Montana
13	Georgia, Illinois, Mississippi, New York (murder II)
14	Alabama, Colorado, Connecticut, Idaho, Iowa, Massachusetts, Minnesota, Missouri, New York (some felonies), North Carolina, North Dakota, Pennsylvania, South Carolina, Tennessee, Utah
15	District of Columbia, Louisiana, Michigan, Nebraska, New Mexico, New York (some felonies), Ohio, Oregon, Texas, Virginia
16	California, Hawaii, Kansas, Nevada, New York, Rhode Island, Washington, Wisconsin

*Age at which a juvenile may be transferred to criminal court by judicial waiver.
†States, District of Columbia, and other federal districts.

Source: Adapted from Linda A. Szymanski, Waiver/Transfer/Certification of Juveniles to Criminal Court: Age Restrictions, Crime Restrictions (Pittsburgh, Pa.: National Center for Juvenile Justice, February 1987), updated.

reasoning that under the parens patriae doctrine the state has every right to protect children from improper upbringing.[36]

Houses of refuge designed to care for the impoverished, "dangerous" street people of the time were based on an earlier English model. In reality, these houses were little more than prisons to which individuals could be sent without trial. The houses of refuge proved a dismal failure. They neither educated nor reformed anybody. In them, children were subjected to harsh discipline.

Reformatories

Massachusetts tried a new approach in 1854, with the creation of the Massachusetts Industrial School for Girls. In a cottage-style setting, surrogate families were created, with the goal of reforming girls who were considered "wayward and delinquent." Other states followed Massachusetts' lead. The problem with this approach was the lack of a judicial determination that a given child had indeed violated the law and therefore was in need of some remedial placement.

The all-important change occurred in Chicago, where Timothy D. Hurley, a judge and former probation officer, and Julia Lathrop, of the Illinois Board of Charities, advocated abandonment of the system that placed child offenders and wayward children in adult jails and prisons and removed children who had been arbitrarily declared wayward from the custody of their parents and placed them in prisonlike institutions. Hurley and Lathrop lobbied for the creation of a juvenile court. With the help of the Catholic Visitation and Aid Society and the Chicago Bar Association, they succeeded. The Illinois legislature created the nation's first juvenile court, in Chicago, in 1899.

The Juvenile Court

The concepts that guided the operation of the Chicago juvenile court and subsequent similar courts were straightforward:

■ All dependent, neglected, and delinquent children under 16 years of age could be brought under the jurisdiction of the juvenile court.

■ Delinquency included any act that, if committed by an adult, would be a crime.

■ The juvenile court did not find youngsters guilty of anything but simply determined their status as dependent, neglected (in a very broad, sweeping sense), or delinquent.

■ The juvenile court judge acted as a surrogate parent, conducting informal proceedings (in contrast to the formal adversarial proceedings in criminal court).

■ Exercising much discretion, the juvenile court judge gave first consideration to the best interest of the child.

■ Dispositions by the court were not punishments; they might include only friendly probation, in the child's own home, or placement in a suitable foster home or training in an industrial school.

There were two problems with this approach. First, the definition of behavior that brought a child under the jurisdiction of the juvenile court was still extremely broad. "Dependency" and "neglect" are vague terms. Nor are these conditions the youngster's fault; they are the parents' fault. Moreover, the concept of delinquency embraced not only acts that would be crimes if an adult committed them but also behavior that would not be considered deviant in adults, such as truancy or running away from home. When dependency and neglect were included in the definition of delinquency, neglect itself became a status offense. A neglected child was by definition delinquent.

Second, while the motivations for the informality of the proceedings in the juvenile justice system were praiseworthy, they led to intolerable abuses. Not all children's rights were violated in all cases, but abuses were frequent. Most juvenile court judges sincerely regarded the informality of their proceedings as in the best interest of the child.[37]

This system dominated until 1967, when the Supreme Court at last ruled that children, too, have rights that are protected by the Constitution. In the case *In re Gault* the Court ruled that virtually all the guarantees of the Fourth, Fifth, and Sixth Amendments, made applicable to the states under the due process clause of the Four-

CRIMINOLOGICAL FOCUS

In re Gault: The Demise of Parens Patriae

On June 8, 1964, in Gila County, Arizona, Mrs. Cook complained to Deputy Sheriff Flagg about obscene phone calls she had received, which she attributed to a neighborhood kid, Gerald Francis Gault, age 15. The deputy sheriff knew Gerry Gault; he was on probation, having been found in the company of another youngster who had lifted a wallet from a woman's handbag.

Deputy Sheriff Flagg promptly went to Gerry's home, arrested him, and placed him in the juvenile detention facility. When Gerry's mother returned home that night and found Gerry gone, she sent her elder son out to find him. He learned from acquaintances that Gerry was in detention. Gerry's mother promptly went to the detention center. She did not get to see Gerry. The deputy told her of Gerry's arrest and informed her that there would be a hearing in juvenile court at 3 P.M. next day. On that day the deputy filed an application with the court noting that Gerry, as a minor, is "in need of the protection of the honorable court, as he is delinquent." The application contained no reference to Mrs. Cook's complaint. The hearing took place before Judge McGhee of juvenile court. Present were Deputy Sheriff Flagg in his capacity as a probation officer, Gerry, and, by chance, his mother and elder brother. Mrs. Cook was absent.

In a formless proceeding Gerry denied ever having made an obscene phone call. The judge returned Gerry to the detention facility. A second hearing was held one week later. Gerry's mother was informed about this hearing by means of a hand-scribbled note that Deputy Sheriff Flagg left at her door. The second hearing was as formless as the first one. There was no complaining witness, and Judge McGhee ruled that none was necessary. The court declared that Gerry's obscene phone call was proved and that if the act were committed by an adult, it would be a misdemeanor subject to a fine of from $5 to $50 and a jail term of up to 2 months. Juveniles, he declared, could not be punished. Judge McGhee then found Gerry to be a habitual juvenile offender, because 3 years earlier Gerry had been accused of the theft of a baseball glove (though he had not been charged with an offense), and declared that Gerry had lied when he denied the accusation. Judge McGhee found Gerry to be a juvenile delinquent, not to be punished but to be sent to a juvenile correctional facility for 6 years—until he reached the age of 21.

After Gerry's parents finally engaged an attorney, the case gained widespread publicity. Everything seemed to have gone wrong in the case. Yet all the appeals courts upheld Judge McGhee's disposition. With the help of civil libertarians and members of some of the most prestigious law faculties, the case reached the United States Supreme Court, 3 years after Gerry had been incarcerated. The Supreme Court's opinion was written by one of the most compassionate men ever to sit on that bench, Justice Abe Fortas. The case was *In re Gault,* and it made history. Children, Fortas wrote, have fully as much right as adults to the protection of the Constitution. Never again would a child be sentenced to 6 years of incarceration for an act that was never proved and that, if proved against an adult, would have warranted a jail term of 2 months.

Source: In re Gault, 387 U.S. 1 (1967).

Questions for Discussion

1. What constitutional rights were denied to Gerry Gault that now must be granted in juvenile court?
2. Does the decision in the Gault case destroy the idea of compassionate informality that had been the hallmark of juvenile court proceedings?

Gerald Gault (center), whose Supreme Court victory guaranteed due process to all future juvenile defendents.

teenth Amendment, must be extended to juveniles.

These guarantees include the right to be informed of the charges, freedom from unreasonable seizure (arrest), the right to have an attorney, and the right to be confronted by and to examine witnesses.[38] Later the Court ruled that proof of juvenile delinquency, like that of a crime charged to an adult, must be established beyond a reasonable doubt. Only the right to a jury trial need not be accorded to juveniles, perhaps to preserve some of the informality of the juvenile court.[39] These decisions subjugated parens patriae to the rule of law and to constitutional due process.

A Junior Criminal Justice System

Juvenile court judges viewed the Supreme Court's decisions with mixed emotions. Some thought the juvenile court movement had come to an end. But as time passed, it became evident that juvenile courts can function well in administering juvenile justice even while abiding by the due process guarantees of the Constitution. There is some evidence, however, that many children and parents do not claim the procedural rights to which they are constitutionally entitled, frequently out of ignorance.[40]

The transformation of juvenile justice proceedings into a junior model of adult criminal justice had a peculiar consequence. If juveniles are to have the rights of adults charged with crime, should they not also have the responsibilities? In 1977 an influential joint committee of the Institute of Judicial Administration at New York University and the American Bar Association formulated a set of standards for juvenile justice.

The committee proposed that juvenile dispositions should be based on the seriousness of the offense, not merely on the court's view of the juvenile's needs.[41] With these standards the punitive movement of the mid-1970s reached juvenile justice. This increased punitiveness manifested itself in four different ways:

1. *Lower age of criminal responsibility.* After New York passed legislation permitting the incarceration of juveniles over the age of 13 for certain serious felonies, other states followed suit. Thus, in most states, the juvenile justice system has become a junior version of the criminal justice system. Only the offenders are junior, however; the rest of the players are not (Table 15.3).

2. *More waivers to (adult) criminal court.* Most states specify an age (16, 17, 18, or 21) below which an offender can be brought before a juvenile court. But most states also have a provision that permits a juvenile court judge to waive jurisdiction and transmit the case to the criminal court. (Table 15.2 indicates the youngest age at which a juvenile may be transferred to criminal

TABLE 15.3 PROVISIONS OF NEW YORK'S JUVENILE OFFENDER LAW

Acts Covered	Ages Affected	Terms of Confinement	
		Minimum	Maximum
Murder 2, excluding felony murder	13–15	5–9 yr.	Life
Murder 2	14, 15	5–9 yr.	Life
Kidnapping 1, Arson 1	14, 15	4–6 yr.	12–15 yr.
Manslaughter 1, Rape 1, Sodomy 1, Burglary 1, Robbery 1, Arson 2, Attempted murder 2, Attempted kidnapping 1	14, 15	1/3 of max.	3–10 yr.
Assault 1, Robbery 2, Burglary 2	14, 15	1/3 of max.	3–7 yr.

Source: Simon I. Singer and David McDowall, "Criminalizing Delinquency: The Deterrent Effects of the New York Juvenile Offender Law," Law and Society Review, 22 (1988): 521–535.

court.) Since the Supreme Court decision in *Breed v. Jones* (1975), such a waiver hearing has been a constitutional right.[42]

In most states less than 5 percent of juvenile cases are in fact waived to criminal court, but the number of waivers has been increasing. In one study of teenage felons and waiver hearings in Virginia, Tennessee, Mississippi, and Georgia, a 104.3 percent increase in waiver hearings was found between 1980 (228) and 1988 (466).[43]

3. *Increasingly formal dispositions.* Over the years dispositions of juveniles have tended to become increasingly formal. In 1972, half of all juvenile cases were referred by police to juvenile court. By 1989, over 80 percent of all cases reached the juvenile court. In 1972, 45 percent of all cases were handled informally within the department, and the suspect was released; by 1987, only 30.3 percent were handled informally. Referral to a criminal court increased from 1.3 percent in 1972 to 5.8 percent in 1989. This is clear evidence of a trend in the direction of greater punitiveness toward juvenile offenders.

4. *Broader legislative exclusion.* The fourth indicator of increased punitiveness is increased legislative exclusion of juveniles from juvenile court adjudication. New York, for example, passed the Juvenile Offender Law of 1978, which abolishes juvenile court jurisdiction for a wide range of crimes, from murder in the second degree to burglary and assault. *Legislative exclusion*—or the grant of jurisdiction to an adult court to adjudicate cases against juveniles for specific offenses—is designed to increase the deterrent effect of the law by providing significant terms of confinement (Table 15.4). At least this is its goal. A recent evaluation of the New York Juvenile Offender Law concluded that there was no appreciable reduction in juvenile crime following its passage. The authors of the evaluation concluded that either the terms were too weak or juveniles were not deterred by its provisions.

The Juvenile Justice Process

Let us now turn to the flowchart for the juvenile justice process (Figure 15.5). Having entered the juvenile justice system, the individual will be processed according to its procedures.

TABLE 15.4 OFFENSES EXCLUDED FROM JUVENILE COURT JURISDICTION*

Excluded Offenses	Jurisdiction[†]
Murder[‡]	Arkansas, Connecticut, Delaware, District of Columbia, Idaho, Illinois, Indiana, Louisiana, Nevada, New York, Ohio, Oklahoma, Pennsylvania, Utah, Vermont
Rape (including criminal sexual conduct of penetration)	Arkansas, Delaware, District of Columbia, Idaho, Illinois, Indiana, Louisiana, New York, Oklahoma, Utah, Vermont
Kidnapping	Delaware, Indiana, Louisiana, New York, Oklahoma, Utah
Burglary	District of Columbia, Louisiana, New York
Armed robbery or robbery	District of Columbia, Idaho, Illinois, Indiana, Louisiana, Maryland, Oklahoma, Utah, Vermont
Other[§]	Arkansas, Colorado, Connecticut, Florida, Idaho, Kansas, Nebraska, Ohio, Rhode Island, Wyoming

*Only criminal courts can try for such crimes by juveniles, provided they have reached minimum age (see Table 15-2).

[†]Only 23 states plus the District of Columbia legislatively exclude certain offenses from juvenile court jurisdiction. Because of the different offense categories, some states are listed more than once.

[‡]This category includes various degrees of criminal homicide, including attempted murder in some states (e.g., Nevada and New York).

[§]This category includes offense categories such as "any offense."

Source: Barry C. Feld, "The Juvenile Court Meets the Principle of the Offense: Legislative Changes in Juvenile Waiver Statutes," *Journal of Criminal Law and Criminology*, 78 (1987): 512–514. Reprinted by special permission of Northwestern University, School of Law.

Entry into the System

It has been said that "citizens . . . largely determine delinquency rates," because it is the citizens' tolerance level and perceptions that determine the decision to call the police.[44] Perceptions and tolerance levels vary from area to area and neighborhood to neighborhood, but on the whole, they are more lenient in the case of juvenile misconduct. We noted earlier that crimes actually committed far outnumber those reported to the police. It appears that as far as crimes committed by juveniles are concerned, the difference is even greater than that in adult crimes because of the reluctance of other juveniles, and of adults who remember their own youth, to bring juvenile misconduct to the attention of the authorities.

Invoking the Juvenile Justice Process

Once juvenile misconduct has been brought to the attention of the authorities, usually the police, the next step is a decision to investigate, to arrest, and to process. There is no uniform standard as to whether the taking of a juvenile into custody is in fact an arrest. In some states it is; in others it is not; and in still others the issue is not clear. But in all states the taking of a juvenile into custody requires compliance with the constitutional mandates of *In re Gault,* including the probable-cause requirement and administration of the *Miranda* warnings.

Generally the police have broad power when a juvenile is taken into custody for reasons other than criminal conduct, such as being in danger, in trouble, or in violation of a juvenile court's order. But police officers are both reluctant and poorly prepared to make decisions in such instances.[45] After an arrest or detention, usually by a patrol officer, the juvenile is ordinarily handed over to a juvenile officer, a member of a specially trained police unit. Such units exercise far broader discretion than their colleagues who process adult criminal cases. They may decide to release a juvenile into the custody of parents or otherwise involve parents, who may be called to the stationhouse to discuss the matter.

Once a juvenile has been taken into custody, the police juvenile unit must also decide, guided by law, whether to process the youngster as an adult offender and take him or her before a mag-

istrate for a first appearance, to choose the juvenile path and take the suspect before a juvenile court judge, or to deal with the case in a less formal manner.

If the case is not informally disposed of by the police or the juvenile probation department, it moves before a juvenile court judge for an intake hearing. In large metropolitan areas the juvenile court judge usually is a specialist in juvenile matters. In the more rural parts of the country the criminal court judge doubles as juvenile court judge.

The juvenile court then decides, on the basis of the report of the intake department (juvenile court officers and probation intake officers), whether sufficient grounds exist for filing a petition requesting an adjudicatory hearing (juvenile court trial), whether the case should be waived to criminal court, whether the juvenile should be transferred to a social agency, or whether the case should be dismissed. Juvenile court judges have broad discretion in making these decisions.

Adjudication

If the juvenile court has retained jurisdiction, the case moves into the adjudicatory hearing, which is equivalent to a trial in criminal court. As we noted earlier, under the terms of *In re Gault* the juvenile is entitled to nearly all the procedural guarantees that protect adults charged with crime.

In the adjudicatory hearing, the juvenile court judge must decide whether the facts warrant a decision in accordance with the petition. If the petition alleges that the juvenile has committed an act which, if committed by an adult, would be a crime or that the juvenile is a status offender by being a truant, a runaway, or ungovernable (or some other such term), and if the facts support the petition, the court will adjudicate the juvenile to be a delinquent.

In order not to stigmatize individuals with the label "delinquent," some states have created such categories as "persons in need of supervision" (PINS), "juveniles in need of supervision" (JINS), "children in need of supervision (CHINS), or "dependent and neglected children," all of which have simply become new labels. Juveniles so charged will be adjudicated as such if the facts warrant this. The judge will then proceed to the

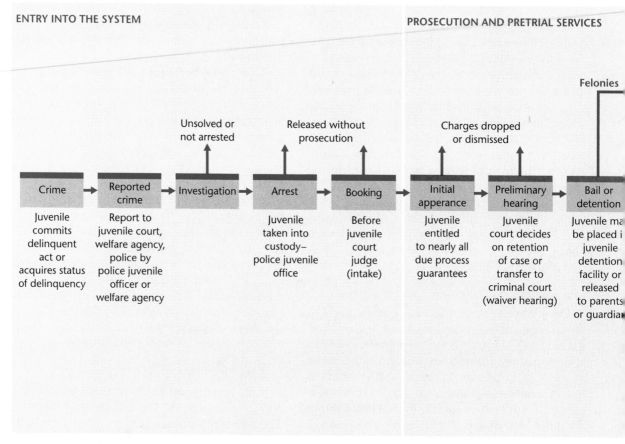

FIGURE 15.5 The juvenile justice process compared with the adult criminal process

second part of the adjudication process, which corresponds to sentencing in criminal court.

The Dispositional Hearing

In finding an appropriate disposition, the court is guided by any relevant information, especially that provided by the juvenile probation officer. The juvenile court judge must reconcile the child's interest with society's interest in being protected from dangerous and disruptive persons; guide delinquent children into a socially acceptable path; set an example for other children on the path of delinquency; make children responsible for their harmful actions; and set an example of love, care, and forgiveness for children who have broken the law.[46]

In choosing a disposition, juvenile court judges have broader discretion than criminal court judges. The judge may choose probation, with numerous conditions; commitment to a juvenile correctional facility; restitution; or fines. Placement in a foster home or in a special program may also be decreed.

Juvenile Corrections

The juvenile court may decide that the only option is to place the juvenile in an institution. There has been considerable debate over whether placement in an institution is ever an appropriate response to juvenile wrongdoing.

Jerome Miller, as head of the Massachusetts juvenile correction system, tried to prove the point by closing down all of the state's juvenile detention facilities.[47] The experiment did not last. Policy makers determined that some juvenile offenders must be segregated for the protection

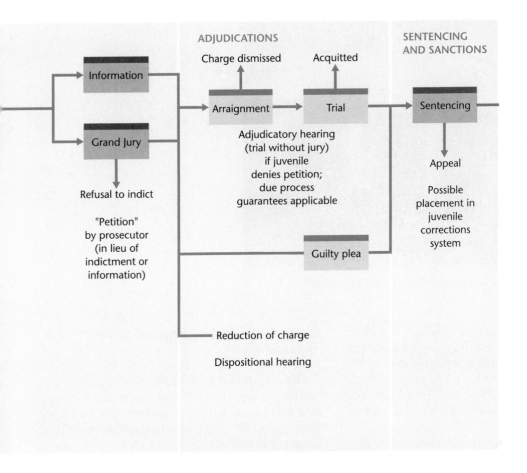

ADJUDICATIONS

SENTENCING
AND SANCTIONS

Charge dismissed   Acquitted

Information

Arraignment → Trial → Sentencing

Grand Jury

Adjudicatory hearing
(trial without jury)
if juvenile
denies petition;
due process
guarantees applicable

Appeal

Refusal to indict

Possible
placement in
juvenile
corrections
system

"Petition"
by prosecutor
(in lieu of
indictment or
information)

Guilty plea

Reduction of charge

Dispositional hearing

of the community. Although researchers continue to demonstrate that the jailing of juvenile offenders has no appreciable effect on the juvenile crime rate,[48] all states maintain facilities for their confinement and hoped-for rehabilitation.

Most inmates of juvenile facilities (74 percent) have committed crimes. Only 12 percent are adjudicated juvenile status offenders, but a surprising 14 percent are juveniles classified as nonoffenders, including dependent, neglected, and abused children. Even more surprising, the total number of residents in juvenile facilities grows by 6 to 9 percent annually.[49]

A federal government survey revealed the following statistics for 1990:

■ 619,181 juveniles were admitted to public detention, correctional, and shelter facilities.

■ 141,463 juveniles were admitted to private facilities.

■ 65,263 juveniles were admitted to adult jails.

■ 9078 juveniles were admitted to state correctional facilities.

The total number of juveniles in custody was 834,985. The number of residents on an average day, however, amounts to only about 99,617, of which about half are long-term residents.[50] Fifty percent of all admissions to juvenile facilities come from only five states—California, Ohio, Texas, Washington, and Florida—which together have only 5 percent of the entire juvenile population of the United States.[51]

The juvenile facilities encompass a wide spectrum: detention centers, training schools, recep-

Giddings (Texas) State School campus housing for juveniles.

tion or diagnostic centers, shelters, ranches, forestry camps or farms, halfway houses, and group homes. Most of the 3036 facilities in the nation are privately operated. Yet the majority of juvenile offenders are being held in public facilities, which are far more security-minded than the private ones.

Juvenile facilities range from serene, campus-like complexes with understanding counselors to sordid, prisonlike establishments. Criminologists have argued that incarceration of juveniles will do more harm than good unless the conditions of detention are radically reformed and the population is kept at a minimum through reduced admissions. This is one of the tasks of the science of criminology.

Arguments about the future of juveniles placed in detention facilities have reached an impasse in the courts. In the case of *Schall v. Martin* (1984) it was argued before the Supreme Court that a New York law permitting the incarceration of juveniles predicted to constitute a danger was unconstitutional because social science cannot make such predictions. In addressing the question, the Supreme Court affirmed its belief "that there is nothing inherently unattainable about a prediction of future conduct."[52] To many researchers it is still apparent that juvenile correctional treatment is largely unsuccessful.[53] This raises the question of whether greater bene-

fits are to be gained by diverting juveniles out of the juvenile justice system.

Diversion Out of the Juvenile System

There is significant attrition in the juvenile system. More than half the total number of juveniles who appear at intake are diverted through dismissal or informal disposition. Of those detained and subsequently adjudicated in 1981, 12 percent had their cases dismissed and 1 percent were transferred to adult court. Two-thirds of those who remained for disposition hearings were placed on probation, and less than 10 percent were sent to a juvenile correctional facility.

A recent depiction of the filtering process separates those cases that are not handled by petition.[54] Of the total number of juveniles charged (1,348,100), slightly more than 20 percent were detained prior to a fact-finding hearing. Of cases handled with a petition, nearly 2 percent were waived to criminal court; 26 percent had the petitions dismissed; in 34 percent the juveniles were placed on probation; and in nearly 14 percent (85,600) they were sent to correctional facilities.

Comparisons of the juvenile and adult attrition rates reveal more significant diversion in the adult criminal justice system. This is remarkable given that the juvenile court was originally designed as a diversion from the adult court. Moreover, literally thousands of diversionary programs were created in the 1970s to filter out juveniles who would "do better" outside the system.

Over the last two decades, some observers have found a wide gap between diversion in theory and diversion in practice. According to some scholars, diversionary programs were originally conceived as alternatives to the formal juvenile justice system—they were to be privately run ("nonlegal"), community-based programs. But most diversionary programs ended up being sponsored by state or local justice agencies. The result seemed to be only a widening of the net of the juvenile justice system—an increase in the reach of state-sponsored social control. Evidence emerged that diversionary programs were in fact sometimes coercive. Finally, to the extent that diversionary programs became government-sponsored, the benefit of using such programs so that children would avoid stigmatization was all but lost.[55]

There is general agreement that our juvenile justice system is far from perfect but that improving it is within our reach.[56] The real problem, however, is not necessarily in the juvenile justice system but rather in the social and economic conditions that produce delinquency in the first place. Reforms, therefore, must aim primarily at the root causes of delinquency.

VICTIMS AND CRIMINAL JUSTICE

Victims of crime play a crucial role in invoking the criminal and juvenile justice processes. An old proverb states: "Where there is no complainant, there is no judge." Victims play an equally significant role at the later stages of the process, as witnesses. Without their testimony, convictions usually cannot be obtained. Until recently, however, the role and plight of victims seemed to have been overlooked by the criminal justice system.

Victims of Crime in History

The plight of the crime victim was recognized by the earliest legal systems. The Code of Hammurabi in the eighteenth century B.C. provided

that the victims of highway robbers had to be compensated for their losses out of the governor's treasury.[57] Until the Middle Ages many acts that are crimes today were considered to be torts—that is, civil wrongs—which entitled the victim to compensation from the wrongdoer. Later on, powerful monarchs claimed compensation for themselves for the harm done to the real victim. Fines to the government replaced compensation to actual victims, who were forced to seek compensation in civil court proceedings.

Not until after World War II was concern for the victim revitalized. In *The Criminal and His Victim*, Hans von Hentig (himself a victim of Nazi persecution) forced us to think of the crucial role of the victim in the criminal justice process.[58] Benjamin Mendelson in 1947 coined the term **victimology,** the scientific study of the victim.[59] The Hungarian-American scholar Stephen Schafer (a victim of Nazi and Stalinist oppression) contributed significantly to victimology in his books *Restitution to Victims of Crime* and *The Victim and His Criminal*.[60] The momentum for focusing on the victim's role in criminal justice processing had been generated,[61] and victimology made rapid progress in theory and practice. Today the study of victimology focuses on five goals:

- To understand and measure the extent and nature of crime as victims perceive them
- To assess the relative risk of victimization
- To appreciate the nature and extent of losses, injuries, and damages experienced by victims of crime
- To study the relation between victim and offender
- To investigate the social reaction of the family, community, and society toward the victim of crime

The literature on victimology has grown significantly, and its impact on the administration of justice has been remarkable. Nevertheless, as the Canadian criminologist Ezzat Fattah has demonstrated, the search continues for a more perfect victimology and more incisive victim assistance.[62]

One of the most practical achievements of victimologists was the development of victimiza-

TABLE 15.5 VICTIMS' RIGHTS: A SUMMARY

Subject	Right of Victims	Enactment
Counseling	To be assured that statements divulged to counselors remain confidential if requested by the defense during the discovery phase of court proceedings	20 states
Evidence	To be assured that defendants cannot benefit from the exclusion of illegally gathered evidence, by having all evidence obtained by the police in good faith declared admissible in trials	1 state
Sentencing	To make statements orally (allocution) or in writing, at sentencing hearing	30 states
Sentence and final disposition	To be notified of the verdict and sentence after the trial and of the final disposition after appeals	35 states
Appeals	To appeal sentences that seem too lenient	1 state
Work release	To be notified if the offender will be permitted to leave the prison to perform a job during specified hours	29 states
✓Notoriety for profit	To have any royalties and fees paid to notorious criminals confiscated and used to repay victims or to fund victim services	42 states
Abuser's tax	To have penalty assessments collected from felons, misdemeanants, and traffic law violators to pay for victim services, compensation, and assistance programs	28 states
✓Parole hearings	To be notified when the prisoner will be appearing before a parole board to seek early release	44 states
Pardon	To be notified if the governor is considering pardoning the offender	27 states
Release of a felon	To be notified when the prisoner is to be released on parole or because the sentence has expired	39 states
Prison escape	To be notified if the prisoner has escaped from confinement	23 states
✓Return of stolen property	To have recovered stolen property that has been held as evidence returned expeditiously by the police or prosecution	43 states
✓Compensation	To be reimbursed for out-of-pocket expenses for medical bills and lost wages arising from injuries inflicted during a violent crime	45 states
Restitution	To receive mandatory repayments from offenders who are put on probation or parole unless a judge explains in writing the reasons for not imposing this obligation	33 states
General rights	To be "read their rights" as soon as a crime is reported or to be provided with written information about all obligations, services, and opportunities for protection and reimbursement	Many local jurisdictions
Case status	To be kept posted about any progress in their cases; to be advised when arrest warrants are issued or suspects are taken into custody	Many local jurisdictions
Employer intercession	To have the prosecutor explain to the complaining witness's employer that the victim should not be penalized for missing work because of court appearances	35 states
Creditor intercession	To have the prosecutor explain to creditors like banks and landlords that crime-inflicted financial losses necessitate delays in paying bills	10 states

TABLE 15.5 VICTIMS' RIGHTS: A SUMMARY (CONTINUED)

Subject	Right of Victims	Enactment
✓ Offender's age	To be assured that juvenile offenders do not escape full responsibility for serious crimes, by having such cases transferred from juvenile court to adult criminal court	50 states
Denial of bail	To be protected from suspects whose pretrial release on bail might endanger them	24 states
Suspect out on bail	To be notified that a suspect arrested for the crime has been released on bail	21 states
✓ Protection from further harm	To be reasonably protected during the pretrial release period from the accused through orders of protection and by increased penalties for acts of harassment and intimidation	46 states
Plea bargaining	To participate or be consulted	13 states
Negotiated plea	To be notified that both sides have agreed to a plea of guilty in return for some consideration	28 states
✓ Court appearances	To be notified in advance of all court proceedings and of changes in required court appearances	41 states
Secure waiting areas	To be provided with courthouse waiting rooms separate from those used by defendants, defense witnesses, and spectators	31 states
Trial	To participate at trial, in person or by writing	33 states
Defenses	To be assured that offenders cannot avoid imprisonment by pleading "not guilty by reason of insanity," through the substitution of "guilty and mentally ill," which requires treatment in a mental institution followed by incarceration in prison	16 states

Source: Based on Andrew Karmen, Crime Victims, 2d ed. (Pacific Grove, Calif.: Brooks/Cole, 1990), p. 332, updated.

tion surveys (Chapter 2), which enable us to estimate more accurately the extent of crime. Analysis of survey data has focused attention on the impact of crime on the victim and has demonstrated the importance of the victim's perception of a criminal event and willingness to report it to the authorities. Victimization studies are now being conducted cross-culturally, benefiting many countries with heretofore inadequate information about their crime problems.

Victims' Rights

The practical impact of victimology on the criminal justice system may be dated from the call by the English magistrate and social reformer Margery Fry for "Justice for Victims" (1957), especially compensation for innocent victims of crime.[63] Within a few years, victim compensation laws were enacted in many countries. As of now, there are such laws in 45 American states. Many

states also enacted a variety of laws intended to ease the lot of victims. Domestic violence and rape crisis centers were created in the late 1960s and early 1970s. These initial efforts were followed by the establishment of victim-witness units, first in the District of Columbia courts and then elsewhere, which ensure respectful treatment for victims and witnesses involved in the criminal justice system. Such units perform a wide variety of services:

- Assisting victims who report crimes
- Responding at the scene of a crime in order to provide crisis counseling
- Providing 24-hour telephone hot-line service to victims and witnesses
- Making emergency monetary aid available to victims
- Providing victims with referral services to appropriate agencies
- Helping victims obtain the return of property

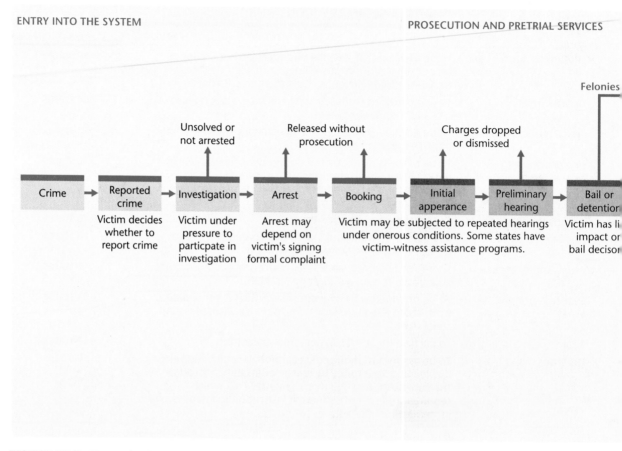

FIGURE 15.6   The path of the victim through the criminal justice process

■ Assisting victims and witnesses throughout their court appearances

Similar programs have been established throughout the country to make it easier for crime victims to participate in the criminal justice process, to secure their participation, and ultimately to provide satisfaction for them. The laws and programs focusing on victims' rights have had a profound impact on the administration of criminal justice, in general, and on the role and plight of victims during the course of the process, in particular. (A summary of legally recognized victims' rights is presented in Table 15.5.)

The Victim's Role in the Criminal Justice Process

Once again we present a flowchart through the criminal justice process, adapted from the one constructed by the President's Commission, but this time geared to the role of the victim (Figure 15.6). The criminal justice process, as we will see, looks quite different from the victim's perspective.

Entry into the System

The victim virtually determines the course of the criminal justice process by his or her willingness to report a victimization and to testify before the authorities, especially at trial.[64] As we noted in Chapter 2, for a wide variety of reasons, many victims are reluctant or unwilling to report their victimization and to participate in the process, yet without a victim's complaint, the process normally cannot start.

Prosecution and Pretrial Services

The victim must appear at a police precinct at least once. The police may have to interview the

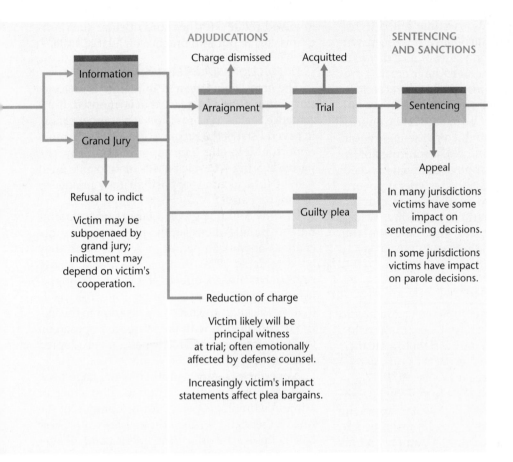

ADJUDICATIONS

SENTENCING
AND SANCTIONS

Information

Grand Jury

Charge dismissed

Acquitted

Arraignment

Trial

Sentencing

Appeal

Refusal to indict

Victim may be
subpoenaed by
grand jury;
indictment may
depend on victim's
cooperation.

Guilty plea

In many jurisdictions
victims have some
impact on
sentencing decisions.

In some jurisdictions
victims have impact
on parole decisions.

Reduction of charge

Victim likely will be
principal witness
at trial; often emotionally
affected by defense counsel.

Increasingly victim's impact
statements affect plea bargains.

victim at home. The victim is likely to have to appear at the district attorney's office to answer the same questions. Accommodations for victims are not comfortable. Interview offices are typically dingy and crowded. Confrontations with the accused, however brief, are disquieting. Actual or anticipated harassment by the perpetrator may instill fear in the victim. Many victims get frustrated and stop showing up for scheduled hearings; many do not appear at the trial.

Adjudication

In most criminal proceedings, a plea negotiation takes the place of a criminal trial. In the past, victims played no role in plea bargaining. More recently the American Bar Association has directed prosecuting attorneys to "make every effort to remain advised of the attitudes and sentiments of victims" before reaching a plea agreement.[65] Several researchers have studied victim

participation in the plea-bargaining process. One study found that only one-third of victims chose to participate, and their participation was minor.[66] Another researcher, by contrast, found victims to be very active in the plea-bargaining process, as demonstrated by the fact that 46 percent of the victims asked for the maximum punishment.[67]

If a case goes to trial, the victim is likely to be called as a witness. Though the defendant, handcuffed and in a holding pen, may be less comfortable and more anxious than the victim-witness, the anxiety of the victim and the lack of comfort in a courthouse corridor can be painful experiences. During the trial the victim is subject to cross-examination by defense counsel, whose strategy it may be to impugn the credibility of the witness.

The victims' rights movement has spurred the development of legislation and services that are responsive to the plight of victims called to testify in court. Several states have increased witness fees from the previous low of $5 a day to as much as $30 a day. Some states have created procedures to notify victims of court proceedings and guarantee them the right to speedy disposition of their cases. Forty-one states and Congress have enacted laws or provided guidelines requiring that victims and witnesses be informed of the scheduling and cancellation of criminal proceedings. Thirty-three states and the federal government permit victims to participate in criminal proceedings by oral or written testimony.[68] These developments have vastly improved the role of the victim in the adjudication process (see Table 15.5).

Sentencing

In the common law tradition the victim has no role in the imposition of a sentence. In 30 states, however, victims now have the right to state their views at sentencing hearings.[69] Yet on average only 10 percent of victims make use of this right. At this stage it is also possible to join the punishment of the offender with the satisfaction of the victim. Ideally, a sentence can be fashioned to satisfy both the victim's sense of outrage and his or her need to be compensated for losses caused by the crime.[70]

In several states, for example, a defendant may be sentenced to a community restitution facility instead of a prison. At a sentencing hearing it can be made clear to a victim who demands a stiff prison sentence for the defendant that such a sentence will not result in compensation for any loss the victim has sustained. A sentence to a community restitution facility, however, guarantees that the offender will make payments to the victim for the harm inflicted. Victims are likely to agree to this seemingly less punitive but more rewarding sentence.

A promising new strategy for involving victims in the sentencing process is the opportunity of reconciling victim and offender in some cases, with or without compensation for the victim.[71] One such victim offender reconciliation program (VORP) began operating in 1992 at the Graterford, Pennsylvania, Correctional Institution and now conducts conferences for the benefit of other practitioners. But the emotional problems involved require further study before such programs can be put into practice on a large scale.[72]

Corrections and Release

The correctional system implements any victim compensation sentence that is imposed. If the sentence makes no provision for compensation, in several states the victim at least has one more opportunity to affect an important decision: the parole hearing.[73] Parole boards tend to give great weight to a victim's opposition to a prisoner's release on parole.

Victims could be given a far greater opportunity to pursue their legitimate interests, especially to obtain compensation for the harm they have suffered. The European criminal justice process has always offered the victim an opportunity to "join" the prosecution. The objective is to have the judge award compensation to the victim in conjunction with the sentence imposed on the offender.[74] American law has not yet adopted this practice.

Nevertheless, great improvements have been made in our system to accommodate victims of crime. Victimology's drive for recognition of the role of the victim in the criminal justice process has had powerful effects in America and all over the world. Undoubtedly it will create even further changes in our criminal justice system as criminology continues to widen its focus to include the victim as well as the offender. The ultimate aim of victimology is, as Senator Joseph Biden put it in his speech on the Brady Bill, on August 11, 1993, "to create a victim-friendly" system of criminal justice.

■ REVIEW

The criminal justice system has been perceived as a system for less than a generation. Like any other system, it has components that are related and interdependent. The criminal justice process begins with the perception that a crime has been committed. After the crime has been reported, laws and standards guide authorities in following up. This may lead to an arrest of a suspect and the presentation of charges. When the facts warrant a grand-jury indictment or a prosecutor's information, the case moves to trial. Yet at this stage a plea agreement may be reached under which the defendant avoids trial and receives a reduced sentence in return for a plea of guilty to a lesser charge or to fewer charges. The conviction rate of defendants who go to trial is high.

The movement through the criminal justice system is not automatic and inevitable. At each stage of the process it is dependent on decisions made by criminal justice officials and by the defendant. These decisions may lead to diversion out of the system at any stage. The criminal justice path has many exits. These multiple exits explain the high attrition rate: only a fraction of the offenders who enter the criminal justice system wind up in corrections.

A juvenile's path through the criminal justice system differs from an adult's. Juveniles are now granted constitutional rights that a generation ago were denied them. But they have also been increasingly subjected to some of the rigors of the adult criminal justice system. Juvenile justice has become punitive.

The recent development of victimology as a subdiscipline of criminology and the emergence of the victims' rights movement have drawn attention to the role and plight of victims. Legislation in most states has facilitated victims' participation in the criminal justice process, eased the burden on victims, and provided compensation for their losses.

■ NOTES

1. See Golan M. Janeksela, "Analysis of Justice Systems," *Criminal Justice Policy Review,* **5** (1991): 114–120; and Alfred Blumstein, "Making Rationality Relevant—The American Society Presidential Address 1992," *Criminology,* **31** (1993): 1–16.
2. President's Commission on Law Enforcement and the Administration of Justice, *The Challenge of Crime in a Free Society* (Washington, D.C.: U.S. Government Printing Office, 1967).
3. Herbert Packer, *The Limits of the Criminal Sanction* (Stanford, Calif.: Stanford University Press, 1968).
4. Michael R. Gottfredson and Don M. Gottfredson, *Decision Making in Criminal Justice: Toward the Rational Exercise of Discretion,* 2d ed. (New York: Plenum, 1988).
5. Ibid., chap. 2.
6. Ibid., chap. 3.
7. *Beck v. Ohio,* 379 U.S. 89 (1964).
8. *Mapp v. Ohio,* 367 U.S. 643 (1961).
9. Comptroller General of the United States, *Impact of the Exclusionary Rule on Federal Criminal Prosecutions* (Washington, D.C.: U.S. General Accounting Office, Apr. 19, 1979); U.S. National Institute of Justice, *The Effects of the Exclusionary Rule: A Study in California* (Washington, D.C.: U.S. Government Printing Office, December 1982). But see Malcolm Richard Wilkey, "The Exclusionary Rule: Costs and Viable Alternatives," *Criminal Justice Ethics,* **1**(2) (1982): 16–27.
10. *Terry v. Ohio,* 392 U.S. 1 (1968).
11. *People v. de Bour,* 40 N.Y. 2d 210 (1976).
12. *Miranda v. Arizona,* 384 U.S. 436 (1966).
13. But there is an exception to this rule: when public safety is at risk, the warning may be postponed. See *New York v. Quarles,* 467 U.S. 649 (1984).
14. *Gideon v. Wainwright,* 372 U.S. 335 (1963), as amplified by, *int. al., Argersinger v. Hamlin,* 407 U.S. 25 (1972), and *Strickland v. Washington,* 446 U.S. 668 (1984) (counsel must be competent). See also Anthony Lewis, *Gideon's Trumpet* (New York: Vintage, 1966).
15. Robert Hermann, Eric Single, and John Boston, *Counsel for the Poor* (Lexington, Mass.: Lexington Books, 1977), esp. p. 153.
16. *United States v. Salerno,* 481 U.S. 739 (1987).
17. Gottfredson and Gottfredson, *Decision Making in Criminal Justice,* chap. 4.
18. Brian E. Forst, J. Lucianovic, and S. Cox, *What Happens after Arrest,* Institute for Law and Social Research publication no. 4 (Washington, D.C.: U.S. Government Printing Office, 1977), p. 67.
19. "Only 3 of every 100 arrests went to trial in 1986, whereas 52 resulted in a guilty plea": U.S. Department of Justice, Bureau of Justice Statistics, *Annual Report, Fiscal 1988* (Washington, D.C.: U.S. Government Printing Office, 1989), p. 49.
20. Federal Rules of Criminal Procedure, Rule 11.
21. Ibid., Rule 6.
22. Forst et al., *What Happens after Arrest,* p. 17.
23. Held constitutional in *Williams v. Florida,* 399 U.S. 25 (1972).
24. See Harry Kalven, Jr., and Hans Zeisel, *The American Jury* (Chicago: University of Chicago Press, 1966).
25. *Apodica v. Oregon,* 406 U.S. 404 (1972). The case involved a homicide that was less than first-degree murder.
26. Alfred Blumstein, Jacqueline Cohen, Susan E. Martin, and Michael H. Tonry, eds., *Research on Sentencing: The Search for Reform,* vol. 1 (Washington, D.C.: National Academy Press, 1983), p. 11.
27. Don Gottfredson and Bridget Stecher, "Sentencing Policy Models," unpublished manuscript, School of Criminal Justice, Rutgers University, 1979.
28. Joan Petersilia, *Expanding Options for Criminal Sentencing* (Santa Monica, Calif.: Rand Corporation, 1987).
29. Hans Toch, *Living in Prison* (New York: Free Press, 1977).
30. Michael R. Gottfredson and K. Adams, "Prison Behavior and Release Performance: Empirical Reality

and Public Policy," *Law and Policy Quarterly*, **4** (1982): 373–391.

31. Gottfredson and Gottfredson, *Decision Making in Criminal Justice*, chap. 8.

32. Allen J. Beck and Bernard E. Shipley, *Recidivism of Young Parolees: Special Report*, for U.S. Department of Justice, Bureau of Justice Statistics (Washington, D.C.: U.S. Government Printing Office, 1987).

33. For a discussion of this study, see Charles Silberman, *Criminal Violence, Criminal Justice* (New York: Random House, 1978), pp. 257–261.

34. Readers interested in the subject may wish to consult William B. Sanders, *Juvenile Delinquency* (New York: Holt, Rinehart & Winston, 1976); G. Larry Mays, *Juvenile Delinquency and Juvenile Justice* (New York: Wiley, 1987); Roy Lotz, Eric D. Poole, and Robert M. Regoli, *Juvenile Delinquency and Juvenile Justice* (New York: Random House, 1985); Larry J. Siegel and Joseph J. Senna, *Juvenile Delinquency: Theory, Practice, and Law* (St. Paul, Minn.: West, 1981); and Arnold Binder, Gilbert Geis, and Bruce Dickson, *Juvenile Delinquency: Historical, Cultural, Legal Perspectives* (New York: Macmillan, 1988).

35. U.S. Department of Justice, Bureau of Justice Statistics, *Criminal Victimization in the United States, 1987* (Washington, D.C.: U.S. Government Printing Office, June 1989), p. 47, table 40.

36. *Ex parte Crouse*, 4 Wharton, Pa., 9 (1838). See Steven L. Schlossman, *Love and the American Delinquent: The Theory and Practice of "Progressive" Juvenile Justice, 1825–1920* (Chicago: University of Chicago Press, 1977).

37. On the problems inherent in the concepts that guide the juvenile justice system, see Sanford Fox, "Juvenile Justice Reform: An Historical Perspective," *Stanford Law Review*, **22** (1970): 1187–1239; and Anthony M. Platt, *The Child Savers: The Invention of Delinquency*, 2d ed. (Chicago: University of Chicago Press, 1977).

38. *In re Gault*, 387 U.S. 1 (1967).

39. *In re Winship*, 397 U.S. 358 (1970); *McKeiver v. Pennsylvania*, 403 U.S. 528 (1971).

40. Norman Lefstein, Vaughan Stapleton, and Lee Teitelbaum, "In Search of Juvenile Justice: *Gault* and Its Implementation," *Law and Society Review*, **3** (1969): 491; H. Ted Rubin, "The Juvenile Court's Search for Identity and Responsibility," *Crime and Delinquency*, **23** (1977): 1–13.

41. Institute of Judicial Administration–American Bar Association, *Juvenile Justice Standards: A Summary and Analysis*, 2d ed., ed. Barbara Danziger Flicker (Cambridge, Mass.: Ballinger, 1982), p. 47.

42. *Breed v. Jones*, 421 U.S. 519 (1975).

43. Dean J. Champion, "Teenage Felons and Waiver Hearings: Some Recent Trends, 1980–1988," *Crime and Delinquency*, **35** (1989): 590–601. See also Dean J. Champion and G. Larry Mays, *Transferring Juveniles to Criminal Courts: Trends and Implications for Criminal Justice* (New York: Praeger, 1991).

44. Richard J. Lundman, Richard E. Sykes, and John P. Clark, "Police Control of Juveniles: A Replication," in *Police Behavior: A Sociological Perspective*, ed. Richard J. Lundman (New York: Oxford University Press, 1980), pp. 130–151.

45. Samuel M. Davis, *Rights of Juveniles: The Juvenile Justice System*, 2d ed. (New York: Clark Boardman, 1980), pp. 3–9.

46. *State ex. rel. D.D.H. v. Dostert*, 165 W.Va. 448, 269 S.E. 2d 401 (1980). See also Institute of Judicial Administration–American Bar Association, *Juvenile Justice Standards*.

47. See Lloyd E. Ohlin, Robert B. Coates, and Alden D. Miller, "Radical Correctional Reform: A Case Study of the Massachusetts Youth Correctional System," *Harvard Educational Review*, **44** (1974): 74–111.

48. Richard Allinson, "There Are No Juveniles in Pennsylvania Jails," *Corrections Magazine*, **9**(3) (1983): 13–20; Paul W. Keve, *The Consequences of Prohibiting the Jailing of Juveniles* (Richmond: Virginia Commonwealth University, 1984). For an evaluation of the closing of a Maryland training school, see Denise C. Gottfredson and William H. Barton, "Deinstitutionalization of Juvenile Offenders," *Criminology*, **31** (1993): 591–611.

49. U.S. Department of Justice, Bureau of Justice Statistics, *Report to the Nation on Crime and Justice*, 2d ed. (Washington, D.C.: U.S. Government Printing Office, 1988), pp. 95, 103, 105.

50. National Council on Crime and Delinquency, *Juveniles Taken into Custody, 1990 Report* (San Francisco: National Council on Crime and Delinquency, 1991), p. 15.

51. Binder *et al*, *Juvenile Delinquency*, p. 529.

52. *Schall v. Martin*, 467 U.S. 253 (1984).

53. Steven P. Lab and John T. Whitehead, "An Analysis of Juvenile Correctional Treatment," *Crime and Delinquency*, **34** (1988): 60–83.

54. See LaMar T. Empey and Mark C. Stafford, *American Delinquency: Its Meaning and Construction*, 3d ed. (Belmont, Calif.: Wadsworth, 1991); and Howard N. Snyder, Terrence A. Finnegan, and John L. Hutzler, *Delinquency, 1981* (Pittsburgh: National Center for Juvenile Justice, 1983), citing Philip Cook and John Laub, "Trends in Child Abuse and Juvenile Delinquency," in *From Children to Citizens, Vol. II: The Role of the Juvenile Court*, ed. Francis X. Hartmann. (New York: Springer Verlag, 1987).

55. See, e.g. James Austin and Barry Krisberg, "Wider, Stronger and Different Nets: The Dialectics of Criminal Justice Reform," *Journal of Research in Crime and Delinquency*, **18** (1981): 165–196; Edwin M. Lemert, "Diversion in Juvenile Justice: What Hath Been Wrought," *Journal of Research in Crime and Delinquency*, **18** (1981): 35–46; and Malcolm W. Klein, "Deinstitutionalization and Diversion of Juvenile Offenders: A Litany of Impediments," in *Crime and Justice*, ed. N. Morris and M. Tonry (Chicago: University of Chicago Press, 1979), pp. 145–200.

56. Barry Krisberg, *Juvenile Justice—Improving the Quality of Care* (San Francisco: National Council on Crime and Delinquency, 1992).

57. See Gerhard O. W. Mueller, "Compensation for Victims of Crime: Thought before Action," *Minnesota Law Review,* **50** (1965): 213–221.

58. Hans von Hentig, *The Criminal and His Victim* (New Haven, Conn.: Yale University Press, 1948).

59. Benjamin Mendelson, "The Origin of the Doctrine of Victimology," *Excerpta Criminologica,* **3** (1963): 239–244.

60. Stephen Schafer, *Restitution to Victims of Crime* (London: Stevens & Sons, 1960); Stephen Schafer, *Victimology: The Victim and His Criminal* (New York: Random House, 1968). See also Gerhard O. W. Mueller and H. H. A. Cooper, *The Criminal, Society, and the Victim,* for Law Enforcement Assistance Administration (Washington, D.C.: U.S. Government Printing Office, 1973).

61. See Symposium, *Minnesota Law Review,* **50** (1965): 211–310. See also Symposium: "Compensation for Victims of Criminal Violence," *Journal of Public Law,* **8** (1959): 191–253, with contributions by G. Williams, J. L. Montrose, F. E. Inbau, F. W. Miller, H. Weihofen, G. O. W. Mueller, and H. Silving.

62. Ezzat Fattah, ed., *Towards a Critical Victimology* (New York: St. Martin's Press, 1992).

63. Margery Fry, "Justice for Victims," *Observer* (London), May 7, 1957, p. 8. See also Margery Fry, *Arms of the Law* (London: Gollancz, 1951). For an assessment of the current state of crime victim compensation, see Robert J. McCormack, "Compensating Victims of Violent Crime," *Justice Quarterly,* **9** (1991): 329–346.

64. See Mary S. Knudten and Richard P. Knudten, "What Happens to Crime Victims and Witnesses in the Justice System?" in *Perspectives on Crime Victims,* ed. Burt Galaway and Joe Hudson (St. Louis: Mosby, 1981), pp. 52–72. See also Wesley G. Skogan, "Citizens' Reporting of Crime: Some National Panel Data," in Galaway and Hudson, *Perspectives on Crime Victims,* pp. 45–51; and Michael J. Hindelang and Michael Gottfredson, "The Victim's Decision Not to Invoke the Criminal Process," in *Criminal Justice and the Victim,* ed. William F. McDonald (Beverly Hills, Calif.: Sage, 1976), pp. 57–58.

65. A. M. Heinz and W. A. Kerstetter, "Victim Participation in Plea Bargaining: A Field Experiment," in *Plea Bargaining,* ed. W. F. McDonald and J. A. Cramer (Lexington, Mass.: Heath, 1979), pp. 167–177. See also American Bar Association, *Pleas of Guilty: Approved Draft* (Washington, D.C.: ABA, February 1979), Standard 14-3, 1(d).

66. William F. McDonald, "The Victim's Role in the American Administration of Criminal Justice: Some Developments and Findings," in *The Victim in International Perspective,* ed. Hans Joachim Schneider (New York: De Gruyter, 1982), pp. 397–407. See also Lis Wieht, "Victim and Sentence: Resetting Justice's Scale," *New York Times,* Sept. 29, 1989, p. B5.

67. U. S. Department of Justice, Bureau of Justice Statistics, *Report to the Nation,* p. 82.

68. Donald J. Hall, "The Role of the Victim in the Prosecution and Disposition of a Criminal Case," in Galaway and Hudson, *Perspectives on Crime Victims,* pp. 318–342.

69. Ibid.

70. Stephen Schafer, "The Victim and Correctional Theory: Integrating Victim Reparation with Offender Rehabilitation," in McDonald and Cramer, *Plea Bargaining,* pp. 227–236.

71. See Dorothy (Edmonds) McKnight, "The Victim-Offender Reconciliation Project," in Galaway and Hudson, *Perspectives on Crime Victims,* pp. 292–298.

72. See Janet Rifkin, "Mediation in the Justice System: A Paradox for Women," *Women and Criminal Justice,* **1** (1989): 41–54.

73. Hall, "The Role of the Victim."

74. See Irene Melup, ed., "UN Regulations on Victims of Crime," *International Review of Victimology,* **2** (1991): 28–72.

16

Enforcing the Law: Practice and Research

KEY TERMS
community policing
constable
frankpledge
justice of the peace
night watchman
police subculture
problem-oriented policing
sheriff
sting operation
team policing
tithing

Crime is rampant. Pickpockets and purse snatchers lurk on every street. To protect their money from muggers, people now carry their wallets on a leather strap around their necks. Just the other day a noted wit said: "Only a fool would go out to dinner without having made his will."[1] The police are sparse in the neighborhoods. The city even installed dummy police officers, at highway intersections and school crossings, to serve as an alert to the presence of law enforcement. Citizens bought locks to protect their homes. You have never seen so many "Beware of Dog" signs! The more affluent hired private security agencies to protect their premises. Public officials don't even ride around in public anymore without security agents in front, in back, and on the sides. Neighborhoods have formed citizens' watch groups. And everybody is upset about the lack of police presence.

What city is being described? Chicago? Washington? New York? Or Denver? Seattle? Dallas? Although it could be any of these or other cities in the United States, this was reported about the Rome of 2000 years ago.

No country or city is capable of ensuring an orderly, secure life for its citizens unless it polices itself. This idea is so ancient that the Greeks used the same word for "city" and for "police": *polis.* Through their presence the police, whether the lictors of ancient Rome or the men and women in blue in modern America, are supposed to maintain peace in the community. But their mere presence cannot prevent crime and disorder unless it is backed by enforcement power. This power cannot be merely reactive; it has to include preventive and protective functions, as well as the right and duty to investigate, to assemble facts, and to prepare these facts for judicial disposition. These duties can be categorized as peacekeeping and crime-fighting functions. Yet as we shall see, relatively little police time is devoted to these duties. Far more time is devoted to social services, such as helping people in distress; answering requests for information; responding to emergencies, disasters, and accidents; and maintaining an orderly traffic flow.

There is general agreement that the police are a multifunction service agency equipped to respond to civic problems and to fight crime. But there is disagreement on the political and social role police should play in a democratic society.

The debate is marked by fear that civil liberties may be lost if the police power to take away personal freedom—by arrest, search, or use of force—is abused. The controversy, which almost prevented the English from creating their first police force in 1829, has surfaced intermittently in the United States since the early nineteenth century. It reached particular intensity in the 1960s, when aggressive policing against demonstrators and minorities resulted in claims that some police agencies were biased and infringed on the rights of citizens.

Their strategic position at the gateway of the criminal justice process, their numerical strength in comparison with that of all other agents of criminal justice, and their constant contact with the public give the police prominence in the criminal justice process.

THE HISTORY OF POLICING

Some cultures can proudly point to ancient documentation for their police. The Egyptians, for example, recruited Nubians for their Medjay police nearly 4000 years ago and established a maritime police about 1340 B.C. We do not even have a record of the existence of our Anglo-Saxon ancestors at that time.

The English Heritage

The earliest records of policing in Anglo-American history can be found in the laws of the Danish king Canute (d. 1035), who governed England in the first quarter of the eleventh century, before the Norman Conquest. In a system called **frankpledge,** members of a **tithing,** an association of ten families, were bound together by a mutual pledge to keep the peace. Every male over age 12 was part of the system. Over time the frankpledge system was strengthened by the establishment of the king's representative, the *reeve,* in each county or shire. The shire reeve, or **sheriff,** presided over the shire's court, executed summonses, and enforced the laws. A force of able-bodied citizens, called a *posse comitatus* (Latin for "power of the county"), assisted the sheriff and could be convened at his command. (The use of sheriff's posses persisted well into the twentieth century in the western and southern United States.)

The Statute of Winchester in 1285 established the office of **constable,** a royal official charged with suppressing riots and violent crimes in each county. By the thirteenth century a night watch system developed in larger towns and cities. The **night watchmen** were untrained citizens who patrolled at night, on the lookout for disturbances. In 1326 the first **justices of the peace** were commissioned. They were untrained men, usually nobles, who investigated and tried minor cases. Law enforcement by sheriffs, constables, hired assistants, justices of the peace, and night watchmen changed very little in England until the eighteenth century.[2]

But then came industrialization and urban growth. The system that had worked in rural and feudal England proved inadequate in the rapidly growing cities. At the beginning of the eighteenth century there was little law and order in London. Henry Fielding (1707–1754), the author of *Tom Jones* and a justice of the peace, led efforts to establish a uniformed, armed standing police force. In response to research conducted by Fielding and reported in his *Enquiry into the Causes of the Late Increase of Robbers* (1751), Parliament granted him funds to recruit England's first professional police force. The experiment failed, and it was not until 1829 that such a system was established.

In that year the Act for Improving the Police in and near the Metropolis was steered through Parliament by England's home secretary (and later prime minister), Sir Robert Peel (1788–1850). This bill established the Metropolitan Constabulary, originally composed of 1000 men. These officers were unarmed but uniformed and well disciplined: they were taught "that there is no qualification more indispensable to a police officer, than a perfect command of temper, never suffering himself to be moved in the slightest degree, by any language or threats that may be used."[3] Sir Robert's officers came to be known as "little Roberts," or "bobbies." The experiment proved such a success in London that by 1856 all counties and boroughs in England were required to have their own professional police.[4]

Despite rising crime rates, urban chaos, and the humanitarian reforms instituted by Peel, some scholars believe that the real reason for the establishment of the English police was not the crime problem but the elite's desire to control the poor. Vagrants and idle persons, after arrest and conviction, could be a source of cheap labor for the Industrial Revolution's large factories.[5]

Policing in the United States

Colonial America used a system of policing much like that of early England. County sheriffs were the principal law enforcement officers. They were supplemented by town marshals, constables, and night watchmen. Sheriffs received no salaries but were paid standard fees for various services (collecting taxes, supervising elections, and so forth).[6] Sheriffs were assisted by deputies, and in case of need they could convene posses composed of ordinary citizens. This system lasted until the early nineteenth century, when the rapid growth of cities brought the need for a better and more formal law enforcement system.[7]

Politics and Policing

In a time of migration and immigration, rapid industrialization, social unrest, hostility toward minorities, and mob violence, American cities organized their first uniformed police forces. In 1838 Boston established its force. New York followed in 1844, and Philadelphia 10 years later. The police were expected to keep the peace, to prevent crime, and to defuse social conflict. Their duties extended to such activities as caring for orphans and derelicts, operating soup kitchens, and maintaining sanitary conditions in overcrowded neighborhoods.

Appointments to the police were made by political bosses. Police commissioners changed with every election, as did many of the men on the force. Often the officers were, in fact, tools of ward politicians. Throughout the nineteenth century, the conduct of the police in the United States was an ongoing scandal. As a group, they were corrupt, powerful, often poorly trained, without standards for admission to the force (not even health or age), unsupervised, and frequently abusive.[8] Police brutality appeared to be tolerated by the middle class because it was used in large measure against social outcasts.

At the turn of the twentieth century, the situation changed. Progressive reformers attacked social and urban problems, including the police. August Vollmer developed the concept of police professionalism. Vollmer's model of police organization and activity, based on crime fighting as the primary role of the police, was not challenged until the 1960s.

The Progressive Era

The Progressives were educated upper- and middle-class Americans determined to stamp out corruption wherever they found it. Among the many places they found it were the police forces. The Progressives worked to professionalize law enforcement by taking it out of politics and introducing modern technology. Their slogan was "The police have to get out of politics, and politics has to be out of the police."[9]

One reformer, Theodore Roosevelt, who accepted the presidency of the New York City Board of Police Commissioners in 1895, immediately effected a change in police standards by failing over half of the applicants on the physical examination and 30 percent on the mental examination in a 10-month period.[10] Despite the many reforms they brought about, some historians of criminology have argued that the Progressives' interest in a more efficient police force was grounded less in a desire to reform than in their fear that newer immigrant groups might be gaining too much power in local government and thus too much control in the cities.

Vollmer and Wilson: Pioneers of Police Professionalization

August Vollmer, who developed the professional model of policing in the early twentieth century, was a first-generation American with a limited education who became one of the most prominent figures in the history of American policing. He began his career in 1904 as police marshal in Berkeley, California. Within 5 years he was made chief of police, a position he held until 1932.

To Vollmer, a professional police force had to be nonpolitical, well recruited, well trained, well disciplined, and equipped with modern technology. Its members had to be part of the civil service, selected and advanced by merit. The police

officers' major role was to fight crime. Vollmer's book *The Police and Modern Society* (1936) remained a guide for police professionals for decades. The American Society of Criminology gave his name to its most prestigious award for outstanding achievement in law enforcement and criminal justice.

Another pioneer in modern policing, Orlando W. Wilson, a student and protégé of Vollmer, stands out for his contribution to the modern management and administrative techniques used in policing. Wilson, who obtained a degree in criminology from the University of California in 1924, became chief of police in Fullerton, California (1924–1928) and Wichita, Kansas (1928–1939). He served as professor of police administration (1939–1960) and as founding dean of the University of California, Berkeley, School of Criminology (1953). He retired in 1967 from his position as superintendent of the Chicago Police Department, which he had transformed from one of the least reputable in the country to one of the very best.

The Wickersham Commission

While the pioneers were professionalizing police forces, several crime commissions at the local, state, and national levels began to investigate the extent of crime and the criminal justice system's response to it. Former attorney general George W. Wickersham was appointed to head the United States National Commission on Law Observance and Enforcement from 1929 to 1932.[11] The commission retained practitioners and academicians to observe and analyze the state of law enforcement in the country, particularly in connection with the futile attempts to enforce the Prohibition laws.

The result of the inquiry was devastating: Many police forces were corrupt, training was superficial, and recruitment was inadequate. Communications, statistics, and information sharing were chaotic. Constitutional guarantees were largely ignored. The report of the Wickersham Commission provided solid evidence that America's early reform efforts had not reached far enough or deep enough.

The crime-fighting model of policing lasted until it was challenged in the 1960s, in the wake of civil unrest. Before we discuss how police

WINDOW TO THE WORLD
Interpol: The International Criminal Police Organization

In 1914 Prince Albert I of Monaco responded to the increasing international mobility of criminals by organizing the First International Criminal Police Congress, which recommended the establishment of an international police force. Founded in 1923, that force evolved into what we now know as the International Criminal Police Organization, called "Interpol" after its telegraphic code name. Membership today stands at 158 states, with a staff of some 300.

As a police organization, Interpol is unique in that it has no police officers. It is, in fact, a complex communications network. It provides information on criminals and handles requests for wanted criminals. Each member state has a police department that serves as the country's National Central Bureau (NCB) for Interpol. The NCB replies to requests from other NCBs and from the Interpol General Secretariat and coordinates large-scale police actions when necessary. In the United States, the U.S. National Central Bureau (USNCB), located in the Department of Justice in Washington, D.C., handles all Interpol requests. The bureau may be asked to locate a fugitive, check a license, or supply a criminal record.(1)

The goals of Interpol are carefully defined:

- To ensure and promote the widest possible mutual assistance between all criminal police authorities, within the limits of the laws existing in the different countries and in the spirit of the Declaration of Human Rights

- To establish and develop all institutions likely to contribute effectively to the prevention and suppression of ordinary law crimes

Interpol is not allowed to undertake "any intervention or activities of a political, military, religious or racial character,"(2) yet it is not always easy to separate "ordinary law crimes" from political crimes. For example, drug crimes are regarded as "ordinary law crimes," and in fact the control of drug-related criminality is one of Interpol's major activities. But traffic in narcotic drugs also can be a highly political affair: it can support some governments and destabilize others. Interpol's annual general assemblies of member states help to draw the boundaries between ordinary and political criminality.

Interpol works to assist member states in preventing the exploitation of children and in devising measures to deal with international organized crime, the firearms and explosives trade, terrorism, the traffic in human beings, missing persons, disaster victim identification, and counterfeiting. Perhaps one of Interpol's most important functions is its continuing activity in the criminal intelligence area—receiving, processing, and disseminating international notices and messages that may lead to crime clearance and arrest of wanted persons in any member state.

Interpol, now headquartered in Lyons, France, has no precinct houses at which a citizen could file a complaint. Unlike any other police organization, Interpol works solely at the intergovernmental level, serving its member states and ultimately benefiting the whole world.

Sources

1. "From the Parc Monceau to the Parc de la Tete d'Or," *International Criminal Police Review* (November–December 1989): 6–8.
2. Richard Bell, "The History of Drug Prohibition and Legislation," *International Criminal Police Review* (September–October 1991): 2–6.

Questions for Discussion

1. Why should ordinary citizens not have the right to file a complaint with Interpol if the crime they wish to report has international dimensions?
2. What stands in the way of Interpol's having its own sworn officers, with power to arrest an international criminal anywhere in the world?

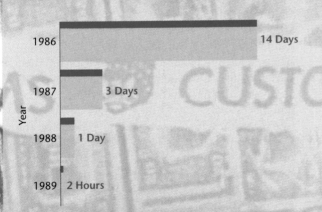

Year	
1986	14 Days
1987	3 Days
1988	1 Day
1989	2 Hours

Response Time to Requests from Member States

departments began to improve their image and try to deal more effectively with the public, let us look at their organizational structure.

LAW ENFORCEMENT AGENCIES

There are more than 20,000 separate law enforcement agencies in the United States. Some 50 of these are at the federal level, about 200 are at the state level, but most of them are at the local level—county, city, town, and village forces. These departments may have only a single officer or as many as 37,000 officers. In 1992, 748,830 full-time law enforcement personnel, including over 544,000 sworn officers, served these agencies.[12]

American policing differs from that found in most other countries in its diversity of forces and lack of central coordination and command. The idea that federal and state police functions are separate is basic to our system of federalism. Even within the states there has always been concern that any central command not only would violate local autonomy but also might put a dangerous concentration of power in the hands of the chief executive. So most policing takes place at the municipal level, where the control rests, for the most part, with an elected police commissioner and an appointed chief, superintendent, or director who handles the administrative responsibilities.

But although there are many levels of public law enforcement agencies, each with specialized units, they often must work together to solve cases. A major narcotics operation, for example, may involve federal agencies like the DEA, the Coast Guard, and the FBI; the state police; county officials; and local police.

Federal Law Enforcement

The framers of the Constitution did not envisage the need for any federal law enforcement agency. But it soon became clear that the federal government needed an enforcement system to perform its mandated functions. The first federal police force to be established was the United States Coast Guard, which in 1790 was assigned the task of policing the coasts to prevent smuggling and ensure the collection of import duties. Other federal police forces were added, particularly after 1870, when the Department of Justice became aware of its law enforcement obligations. The federal agency with the broadest range of duties is the FBI.

The Federal Bureau of Investigation

In 1908 President Theodore Roosevelt, angered by Congress's failure to adopt legislation to regulate political and business corruption, established the Department of Justice's Bureau of Investigations. Initially the bureau was staffed by 35 employees. They were empowered to investigate bankruptcy fraud, antitrust violations, and other violations of federal law.

During the late 1920s—the heyday of Prohibition—citizens became frustrated by the inability of local and state law enforcement agencies to stem the growth of organized crime. Incidents such as the Lindbergh kidnapping added to this frustration. But at that point the bureau had no authority to investigate or apprehend fleeing felons who crossed state lines.

In the face of arguments favoring establishment of a national, or federal, police force, J. Edgar Hoover, whom President Calvin Coolidge had appointed to head the bureau in 1924, argued that state and local police should retain their own jurisdictions and sovereignty but that new federal legislation was needed to give the bureau jurisdiction over criminals who operate across state lines. In 1934 Congress passed such legislation. One year later, in 1935, the bureau adopted a new name—the Federal Bureau of Investigation.

Over the years the FBI has played a highly publicized role in the investigation and capture of such criminals as Baby Face Nelson, Doc Barker, John Dillinger, Pretty Boy Floyd, Al Capone, Bonnie Parker, and Clyde Barrow. Under Hoover, the FBI acquired its sterling image as the chief investigative branch of the Department of Justice. This image was tarnished in the 1960s when it was revealed that FBI agents had been wiretapping national leaders, including Martin Luther King, Jr.; opening mail; and discrediting political radicals as "enemies of the government."[13] In the 1990s charges of racial discrimination and harassment have plagued the

FBI agents securing evidence at the World Trade Center bombing, New York, February 1993.

bureau. But the FBI's reputation has been largely restored through more enlightened leadership. The orientation of the bureau has changed; now it focuses on white-collar crime, public corruption, organized crime, drug offenses, and terrorism.

In 1991, the bureau, headquartered in Washington, D.C., had 10,036 special agents and 12,896 civilian employees in 59 field offices around the United States. The FBI Laboratory and Forensic Science Research and Training Center has stayed at the forefront of technology and training. In 1982 the laboratory conducted nearly 800,000 scientific investigations; by 1985 that number had almost doubled.[14] The FBI holds the fingerprints of more than 181 million people. In addition, the bureau maintains one of the main sources of crime statistics, the Uniform Crime Reports (Chapter 2).

In 1967 the FBI initiated the National Crime Information Center (NCIC), a computerized data base that collects information on criminals and makes it accessible to law enforcement agencies in all 50 states. More than 900,000 transactions are processed each day. The NCIC also supplies information on stolen guns, stolen vehicles, and wanted persons. The FBI plays a role in police training as the administrator of the National

Police Academy, located at the U.S. Marine Corps base in Quantico, Virginia. The academy trains all its own agents and is responsible for the professional education of more than 1000 state and local law enforcement administrators every year.

Other Federal Law Enforcement Agencies

The Department of Justice maintains other agencies that also fulfill law enforcement duties:

■ The *Drug Enforcement Administration (DEA)*, which is charged with the enforcement of laws controlling the use, sale, and distribution of narcotics and other controlled substances

■ The *Immigration and Naturalization Service (INS)*, which has the dual authority of policing U.S. borders to prevent aliens from entering illegally and overseeing the admission, naturalization, exclusion, and deportation of aliens

■ The *United States Marshal Service*, which provides protection for relocated witnesses and administrative support and security services for federal district courts and the U.S. courts of appeals.

Most of the other departments of the federal government operate law enforcement agencies as well. The Treasury Department maintains a law enforcement agency within the Internal Revenue Service (IRS). The Treasury also operates the Secret Service, which protects governmental officials and investigates forgery and counterfeiting, and the Bureau of Alcohol, Tobacco, and Firearms (ATF), which enforces federal laws regulating the importation, distribution, and use of alcohol, tobacco, and firearms. The Department of Transportation is responsible for the U.S. Coast Guard (in peacetime). The Federal Trade Commission (FTC), the Securities and Exchange Commission (SEC), the Department of Labor, and the United States Postal Service all maintain their own law enforcement agencies.

State Police

In 1835 the first state police agency, the Texas Rangers, was established. Its primary purpose was to control the Mexican border. Thirty years later Massachusetts created a similar force. It was not until the turn of the twentieth century that states across the country followed suit—Connecticut in 1903, Arizona and Pennsylvania in 1905, New Jersey in 1921. The Pennsylvania Constabulary (state police) became a model for the nation. It is a highly centralized, quasi-military force, which had to overcome its initial reputation as being an antilabor, pro-big-business police.

Today all states except Hawaii have their own state police forces, whose primary function is to control traffic on the highways. These forces also fill gaps in rural and suburban policing, respond to the statewide mobility of crime (for example, by pursuing offenders crossing jurisdictional boundaries), aid in crowd control, and provide centralized services for local police forces (tracing stolen cars, statewide record keeping, laboratory assistance). Distrust of centralized police power has generally kept state police forces from assuming any duties of local officials.

County Police

The sheriff's office, at the county level, is responsible for countywide policing outside municipal-

ities. In Westerns, the sheriff is portrayed as a tough, fearless, fair, and incorruptible official, clearly distinguishable by his "tin star" and his agility with pistols. He was indeed a powerful figure on the frontier. During the westward expansion in the nineteenth century, the sheriff was often the only legal authority over vast areas.

Today sheriff's departments range from small offices with an appointed sheriff to large departments staffed by trained, professional personnel (as in Los Angeles County, California). Most sheriff's forces perform functions that extend beyond crime prevention and control to such traditional county services as tax assessment and collection, court duty, jail administration, inspection services, the serving of court orders, and the overseeing of public buildings, highways, bridges, and parks. In some places the sheriff may even serve as the coroner.

Municipal Police

In modern urban America, as in urbanized ancient Greece, the city is the societal unit with which most people identify. Its most visible government representatives are the municipal police. Citizens rely on the police for advice, service, and protection around the clock. No wonder, then, that municipal police forces are among the largest governmental employers and account for so large a proportion of the budget. Local police forces account for more than three-quarters (76.8 percent) of the total employment in police agencies at all levels of government.[15] A recent survey estimated that 11,989 local police agencies employed approximately 494,000 people, including 376,000 sworn officers.[16]

The distribution of personnel is very lopsided, however, ranging from departments with one or two employees to the New York City Police Department, with a force of over 37,000 law enforcement employees in 1991, the largest in the country. Ninety-one percent of all police departments employ fewer than 50 people, and more than half employ fewer than 10. Big-city departments account for less than 1 percent of the total number of agencies, but their employees constitute approximately 23 percent of total police employment at the local level.[17]

The sheer size of some of the larger departments is intimidating. New York City has a police payroll of over $144 million; Chicago, of over $40 million; and Los Angeles, of $37 million.[18] Yet fiscal management, with its constant crises, revenue shortfalls, and budget-cutting exercises, is only one of the many challenges facing a police department. Controlling crime, controlling officers, and facing constant pressures from all segments of society make the management of large urban departments one of the most difficult governmental tasks.

The limited size of small-town departments means that they differ from their big-city counterparts in several ways. Officers who work in small departments usually work as generalists, and there is a much less formal chain of command than that found in the large municipal departments. The chief of police might be found on patrol, and a detective might be making traffic stops. These departments also usually have a smaller proportion of civilian employees than do those in cities.[19] City residents would probably be surprised to realize that the continuous presence and round-the-clock availability of police officers to which they are accustomed is not the norm in many departments. Agencies staffed by as few as one or two officers simply cannot provide service 24 hours a day, 7 days a week.[20]

The small-town police officer has sometimes been depicted in popular culture as a good-natured figure whom nobody takes very seriously as a law enforcement officer. Some recent research, however, suggests that in fact investigative effectiveness, as measured by clearance rates, is greater in smaller departments than in larger ones.[21] Additional research is required before we can conclude that small-town police are more effective than those in large cities and, if they are, before we can determine what factors account for the difference.

Special-Purpose Police

Throughout the country, agencies that are not part of the local department possess police powers within specified jurisdictional limits that may cut across political boundaries. Special police forces include transit police, public housing police, airport police, public school police, and park police. Special police forces were often regarded as inferior to municipal forces. Indeed, some of them started out as guard services. By now, however, most special forces are as well recruited and trained as their municipal counterparts. Some have better training, given the highly specialized nature of their duties. The New York–New Jersey Port Authority Police, for example, has some of the highest standards of recruitment, training, and performance.

Several of the special police forces are quite large. America's five largest special police forces operate in the New York metropolitan area, with over 10,000 sworn officers. The New York City Transit Authority Police, for instance, has 3900 officers who patrol approximately 250 miles of subways used by more than 3 million riders daily. The size of this force makes it not only the largest special police force in the United States but also one of the ten largest police departments of any kind.

Private Police

Security guards, alarms, closed-circuit surveillance systems, and antitheft devices are everywhere in American life today. At work, at home, or at leisure, Americans are now the object of surveillance or protection furnished by the private security industry more often than at any previous time. Clifford Shearing and Philip Stenning, who have written extensively on the subject, note that the widespread acceptance of private police, or private security, has significantly extended the reach of social control.[22] Given the extent and significance of this phenomenon, any discussion of policing in the United States would be incomplete without reference to private security forces, even though they are not part of the publicly financed system of law enforcement.[23]

Private security today includes guard and patrol services, private investigators, alarm companies, armored-car and -courier services, and security consulting services for loss-prevention strategies, computer security systems, and executive-protection strategies. Private security forces even provide protection to entire communities, and some compare very favorably with the public police in surrounding neighborhoods in terms of crime prevention and lower levels of fear of crime.[24]

AT ISSUE
Private Policing

Most people do not realize that we depend more on private services for our security than on public police officers. According to a 1990 National Institute of Justice study, the number of people employed in the nation's private security companies is approximately twice the number in official law enforcement agencies, and private spending on security outweighs law enforcement budgets by 73 percent.(1,2)

Private policing, or private security, assumed a major role during the westward movement of our nation. Express companies carried valuable cargo under the protection of armed guards. One name that stands out in the history of private policing in the United States is Allen Pinkerton, who started the private detective business in America. During the Civil War he set up the Union Army's successful espionage system. After the war Pinkerton's agents became the tools of management in labor disputes. The brutal force used by "the Pinkertons" to break strikes became notorious.

Private policing grew after World War II. Industrial plants were involved in the production of nuclear weapons and rocketry; the cold war was in progress, and there was a need to protect dangerous industrial activities against espionage, sabotage, or accident. Public law enforcement was not able to keep up with the demand for protection. Private enterprises, even housing developments, had to provide for their own protection. This was fertile ground for the growth of the private security business.(3,4)

Today, the industry includes security guards, alarm and surveillance system businesses, consultants, private investigators, and armored-car and -courier services. The number of private security employees in the United States is expected to reach 2 million by the year 2000.(1,2)

In an effort to ensure reasonably accountable and at least semiprofessional protection, in the 1980s many states and municipalities passed legislation and ordinances to regulate the private security industry. State and municipal agencies may require the licensing and bonding of private security personnel. Contract security agencies have upgraded their recruitment and educational standards.

Much remains to be done to bring private security under public control. "Who are they accountable to?" asks the director of the New York Civil Liberties Union. "I foresee private groups will do things that public law enforcement can't do constitutionally."(1) And some criminologists are concerned that in the long run the notion that all citizens should be equally protected by the police will suffer. All evidence suggests that private policing will continue to grow, but not without problems.

Sources

1. Ralph Blumenthal, "Private Guards Cooperate in Public Policing," *New York Times*, July 13, 1993, p. B1.
2. William C. Cunningham, John J. Strauchs, and Clifford W. Van Meter, *Private Security Trends, 1970 to the Year 2000: The Hallcrest Report II* (Boston: Butterworth-Heinemann, 1990).
3. Milton Lipson, *On Guard—The Business of Private Security* (New York: Quadrangle, 1975).
4. Charles P. Nemeth, *Private Security and the Investigative Process* (Cincinnati, Ohio: Anderson, 1992).

Questions for Discussion

1. Do you think those who can afford the extra protection provided by private security should be allowed to have it?
2. Do you see any problems with simply firing an accused embezzler, as might happen if the crime is discovered by a private security employee, instead of handing him or her over to the criminal justice system?

Private security guard using multi-image closed-curcuit TV sets to monitor a large high-tech manufacturing facility in Irvine, California.

The costs of private security were approximately $52 billion in 1990,[25] while the most recent (1988) expenditure figures for police protection at all levels of government amounted to only about $32 billion.[26] Estimates for 1990 indicated that 1.5 million people worked in private security, approximately twice as many as were employed by public law enforcement agencies (Figure 16.1).[27] Many of those employed in private security have a background in public law enforcement. In fact, research conducted for the National Institute of Justice indicated that almost one-quarter (24 percent) of public police personnel also work off-duty in private security.[28]

The widespread use of private security forces has raised a number of issues. One is the fitness of security personnel, especially of guards. Training is usually minimal, and few states had standards until recently. Worldwide concern about the quality of private policing was expressed in 1975, when the Fifth United Nations Congress on the Prevention of Crime and the Treatment of Offenders called for "public controls" in the nature of "licensing, screening and the requirement of basic qualifications."[29]

Another concern is the question of equity. Is it fair for those who can afford it to have more protection than those who cannot? One reason for public police is to provide equal protection to all; the idea that the wealthy can buy added services seems to violate this principle and raises troubling questions about the willingness of the wealthy to support tax-financed public police.[30] The employment of off-duty police officers (an estimated 166,000) by private security companies also raises a number of issues, including questions of police department liability for the actions of its officers while engaged in private duty, potential tarnishing of the image of police if officers give the appearance of serving private interests only, and the possibility of conflicts of interest.[31]

COMMAND STRUCTURE

A prototype for a well-organized municipal police department, developed by the President's Commission on Law Enforcement and the Administration of Justice, has become the model for urban agencies (Figure 16.2). A department performs basically two types of functions: line functions (bureaus of operational services, of investigative services, of technical services) and nonline functions (administration and technical service bureaus).

Line functions include patrol duties, investigation, traffic control, and various specialized services (juvenile, vice, domestic dispute). Most officers are assigned to patrol duties. The *nonline functions* include the staff duties that one finds in most large organizations, public or private, such as planning, research, administration and training, budgeting, purchasing, public relations, inspections. Nonline functions also increasingly include the complex tasks of supporting line functions with high-tech services in communications, identification, laboratory work, and data processing, as well as such routine services as building and grounds maintenance, repair services, supply provisioning, and jail administration.

Police departments are not democratic organizations. They are organized largely along the lines of a military command, with military ranks and insignia. Patrol officers are responsible to

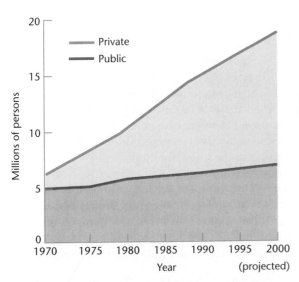

FIGURE 16.1 The growth of private and public police, 1970–2000

Source: Robert J. Fisher and Gion Green, *Introduction to Security,* 5th ed. (Stoneham, Mass.: Butterworth-Heinemann, 1992).

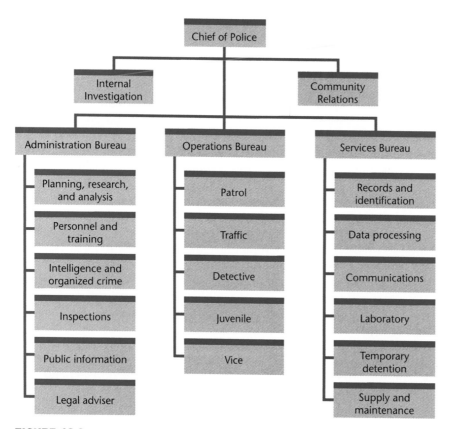

FIGURE 16.2 One form of a well-organized municipal police department

Source: The President's Commission on Law Enforcement and the Administration of Justice, *Task Force Report: The Police* (Washington, D.C.: U.S. Government Printing Office, 1967), p. 47.

their sergeants, sergeants to lieutenants, lieutenants to captains, captains to inspectors, inspectors to their chief or director. The structure of operational units is similar to that of other governmental departments. A bureau is at the highest level (a bureau of police within a department of public safety, for instance); divisions (such as a criminal investigation division) are at the next lower level; and sections and/or units are at the lowest level (the art theft unit, for example). The goal of this type of organization is efficient performance. The day-to-day and night-to-night operations of line officers are carried out in shifts, or watches, usually of 8 consecutive hours but often lasting longer.

Operations Bureau: Patrol

Patrol officers on the beat are usually the first law enforcement persons on the scene of a crime. They conduct the initial search, block off the crime scene for later investigation, interview victims and witnesses, and make a report of the facts. Small police agencies may have only patrol officers. In larger agencies, the patrol unit is made up of about two-thirds of the officers.

The functions of this unit are to deter crime by the presence of officers on the street, to check on suspicious activities, to respond to calls for aid, to enforce laws, and to maintain order. The public is more familiar with patrol officers than with officers of other units because the former are the ones who walk or cruise the neighborhoods, and constantly come into contact with residents. The patrol officer on the beat is very important to the relations between the police and the community.

Operations Bureau: Investigation

With only a few clues, a magnifying glass, a bumbling friend, and a good bit of intuition, Sherlock Holmes always solved the crime. Television and motion pictures have promoted the romanticized version of the detective as a tough "loner" stalking suspects until they end up in handcuffs or dead after a hair-raising shootout. In reality, however, the role of the detective is quite different. Most detectives are trained in modern investigative techniques and in the laws of evidence and procedure. They interact with many other individuals or police units, such as the traffic, vice, juvenile, and homicide divisions. And they spend most of their time on rather routine chores involving quite a bit of paperwork and not much excitement.

Detectives, however, occupy a more prestigious position in a police department than do patrol officers. They receive better salaries, they have more flexible hours, they do not wear uniforms, and they can act more independently. After a crime is reported, detectives investigate the facts in order to determine whether a crime has been committed and whether they have enough information to indicate that the case warrants further investigation. If a full-scale investigation is undertaken, detectives reinterview witnesses, contact informants, check crime files, and so on.

Modern detective work sometimes includes **sting operations,** which are undercover operations in which police pretend to involve themselves in illegal acts to trap a suspect. They may pose as fences in order to capture thieves or as wealthy businesspeople offering money to those suspected of taking bribes. Sting operations have been highly criticized by researchers, who find that this particular method borders on illegal entrapment.[32] However, there is an important legal and psychological difference between a sting operation—or, for that matter, a *decoy operation,* in which a police officer poses as a vulnerable victim—on the one hand, and an entrap-

"Notice all the computations, theoretical scribblings, and lab equipment, Norm. ... Yes, curiosity killed these cats."

ment, on the other. *Entrapment* involves police conduct in which an originally unwilling person is actively induced to commit a crime. That is illegal, as the U.S. Supreme Court has ruled.[33]

The Rand Corporation has studied how efficient detectives are at clearing cases. Data from 153 large detective bureaus demonstrated that too much time was spent on paperwork and too little on detecting.[34] Another analysis of 5336 cases reported to suburban police departments reached a similar conclusion: the solution of most crimes does not require detective work.[35] But a Police Executive Research Forum (PERF) study had contradictory findings: data on 3360 burglaries and 320 robberies in De Kalb County, Georgia; St. Petersburg, Florida; and Wichita, Kansas, show that both initial investigation by patrol officers and follow-up work by detectives are necessary to find suspects.[36]

Specialized Units

Metropolitan police departments have specialized units to deal with specific kinds of problems. The traffic unit, for example, is responsible for investigation of accidents, control of traffic, and enforcement of parking and traffic laws. Since police departments have neither the resources to enforce all traffic laws nor the desire to punish all violators, they have a policy of selective enforcement: they target specific problem intersections or highways with high accident or violation rates for stiffer enforcement. Traffic law enforcement has an important influence on community relations because of the amount of contact with the public that this task requires. Most large city departments also have a vice squad. It enforces laws against such activities as gambling, drug dealing, and prostitution. This type of work requires undercover agents, informants, and training in the legal procedures that govern their duties.

Nonline Functions

Every department also needs administrators to recruit officers, to plan, to run the budget, to keep records, and to teach. The training of officers has gained particular significance. Today all police agencies have training programs, and in each state there is a Police Officer Standards and Training (POST) Commission that sets mandatory minimum requirements for training. As yet there is a great deal of difference among the states. Some mandate 16 weeks of training; others require only 3 weeks. Depending on the length of time, training programs range from basic training (handling of weapons) to academic courses.[37] Before 1969, only ten states required preservice training for their officers.[38]

POLICE FUNCTIONS

The police have three categories of functions: law enforcement, order maintenance, and community service. As the most highly visible members of the criminal justice system, local police play a major role in instilling a sense of security among citizens and in maintaining good relations between the police and the community. During the civil unrest of the 1960s, police departments began to look for ways to improve their image in order to establish better relations with the public. Police administrators realized that officers had to do more than just enforce the law; they needed to concentrate on maintaining order and providing services as well.

Law Enforcement

The law enforcement function, which involves intervention in situations in which the law has been broken, predominated well into the 1960s, under the strong influence of Vollmer, Wilson, and their like-minded contemporaries. Crime was to be controlled by concentration on serious offenses, and police performance was assessed by the number of felony arrests. There was not much concern about routine, minor violations, like public drunkenness and groups of noisy teenagers.

Crime was to be suppressed in the most efficient way possible, and that way depended on maximum coverage of an officer's beat. A beat, the argument ran, was covered better in a car than on foot, and one-officer cars were twice as efficient as two-officer cars. So police departments shifted from foot patrol to car patrol and made large investments in communications equipment.

As depersonalized as the car-patrol beats

became, they were made even more so by frequent rotation in an effort to minimize the corruption that might tempt officers if they got to know their constituents too well. The result of all these changes, suggest James Q. Wilson and George Kelling, was that the personal relationship between the people in the neighborhood and the cop of former days was lost.[39] But not all criminologists agree with Wilson and Kelling. Samuel Walker, for example, contends that the "good old days" of policing never existed. When communications were primitive, officers could avoid supervision, neglect their responsibilities, and engage in corrupt practices.

Walker also points out that at the same time that police were put into patrol cars to depersonalize the system, the widespread use of the telephone increased the number of contacts with individuals. When police were on foot patrol, they had more in-person contact with people, but mainly in public places. They seldom went into private homes, for the good reason that a person in trouble at home had no way to call for help.[40] Empirical studies have confirmed the importance of the telephone. It is estimated that when citizens ask for police help, close to 90 percent of the requests are made by phone.[41]

Order Maintenance

Several researchers have studied police work, usually by observing police on duty or by reviewing and categorizing the nature of the incidents with which police officers deal, based on the calls they receive and the incident reports they file. Specific numbers may vary, but analyses of the types of incidents reveal that the majority usually do not involve law enforcement (Figure 16.3). Egon Bittner, for instance, found that patrol officers average about one arrest per month. Many of the calls relate to what has been called order maintenance, peacekeeping, or conflict management (for example, dispersing a group of rowdy teenagers or warning an aggressive panhandler to move on).[42] In maintaining order, officers usually can exercise discretion in deciding whether a law has been broken.

Wilson and Kelling described this police function in an article titled "Broken Windows: The Police and Neighborhood Safety."[43] Though literally "broken windows" refers to the run-down, burned-out, deteriorated conditions of buildings in many inner-city neighborhoods, the phrase has a symbolic meaning as well. It refers to the quality of life in a neighborhood and the attitudes of the people who live in it. According to Wilson and Kelling, as policing in America became more professional, increasing emphasis was placed on crime fighting (the law enforcement model) and less on the type of policing that enhances harmonious relationships within the community, reduces fear of crime, and fosters cooperation between citizens and police (the order maintenance function).[44]

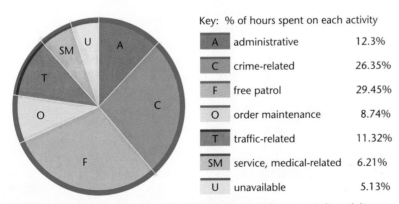

FIGURE 16.3 Police workload in Wilmington, Delaware: Unit activity file

Source: Jack R. Greene and Carl B. Klockars, "What Police Do," in *Thinking about Police,* 2d ed., Carl B. Klockars and Stephen D. Mastrofski (New York: McGraw-Hill, 1991), pp. 273–274, 279.

CRIMINOLOGICAL FOCUS
Police and the Homeless

The problems of the homeless in the United States create a dilemma for police officers. Many citizens, offended by the presence of homeless men and women on city streets or frightened by aggressive panhandling, call the police for help. The homeless, however, have a legitimate right to be in public places, and in many jurisdictions asking people for money is not illegal. The police have to try to satisfy the public's demand for the appearance of public order without abridging the rights of the homeless, who also are part of the public.

Recent court decisions and changes in regulations have changed police responsibilities and limited officers' range of responses to homeless people. In 1992, a New York State law prohibiting begging on the streets was declared unconstitutional, and the police were explicitly told not to order beggars to "move along."(1) A 1993 federal appeals court decision upheld the judgment that New York's statute against "loitering for the purposes of begging" was unconstitutional.

In Miami, a federal district court judge has ordered the city to create "safe zones" where homeless people can sleep, bathe, prepare food, and eat without being arrested; the judge noted that "arresting the homeless for harmless, involuntary, life-sustaining acts" violated the Constitution.(2) The lawsuit had originated in complaints by three homeless men that the city was using ordinances on disorderly conduct, curfew, vagrancy, and loitering to keep homeless people out of public areas.

While police department policies with respect to the homeless have become more compassionate and individual officers have switched from law enforcement to service roles, a new problem has surfaced that threatens a reversal: the increasing involvement of the homeless in serious felonies, both as perpetrators and as victims. In Santa Monica, a study showed that approximately half of all serious felonies in the first half of 1990 were committed by homeless people—often against other homeless people.

Recent city and police department decisions may help resolve the difficulties of the homeless. For example, Santa Monica's police department has begun the Homeless Enforcement Liaison Program (HELP), in which two experienced officers are assigned to work only with transient-related crimes. Plans include identifying the most conspicuous criminals among the homeless and arresting them, adding more officers to HELP, and working closely with the city attorney's office.

A Santa Monica police lieutenant summed up the problems all police face with regard to the homeless:

> Unlike drugs, there is no clearly defined public consensus as to whether a law enforcement problem truly exists concerning the homeless, and assuming that it might, what ought to be done about it. The idea of using police force to drive the homeless out of town is emotionally appealing to some segments of the resident population, but it ultimately presents grave moral and constitutional conflicts."(3)

Sources
1. Douglas Martin, "Speech Is Just One Part of Begging," *New York Times,* Oct. 4, 1992, p. 21.
2. Larry Rohter, "Judge Orders 'Safe Zones' for Homeless," *New York Times,* Nov. 18, 1992, p. A10.
3. Barney Melekian, "Police and the Homeless," *FBI Law Enforcement Bulletin,* **59** (November 1990): 1–7.

Questions for Discussion
1. Should the police take a more active role in providing accommodations for homeless people?
2. How should police respond to the increasing role of the homeless as both crime victims and offenders?

A teen runaway sleeping in an alley in Hollywood, California.

Community Service

As the government's frontline response to social problems and emergencies, the police are called on to provide service to those members of the community who, by reason of personal, economic, social, or other circumstances, are in need of immediate aid.[45] Their duties bring them in contact with knife and gunshot wounds, drug overdoses, alcoholic delirium, and routine medical problems from heart attacks to diabetic comas. They return runaway children to their parents and remove cats from trees. Research done in a city of 400,000 found, in fact, that social service and administrative tasks accounted for 55 percent of officers' time; crime fighting accounted for 17 percent.[46] Another study found that of 18,000 calls to a Kentucky police department over a 4-month period, 60 percent were for information, 13 percent concerned traffic, 2.7 percent dealt with violent crime, and 1.8 percent involved property crime.[47]

THE POLICE AND THE COMMUNITY

The successful performance of the law enforcement, order maintenance, and community service functions requires that the police have the trust and cooperation of the public. The manner in which the police perform these three functions, especially order maintenance and community service, determines the community's respect for and trust in its police. If such respect exists, citizens are much more likely to assist the police in their law enforcement function. Yet good police-community relations had all but vanished during the era of professionalization. This became apparent during the late 1960s and early 1970s when citizens, especially in inner-city ghetto areas, rebelled against government policy in general and law enforcement in particular. The revolts prompted large-scale efforts to restore police-community relations.

Community Policing

The most widely accepted strategy for improving police-community relations is that of community policing. **Community policing** generally consists of programs and policies based on a partnership between the police and the community they serve. Some observers have used the term "community wellness" to describe the philosophy behind this kind of policing.[48] The emphasis is on working in collaboration with residents to determine community needs and the best way to address them and to involve citizens as "co-producers of public safety."[49] Among the goals of community policing are a reduction in fear of crime, the development of closer ties with the community, the engagement of residents in a joint effort to prevent crime and maintain order, and an increase in the level of public satisfaction with police services. Many types of programs have been described as community policing, including increased use of foot patrol, storefront police stations, community surveys, police-sponsored youth activities, and Neighborhood Watch programs.[50]

The idea of community policing is neither new nor unique to the United States. Several countries have much more active programs than we have in this country. In Japan, for example, officers are stationed in a mini-police station (called a *koban*) in each neighborhood. They receive complaints, search for runaways, patrol on bike or foot, and provide security through constant contact. The *koban* has a reception room, a small kitchen, an interview area, and a lost-and-found service; it serves the important function of soliciting recommendations for what the police might do to help the community.[51] Norway and Singapore also have such mini-police stations.[52]

The idea behind this approach is that communities have different needs and priorities that the police have to be aware of if efforts to prevent crime are to be effective. New York City established the Community Patrol Officers (CPO) program in July 1984. Individual officers were taken from their routine line duties and appointed CPOs. A CPO was to make rounds, on foot, and "to function as a planner, problem solver, community organizer, and information link between the community and the police."[53]

The CPO evaluation project conducted by the Vera Institute focused on the functioning of CPOs in relation to the command structure of normal policing. It concluded that if the program was to work, changes would need to be made in

Successful community policing in America's many different ethnic neighborhoods requires officers who know and understand the culture.

traditional operational functioning—changes that would take into account the aspirations of the residents, the diversity of their problems, and the resources in the neighborhoods patrolled.[54]

Team Policing

In the early 1970s a strategy called **team policing** became a popular way to enhance contacts between citizens and police. Team policing was a response to the riots in the inner cities, the perception of the police as an army of occupation, and the limited familiarity on the part of officers with the needs of the neighborhoods they served. It was hoped that if the image of the police was changed from that of enemy to that of friend, law enforcement activities would be a great deal more effective.

In team policing, a team of officers, rather than individual officers, carries out the policing responsibilities. The team, a group of officers and a supervisor, is in charge of a specific neighborhood on a 24-hour basis. Team members decide how to divide up the work, what methods to use to cover an area, and how to maximize communication with community members. The communication is accomplished by a variety of means,

including meetings between community leaders and team representatives, storefront mini-police stations that encourage citizens to drop in, and programs in which community volunteers work as block watchers to report suspicious situations. Team members meet regularly to discuss neighborhood problems, to keep each other informed, and to decide on common policy.

Like most innovations, team policing has its advocates and its critics. Some observers say that it has neither prevented crimes nor increased the number solved.[55] Others question whether it really differs much from routine patrol activities.[56] Nevertheless, other experts argue, team policing has indeed helped to encourage crime control through better police-community relations.[57]

Problem-Oriented Policing

Another way in which police can enhance community relations is through **problem-oriented policing.** In this approach police work with citizens to identify and respond to community problems. Herman Goldstein warns that police too often focus on specific incidents. Their object is to get to places fast, to stabilize the situation, and to get back into service quickly. Most administrators want their officers available to respond to emergency calls as rapidly as possible. But, argues Goldstein, police cannot reduce or prevent crime this way. They need to be more problem-oriented and less incident-oriented. They should analyze local social problems, help to design solutions, advocate programs to change the situation, and monitor effects.[58]

Goldstein's approach has been tried in many communities. In Madison, Wisconsin, police were called regularly to deal with people behaving strangely at a shopping mall. The press characterized the mall as a haven for vagrants and put their number at 1000. The public began to stay away. Business suffered. The police looked into the problem and discovered that the individuals in question had been under psychiatric supervision and were disruptive when they did not take their medication. The police worked with mental-health professionals to set up better supervision. Within a short time the problem was solved, customers returned, and business went back to normal.

In 1982 the Baltimore County Police Department created three teams of officers to solve recurring problems. The teams, called Citizen-Oriented Police Enforcement (COPE) teams, worked with local patrol officers to pinpoint conditions that appeared to be creating problems. For example, each spring burglaries increased, and one item, baseball gloves, was consistently stolen. When a program was instituted to provide baseball equipment to low-income families, the burglary rate fell significantly.[59]

Foot Patrol

Another effort to improve police–community relations involved the reintroduction of the pre–World War II practice of "walking the beat." It was felt that patrol cars isolated officers from citizens and that if police were put back on the streets, people would get to know them and feel a greater sense of security.[60] A number of cities, including Houston, Newark, and Flint, Michigan, carried out experiments to test the effectiveness of foot patrol. They found that crime rates generally did not go down significantly, but citizen fear of crime did. Moreover, better citizen cooperation resulted in more job satisfaction among officers and fewer calls for assistance.[61]

Preventive Patrol

It has long been argued that preventive patrol, which entails an increase in police presence and visibility, deters criminals from committing crimes and thereby reduces citizen fear and fosters good police-community relations. Between October 1, 1972, and September 30, 1973, the Kansas City Police Department conducted the Kansas City Preventive Patrol Experiment. Fifteen police beats covering a population of close to 150,000 inhabitants were divided into three sections. Each section was subjected to a different type of patrol: intensified routine patrol (two to three times more officers were on the beat), decreased patrol (officers came into the area only when they were called for service), and routine patrol (the area maintained its usual number of police).

The results were unexpected: increased patrol levels had no effect on crime rates, citizens' fear of crime, citizens' satisfaction with police, or the amount of time it took to respond to calls.[62] Lawrence Sherman and David Weisburd decided to replicate the Kansas City study but with a different focus. They argued that allocating more police to entire neighborhoods did not have a deterrent effect because not all areas of a neighborhood are at high risk for crime. The police presence, rather than being distributed over the whole neighborhood, should be intensified in hot spots, particular places within neighborhoods that are the source of the most calls to the police. In Minneapolis, for example, 5 percent of the locations were the sources of 64 percent of the calls.[63] Sherman and Weisburd are now testing the effects of an increased police presence in 110 hot spots in this city.[64]

Police-Community Relations Programs

A final strategy for enhancing public perception of the police consists of police-community relations programs. These programs do not change the basic method of policing; but by reaching out into the community, they have had good results:

■ Increased likelihood of citizen cooperation in providing information to assist in law enforcement

■ More voluntary compliance with the law

■ Improved relations with minority groups[65]

■ Community support for budget appropriations in an environment of competing demands[66]

A recent inventory of programs in different jurisdictions showed that department-sponsored activities include "ride-along" programs in which citizens accompany the police on patrols, citizenship awards, citizen citation programs to recognize meritorious acts, liaison programs with the clergy, police headquarters tours, and public-speaking programs.[67]

THE RULE OF LAW IN LAW ENFORCEMENT

National investigative commissions in the 1930s and again in the 1960s found American policing to be defective in six distinct areas:

■ Constitutional due process

■ Civil rights

■ Use of deadly force and police brutality

■ Abuse of discretion

■ Corruption

■ Police-community relations

Restoration and maintenance of the rule of law to which the American system of government is devoted required reforms in all these areas.

Constitutional Due Process

Largely as a result of the demonstrated systematic lawlessness of some police officers, the United States Supreme Court, under the leadership of Chief Justice Earl Warren, played the leading role in the reform movement. In case after case the Supreme Court reversed convictions that had been obtained in violation of constitutional restraints. The provisions in the Bill of Rights, which had been applied only to federal law enforcement, were extended to cover state actions as well through the Fourteenth Amendment, which guarantees that no one shall be deprived of life, liberty, or property without due process of law (Chapter 15). These rights include protection against unreasonable searches and seizures (Fourth Amendment), protection against self-incrimination (Fifth Amendment), and the right to counsel (Sixth Amendment). Some people hailed the Court's decisions; others decried them as handcuffing the police in their efforts to enforce the law.

Civil Rights

In the 1960s, American policing also suffered from increasing tensions between black citizens who demanded their civil rights and police who tried to maintain the status quo. Police officers gave the appearance of a force removed from the community, encapsulated in a professional cocoon, insensitive to community moods and needs. This was especially the case in the inner cities.

On July 16, 1964, a white New York City officer shot and killed a black teenager. Demonstrators marched to the Twenty-Eighth Precinct headquarters, and 2 days of rioting followed. The rioting spread to Rochester, Jersey City, and Philadelphia, and in the next year to Los Angeles, Chicago, and San Diego. Then Cleveland, San Francisco, Atlanta, Detroit, and Newark were affected. In the same years, college students were demonstrating against the Vietnam war. In all cases, the police were called in to restore order, a process that culminated in many confrontations and some deaths.

During these years of turmoil, in 1966, Lyndon B. Johnson established the President's Commission on Law Enforcement and the Administration of Justice. The commission reported findings of racism, unequal justice, and police brutality. This report led to the enactment of the Omnibus Crime Control and Safe Streets Act of 1968, which created the Law Enforcement Assistance Administration (LEAA). During its brief existence (1967–1982) the agency spent $7 billion in an effort to upgrade law enforcement and criminal justice in the United States.

Though the LEAA has been criticized for its vast expenditures on hardware and on speculative research and development, among other things, it has also been praised for its enormous positive effects on American criminal justice.[68] LEAA funds established advanced training in law enforcement and criminal justice and, directly and indirectly, resulted in the creation of more than 600 academic programs of criminal justice in the United States.

Use of Deadly Force and Police Brutality

In *Tennessee v. Garner* the United States Supreme Court was confronted with a tragic situation. A father was suing a Memphis police officer, as well as governmental agencies, for the loss of the life of his 17-year-old son. The son, according to the undisputed facts, had burglarized a home. The police responded instantly to the homeowner's call. An officer spotted the suspect fleeing across the backyard and ordered him to stop. The officer saw that the suspect was unarmed. The youngster made an effort to jump over a high fence. The officer shot and killed him. The common law rule of England and the United States, as well as the law of Tennessee, had always been that the police may use deadly force to stop a fleeing felon whether or not he or she is in pos-

session of a weapon. The officer had acted properly when he shot and killed the suspect, and the Supreme Court found that the officer could not be prosecuted or sued for wrongful death.

The Court reached a different conclusion, however, with respect to governmental liability. The Court reasoned that when all felonies in England were capital crimes, perhaps such a rule on the use of deadly force made sense, because an offender found guilty at trial could be sentenced to death. But the taking of the life of a suspect who, if convicted, might receive only a relatively short prison sentence makes no sense and constitutes an unreasonable seizure of the person in violation of the Fourth Amendment.

The Police Foundation was allowed to file an *amicus curiae* ("friend of the court") brief in which it supported abandonment of the harsh common law rule. The brief demonstrated through research that the shoot-to-kill rule for fleeing felons does not prevent crime or enhance the protection of police officers and thus is unreasonable as a law enforcement tool. Consequently, the Supreme Court overturned the common law rule as violating the due process clause of the Fourteenth Amendment.[69]

Deadly force may not be used unless it is nec-

The unpopularity of the decision in a trial of a police officer for use of deadly force spawned attacks against law enforcement in Teaneck, New Jersey, where the incident happened.

essary to prevent the escape of a suspect who the officer has probable cause to believe poses a significant threat of death or serious injury to the officer or others. As we noted, use of deadly force by police officers has been a major issue in police-minority relations. James J. Fyfe writes, "As most police recruits learn in the academy, the cop on the street . . . carries in his holster more power than has been granted the Chief Justice of the Supreme Court."[70] If this power is used improperly, it can lead to riots, more deaths, litigation against the police, and the downfall of entire city administrations.

The issue had been confronted by two presidential commissions, the Commission on Civil Disorders (1968) and the President's Commission on Law Enforcement and the Administration of Justice (1967). Both had suggested that use of deadly force was the immediate reason for urban riots. Before the work of these commissions, little had been done in the way of empirical research.[71] Since then a number of scientists have studied the issue. John Goldkamp explains that there are two conflicting perspectives. Some people claim that the disproportionately high number of minority persons shot and killed by police can be explained by the irresponsible use of deadly force by some police officers and the differential administration of law enforcement toward minorities. Others claim that the disproportionately high number of minority persons shot and killed by police can be explained by disproportionately high arrest rates among minorities for crimes of violence.[72]

There is evidence to support both claims. Catherine Milton and her associates point out that 70 percent of the people shot by police in the seven cities that they studied were black, although blacks made up about 39 percent of the population.[73] Betty Jenkins and Adrienne Faison showed that 52 percent of the persons killed by police over a 3-year period were black and 21 percent Hispanic.[74] Paul Takagi sums up this side of the controversy: "The news gets around the community when someone is killed by police. It is part of a history—a very long history of extralegal justice that included whippings and lynchings."[75]

The other side of the argument—that larger proportions of minority individuals are shot by police because they live in high-crime areas, are more likely to own guns, and more often commit violent crime—also finds support. James Fyfe's study of New York City shootings, for example, showed that in many incidents in which a shooting took place, police officers themselves were killed or wounded. He also found that minorities were more likely than whites to be involved in incidents in which guns were used.[76]

Official inquiries and empirical studies of police use of deadly force continue. Lawrence Sherman maintains that there have been some positive developments. Data obtained from surveys of killings of civilians by police in 59 cities between 1970 and 1984 show that such killings have decreased by 50 percent.[77] Nonetheless, even with improved training, controversial incidents will still happen, often polarizing an entire county or city. For example, on April 10, 1990, a black teenager, Phillip Pannell, was shot and killed by a white Teaneck, New Jersey, police officer. The shooting resulted in riots throughout Teaneck and polarized Bergen County, New Jersey, for nearly 2 years.[78]

The use of uncalled-for deadly or overwhelming physical force against persons, frequently suspects, who are deemed not to respect the power of the police is what we call *police brutality.* Who can forget the image of Rodney King being beaten mercilessly, without any apparent reason, by four Los Angeles police officers?[79] But Los Angeles is not an exception. A similar amateur videotape recorded a beating inflicted by a Trenton, New Jersey, police officer on Thomas Downing, who had simply inquired why his stepson was being arrested.[80]

Force must be used in law enforcement, but democracies always put limits on that use. The best-known abuse historically was probably the "third degree"—torture for the purpose of extracting a confession. Torture by police may be rare in the United States today, but it remains a significant problem in many countries around the world, even with the adoption of the United Nations Code of Conduct for Law Enforcement Officials, which prohibits all police abuses.[81] We have a long way to go before the ideals found in that code guide police practice in every nation.

Abuse of Discretion

Yet another defect in the functioning of American policing has been and still is the potential abuse of discretion in making decisions about whom to arrest. How does police discretion work in the case of young, poor, minority males? While discretionary power may indeed be regulated officially, the reality of the patrol situation is such that officers have considerable autonomy.

Several studies show that the discretionary nature of police decision making discriminates against blacks.[82] But there is no clear-cut pattern: Some researchers conclude that the neighborhood is the best predictor of arrest. Police make more arrests in low-income areas.[83] Others clarify the importance of neighborhood by adding that in black communities police are more punitive toward whites than blacks. The reverse is also true. In predominantly white neighborhoods, police are more punitive to black offenders.[84]

Other determinants of racial disparity in arrests are revealed by an array of studies that have examined such factors as income differences between neighborhood residents and suspects, personal characteristics of the victim, the demeanor (attitude and appearance) of the suspect, real differences in rates of offending, and the choice of the people who make the complaints (blacks more often than whites request that an officer make an arrest).[85]

Christy Visher found that police are more likely to arrest a woman whose attitudes and actions differ from the stereotype of a "lady" and that older white women are less likely to be arrested than young black women.[86] Marvin Krohn and his colleagues disagree. In a study conducted between 1948 and 1976 involving 10,723 police contacts, they found a trend toward more equal treatment of girls (compared with boys) for juvenile misdemeanors and of women (compared with men) for both misdemeanors and felonies.[87]

Many efforts have been made to control police abuse of discretion. The courts have placed limits on what police are permitted to do when they investigate and question suspects. Police administrators have tried to establish guidelines for police behavior in the field. But the task is difficult. Police officers perform a wide variety of duties under a wide range of conditions. We have little detailed information on what factors actually influence their decisions.

Corruption

At the turn of the century the Progressives thought that the civil service system would eliminate corruption and incompetence among the police. Yet after a century of reforms, police corruption persists. In the early 1970s a New York City police lieutenant, then sergeant, David Durk, and his partner, Detective Frank Serpico, discovered massive corruption among fellow officers and superiors. They collected the evidence and reported it to higher authorities within the department. Neither there nor at the highest level of the department was any action taken. Durk and Serpico ultimately reported their findings directly to the mayor. Still nothing happened. In frustration they released their information to the press. Durk and Serpico were attacked by fellow officers for "dirtying their own nest," "washing dirty laundry in public," "tarnishing their shields," and worse. The result of their revelations was the creation of the Knapp Commission, which unraveled the existing police corruption in New York City and recommended measures to avoid it in the future.[88]

The term "corruption" covers a wide range of conduct patterns. The Knapp Commission itself distinguished—in typical police jargon—between "meat eaters," who solicit bribes or actually cooperate with criminals for personal gain, and "grass eaters," who accept payoffs for rendering police services or for looking the other way when action is called for. Subsequent empirical and analytical studies have provided additional classifications and descriptions of police misconduct, including soliciting and accepting bribes, dereliction of duty, and street crime offenses such as larceny, embezzlement, and coercion.[89]

Despite the efforts of the Knapp Commission in 1972 and the National Advisory Commission on Criminal Justice Standards and Goals in 1973, corruption continues. According to experts, corruption may even be more serious now than it was in the 1970s.[90] In 1988 more than 100 Miami police officers were implicated in corrupt drug-related activities. A federal grand jury indicted ten of them for their involvement in a $13 million theft of cocaine from a boat anchored in the Miami River. A Philadelphia officer who was heading a corruption investigation was given an 18-year prison sentence on evidence that he received $50,000 a month from operators of illegal electronic poker machines.[91]

The ancient Romans had a phrase, *Quis enim custodiet custodes?*—"Who then watches the watchmen?" Modern policing relies on internal and external controls to maintain its professionalism and its integrity. We have discussed some of the external controls. The court system, especially the Supreme Court, plays a role in policing the police by holding law enforcement activities to strict constitutional standards.

Another external-control mechanism is the civilian police review boards that were established to fulfill a review function. From the outset, however, they were opposed both by police unions (such as the Fraternal Order of Police) and by management organizations (such as the International Association of Chiefs of Police). The boards were short-lived in Philadelphia and New York. Voters in other cities defeated proposals to establish such boards; and both the 1967 President's Commission on Law Enforcement and the Administration of Justice and the 1973 National Advisory Commission on Criminal Justice Standards and Goals opposed them as being unworkable and detrimental to morale within departments. Nevertheless, by 1993, 30 of the nation's 50 largest cities had established civilian review boards, and New York City had reactivated its civilian review board.[92]

Many police departments rely on internal controls to police themselves. If internal controls are to be effective, experts argue, law enforcement professionals need to change their thinking about self-policing. In the past, departmental whistleblowers were regarded with derision. Such attitudes need to be replaced by intolerance toward those who abuse the public trust and the power of the shield by engaging in abuses, corruption, and other forms of criminality. Studies indicate, however, that more officers than not are unwilling to report misconduct by other officers.[93] This raises the question of whether there is anything special or different about the personality of police officers and the culture in which they function that sets them apart from the rest of the population.

POLICE OFFICERS AND THEIR LIFESTYLE

If we want to answer the above question, we must find out who it is police departments accept into their ranks. We must then understand the police culture in which the officers live and function.

Qualifications

Most departments require that new recruits be in good physical condition, have no criminal record, and have a high school diploma. Other criteria for selection, used to varying degrees by different departments, are a written exam (78 percent), an interview (97 percent), a lie detector test (40 percent), weight and height standards (42 percent), and a background check (99 percent). Some require intelligence and psychological tests also (68 percent).[94] About 10 percent require some college education, and less than 1 percent a college degree. Nevertheless, by 1988, 65.2 percent of all sworn officers had 1 or more years of college education.[95]

The question of whether police officers should have a college degree, although it has been recommended by national commissions since 1931, is still controversial. In a survey of law enforcement agencies conducted by the Police Executive Research Forum and supported by the Ford Foundation, some consistent themes emerged. Those in favor of higher education argued that college-educated officers:

Communicate better with the public
Show more initiative
Write better reports
Make better decisions
Have greater sensitivity to minorities
In general, perform better[96]

Those who questioned higher-education requirements for police officers argued that college-educated officers:

Might leave police work
Are more prone to question orders
Expect preferential treatment
Cause animosity within the ranks
Feel dissatisfied with the job[97]

Changing Composition of the Police Force

The political and social crises of the 1960s challenged Americans to reaffirm their commitment to equality before the law. Title VII of the Civil Rights Act of 1964 prohibited the private sector from discrimination in employment on the basis of race, gender, religion, or national origin. In 1972, the Equal Employment Opportunity Act amended the Civil Rights Act to include the public sector. The 1972 act also required that federal agencies develop affirmative action programs. Besides federal legislation, state and local laws prohibit discrimination on the basis of race, national origin, religion, and gender. Two states and over sixty cities go even further by prohibiting discrimination on the basis of sexual preference.[98]

These social and legal changes have had a major impact on the composition of the police force (Figure 16.4). First, the laws made it easier for individuals to bring employer discrimination suits against police agencies. Many did. In fact, over the last 20 years, most of the largest police departments in the country have been sued. Second, to comply with federal guidelines, police departments had to make an effort to attract minority and female applicants.[99] And third, the community has continued to put pressure on the police administration to make policy changes with respect to the recruitment of minorities.

Minority Groups in Policing

The first minority police officer was hired in Washington, D.C., in 1861.[100] By 1940, only 1 percent of all police officers in the United States came from minority groups; in 1950, only 2 percent.[101] Nicholas Alex wrote in *Black in Blue* (1969) that black officers were pressured in two

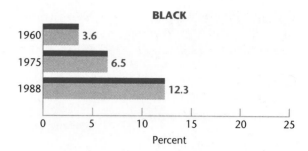

BLACK

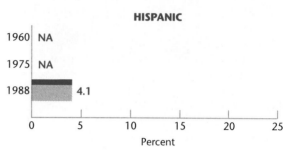

HISPANIC

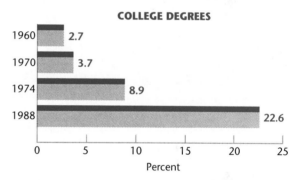

COLLEGE DEGREES

FIGURE 16.4 The changing profile of the American police officer

Source: Samuel Walker, *The Police in America*, 2d ed. (New York: McGraw-Hill, 1992), p. 303.

ways: by racism on the part of white colleagues and by the expectation of black citizens that they would get a break from a black officer.[102]

Changes began to occur in the 1960s. Civil unrest at the time showed that if police officers were recruited from a limited segment of the overall population, there was a risk of alienating those groups that were not represented in law enforcement.[103] Recruitment drives to hire minorities began in most major metropolitan police departments. The issue was highly controversial during the initial phase, and progress has been slow.[104] In the face of outright discrimination in examination and appointment procedures, court action had to be resorted to in many

In the early 1990s, women constituted about 10 percent of sworn officers.

instances to open the doors to blacks and Hispanics who wanted to join the ranks.

By 1982 the overall percentage of minorities in the police force was 7.6 percent.[105] In Washington, D.C., where 70.3 percent of the population was black, over half of the officers came from the black community. In Detroit, blacks accounted for two-thirds of the total population and one-third of the police officers. Recruitment and retention of Hispanic officers likewise increased slowly. By 1980, Hispanic officers accounted for 7.2 percent of the police department of New York City, where the Hispanic population was 19.9 percent of the total. In Los Angeles the percentage of Hispanic officers was 13.6 percent, while that of the Hispanic population was 27.5 percent.[106]

Although changes have occurred—many

police departments are headed by blacks, for example—the ethnic problem has not yet been resolved.[107] Well-founded discrimination suits continue to be brought by minority-group officers. In 1989 Hispanic police officers in New York City complained about discrimination in the promotion of patrol officers to sergeants.[108] The Federal Bureau of Investigation, found by a federal court to have engaged in discriminatory practices, is revamping its practices so as to be in compliance with the Equal Employment Opportunity Act of 1972. This act prohibits discriminatory hiring practices by state and local governments. It also prohibits job discrimination against women.

Women in Policing

The First American woman to serve as a sworn police officer was Lola Baldwin, who joined the Portland, Oregon, police department in 1905. Like the few police matrons of the nineteenth century, she dealt primarily with women and children. In fact, she was originally granted the police power so that she could manage women and children at the Ohio State Exposition. Five years later, in 1910 in Los Angeles, Alice Stebbin Wells became the first officially classified policewoman, assigned to "supervising and enforcing laws concerning dance halls, skating rinks, and theaters; monitoring billboard displays; locating missing persons; and maintaining a general bureau for women seeking advice on matters within the scope of the police department."[109] In 1915 she founded the International Association of Police Women.

More than 60 police departments had women on their staffs by 1919; 145 had women by 1925. But women's police roles remained restricted. Women did not attain patrol officer status until the 1960s. There were no female sergeants until 1965, after a successful lawsuit against New York City.[110] With the emergence of the drive for the equality of women in the late 1960s and early 1970s and the passage of Title VII of the Civil Rights Act of 1972, many departments began to recruit women. Others resisted. Serious obstacles and stereotypes had to be overcome: that women were physically weak, irrational, and illogical; that they lacked the toughness needed to deal with work on the streets. Some people argued that the association of female with male officers

TABLE 16.1   WOMEN POLICE OFFICERS IN THE UNITED STATES, 1971–1992

Year	Total No. of Police Officers	Women Police Officers	
		Number	Percent of Police Force
1971	225,474	3,156	1.4
1972	269,420	4,041	1.5
1973	276,808	4,705	1.7
1974	286,973	5,739	2.0
1975	292,346	6,130	2.1
1976	287,448	6,898	2.4
1977	293,017	7,911	2.7
1978	294,579	9,426	3.2
1979	296,332	10,371	3.5
1980	294,181	11,178	3.8
1981	297,324	13,082	4.4
1982	298,334	14,021	4.7
1983	304,012	15,504	5.1
1984	309,960	17,357	5.6
1985	312,713	19,388	6.2
1986	318,484	21,338	6.7
1987	320,959	22,788	7.1
1988	325,095	24,362	7.5
1989	496,753	41,197	8.3
1990	523,262	45,001	8.6
1991	535,629	48,207	9.0
1992	544,309	49,532	9.1

Source: Uniform Crime Reports relevant to each year.

would cause complications in both job and family life.

By 1980, according to the Uniform Crime Reports, the number of policewomen was still low—under 4 percent of all officers. By 1991 that proportion had more than doubled, to 9 percent (Table 16.1). Most recent surveys of personnel practices have found that eligibility criteria and mechanisms used to recruit, screen, and select candidates have changed dramatically, enlarging the pool of eligible women. This change appears to be happening worldwide, not just in the United States, according to an international survey sponsored by the United Nations.[111]

Despite the advances that women have made in policing, they are still not fully accepted by their male colleagues or the public. Most of the resistance stems from the belief that the physical strength of women does not allow them to perform well in violent situations.[112] Responding to these concerns, many police departments continue to assign women to clerical duties or to specific types of problems, such as domestic disputes and runaways. Research has demonstrated, however, that these fears are un-

grounded. Female officers make almost as many successful arrests as male officers, their overall work performance has been rated extremely satisfactory by superiors, their level of strength is well within the acceptable range for the profession, and they may be more pleasant and respectful with the public than their male counterparts.[113]

As regards the way policewomen perceive themselves, it appears that they enter the force self-confident and a bit idealistic but gradually become disillusioned by others' beliefs that they are flirtatious and ineffective.[114] In sum, policewomen have indeed made their mark on the police force, but it may be some time before their male colleagues accept them as equal partners.

The Police Subculture

While there continue to be many differences—in numbers, seniority, and positions, for example—between black, Hispanic, and female police officers, on the one hand, and white male police officers, on the other, one thing that they all have in common is job-related stress. Where their police work is concerned, they rely heavily on each other as partners.

Michael K. Brown describes how police officers stick together when they work the streets because of the constant stress and anxiety that goes along with the job. These working conditions, plus the entry requirements, training, citizen expectations, and behavioral norms (officers are required to be respectful yet to be in control of a situation, for instance) combine to produce a similarity of values—a **police subculture.**[115]

The process of socialization into the culture begins as soon as new recruits enter the academy. They get to know not only the formal rules of policing but also the informal norms that a person has to abide by in order to be accepted into the group. They learn very quickly that loyalty—the obligation to support a fellow officer—is the first priority. Respect for police authority, honor, individualism, and group solidarity also rank high among esteemed values.[116]

One of the primary reasons for the existence of a subculture that is characterized by very strong in-group ties is the nature of police work. Officers often view the external community as hostile and threatening. They are caught in a bind. Their job calls for them to discipline the people they serve, and they are allowed to use force to do it. The police uniform also isolates officers. Easily recognizable, they are constantly approached by people who know what is going on and want to tell them about it or who want to complain.

When they are off duty, police officers also tend to isolate themselves from the community, spending most of their time with other officers and their families. William Westley says that police officers are isolated from the rest of society behind a "blue curtain."[117] Police officers are often viewed as suspicious, authoritative, and cynical.[118] Their working environment may be responsible for the development of these traits.[119] Police work is potentially dangerous, so officers need to be constantly aware of what is happening around them. At the academy they are warned about what happens to officers who are too trusting. They learn about the many officers who have died in the line of duty because they did not exercise proper caution. It would be surprising if they did not become suspicious.

As George Kirkham, police officer and professor, argues: "Chronic suspiciousness is something that a good cop cultivates in the interest of going home to his family each evening."[120] The second trait, authoritativeness, is another response to the police working environment. Uniforms, badges, and guns signify authority. But even more important is the fact that officers need to gain immediate control of potentially dangerous situations in order to do their job.

And what about cynicism? In a study of 220 New York City police officers, Arthur Niederhoffer found that 80 percent of the new recruits believed that the department was a smoothly operating, effective organization. Within a couple of months, fewer than one-third still held that belief. Moreover, cynicism increased with length of service and among those of the more highly educated who did not get promoted.[121]

The working environment that we have described quite often leads to stress, which results in emotional and physical problems. A study of 2300 officers in 20 departments found that 37 percent had serious marital problems, 36 percent suffered physical ailments, 23 percent abused alcohol, 20 percent indicated problems among their children, and 10 percent abused drugs.[122] Since the 1970s there has been increasing concern over these stress-related problems. Many departments, especially the large ones, are trying to provide more medical attention, more psychological counseling, and a greater range of disability and retirement benefits and to give higher priority to community-oriented policing, which lessens tension between officer and citizenry.[123]

■ REVIEW

In tenth-century England, policing was done by all males over age 12, who were bound to keep the peace and track down criminals. Through the centuries the system became more formal, with sheriffs, night watchmen, and justices of the peace. It was not until 1829 that the first professional police force came into existence in England. Colonial America adopted a similar system.

Today there are more than 20,000 separate public law enforcement agencies in the United States. About 50 are federal, some 200 are state, and all the rest are local. But although there are many levels of law enforcement agencies, each with specialized units, they often work together on major operations. The federal agency with the broadest range of duties is the FBI. At the state level, all states except Hawaii have centralized, quasi-military forces. At the county level, the sheriff's office is responsible for countywide policing outside municipalities. Municipal police forces range in size from small-town one- or two-person departments to the New York City department, which with over 37,000 employees is the largest in the country. There are also specialized police forces, like housing police, and a growing number of private security police.

Police departments are organized largely along the lines of a military command, with units that parallel those of other government departments: bureaus, divisions, and sections or units. Police perform three categories of functions: law enforcement, order maintenance, and community service. Because the focus on crime fighting and law enforcement tended to alienate police from the community, the social unrest of the 1960s resulted in a great deal of tension and distrust of the police. Departments sought ways to change their image by using innovative policing methods like community policing, team policing, foot and bicycle patrols, and problem-oriented policing.

Defects in the functioning of American police forces, in addition to community relations, include maintenance of the rule of law (due process protections and civil rights), use of deadly force and brutality, abuse of discretion, and corruption.

Departments also sought to broaden their community base by recruiting members of various ethnic and minority groups, including women. Today the composition of American police forces is changing rapidly. But although there continue to be many differences in numbers, seniority, and position, for example, between black, Hispanic, and female police officers, on the one hand, and white male officers, on the other, they all have in common the stress of their jobs. They rely heavily on one another at work and tend to spend most of their off-duty time with other officers and their families.

■ NOTES

1. Based on Martin A. Kelly, "Citizen Survival in Ancient Rome," *Police Studies*, **11** (1988): 195–201, a delightful historical police vignette, which we recommend to all our readers. The quote is from Juvenal (A.D. 40–120).
2. See Daniel Devlin, *Police Procedure, Administration, and Organization* (London: Butterworth, 1966).
3. Metropolitan Police Force, *Instruction Book* (London, 1829), as quoted in William H. Hewitt, Robert S. Getz, and Oscar H. Ibele, *British Police Administration* (Springfield, Ill.: Charles C. Thomas, 1965), p. 32.
4. Patrick Pringle, *Hue and Cry: The Story of Henry and John Fielding and the Bow Street Runners* (New York: Morrow, 1965).
5. Drew Humphries and David F. Greenberg, "The Dialectics of Crime Control," in *Crime and Capitalism: Readings in Marxist Criminology*, ed. David Greenberg (Palo Alto, Calif.: Mayfield, 1981), pp. 209–254.
6. Samuel Walker, *Popular Justice: A History of American Criminal Justice* (New York: Oxford University Press, 1980), p. 18.
7. Roger Lane, *Policing the City: Boston, 1822–1885* (Cambridge, Mass.: Harvard University Press, 1967), p. 26.
8. Walker, *Popular Justice*, pp. 61–62.
9. George F. Cole, *The American System of Criminal Justice* (Pacific Grove, Calif.: Brooks/Cole, 1989), p. 177.
10. Samuel Walker, *A Critical History of Police Reform* (Lexington, Mass.: Lexington Books, 1977), pp. 45–46; Bruce Smith, *Police Systems in the United States*, rev. ed. (New York: Harper, 1949). For a complete discussion of Theodore Roosevelt as police commissioner, see Jay Stuart Berman, *Police Administration and Progressive Reform: Theodore Roosevelt as Police Commissioner of New York* (New York: Greenwood, 1987).
11. National Commission on Law Observance and Enforcement, *Report on Lawlessness in Law Enforcement*, no. 11 (Washington, D.C.: U.S. Government Printing Office, 1931).
12. Figures are based on the U.S. Department of Justice, Federal Bureau of Investigation, Uniform Crime Reports, 1992 (Washington, D.C.: U.S. Government Printing Office, 1993). Also see Sue A. Lindgren, *Justice Expenditure and Employment, 1990* (Washington, D.C.: U.S. Department of Justice, Bureau of Justice Statistics, 1992).
13. Walker, *Popular Justice*, p. 238.
14. Donald A. Torres, *Handbook of Federal Police and Investigative Agencies* (Westport, Conn.: Greenwood, 1985), pp. 135–144.

15. Lindgren, *Justice Expenditure and Employment, 1990.*

16. Brian Reaves, *Profile of State and Local Law Enforcement Agencies, 1987* (Washington, D.C.: U.S. Department of Justice, Bureau of Justice Statistics, 1989).

17. Uniform Crime Reports.

18. U.S. Department of Justice, *Justice Expenditure and Employment, 1988,* table 20.

19. See John P. Crank, "Civilianization in Small and Medium Police Departments in Illinois, 1973–1986," *Journal of Criminal Justice,* **17** (1989): 167–177.

20. Victor H. Sims, *Small Town and Rural Police* (Springfield, Ill.: Charles C. Thomas, 1988).

21. Gary W. Cordner, "Police Agency Size and Investigative Effectiveness," *Journal of Criminal Justice,* **17** (1989): 145–155.

22. Clifford D. Shearing and Philip C. Stenning, "Private Security: Implications for Social Control," *Social Problems,* **30** (1983): 493–506.

23. For a brief history of the private security industry, see Milton Lipson, *On Guard—The Business of Private Security* (New York: Quadrangle, 1975); and Robert D. McCrie, "The Development of the U.S. Security Industry," *Annals of the American Academy of Political and Social Science,* **498** (1988): 23–33.

24. William F. Walsh and Edwin J. Donovan, "Private Security and Community Policing: Evaluation and Comment," *Journal of Criminal Justice,* **17** (1989): 187–197.

25. William C. Cunningham, John J. Strauchs, and Clifford W. Van Meter, *Private Security Trends, 1970 to the Year 2000: The Hallcrest Report II* (Boston: Butterworth-Heinemann, 1990).

26. Lindgren, *Justice Expenditure and Employment, 1990,* p. 3.

27. Cunningham et al., *Private Security Trends.*

28. William C. Cunningham and Todd H. Taylor, *Crime and Protection in America: A Study of Private Security and Law Enforcement Resources and Relationships—Executive Summary* (Washington: D.C.: National Institute of Justice, 1985); Charles P. Nemeth, *Private Security and the Investigative Process* (Cincinnati, Ohio: Anderson, 1992).

29. Fifth United Nations Congress on the Prevention of Crime and the Treatment of Offenders, *Report Prepared by the Secretariat,* A/Conf. 56/10 (New York: United Nations, 1976), p. 29.

30. See Hubert Williams, "Trends in American Policing: Implications for Executives," *American Journal of Police,* **9** (1990): 139–149.

31. Albert J. Reiss, Jr., "Private Employment of Public Police," *NIJ Reports* (Washington, D.C.: National Institute of Justice, 1988), pp. 2–6.

32. C. Cotter and J. Burrows, *Proper Crime Program, A Special Report: Overview of the STING Program and Project Summaries,* for U.S. Department of Justice (Washington, D.C.: U.S. Government Printing Office, 1981); Gary Marx, "The New Police Undercover Work," *Urban Life,* **8** (1980): 399–446; Carl B. Klockars, "Jonathan Wild and the Modern Sting," in *History and Crime: Implications for Criminal Justice Policy,* ed. James C. Inciardi and Charles Faupel (Beverly Hills, Calif.: Sage, 1980), pp. 225–260; Henry W. Prunckun, "It's Your Money They're After: Sting Operations in Consumer Fraud Investigations," *Police Studies,* **11** (1988): 190–194; Clarence Dickson, "Drug Stings in Miami," *F.B.I. Law Enforcement Bulletin* (January 1988): 1–6.

33. *Sherman v. United States,* 356 U.S. 369 (1958).

34. Peter Greenwood and Joan Petersilia, *The Criminal Investigation Process:* vol. 1, *Summary and Policy Implications* (Santa Monica, Calif.: Rand Corporation, 1975).

35. Mark T. Willman and John Snortum, "Detective Work: The Criminal Investigation Process in a Medium-Sized Police Department," *Criminal Justice Review,* **9** (Spring 1984): 33–39.

36. John E. Eck, *Solving Crimes: The Investigation of Burglary and Robbery* (Washington, D.C.: Police Executive Research Forum, 1983). For a study of factors that influence time spent on investigation of burglaries and robberies see Steven G. Brandl, "The Impact of Case Characteristics on Detectives' Decision Making," *Justice Quarterly,* **10** (1993): 395–415.

37. Kenneth E. Christian and Steven M. Edwards, "Law Enforcement Standards and Training Councils: A Human Resource Planning Force in the Future," *Journal of Police Science and Administration,* **13** (1985): 1–9. For changes over time in police training, see Thomas M. Frost and Magnus J. Seng, "Police Recruit Training in Urban Departments: A Look at Instructors," *Journal of Police Science and Administration,* **11** (1983): 296–302. For a methodology of police training evaluation, see Richard A. Talley, "A New Methodology for Evaluating the Curricula Relevancy of Police Academy Training," *Journal of Police Science Administration,* **14** (1986): 112–120. For a discussion of police academy instructors currently teaching in America, see Bruce L. Berg, "Who Should Teach Police: A Typology and Assessment of Police Academy Instructors," *American Journal of Police,* **9** (1990): 79–100.

38. Samuel Walker, *The Police in America* (New York: McGraw-Hill, 1983), p. 265.

39. James Q. Wilson and George L. Kelling, "Broken Windows: The Police and Neighborhood Safety," *Atlantic Monthly* (March 1982): 29–38; Mark H. Moore and George L. Kelling, "To Serve and Protect: Learning from Police History," *Public Interest,* **70** (Winter 1983): 49–65.

40. Samuel Walker, "'Broken Windows' and Fractured History: The Use and Misuse of History in Recent Police Patrol Analysis," *Justice Quarterly,* **1** (1984): 76–90.

41. Albert Reiss, Jr., *The Police and the Public* (New Haven, Conn.: Yale University Press, 1971), p. 11.

42. See, e.g., James Q. Wilson, *Varieties of Police Behavior* (Cambridge, Mass.: Harvard University Press, 1968); Eric J. Scott, *Calls for Service: Citizen Demand and Initial Police Response* (Washington, D.C.: U.S. Government Printing Office, 1981); Steven P. Lab,

"Police Productivity: The Other Eighty Percent," *Journal of Police Science and Administration,* **12** (1984): 297–302; and Reiss, *The Police and the Public.* See also David H. Bayley and James Garofalo, "The Management of Violence by Police Patrol Officers," *Criminology,* **27** (1989): 1–25.

43. Wilson and Kelling, "Broken Windows."

44. George L. Kelling, "Order Maintenance, the Quality of Urban Life, and Police: A Line of Argument," in *Police Leadership,* ed. William A. Gelles (Chicago: American Bar Association, 1985), p. 297.

45. Reiss, *The Police and the Public,* pp. 70–72.

46. John Webster, "Police Task and Time Study," *Journal of Criminal Law, Criminology, and Police Science,* **61** (1970): 94–100.

47. J. Robert Lilly, "What Are the Police Now Doing?" *Journal of Police Science and Administration,* **6** (1978): 51–60. See also Wilson, *Varieties of Police Behavior,* chap. 7; Egon Bittner, *The Function of the Police in Modern Society* (Chevy Chase, Md.: National Institute of Mental Health, 1970).

48. Robert C. Wadman and Robert K. Olson, *Community Wellness: A New Theory of Policing* (Washington, D.C.: Police Executive Research Forum, 1990). See also Mark H. Moore, "Problem-Solving and Community Policing," in *Crime and Justice: A Review of Research,* vol. 15, ed. M. Tonry and N. Morris (Chicago: University of Chicago Press, 1992), pp. 99–158; and Patrick V. Murphy, "Organizing for Community Policing," in *Issues in Policing: New Perspectives,* ed. John W. Bizzack (Lexington, Ky.: Autumn Press, 1992), pp. 113–128.

49. Gary W. Cordner and Robert C. Trojanowicz, "Patrol," in *What Works in Policing? Operations and Administration Examined,* ed. Gary W. Cordner and Donna C. Hale (Highland Heights, Ky., and Cincinnati, Ohio: Academy of Criminal Justice Sciences and Anderson, 1992), p. 11.

50. Jerome H. Skolnick and David H. Bayley, *Community Policing: Issues and Practices around the World* (Washington, D.C.: National Institute of Justice, May 1988). See also David Weisburd, Jerome McElroy, and Patricia Hardyman, "Challenges to Supervision in Community Policing: Observations on a Pilot Project," *American Journal of Police,* **7** (1988): 29–50; and Jerome E. McElroy, Colleen A. Cosgrove, and Susan Sadd, *CPOP, The Research: An Evaluative Study of the New York City Community Patrol Officer Program* (New York: Vera Institute of Justice, 1990).

51. Freda Adler, *Nations Not Obsessed with Crime* (Littleton, Colo.: Fred B. Rothman, 1983), p. 101.

52. Skolnick and Bayley, *Community Policing,* p. 8.

53. David Weisburd, Jerome McElroy, and Patricia Hardyman, "Challenges to Supervision in Community Policing: Observations on a Pilot Project," *American Journal of Police,* **7** (1988): 29–50.

54. David Weisburd and Jerome E. McElroy, "Enacting the CPO Role: Findings from the New York City Pilot Program in Community Policing," in *Community Policing: Rhetoric or Reality?,* ed. Jack R. Greene

and Stephen D. Mastrofski (New York: Praeger, 1988), pp. 89–101. For a discussion of communication between police chiefs and their constituents, see William A. Geller, ed., *Police Leadership in America: Crisis and Opportunity* (New York: Praeger, 1985). For a discussion of the use of consumer surveys to evaluate the job that police are doing, see Frank F. Furstenberg, Jr., and Charles F. Wellford, "Calling the Police: The Evaluation of Police Service," *Law and Society Review,* **7** (1973): 393–406. For the importance of soliciting and evaluating citizen requirements, problems, and expectations of police, see R. M. Patterson, Jr., and Nancy K. Grant, "Community Mapping: Rationale and Considerations for Implementation," *Journal of Police Science and Administration,* **16** (1988): 136–143.

55. William J. Bopp, *Police Personnel Administration* (Boston: Holbrook, 1974), pp. 48–51.

56. Lawrence W. Sherman, Catherine H. Milton, and Thomas V. Kelly, *Team Policing: Seven Case Studies* (Washington, D.C.: Police Foundation, 1973).

57. John P. Kenney, *Police Administration* (Springfield, Ill.: Charles C. Thomas, 1972).

58. Herman Goldstein, *Problem-Oriented Policing* (New York: McGraw-Hill, 1990), pp. 14–31.

59. Gard W. Cordner, "The Baltimore County Citizen-Oriented Police Enforcement (COPE) Project: Final Evaluation," paper presented at the American Society of Criminology, San Diego, 1985.

60. Hubert Williams and Antony M. Pate, "Returning to First Principles: Reducing the Fear of Crime in Newark," *Crime and Delinquency,* **33** (1987): 53–70.

61. *The Effects of Police Fear Reduction Studies: A Summary of Findings from Houston and Newark* (Washington, D.C.: Police Foundation, 1986); *The Newark Foot Patrol Experiment* (Washington, D.C.: Police Foundation, 1981); Lee P. Brown and Mary Ann Wycoff, "Policing Houston: Reducing Fear and Improving Service," *Crime and Delinquency,* **33** (1987): 71–89; Frans Willem Winkel, "The Police and Reducing Fear of Crime: A Comparison of the Crime-Centered and the Quality of Life Approaches," *Police Studies,* **11** (1988): 183–189.

62. George L. Kelling, *What Works—Research and the Police, Crime File Study Guide,* for U.S. Department of Justice, National Institute of Justice (Washington, D.C.: U.S. Government Printing Office, 1988); George L. Kelling, Antony Pate, Duane Dieckman, and Charles E. Brown, *The Kansas City Preventive Patrol Experiment: A Summary Report* (Washington, D.C.: Police Foundation, 1974). See also David F. Greenberg, Ronald C. Kessler, and Colin Loftin, "The Effect of Police Employment on Crime," *Criminology,* **21** (1983): 375–394; Charles R. Wellford, "Crime and the Police: A Multivariate Analysis," *Criminology,* **12** (1974): 195–213; Craig Uchida and Robert Goldberg, *Police Employment and Expenditure Trends,* for U.S. Department of Justice, Bureau of Justice Statistics (Washington, D.C.: U.S. Government Printing Office, 1986); and Colin Loftin and David

McDowall, "The Police, Crime, and Economic Theory: An Assessment," *American Sociological Review*, **47** (1982): 393–401.

63. Lawrence W. Sherman, *Repeat Calls to Police in Minneapolis* (Washington, D.C.: Crime Control Institute, 1987).

64. Personal communication from David Weisburd. See also David Weisburd, Lisa Maher, Lawrence Sherman, Michael Buerger, Ellen Cohn, and Anthony Petrosino, "Contrasting Crime-General and Crime-Specific Theory: The Case of Hot Spots in Crime," paper presented to the American Sociological Association, San Francisco, 1989.

65. For recent surveys of attitudes of minority-group members toward the police, see James R. Davis, "A Comparison of Attitudes toward the New York City Police," *Journal of Police Science and Administration*, **17** (1990): 233–243; and Komanduri S. Murty, Julian B. Roebuck, and Joann D. Smith, "The Image of the Police in Black Atlanta Communities," *Journal of Police Science and Administration*, **17** (1990): 250–257.

66. See Earl M. Sweeney, *The Public and the Police: A Partnership in Protection* (Springfield, Ill.: Charles C. Thomas, 1982); and Louis A. Radelet, *The Police and the Community* (New York: Macmillan, 1986).

67. Thomas A. Johnson, Gordon E. Misner, and Lee P. Brown, *The Police and Society: An Environment for Collaboration and Confrontation* (Englewood Cliffs, N.J.: Prentice-Hall, 1981). See also Fred I. Klyman and Joanna Kruckenberg, "A National Survey of Police-Community Relations Units," *Journal of Police Science and Administration*, **7** (1979): 72–79. For the importance of municipal police organization to police–community relations, see Thomas A. Johnson, *A Study of Police Resistance to Police Community Relations in a Municipal Police Department* (Ann Arbor, Mich.: University Microfilms, 1971).

68. See Richard S. Allinson, "LEAA's Impact on Criminal Justice: A Review of the Literature," *Criminal Justice Abstracts*, **11** (1979): 608–648.

69. *Tennessee v. Garner*, 471 U.S. 887 (1985).

70. James J. Fyfe, "Police Use of Deadly Force: Research and Reform," *Justice Quarterly*, **5** (1988): 165–205.

71. With the exception of, e.g., Gerald D. Robin, "Justifiable Homicide by Police Officers," *Journal of Criminal Law, Criminology, and Police Science*, **54** (1963): 225–231, and American Civil Liberties Union, *Police Power vs. Citizens' Rights* (New York: American Civil Liberties Union, 1966).

72. John S. Goldkamp, "Minorities as Victims of Police Shootings: Interpretations of Racial Disproportionality and Police Use of Deadly Force," *Justice System Journal*, **2** (1976): 169–183. For the association between economic inequality and police-caused homicides, see Johnathan R. Sorensen, James W. Marquart, and Deon E. Brock, "Factors Related to Killings of Felons By Police Officers: A Test of the Community Violence and Conflict Hypothesis," *Justice Quarterly*, **10** (1993): 417–440.

73. Catherine Milton, J. W. Halleck, J. Lardner, and G. L. Abrecht, *Police Use of Deadly Force* (Washington, D.C.: Police Foundation, 1977).

74. Betty Jenkins and Adrienne Faison, *An Analysis of 248 Persons Killed by New York City Policemen* (New York: Metropolitan Applied Research Center, 1974).

75. Paul Takagi, "Death by Police Intervention," in *A Community Concern: Police Use of Deadly Force*, ed. R. N. Brenner and M. Kravitz (Washington, D.C.: U.S. Government Printing Office, 1979), p. 34.

76. James J. Fyfe, "Race and Extreme Police-Citizen Violence," in *Race, Crime, and Criminal Justice*, ed. R. L. McNeely and C. E. Pope (Beverly Hills, Calif.: Sage, 1981), pp. 89–108. See also Arnold Binder and Peter Scharf, "Deadly Force in Law Enforcement," *Crime and Delinquency*, **28** (1982): 1–23; and Reiss, *The Police and the Public*.

77. Lawrence W. Sherman, *Citizens Killed by Big City Police, 1970–1984* (Washington, D.C.: Crime Control Institute, Crime Control Research Corporation, 1986).

78. Anthony Desletano et al., "NJ Cop Innocent: Slain Teen's Mom Falters after Verdict," *Newsday*, July 12, 1992, p. 3; John Kifner, "Evidence Shows Youth's Hands Up when Teaneck Officer Killed Him," *New York Times*, Aug. 2, 1990, p. 1.

79. The four officers whom a videotape showed beating the black driver were acquitted. Thereupon the Los Angeles riots occurred, resulting in over 50 deaths and the destruction of nearly $1 billion worth of property. See Carl E. Pope and Lee E. Ross, "Race, Crime and Justice: The Aftermath of Rodney King," *Criminologist*, **17** (1992): 1–10.

80. Jerry Gray, "In Police Brutality Case, One Videotape but Two Ways to View It," *New York Times*, Dec. 13, 1991, p. B7. A jury subsequently found the police officers not guilty of official misconduct; see "Videotape Discounted in Beating," *New York Times*, Feb. 20, 1993, p. A25. But two of these officers were subsequently found guilty in federal court of having abused King's constitutional rights. In August 1993, King himself was again arrested on a drunk-driving charge, having smashed his car into a wall while under the influence of alcohol.

81. U.N. General Assembly Resolution 34/169, Dec. 17, 1979. On the difficulties of research on police violence, see Jeffrey Ian Ross, "The Outcomes of Public Violence: A Neglected Research Agenda," *Police Studies*, **15** (1992): 1–12.

82. Cecil L. Willis and Richard H. Wells, "The Police and Child Abuse: An Analysis of Police Decisions to Report Illegal Behavior," *Criminology*, **26** (1988): 695–716; John R. Hepburn, "Race and the Decision to Arrest: An Analysis of Warrants Issued," *Journal of Research in Crime and Delinquency*, **15** (1978): 54; Douglas A. Smith and Christy A. Visher, "Street-Level Justice: Situational Determinants of Police Arrest Decisions," *Social Problems*, **29** (1981): 167–177; Dale Dannefer and Russell K. Schutt, "Race

and Juvenile Justice Processing in Court and Police Agencies," *American Journal of Sociology*, **87** (1982): 1113–1132.

83. Carl Werthman and Irving Piliavin, "Gang Members and the Police," in *The Police: Six Sociological Essays*, ed. David Bordua (New York: Wiley, 1967), pp. 75–83.

84. Dennis D. Powell, "Race, Rank, and Police Discretion," *Journal of Police Science and Administration*, **9** (1981): 383–389.

85. Douglas Smith and Jody Klein, "Police Control of Interpersonal Disputes," *Social Problems*, **21** (1984): 468–481; Richard C. Hollinger, "Race, Occupational Status, and Pro-Active Police Arrest for Drinking and Driving," *Journal of Criminal Justice*, **12** (1984): 173–183; Douglas A. Smith, Christy A. Visher, and Laura A. Davidson, "Equity and Discretionary Justice: The Influence of Race on Police Arrest Decisions," *Journal of Criminal Law and Criminology*, **75** (1984): 234–249; Donald Black, "The Social Organization of Arrest," *Stanford Law Review*, **23** (1971): 1087–1098; Alfred Blumstein, "On the Racial Disproportionality of United States' Prison Populations," *Journal of Criminal Law and Criminology*, **73** (1982): 1259–1281; Richard J. Lundman, Richard E. Sykes, and John P. Clark, "Police Control of Juveniles: A Replication," *Journal of Research in Crime and Delinquency*, **15** (1978): 74–91.

86. Christy A. Visher, "Gender, Police Arrest Decisions, and Notions of Chivalry," *Criminology*, **21** (1983): 5–28.

87. Marvin D. Krohn, James P. Curry, and Shirley Nelson-Kilger, "Is Chivalry Dead?: An Analysis of Changes in Police Dispositions of Males and Females," *Criminology*, **21** (1983): 417–437. See also Imogene L. Moyer, "Police/Citizen Encounter: Issues of Chivalry, Gender and Race," in *The Changing Roles of Women in the Criminal Justice System*, ed. Moyer (Prospect Park, Ill.: Waveland, 1992), pp. 69–80.

88. Commission to Investigate Allegations of Police Corruption and the City's Anticorruption Procedures (New York City; Whitman Knapp, chairman), *Commission Report* (1972); *Knapp Commission Report on Police Corruption* (New York: Braziller, 1973).

89. Herman Goldstein, *Police Corruption: A Perspective on Its Nature and Control* (Washington, D.C.: Police Foundation, 1975); Lawrence Sherman, *Police Corruption: A Sociological Perspective* (Garden City, N.Y.: Doubleday, 1974); Ellwyn Stoddard, "Blue Coat Crime," in *Thinking about Police: Contemporary Readings*, ed. Carl Klockars (New York: McGraw-Hill, 1983), pp. 338–349; Michael Johnston, *Political Corruption and Public Policy in America* (Monterey, Calif.: Brooks/Cole, 1982), p. 75.

90. Robert J. McCormack, "Confronting Police Corruption: Organizational Initiatives for Internal Control," in *Managing Police Corruption: International Perspectives*, ed. Richard H. Ward and Robert McCormack (Chicago: Office of International Crim-

inal Justice, University of Illinois at Chicago, 1987), pp. 151–165.

91. Cole, *The American System of Criminal Justice*, p. 277.

92. Maria Newman, "Report Details Variations in Police Review Boards," *New York Times*, Jan. 10, 1993, p. 26. On the question of the relationship between the type of civilian oversight and community satisfaction, see Samuel Walker and Vic Bumphus, *A National Survey of Civilian Oversight of the Police* (Omaha: University of Nebraska at Omaha, 1991). See also Andrew J. Goldsmith, *Complaints against the Police* (Oxford, England: Clarendon, 1991).

93. William Westley, *Violence and the Police* (Cambridge, Mass.: M.I.T. Press, 1970); Paul Chevigny, *Police Power: Police Abuses in New York City* (New York: Pantheon, 1969); Sherman, *Police Corruption: A Sociological Perspective*.

94. Jack Aylward, "Psychological Testing and Police Selection," *Journal of Police Science and Administration*, **13** (1985): 201–210.

95. David L. Carter, Allen D. Sapp, and Darrell W. Stephens, *The State of Police Education: Policy Direction for the 21st Century* (Washington, D.C.: Police Executive Research Forum, 1989), p. 38. See also James J. Fyfe, "Police Personnel Practices," *Baseline Data Reports* (Washington, D.C.: International City Management Association), **15**(1) (1983). For a discussion of a New York City Police Department program (the Police Cadet Corps) designed to attract college students to careers as police officers, see Antony M. Pate and Edwin E. Hamilton, *The New York City Police Cadet Corps: Final Evaluation Report* (Washington, D.C.: Police Foundation, 1991).

96. Carter et al., *The State of Police Education*. See also Lee H. Bowker, "A Theory of Educational Needs of Law Enforcement Officers," *Journal of Contemporary Criminal Justice*, **1** (1980): 17–24. For a discussion of the best type of college education for law enforcement officers, see Lawrence W. Sherman and Warren Bennis, "Higher Education for Police Officers: The Central Issues," *Police Chief*, **44** (August 1977): 32. See also Lawrence Sherman et al., *The Quality of Police Education* (San Francisco: Jossey-Bass, 1978).

97. Elizabeth Burbeck and Adrian Furnham, "Police Officer Selection: A Critical Review of the Literature," *Journal of Police Science and Administration*, **13** (1985): 58–69.

98. Samuel Walker, *The Police in America*, 2d ed. (New York: McGraw-Hill, 1992), p. 313.

99. Candice McCoy, "Affirmative Action in Police Organizations: Checklist for Supporting a Compelling State Interest," *Criminal Law Bulletin*, **20** (1984): 245–254; Timothy Stroup, "Affirmative Action and the Police," in *Police Ethics: Hard Choices in Law Enforcement*, ed. W. C. Heffernan and Timothy Stroup (New York: John Jay, 1985). See also Isaac C. Hunt, Jr., and Bernard Cohen, *Minority Recruiting in the New York City Police Department* (New York: Rand Institute, 1971).

100. Jack L. Kuykendall and David E. Burns, "The Black

Police Officer: An Historical Perspective," *Journal of Contemporary Criminal Justice,* **1** (1986): 4–12.

101. Fyfe, "Police Personnel Practices."

102. Nicholas Alex, *Black in Blue: A Study of the Negro Policeman* (New York: Appleton-Century-Crofts, 1969).

103. Bruce L. Berg, Edmond J. True, and Marc G. Gertz, "Police, Riots, and Alienation," *Journal of Police Science and Administration,* **12** (1984): 186–190.

104. See U.S. Commission on Civil Rights, *Who Is Guarding the Guardians?: A Report on Police Practices* (Washington, D.C.: U.S. Government Printing Office, 1981).

105. Fyfe, "Police Personnel Practices."

106. Data supplied by the Police Foundation.

107. Ellen Hochstedler, "Impediments to Hiring Minorities in Public Police Agencies," *Journal of Police Science and Administration,* **12** (1984): 227–240.

108. David E. Pitt, "Racial Tensions in Police Ranks Work Three Ways Now," *New York Times,* Feb. 19, 1989, p. E6.

109. Daniel J. Bell, "Policewomen: Myths and Reality," *Journal of Police Science and Administration,* **10** (1982): 112–120. On the history of women in policing, see Jenis Appier, "Preventive Justice: The Campaign for Women Police, 1910–1940," *Women and Criminal Justice,* **4** (1992): 3–36.

110. Samuel S. Janus, Cynthia Janus, Leslie K. Lord, and Thomas Power, "Women in Police Work—Annie Oakley or Little Orphan Annie?" *Police Studies,* **11** (1988): 124–127; Susan E. Martin, *Women on the Move?: A Report on the Status of Women in Policing* (Washington, D.C.: Police Foundation, 1989).

111. United Nations report, A/Conf. 121/17, July 1, 1985, with a comprehensive analysis of women in law enforcement by Edith Flynn, who served as U.N. consultant on the topic.

112. Kenneth W. Kerber, Steven M. Andes, and Michele B. Mittler, "Citizen Attitudes Regarding the Competence of Female Police Officers," *Journal of Police Science and Administration,* **5** (1977): 337–347. On the variegated forms of gender discrimination, see Inger J. Sagatun, "Gender Discrimination in Criminal Justice: Relevant Law and Future Trends," *Women and Criminal Justice,* **2** (1990): 63–81. For comparative discussion, see M. Natarajan, "A Comparative Analysis of Women Police in India," *International Journal of Comparative and Applied Criminal Justice* (1994).

113. Merry Morash and Jack Greene, "Evaluating Women on Patrol: A Critique of Contemporary Wisdom," *Evaluation Review,* **10** (1986): 230–255. A study of patrol teams in New York City found policewomen less likely to injure citizens or to be injured; see Sean Grennan, "Findings on the Role of Officer Gender in Violent Encounters with Citizens," *Journal of Police Science and Administration,* **15** (1988): 78–85. A Texas and Oklahoma study found arrest rates of male and female officers almost alike; see James A. Davis, "Perspectives of Policewomen in Texas and Oklahoma," *Journal of Police Science and*

Administration, **12** (1984): 395–403. See also Robert J. Homant and Daniel B. Kennedy, "Police Perceptions of Spouse Abuse: A Comparison of Male and Female Officers," *Journal of Criminal Justice,* **13** (1985): 29–47; Michael T. Charles, "Women in Policing: The Physical Aspects," *Journal of Police Science and Administration,* **10** (1982): 194–205; James A. Davis, "Perspectives of Policewomen in Texas and Oklahoma," *Journal of Criminal Justice,* **13** (1985): 49–64; and Peter Bloch and Deborah Anderson, *Police Women on Patrol: Final Report* (Washington, D.C.: Urban Institute, 1974).

114. Sally Gross, "Women Becoming Cops: Developmental Issues and Solutions," *Police Chief,* **51** (January 1984): 32–35.

115. Michael K. Brown, *Working the Street* (New York: Russell Sage, 1981).

116. William A. Westley, *Violence and the Police: A Sociological Study of Law, Custom, and Morality* (Cambridge, Mass.: M.I.T. Press, 1970), p. 226.

117. Ibid.

118. Arthur Niederhoffer, *Behind the Shield: The Police in Urban Society* (Garden City, N.Y.: Doubleday, 1967); Richard Lundman, *Police and Policing* (New York: Holt, Rinehart & Winston, 1980); Jerome H. Skolnick, *Justice without Trial* (New York: Wiley, 1966); John P. Crank, Robert M. Regoli, Eric D. Poole, and Robert G. Culbertson, "Cynicism among Police Chiefs," *Justice Quarterly,* **3** (1986): 343–352. For different "types" of officers, see William F. Walsh, "Patrol Officer Arrest Rates: A Study of the Social Organization of Police Work," *Justice Quarterly,* **3** (1986): 271–290.

119. Some people believe police work attracts individuals with these characteristics. See Milton Rokeach, Martin Miller, and John Snyder, "The Value Gap between Police and Policed," *Journal of Social Research,* **27** (1971): 155–171; and James Teevan and Bernard Dolnick, "The Values of the Police: A Reconsideration and Interpretation," *Journal of Police Science and Administration,* **1** (1973): 366–369.

120. George Kirkham, "A Professor's Street Lessons," in *Order under Law,* ed. R. Culbertson and M. Tezak (Prospect Heights, Ill.: Waveland, 1981), p. 81.

121. Niederhoffer, *Behind the Shield.* For changes over time attributed to occupational socialization, see Jesse L. Maghan, "The 21st-Century Cop: Police Recruit Perceptions as a Function of Occupational Socialization," Ph.D. dissertation, City University of New York, 1988.

122. John Blackmore, "Are Police Allowed to Have Problems of Their Own?" *Police Magazine,* **1** (1978): 47–55. See also Clement Mihanovich, "The Blue Pressure Cooker," *Police Chief,* **47** (February 1980): 20–21; Mary Hageman, "Occupational Stress and Marital and Family Relationships," *Journal of Police Science and Administration,* **6** (1978): 402–416; Francis T. Cullen, Terrence Lemming, Bruce G. Link, and John F. Wozniak, "The Impact of Social Supports on Police Stress," *Criminology,* **23** (1985): 503–522; W.

Clinton Terry III, "Police Stress: The Empirical Evidence," *Journal of Police Science and Administration,* **9** (1981): 61–75; T. E. Malloy and G. L. Mays, "The Police Stress Hypothesis: A Critical Evaluation," *Criminal Justice and Behavior,* **11** (1984): 197–226; B. A. Vulcano, G. E. Barnes, and L. J. Breen, "The Prevalence and Predictors of Psychosomatic Symptoms and Conditions among Police Officers," *Psychosomatic Medicine,* **45** (1983): 277–293; R. C. Trojanowicz, *The Environment of the First-Line Police Supervisor* (Englewood Cliffs, N.J.: Prentice-Hall, 1980); W. Clinton Terry III, "Police Stress as a Professional Self-Image," *Journal of Criminal Justice,* **13** (1985): 501–512; Katherine W. Ellison and John L. Genz, *Stress and the Police Officer* (Springfield, Ill.: Charles C. Thomas, 1983); William H. Kroes, *Society's Victims—The Police,* 2d ed. (Springfield, Ill.: Charles C. Thomas, 1985). An entire organization devoted to the study of police stress (the International Law Enforcement Stress Association) has been founded; it publishes its own journal, *Police Stress.*

123. Jack R. Greene, "Police Officer Job Satisfaction and Community Perceptions: Implications for Community-Oriented Policing," *Journal of Research in Crime and Delinquency,* **26** (1989): 168–183.

17
The Nature and Functioning of Courts

KEY TERMS
arraignment
certiorari, writ of
challenges for cause
defense counsel
deterrence
habeas corpus
indictment
information
just deserts
motions
peremptory challenges
plead
prosecutor
rehabilitation
retribution
selective incapacitation
voir dire

"I got arraigned before the judge and got ten thousand dollars bail, and then I stayed in jail ever since then."

"Now, did you intend to plead not guilty to this charge?"

"Yes, I was gonna plead not guilty."

"So you were arraigned: they gave you a bond you can't make; so you're back in jail."

"Right."

"What happens then?"

"I just stayed there and kept going back and forth to court."

"What did you go to court for?"

"For the same charge."

"What was happening?"

"The lawyer didn't seem to be doing nothin. Every time I'd go there he would—he wouldn't, he wasn't sayin nothin."

"He was a public defender?"

"Yes."

"Did you appear in circuit court? Did you have the probable cause hearing?"

"Naw, he said it's better not to have it."

"So you were bound over?"

"Yes. To high court."

"So you had a different public defender in superior court?"

"Yes, I had a different one there."

"Now, when was the first time you met him?"

"It was about three months."

"You were taken over to superior court, and you met the public defender?"

"Yes. See, I had started off with Moore; then they switched me to some other guy. And none was takin interest in—"

"Did any of them come visit you in jail?"

"Naw."

"The only time you saw them was in the bullpen or around court?"

"Yes."

"Did you eventually plead guilty?"

"Yes, he told me, 'With your record and stuff, you'd better plead guilty.'"

"Who told you that?"

"The lawyer."[1]

Courts of law are entrusted with the responsibility for resolving controversies arising under civil law and determining the guilt or innocence of a party charged with the violation of a criminal law. To an ordinary citizen charged with a crime, the experience of going to court can be confusing, frightening, and frustrating. Courts follow legal rules and procedures that only lawyers and judges fully understand. The court system is intricate and often complex. Defendants are frightened because they experience a loss of control over their own destiny. The experience is frustrating because the court system does not always function as effectively as it should. In many jurisdictions delay is inevitable. Bargains and deals made by prosecutor and defense counsel are common. Bias, discrimination, and arbitrariness are just part of the system.

In this chapter we will examine the structure, function, rules, and procedures of courts. We will review their origins, the various types of court systems, the trial court process, and issues relating to the sentencing of convicted offenders.

THE ORIGINS OF COURTS

The word "court" is derived from the Latin of classical Rome (a contraction of *co*, meaning together, and *hortus*, meaning garden or yard). Later, emperors, kings, dukes, and other nobles had estates or castles that were referred to as "courts"—the court of the king of England, the court of the queen of Spain, and so on. Important business was conducted at the court, including the business of resolving disputes and adjudging the guilt or innocence of persons accused of crime.

The earliest trial methods seem very strange to us today. In trial by combat, for example, the accuser and the accused, or their hired professional fighters, fought on foot or on horseback and in armor until God picked the winner. Trial was a game at court, very much like games played on basketball courts and tennis courts. What all these court games have in common is the fact that they are played in established public places, in accordance with established rules, and are judged by umpires or judges in the presence of the public. A nineteenth-century English cartoonist captured the spirit of an Anglo-American trial court proceeding when he depicted it as if it were a game of tennis. Opposing counsel bounce their arguments back and forth in front of the judge, who makes sure that the game is being played according to the rules. When the game is over, he pronounces the winner.

An American jurist and philosopher, Jerome Frank, has questioned the American "game" approach to the resolution of disputes in court.[2] Such an approach encourages advocates for the people or state (prosecutors) and for the defendant (defense counsel) to adopt and argue extreme positions. A judge is thus required to mediate between two inconsistent and often incompatible interpretations of fact and law. Is the truth really discovered when opposing counsel for the prosecution and defense argue it out, sometimes overstepping the bounds of propriety? Defenders of Anglo-American trial theory hold that a contest between combatants in open court will indeed resolve the issues fairly.

Some changes have been made in criminal procedure over the centuries, but the basic idea still holds: Anglo-American criminal trials are a game played by competitors; the players are combatants defending opposing positions, they are adversaries, and it is at court that the contest is fought out.

THE U.S. COURT SYSTEM

The basic premises of the Anglo-American criminal process were well established in the fifteenth and sixteenth centuries and were ready to be imported into the North American colonies in the seventeenth century. The American colonies followed the British common law model. The courts of the colonies were common law courts, applying the common law of England with certain limitations that contributed to the drive for independence. When independence was declared, these courts became common law courts of the several states, subject only to the laws of the state legislatures. They still are: we have 50 state court systems in the United States.

The courts of these 50 jurisdictions are common law courts, the heirs of the common law of England as of 1776, applying the law in the common law fashion, as modified and amplified by state legislatures. There is, however, one big difference. In forming the United States, the original colonies granted the federal government the right to make and enforce, through federal courts, those laws that Congress was empowered to make. Consequently, we have two legal systems, one implemented by the state courts and another implemented by the federal courts.

State Courts

Most states have three distinct levels of courts of law: courts of limited or special jurisdiction, courts of general jurisdiction, and appellate courts (see Figure 17.1).

Courts of Limited or Special Jurisdiction

Courts of limited jurisdiction are limited by law as to the kinds of cases they can hear. Every

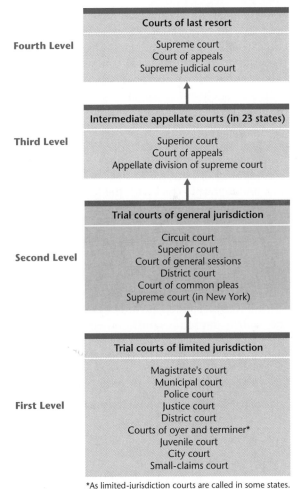

*As limited-jurisdiction courts are called in some states.

FIGURE 17.1 State court systems

Source: Adapted from Abraham S. Blumberg, *Criminal Justice: Issues and Ironies* (New York: New Viewpoints, 1979), p.150.

town or city is likely to have a court with a justice of the peace, magistrate, or judge, not necessarily trained in law, who handles minor criminal cases (misdemeanors or violations), less serious civil suits (involving small sums of money), traffic and parking violations, and health law violations. These courts are called municipal courts, justice of the peace courts, and magistrate's courts. Courts of special jurisdiction include family courts, juvenile courts, and probate courts (which deal with estate matters).

Courts of General Jurisdiction

At the next state level are the courts of general jurisdiction. These are a state's major trial courts. They have regular jurisdiction over all cases and controversies involving civil law and criminal law. Courts of general jurisdiction are county courts or, in less populous states, courts of a region that includes several counties. These are called superior courts or district courts. The judges of such courts are law school graduates, often with extensive experience at the bar. They are elected or appointed. In criminal cases, the law grants a defendant the right to a jury trial. When a defendant chooses a jury trial, the court is composed of a judge, to deal with matters of law, and a jury, to deal with the facts of the case and to apply to them the law as laid down by the judge.

Appellate Courts

All states have developed elaborate procedures of appeal for parties who are unsuccessful at trial. In some states the only appellate court is the state's supreme court; others provide an intermediate court of appeals. A person convicted of a crime has the right to appeal to an appellate court and ultimately to the court of last resort, the state supreme court, whenever the trial court is alleged to have erred on a point of law.

Federal Courts

The primary function of the federal courts is to apply and enforce all federal laws created by Congress. These statutes include a large body of federal criminal laws, which range from violations of the Migratory Bird Act to treason and piracy. Most of the federal criminal laws can be found in Title 18 of the U.S. Code. The federal courts have a second and perhaps even more important function: they are continually called upon to test the constitutionality of federal and state legislation and of court decisions.[3] For example, can a state pass and enforce a statute making it a criminal offense for black and white citizens to intermarry? In *Loving v. Virginia* (1967) the Supreme Court of the United States ruled no.[4] The states cannot create such a crime because it violates the equal protection clause of the Fourteenth Amendment to the U.S. Constitution.

In other words, the Supreme Court (a federal court) has the power to hold as a matter of law that a state cannot enact a statute that violates the U.S. Constitution. Consider another example: Can a state court receive in evidence at trial an object seized by state or local law enforcement officers in violation of the Fourth Amendment to the U.S. Constitution, which protects citizens against unreasonable searches and seizures? The Supreme Court ruled that doing so would be a violation of the due process guarantee of the Fourteenth Amendment, which protects all people in the United States.[5] Thus federal courts often ensure that citizens are afforded the rights that the U.S. Constitution guarantees them. And just as in the state systems, there are several levels of federal courts.

Federal Magistrates

At the lowest level of jurisdiction are the federal magistrates, formerly called United States commissioners. The magistrates not only have trial jurisdiction over minor federal offenses but also have the important right to issue warrants, such as arrest warrants.

United States District Courts

The trial courts in the federal system, called United States district courts, have both civil and criminal jurisdiction. There are 94 federal district courts, including those in Guam, the Virgin Islands, the northern Marianas, and Puerto Rico. Every state has at least one such court, and the populous states have more than one. A total of 576 presidentially appointed judges sit in these courts.

United States Circuit Courts of Appeals

An appeal of a conviction in a federal district court is heard by a United States Circuit Court of Appeals. There are 13 appeals courts in the country: one in each of 11 areas (circuits) of the country plus one in the District of Columbia and another, also in Washington, D.C., called the Federal Circuit. It handles appeals that originate anywhere in the country when they pertain to such matters as patents and copyrights, some tax disputes, and suits against the federal government. There are 156 federal appeals court judges.

The original designation of states included within the federal circuits was made when most of the business of the federal courts was in the populous East and in the Midwest (Figure 17.2). With shifts in population to the West Coast, the Ninth Circuit, which covers a vast area, now has more business than any of the other courts.

The Supreme Court of the United States

The Supreme Court of the United States occupies a unique position in our system of government. It is the highest level of the third branch of government, the judiciary, and occupies a place of honor not equaled in any other country. Its chief justice is not just the chief justice of the Supreme Court but the chief justice of the United States. The chief justice and the eight associate justices are appointed by the president of the United States, with the advice and consent of the Senate.

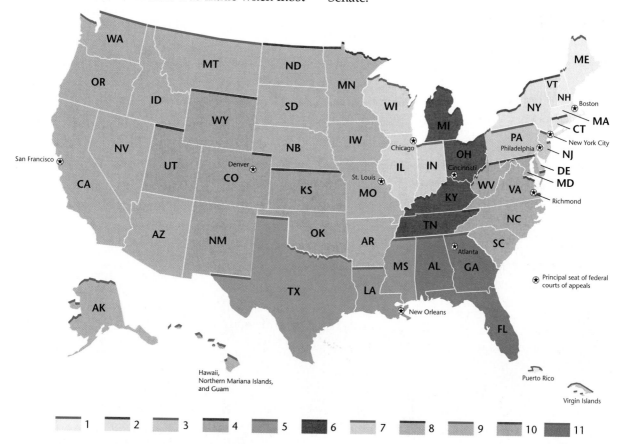

FIGURE 17.2 United States Circuit Court of Appeals

WINDOW TO THE WORLD
Judging at the World Level

In the nearly 50 years of its existence, the International Court of Justice—commonly known as the World Court—has handed down more than 115 decisions in cases and advisory proceedings. Established by the Charter of the United Nations (Article 92) of June 26, 1945, the International Court of Justice hears cases ranging from the disposition of a Belgian-Canadian electricity franchise in Barcelona to United States–Nicaraguan relations.

All member states of the United Nations are automatically parties to the World Court, but states seeking to litigate do not need to be U.N. members if they have accepted the court's jurisdiction in general or for a particular case. The World Court is able to resolve conflicts only when the parties involved agree to abide by its decisions. Its 15 judges are elected by the General Assembly of the United Nations and the Security Council.

The Problem of International Crime

The biggest shortcoming of the World Court, in the view of many political leaders and scholars, is that it has no power, or jurisdiction, to try persons charged with crimes under international law, such as war crimes. At the end of World War II two international tribunals tried German and Japanese war criminals, but these were temporary courts. Even the war crimes tribunal established in 1993 by the U.N. Security Council to deal with war crimes committed in the former Yugoslavia is only a temporary court.[1,2]

However, after several decades of effort, the International Law Commission, a United Nations body, has completed the draft of a statute setting up a permanent international criminal court. The statute was debated by the General Assembly in its 1993 session, but final action was not taken.[3]

One significant problem remains: Who enforces international court rulings—and how? How can indicted international criminals be brought to justice? One way is through the stigma of indictment. An indictment is a potent tool, since it is an accusation based on evidence that will likely convict the person in a court of law. In the ordinary course of events, an indictment is followed by an arrest warrant. In the case of international crimes, such a warrant could be issued to be executed anywhere in the world, therefore effectively confining the indicted person to the territory under his or her control.[4]

Sources
1. Thomas M. Franck, *Judging the World Court: A Twentieth Century Fund Paper* (New York: Priority Press, 1986).
2. Resolution of the U.N. Security Council, S/RES/808, Feb. 22, 1993.
3. International Law Commission, "Revised Report of the Working Group on the Draft Statute for an International Criminal Court," A/CN.4/L.490, July 19, 1993, and "Addendum, Draft Statute for an International Tribunal and Commentaries Thereto," A/CN.4/L.490/Add. 1, July 19, 1993.
4. Gerhard O. W. Mueller, "Two Enforcement Models for International Criminal Justice," in *Études en L'Honneur de Jean Graven* (Geneva: Libraire de l'Université, 1969), pp. 106–115.

Questions for Discussion
1. What would public order in the United States be like if American courts operated as the existing World Court does—if conflicts could be resolved only when the parties involved in a case agreed to abide by the court's decision?
2. How would an international criminal court deal with accused war criminals who are still engaged in combat?

The International Court of Justice in session at the Hague.

The nine justices of the United States Supreme Court, which in the 1994 term included two women, Sandra Day O'Connor and Ruth Bader Ginsburg. Standing from left, Justices Thomas, Kennedy, Souter, and Ginsburg. Seated, Justices O'Connor and Blackmun, Chief Justice Rehnquist, Justices Stevens and Scalia.

The United States Supreme Court is the ultimate authority in interpreting the Constitution as it applies to both federal and state law; it also is the final authority in interpreting federal law. Thus, both federal and state cases may reach the Supreme Court.

Interaction between State Courts and Federal Courts

It is important not to view state and federal court systems as wholly independent or mutually exclusive. A legal controversy that arises in a state court may raise matters of federal law, such as constitutional questions. In such a case, a federal court may be asked to hear the case.

Suppose that on the tip of an anonymous informer, with no other corroborating evidence, a local magistrate issues a warrant authorizing the search of a college dormitory room for marijuana. Let us further suppose that a small bag of marijuana is found in the drawer of a desk that is used by two students. Both are arrested, tried in a local court, and convicted of the crime of possession of a controlled substance. Defense counsel claims that the search warrant was illegally issued, because it was not based on the legally required evidence showing probable cause that a

crime was committed. Therefore, the evidence, the marijuana, should never have been admitted in court. Let us suppose that the state trial judge does not agree with this defense.

Appeal and the Writ of Certiorari

The students decide to appeal their conviction, claiming that the trial judge committed a legal error by not excluding the evidence. Suppose that the state court of appeals (if there is one) rules against the students. They next appeal to the state supreme court. If the state supreme court rejects the argument as well, the next option is to appeal to the United States Supreme Court. The basis of this appeal is that the federal constitutional right to be free from search and seizure except on a warrant issued on the basis of probable cause (Fourth Amendment) was violated. This option is exercised by an application for a **writ of certiorari,** a document issued by a higher court (in this case the U.S. Supreme Court) directing a lower court (the state supreme court) to send to it the records of a case.

The Supreme Court may accept this case because it has established the rule that a search warrant issued on the basis of an unreliable informant's tip does not meet the reasonableness and probable-cause requirements of the Fourth

Amendment.[6] But the U.S. Supreme Court gets thousands of appeals and applications for writs of certiorari every year; it can consider only very few. Normally the Court chooses to review a case only if it involves a substantial unresolved constitutional question, particularly one on which the findings of the various federal courts of appeals have diverged.

Habeas Corpus

Having been denied a writ of certiorari by the United States Supreme Court, the students may then apply for a writ of **habeas corpus** at the federal district court. Historically, under the common law of England, a prisoner's detention could be tested by a judicial writ (command) to a jailer for an inquiry. Written in Latin, the writ contained the crucial words "habeas corpus," which mean "you have the body [person] of." The text of the writ concluded with a request to produce the prisoner before the reviewing judge and to explain by what lawful authority the prisoner is being detained.[7] Used throughout the history of Anglo-American law, such inquiries still determine whether the Constitution was violated during the trial that resulted in the conviction that led to the imprisonment.

In our hypothetical case, until 1976, the students could have applied to the federal district court for a writ of habeas corpus. But in that year the Supreme Court held that the writ was no longer available in Fourth Amendment search-and-seizure cases because the federal courts were so flooded with applications for the writ that they could not manage the caseload.[8] Whenever the alleged constitutional violation pertains to issues other than search and seizure, the writ is still available.

If the district court denies the writ of habeas corpus, the prisoner can appeal that decision to a U.S. circuit court of appeals. If that court does not overrule the district court, the prisoner can appeal again to the U.S. Supreme Court. Figure 17.3 depicts the entire process.

Lawyers in the Court System

In every criminal case an attorney represents the government, whether county, city, or state. That attorney is called a **prosecutor.** On the other side of the case is the lawyer who has been retained by the person charged with an offense or who has been assigned by the court if the defendant is

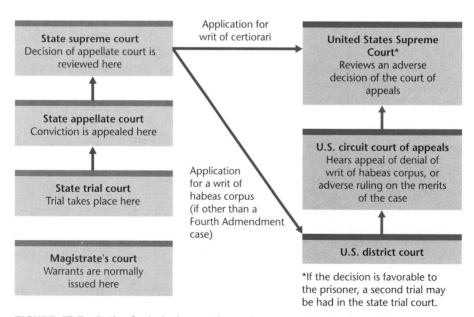

FIGURE 17.3 Path of criminal cases through state and federal appeals processes

If the decision is favorable to the prisoner, a second trial may be had in the state trial court.

Deputy District Attorney Janet Moore delivering a rebuttal during the Reginald Denny beating trial in Los Angeles, September 30, 1993.

indigent. That attorney is called the **defense counsel.**

Prosecutors and Their Duties

Prosecutors are government officials who represent the people of a particular jurisdiction. They may be appointed or elected. Prosecutors are responsible for some of the most important initial responses to crime. They screen suspects arrested by the police, decide whether or not to press charges, argue the case on behalf of the government, and often make recommendations regarding sentencing. More than 8000 state and local agencies are involved in prosecution. They include the offices of district attorney, city corporation counsel, and state attorney general. Federal crimes are prosecuted by United States Attorneys, who are appointed by the president.

Prosecutorial Discretion

Prosecutors can exercise a variety of options that have far-reaching effects on an individual's freedom, life, property, reputation, and well-being. This power is unmatched by that of any other official in the American criminal justice system. Prosecutors are relatively free to choose their causes, cases, and targets for prosecution.[9] They have complete discretion in three areas of pretrial decision making: (1) whether or not to file a criminal charge, (2) how to set the level of seriousness of the offense to be charged, and (3)

when to cease prosecution.[10] In most jurisdictions, prosecutors are empowered by statute to "prosecute for all offenses." As the legal scholar Abraham S. Goldstein has noted, however, this exclusive authority to prosecute does not confer an obligation to do so in every case.[11] Prosecutors have discretion in the way they handle cases.

Prosecutorial Roles

Prosecutors play a variety of functional and occupational roles, which are not necessarily identified by law. Abraham Blumberg has identified several such roles:

■ *Collection agent:* In smaller communities, prosecutors collect and dispense money to cover debts, such as family support payments, proceeds from bad checks, and debt arising from fraud.

■ *Dispenser of justice/power broker–fixer:* Prosecutors weigh the available penalties associated with certain charges and, by using their discretion, dispense justice. In political situations, they mediate between disputants by the use and threat of sanctions.

■ *Political enforcer:* A prosecutor may prosecute a case for reasons and purposes other than a desire to achieve a just conviction—perhaps for vengeance or notoriety, to deter certain conduct, or to damage a reputation.

■ *Overseer of police:* The prosecutor is also known to act as a magistrate, continually reviewing the work of the police.[12]

Defense Counsel

All persons accused of a crime for which jail or prison is the possible penalty have a right to counsel under the Sixth Amendment to the U.S. Constitution.[13] A defense attorney ensures that the legal rights of an accused person are fully protected at every stage in the criminal justice process. Defendants who can afford counsel retain an attorney of their choice or, very rarely, choose to represent themselves. An accused person who is unable to afford an attorney may be represented free of charge by counsel coming from any of three sources, depending on the jurisdiction:

■ *A public defender program:* Statewide and local public defenders belong to public or private nonprofit organizations that provide free legal counsel.

■ *An assigned-counsel system:* Judges appoint attorneys who are in private practice as they are needed.

■ *A contract system:* Contracts are awarded to bar associations, private law firms, or individual attorneys who agree to provide legal counsel on a regular basis.

THE ROLE OF THE TRIAL JUDGE

In discussing the criminal justice process, we noted the important role judges play during proceedings before trial. They grant release at various stages, preside over first appearances of arrested persons in court and over preliminary hearings, issue orders and rule on motions, accept plea bargains, impanel grand juries, and instruct juries in their tasks.

The role traditionally associated with a judge is that of a person who presides over trials.

Arraignment

A trial begins with the **arraignment,** a formal proceeding in open court at which the grand jury hands down its indictment. Not all states, how-

ever, require a grand-jury indictment to initiate prosecutions.

At the arraignment, in the presence of the defendant and the defense counsel, the person named in the **indictment** (accusation by the grand jury) or **information** (accusation by the prosecutor) is asked to **plead** to the charge. The defendant has two or sometimes three options:

■ The defendant may plead *guilty* to the charges contained in the various counts of the indictment, thereby admitting all the facts alleged to have occurred, as well as their legal implications. Under those circumstances no trial need take place. The trial judge need only make certain that the pleas have been advisedly taken and that the facts indeed support the guilt of the defendant. The judge may then accept the plea of guilty and sentence the offender.

■ The defendant may plead *not guilty,* thereby denying everything and putting on the prosecution the burden of proving beyond a reasonable doubt all the facts alleged in the indictment.

■ In most jurisdictions, the defendant may also plead *no contest,* or *nolo contendere,* with the approval of the prosecution and the court. By this plea the defendant admits criminal liability for the purposes of the immediate proceeding only. This procedure has the practical advantage of avoiding the implications of guilt in other proceedings (a civil suit for damages, for example).

Pretrial Motions

Counsel for either side, defense or prosecution, may make a multitude of **motions,** or official requests to the judge, at any appropriate moment from arrest until after the trial is over. The majority of such motions are made before trial; each requires a hearing and sometimes a separate minitrial. Among the many types of motions are the following:

■ A motion for a severance, by which a defendant claims that it would be prejudicial to his or her case to be tried together with other defendants charged in the indictment

■ A motion for a change of venue, which is made when pretrial publicity makes it impossible to get a fair trial in the county where the crime was committed

- A motion to quash the indictment on the grounds that the evidence presented is insufficient to establish probable cause
- A motion for a sanity hearing, which is made when the defendant claims that mental illness deprives him or her of legal responsibility
- A motion to suppress illegally obtained evidence
- A motion for discovery of evidence in the hands of the prosecution
- A motion to dismiss the case for want of adequate evidence or some other cause

Release Decisions

Once again the trial judge must decide whether to release the defendant, this time for the period between the arraignment and the main phase of the trial—a period that may last weeks. The decision has far-reaching consequences, summarized by the President's Commission on Law Enforcement and the Administration of Justice:

> The importance of this decision to any defendant is obvious. A released defendant is one who can live with and support his family, maintain his ties to his community, and busy himself with his own defense by searching for witnesses and evidence and by keeping close touch with his lawyer. An imprisoned defendant is subjected to the squalor, idleness, and possible criminalizing effect of jail. He may be confined for something he did not do; some jailed defendants are ultimately acquitted. He may be confined while presumed innocent only to be freed when found guilty; many jailed defendants, after they have been convicted, are placed on probation rather than imprisoned. The community also relies on the magistrate for protection when he makes his decision about releasing a defendant. If a released defendant fails to appear for trial, the law is flouted. If a released defendant commits crimes, the community is endangered.[14]

The various types of pretrial release are summarized in Table 17.1

In view of the large number of indigent defendants today, is it reasonable to base release decisions on financial means? A movement to ensure fairness in bail decisions began in the early 1960s in response to the perception of discrimination against defendants who could not afford bail. The Manhattan Bail Project, sponsored by the Vera Institute of Justice, found that it was possible to minimize no-shows and to predict with reasonable accuracy whether an accused would return to court on the basis of the person's offense history, family ties, and employment record. The project's early findings revealed a low default rate.

Through the 1960s and early 1970s, similar programs flourished throughout the country. Perhaps the most promising reform attempt may be credited to the criminologist John Goldkamp, who, with the assistance of Michael Gottfredson, designed uniform guidelines for bail decision makers (see Figure 17.4).[15] By creating a two-dimensional grid on which they could plot the severity of the offense against a series of variables, such as type of crime, number of arrests, age, and community ties, these criminologists enabled judges to reduce significantly the disparities in decisions regarding bail.

Despite efforts to make the bail system equitable, the tide has shifted toward placing restraints on pretrial release and instituting provisions for pretrial detention. Many states now place significant restrictions on pretrial release decisions. Some jurisdictions, such as Washington, D.C., have instituted preventive detention statutes that authorize judges to deny bail to apparently dangerous offenders and keep them in custody. In fact, the Bail Reform Act of 1984 permits preventive detention in the federal system where "no condition or combination of conditions will reasonably assure the appearance of the person as required and the safety of any other person, and the community."[16]

Plea Bargaining

The arraignment gives prosecutor and defense counsel their last significant opportunity to offer the court a negotiated plea. As we noted in Chapter 15, the majority of defendants prefer to plead guilty to a lesser charge at any step of the process before trial. The inclination to make such a bargain is particularly great at arraignment, when the defendant may realize he or she stands a good chance of being convicted. Though an acquittal cannot be ruled out, the near certainty of a significant period of incarceration if con-

TABLE 17.1   TYPES OF PRETRIAL RELEASE

Financial Bond	Alternative Release Options
Fully secured bail: The defendant posts the full amount of bail with the court.	*Release on recognizance (ROR):* The court releases the defendant on his promise that he will appear in court as required.
Privately secured bail: A bondsman signs a promissory note to the court for the bail amount and charges the defendant a fee for the service (usually 10% of the bail amount). If the defendant fails to appear, the bondsman must pay the court the full amount. Frequently the bondsman requires the defendant to post collateral in addition to the fee.	*Conditional release:* The court releases the defendant subject to his following of specific conditions set by the court, such as attendance at drug treatment therapy or staying away from the complaining witness.
Percentage bail: The courts allow the defendant to deposit a percentage (usually 10%) of the full bail with the court. The full amount of the bail is required if the defendant fails to appear. The percentage bail is returned after disposition of the case, although the court often retains 1% for administrative costs.	*Third-party custody:* The defendant is released into the custody of an individual or agency that promises to ensure his appearance in court. No monetary transactions are involved in this type of release.
Unsecured bail: The defendant pays no money to the court but is liable for the full amount of bail should he fail to appear.	

Source: U.S. Department of Justice, Bureau of Justice Statistics, Report to the Nation on Crime and Justice: The Data (Washington, D.C.: U.S. Government Printing Office, 1983) p. 58.

victed is an incentive to bargain or negotiate. Statistics support such considerations. While the conviction rate in felony cases that go to trial varies from jurisdiction to jurisdiction, it is generally high. Prosecutors are concerned about the expense of a trial, a shortage of staff, and perhaps a long wait for available courtroom space and a trial judge. A study of 26 jurisdictions found a median conviction rate of 73 percent.[17]

The National Advisory Commission on Criminal Justice Standards and Goals recommended in 1971 that the practice of plea bargaining be abolished: "As soon as possible, but in no event later than 1978, negotiations between prosecutors and defendants—either personally or through their attorneys—concerning concessions to be made in return for guilty pleas should be prohibited."[18] According to the commission, abolishing plea bargaining would remove the incentive for prosecutors to charge an offender with a crime more serious than they expect to be able to prove; it would increase the number of trials only insignificantly; and, most important, it would increase the rationality and fairness of the criminal trial process.[19]

Abolition of plea bargaining would also restore the constitutional right to a trial by jury, which defendants are now manipulated into giv-

ing up. It would prevent the prosecution from achieving victory on the basis of insufficient or even illegally obtained evidence, which it can currently hide in a plea bargain.

But would the elimination of plea bargaining really have only an insignificant effect on the caseloads of judges, juries, prosecutors, and defense counsel? Only a 10 percent increase in trials, some experts claim, might cause the court apparatus to stop functioning.[20] But it also has been argued, on the basis of the experience of the few jurisdictions that have abolished plea bargaining—Alaska, New Orleans, El Paso, Blackhawk County in Iowa, Maricopa County in Arizona, Oakland County in Michigan, and Multnomah County in Oregon—that most defendants who consider themselves guilty will plead guilty anyway in the hope of a lighter sentence.[21]

This hypothesis, however, is largely untested. Rather than abolish plea bargaining, most jurisdictions have made it more open, more regulated, and fairer. The Supreme Court has insisted that the voluntariness of the plea and an understanding of its implications must be demonstrated in open court and that the prosecution must stick to its part of the bargain.[22] In federal courts the plea-bargaining process has actually been turned into a minitrial, consisting of such an

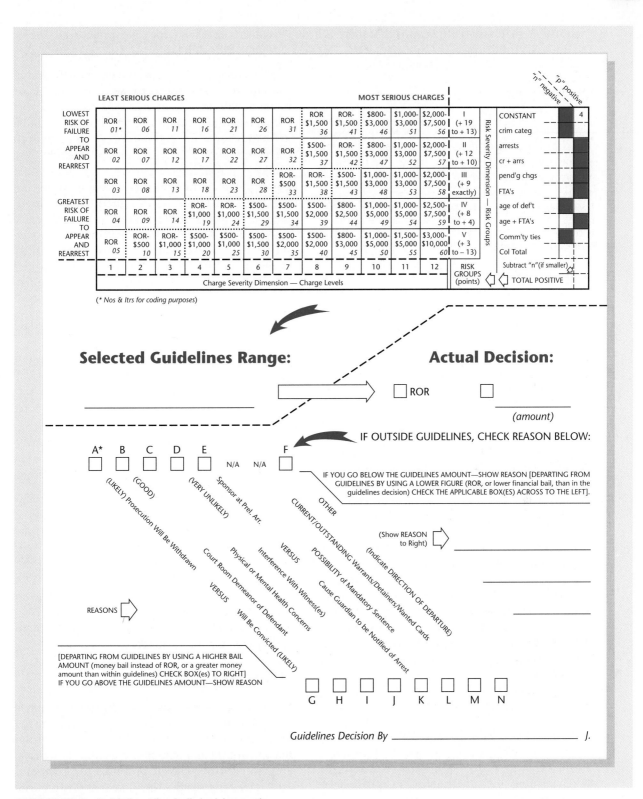

FIGURE 17.4 Guidelines for bail decision makers

Source: John Goldkamp and Michael Gottfredson, *Judicial Decision Guidelines for Bail: The Philadelphia Experiment* (Washington, D.C.: National Institute of Justice, 1983).

"inquiry as shall satisfy [the court] that there is a factual basis for the plea."[23]

THE TRIAL

Trial courts are established to find and express the communal judgment under law as to the guilt or innocence of an accused person. The public, in whose name the judgment is rendered, is supposed to participate actively in the process. Indictments read "The People of the State of . . . versus John Doe or Jane Roe."

What specifically is meant by "the people"? One answer is that the judge, who is elected by the people or appointed by somebody who was elected by the people, represents a consensus of the people. When an indictment is handed down and a jury trial held, the people are directly represented by a cross section of the community participating in the grand jury that indicts the defendant and the trial jury that tries the defendant. Any citizen is allowed into the courtroom to witness the proceedings, and seats for spectators are provided. Indeed, in pioneer days, trial day at the county seat was major entertainment. In some states, television coverage of court proceedings has taken the place of direct and total community participation.

Selecting the Jury: Voir Dire

After a plea of not guilty, the first step is the impaneling of the jury, which is called the *petit*, or *petty*, jury, in contrast to the grand jury. Twelve is the traditional number of trial jurors. Some states use fewer jurors for trials involving crimes of lesser seriousness. Ordinarily several alternate jurors are selected to take the place of any juror who might become disabled during the trial.

Jury selection is usually guided by three objectives. Attorneys have to:

■ Determine whether prospective jurors meet the minimum qualifications to sit as jurors (age and residency requirements)

■ Determine the impartiality of prospective jurors

■ Obtain sufficient information on prospective jurors to enable the attorneys to exclude "for cause" any who may be prejudiced for or against the defendant

The process by which lawyers and the judge examine a prospective juror to determine his or her acceptability is known as **voir dire.** Attorneys for each side attempt to pick jurors who might be just a little more understanding or sympathetic to their arguments. They can exclude people they think will be unsympathetic by means of **peremptory challenges,** or objections to potential jurors for which no explanation is required. Each side has a certain number of such challenges; usually the defense has more than the prosecution. Either side may use an unlimited number of **challenges for cause,** which are intended to keep persons with a conflict of interest off the jury. A person related by birth or by marriage to any of the parties connected with the case, for example, would almost certainly be challenged for cause.

Jury selection has yet another aspect: Skilled attorneys believe they can subliminally inject certain biases into potential jurors to ensure that evidence introduced at trial will be understood in a particular way. In a sense, they attempt to create sympathetic understanding for the position of the prosecution or the defense, as the case may be. The psychologists David Suggs and Bruce Sales, however, have noted:

> [S]uggestions from the legal literature [on ways to ensure sympathetic jurors] for the most part are based on hypotheses and folklore. Very little, if any, empirical work has been performed to substantiate the reliability and validity of the [jury selection] techniques proposed by legal writers.[24]

Nevertheless, consulting firms make their services available to attorneys, to assist them in selecting sympathetic jurors.

The Proceedings

Once a jury has been chosen or the defendant has waived a jury trial and consented to a trial by the judge alone, proceedings begin. The prosecution makes an opening statement, outlining the case and previewing what it proposes to prove and how. The defense may then make or postpone its opening statement. It is the prosecution's burden to introduce the evidence against the defendant. All evidence necessary to prove the case must be

AT ISSUE
New Witness in Court: The Camcorder

The 1991 videotaping of the Los Angeles Police Department officers' brutalization of Rodney King may not have been the first time private citizens caught crime on camera, but it certainly was the one that shook the country and the world. There have been other such video recordings since then, and there will be more. Several million camcorders—videotape camera recorders—are in the hands of ordinary Americans, and they record everything from weddings and puppet plays at kids' birthday parties to crimes, police behavior at crime scenes, and natural disasters.

Sometimes it is a television network whose camera catches an event on tape. Police departments now often and readily grant permission to the news media to ride "shotgun" in squad cars and capture police events on tape, and shows featuring "live-action" segments are popular with the public. But more and more, it is individuals who are using video cameras to document prostitution, drug deals, car thefts, police brutality, and other crimes.

Although video cameras can catch crime on tape, we should not think that their increasing use will solve all crime problems. These cameras record only what the operator zeros in on. They do not catch what is outside the range of the lens or the microphone, nor do they necessarily catch what is outside the reach of the law. The difficulties in using videotapes were shown in the aftermath of the Los Angeles riots in 1992, as noted by a reporter for the *New York Times*:

> A joint local-Federal team . . . spent weeks poring over hundreds of feet of videotape and hundreds of photographs. . . .
> The pictures show hordes of people running amok, but only a few prosecutions have resulted.(1)

Despite the "miles" of videotape available to police for identifying suspects, most of it recorded by trained camera operators for news agencies, there have been significant problems in using it effectively as evidence. Recorded images may show deceptive or baffling angles; shades and shadows may be hard

to interpret. Three-dimensional human faces, caught in the middle of an active expression and made two-dimensional, may be hard to recognize. Prodded by persuasive lawyers, juries may come to disregard a videotape entirely.(2) Problems in interpreting recorded images and demonstrating their validity as evidence may be even worse when the camera operators are private citizens with no training in videotaping.

Despite such problems, the advent of the camcorder has the potential to change police behavior and the world of crime:

> When it premiered last March, CamNet—America's first all-camcorder network—became a sort of non-establishment C-SPAN. While cable-supported C-SPAN covers power in Washington, CamNet's army of unpaid photographers serves up raw, and often fascinating, scenes from the fringe that the traditional news media frequently ignore. . . . It's difficult to keep secrets when everyone has a camera. . . . As the Rodney King video showed, even government officials can't fight the power that ordinary citizens can wield with a tiny camcorder.(3)

Sources
1. Seth Mydans, "Wheels of Justice Lurch after Los Angeles Riots," *New York Times*, Oct. 13, 1992, p. A8.
2. "Videos of LA Riots Useful in Investigation," National Public Radio's Weekend Edition, May 23, 1992, 53d story.
3. "Video Power to the People: CamNet, America's First All-Camcorder Channel, Shows Life on the Fringe," *TV Guide*, Nov. 28, 1992, p. 19.

Questions for Discussion
1. Camcorders in private hands may provide a useful source of evidence in court. Do you think this will have a positive impact on police behavior and on crime?
2. Should it be made a special offense for police to destroy a camcorder or its tape when a police event has been recorded?

A videotaping patrol as part of the neighborhood crime watch.

introduced in court directly and in compliance with the rules of evidence.

Evidence

The rules of evidence have evolved over centuries. One prominent rule says that hearsay cannot be used because, when information is repeated, it tends to become distorted. The exclusionary rule prohibits the introduction of any evidence that does not meet the strict standards of the law of evidence.[25] But the exclusionary rule is also used to keep out of court evidence that was obtained in violation of constitutional rights. For example, if a suspect is not given the *Miranda* warnings, any evidence obtained through police-initiated questioning after arrest may be excluded from trial. On constitutional issues, the exclusionary rule, for example, is a legal standard that binds not only the federal courts but all state courts as well.[26]

Evidence found as a result of illegally received information cannot be introduced as evidence at trial either. It is regarded as "the fruit of the poisonous tree" and thus is tainted.[27] The Supreme Court has made exceptions to the constitutional exclusionary rule, for example, by creating the "inevitable discovery" rule. Under this rule, evidence obtained in violation of a constitutional prohibition is admissible if it would have been discovered anyway.[28]

During the entire evidentiary stage of the trial, the defense watches the prosecution carefully, objecting immediately when it appears that one of the rules of evidence may have been violated. If the breach of the rule is so grave that the defendant's chance of a fair trial has been prejudiced, the defense may even move for a mistrial. If that motion is granted, the prosecution will have to start over again before a new jury. The judge rules on all motions and objections. If the judge rules against the defendant, defense counsel will have the ruling placed on record as a potential cause to appeal a verdict and judgment of guilty. Every witness called by either party is subject to cross-examination by the other party.

When the prosecution has completed its case, the defense has several options. If the evidence against the defendant is poor, the defense may move for a directed verdict of acquittal or a motion to dismiss. A *directed verdict* is a verdict pronounced by the judge. A *motion to dismiss* is a request that the proceedings be terminated. The defense can also address the jury in a postponed opening statement to influence an acquittal.

But the defense is more likely to present its own evidence—alibi witnesses, expert witnesses, character witnesses, even the defendant. The defendant is under no obligation to testify in his or her own behalf, and any defendant who does testify is subject to cross-examination by the prosecution.

The Task of the Jury

In the normal course of a trial, after both sides have presented their evidence, closing arguments are presented by the defense and the prosecution. The jurors then must apply the law to the facts that they have heard and determine the guilt or innocence of the defendant. So that they may do so responsibly, the judge gives them instructions—directions concerning the way they should go about deciding the case. Often both the prosecution and the defense will offer the judge instructions on the law that they propose should be given to the jury.

Defense and prosecution usually differ on how the jury should be instructed, especially on how the instructions should be phrased. Once again the judge takes ultimate responsibility for instructing the jury and may even prefer his or her own version of the instructions to those offered by defense and prosecution. If the defense counsel objects to the proposed instructions on grounds of law, the objections are noted for a potential appeal.

After receiving their instructions, the jurors retire to the jury room for their deliberations, which are guided by a foreman—one of their number whom they select to preside over their deliberations. The majority of juries have little difficulty in arriving at a verdict: guilty, not guilty, guilty of the crime charged in a lesser degree, or guilty of some but not all of the crimes charged. Some juries, however, do have difficulty reaching a verdict. In the celebrated "preppy murder case" (*People v. Chambers*), the jury wavered for 9 days between overwhelming majorities for and against the defendant, until defense and prosecution both realized the dilemma and agreed on a plea bargain, thus taking the jury out of the picture.[29]

Public defender Wil Smith addresses the jury in a trial in Portland, Oregon.

Jury Decision Making

For several decades psychologists have studied juror decision making, courtroom testimony, and eyewitness identification and testimony.[30] In examining the power of eyewitness testimony, psychologist Elizabeth Loftus conducted a mock-trial experiment in which subjects played the roles of jurors, listened to testimony, and were asked to reach a verdict. The mock jurors received a detailed description of a grocery store robbery in which the store's owner and grand-daughter were killed.

Loftus presented three versions of the evidence. One group of subjects was informed that there was no eyewitness, only circumstantial evidence. The second group was told a store clerk had testified that the defendant shot the two victims. The third group was told of the store clerk's identification but was informed that on cross-examination his testimony was discredited because he had not been wearing his glasses and his eyesight was poor. Eighteen percent of the first group found the defendant guilty, 72 percent of the second group, and 68 percent of the third group. The results of this research suggest that eyewitness testimony, even if contradicted or impeached, can be very persuasive to jurors.

Psychologists have also studied the influence of personal prejudice and expectations on the validity of eyewitness accounts. To address this question, Albert H. Hastorf and Hadley Cantrill showed a film of a football game between Dartmouth and Princeton to students at each school and asked them to note the number of infractions. Princeton students reported twice as many infractions by Dartmouth as their own team had made, and twice the number that Dartmouth students noted about their own team.[31] This study and the hundreds that followed it demonstrate the weakness of eyewitness accounts. Consider the findings of just a few of these other studies:

- The accuracy of older eyewitnesses is reduced in certain situations.[32]
- Both whites and blacks do better at identifying suspects of their own race.[33]
- Experience in recalling details of events witnessed (such as a police officer might have) does not necessarily improve recall.[34]
- The credibility of a witness is increased significantly by a display of confidence.[35]

There is a large body of research evaluating the process of juror decision making and whether or not extralegal issues influence jurors. Studies

"Your Honor, we the jury blame the victim."

have demonstrated that jurors are sometimes influenced by their own personal characteristics (age, race, gender, occupation) and by the characteristics of defendant and victim. In fact, mock jurors who evaluated the culpability of attractive versus unattractive defendants charged with identical crimes ascribed greater guilt to the unattractive ones.[36] Other studies that considered the character of the victim found that such variables as marital status, unorthodox lifestyle, and past sexual experience can play a role in jurors' decision making.

If class and race affiliation appear to influence jurors' verdicts, then the question becomes: What is a jury of one's peers? Must race and social status be reflected in the composition of a jury? Are we headed for a jury quota system? The jury verdicts in cases that led to and arose out of the 1992 Los Angeles race riots may make such questions vital in the future.

SENTENCING: TODAY AND TOMORROW

Sentencing has been characterized as the most controversial of all the stages in the criminal justice process.[37] This is not surprising. At earlier stages the defendant benefits from the presumption of innocence, and certain safeguards are built into the adversarial system: due process, fundamental fairness, and impartiality. Once the defendant is convicted, however, the focus shifts away from these concerns to the imposition of punishment.

Judges can choose from a variety of sentencing options, ranging from the death penalty to the imposition of a fine:

- *Death penalty:* In 37 jurisdictions, judges may impose a sentence of death for any offense designated a capital crime, most commonly murder.

- *Incarceration:* A defendant may be sentenced to serve a term in a state or federal prison or in a local jail.

- *Probation:* A defendant may be sentenced to a period of community supervision with special limitations. Violation of these conditions may result in incarceration.

- *Split sentence:* A judge may split the sentence between a period of incarceration and a period of probation.

- *Restitution:* An offender may be required to provide financial reimbursement to cover the cost of a victim's losses.

- *Community service:* A judge may require an offender to spend a period of time performing public service work.

- *Fine:* The offender may be required to pay a certain sum of money as a penalty and/or as an alternative to or in conjunction with incarceration.

What determines which option will be chosen? More often than not, judges are given discretion and thus are guided by their own sentencing philosophy. Their discretion may be limited by a statute that prescribes a prison term of a specified length or a range of prison terms. Before we consider the various limits and guidelines, we need to review the most prominent philosophies of punishment: incapacitation, deterrence, retribution, rehabilitation, and just deserts.

Incapacitation

"Lock 'em up and throw away the key" reflects the belief that, given the frequency with which offenders commit crime, society is best off when criminals are incarcerated for long periods of time—or incapacitated. Yet long sentences may be unjust, unnecessary, counterproductive, and inappropriate:

■ They are unjust if other offenders who have committed the same crime receive shorter sentences.

■ They are unnecessary if the offender is not likely to offend again.

■ They are counterproductive whenever prison increases the risk of habitual criminal behavior.

■ They are inappropriate if the offender has committed an offense entailing insignificant harm to the community.

Research evidence on incapacitation is equivocal. Joan Petersilia and Peter Greenwood, for example, suggest that the crime rate could be reduced by as much as 15 percent if every convicted felon were imprisoned for 1 year.[38] Earlier investigations provided widely different estimates. Revel Shinnar and his colleagues projected that an 80 percent reduction in violent crime rates was possible if everyone convicted of a violent crime served 5 years in prison. Another study, however, concluded that only a 4 percent reduction would result from that policy.[39]

Most of the empirical research in the area of incapacitation focuses on criminal behavior that persists over many years. Such research examines how criminal careers begin, how they progress, and why they terminate. As we saw in Chapter 2, Marvin Wolfgang and his associates determined that two-thirds of all violent crimes

and more than one-half of all crimes were committed by 6 percent of the birth cohort they investigated. This evidence, in conjunction with Peter Greenwood's findings that recidivists often manage to stay out of prison by plea bargaining, suggests that if prosecutors could identify recidivists and prosecute them vigorously, and if judges imposed long prison sentences on them, serious crime might be reduced significantly.

Some believe that a policy of **selective incapacitation**—that is, the targeting of high-risk, recidivist offenders for prosecution and incarceration—may be worth pursuing.[40] Implementation of such a policy, however, is limited by the state of criminological research. In the words of Joan Petersilia and her colleagues::

> For an incapacitative crime control strategy to be effective, we need to know, first, whether there is a group of offenders who commit large numbers of offenses over a substantial period, and second, whether we can identify them. The first condition can be met. There is a small group of persistent offenders. . . . The second condition—ability to predict—cannot now be met.[41]

There are other problems as well, such as the false identification of high-risk offenders (false positive) and the release of defenders mistakenly labeled as low-risk (false negative).

Deterrence

The theory of **deterrence** holds that fear of punishment will cause potential offenders to refrain from committing crimes. According to Philip Cook, if we disbanded all law enforcement agencies and removed all sanctions from the penal laws, the result would be "a crime wave of unprecedented proportions."[42] The very existence of the criminal justice system, he argues, has a strong general deterrent effect, civilizing many people who otherwise would not be civil.

Researchers have investigated instances in which policing was terminated and others in which policing was significantly strengthened. A classic example of the former situation occurred in Denmark in 1944, when the German occupation forces arrested the entire Danish police force. An examination of insurance claims showed that fraud crimes and embezzlement did not increase but that larcenies and burglaries rose tenfold.[43] During a strike by the Montreal police force in

1969, crimes of revenge and vandalism increased significantly.[44] Yet research on the effect of police strikes in the 1970s on the crime rates of 11 American cities provided very little support for the hypothesis that removal of the police presence raises crime rates.[45]

The evidence on the effects of intensified policing is no clearer. In 1982, New York City's Transit Police force was strengthened to combat subway crime. Additional officers were posted in subway stations on virtually all trains between 8 P.M. and 4 A.M. The results were inconclusive.[46] Researchers have studied the effects of increasing the threatened punishments for some crimes. Massachusetts mandated a minimum prison term of 1 year for carrying a firearm without a permit. This law had a measurable deterrent effect.[47] But the deterrent effect of criminal sanctions is limited.

In a study of deterrence by the Criminal Law Education and Research Center at New York University, three types of warning stickers were attached to parking meters in three comparable areas. One sticker threatened a $50 fine for the use of slugs in parking meters. The second threatened a $250 fine and 3 months' imprisonment. The third threatened a $1000 fine and 1 year in prison. Slug use decreased substantially where the threatened sanction was lowest and thus realistic. The highest sanction appeared so unrealistic that slug use actually increased, although only slightly. In another area, where newly installed parking meters had coin-view windows that revealed what had been inserted into the meter, slug use decreased substantially.[48]

Overall, research on deterrence is still inconclusive, largely because the opportunities for making controlled studies are extremely limited but also because some crimes and some criminals are more easily deterred than others.[49] It is important to note that deterrence assumes rational choice. Supporters of deterrence-based strategies argue that criminals weigh the relative benefits and risks of engaging in crime and choose not to do so because they are deterred by a greater chance of being caught.

Retribution

In many preliterate societies victims retaliated fiercely against anybody or anything that had caused them harm—another person, an animal, a tree. In early literate societies such uncontrolled revenge gave way to a measured response to wrongdoing. In the Mosaic laws we find a limitation on revenge: the punishment should be comparable to the harm inflicted ("an eye for an eye"). This *lex talionis* ("retaliation law") marks the birth of the idea of **retribution**.[50]

Under the retributive system of the nineteenth and early twentieth centuries, all punishments were determined by legislative act, and the judge had little choice in sentencing. Every type of crime was given a fixed punishment. In fixing these punishments, legislatures took into account the perceived gravity of each type of crime. Thus murder commanded a more severe punishment than robbery, and robbery a more severe punishment than larceny.

In the early part of this century attitudes began to change. This was a period of great expectations, of great advances in medicine and in psychology. Especially in the United States, anything seemed possible, even changing criminals into law-abiding citizens. In this climate the classical retributive idea of punishment seemed to be inherently flawed. The idea of punishment as retribution was based on the assumption that all offenders who had violated the same provision of the penal law were alike and thus deserved the same punishment. But behavioral scientists point out that no two offenders who have committed the same crime are completely alike in capacity, depravity, intelligence, and potential for rehabilitation.

Rehabilitation

Dissatisfaction with retribution led to a new emphasis on the rehabilitative ideal. As a sentencing strategy or option, **rehabilitation** is based on the premise that through correctional intervention (educational and vocational training and psychotherapeutic programs), an offender may be changed and returned to society as a productive citizen. Punishment now became individualized: the court could select a sentence ranging from a minimum to a maximum length of incarceration or impose an indeterminate sentence. The parole board was established to decide when the convicted person should be released and under what conditions.

Although correctional systems did experiment with rehabilitation, more often than not the efforts were perfunctory. Yet judges believed in the promise of rehabilitation and sentenced offenders accordingly. In the 1970s, researchers increasingly attacked the rehabilitative ideal as a failure. In 1974 Robert Martinson wrote: "[W]ith few and isolated exceptions, the rehabilitative efforts that have been reported so far have had no appreciable effect on recidivism."[51] After Martinson's devastating analysis, a number of criminologists and research organizations responded with comparable findings and conclusions.[52] The result was a temporary vacuum in sentencing theory. In practice, however, most states had adopted the sentencing policies of the Model Penal Code and tried to abide by them.

Model Penal Code Sentencing Goals

The Model Penal Code describes the general purposes of the provisions governing the sentencing of offenders as follows:

1. To prevent and condemn the commission of offenses.
2. To promote the correction and rehabilitation of offenders.
3. To ensure the public safety by preventing the commission of the offenses through the deterrent influence of sentences imposed and the confinement of offenders when required in the interest of public protection.
4. To safeguard offenders against excessive, disproportionate, or arbitrary punishment.
5. To give fair warning of the nature of the sentences that may be imposed on conviction of an offense.
6. To differentiate among offenders with a view to a just individualization in their treatment.
7. To advance the use of generally accepted scientific methods and knowledge in sentencing offenders.[53]

Thus the Model Penal Code set as goals the prevention of crime through deterrence and incapacitation; condemnation of the commission of offenses, which may be called *vindication* of the law; correction and rehabilitation of the offender; and retribution if sentences are properly individualized.

These sentencing objectives have been with us for a long time. Each objective has been given more or less emphasis at various times. As we have noted, some have been supported or even partially validated by research. The difficulty comes in trying to combine objectives. Legislatures, in providing appropriate punishments for the various offenses in the code, are supposed to consider the interplay of the multiple goals. Judges, acting within the legislative framework, likewise are supposed to consider all the goals when they mete out individual sentences. But the goals are not necessarily compatible; in fact, they may be contradictory. For example, a long prison term may be necessary to remove an offender from society (incapacitation), but a long prison sentence can be incompatible with the goal of rehabilitation.

Just Deserts

In the wake of the perceived failure of rehabilitation, the wide differences in sentences for like crimes under indeterminate sentencing laws became apparent. Andrew von Hirsch, Richard Singer, and other scholars began to promote a return to retribution.[54] Their model is called **just deserts.** Underlying the concept of just deserts is the proposition that the punishment must be based on the gravity of the offense and the culpability of the perpetrator.

Utilitarian aims, such as general or individual deterrence, incapacitation, and rehabilitation, can only result in variations among the sentences imposed on offenders who deserve identical punishment. Moreover, it can be established that such extralegal factors as the characteristics of judges, race, socioeconomic status, sex, age, geographic area of the trial, and type of defense counsel cause wide differences in sentences imposed.[55] Just-deserts advocates further hold that courts simply do not have the capacity to discriminate between those who can be deterred, reformed, or incapacitated and those who cannot. Parole boards likewise have been found to be poorly prepared to make sound decisions as to which offenders are good risks for release and which are not.

The system of rehabilitation was based on the capacity of prisons—"correctional" institutions—to correct or rehabilitate, but they did not do so in most cases. There is therefore no choice but to return to retribution, which at least guarantees just or like sentences for like crimes. Any rehabilitative efforts in prisons should be made only within the terms of the fixed sentence and with the consent of the convicted person.[56]

The just-deserts approach has been successful in minimizing disparity in sentences and in curbing judicial arbitrariness. But it has its problems as well: It has been blamed for prison overcrowding. It has been attacked for insensitivity to the social problems that lead a large proportion of offenders to crime. It has been criticized for refusal to acknowledge the fact that education, in the broadest sense, can affect values, attitudes, and behavior. It also has been called unscientific because of its rejection of scientific efforts to identify the types of offenders whose leanings toward crime are said to be demonstrable.

Critics have complained that the just-deserts concept is superficial in its rejection of the rehabilitative ideal: it ignores the fact that rehabilitation has been condemned on the basis of flawed evaluations. Recently, legislatures and courts have demonstrated a willingness to search for new sentencing policies that take into account the scholarly disputes over the rehabilitative ideal, the incapacitative approach, and just deserts and yet also satisfy the popular demand for effective means of coping with crime.

Sentencing Limits and Guidelines

Presumptive and Mandatory Sentencing

The federal courts and at least 12 state court systems have judges who are virtually deprived of the power to determine the lengths of sentences.[57] The law determines what the punishment ought to be, often by a *presumptive* (presumed to be most appropriate) sentence. The length of such a sentence is regulated by statute—there is a definite sentence for each class of crimes, and it cannot ordinarily be adjusted for mitigating or aggravating circumstances. In some limited cases a judge may modify the sentence slightly on the basis of such circumstances, provided the reasons are detailed in a written explanation. When sentences are *mandatory*, judges have no discretion to alter them. Thus presumptive and mandatory sentencing leaves judges with little power to respond to the needs

of the individual offender. More recently this situation has been eased somewhat by the institution of sentencing guidelines.

Sentencing Guidelines

Sentencing guidelines provide a relatively fixed punishment that corresponds with prevailing notions of harm and allows for upward or downward adjustment on the basis of specific aggravating or mitigating circumstances.[58] In the United States, the movement toward sentencing guidelines began with a plea by federal district judge Marvin E. Frankel in 1972 for an independent sentencing commission to study sentences and assist in the formulation and enactment of detailed guidelines for use by judges.[59] Since then a number of states have adopted guidelines, and several have created *sentencing commissions,* which are independent agencies authorized by state legislatures to create guidelines. In 1984 the United States Sentencing Commission was established by Congress, and in 1987 it delivered its guidelines for the sentencing of individual defendants. In November 1991, Congress adopted guidelines proposed by the Sentencing Commission for organizations, especially for corporations.[60]

At the heart of all guidelines is a sentencing grid, most often in the form of a matrix, in which a ranking of the severity of the offense is combined with a defendant's criminal history or other characteristics to arrive at a recommended sentence or sentence range (Figure 17.5). Guidelines usually allow for mitigating or aggravating circumstances associated with the specific offense. They typically indicate which offenses should be sanctioned by a prison term (the "in/out" decision) and the length of the sentence.

A judge simply calculates a defendant's history and the severity of the offense, plus or minus mitigating or aggravating circumstances (where allowed), and, with the exactness of a computer, has a sentence to impose. In practice, some guidelines can be fairly complicated to use because of the number of factors that must be included in calculating the sentence. Every U.S. probation office and U.S. attorney's office has been provided with a computer program to assist in calculating recommended sentences in accordance with the federal sentencing guidelines.[61]

CRIMINOLOGICAL FOCUS
The Mandatory Sentence Debate

Widespread outrage at revolving door practices that freed convicted criminals before they served their entire sentences led to mandatory sentences. Many of these laws contain a strong presumption in favor of incarceration for even first-time and petty offenders. The result—and we are only now beginning to see the full effects—has been soaring numbers of people under correctional supervision for longer periods of time.(1)

Mandatory minimum laws, passed during the "War on Crime" in the 1980s, take sentencing out of the hands of the judge and provide for fixed periods of "straight time" for various crimes, with no chance of parole. Aimed primarily at drug offenses, these laws are widely blamed for the prison overcrowding of the 1990s. For example, federal statutes passed in the mid-1980s created a mandatory 5-year minimum sentence for possession of 5 grams of crack cocaine. The number of inmates in federal prisons has doubled since 1986, and six of every ten inmates are in on drug charges; more than half of those are first offenders.(2)

U.S. Attorney General Janet Reno wants to change that. Due to prison overcrowding, mandatory minimums can result in the early release of inmates with long records of violent crimes, while first offenders serve out their mandatory sentences. "I'm getting input from judges and the entire criminal justice community that their hands are tied," Reno says. "[There are] low-level, non-violent people serving 10- to 15-year mandatory minimum sentences in the federal system."(1)

What would she do about it? Reno would like to bring drug offenders into the community through an "intensive supervision" program. She helped develop an approach in Dade County, Florida,

that treats offenders as individuals and tracks their progress daily, provides such close supervision that someone knows where each offender is each hour of the day, and gives judges power to move offenders in and out of jail as needed.(1) And with the passage of new sentencing guidelines in 1993, Florida became one of the first states to back away from mandatory sentencing. The legislation has provided longer prison terms for violent criminals and eliminated mandatory sentences for many lesser crimes.(3)

While Reno expects significant resistance to the idea of letting drug offenders go back out on the streets, her agenda fits well with the just-deserts rationale: all penalties should be proportional to the seriousness of the crime for which the person is convicted.(4) That means a 19-year-old, nonviolent, first-offender crack courier should not get a mandatory 5-year sentence. The just-deserts rationale can be implemented through legislatively mandated penalties, but sentencing guidelines, based

almost entirely on the seriousness of crimes, overcome the problem of the political influences that dominate legislative decisions.

Sources
1. John Hanchette, "Crime and the Cost of Punishment—Reno Puts Prison Crisis Blame on Mandatory Minimum Sentences," Gannett News Service, June 13, 1993. The extract is from John Dilulio, Princeton University, as quoted by Hanchette.
2. "Mandatory-Minimum Sentencing Laws—Time for Repeal?" Cable News Network, News, July 5, 1993, Transcript 351-2.
3. "With Prison Costs Rising, Florida Ends Many Mandatory Sentences," *New York Times*, May 29, 1993, p. 5.
4. Andrew von Hirsch, *Doing Justice* (Boston: Northeastern University Press, reprint edition, 1986).

Questions for Discussion
1. Have the mandatory minimum laws had an appreciable impact on the drug problem in the United States?
2. Do you think a first-time drug offender should be let back out on the streets under supervision, as Reno proposes?

Attorney General Janet Reno during her confirmation hearing, March 1993.

Types of Guidelines

There are two types of sentencing guidelines: voluntary and presumptive. *Voluntary* guidelines are created by the judiciary rather than mandated by the legislature. They are sometimes referred to as "descriptive guidelines" because they describe, rather than prescribe, recommended sentences. Denver developed a voluntary system in 1976; subsequently it was tried in other cities, such as Newark, Chicago, and Phoenix. Michigan, Massachusetts, and New Jersey pioneered use of voluntary systems on a statewide basis. Such voluntary systems have been tried at the state or local level in almost every state. However, evaluations have shown that they have had little effect on judges' sen-

tencing patterns, and interest in them seems to have diminished.[62]

The other form of sentencing guideline is referred to as *presumptive* because the appropriate sentence for an offender is presumed to fall within the range of sentences specified by the guidelines. Judges are expected to choose from a range of available sentences, and all deviations must be documented in writing. The federal sentencing guidelines and those of Minnesota, Pennsylvania, and Washington are all considered presumptive schemes.

Pennsylvania's system, unlike the others, still allows for indeterminate sentences because the sentencing commission sought to incorporate a rehabilitative philosophy into its guidelines,

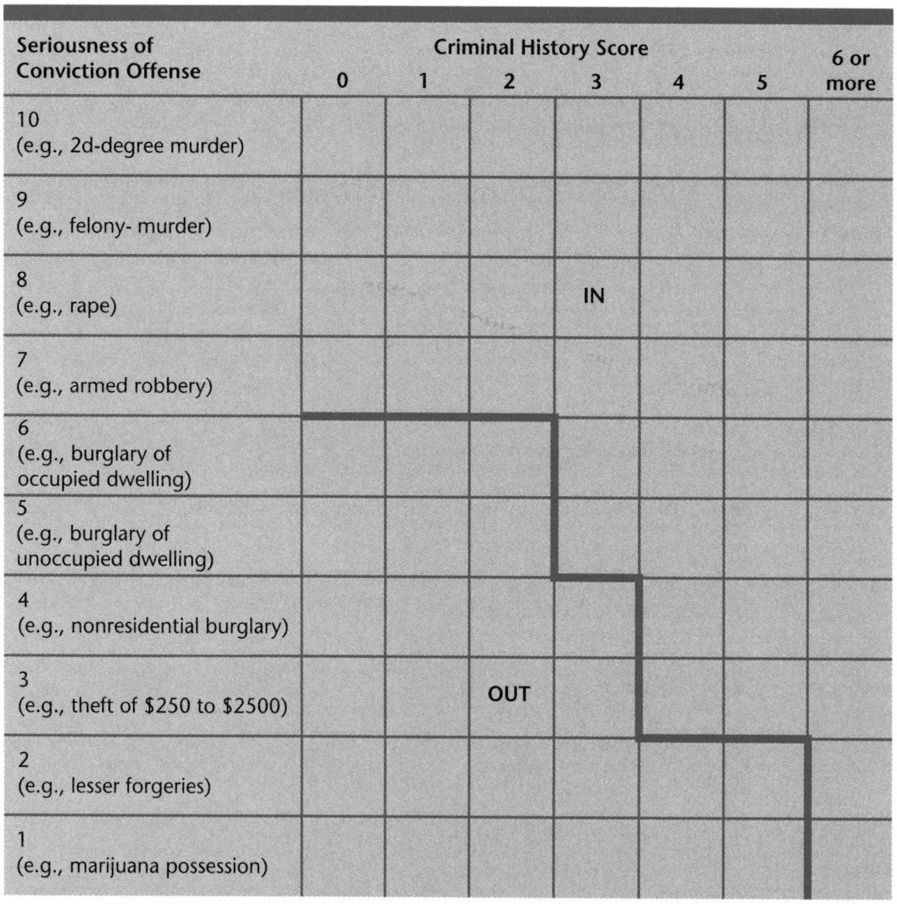

Seriousness of Conviction Offense	Criminal History Score						6 or more
	0	1	2	3	4	5	
10 (e.g., 2d-degree murder)							
9 (e.g., felony- murder)							
8 (e.g., rape)			IN				
7 (e.g., armed robbery)							
6 (e.g., burglary of occupied dwelling)							
5 (e.g., burglary of unoccupied dwelling)							
4 (e.g., nonresidential burglary)							
3 (e.g., theft of $250 to $2500)			OUT				
2 (e.g., lesser forgeries)							
1 (e.g., marijuana possession)							

FIGURE 17.5   The dispositional line on Minnesota's sentencing grid

Source: Andrew von Hirsch, Kay A. Knapp, and Michael Tonry, *The Sentencing Commission and Its Guidelines* (Boston: Northeastern University Press, 1987) p. 91.

along with goals related to deterrence, incapacitation, and just deserts. For offenders in Pennsylvania who are to be incarcerated, the judge must specify a minimum and a maximum sentence chosen from a wide range allowed in the guidelines. The parole board then decides the actual release date. Minnesota and Washington, emphasizing a retributive approach, have made the range for a given offense narrower than that in Pennsylvania.[63]

Some Criticisms

Sentencing commissions and sentencing guidelines both have met with significant resistance, perhaps because the state commissions are independent of the judicial and the legislative branches. Some of the proposed guidelines or recommendations were simply rejected by the legislatures.[64] The Connecticut commission developed a guidelines system but went on record as strongly opposed to its adoption and instead recommended statutory determinate sentences.[65] At the federal level, opposition to individual guidelines came chiefly from the judges themselves.

The federal guidelines for individuals took effect on November 1, 1987, but many judges found them unconstitutional. They reasoned that, since the U.S. Sentencing Commission was created by Congress, the guidelines were a violation of the separation of powers. In January 1989, the United States Supreme Court upheld the constitutionality of the U.S. Sentencing Commission and the guidelines.[66] Between the time the guidelines went into effect and this Supreme Court decision, more than 150 federal district judges refused to use the guidelines on the grounds that they might be unconstitutional. An evaluation of the initial use of the guidelines at the federal level showed that lawyers also opposed them. Only probation officers, who are responsible for preparing presentence investigation reports, seemed to have mastered the intricacies of the system.[67]

Like statutory determinate sentencing schemes, guidelines represent an attempt to overcome the inequities and uncertainties associated with indeterminate sentences. Critics of presumptive sentencing guidelines, however, fear that their use will lead to harsher sentences and make the already serious problem of prison overcrowding worse. Others suggest that discretion in sentencing will simply move from the judge to the prosecutor. Defendants will seek bargains that move their charges to the "out" side of the in/out line or to a location on the sentencing grid that carries a more lenient sentence. The pressure to bargain will also lead defendants to avoid trials. Finally, some are concerned that judges will simply ignore the guidelines.

CAPITAL PUNISHMENT

A judge's most awesome sentencing alternative for those convicted of a capital crime is the imposition of the death sentence. Capital punishment is a controversial issue, and one that poses particular challenges to the judiciary. After all, it is the only sentence that, once executed, is irreversible and final: it deprives the convicted person of an ultimate appeal.

Daniel Frank's execution in 1622 was the first on record in America. He was executed in the colony of Virginia for the crime of theft.[68] Scholars have estimated that since that year, between 18,000 and 20,000 people in America have suffered state-sanctioned execution for crimes including train wrecking, aggravated murder, and rape.[69] (The latest estimate puts the total at 14,570.)[70] Countless others have died at the hands of lynch mobs.[71] During the last century, Western countries have employed six methods of execution: firing squad, lethal gas, hanging, decapitation by ax or guillotine, electrocution, and lethal injection. Decapitation is the only one of these methods that has never been used in the United States.

Since 1976, when the death penalty was reinstated in the United States after a short moratorium, 210 convicted criminals have been executed (Figure 17.6). Thirty-six states and the federal government now have death penalty laws in effect.

The arguments surrounding capital punishment are deceptively simple. What makes them deceptive is that abolitionist or retentionist views of the death penalty often influence assessments of the penalty's utility and effectiveness. Abolitionists find little empirical evidence of a deter-

A death penalty protest at the state capitol in Austin, Texas, in 1991.

rent effect, and retentionists claim that sophisticated studies can be conducted only after executions have been resumed at a steady pace. They argue, in other words, that it is impossible to tell whether deterrence is fact or fiction until we execute all inmates sentenced to death.

The Deterrence Argument

Social scientists have long debated whether and to what extent executions deter murder. The debate focuses on two questions: Do would-be murderers decide not to kill out of fear of being put to death? If the threat of execution is in fact a deterrent, would the threat of life imprisonment be just as effective?

The results of studies designed to answer these questions are inconclusive. Thorsten Sellin, Hans Zeisel, William C. Bailey, and Ruth D. Peterson, for example, have found little evidence that homicide rates are affected by executions.[72] On the other hand, Isaac Ehrlich, an economist, has found what does appear to be a deterrent effect: specifically, that each execution prevents between 8 and 20 murders.[73] His study, however, has been criticized on a number of methodological grounds.

Recent research on the deterrent effect of the death penalty has focused on the relationship between publicity about executions and homi-

cide rates. If deterrence works, the argument goes, then publicized executions should result in lower numbers of murders because of greater awareness of the risk of being sentenced to death. Here again, the results of research are not clear: some studies show that publicity does have some deterrent effect (although much weaker than other factors associated with the homicide rate),[74] and others conclude that neither newspaper nor television coverage of executions has had any deterrent effect.[75]

The legal scholar Charles L. Black has noted that it is extremely difficult to design methodologically sound deterrence studies. How can we estimate the number of people who did not commit murder in a jurisdiction with a death penalty or in one without a death penalty? How can we know that a would-be killer decided against the act of murder? According to Black:

> After all possible inquiry, we do not know, and for systematic and easily visible reasons cannot know, what the truth about this "deterrent" effect may be. A "scientific"—that is to say, a soundly based—conclusion is simply impossible, and no methodological path out of this tangle suggests itself.[76]

The Discrimination Argument

In the early 1970s Marvin Wolfgang and Mark Riedel identified an anomaly in the use of the

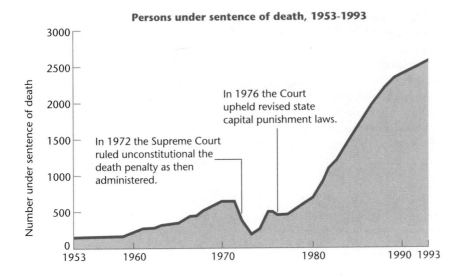

Persons under sentence of death, 1953-1993

In 1976 the Court upheld revised state capital punishment laws.

In 1972 the Supreme Court ruled unconstitutional the death penalty as then administered.

Persons executed, 1930-1993 (4016)

FIGURE 17.6   Death sentences and executions in the United States

Source: Capital Punishment 1992, Bureau of Justice Statistics Bulletin (Washington, D.C.: U.S. Government Printing Office, December, 1993).

death penalty. Since the 1950s it had become clear that death sentences in some southern states had been given disproportionately to blacks convicted of the rape of white women. Wolfgang and Riedel noted: "Of the 3,859 persons executed for all crimes since 1930, 54.6 percent have been black or members of other racial minority groups. Of the 455 executed for rape alone, 89.5 percent have been non-white."[77]

Though the discrimination question has been at the core of legal challenges to the constitutionality of many death sentences, it remained in the background until the legal scholar David Baldus and his colleagues conducted a comprehensive and methodologically sound analysis of discrimination in capital sentencing in Fulton County, Georgia.[78] This study, which clearly demonstrated that a black defendant is 11 times more likely to be sentenced to death for killing a white person than is a white for killing a black, was presented to the United States Supreme Court in *McKlesky v. Kemp* (1985).[79]

Warren McKlesky asked the Supreme Court to invalidate the Georgia capital punishment statute because of this proven discrimination. The Court refused to do so because defense attorneys had not shown that McKlesky himself had been discriminated against. Further, the

Court ruled that if there is such racial bias, it is at a tolerable level. But a level that is tolerable is difficult to specify. For over 50 years research on sentencing disparity has found racial discrimination in both capital and noncapital cases. This does not suggest that all judges discriminate; rather, some judges discriminate and some do not.[80] Furthermore, differences based on race are not just the result of judicial decision making. Research has found evidence indicating that prosecutors are more likely to request the death penalty for black killers of white people.[81]

Other Arguments

Other arguments have been advanced for and against the death penalty. They are based on everything from religious concerns to a calculation of the cost of imprisonment. Table 17.2 lists

TABLE 17.2 ARGUMENTS AGAINST AND FOR THE DEATH PENALTY

Arguments	Rationales
Against	
Arbitrary-use argument	With over 2600 inmates on death row, the process by which an inmate is selected to die is entirely arbitrary; it is not determined by the seriousness of the crime committed or any other objective measure.
Mistakes argument	Studies have documentd cases in which individuals were wrongly convicted and thus executed in error.* It is impossible to be entirely certain that a person is truly guilty. Are we willing to permit mistakes?
Religious argument	Organizations representing most of the major religions have called for an end to the death penalty. Interreligious task forces have voiced concern over issues of ethics and guilt in the putting to death of human beings.
Cost-benefit argument	The cost of appeals and maintenance of a person on death row is higher than the cost of maintaining a prisoner sentenced to life imprisonment—approximately $3 million.
Risk argument	Convicted murderers behave well in prison and, if paroled, rarley commit violent offenses.
Morality argument	Examinations of the relation between moral development and attitudes toward capital punishment show that the more developed one's sense of morality, the less likely one is to favor the death penalty.
For	
Economic argument	The cost of maintaining an inmate in prison for life places an unfair burden on taxpayers and the state.†
Retribution argument	Any individual who kills another human being must pay for the crime.
Community protection argument	It is always possible that a person on death row may escape and kill again or may kill another inmate or a correctional officer. Thus the community cannot be fully protected unless the person is executed.‡
Public opinion argument	Standards of decency, the criteria by which courts judge the humaneness of a punishment, are continually evolving. Two decades ago public opinion was not in favor of the death penalty. Today three-quarters of Americans favor capital punishment.

*Hugo Adam Bedau and Michael J. Radelet, "Miscarriages of Justice in Potentially Capital Cases," *Stanford Law Review* 40 (1987): 21–129.

†Actually, the cost of appeals and maintenance of a person on death row is far higher than the cost of maintaining a prisoner sentenced to life imprisonment—approximately $3 million. See Andrew P. Malcolm, "Capital Punishment Is Popular, but So Are Its Alternatives," *New York Times*, Sept. 10, 1989, p. E4.

‡Thorsten Sellin's research demonstrated that this argument is specious. Convicted murderers behave exceedingly well in prison and, if released, have very good parole records. Repeat homicides are statistically rare. See Sellin, *The Death Penalty* (Philadelphia: American Law Institute), pp. 69–79.

these arguments and gives the rationales for them.

The Future of the Death Penalty

The number of people sentenced to death grew more than three times between 1980 and 1990. In 1990, 2 percent of offenders convicted of homicide were given sentences of death. With public support for the death penalty and increasing calls for politicians to "get tough" on crime, the death penalty in America is likely to continue for the foreseeable future.[82] Furthermore, recent Supreme Court decisions indicate growing impatience with the number of appeals traditionally granted a death-row inmate, and legislation has been introduced in Congress to limit the number of these appeals.

Of the world's major industrialized nations, only the United States, Japan, and South Africa retain the death penalty. Much of the rest of the world shows an opposite trend: between 1965 and 1990, 25 countries abolished the death penalty altogether and 10 abolished it for "ordinary crimes" (crimes other than those under military codes or those enforced in time of war). The only country in Europe that retains the death penalty in practice is Turkey (Belgium, Ireland, and Greece also retain the death penalty but do not use it in practice). The trend in the former communist countries is toward abolition.[83]

The lessons learned from the countries where capital punishment has been abolished might be useful in this country when the future of the death penalty is discussed. The deterrence argument would predict that homicide rates should go up when the death penalty is abolished. An analysis of murder rates in 14 abolitionist nations showed that homicide rates actually declined after abolition.[84]

■ REVIEW

Since earliest times society has used courts to resolve disputes among individuals and between a society and its members. With the emergence of government under strong rulers, the establishment of courts became a sovereign prerogative. In the common law family of legal systems, to which the United States belongs, the adversary system prevails. In criminal cases the prosecution, as one of the adversaries, presents evidence against the defendant in an effort to establish guilt beyond a reasonable doubt. The defendant, as the other adversary, has the right to contest the prosecution's evidence. The judge ensures the fairness of the proceedings.

The United States has two legal systems, one implemented by the state courts and the other implemented by the federal courts. In most of the 50 state systems, there are three distinct levels of courts of law: courts of limited or special jurisdiction, courts of general jurisdiction, and appellate courts. The federal system has several levels as well: federal magistrates, United States district courts, United States circuit courts of appeal, and the United States Supreme Court.

In the United States criminal cases are tried in state courts when the crime charged is one that violates state law and in federal courts when a violation of federal law is charged. Both state and federal convictions may be appealed within each system, with federal review of state cases when certain federal constitutional issues are raised.

The roles and decision-making processes of all participants in the criminal process—defendants and defense counsel, prosecutors, judges and jurors—have been subjected to increasing scientific scrutiny. The research reveals that the system does not measure up to expectations. Plea bargaining, in particular, undermines confidence in the court process, yet it may well be the only way to deal with vastly increased caseloads that make it impossible to grant a jury trial in most cases.

Legislative and judicial policies in sentencing convicted offenders are currently in turmoil. Evidence of grossly disproportionate punishments meted out for comparable offenders has led to large-scale abandonment of the rehabilitative goal in sentencing and to a return of the retributive (just-deserts) and incapacitative approaches. But sentencing policies continue to change, with some signs of a rebirth of the rehabilitative goal. At the moment, many states operate with sentencing guidelines that seek to curb abuses of judicial discretion, incorporate just-deserts ideas, and allow some degree of flexibility for aggravating and mitigating circumstances.

Capital punishment as a sentencing option remains a problem for policy makers and the general public. The United States is the only major western democracy to have returned to capital punishment, without any clear evidence that it promotes public safety.

■ NOTES

1. Jonathan D. Casper, *American Criminal Justice: The Defendant's Perspective* (Englewood Cliffs, N.J.: Prentice-Hall, 1972).

2. See, e.g., Jerome Frank, *Courts on Trial: Myth and Reality in American Justice* (Princeton, N.J.: Princeton University Press, 1949).

3. In the epochal case *Marbury v. Madison*, 1 Cr. 137 (1803), the Supreme Court, in an opinion by Chief Justice John Marshall, established the power of judicial review over all legislation and thus the primacy of the judiciary in our system of government.

4. *Loving v. Virginia*, 388 U.S. 1 (1967).

5. *Mapp v. Ohio*, 367 U.S. 643 (1961).

6. *Draper v. United States*, 358 U.S. 307 (1961). The *Draper* rule was modified in *Illinois v. Gates*, 462 U.S. 213 (1983), upholding the issuance of a search warrant even on the basis of an anonymous informant's tip as long as, under all the circumstances, the magistrate had a "substantial basis for concluding . . . that probable cause existed."

7. "Praecipibus tibi quod *corpus* A.B. in custodia vestra detentum, ut dicitur, una cum causa captionis et detentionis suae, quocumque nomine idem A.B. censeatur in eadem *habeas* coram nobis apud Westm." (emphasis added). Freely translated: Inasmuch as you are detaining the person A.B., we instruct you to deliver the said A.B. to us at Westminster and to tell us the reason for his capture and detention.

8. In *Stone v. Powell*, 428 U.S. 465 (1976), the court ruled that in Fourth Amendment cases (search and seizure), federal habeas corpus is not available to a state prisoner when the alleged due process violation has been fully and fairly litigated in the state court system.

9. See, e.g., Elizabeth Anne Stanko, "The Impact of Victim Assessment on Prosecutor's Screening Decisions: The Case of the New York County District Attorney's Office," *Law and Society Review*, 16 (1982): 225–239; James Eisenstein and Herbert Jacob, *Felony Justice: An Organizational Analysis of Criminal Courts* (Boston: Little, Brown, 1977); W. Boyd Littrell, *Bureaucratic Justice: Police, Prosecutors, and Plea Bargaining* (Beverly Hills, Calif.: Sage, 1979); Victoria Swigert and Ronald A. Farrell, *Murder, Inequality, and the Law* (Lexington, Mass.: Heath, 1976); Frank Miller, *Prosecution: The Decision to Charge a Suspect with a Crime* (Boston: Little, Brown, 1969); Martha Myers and John Hagan, "Private and Public Trouble: Prosecutors and the Allocation of Court Resources," *Social Problems*, 26 (1979): 439–451; and David Neubauer, "After the Arrest: The Charging Decision in Prairie City," *Law and Society Review*, 8 (1974): 495–517.

10. Celesta A. Albonetti, "Prosecutorial Discretion: The Effects of Uncertainty," *Law and Society Review*, 21 (1987): 291–313.

11. Abraham S. Goldstein, *The Passive Judiciary: Prosecutorial Discretion and the Guilty Plea* (Baton Rouge: Louisiana State University Press, 1981).

12. Abraham S. Blumberg, *Criminal Justice: Issues and Ironies* (New York: New Viewpoints, 1979), p. 123.

13. *Gideon v. Wainright*, 375 U.S. 335 (1963); *Argersinger v. Hamlin*, 407 U.S. 25 (1972).

14. President's Commission on Law Enforcement and the Administration of Justice, *Task Force Report: Courts* (Washington, D.C.: U.S. Government Printing Office, 1967), p. 131.

15. John S. Goldkamp, *Two Classes of Accused: A Study of Bail and Detention in American Justice* (Cambridge, Mass.: Ballinger, 1979).

16. Bail Reform Act of 1984, 18 U.S.C. §§3141–3150 (1984).

17. U.S. Department of Justice, Bureau of Justice Statistics, *Report to the Nation on Crime and Justice* (Washington, D.C.: U.S. Government Printing Office, 1988), p. 24.

18. National Advisory Commission on Criminal Justice Standards and Goals, *A National Strategy to Reduce Crime* (Washington, D.C.: U.S. Government Printing Office, 1971), p. 43.

19. See Douglas Smith, "The Plea Bargaining Controversy," *Journal of Criminal Law and Criminology*, 77 (1986): 949–967.

20. Barbara Boland, *Prosecution of Felony Arrests*, for Bureau of Justice Statistics (Washington, D.C.: U.S. Government Printing Office, 1986).

21. Teresa Carns and John Kruse, *Alaska's Plea Bargaining Ban Re-evaluated: Executive Summary* (Anchorage: Alaska Judicial Council, 1991); Malcolm D. Holmes, Howard C. Daudistel, and William A. Taggart, "Plea Bargaining Policy and State District Court Caseloads: An Interrupted Time Series Analysis," *Law and Society Review*, 26 (1992): 139–159; William McAllister, James Atchinson, and Nancy Jacobs, "A Simulation Model of Pretrial Felony Case Processing: A Queuing System Analysis," *Journal of Quantitative Criminology*, 7 (1991): 291–314.

22. *Boykin v. Alabama*, 395 U.S. 238 (1964); *Santobello v. New York*, 404 U.S. 257 (1971).

23. Rule 11(f), Federal Rules of Criminal Procedure. See also Samuel Walker, *Taming the System: The Control of Discretion in Criminal Justice, 1950–1990* (New York: Oxford University Press, 1993).

24. David Suggs and Bruce Sales, "The Art and Science of Conducting the Voir Dire," *Professional Psychology*, 9 (1978): 362–388.

25. *Mapp v. Ohio*, 367 U.S. 643 (1961).

26. The *Mapp* decision made the Fourth Amendment's exclusionary rule applicable to the states through the Fourteenth Amendment's due process clause. See n. 5 above.

27. See, e.g., *Wong Sun v. United States*, 371 U.S. 471 (1923); and *People v. Defore*, 242 N.Y. 13 at 21 (1926).

28. *Nix v. Williams*, 467 U.S. 431 (1984).

29. Linda Wolfe, *Wasted: The Preppie Murder* (New York: Simon & Schuster, 1989).

30. See Reid Hastie, *Inside the Jury* (Cambridge, Mass.: Harvard University Press, 1983); Elizabeth F. Loftus, "Reconstructing Memory: The Incredible Eyewitness," *Psychology Today* (August 1974): 116–119; Elizabeth F. Loftus, "Leading Questions and the Eyewitness Report," *Cognitive Psychology*, **7** (1975): 560–572; Elizabeth F. Loftus, *Eyewitness Testimony* (Cambridge, Mass.: Harvard University Press, 1979); Elizabeth F. Loftus, "Eyewitness Testimony: Psychological Research and Legal Thought," in *Crime and Justice: An Annual Review of Research*, vol. 3, ed. Michael Tonry and Norval Morris (Chicago: University of Chicago Press, 1981), pp. 105–151; Elizabeth F. Loftus and James M. Doyle, *Eyewitness Testimony: Civil and Criminal* (New York: Kluwer, 1987); and Elizabeth F. Loftus and G. Zanni, "Eyewitness Testimony: The Influence of the Wording of a Question," *Bulletin of the Psychonomic Society*, **5** (1975): 86–88.

31. Albert H. Hastorf and Hadley Cantrill, "They Saw the Game: A Case Study," *Journal of Abnormal and Social Psychology*, **49** (1954): 129–134.

32. J. C. Bartlett and J. E. Leslie, "Aging and Memory for Faces versus Single Views of Faces," *Memory and Cognition*, **14** (1986): 371–381.

33. Kenneth A. Deffenbacher and Elizabeth F. Loftus, "Do Jurors Share a Common Understanding Concerning Eyewitness Behavior?" *Law and Human Behavior*, **6** (1982): 15–30.

34. J. C. Yuille, "Research and Teaching with Police: A Canadian Example," *International Review of Applied Psychology*, **33** (1984): 5–23.

35. R. K. Bothwell, J. Brigham, and M. A. Piggott, "An Exploratory Study of Personality Differences in Eyewitness Memory," *Journal of Social Behavior and Personality*, **2** (1987): 335–343.

36. C. A. Visher, "Juror Decision-Making: The Importance of Evidence," *Law and Human Behavior*, **11** (1987): 1–17.

37. See Gerhard O. W. Mueller, *Sentencing: Process and Purpose* (Springfield, Ill.: Charles C. Thomas, 1977).

38. See, e.g., Joan Petersilia, Peter Greenwood, and Marvin Lavin, *Criminal Careers of Habitual Felons*, for LEAA (Washington, D.C.: U.S. Government Printing Office, 1978).

39. Revel Shinnar and S. Shinnar, "The Effects of the Criminal Justice System on the Control of Crime: A Quantitative Approach," *Law and Society Review*, **9** (1975): 581–611.

40. See, e.g., Peter Greenwood, *Selective Incapacitation* (Santa Monica, Calif.: Rand Corporation, 1982).

41. Petersilia et al., *Criminal Careers of Habitual Felons*, p. 5.

42. Philip Cook, "The Demand and Supply of Criminal Opportunities," in *Crime and Justice*, vol. 7, ed. Michael Tonry and Norval Morris (Chicago: University of Chicago Press, 1986).

43. Johannes Andenaes, *Punishment and Deterrence* (Ann Arbor: University of Michigan Press, 1974), p. 51.

44. William G. Bailey, ed., *The Encyclopedia of Police Science* (New York: Garland, 1989), p. 600.

45. Edwin H. Pfuhl, Jr., "Police Strikes and Conventional Crime," *Criminology*, **21** (1983): 489–503.

46. Ari L. Goldman, "In Spite of Dip, Subway Crime Nears a Record," *New York Times*, Nov. 20, 1982, pp. 1, 26.

47. James A. Beha II, "And Nobody Can Get You Out: The Impact of a Mandatory Prison Sentence for the Illegal Carrying of a Firearm on the Administration of Criminal Justice in Boston," *Boston University Law Review*, **57** (March 1977): 96–146.

48. Robert P. Barry, "To Slug a Meter: A Study of Coin Fraud," *Criminology* **4** (1969): 40–47; John F. Decker, "Curbside Deterrence," *Criminology*, **10** (1972): 127–142.

49. Scott Decker, Richard Wright, and Robert Logie, "Perceptual Deterrence among Active Residential Burglars: A Research Note," *Criminology*, **31** (1993): 135–147; Steven R. Burkett and David A. Ward, "A Note on Perceptual Deterrence, Religiously Based Moral Condemnation, and Social Control," *Criminology*, **31** (1993): 119–134; David Ward and Charles R. Tittle, "Deterrence or Labeling: The Effects of Informal Sanctions," *Deviant Behavior*, **14** (1993): 43–64; Carol Veneziano and Louis Veneziano, "The Relationship between Deterrence and Moral Reasoning," *Criminal Justice Review*, **17** (1992): 209–218; Ronet Bachman, Raymond Paternoster, and Sally Ward, "The Rationality of Sexual Offending: Testing a Deterrence/Rational Choice Conception of Sexual Assault," *Law and Society Review*, **26** (1992): 343–372; Kirk R. Williams and Richard Hawkins, "Wife Assault, Costs of Arrest, and the Deterrence Process," *Journal of Research in Crime and Delinquency*, **29** (1992): 292–310; Mitchell B. Chamlin, Harold G. Grasmick, and Robert J. Bursik, Jr., "Time Aggregation and Time Lag in Macro-Level Deterrence," *Criminology*, **30** (1992): 377–395; Sally S. Simpson and Christopher S. Koper, "Deterring Corporate Crime," *Criminology*, **30** (1992): 347–375; Joan McCord, "Deterrence of Domestic Violence: A Critical View of Research," *Journal of Research in Crime and Delinquency*, **29** (1992): 229–239; Chester L. Britt III, Michael R. Gottfredson, and John S. Goldkamp, "Drug Testing and Pretrial Misconduct: An Experiment on the Specific Deterrent Effects of Drug Monitoring Defendants on Pretrial Release," *Journal of Research in Crime and Delinquency*, **29** (1992): 62–78; Jeff T. Casey and John T. Scholz, "Beyond Deterrence: Behavioral Decision Theory and Tax Compliance," *Law and Society Review*, **25** (1991): 821–843; Daniel Nagin and Raymond Paternoster, "The Preventive Effects of the Perceived Risk of Arrest: Testing an Expanded Conception of Deterrence," *Criminology*, **29** (1991): 561–587; David McDowall, Alan Lizotte, and Brian Wiersema, "General Deterrence through Civilian Gun Ownership," *Criminology*, **29** (1991): 541–559; Lawrence W. Sherman, Janell D. Schmidt, Dennis P. Rogan, et al., "From Initial Deterrence to Long-Term Escalation: Short Custody Arrest for Poverty Ghetto Domestic

Violence," *Criminology,* **29** (1991): 821–850; Ruth D. Peterson and William C. Bailey, "Felony Murder and Capital Punishment: An Examination of the Deterrence Question," *Criminology,* **29** (1991): 367–395.

50. Immanuel Kant, *Critique of Pure Reason* (1781).

51. Robert Martinson, "What Works? Questions and Answers about Prison Reform," *Public Interest,* **35** (Spring 1974): 25. See also James Q. Wilson, "'What Works?' Revisited: New Findings on Criminal Rehabilitation," *Public Interest,* **61** (Fall 1980): 1.

52. See Francis T. Cullen, Edward J. Latessa, and Velmer S. Burton, Jr., "The Correctional Orientation of Prison Wardens: Is the Rehabilitative Ideal Supported?" *Criminology,* **31** (1993): 69–92; Grant E. Coulson and Verna Nutbrown, "Properties of an Ideal Rehabilitative Program for High-Need Offenders," *International Journal of Offender Therapy and Comparative Criminology,* **36** (1992): 203–208; David Shichor, "Following the Penological Pendulum: The Survival of Rehabilitation," *Federal Probation,* **56** (1992): 19–25; and H. R. De Luca, Thomas J. Miller, and Carl F. Wiedemann, "Punishment vs. Rehabilitation: A Proposal for Revising Sentencing Practices," *Federal Probation,* **55** (1991): 37–45.

53. Model Penal Code, sec. 1.02(b).

54. Andrew von Hirsch, *Doing Justice: The Choice of Punishments* (New York: Hill & Wang, 1976). And see Andrew von Hirsch, *Past or Future Crimes: Deservedness and Dangerousness in the Sentencing of Criminals* (New Brunswick, N.J.: Rutgers University Press, 1985).

55. Willard Gaylin, *Partial Justice* (New York: Knopf, 1974).

56. Norval Morris, *The Future of Imprisonment* (Chicago: University of Chicago Press, 1974).

57. Michael Tonry, "Mandatory Penalties," in *Crime and Justice: A Review of Research,* vol. 16, ed. Tonry (Chicago and London: University of Chicago Press); David W. McDowall, Colin Loftin, and Brian Wiersema, *A Comparative Study of the Preventive Effects of Mandatory Sentencing Laws for Gun Crimes* (Washington, D.C.: U.S. Government Printing Office, 1992); U.S. Sentencing Commission, *Special Report to the Congress: Mandatory Minimum Penalties in the Federal Criminal Justice System* (Washington, D.C.: U.S. Government Printing Office, 1991).

58. Contemporary sentencing guidelines are neither novel nor unique. Mosaic law (Exodus 21) (*lex talionis*) graded the punishment in accordance with the harm done. The Germanic Codes (*Leges Barbarorum,* 500–1100 A.D.) had similar provisions. Nineteenth- and twentieth-century penal codes (starting with the French of 1810) have more or less binding guidelines or postulates adjusting the severity of the punishment to the harm done (e.g., loss of a limb or an eye). Most notable is the current Spanish Penal Code (of Dec. 23, 1944), which provides in Article 9 for a list of mitigating circumstances, in Article 10 for aggravating circumstances, and in Articles 58 through 67 for the interrelation between aggravating and mitigating circumstances.

59. Marvin E. Frankel, *Criminal Sentences* (New York: Hill and Wang, 1973).

60. Sally S. Simpson and Christopher S. Koper, "Deterring Corporate Crime," *Criminology,* **30** (1992): 347–373. See also Andrew von Hirsch, Kay A. Knapp, and Michael Tonry, *The Sentencing Commission and Its Guidelines* (Boston: Northeastern University Press, 1987); and William S. Laufer, "Culpability and the Sentencing of Corporations," *Nebraska Law Review,* **71** (1992): 1049–1094.

61. See Eric Simon, Gerry Gaes, and William Rhodes, "ASSYST—The Design and Implementation of Computer-Assisted Sentencing," *Federal Probation,* **55** (1991): 46–55.

62. See Michael Tonry, "The Politics and Processes of Sentencing Commissions," *Crime and Delinquency,* **37** (1991): 307–329. See also Alfred Blumstein, Jacqueline Cohen, Susan E. Martin, and Michael H. Tonry, *Research on Sentencing: The Search for Reform* (Washington, D.C.: National Academy Press, 1983); and Joann L. Miller, Peter H. Rossi, and Jon E. Simpson, "Felony Punishments: A Factorial Survey of Perceived Justice in Criminal Sentencing," *Journal of Criminal Law and Criminology,* **82** (1991): 396–422.

63. See John H. Kramer, Robin L. Lubitz, and Cynthia A. Kempinen, "Sentencing Guidelines: A Quantitative Comparison of Sentencing Policies in Minnesota, Pennsylvania, and Washington," *Justice Quarterly,* **61** (1989): 565–587.

64. For a complete account of the fate of New York's sentencing commission, see Pamala L. Griset, *Determinate Sentencing: The Promise and the Reality of Retributive Justice* (Albany: State University of New York Press, 1991).

65. Michael Tonry, "Sentencing Guidelines and Their Effects," in von Hirsch, Knapp, and Tonry, *The Sentencing Commission,* pp. 16–43; Laura Lein, Robert Rickards, and Tony Fabelo, "The Attitudes of Criminal Justice Practitioners toward Sentencing Issues," *Crime and Delinquency,* **38** (1992): 189–203.

66. *Mistretta v. U.S.,* 488 U.S. 361 (1989).

67. Stephen J. Schulhofer and Ilene H. Nagel, "Negotiated Pleas under the Federal Sentencing Guidelines: The First Fifteen Months," *American Criminal Law Review,* **27** (1989): 231–288.

68. Sara T. Dike, "Capital Punishment in the United States, Part I: Observations on the Use and Interpretation of the Law," *Criminal Justice Abstracts,* **13** (1981): 283–311; Hugo A. Bedau, *The Death Penalty in America* (New York: Oxford University Press, 1984).

69. William Bowers, *Executions in America* (Lexington, Mass.: Lexington Books, 1974).

70. Victoria Schneider and John Ortiz Smykla, "A Summary Analysis of *Executions in the United States: 1608–1978: The Espy File,*" in *The Death Penalty in America: Current Research,* ed. Robert M. Bohm (Cincinnati, Ohio, and Highland Heights, Ky.: Anderson and Academy of Criminal Justice Sciences, 1991), pp. 1–20.

71. Sandra Nicolai, Karen Riley, Rhonda Christensen,

Patrice Stych, and Leslie Greunke, *The Question of Capital Punishment* (Lincoln, Neb.: Contact, 1980).

72. Thorsten Sellin, *The Death Penalty* (Philadelphia: American Law Institute, 1959); Thorsten Sellin, *Capital Punishment* (New York: Harper & Row, 1967); Thorsten Sellin, *The Penalty of Death* (Beverly Hills, Calif.: Sage, 1980); Hans Zeisel, "The Deterrent Effect of the Death Penalty: Facts v. Faith," in *The Supreme Court Review*, ed. P. E. Kurland (Chicago: University of Chicago Press, 1976), pp. 317–343; William C. Bailey, "A Multivariate Cross-Sectional Analysis of the Deterrent Effect of the Death Penalty," *Sociology and Social Research*, **64** (1980): 183–207; Ruth D. Peterson and William C. Bailey, "Murder and Capital Punishment in the Evolving Context of the Post-*Furman* Era," *Social Forces*, **66** (1988): 774–807; Raymond Paternoster, *Capital Punishment in America* (New York: Lexington Books, 1991); Louis D. Bilionis, "Moral Appropriateness, Capital Punishment, and the 'Lockett' Doctrine," *Journal of Criminal Law and Criminology*, **82** (1991): 283–333; Robert M. Bohm, Louise J. Clark, and Adrian F. Aveni, "Knowledge and Death Penalty Opinion: A Test of the Marshall Hypotheses," *Journal of Research in Crime and Delinquency*, **28** (1991): 360–387.

73. Isaac Ehrlich, "The Deterrent Effect of Capital Punishment: A Question of Life and Death," *American Economic Review*, **65** (1975): 397–417. For discussions demonstrating that convicted murderers, if paroled, rarely commit violent offenses, see Sellin, *The Death Penalty*, pp. 69–79; Gennaro F. Vito, Pat Koester, and Deborah G. Wilson, "Return of the Dead: An Update on the Status of *Furman*-Commuted Death Row Inmates," in Bohm, *The Death Penalty in America*, pp. 89–99; and James W. Marquant and Jonathan R. Sorensen, "Institutional and Post-Release Behavior of *Furman*-Commuted Inmates in Texas," *Criminology*, **26** (1988): 677–693. See also Thomas J. Keil and Gennaro F. Vito, "Fear of Crime and Attitudes toward Capital Punishment: A Structures Equation Model," *Justice Quarterly*, **8** (1991): 447–464; and Robert M. Bohm, "Retribution and Capital Punishment: Toward a Better Understanding of Death Penalty Opinion," *Journal of Criminal Justice*, **20** (1992): 227–236.

74. See Steven Stack, "Publicized Executions and Homicide, 1950–1980," *American Sociological Review*, **52** (1987): 532–540; and David J. Phillips, "The Deterrent Effect of Capital Punishment: New Evidence on an Old Controversy," *American Journal of Sociology*, **86** (1980): 139–148.

75. See William C. Bailey and Ruth D. Peterson, "Murder and Capital Punishment: A Monthly Time-Series Analysis of Execution Publicity," *American Sociological Review*, **54** (1989): 722–743; William C. Bailey, "Murder, Capital Punishment, and Television: Execution Publicity and Homicide Rates," *American Sociological Review*, **55** (1990): 628–633; and Peterson and Bailey, "Felony Murder and Capital Punishment."

76. Charles L. Black, *Capital Punishment: The Inevitability of Caprice and Mistake* (New Haven, Conn.: Yale University Press, 1984); Herb Haines, "Flawed Executions, The Anti-Death Penalty Movement, and the Politics of Capital Punishment," *Social Problems*, **39** (1992): 125–138.

77. Marvin Wolfgang and Mark Riedel, "Race, Judicial Discretion, and the Death Penalty," *Annals of the American Academy of Political and Social Sciences*, **407** (1973): 119–133. See also Joseph E. Jacoby and Raymond Paternoster, "Sentencing Disparity and Jury Packing: Further Challenges to the Death Penalty," *Journal of Criminal Law and Criminology*, **73** (1982): 379–387; Joseph E. Jacoby, "The Deterrence and Brutalizing Effects of the Death Penalty," in *The Death Penalty in South Carolina*, ed. Bruce L. Pearson (Columbia, S.C.: Acluse Press, 1981); Robert L. Young, "Race, Conceptions of Crime and Justice, and Support for the Death Penalty," *Social Psychology Quarterly*, **54** (1991): 67–75; and Elizabeth Rapaport, "The Death Penalty and Gender Discrimination," *Law and Society Review*, **25** (1991): 367–383.

78. David Baldus, Charles Pulaski, and George Woodworth, "Comparative Review of Death Sentences: An Empirical Study of the Georgia Experience," *Journal of Criminal Law and Criminology*, **74** (1983): 661–678.

79. *McKlesky v. Kemp*, 478 U.S. 109 (1985). For a recent study, see Thomas J. Keil and Gennaro F. Vito, "Race and the Death Penalty in Kentucky Murder Trials: An Analysis of Post-*Gregg* Outcomes," *Justice Quarterly*, **7** (1990): 189–207. On the overall use of social science data by the Supreme Court in capital cases, see James R. Acker, "Social Science in Supreme Court Death Penalty Cases: Citation Practices and Their Implications," *Justice Quarterly*, **8** (1991): 422–446.

80. Blumberg, *Criminal Justice*.

81. See Raymond Paternoster, "Prosecutorial Discretion in Requesting the Death Penalty: A Case of Victim-Based Racial Discrimination," *Law and Society Review*, **18** (1984): 437–478; Michael L. Radelet and Glenn L. Pierce, "Race and Prosecutorial Discretion in Homicide Cases," *Law and Society Review*, **19** (1985): 587–621; Thomas J. Keil and Gennaro F. Vito, "Race, Homicide Severity, and Application of the Death Penalty: A Consideration of the Barnett Scale," *Criminology*, **27** (1989): 511–535; and Paige H. Ralph, Jonathan R. Sorensen, and James W. Marquart, "A Comparison of Death-Sentenced and Incarcerated Murderers in Pre-*Furman* Texas," *Justice Quarterly*, **9** (1992): 185–209.

82. Robert M. Bohm, Louise J. Clark, and Adrian F. Aveni, "The Influence of Knowledge on Reasons for Death Penalty Opinions: An Experimental Test," *Justice Quarterly*, **7** (1990): 175–188.

83. Roger Hood, *The Death Penalty: A World-Wide Perspective* (New York: Oxford University Press, 1989); Dennis Wiechman, Jerry Kendall, and Ronald Bae, "International Use of the Death Penalty," *International Journal of Comparative and Applied Criminal Justice*, **14** (1990): 239–260.

84. Hugo Adam Bedau, *Death Is Different* (Boston: Northeastern University Press, 1987).

18

A Research Focus on Corrections

KEY TERMS
conjugal visits
corrections
employment prisons
fee system
good-time system
inmate code
intensive-supervision probation (ISP)
parole
penitentiary
prisonization
probation
rehabilitation
shock incarceration (SI)

To the uninitiated observer, the sentencing of the convicted person is the end of the judiciary's role in the process of reacting to crime and the beginning of the role of the executive branch of government—the execution of the court-imposed sentence. Such a view was official doctrine as late as 1958, when Justice Felix Frankfurter, in *Gore v. United States,* pronounced that "in effect, we are asked to enter the domain of penology. . . . This Court has no such power."[1]

Much has changed since then. Prisoners have acquired the right to appeal judgment and sentence and the conditions of their confinement. In many states, courts have intervened by ordering changes in the way sentences are being executed. In some jurisdictions the courts have actually assumed control and management of prison systems, through court-appointed masters. The tasks of the courts never end. From the moment a sentence has been imposed until the last minutes of its execution, the courts have the power and duty to intervene in the correctional system. Courts and corrections may be separate organizational entities and represent different branches of government, yet they are quite interdependent, in that corrections executes and implements the orders of courts—the sentences—in compliance with standards of law.

There was yet another anachronism in Frankfurter's pronouncement. He referred to penology as the domain of those who deal with offenders after sentence has been imposed. *Penology* was a term used in the nineteenth century and the first half of the twentieth to describe the science of applying punishment for retributive or utilitarian purposes. Today criminologists speak of **corrections** when they refer to the implementation and execution of sentences imposed by courts, and to the system that administers those sentences. The switch was more than a change of name; it was a change of outlook and approach, from a punitive to a rehabilitative philosophy.

The meaning of "corrections" varies with the context. Professors make corrections on term papers. Eyeglasses or contact lenses make corrections in vision. Ignorance may be corrected by education. In each of these contexts, "correction" implies some form of improvement. After centuries of exploiting and punishing criminals, the penologists of the nineteenth century concluded that criminals needed correction more than punishment. "Penologists" became "correctional specialists," and the "penal system" became a "correctional system."

PUNISHMENT AND CORRECTIONS: A HISTORICAL OVERVIEW

From Antiquity to the Eighteenth Century

It is common to equate corrections with a prison system. That equation is not accurate today, nor was it ever accurate in the past. Nomadic people have no prisons, because buildings cannot be carried on the trek. Yet nomadic people do have means of correcting or punishing offenders. The Romans, once nomads, did not use prisons for punishment even after they settled and built the city and state of Rome. Roman criminals were punished primarily by being sentenced to hard labor for a specified period of time or for life. The Romans also had capital punishment of various forms for very serious crimes that offended not only the Roman state but also the gods. Prisons were simply places of detention for offenders awaiting trial or criminals about to be transported to the place where their sentence was to be carried out.

The limited information we have about Germanic punishment comes from the Roman historian Tacitus, who reported in the first century A.D. that the ancient Germans hanged traitors and deserters. Cowards were drowned in swamps. The Goths, a nomadic Germanic people, declared a convicted offender to be a wolf and sent him to the forest to live if he could. Under Germanic law, however, most wrongs were compensated by money or property to which, in serious cases, a fine could be added.

From the fifth to the eleventh centuries, under Germanic law homicides were dealt with by *blood feuds,* revenge killings by the victimized family against the offender's family. These feuds were not viewed as private revenge. In fact, the law demanded and sanctioned the feud as punishment. But the feud was lawful only if it was completed in a timely manner and if it did not exceed in measure the harm done. Any revenge committed thereafter or any that exceeded the limit was considered to be unlawful and would lead to legal proceedings.[2] Some unlawful killings could also be compensated by payment of *wergeld*, money to compensate for the loss of a warrior.[3]

The late Middle Ages in Europe were marked by the emergence of strong rulers who gained increasing control over the punishment of wrongdoers. Punishment, except that inflicted within the family, became a function of the state. By converting compensation money into fines and by claiming the estates of persons sentenced to death, rulers enriched themselves. Consequently, the number of capital offenses and of executions increased sharply. During the reign of Henry VIII in England (1509–1547), the number of executions rose rapidly, though not to the 72,000 that some writers have claimed.[4]

The forms of punishment became ever more cruel. Those sentenced to death were hanged, burned at the stake, drawn and quartered, disemboweled, boiled, broken on the wheel, stoned to death, impaled, drowned, pressed to death in a spiked container, and torn by red-hot tongs. Noncapital punishments also rose to a level of unprecedented cruelty; prisoners were branded, dismembered, flogged, and tortured, even for offenses that today are considered trivial. This state-sanctioned brutality apparently did not reduce the crime rate, but it did condition the population to accept cruelty as part of daily life.

During the reign of Queen Elizabeth I (1558–1603) the English began to experiment with additional forms of punishment. In 1598 galley slavery was introduced.[5] Queen Elizabeth characterized it as a "more merciful" form of punishment.[6] Many city-states on the Continent also used this form of punishment, selling their prisoners as galley slaves to the fleets of Italian city-states.[7] Slave galleys were maintained by France, Spain, Denmark, and other European countries well into the eighteenth century. Conditions on the galleys were anything but merciful. Chained to crowded rowing benches, exposed to all kinds of weather conditions, whipped by brutal overseers, and fed on hard rations, the galley slaves often welcomed death.

Imprisonment was not a principal means of punishment in England or on the Continent. The penal code of the Holy Roman emperor Charles V (1532) mentions punitive incarceration only once. Gradually, however, incarceration evolved from the practice of forced labor, a popular punishment because it supplied rulers with cheap workers. It was necessary to confine forced laborers at night in secure places. Ultimately, imprisonment came to be the primary punishment and forced labor the secondary punishment. By the mid-sixteenth century, the old English castle of Bridewell had been converted into a "house of occupations, or rather a house of correction—for repression of the idle and sturdy vagabond and common strumpet."[8] "Bridewells" were later established in all the counties of England.

Reformers in other countries created similar

A 17th century depiction of the classical forms of punishment, including hanging, breaking on the wheel, burning at the stake, decapitation, casting adrift, and whipping.

institutions. The Dutch, for example, established a *tuchthuis*, a house of discipline, in 1589. Germany, Denmark, and Sweden soon followed. The purpose of imprisonment was to make offenders useful members of the community through hard labor and religious worship. But soon after prisons were established, they became overcrowded. The English addressed the problem by establishing the prison hulk. Decommissioned and deteriorated warships were converted into prisons, most of which were docked in the river Thames. In the 1840s the British government had about 12 hulks that housed up to 4000 inmates.[9]

Hulks made no contribution to the correction of offenders. They offered no opportunity for work or exercise. They were overcrowded, insanitary places of confinement, with high death rates due to communicable diseases. Today the world community is in agreement that at least prisoners of war should not be confined on prison ships.[10] Yet New York City recently commissioned a fleet of prison barges and decommissioned ferry boats as prisons for ordinary criminals.

The Bridewells and the houses of correction never measured up to the ideals of the reformers. In fact, they became slave-labor camps in which the offenders' cheap labor contributed to the wealth of the rulers. In 1832 prison inmates still worked on treadmills, holding on to a wooden bar above their heads and treading steadily as the steps went round to produce power to move millstones.[11] In the eighteenth century England invented yet another way to deal with convicted persons: it sentenced them to be "transported" to the colonies. Virginia and the other southern colonies received many such persons who labored for the development of towns and plantations. After the American colonies won their independence, England transported offenders to Australia, which is proud to acknowledge its debt to their labor.[12]

Punishment in the New World

The first settlers of New England were Puritans opposed to the primacy of the Church of England. Rejecting English law, they nevertheless imported the English means of punishment, including the stocks and the pillory. Their religious beliefs were similar to those of the Calvin-

ists of the Netherlands, the country in which the *Mayflower* group prepared for the crossing to America. The *tuchthuis,* which they saw in the Netherlands, must have stuck in their minds as a means of correcting wrongdoers.

It was not in New England, however, but in Pennsylvania that the American correctional movement began. It started there with William Penn's "Great Law" of December 4, 1682, which provided for the establishment of houses of correction. Penn's law restricted corporal and capital punishment, though it retained whipping for the more severe offenses.[13]

After the colonies declared their independence, Pennsylvania continued the liberal spirit of William Penn. In Philadelphia the physician William Rush (1745–1813) took up the cause of penal reform. He worked to abolish capital punishment and to introduce penitentiaries. Rush helped organize the Pennsylvania Society for the Abolition of Slavery, and he became instrumental in the creation of the Philadelphia Society for Alleviating the Miseries of Public Prisons (1787). As a result, a small **penitentiary** wing was added to the Walnut Street Jail in 1790. Extended solitary confinement in a cell, it was thought, would bring the offender to penitence. Even at work prisoners were not allowed to communicate with one another.

The Quaker idea of penitence and labor in lieu of capital punishment seemed persuasive. For a few years after the creation of the Walnut Street penitentiary wing, the crime rate appeared to drop. New York (1791), Virginia (1800), Kentucky (1800), New Jersey (1798), and other states later adopted the penitentiary concept and reduced the use of capital punishment. These reforms reflected the Quaker philosophy of redemption through penitence. They must also be viewed as an extension of the Enlightenment reforms advocated by Cesare Beccaria in Italy and by John Howard, Jeremy Bentham, and Elizabeth Fry in England (Chapter 3).

The Pennsylvania System: Separate Confinement

Although the experiment at first seemed to be successful, barely a decade after the penitentiary wing was constructed at the Walnut Street Jail, the visiting committee of the Philadelphia Soci-

Short Answer Questions for Final

1. What are the major phases of a generalized system of justice? Briefly indicate the function of each phase.

2. Discuss the use of discretion. How and why does it occur?

3. What are some of the organizational and structural pressures that influence police conduct?

4. What are some of the consequences of organizational and structural pressures on police officers?

5. Present as many different possibilities for controlling the conduct of the police as you can. (List and number, explain if necessary.)

6. What are some of the problems involved in eliminating corruption, brutality, rule-breaking, and abusive procedures in police agencies?

7. Discuss the functioning of the bail system and alternatives to it.

8. What are the responsibilities and discretionary powers of the prosecutor.

9. What is negotiated justice or plea bargaining? Explain its operation and consequences for the legal system using perspectives emphasizing (1) theory, (2) fact, and (3) value.

10. Briefly describe at least three theories of (rationales for) punishment discussed in either the readings or the lectures.

11. What are the basic types of punishment used in connection with the criminal law?

Conflict Theory	Consensus Theory	Deviance/Deviant Behavior	Due Process	
Equal Protection	Labeling Theory	Karl Marx	Renology	Pseudo patients
Radical Criminology	Richard Quinney	Rusche and Kirchheimer	Social	
Interactionists	Socioeconomic Status			

Bobbies	Deadly Force	Exclutionary Rule	Knapp Commission	Miranda
Warnings	Negotiated Justice	Order Maintenance	Parens Patrise	
Plea Bargaining	Police Subculture	Prima Facie Case	Probable Cause	
Reasonable Suspicion	Sheriff	Victimology	Wickersham Commission	

Assigned Counsel	Bail Reform Act	Capital Punishment	Community	
Policing	Constable Magistrate	Courts of General Jurisdiction	Courts of Limited	
Jurisdiction	Cross-examination	Defendant	Defense Counsel	Deterrence
Federal Courts	Guilty Plea	Guilty Plea	Habeas Corpus	Incapacitation
Just Deserts	Justice of the Peace	Manhattan Bail Project	Night Watchman	
Peremptory Challenge	Problem Oriented Policing	Public Defender	Rehabilitation	
Restitution	Sting Operation	Team Policing	US Supreme Court	
Arraignment	Certiorari, writ of	Challenges for Cause	Defense Counsel	
Deterrence	Forensic Hospitals	Indictment	Information	Jails	Motions
Plead	Prisons	Prosecutor	Recidivism	Restitution	Selective Incapacitation
Voir Dire	Determinate Sentencing	Mandatory Sentencing		

Auburn System	Boot Camp Programs	Congregate Labor	Conjugal Visits	
Corrections	Custody Levels	Good Time	Incarceration	Inmate Code	Intensive
Supervision Probation	John Augustus	John Howard	Medical Model	
Parole	Penitentiary	Pennsylvania System	Prison Culture	Prisoner's Rights
Prisonization	Probation	Reformatory Movement	Rehabilitation	Shock Incarceration

ety for Alleviating the Miseries of Public Prisons reported "Idleness, Dirt, and Wretchedness" in the facility.[14] These conditions were the result of overcrowding and management's failure to cope with it. Prisoners were not at all penitent, useful labor could not be provided, and the authorities were unable to maintain the institution in a condition conducive to the improvement of prisoners.

New solutions were sought—better prisons, with better conditions and better management. Dr. Rush was in the forefront of the search. After his death in 1813 and after much lobbying by the Philadelphia Society, the Pennsylvania legislature approved the construction of two new penitentiaries, the Western in Pittsburgh and the Eastern in Philadelphia. They received their first inmates in 1826 and 1829, respectively.

The Western Penitentiary was a round building, permitting control of all cells from a central point. It was constructed more sturdily than any fortress then in existence. The prisoners were housed in small, tomblike cells that were furnished with Bibles. They had to work in their cells and were permitted only 1 hour of exercise daily. Even then they were not allowed to communicate with one another. The system proved disastrous: anxiety increased; psychoses were rampant. The prison soon had to be rebuilt at great cost to allow some daylight into the cells. The Eastern Penitentiary functioned along similar lines. Solitary confinement, work in cells, religious instruction, and penitence were the principal features. Yet harsh discipline was not tolerated.

The Auburn System: Congregate Labor

An alternative approach to imprisonment was developed in New York at the Auburn Penitentiary. Silence and labor, key features of the Pennsylvania system, were adopted. But one innovation was added—congregate labor. Younger offenders were permitted to work and eat in groups, although they were not allowed to talk to or even to glance at one another. Since the Pennsylvania system, which permitted inmates to work only in their cells, also proved extremely expensive, most states adopted the Auburn system. Congregate labor was cost-beneficial. Many penitentiaries even made a profit. European countries, which studied both American models, opted mostly for Pennsylvania's system, which was endorsed by the World's First International Prison Congress, held at Frankfurt, Germany, in 1846.

The Reformatory Movement

After the Civil War, Americans became disenchanted with both types of penitentiaries. Penitence rarely resulted from incarceration. Brutality and corruption were common. Operating costs rose. In 1870 a group of prison administrators met in Cincinnati to discuss their problems. These corrections leaders included Gaylord Hubbell, warden of Sing Sing Prison in New York; Enoch C. Wines, secretary of the New York Prison Association; Franklin Sanborn, Massachusetts correctional administrator; and Zebulon Brockway, of the Michigan House of Corrections, Detroit. The group enthusiastically adopted the reform ideas of two English penal reformers, Captain Alexander Maconochie and Sir Walter Crafton.

Maconochie and Crafton had called for an end to the vindictive imposition of suffering and embraced the ideas of treatment, moral regeneration, and reformation. The approach had to be scientific, starting with classification of inmates. Sentences had to be indeterminate, and release was to be the reward for having reformed in the "reformatory." The new reform spirit was to be kept alive by the National Prison Association, founded at that conference. Within a few years, nearly all states had constructed reformatories, primarily for younger prisoners. The Elmira Penitentiary in New York (1876) was used as a model. Optimism disappeared, however, as it became apparent that reformatories did not reform.[15]

The Medical Treatment Model

After World War I a new corrections philosophy appeared. During the war draftees had been subjected to psychological testing. Psychiatry was widely accepted as a means of dealing with individual and social problems. Psychiatrists (especially psychoanalysts) and psychologists became involved in the treatment of criminals and the reform of the penal system. Individual and group therapy was practiced in American prisons. This medical model flourished until World War II.

Despite the good intention of treating inmates as if they were medical patients, conditions of imprisonment changed very little. Inmates were permitted to leave their cells only for exercise, congregate work, chapel, therapy, and meals. Silence was enforced. Movements from cell to yard, to mess hall, to chapel took place in controlled groups that marched in lockstep. A particularly harsh form of military discipline had taken over. Indeed, many members of the prison staff were recruited from the military. The slightest infraction of the rules was severely punished, often by flogging.

After World War II the medical model lingered on under such rubrics as the therapeutic approach and the rehabilitative model. California was the leader in this movement, but nearly all states instituted group and individual therapy programs, counseling services, and behavior modification programs of various sorts, including shock therapy and revulsion therapy. Many of these programs raised serious civil liberties issues. Most were underfunded and inade-quately staffed. They reached only a small number of inmates, and the results were disappointing.

Community Involvement

At the same time American corrections experienced yet another change. With the realization that prisons did not rehabilitate offenders and at best rendered them fit to survive in a prison environment, efforts were made to integrate the offender into the community. Representatives of the community came into prisons, and offenders were diverted out of prisons. Increasing use was made of probation, parole, and halfway houses. Later on work-release and community projects became popular. Yet in all these approaches prisoners were simply the objects of the system and had to take what came to them.

The Prisoners' Rights Movement

The mid- and late 1960s witnessed rapid social change all over the world. In the United States minority groups demanded equality, women wanted equal treatment in public and private

Attica after the 1971 uprising: inmates ordered to lie down in the yard prior to a skin search. As the area became crowded, they were made to crawl away from the door on their bellies, hands locked behind their heads, to make room for more.

life, students rebelled against complacent educational systems, and the young rebelled against their elders. Prisoners, too, demanded their rights. But the correctional system was not prepared to respond. A riot broke out on September 9, 1971, at New York's Attica State Prison, an institution holding 2200 inmates. Prisoners took over most of the facility and held correctional officers as hostages. Governor Nelson Rockefeller ordered an attack by the state police. Helicopters dropped bombs and gas canisters. After 4 days and 43 deaths, "peace" was restored.[16]

Why had prisoners revolted? As a list of their demands revealed, they had been denied many of the fundamental rights guaranteed them under the Constitution. Douglas J. Besharov and G. O. W. Mueller compared the list of demands by the inmates with the United Nations Standard Minimum Rules for the Treatment of Prisoners, to which all countries, including the United States, had agreed. These standards pertain to diet, the handling of complaints, hygiene, religious freedom, contact with the outside world, treatment, education, legal assistance, recreation, medical treatment, minority-group personnel, inmate funds, resentencing and parole, and discipline. Most of the prisoners' demands were justified by the minimum standards guaranteed to them.[17]

The Attica experience was a shock to administrators. Prisoners' rights litigation had been initiated in the early 1960s, but the Attica rebellion opened the floodgates to lawsuits by prisoners testing not only the right of access to the courts but the particular conditions of their confinement.[18] Until the middle of the twentieth century, the penal codes of many states provided that felony imprisonment amounted to civil death: the felon lost virtually all civil rights, including the right to vote; the spouse of the prisoner was even entitled to have the marriage annulled.

The courts did not interfere with the management of prisons. In 1951 a federal circuit court ruled in the case of the "Birdman of Alcatraz," a prisoner who had become a highly respected ornithologist in prison, that "it is not the function of the courts to superintend the treatment and discipline of persons in penitentiaries."[19] This was called the "hands-off" doctrine.

In the 1960s the National Prison Project of the American Civil Liberties Union, the NAACP Legal Defense and Educational Fund, and the Legal Services of the federal government's Office of Economic Opportunity, as well as countless volunteers from the legal profession and hundreds of self-trained jailhouse lawyers, succeeded in overturning the hands-off doctrine. Since then, hundreds of decisions establishing various rights have been handed down. Prisoners now have the right to humane living conditions, legal assistance and law libraries, and freedom of religious practice. The rights guaranteed by the Constitution were finally granted to prisoners.[20]

Prisoners' rights litigation had a profound impact on the American correctional system. Some correctional administrators welcomed these decisions. Under court order, or the threat of court order, they could finally make improvements they had long considered necessary. Others regarded court-ordered changes in prison management as undue interference with their authority (see Table 18.1).

During the 1980s and 1990s the number of suits reaching the Supreme Court has declined, for several reasons: (1) The Supreme Court has taken a more restrictive view of such litigation. (2) Prison administrators, whether directly affected by lawsuits or not, have made an effort (although often unsuccessful) to comply with mandated standards. (3) Many prison systems have set up alternative means to improve relations, such as grievance procedures, mediation, and review boards. (4) While trial courts have been as busy ruling for prisoners' rights as ever, most administrators prefer not to take the costly route of appeal. (5) Most state correctional systems have been under court order to improve conditions of confinement. In many cases, court-appointed special masters with expertise in corrections are monitoring compliance with court orders.

CORRECTIONS TODAY

The prisoners' rights movement was one of two factors that changed the nature of American corrections. The other was the rebirth in the mid-1970s of the retribution philosophy in the form of

TABLE 18.1   BENCHMARKS IN RIGHTS FOR PRISONERS

Year	Case	Ruling
1958	*Gore v. United States*, 357 U.S. 386	*The hands-off doctrine:* The court has no right to enter the domain of penology.
1964	*Cooper v. Pate*, 378 U.S. 546	*End of the hands-off doctrine:* Prisoners may bring civil action for violation of their civil rights under the Civil Rights Act of 1871.
1964	*Rouse v. Cameron*, 373 F. 2d 452 (D.C. Cir.)	*Right to treatment:* A person incarcerated for "treatment" has a right to such treatment; otherwise, he or she must be discharged.
1968	*Lee v. Washington*, 390 U.S. 333	*Equal protection (Fourteenth Amendment):* Racial discrimination in prison is unconstitutional.
1969	*Johnson v. Avery*, 393 U.S. 499	*Right to legal defense:* Prisoners have a right to assistance from jailhouse lawyers.
1970	*Goldberg v. Kelly*, 397 U.S. 254	*Due process rights (Fourteenth Amendment):* Prisoners have a right to due process when threatened with a loss resulting from arbitrary or erroneous official decisions.
1972	*Cruz v. Beto*, 405 U.S. 319	*Freedom of religion (First Amendment):* Religious freedom must be granted equally to inmates of all faiths.
1974	*Wolff v. McDonnell*, 418 U.S. 539	*Due process in disciplinary proceedings:* When faced with serious disciplinary action, prisoners are entitled to procedural due process.
1974	*Procunier v. Martinez*, 416 U.S. 396	*Freedom of speech (First Amendment):* Prisoners' mail may be opened only by "legitimate," "least-restrictive" means. Relative freedom from censorship.
1976	*Estelle v. Gamble*, 429 U.S. 97	*Medical treatment:* Deliberate indifference to prisoners' serious medical needs is cruel and unusual punishment.
1977	*Bounds v. Smith*, 430 U.S. 817	*Legal assistance:* Prison law libraries must be adequately staffed to provide legal assistance to inmates in need.
1978	*Hutto v. Finney*, 437 U.S. 678	*Prohibition of cruel and unusual punishment (Eighth Amendment):* Confinement in a segregation cell for 30 days is cruel and unusual punishment. (Totality of circumstances test.)
1992	*Hudson v. McMillian*, 112 S. Ct. 995, 117 L. Ed. 2d 156	*Use of excessive force:* Beating of a prisoner by guards, or use of excessive force, may constitute cruel and unusual punishment even if not resulting in serious injury.

Source: Based on Geoffrey P. Albert, ed., Legal Rights of Prisoners (Beverly Hills, Calif.: Sage, 1980).

the just-deserts model. This rebirth had an immediate effect on corrections. As sentencing became oriented toward punitive and proportionate prison sentences, corrections became punitive and custodial. Most rehabilitation programs, already discredited, were abandoned. Prisoners were "doing time" in proportion to the gravity of their crime. They were not incarcerated to be rehabilitated or to be reformed.

This more punitive attitude toward offenders had an unfortunate consequence: legislators passed more punitive sentencing laws, and parole boards became more reluctant to grant parole or were abolished altogether. Table 18.2

identifies the significant stages in the evolution of corrections and their relation to important criminological phenomena.

Types of Incarceration

There are two categories of prison facilities: detention facilities and correctional facilities. *Detention facilities* normally do not house convicted persons; they are not, technically, correctional facilities. They house persons arrested and undergoing processing, awaiting trial, or awaiting transfer to a correctional facility after conviction. *Correctional facilities* include county jails and state and federal prisons. In county jails, persons convicted of misdemeanors normally serve sentences of not more than 1 year. State and federal prisons house persons sentenced for felonies to terms of longer than 1 year.

But there are numerous exceptions to the rules. Many jails operated by counties and cities serve two purposes: they house persons awaiting trial or transfer, and they also hold those serving misdemeanor sentences. Moreover, since a large number of state prisons are overcrowded, many states have found it necessary to house in county jails those sentenced to state prison for felonies. Local variations cloud the distinctions even further. Riker's Island in New York City serves not only as the jail for all the boroughs of the city but also as a prison for offenders serving longer state sentences. Finally, a few states call some of their prisons "houses of detention."

Jails

Criminologists generally consider the conditions in jails to be inferior to those in prisons. Most jails are not sanitary, have few services or programs for inmates, and do not separate dangerous from nondangerous prisoners.[21] They are often overcrowded and underfunded.[22]

There are 3338 jails in the United States. A jail in one state may be as large as the entire prison system of another state. The men's central jail of Los Angeles has a rated capacity of 5136 inmates; it usually holds more. Cook County Jail in Chicago has a rated capacity of 4600. Many jails in rural counties, by contrast, are small and operate under a **fee system,** by which the county gov-

ernment pays a modest amount of money for each prisoner per day. That amount usually constitutes the entire operating budget of the jail. As a result, there are movements to create central jails for neighboring counties, which can then share the cost of operation.

The movement to deinstitutionalize mental patients, begun in the 1960s, added an additional burden to the criminal justice system, especially to jails. It was demonstrated in a study of county jails in New Jersey that 10.9 percent of inmates had a history of mental hospitalization. That figure did not include inmates who were confined on special tiers reserved for those exhibiting grossly bizarre, irrational, or violent behavior patterns that the jail staff considered a threat to researchers.[23] The inmates on the segregated tiers were even more likely to have some history of mental institutionalization.

Jail staff, whether law enforcement or corrections employees, cannot be expected to have the expertise required to deal with such a massive problem.[24] Experts argue that if public policy dictates that jails deal with emotionally disturbed and mentally ill offenders, a far better program of identification, diagnosis, crisis intervention, and case management at release is called for.[25]

Prisons

Whatever they are called, whether state or federal prisons, penitentiaries, or correctional institutions, prisons for the most part have had better management than jails and better education, recreation, and employment programs.[26] But this is not surprising. After all, prisons are larger, have many more inmates, and thus have much bigger budgets. A prison normally has three distinct custody levels for inmates, based on an assessment of their perceived dangerousness:

■ *Maximum security prisons* are designed to hold the most dangerous and aggressive inmates. They have high concrete walls or double-perimeter fences, gun towers with armed guards, and strategically placed electronic monitors.

■ *Medium security prisons* house inmates who are considered less dangerous or escape-prone than those in maximum security facili-

TABLE 18.2   SIGNIFICANT STAGES IN THE EVOLUTION OF CORRECTIONS

Time Frame	Culture: Socio-Economic - Political Development	Theory of Crime Causation	Intervention Modes
Prehistoric, pre-literate, Stone Age	Clans, tribes of hunter-gatherers, early agriculture	Fate, spirits	Sacrifices to spirits, appeasement, outlawry
Starting around 3500 B.C.	Near-Eastern cities and kingdoms, commerce and agriculture	Personal motivation, rebellion	Elaborate rituals, capital punishment, compensation
Ca. 1200 B.C.	Ancient Israelites	Personal wrongdoing, offending God	Talionic punishment (an eye for an eye)
Ca. 1110 B.C.–A.D. 375	Graeco-Roman (classical period)	Ranging from fate (deities) to personal guilt (free will, pleasure/pain)	Severe punishments, slave labor (mines, galleys), capital and corporal punishment
Starting in A.D. 30	Christianity, church leaders, feudal lords, agriculture, commerce	Disobedience to God, sin, the devil	Capital punishment, penance, fines, shaming
A.D. 400–1500	Europe, Middle Ages (Inquisition, beginning 12th century)	Rebellion against the Lord and the lords, the devil	Blood feuds, capital punishment, cruel and severe, galley slavery
A.D. 1500–1800	Age of discovery and commercial expansion; development of sovereign states	Personal responsibility, laziness, bad habits, rebellion	Galley slavery, capital punishment, disfigurement, beginning of houses of correction (Netherlands, England), transportation to penal colonies
Late 18th century	American and French Revolutions, Age of Enlightenment	Free will: Beccaria, Bentham, the Classical School	Fixed & proportionate punishments, decrease of capital punishment, imprisonment, transportation, fines
19th century	Industrial Revolution, rise of middle class	Social problems (Marx, Engels); free will theory continues	Incarceration for reformation, control; work houses, penitentiaries, probation, parole, juvenile court
Late 19th century	Evolutionism (Darwin), the scientific age	Positivist School (Lombroso), the born criminal	Control, imprisonment and community sentences, classification of convicts
First quarter, 20th century	The rise of psychology and psychiatry	Lombroso's theory disproven (Goring); biological-psychological factors	Individualized punishments, start of indeterminate prison sentences
Mid-20th century	From depression to recovery, era of world wars	Sociological, ecological factors and learning theory	Individualized sentencing, beginning of treatment approach, side-by-side with harsh imprisonment

TABLE 18.2 SIGNIFICANT STAGES IN THE EVOLUTION OF CORRECTIONS (CONTINUED)

Time Frame	Culture: Socio-Economic - Political Development	Theory of Crime Causation	Intervention Modes
Third quarter, 20th century	Civil rights movement and due process revolution	Strain, culture deviance, sub-culture theory	The treatment approach: rehabilitation
Fourth quarter, 20th century	Rapid socio-economic development, worldwide internationalization (esp. of culture)	Labelling theory, radical theory, conflict and social control theories	Away from treatment approach, social intervention, return to retribution (fixed, mandatory sentences); return to social intervention and treatment, tough alternative sentences

ties. These less imposing structures typically have no outside wall, only a series of fences. Many medium security inmates are housed in dormitories rather than cells.

■ *Minimum security prisons* hold inmates who are considered the lowest security risks. Very often these institutions operate without armed guards and without perimeter walls or fences. The typical inmate in such an institution has proved to be trustworthy in the correctional setting, is nonviolent, and/or is serving a short prison term.

The Size and Cost of the Correctional Enterprise

The correctional enterprise encompasses a very large number of people and requires a huge budget. In 1992 there were 883,593 prisoners in about 640 state and federal prisons, the highest number in our history. There were also 441,889 persons in locally administered jails.[27] If we add the number of children in custody, which stood at 99,617,[28] over 1.4 million persons were incarcerated in the United States, or about 1 in every 180 residents.

That figure does not include the 37,842 persons arrested daily for Index crimes or the many more arrested for misdemeanors and disorderly charges. Most of these were being detained on any given day (usually for several days) in the country's 13,500 police lockups, holding pens, and other local facilities operated by police and sheriff's departments.[29]

Most of the prisoners are male. State and federal correctional facilities held only 50,409 female prisoners in 1992, as compared with 833,184 male prisoners. Since 1981 the number of women incarcerated has risen from 4.2 to 5.7 percent of the total prison population.

In addition to offenders in correctional institutions, there are those who are sentenced to non-institutional, or community, corrections. Principally, these are persons on probation, which provides for the sentence to be served in the community in lieu of imprisonment, and on parole, which permits a convict to serve the tail end of a prison sentence in the community. On January 1, 1991, 1,917,865 adults were on probation and 497,391 on parole. Consequently, an estimated 3.8 million adult men and women, or an estimated 1 in 65 U.S. residents age 18 or older, were being serviced by the correctional system.[30]

Our rate of incarceration—426 imprisoned in prisons and jails per 100,000 of our population—is higher than that in any other country. It has far outstripped the rate in South Africa (333) and in the former Soviet Union (268 prisoners and work-camp inmates). The rate of incarceration in the Netherlands (40 per 100,000) is only 8 percent that of the United States. (See Figure 18.1.)

In 1991 the cost of running the entire federal and state correctional enterprise was over $18.1

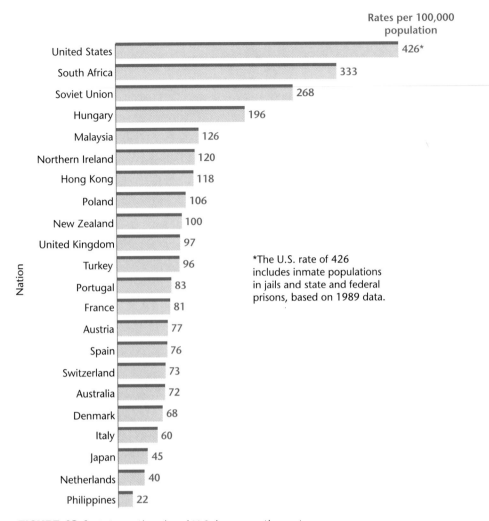

FIGURE 18.1 International and U.S. incarceration rates

Source: Americans behind Bars: A Comparison of International Rates of Incarceration (Washington, D.C.: The Sentencing Project, 1991). Reprinted with permission.

billion. This may sound like a lot of money, but it is actually only 1 percent of all government spending. While there is considerable variation among the states, on average prison officials report that it costs about $20,000 a year to house, feed, clothe, and supervise a prisoner. Because this estimate does not include indirect costs, the true annual expenditure probably exceeds $30,000 per prisoner.

The other significant cost is construction. We divide the total construction cost of any one institution by the number of prisoners it houses to get the cost per "bed." This cost may be as low as $7000 per year for a minimum security prisoner

to as high as $155,000 for a maximum security prisoner. (The comparable cost 50 years ago was between $4000 and $6000.) Of course, the annual cost of incarcerating just one offender varies from state to state.

The Problem of Overcrowding

At a recent international conference of criminal justice specialists, a Japanese correctional administrator asked, "With half of our prison cells being empty and our prisoner population declining, do I have a future in my chosen profession, corrections?" American corrections specialists do not have that worry. The U.S. prison population has been increasing since the early 1970s, and the rise does not appear to be related to crime rates. For example, the Index crime rate dropped steadily between 1980 and 1984, while incarceration rates continued to go up (Figure 18.2).

Some experts argue that incarceration rates rose because punitiveness increased, perhaps fueled by fear of drug crime and crime in general, supported by increasing media attention to crime. Once this fear was generated, it had a snowball effect. Scholars began to argue in favor of punitiveness, against the rehabilitative idea, and in support of just deserts. These arguments prompted legislative programs that severely curtailed judicial discretion in sentencing by mandating specific sentences for specific crimes.

An alternative hypothesis seeks to explain the escalating prison population in demographic terms. The most crime-prone population group is made up of 18- to 25-year-old males, a group whose numbers have grown rapidly since 1960. But this explanation is not entirely satisfactory, since the increase in the prison population was greater than the increase in the prison-prone population group.[31]

Charles F. Wellford and Laure Weber Brooks found that a number of factors accounted for the rise in the prison population. Between 1970 and 1979, for example, 54 to 76 percent of the rise could be explained by changes in demographic, structural, and legal (tougher sentencing laws) characteristics, strongly associated with regional location in the South, the percentage of the population age 18 to 29, unemployment rates, and changes in prison capacity and use of parole.[32]

The enormous prison overcrowding over the last two decades contributed significantly to the increase in prisoners' rights litigation. The populations of institutions in 29 state and local jurisdictions currently exceeded the institutions' capacity. All jurisdictions are nearing their breaking points. The National Prison Project of the American Civil Liberties Union has reported that as of January 1, 1992, 40 states, the District of Columbia, Puerto Rico, and the Virgin Islands were under some form of court order to reduce prison populations.[33]

On federal litigation arising out of this "crisis in corrections," Stephen D. Gottfredson and Sean McConville noted:

> The issue of crowding and other atrocious conditions is central to the overwhelming majority of these suits, and under present interpretation, the U.S. Constitution forbids the kind of treatment prison inmates in almost all states presently receive. Most of these states have been unable to meet the terms of the court orders, and despite action (such as refusals to accept new prison admissions or wholesale release of inmates), the situation in most jurisdictions is daily getting worse. As a result, we are facing a far-reaching constitutional crisis.[34]

Prison Culture and Society

For over half a century social scientists have studied the prison as a social entity with its own traditions, norms, language, and roles. Inmates constitute a unique social group. They live together, but not voluntarily. They live in extremely close quarters, often sharing all space other than a bed. They must stay in the group even if they fear for their safety.

The Deprivation Model

Some experts argue that the traditions, norms, languages, and roles that develop in prison result from the deprivations of prison life (the *deprivation model*). Donald Clemmer, who has described

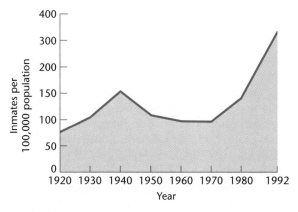

FIGURE 18.2 U.S. prison incarceration rates, 1930–1992

Source: U.S. Department of Justice, Bureau of Justice Statistics, *Report to the Nation on Crime and Justice,* 2d ed. (Washington, D.C.: U.S. Government Printing Office, 1988), p. 104; *Prisoners in 1992,* Bureau of Justice Statistics Bulletin (Washington, D.C.: U.S. Government Printing Office, May 1993).

In an overcrowded facility in the Cook County, Illinois, jail, prisoners sleep on mattresses on the gym floor.

the prison subculture and how inmates adapt to it, uses the term **prisonization** to describe the complex process by which new inmates learn the ways of the prison society and what is expected of them. Inmates are first reduced in status from civilians to anonymous figures, numbers in a common uniform, subject to institutional rules and the prison's rigid hierarchy. After a while they begin to accept the inferior role; to take on new habits of eating, sleeping, and working; and to learn that they do not owe anything to anybody for their subsistence.[35]

Building on Clemmer's work, Gresham M. Sykes described the "pains of imprisonment" new inmates suffer.[36] First, inmates are deprived of liberty and cut off from friends and family. The results are lost emotional relationships, boredom, and loneliness. Second, inmates are deprived of goods and services. While it is true that an inmate will get "three squares and clean sheets," the standard of living inside a prison is very low. Prisoners have no chance to retain or to obtain material possessions.

Third, inmates are deprived of heterosexual relations. Criminologists have identified a number of psychological problems that result from this deprivation. The worst of these problems

expresses itself in the homosexual enslavement of younger prisoners by older, aggressive inmates. For heterosexual inmates the deprivation of a partner of the opposite sex is one of the worst forms of punishment. Precisely for that reason, many correctional systems have instituted programs of **conjugal visits,** allowing inmates to have contact with loved ones and family. At the Eastern Correctional Facility in Napanoch, New York, inmates are given the opportunity to stay with their spouse for 44 hours every 3 or 4 months.[37]

Fourth, convicts are deprived of personal autonomy. Their lives are regulated and controlled 24 hours a day. But the control by corrections staff is selective. Staff are likely to look the other way when prisoners enforce, often brutally, their own code of conduct among themselves. The fifth pain of imprisonment is the deprivation of security. When a prisoner shares a small space with other inmates, some of whom are likely to be violent, aggression, violence, and sexual exploitation are inevitable.

To cope with these pains of imprisonment, an inmate needs to live by the **inmate code,** a set of rules that reflect the values of the prison society ("Don't interfere with inmate interests," "Don't trust the guards," "Don't weaken," and so on).[38] The prison culture is a distinct culture that develops because of the nature of confinement.

The Importation Model

Clarence Schrag has offered an opposing explanation of prison cultures. In his view, the values found within the prison are precisely those values found on the streets from which the offenders come.[39] This model, called the *importation model*, suggests that the inmate subculture is not formed within the prison but is brought in from the outside.

Research Studies

Many researchers have tested the ideas of Clemmer, Sykes, and Schrag. Charles W. Thomas, for example, found support for the importation model.[40] Stanton Wheeler tested Clemmer's prisonization concept empirically and found that prisonization follows a U-shaped pattern during a period of incarceration: it is mild at the beginning, increases in intensity, and then decreases as release becomes imminent.[41] More recent research on Swedish prisoners by Ulla V. Bondeson comes to the opposite conclusion: prisonization, with all its detrimental aspects, increases with the length of the term. She concludes that prisons are schools of crime.[42]

The psychologist Hans Toch and his colleagues determined that most inmates serve trouble-free terms and that prison misbehavior is characteristic of youthful offenders sentenced to long terms. Misbehavior dissipates as prisoners age. To Toch, the goal of any prison system is to reduce violence through the creation of a climate that defuses it and to deal with residual violence through a person-centered approach.[43] The anthropologist Mark S. Fleisher's research on life in the Lompoc Federal Penitentiary in California supports Toch's hypothesis. An institutional culture that fosters and rewards peace and quiet can maintain a peaceful prison life, even for violent offenders.[44]

Reformers traditionally have been concerned with the physical environment in which prisoners serve their sentences. They have expressed the belief that prisoners cannot be reformed unless they are provided with more decent, more humane, and more refined settings. The findings of a study by James F. Houston, Don C. Gibbons, and Joseph F. Jones contradict this premise. The physically more attractive settings and facilities of a new jail made prisoners feel no better about their surroundings and made the correctional staff feel only slightly better.[45]

The modern prison, according to James Jacobs, can be understood only in terms of the interaction between the institution and the larger society. He claims that there are still unique conditions in the prison environment which require special adaptation (as described by Clemmer and Sykes), but that the isolation of inmates from the world outside the prison walls is decreasing. Television, radio, newspapers, more visitation, and increased legal representation account for the changes. Jacobs says the idea that "prison subculture" means a group that is "isolated, separate, and opposed to the dominant culture" may no longer be true.[46]

Some researchers argue that changes in the prison population since the 1960s have created a new prison society. Contemporary prisons now house a more heterogeneous group of inmates, and it appears that a single inmate code for the whole population no longer exists. Race plays the dominant role in inmate relationships.[47] In many state prison systems competition among black, Hispanic, Native American, and white power blocs often leads to alliances that resemble international treaties among nations. Robert G. Leger concludes:

> Whites, who represent the dominant race outside prison, find themselves [to be] a distinct minority group on the inside. Whites' apparent realization of their minority position seems to affect their perception of their living space, levels of aggression, and attitudes towards the dominant racial group— blacks.[48]

Leo Carroll's *Hacks, Blacks, and Cons* also identified race as a crucial factor in inmate social relationships. In 1980, John Irwin's study *Prisons in Turmoil* showed how the social structure of California prisons was divided into white, black, and Hispanic groups. Hostile racial gangs emerged with links to their old gangs outside the walls.[49]

Prison Violence

The new prison society is characterized by increased violence. On February 2, 1980, the New Mexico Penitentiary in Santa Fe exploded in the most violent and destructive riot since 43 inmates and hostages were killed at Attica in 1971. In Attica, the disturbance was tightly controlled by a small group of powerful inmates; the New Mexico inmates were leaderless and out of control. Fourteen guards were held hostage while hundreds of prisoners roamed the prison smashing and burning everything in sight. At least seven of the hostages were severely beaten and several were repeatedly raped.

But the inmates reserved the brunt of their rage for each other. Thirty-three inmates were killed, some after being brutally tortured and mutilated. As many as 200 other inmates were beaten and raped. The terror was so pervasive and uncontrolled that the majority of 1136 inmates fled and sought safety among the state police and National Guard personnel ringing the penitentiary. The level of inmate-to-inmate violence was unprecedented.

When the riot was over, officials acknowledged that the New Mexico corrections system had long been neglected. Maximum-custody inmates, including some labeled psychotic, were mixed with young and vulnerable first offenders, often in dormitories holding as many as 90 men each.[50]

The increasing violence in prisons has been attributed to the younger age of inmates, warring racial groups, and the transfer of the subculture of violence from the streets into the prison.[51] Lee Bowker adds the easy availability of deadly weapons, the mixing of violence-prone with nonviolent inmates, the level of tension, and inadequate supervision.[52]

Prison Gangs

Over the past 30 years prison gangs have evolved from small groups of inmates associated for mutual protection into self-perpetuating criminal gangs with the characteristics of organized-crime syndicates. The first prison gang, the Gypsy Jakers, started at Washington State penitentiary, Walla Walla, in 1950. In the 1960s, racial turmoil in American society spilled into the prisons, sometimes resulting in inmate race wars. Gangs provided protection for their members. At San Quentin, for example, there were the Aryan Brotherhood, supposedly created to protect white inmates; the Black Guerrilla Family, a militant gang associated with the Black Panther party; the Mexican Mafia, with members from East Los Angeles; and their bitter rivals, the Nuestra Familia, consisting of rural Chicanos.

Gangs developed in Illinois in the late 1960s, and by the 1970s and 1980s prison gangs had spread throughout the country. A recent report indicates that there are prison gangs in the federal system and in 32 state jurisdictions.[53] Most gang members are in Illinois (5300), Pennsylvania (2400), and California (2050).

Correctional Officers

Prison life is largely determined by the interactions among the prisoners themselves. The role of correctional officers appears secondary. The popular perception is that the correctional staff must control prisoners by brute force. Yet officers rarely carry weapons inside the prison because inmates might take the weapons away from them if they did.

Controlling Inmates

Correctional officers survive by earning respect and resorting, when necessary, to unarmed coercion. James W. Marquart designed an innovative study to address this issue. In order to understand inmate coercion, Marquart became a correctional officer for 19 months in a prison housing nearly 3000 inmates. He worked throughout the institution, collecting data on social control and order. He was able to observe how the guards meted out official and unofficial punishments, coopted inmate elites to act as prisoner correctional officers, cultivated snitches, and engaged in other activities.

Marquart developed relations with more than 20 key informants, who helped him interpret events. His research revealed the following on officers' use of force:

[G]uard violence was not idiosyncratic nor a form of self-defense and was relatively unprovoked. Instead, force was used against inmates as a means of physical punishment by a small but significant percentage of the guards. These officers were primarily hall officers and sergeants with relatively low-ranking positions in the guard hierarchy. It also demonstrated that force served not only as a control mechanism, but also induced group cohe-

Corrections officer at work: Perimeter duty at the East Jersey Prison, New Jersey.

sion, maintained status and deference, and facilitated promotions.[54]

Types of Correctional Officers

The life of a correctional officer is not easy. In some communities, such as Moundsville, West Virginia, and Elmira, New York, it is a tradition for sons, and now daughters as well, to follow in a father's footsteps and seek employment with the state correctional authority. In many towns the prison is the principal employer. Most guards, however, take the job for lack of better opportunities.

The stressful quality of the job determines the types of personalities that serve in correctional institutions. Kelsey Kaufman describes five types, based on their attitudes toward the inmates and the other officers:

Pollyannas (optimists): Positive toward both groups
Burnouts: Negative toward both groups
Functionaries: Ambivalent toward both groups
Hard asses: Negative toward inmates, positive toward officers
White hats: Positive toward inmates, negative toward officers.[55]

Barbara A. Owen found that at San Quentin, in California, correctional officers are molded by the interactions between themselves and prisoners and among themselves. She ranks the personality types on a continuum:

John Waynes (disciplinarians)
Wishy-washy
Lazy/laid back
All right
Dirty officers[56]

Programs in Penal Institutions

With this understanding of prison life and institutional culture, it is possible to assess contemporary programs in American corrections: labor, treatment, and rehabilitation.

Labor

The overpowering demand to save taxpayers' money has led to massive programs to employ prisoners for profit. We have seen that in antiquity prisoners were exploited as cheap labor on ships. In the nineteenth century, American prisoners were farmed out to private entrepreneurs. The products of the prisoners' labor were sold at a profit, which was shared by the entrepreneur and the state. In Alabama until 1862, Burrows, Holt & Company used prison labor for the manufacture of "sack, blinds, doors, russet, brogans, cabinet furniture, wagons, wheat fans, well buckets, five and ten gallon kegs."[57] Alabama was still leasing inmates to private mining companies as recently as 1928.

When the lease system was abolished in the 1920s, the legislatures of southern states enacted statutes permitting the state highway authorities to use prison labor in chain gangs on the roads. Several southern states established plantation prisons, where, to save money, armed prisoner "trusties" replaced guards. Conditions were brutal.

The exploitation of prison labor came to a gradual halt in the early 1930s when federal legislation prohibited the interstate sale of prison-made goods.[58] In some states administrators disregarded federal restraints and defiantly maintained their own prison industries. In other states, however, prison labor was restricted to government services, such as the manufacture of license plates and the repair of state vehicles. But there was not enough of this kind of work to keep all inmates busy, and many prisoners spent their days in idleness.

In the 1970s prison administrators once again realized the potential profitability of prison industries. The U.S. Department of Justice now certifies state prison systems that have met certain standards and authorizes them to ship prison-made goods in interstate commerce. At present the resistance to inmate labor has lessened. In fact, more than 30 private-sector industry projects are in operation. Companies such as Best Western International (hotels), Wahlers Company (office furniture), and Utah Printing and Graphics have set up shops in prisons around the country. Prisoners manufacture disk drives, airplane parts, light metal products, and condensing units. Many prisoners also operate computer terminals. In several states, private, nonprofit corporations operate all or parts of prison industries. The wages paid to most prisoners, however, are less than those paid to free workers.[59]

Among the states that have successfully experimented with productive prison labor are New York and Florida. New York State created Corcraft, a corporation empowered to run its prison industries. It has proved economically beneficial for the state, and jobs displaced in the private sector were more than offset by new civilian employment opportunities created by Corcraft.[60] Florida created Prison Rehabilitative and Diversified Enterprises (PRIDE), a nonprofit corporation that since 1982 has operated all prison industries at double the income that was made before it took over. It has increased prisoner employment rates by 70 percent and seemingly lowered the recommitment rate for prisoners who participate in the program.[61]

A lowered recommitment rate, however, may be due to factors other than the programs themselves. Kathleen E. Maguire, Timothy J. Flanagan, and Terence P. Thornberry compared the recidivism rate of former prisoners who had participated in prison industry programs with that of nonparticipants. They found that when differences among the two groups in regard to other characteristics associated with imprisonment were taken into account, the rates were virtually identical.[62]

The question of prison labor is intricate and bothersome. The return to prison industry seemed to offer a means to deal with the budget crisis in which American corrections found itself. As yet there is no indication that the correctional system can be made to pay for itself by prison industry. It is doubtful as well that useful work in a commercial industry can prepare prisoners for gainful employment in free society. Moreover, troublesome questions persist about such issues as compensation, industrial safety, unionization, and the absence of benefits.

Treatment and Rehabilitation

Few criminologists disagree about the need for prisons. But many also generally agree that the number of people imprisoned is far greater than necessary. They disagree about the criteria for determining which inmates should be incarcerated and which should not.

Progressive criminologists regard the principal objective of the correctional system to be *reformation,* the voluntary, self-initiated transformation of an individual, lacking in social or vocational skills, into a productive, normally functioning citizen. Offenders are, according to this view, in need of rehabilitation. They may be psychologically disturbed, addicted to alcohol or drugs, or simply lacking in the basic skills necessary to survive in a complex society. They therefore need educational, psychological, and vocational programs.

Other criminologists have little faith in rehabilitation programs or are philosophically opposed to the emphasis on treating and correcting behavior. With the recent focus on retribution and just deserts, some criminologists have promoted the incarceration of offenders in humane conditions with few efforts to change them, either through work or through involvement in therapeutic programs. But even those opposed to compulsory rehabilitation would not deny prisoners the right to participate in voluntary programs.

Rehabilitation has been broadly defined as the result of any social or psychological intervention intended to reduce an offender's further criminal activity.[63] By this standard, the true test of success is noninvolvement in crime following participation in an intervention program. This is why criminologists traditionally have examined recidivism (repeat offenses) rates of offenders who have and have not been exposed to rehabilitative intervention. Supporters of rehabilitation hope to see lower recidivism rates, while those who seek warehousing of inmates anticipate no such change. Three types of programs are typically in use in prisons in the United States: psychological (psychotherapy and behavior therapy), educational (general equivalency diploma), and vocational (for example, food preparation) programs.

Evaluation of Rehabilitation

Innovative rehabilitation programs are generally begun with great enthusiasm; then disillusion sets in when they are subjected to critical examination. Most programs promise more than they can deliver, as new evaluation techniques have demonstrated. In 1964 Daniel Glaser established that vocational rehabilitation programs have virtually no effect on postrelease behavior.[64] In 1966, after evaluating 100 correctional treatment programs, Walter C. Bailey concluded that "evidence supporting the efficacy of correctional treatment is slight, inconsistent and of questionable reliability."[65] Roger Hood came to similarly disappointing conclusions in England.[66] James Robison and Gerald Smith evaluated California correctional and treatment programs and found inconclusive evidence of success.[67]

Freda Adler and her colleagues, after evaluating all Pennsylvania drug treatment programs, including all prison-based programs, concluded that virtually none could claim any significant successes and that the system as a whole was in a chaotic condition largely due to financial limitations.[68] The most devastating evaluation was that by Douglas Lipton, Robert Martinson, and Judith Wilks, published in 1975, with a preview article proclaiming that nothing works.[69] As a result, the treatment philosophy was discredited, programs were dismantled, and the vacuum in corrections was filled by the just-deserts approach.

Later some criminologists scrutinized Martinson's evaluations and found them methodologically flawed.[70] Martinson himself recanted to some extent and later confirmed that some programs have some success in curbing recidivism.[71] Paul Gendreau and Robert R. Ross presented impressive evidence of successful treatment programs.[72] After a thorough review of treatment programs initiated between 1981 and 1987, they concluded:

> [I]t is downright ridiculous to say "nothing works." This review attests that much is going on to indicate that offender rehabilitation has been, can be, and will be achieved.[73]

Their analysis of biomedical, diversion, family intervention, education, get-tough, and work programs gives reason for hope. The expectation that appropriate efforts may yield some success in changing recidivism rates has been rekindled.[74] In their recent study of the psychology of criminal behavior, Nathaniel Pallone and James Hennessy conclude that the future of rehabilitation will be found in models of education and reeducation developed for behavior therapy. These approaches seek incremental changes in behavior through incentives and disincentives.[75]

At present criminologists are ambivalent about the future of the rehabilitative approach; they agree only that therapy can never again be forced. Integration of the treatment approach with the widely accepted just-deserts model seems hard to achieve. Matching offenders with available treatment programs has been difficult in the past and will continue to be a problem. Above all, criminologists are wary of viewing treatment as the solution to the crime problem. The approach nevertheless is gaining support because, as Francis Cullen and Karen Gilbert aptly remark, it is "the only justification of criminal sanctioning that obligates the state to care for an offender's needs or welfare."[76] It is a humanitarian approach.

Medical Problems: AIDS and TB

When the rehabilitative model was created, and even as late as 1982, when Cullen and Gilbert

CRIMINOLOGICAL FOCUS
Health Problems in Prison

Prisoners are subject to all the routine medical problems everyone encounters, but they also may have special and more profound problems caused by close living and confinement. In early 1992, 23 percent of New York prison inmates and 6 percent of staff tested positive for tuberculosis, compared with a national rate of only 4 percent. Tuberculosis is a typical prison disease, an airborne infection that spreads through repetitious exposure in poorly ventilated spaces.(1)

Acquired immune deficiency syndrome (AIDS) poses an even greater danger. Because of the higher concentration among inmates of people with histories of high-risk behaviors for contracting the disease, particularly IV drug use, the incidence of AIDS is 202 per 100,000 in correctional facilities versus 14.65 per 100,000 in the general population—nearly 14 times higher.(2) In some correctional systems AIDS is now the leading cause of death.

With no cure for AIDS and no vaccine to protect against the virus that causes it, long-term health care for infected inmates and long-range plans for minimizing transmission are important. The fear of contagion is great, both among prison guards and among inmates, raising questions about isolation or quarantine of AIDS-infected prisoners. There is little risk of HIV infection through assault and none through casual contact, but correctional officers often are afraid of dealing with HIV-infected inmates.

AIDS patients suffer mental distress as well as physical problems, and their psychological needs can affect other inmates and prison officials. Indeed, mental illnesses in general pose a special and costly challenge for correctional services. Every state operates one or more facilities for mentally ill offenders, and prison and jail inmates often migrate between correctional and mental-health facilities. Over half the inmates in the mental-health facilities of correctional systems are prisoners who have become mentally ill in prison.(3)

Do the realities of prison overcrowding and inadequate budgets that contribute to health problems in prison constitute "deliberate indifference to serious medical needs of prisoners" and so violate the Eighth Amendment? If the current AIDS crisis and other health problems continue, we may have the opportunity to find out.

Sources
1. Lisa Belkin, "23% of State Prisoners Test Positive for TB," *New York Times,* Mar. 31, 1992, p. B4; Mireya Navairro, "As Suspects Wait, the Fear of Tuberculosis Rises," *New York Times,* Jan. 30, 1992, pp. B1, B2.
2. Theodore M. Hammett and Saira Moini, *Update on AIDS in Prisons and Jails,* National Institute of Justice AIDS Bulletin (U.S. Department of Justice, September 1990).
3. U.S. Bureau of Justice Statistics, *Report to the Nation on Crime and Justice* (Washington, D.C.: U.S. Government Printing Office, 1983), p. 68.

Questions for Discussion
1. The French correctional system has special institutions for the handicapped and other groups. Should we follow this model?
2. In 1993, two Supreme Court justices dissented from a majority view, saying that the "cruel and unusual punishments" prohibited by the Eighth Amendment do not extend to deprivations that are not part of a prisoner's sentence. Do you agree?

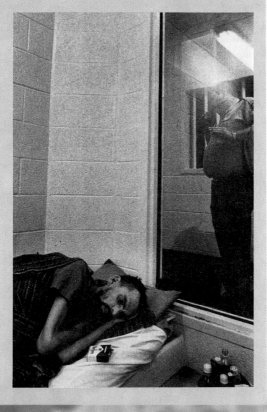

In 1990 AIDS sufferer Patrick McGuire spent his final months in prison after an arrest for breaking and entering when area hospitals refused to treat him because of his past behavior.

spoke of the state's obligation to care for offenders' needs and welfare, nobody could anticipate the enormous financial burden that the acquired immune deficiency syndrome (AIDS) crisis would impose on corrections. In 1991, 17,479 federal and state prisoners were infected with the human immunodeficiency virus (HIV) that causes AIDS. Of HIV-positive inmates, 9.6 percent had confirmed AIDS. Of the 1863 deaths of prisoners in 1991, 528 (28%) were due to AIDS.[77]

The cost of caring for a terminal AIDS patient has been estimated to be $500,000. There are large management problems as well. AIDS patients are shunned by other prisoners and by officers. In a recent case (*Dow v. State of New York*), $5.4 million in damages was awarded to a 42-year-old nurse who tested positive for HIV after being jabbed by an intravenous needle that came loose while she tried to restrain an AIDS-infected inmate being treated in a community hospital. Nurses testified that they had screamed 50 times for help from correctional officers who were standing in the doorway and did nothing.[78]

How can the system control prisoners dying of AIDS, who have nothing to lose? Prison hospitals are not equipped to provide adequate care for terminal patients. Placement in community hospitals poses grave risks. Successful treatment programs have not yet been established, and system officials are still searching for solutions.

The recent spread of tuberculosis (TB) among inmates has become another major health problem. In early 1992, 23 percent of New York prison inmates and 6 percent of staff tested positive for TB. (The national TB rate is 4 percent.) TB is a typical prison disease, an airborne infection that spreads through repetitious exposure in poorly ventilated spaces.[79] Prisons are challenged to provide isolation wards for those affected and to improve ventilation for all prisoners. There is also the danger of infection for the community at large from released TB-infected offenders.

Women in Prison

Most prisons are male institutions in which male offenders are guarded and receive services from a male staff. Until the mid-nineteenth century there were no separate prisons for women in the United States. The relatively few women prisoners were housed in male institutions, though usually in segregated sections. The first prison for women was opened in 1835 at Mt. Pleasant, New York, next to and under the supervision of Sing Sing Prison for men. Indiana started the next prison for women in 1873. During most of the twentieth century, women were imprisoned exclusively in women's prisons. These institutions tend to be smaller and less threatening in appearance and operation than male prisons (for example, no high walls or guard towers, and less regimentation). Yet, being smaller, they also lack many of the facilities of male institutions.

Currently, the population in women's prisons resembles that in men's prisons. Prisoners come predominantly from the uneducated, urban, poor sections of the population. Women in prison often adapt to prison life by creating surrogate families among themselves. These kinship networks provide mutual support and stable relationships and help to alleviate the deprivation caused by separation from their real families.

Investigators disagree on the extent and nature of homosexual relationships in women's prisons. Imogene Moyer argues that situations differ depending on factors specific to various institutional settings—separation of prisoners, average time served, and amount of supervision.[80] Informal social structures differ in a number of ways from those in male prisons: First, Edna Erez argues that an antiauthority inmate code does not appear to exist in women's prisons.[81] Second, unlike those in male prisons, homosexual relationships among women appear to be voluntary.

Programs available in women's prisons are also different from those in male prisons. They tend to emphasize society's traditional stereotype of "women's work": cooking, sewing, cosmetology, and office work, to which more recently computer programming has been added.

There is an additional burden on women in institutions. More than 76 percent of women prisoners are mothers. They leave behind an estimated 167,000 children.[82] Many give birth in prison. The mother–child relationship poses problems the correctional system has not resolved. Programs for mother–child contact are woefully inadequate; mothers may keep their newborns only for a few weeks, and children's visits are typically limited because of the distance from the children's homes and the restricted visiting hours.

Nearly a century and a half after the first U.S. prison for women was opened, an effort to use facilities in a cost-effective manner led to the establishment of the first co-correctional institutions, sometimes referred to as co-ed prisons, in which men and women, segregated at night, participate in joint daytime programs of work, recreation, and meals. Physical contact is limited to hand holding. Infraction of the rules leads to transfer to separate institutions. The federal system has played a leading role in operating co-correctional prisons; nearly two-thirds of federal women offenders serve their sentences in such facilities. For the country as a whole, however, the majority of the women prisoners are serving their time in institutions for women.

Privatization of Corrections

So far we have viewed punishment as the prerogative of the state, and the correctional system as a governmental institution for dealing with convicted offenders. This state monopoly of the penal system has existed since the Middle Ages. In the current era of free enterprise, state monopolies in many areas of government are gradually giving way to private enterprise. The delivery of letters is no longer exclusively in the hands of the U.S. Postal Service; much of it has been taken over by private courier companies. A great deal of government's police function has been taken over by private security firms. A similar movement is discernible in corrections.[83]

Frustration over the low success rates of prisons, usually measured by recidivism rates, coupled with incredibly high expense to the taxpayers, has prompted policy makers to search for alternatives to government-operated prisons. One is to turn over the administration of prisons to private entrepreneurs, who expect to run prisons at a profit.[84] The first private-enterprise prison was established in 1975, when RCA, under contract with the Commonwealth of Pennsylvania, opened a training school for delinquents in Weaversville. When James O. Finck-

enauer evaluated this facility, he found it "better staffed, organized, and equipped than any other program of its size" that he knew.[85] By 1993, approximately 18,800 adults were incarcerated in 55 privately run prisons.[86]

Although it still has not been conclusively shown that private facilities are indeed more cost-beneficial than public ones, privatization is continuing. This movement raises some troubling questions, which have been summarized by Ira P. Robbins:

What standards will govern the operation of the institution?
Who will monitor the implementation of the standards?
Will the public still have access to the facility?
What recourse will members of the public have if they do not approve of how the institution is operated?
Who will be responsible for maintaining security if the private personnel go on strike?
Where will the responsibility for prison disciplinary procedures lie?
Will the company be able to refuse to accept certain inmates, such as those who have contracted AIDS?
What options will be available to the government if the corporation substantially raises its fees?
What will happen if the company declares bankruptcy or simply goes out of business because there is not enough profit?[87]

These questions underline the legal problems inherent in privatization.[88] The most disturbing and basic question that must be addressed is whether the sovereign right of the people, as represented by their government, to punish those found guilty of violating the people's code should ever be transferred to private hands.[89]

A report prepared for the National Institute of Justice, based on a survey of private-sector corrections in all states, is fairly optimistic about the future of private prisons:

■ Idleness is reduced at low cost.

■ Prisons have access to private-sector economic expertise.

■ The prison environment is improved.

■ Prisoners may earn real wages and obtain vocational training useful after their release.

■ Taxpayers benefit because the wages of prisoners help offset the cost of incarceration.

■ Victims have a better chance of obtaining compensation out of prisoners' earnings.[90]

As for the inmates themselves, by and large they do not care who runs the prison.[91] The general reluctance to accept the concept of private correctional institutions may perhaps be offset by a reminder that noninstitutional corrections owes its origin largely to private entrepreneurship, private concern for offenders, and community action in caring for convicted offenders in the community itself.

COMMUNITY ALTERNATIVES

The public equates punishment and corrections with prisons and jails. Incarceration is, in fact, the most painful, enduring contemporary punishment. In terms of the number of sentenced offenders, however, incarceration is far less significant than noninstitutional control of offenders through probation, parole, and other alternatives to confinement.

Probation

John Augustus, born in Woburn, Massachusetts, in 1784, moved to Lexington at the age of 21, learned the shoemaking trade, and by 1827 had become a successful craftsman in Boston. He often visited the courts, where he was appalled by what he saw. Judges filled the jails with petty criminals simply because the miscreants could not pay the small fines imposed. So Augustus stepped forward to pay the fines himself. Sheldon Glueck, nearly a century later, described how John Augustus worked:

> His method was to bail the offender after conviction, to utilize this favor as an entering wedge to the convict's confidence and friendship, and through such evidence of friendliness as helping the offender to obtain a job and aiding his family in various ways, to drive the wedge home. When the defendant was later brought into court for sentence, Augustus would report on his progress toward reformation, and the judge would usually fine the convict one cent and costs, instead of committing him to an institution.[92]

John Augustus promoted his new approach through his Washington Total Abstinence Society, and the Boston courts endorsed the idea. Thus was born the concept of **probation,** the release of a prison-bound offender into the community under the supervision of a trustworthy person and bound by certain conditions, such as not to violate the law, not to leave the jurisdiction, and to maintain employment. Probation was greeted as a welcome alternative to prisons in the mid-nineteenth century, when the demand for prison space was greater than the supply, the first disenchantment about the capacity of penitentiaries to reform their inmates had set in, and the exorbitant cost of imprisonment was first perceived.

The purpose of probation has always been to integrate offenders, under supervision, into law-abiding society. By 1956 all states had established a probation system. Most operate throughout a county, but some are statewide.[93] Probation is now one of the most widely used correctional dispositions. In fact, approximately four times as many offenders are placed on probation as are sent to prison.

Probation serves the dual purpose of protecting the community through continued court supervision and rehabilitating the offender. Only minor restrictions are imposed on the probationer's life. The benefits of probation are great: (1) not all types of offenses are serious enough to require costly incarceration; (2) probationers can obtain or maintain employment and pay taxes; and (3) offenders can care for their families and comply with their other financial responsibilities without becoming burdens on the state.

As we noted in Chapter 17, the trial judge, in order to determine a convicted defendant's eligibility for probation, requests a presentence investigation (PSI) report. This report is prepared by a probation officer, who focuses on such factors as the nature of the offense (violent or nonviolent), the defendant's version of the offense, prior criminal record, employment history, family background, financial situation, health, religious involvement, length of current residence, and community ties.[94] On the basis of such factors, the judge then decides whether to impose a prison sentence or probation.

The probation concept as it works in practice

WINDOW TO THE WORLD
Volunteers in Probation

Over 48,000 Japanese proudly wear this little medal:

These are the voluntary probation officers, or *hogoshi,* who donate their time and energy to assisting probationers. The idea of probation was unknown to the Japanese prior to the American occupation after World War II, when several features of the American criminal justice system were introduced. Foremost among them was probation, which was established by the Offenders Rehabilitation Law of 1949.

With no tradition of probation in Japan and no professionals available, the idea that volunteer probation officers would do the job was anticipated from the very beginning. Article I of the Offenders Rehabilitation Law states:

> The objective of this law is to protect society and promote individual and public welfare by aiding the reformation and rehabilitation of offenders . . . and facilitating the activities of crime prevention. All the people are required to render help according to their position and ability, to accomplish the objective mentioned.(1)

Since then, citizen-run parole and probation have come to occupy an important position in the Japanese criminal justice system:

> Offenders rehabilitation services occupy the final position in the current criminal justice system. . . . [T]he parole and probation sys-

tems have the fundamental characteristic that the offenders are supervised actively and their rehabilitation is strongly promoted. The Japanese parole and probation systems aim at the offenders' rehabilitation and reintegration into society. We call that system "*kosei-hogo*" in Japanese.(2)

The volunteers for offender rehabilitation, recruited from all walks of life, were 80,000 strong when the system began. Now, because of low crime rates in Japan and the availability of more professionals, the number of volunteer probation officers has leveled off at approximately 48,000. Each leaves home for a weekend day or an evening or two to visit probationers. Visits and interviews typically take place twice a month, and the volunteers may assist their probationers with housing problems, employment, medical care, adjustment to living with their families, and other aspects of life.

"Volunteer probation officer" is an honorable position in Japan, and not everyone is accepted. Eligibility depends on patience, intelligence, kindness, and a good reputation. In some respects, the problems of the Japanese volunteers are similar to those faced by American probation officers; in other ways, the lot of the Japanese volunteer probation officer is easier. Japan is a high-employment country, which makes it much easier to find jobs for probationers. Public health services are far more accessible in Japan than in the United States. And the fact that the whole country is served by the same criminal justice organization also helps the Japanese volunteers. Probation and parole are handled by the same service.

The use of volunteers in Japan's probation and parole system is not without problems. But as criminologist William Clifford notes, "The system has stood the test of time."(1)

Sources
1. William Clifford, *Crime Control in Japan* (Lexington, Mass.: Lexington Books, 1976), pp. 100–107.
2. Mitsugu Nishinsukama, "The Development of Non-institutional Treatment for Criminal Offenders in Japan," *UNAFEI Resource Material Series* (Tokyo, Japan), **36** (1989): 124–130.

Questions for Discussion
1. What stands in the way of combining probation and parole in the same service in the United States as the Japanese have done in Japan?
2. What complications might arise in the United States if the probation system were to switch to using more volunteer probation officers than professionals?

has two major flaws. First, judges generally do not have the time, the information, or the capacity to determine whether a given offender is a good prospect for probation. They frequently view probation simply as a means of limiting the prison population by keeping less serious offenders out of prison or jail. Second, the probationer (the person put on probation) does not have the assistance and guidance John Augustus considered essential for success. There are 30,606 probation officers in the United States, each with an average caseload of 115 probationers at any given moment. Some officers supervise many more.[95] And the cases are constantly changing.

Under such circumstances, the officer has no chance to provide guidance and assistance. We would expect failure rates to be very high, but this is not the case. A 17-state survey of felons sentenced to probation in 1986 shows that within 3 years, only 20 percent were rearrested for violent crimes.[96]

The unmet challenge is to exclude from routine probation those 20 to 23 percent of offenders who do constitute a danger. Better presentence screening may provide an answer, since probationers (except property offenders) for whom the PSI recommends probation are less likely to offend than those placed on probation against the investigator's recommendation.

Treatment programs in general and probation programs in particular depend greatly on the personality of the person providing the service. The relative success of probation programs may be attributable to the people who have joined the probation service. An evaluation of the Massachusetts probation system found the quality of probation staff to be outstanding, with a strong and common desire to ensure public safety while providing support for offenders.[97] Probation officers have relatively low levels of job stress. They like what they are doing, except for the endless preoccupation with administrative procedures.[98]

Parole

The concept of parole was introduced about the same time as that of probation. In the 1840s Captain Alexander Maconochie adminstered an English penal colony on Norfolk Island, a speck of land in the Pacific Ocean, 900 miles east of Australia. He observed:

[A] man under a time sentence thinks only how he is to cheat that time and while it away; he evades labor, because he has no interest in it whatsoever, and he has no desire to please the officers under whom he is placed, because they cannot serve him essentially; they cannot in any way promote his liberation.

Maconochie created a "scheme of marks awarded for industry, labor, and good conduct, [which] gave prisoners an opportunity to earn their way out of confinement."[99] Release from confinement proceeded through several stages of ever-greater freedom from control.

On the surface, **parole** may appear to be similar to probation. Both programs provide periods in which an offender lives in the community instead of serving time in a prison. Both programs require that the person be under supervision to ensure his or her good conduct. When the condition is violated, confinement results. But here the similarity ends (see Table 18.3).

The idea of parole was introduced in the United States at the first National Prison Association Congress in Cincinnati in 1870. Warden Zebulon Brockway of the Elmira Reformatory began using parole in 1876. Promising offenders were released into the care of private reform groups before their terms had expired. Later on, correctional officers were assigned to supervise the parolees. By 1900 20 states and the federal government had parole systems in place. Ultimately all jurisdictions instituted parole.

Parole success rates have never been great. Perhaps parole is granted too late. Don M. Gottfredson and his colleagues at the National Council on Crime and Delinquency found that success on parole diminishes as the length of time served in prison increases.[100] In 1990 only 45 percent of parolees had completed their terms successfully.[101] The high failure rate is not the only reason parole has come under attack in recent years. First, parole is supposed to be a reward for rehabilitation in prison, yet prisons do not rehabilitate inmates. Thus prisoners are denied rewards because of the prison's failure. Second, the parole system has long been plagued by a lack of valid criteria that parole boards can use when they decide whether to release a prisoner. Though 19 jurisdictions have had guidelines for parole decisions since federal guidelines were instituted in 1973, parole decision making

TABLE 18.3   PROBATION VS. PAROLE

Probation	Parole
An offender is sentenced to a period of probation *in lieu of prison.*	A prisoner is *released from prison* and placed on parole.
Probation is a front-end measure.	Parole is a tail-end measure.
The court imposes the sentence of probation.	A parole board grants release on parole.
The court retains jurisdiction.	A parole board retains jurisdiction.
A probation officer is an officer of the court and is employed by a county or district.	A parole officer is a state officer employed by the state government.
Probation is an alternative sentence for less serious cases.	Originally serious offenders earned parole through good conduct in prison.
Eligibility depends on a favorable PSI report.	Eligibility depends on successful service of a specific part of the prison sentence.

nevertheless remains a mysterious process that increases the anxiety of inmates.

The system is also criticized because it is subject to political manipulation and lobbying. For example, the governor may pressure the parole board to grant more parole releases when prisons are overcrowded. Lobbyists may exert pressure against a parole decision when a notorious convict comes up for parole. Parole, like probation, depends for its success on assistance and supervision. Yet caseloads are so great that such assistance is not available in the ordinary case.[102]

In a broad attack on the parole system, Andrew von Hirsch and Kathleen J. Hanrahan argued for its abolition. The decision to release an offender, they say, should not be based on questions of treatment or likelihood of offending again; rather, prison time should be correlated with responsibility for the current offense. Parole supervision and the potential for revocation of parole disturb von Hirsch and Hanrahan particularly on grounds of fairness and appropriateness. They propose instead a fixed release date, rather than one that can change after a large portion of the sentence has been served.[103]

These criticisms have led some jurisdictions to terminate discretionary releases by parole boards. They have substituted mandatory release, either through determinate sentencing (Alaska, Arizona, Colorado, Indiana, Maine, Missouri, New Jersey, New Mexico, North Carolina, Tennessee) or through parole guidelines (Florida, Georgia, Hawaii, Louisiana, Maryland, Michigan, New York, Ohio, Oregon, Rhode Island, South Carolina, Virginia, Washington,

West Virginia, Wisconsin, and the federal system). Some jurisdictions use both methods (California, Minnesota, Pennsylvania), and some have returned to the "good-time" system.[104]

The **good-time system** entails a procedure by which the length of the sentence is shortened by specific periods if the prisoner performs in accordance with the expectations of prison authorities. Many risks, especially to public safety, may inhere in the good-time system, and much has yet to be learned about it before it can be considered a sensible means of dealing with prison overcrowding.[105] An opinion survey has found strong public approval for the use of good time and community-based corrections; construction of more prisons received only moderate support; and shortening sentences and increasing parole boards' authority were disapproved.[106]

The Search for Cost-Beneficial Alternatives

Probation and parole have always been regarded as cost-beneficial alternatives to imprisonment.[107] As we noted, however, their success rates are mixed. In an era when drug-related and other crimes of violence are increasing, policy makers and the public view routine probation and parole as unsuitable solutions to the problem of prison overcrowding. Conservative legislators have generally been willing to fund the construction of new prisons, but construction costs and the frequency with which new facilities have to be built have put such a strain on state budgets that many conservatives have joined their liberal colleagues in opposing the expansion of the prison system.

The search has begun for cost-beneficial alternatives consistent with the public's demand for security and the punitive philosophy that marks the current era.[108] The search has focused on penal or correctional measures that:

■ Are less costly than confinement in a prison or jail

■ Are not perceived by the population as a cop-out, a lessening of the message conveyed by a jail or prison term

■ Do not pose a threat to the community

■ Do not have the negative effect on offenders that prison terms normally entail, but may actually benefit the offenders, their families, and their communities

Experimentation has shown some promising possibilities, among them intensive-supervision programs, home confinement programs, shock programs, restitution programs, fines, and community service programs.

Intensive-Supervision Probation

As originally conceived, probation programs were aimed at prison-bound offenders for whom it was thought that safety considerations did not require confinement and for whom association with others in confinement would do more harm than good. Traditional probation required intensive supervision, but such supervision has become impossible because the number of probationers is so enormous. Some states continue to use token or routine probation for low-risk cases, but many have introduced **intensive-supervision probation (ISP)** for those who do not qualify for routine probation.

The experience of the New Jersey ISP program has been particularly encouraging. The New Jersey program, directed by the Administrative Office of the Courts since 1983, is designed to handle 500 offenders, the equivalent of the population of one prison. Only nonviolent offenders are eligible for the program, so it excludes robbers, murderers, and all sex offenders. Those who want to be considered for the program must apply after 30 days and before 60 days from the day of imprisonment. This period is considered to be desirable for shock incarceration.

Each applicant must develop a personal plan, describing his or her own problems, plans, community resources, and contacts. A community sponsor must be identified with whom the offender will live during the early months after release and who will help the offender to fulfill the program's objectives. Applicants must also identify several other people in the community who can be relied on for help. These people are called the *network team.*

The offender's ISP plan and the persons identified in it are closely checked. All information is placed before the ISP screening board, which includes the ISP director, correctional staff, and community representatives. If the screening board's decision is positive, the application goes to a three-judge resentencing panel. A positive decision by this panel results in a 90-day placement in the ISP program; the placement is renewable after 90 days. Each participant must serve a minimum of 1 year in the program, including time on parole after release, during which period he or she is on bench warrant status and thus subject to immediate arrest should a violation occur.

Program conditions are punitive and onerous, centering on employment and hard work. They include the following:

■ At least 16 hours of community service per week

■ Multiple weekly contacts with the ISP officer and the community sponsor

■ Maintenance of a daily diary detailing accomplishments

■ Immediate notification of the ISP officer of any police contact or arrest

■ Participation in weekly counseling activities, if ordered

■ Maintenance of employment or participation in a vocational training program

■ Participation in any treatment program (for example, drug, alcohol) designated by the ISP officer

■ Adherence to curfew requirements (normally 10 P.M. to 6 A.M.)

■ Subjection to electronic monitoring, if ordered

■ Payment of all obligations, such as the cost of

electronic monitoring ($5 to $18 daily), court costs, fines, victim compensation payments, and child support, to the extent ordered by the court

The failure rate in the New Jersey program has been far lower than anybody expected. Only 5 percent of ISP participants committed a felony during the average 18 months of the program's duration. This rate is considered a success rate, as it tends to prove that intensive supervision is capable of detecting those who may abuse the privilege of participating in the ISP program.

Among the program's greatest benefits are these:

■ Rather than costing the state $17,000 per year, ISP costs $7000, thus saving the state $10,000 per offender per year.

■ The offender earns a living, pays taxes, and pays the cost of electronic monitoring, fines, fees, and other obligations.

■ Though it is too soon to make definite pronouncements, there is an indication that ISP program participants can do better after discharge than comparable prison inmates, thus saving the community some of the costs of crime.[109]

New Jersey's program is particularly punitive and demanding and thus more costly than any other state's ISP program. The Illinois program, for instance, aims at offenders who constitute a lesser risk and costs only $2500 per person. ISP programs in some other jurisdictions have proved to be similarly cost-beneficial (see Figure 18.3). The ISP program in Montgomery County (Dayton), Ohio, was found to be operating at an acceptable level for a program of its kind.[110] But evaluation of a similar Ohio county program indicated that it did not lower recidivism rates.[111] Results of effectiveness evaluations of ISP programs in other jurisdictions are inconclusive.[112]

Intensive Supervision of Parolees

Intensive supervision appears to be effective and cost-beneficial for offenders who are eligible for parole but who might pose undue risks and are therefore denied release on routine parole. In such cases, release into an intensive-supervision parole program, structured along the same lines

as front-end programs, frees prison bed space and provides the same financial rewards to the community as front-end programs. New Jersey's Intensive Supervision and Surveillance Program (ISSP), operated by the Bureau of Parole, assigns high-risk offenders to ISSP for 90 days. Following a case evaluation, the parolee may then be assigned to standard parole. As of 1991, 46,586 parolees around the United States were under intensive supervision. Judgment on the effectiveness of these types of programs awaits further research.[113]

Home Confinement Programs

In view of the high cost of incarcerating a criminal in a public prison, many state administrators have thought it cheaper to "imprison" a person at a place where the "rent" is cheaper. The person's home, or an alternative such as a group home or shelter, has been viewed as a viable option. Thus was introduced the concept of *house arrest*, to which some 50,000 American offenders have already been sentenced.

> House arrest is a sentence imposed by the court whereby offenders are legally ordered to remain confined in their own residences for the duration of their sentence. House arrestees may be allowed to leave their homes for medical reasons, employment, and approved religious services. They may also be required to perform community service and to pay victim restitution and probation supervising fees. In selected instances, electronic monitoring equipment may be used to monitor an offender's presence in a residence where he or she is required to remain.[114]

Technical problems in the original electronic monitoring systems had caused some initial difficulties, but these have now been largely resolved. As to psychological difficulties, it appears that other householders can accept their family member's house arrest, but many people have a civil libertarian aversion to electronic monitoring of human beings.[115] Michigan, Nevada, and Oklahoma have experimented with residential confinement programs whose participants are drawn from the prison population. Most states with such programs use them for diversion from prison.

In the Maryland program, which has operated successfully for several years, the sentencing

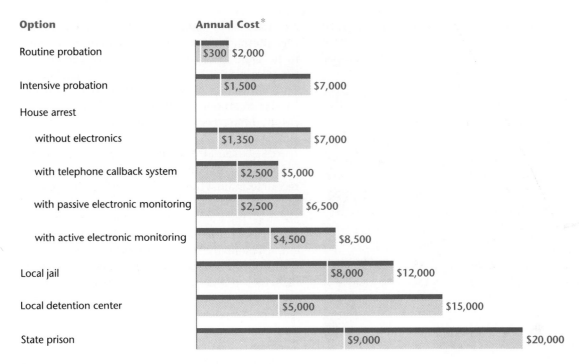

Option	Annual Cost*
Routine probation	$300 – $2,000
Intensive probation	$1,500 – $7,000
House arrest	
without electronics	$1,350 – $7,000
with telephone callback system	$2,500 – $5,000
with passive electronic monitoring	$2,500 – $6,500
with active electronic monitoring	$4,500 – $8,500
Local jail	$8,000 – $12,000
Local detention center	$5,000 – $15,000
State prison	$9,000 – $20,000

*Dollar amounts indicate range of annual costs.

FIGURE 18.3 Annual cost of sentencing options, exclusive of construction costs

Source: Joan Petersilia, *Expanding Options for Criminal Sentencing* (Santa Monica, Calif.: Rand Corporation, 1987), p. 32.

judge, together with the Department of Corrections, makes the decision to use the defendant's home rather than a prison cell as the place of confinement. This double-approval requirement is designed to ensure that dangerous or high-risk offenders are not placed in the program. The total cost of the Prince Georges County, Maryland, home detention program, including staff, transportation, and equipment, is $7 per day per prisoner, contrasted with the $45 it costs to maintain a prisoner in the county detention center for a day. In the first 2 years of this program, 188 offenders successfully completed their period of confinement on home detention, at savings to the county of well over $1 million.

The advantages of home confinement programs are that they are seen as sufficiently punitive, that the retribution and deterrence goals of punishment are satisfied, and that the offender is still allowed to maintain employment as well as close family ties, which can be particularly important when the family includes young chil-

dren. But it is too early to claim that home programs are a total success.[116]

Shock Programs

Both under retribution theory of the past and under the current just-deserts theory, punishment is measured by the length of time to be spent in confinement, a period determined by the gravity of the offense and the guilt or culpability of the perpetrator. Some corrections specialists believe that punishment should also be measured by the punitiveness and severity of incarceration. Thus the intensity of a short, sharp shock incarceration may be as severe as a longer, "easy-time" confinement in a prison. Moreover, the shorter incarceration may avoid the detrimental prisonization effects of a longer prison sentence.

Shock incarceration (SI) attempts to "shock" offenders out of criminal behavior by subjecting them to short periods (90 to 180 days) of intense drills, hard work, and character-building exer-

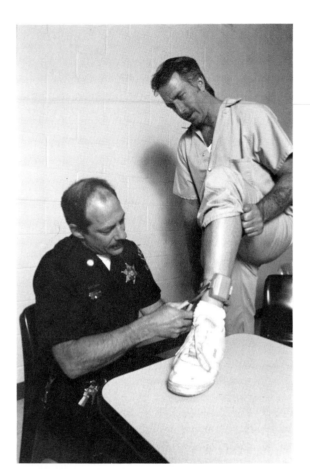

An electronic monitoring device is attached to an offender's ankle.

cises. Some ISP programs include shock incarceration; other types of programs are based entirely on the shock model. Similar to marine corps or army training, shock programs are sometimes referred to as "boot camps."

Boot camp programs are politically attractive because they are cost-effective and demonstrate to the public that offenders are undergoing an intense disciplinary experience. Their popularity has spread across the country. The programs have been used only for young (under age 30) male offenders, but this group traditionally constitutes two-thirds of all inmates. It may be too early to assess the value of boot camps to the correctional system, but the legislatures of several states—including Oklahoma (first SI program), Georgia, Connecticut, New York, Mississippi, Louisiana, Michigan, Florida, Colorado, and Nevada—have been willing to experiment with this alternative form of confinement. It remains to be seen whether American boot camps will produce disciplined and productive members of the community.[117] In several European countries, similar treatment programs have had little success and have been discontinued.[118]

Restitution Programs

In theory, victims of crime always have some recourse against their victimizers, traditionally in the form of a civil suit. Most offenders, however, are too poor to pay damages. Incarceration aggravates the situation by depriving them of the employment that could provide the money for restitution. Policy makers have begun to recognize this problem. Restitution programs have become increasingly popular since 1973, when a team of American corrections specialists visited Radbruch Haus, a former prison in Frankfurt, Germany, that had been converted into an employment-detention facility.

Half of the district's prison inmates had been selected at random to reside in this no-security facility. They were obligated to go to work every day. Their wages were carefully budgeted by correctional staff (guards retrained as accountants) to pay for court costs, confinement costs, victim restitution, support of their families, transportation to work, and so forth. The walkaway rate was low. Inmates who did walk off were placed in a secure prison.[119]

Among the American visitors was Kenneth C. Schoen, who, as head of the Minnesota correctional system, pioneered the first American restitution program at the Minnesota Restitution Center. Offenders lived at a community correctional center after making a contractual agreement with the victim, which itemized the amount, schedule, and form of restitution.

By now several jurisdictions have experimented successfully with **employment prisons,** or minimum security restitution centers. Low-risk offenders bound for prison may be placed in such facilities, which are usually located in or near the cities where they live and work. At night, the prisoners must remain in the facility. During working hours, they pursue their employment. Wages are administered by the correctional staff and applied to the cost of incarcer-

AT ISSUE
Boot Camp: A Military Option for Corrections

A new type of incarceration attempts to "shock" offenders out of criminal behavior by subjecting them to short periods (90 to 180 days) of intense marine corps–style drills, hard work, absence of spare time, and character-building exercises: in other words, a sort of boot camp for prisoners. Young prison-bound convicts, most of them undisciplined high school dropouts with histories of alcohol and drug abuse, are selected for these programs, called Regimented (or Regimental) Inmate Discipline (RID).

The first such program was established in Oklahoma in 1983. Along with the usual strict discipline and drill of all RID programs, inmates there spend several hours daily in educational, vocational, drug abuse, and counseling programs. Inmates go from the program to probation or to a halfway house.(1) A similar program in Georgia subjects inmates to 8 hours a day of hard labor in addition to the usual boot camp activities. Some boot camps include more extensive therapy programs or community service experiences.(2)

Boot camp programs have been used only for young male offenders, but this group traditionally constitutes two-thirds of all inmates. The Oklahoma RID program has a success rate (individuals crime-free 12 months after discharge) of 85 percent.

Boot camp programs have been attacked as creators of "Rambos," but the use of such programs in the United States is too new a phenomenon to allow us to judge. Perhaps the experience of other countries can give insights into the effects of boot camp programs. Germany's thorough militarization until 1918 extended to the prison system, where inmates wore military-style uniforms, marched in lockstep from place to place, and had orders barked at them by drill sergeants. Their education was confined to military manuals. One prisoner's story—that of "the captain of Koepenik"—has been retold in several books and movies. Upon discharge, the prisoner bought himself an infantry captain's worn uniform in a secondhand clothing store, changed into the uniform in the men's room of the railroad station, and emerged as a man of authority. He promptly assumed command of a passing platoon of soldiers, marched them to city hall, arrested the mayor, and retrieved his confiscated passport—all this just so he could get out of the country.

It may be too early to assess the value of boot camps to the correctional system in the United States, but the proposed federal budget for 1994–1995 envisages increased federal contributions for state boot camp programs. The faith of politicians in these programs, demonstrated by their willingness to fund them, is surprising in view of the lack of evaluation research. It remains to be seen whether American boot camps will produce disciplined and productive members of the community, Rambos, mercenaries, or captains of Koepenik.

Sources

1. Dale Parent, *Shock Incarceration: An Overview of Existing Programs* (Washington, D.C.: National Institute of Justice, 1989).
2. New York State Division of Parole, *Shock Incarceration: One Year Out of 3* (prepared by the New York Office of Policy Analysis and Information, August 1989); *New Haven Register,* Nov. 10, 1989, p. 15.

Questions for Discussion

1. Do you think the addition of educational and counseling sessions to the boot camp–style discipline of RID programs serves to dilute the "shock effect" or to prevent inmates from becoming captains of Koepenik?
2. Would you expect boot camp graduates to continue on their careers crime-free for longer than 1 year after release, or will the effect of the boot camp experience wear off with time?

New participants in the Sumter County Correctional Institute "Boot Camp" program arrive at their barracks, Bushnell, Florida.

ation and to all other financial obligations, including compensation to the victim when it has been ordered.

Research has confirmed the feasibility and success of restitution programs. Burt Galaway reviewed the development of restitution programs and research on them from the 1970s through 1988. He concluded:

■ Restitution programs are feasible in both juvenile and adult correctional systems.

■ Victims and the public at large strongly support restitution programs.

■ Restitution may achieve the utilitarian goal of punishment as well as the goal of ensuring just deserts.[120]

Research conducted in Canada, however, established that restitution programs there have a much higher rate of failure. Yet even there, only one-quarter of the offenders fail to live up to their restitution orders.[121]

Straight Fines, Day Fines, and Community Service

Forced labor to pay the treasury and fines to reimburse the government for its trouble in dealing with or punishing an offender have been part of the system since the Middle Ages. Most offenders today are too poor to pay fines. Even a dollar is a lot for a person who has no income. A *straight fine* can be a burden to a factory worker but no burden to a manager. A fixed sum of money means different things to persons in different income brackets.

To compensate for income differentials among offenders, the Nordic countries (Sweden, Denmark, Norway, Finland, and Iceland) have long used the *day-fine system,* according to which the amount of the fine is measured in days of earnings. For a drunk-driving offense, the fine may be 10 days' earnings. For the corporate executive, this fine may amount to ten times $500, or $5000; for a factory worker it may amount to ten times $50, or $500. This scheme, which approximates that of the graduated income tax, helps the public treasury. The offender is in the community and is able to meet other obligations, such as supporting children and making car payments. And the offender is not subjected to prisonization.

Fines are predicted to play a far greater role in

American corrections than they have done in the past. In view of the large number of unemployed and unemployable minor offenders, however, fines have their limitations. Whether vocational training can bring these people into the group of finable offenders is yet to be seen.

When the payment of money is inappropriate, an order of *community service* may be an alternative. One of the first jurisdictions in the United States to use community service orders was Alameda County, California. In October 1966 the Alameda County court agreed to permit misdemeanants to serve their sentences as volunteers for community organizations. Since then, thousands of minor offenders have served time by performing many hours of service for health and welfare organizations.

The benefits of such programs are clear:

■ Offenders have opportunities to engage in constructive activities.

■ Offenders may undergo a change of attitude through the experience of volunteer work.

■ Community service is a sentence uniquely appropriate to indigent offenders.

■ It can also be an appropriate sentence for persons in higher income brackets whose offenses merit a public humbling.

Evaluation of Community Alternatives

Prison overcrowding in America has become such a problem both socially and financially that the established system can no longer cope with it. Many legislatures tolerated prison construction and extension of the capacity of existing penal institutions for a while. Then a countertrend set in. As both liberal and conservative legislators became reluctant to commit ever-increasing portions of state budgets to prison expansion, criminologists were challenged to devise cost-beneficial alternatives to incarceration and the standard forms of probation and parole that also met the contemporary demand for punitiveness and public security.

In an amazingly short time, several such alternatives were developed and instituted in various states. Heralded as cost-beneficial, punitive, and secure, these programs were accepted at face value and replicated in other states on very little evidence of success in achieving the stated goals. We have pointed to some of the early evaluations, fully aware that they do not provide an accurate measure of the success of these programs.[122]

■ REVIEW

Throughout history systems of punishment have often served the economic purposes of the state, first as a source of slave labor, later as a source of fines. During the last two centuries many well-meaning efforts by reformers to rehabilitate offenders turned out to be fruitless, but they shaped the correctional system into the form it has today, a mix of punishment and reform efforts.

Prison overcrowding is a particularly American phenomenon, resulting from punitiveness fueled by the drug problem and its corresponding violence. The traditional forms of alternative corrections, probation and parole, are still used, but recognition of their limitations has led to the development of innovative forms of intermediate corrections, such as intensive-supervision programs, home confinement, shock programs, restitution, fine systems, and community service programs.

Having recently gone through a period in which the need for rehabilitation nearly determined the measure of punishment, and after a brief return to straight time (the just-deserts movement), we seem to be headed for a new era in which the measure of punishment is likely to include also the need to protect society, the need to compensate society for losses due to crime, and the need to compensate victims of crime for their losses.

■ NOTES

1. *Gore v. United States,* 357 U.S. 386 (1958), at 393.
2. Rudolf His, *Deutsches Strafrecht bis zur Karolina* (Munich and Berlin: R. Oldenbourg, 1928), pp. 58–60.
3. Georg Rusche and Otto Kirchheimer, *Punishment and Social Structure* (New York: Columbia University Press, 1939), p. 9. The book has a foreword by Thorsten Sellin.
4. Thorsten Sellin, "Two Myths in the History of Capital Punishment," *Journal of Criminal Law and Criminology,* **50** (1959): 114–117.
5. Thorsten Sellin, *Slavery and the Penal System* (New York: Elsevier, 1976), p. 54.
6. George Ives, *A History of Penal Methods* (1914; Montclair, N.J.: Patterson Smith, 1970), p. 104.
7. Sellin, *Slavery and the Penal System,* pp. 54–55.
8. Ibid., p. 71.
9. Ibid., pp. 77, 101.
10. Geneva Convention Relative to the Treatment of Prisoners of War, Aug. 12, 1949, art. 22.
11. Sellin, *Slavery and the Penal System,* p. 101.
12. It is estimated that 100,000 offenders were transported from England to the American colonies and Australia over a period of nearly 200 years. See J. J. Tobias, *Nineteenth-Century Crime: Prevention and Punishment* (Newton, Mass.: David & Charles, 1972); and C. R. Henderson, *Penal and Reformatory Institutions* (New York: Charities, 1910).
13. Graeme R. Newman, *The Punishment Response* (Philadelphia: Lippincott, 1978), p. 121.
14. Harry Elmer Barnes and Negley K. Teeters, *New Horizons in Criminology,* rev. ed. (New York: Prentice-Hall, 1945), p. 505.
15. See Alexander W. Pisciotta, "A House Divided: Penal Reform at the Illinois State Reformatory, 1891–1915," *Crime and Delinquency,* **37** (1991): 165–185.
16. *Attica: The Official Report of the New York Special Commission on Attica* (McKay Commission report) (New York: Bantam, 1972). For an analysis of conditions leading to prison riots and management proposals for the future, see Edith E. Flynn, "From Conflict Theory to Conflict Resolution: Controlling Collective Violence in Prisons," *American Behavioral Scientist,* **23** (1980): 745–776. For an overall account of prison riots, see Bert Useem and Peter Kimball, *States of Siege: U.S. Prison Riots, 1971–1986* (New York: Oxford University Press, 1989).
17. "Standard Minimum Rules for the Treatment of Prisoners," in *Human Rights: A Compilation of International Instruments,* Center for Human Rights (New York: United Nations, 1988), pp. 190–209; Douglas J. Besharov and Gerhard O. W. Mueller, "The Demands of the Inmates of Attica State Prison and the United Nations Standard Minimum Rules for the Treatment of Prisoners: A Comparison," *Buffalo Law Review,* **21** (1972): 839–854.
18. In *Cooper v. Pate,* 378 U.S. 546 (1964), the Supreme Court declared that prisoners may sue "the system" for infringement of their civil rights under the Civil Rights Act of 1871. For an account of the prisoners' rights movement, see James B. Jacobs, *New Perspectives on Prisons and Imprisonment* (Ithaca, N.Y.: Cornell University Press, 1983); Geoffrey P. Repert, ed., *Legal Rights of Prisoners* (Beverly Hills, Calif.: Sage, 1980); and Penelope D. Clute, *The Legal Aspects of Prisons and Jails* (Springfield, Ill.: Charles C Thomas, 1980).

19. *Stroud v. Swope,* 187 F. 2d 850 (9th Cir. 1951).

20. For a discussion of court treatment of women inmates' rights claims, see Barbara B. Knight, "Women in Prison as Litigants: Prospects for Post-prison Futures," *Women and Criminal Justice,* 4 (1992): 91–116.

21. Hans Mattick, "The Contemporary Jail in the United States," in *Handbook of Criminology,* ed. Daniel Glaser (Chicago: Rand McNally, 1974).

22. Michael T. Charles, Sesha Kethineni, and Jeffrey L. Thompson, "The State of Jails in America," *Federal Probation,* **56** (1992): 56–62. See also Wayne N. Welsh, Henry N. Pontell, Matthew C. Leone, and Patrick Kinkade, "Jail Overcrowding: An Analysis of Policy Makers' Perceptions," *Justice Quarterly,* **7** (1990): 339–370. For an historical description, see Lois A. Guyon and Helen Fay Greer, "Calaboose: Small Town Lockup," *Federal Probation,* **54** (1990): 58–62.

23. Freda Adler, "Jails as a Repository for Former Mental Patients," *International Journal of Offender Therapy and Comparative Criminology,* **30** (1986): 225–236.

24. See John J. Gibbs, "Symptoms of Psychopathology among Jail Prisoners: The Effects of Exposure to the Jail Environment," *Criminal Justice and Behavior,* **14** (1987): 288–310; and John R. Belcher, "Are Jails Replacing the Mental Health System for the Homeless Mentally Ill?" *Community Mental Health Journal,* **24** (1988): 185–195, recommending changes in the mental-health system to prevent the criminalization of the homeless mentally ill.

25. Henry J. Steadman, Dennis W. McCarty, and Joseph P. Morrissey, *The Mentally Ill in Jail: Planning for Essential Services* (New York: Guilford, 1989). See also Peter Finn, "Coordinating Services for the Mentally Ill Misdemeanor Offender," *Social Service Review,* **63** (1989): 127–141.

26. The literature on imprisonment is vast. For some of the challenging assessments (besides those mentioned elsewhere in this section), see Benedict S. Alper, *Prisons Inside Out* (Cambridge, Mass.: Ballinger, 1974); and Richard Hawkins and Geoffrey P. Alpert, *American Prison Systems: Punishment and Justice* (Englewood Cliffs, N.J.: Prentice-Hall, 1989).

27. Darrell K. Gilliard, *Prisoners in 1992,* Bureau of Justice Statistics Bulletin (Washington, D.C.: U.S. Government Printing Office, May 1993); Allen J. Beck, Thomas P. Bonczar, and Darrel K. Gilliard, *Jail Inmates, 1992,* Bureau of Justice Statistics Bulletin (Washington, D.C.: U.S. Government Printing Office, August 1993).

28. National Council on Crime and Delinquency, *Juveniles Taken into Custody, 1990 Report* (San Francisco: NCCD, 1991).

29. Todd R. Clear and George F. Cole, *American Corrections* (Monterey, Calif.: Brooks/Cole, 1986), p. 198.

30. George M. Camp and Camille Graham Camp, *The Corrections Yearbook 1991: Probation and Parole* (South Salem, N.Y.: Criminal Justice Institute, 1991), p. 3.

31. See Clear and Cole, *American Corrections,* p. 279.

32. Charles F. Wellford and Laure Weber Brooks, *Correlates of Incarceration Rates: Explaining the Pattern of Incarceration between 1970 and 1979* (College Park: Institute of Criminal Justice and Criminology, University of Maryland, 1984). For overcrowding and policy change, see Franklin E. Zimring and Gordon Hawkins, *Prison Population and Criminal Justice Policy in California* (Berkeley, Calif.: Institute of Governmental Studies Press, 1992).

33. National Prison Project, "Status Report: State Prison and the Courts," *Corrections Digest,* Mar. 19, 1992, pp. 3–9, and Apr. 1, 1992, pp. 2–6.

34. Stephen D. Gottfredson and Sean McConville, eds., *America's Correctional Crisis: Prison Populations and Public Policy* (New York: Greenwood, 1987), p. 3, with contributions by Barton L. Ingraham and Charles F. Wellford, Todd R. Clear and Patricia Harris, Ralph B. Taylor, Joan Mullen, Eryl Hall Williams, Don Gottfredson, Alfred Blumstein, Alan T. Harland, and Philip W. Harris and M. Kay Harris. For overcrowding problems of jails, see John M. Klofus, "The Jail and the Community," *Justice Quarterly,* **7** (1990): 69–102. See also Sandra Evans Skovron, Joseph E. Scott, and Francis T. Cullen, "Prison Crowding: Public Attitudes toward Strategies of Population Control," *Journal of Research in Crime and Delinquency,* **25** (1988): 150–169.

35. Donald Clemmer, *The Prison Community* (New York: Holt, Rinehart & Winston, 1965).

36. Gresham M. Sykes, *The Society of Captives: A Study of a Maximum Security Prison* (Princeton, N.J.: Princeton University Press, 1958).

37. J. Q. Burstein, *Conjugal Visits in Prison: Psychological and Social Consequences* (Lexington, Mass.: Lexington Books, 1977); Ann Goetting, "Conjugal Association in Prison: Issues and Perspectives," *Crime and Delinquency,* **28** (1982): 52–71; Randolph Davis, "Education and the Impact of the Family Reunion Program in a Maximum Security Prison," *Journal of Offender Counseling, Services, and Rehabilitation,* **12** (1988): 153–159. See also Laura T. Fishman, "Treacherous Trysts, Tender Trade: Prisoners' Wives as Contacts and Contraband Carriers," *Women and Criminal Justice,* **2** (1991): 45–70.

38. Gresham M. Sykes and Sheldon L. Messinger, "The Inmate Social System," in *Theoretical Studies in Social Organization of the Prison,* ed. Richard A. Cloward et al. (New York: Social Science Council, 1960).

39. Clarence Schrag, "Some Foundations for a Theory of Corrections," in *The Prison: Studies in Institutional Organization and Change,* ed. Donald R. Cressey (New York: Holt, Rinehart & Winston, 1961). For a comparative analysis, see William G. Archambeault and Charles Fenwick, "A Comparative Analysis of Culture, Safety, and Organizational Management Factors in Japan and U.S. Prisons," *Prison Journal,* **68** (1988): 3–23.

40. Charles W. Thomas, "Prisonization or Resocialization: A Study of External Factors Associated with the Impact of Imprisonment," *Journal of Research in*

Crime and Delinquency, **10** (1973): 13–21.

41. Stanton L. Wheeler, "Socialization in Correctional Institutions," in *Handbook of Socialization Theory and Research,* ed. D. A. Goslin (Chicago: Rand McNally, 1969). For adjustment to prison, see Kevin N. Wright, "A Study of Individual, Environmental, and Interactive Effects in Explaining Adjustment to Prison," *Justice Quarterly,* **8** (1991): 216–242.

42. Ulla V. Bondeson, *Prisoners in Prison Societies* (New Brunswick, N.J.: Transaction, 1989). For a discussion of the failure of prisons, see Gerhard O. W. Mueller, "Economic Failures in the Iron Womb: The Birth of Rational Alternatives to Imprisonment," in *Sentencing: Process and Purpose,* ed. Mueller (Springfield, Ill.: Charles C. Thomas, 1977), pp. 110–143.

43. Hans Toch, Kenneth Adams, and Douglas J. Grant, *Coping: Maladaptation in Prisons* (New Brunswick, N.J.: Transaction, 1989). See also Ester Heffernan, *Making It in Prison: The Square, the Cool, and the Life* (New York: Wiley-Interscience, 1972), for an analysis of adaptation processes in women's prisons.

44. Mark S. Fleisher, *Warehousing Violence* (Newbury Park, Calif.: Sage, 1989). See also Albert K. Cohen, George F. Cole, and Robert G. Bailey, eds., *Prison Violence* (Lexington, Mass.: Lexington Books, 1976).

45. James F. Houston, Don C. Gibbons, and Joseph F. Jones, "Physical Environment and Jail Social Climate," *Crime and Delinquency,* **34** (1988): 449–466.

46. James B. Jacobs, "Prisons: Prison Subculture," in *Encyclopedia of Crime and Justice,* ed. Sanford H. Kadish (New York: Free Press, 1983), p. 1224.

47. Frank S. Pearson, "Evaluation of New Jersey's Intensive Supervision Program," *Crime and Delinquency,* **34** (1988): 437–448.

48. R. G. Leger, "Perception of Crowding, Racial Antagonism, and Aggression in a Custodial Prison," *Journal of Criminal Justice,* **16** (1988): 167–181, at p. 178.

49. John Irwin, *Prisons in Turmoil* (Boston: Little Brown, 1980); Leo Carroll, *Hacks, Blacks and Cons: Race Relations in a Maximum Security Prison* (Lexington, Mass.: Lexington Books, 1974).

50. Michael S. Serrill and Peter Katel, "New Mexico: The Anatomy of a Riot," *Corrections Magazine,* **6** (1980): 6–7. For causes of riots, see Randy Martin and Sherwood Zimmerman, "A Typology of the Causes of Prison Riots and an Analytical Extension to the 1986 West Virginia Riot," *Justice Quarterly,* **7** (1990): 711–737.

51. Marvin E. Wolfgang and Franco Ferracuti, *The Subculture of Violence* (London: Tavistock, 1967). For a study of violence in female prisons, see Richard H. Anson and Barry W. Hancock, "Crowding, Proximity, Inmate Violence, and the Eighth Amendment," *Journal of Offender Rehabilitation,* **17** (1992): 123–132: and Candace Kruttschnitt and Sharon Krmpotich, "Aggressive Behavior among Female Inmates: An Exploratory Study," *Justice Quarterly,* **7** (1990): 369–389. Lenore M. J. Simon, "Prison Behavior and the Victim-Offender Relationship Among Violent Offenders," *Justice Quarterly,* **10** (1993): 489–506.

52. Lee H. Bowker, "Victimizers and Victims in American Correctional Institutions," in *Pains of Imprisonment,* ed. Robert Johnson and Hans Toch (Beverly Hills, Calif.: Sage, 1982), p. 64; Peter Kratcoski, "The Implications of Research Explaining Prison Violence and Disruption," *Federal Probation,* **52** (1988): 27–32; Martin and Zimmerman, "A Typology of the Causes of Prison Riots." See also Edith E. Flynn, "From Conflict Theory to Conflict Resolution: Controlling Collective Violence in Prison," *American Behavioral Scientist,* **23** (1980): 745–776.

53. George M. Camp and Camille Graham Camp, *Prison Gangs,* U.S. Department of Justice (South Salem, N.Y.: Criminal Justice Institute, 1985).

54. James W. Marquart, *Cooptation of the Kept: Maintaining Control in a Southern Penitentiary* (Ann Arbor, Mich.: University Microfilms, 1983).

55. Kelsey Kaufman, *Prison Officers and Their World* (Cambridge, Mass.: Harvard University Press, 1988).

56. Barbara A. Owen, *The Reproduction of Social Control: A Study of Prison Workers at San Quentin* (New York: Praeger, 1988). For a discussion of women officers in male prisons, see Linda L. Zupan, "The Progress of Women Correctional Officers in All-Male Prisons," in *The Changing Roles of Women in the Criminal Justice System,* ed. Imogene L. Moyer (Prospect Park, Ill.: Waveland, 1992, pp. 323–343; and Lynn Zimmer, "Solving Women's Employment Problems in Corrections: Shifting the Burden to Administrators," *Women and Criminal Justice,* **1** (1989): 55–79. For a discussion of men guarding women, see Linda L. Zupan, "Men Guarding Women: An Analysis of the Employment of Male Correction Officers in Prisons for Women," *Journal of Criminal Justice,* **20** (1992): 297–309. For female correctional officers' perceptions about performance, see Joanne Belknap, "Women in Conflict: An Analysis of Women Correctional Officers," *Women and Criminal Justice,* **2** (1991): 89–115. See also Kevin N. Wright and William G. Saylor, "Male and Female Employees' Perceptions of Prison Work: Is There a Difference?" *Justice Quarterly,* **8** (1991): 504–524.

57. Sellin, *Slavery and the Penal System,* p. 143.

58. Barnes and Teeters, *New Horizons in Criminology,* p. 702.

59. Clear and Cole, *American Corrections,* pp. 333–338.

60. Institute for Economic and Policy Studies, *The Economic Impact of Corcraft Correctional Industries in New York State* (Alexandria, Va.: 1988).

61. Florida House of Representatives, Committee on Corrections, *Probation & Parole, Oversight Report on PRIDE* (Tallahassee, 1988). See also Dianne Carter, "The Status of Education and Training in Corrections," *Federal Probation,* **55** (1991): 1723.

62. Kathleen E. Maguire, Timothy J. Flanagan, and Terence P. Thornberry, "Prison Labor and Recidivism," *Journal of Quantitative Criminology,* **4** (1988): 3–18.

63. L. Sechrest, S. O. White, and E. D. Brown, eds., *The*

Rehabilitation of Criminal Offenders: Problems and Prospects (Washington, D.C.: National Academy of Sciences, 1979). For an examination of the role of religion in prison, see James M. Day and William S. Laufer, eds., *Crime, Values and Religion* (Norwood, N.J.: Ablex, 1987); and Byron R. Johnson, "Religious Commitment within the Corrections Environment: An Empirical Assessment," in *Crime, Values and Religion*, ed. Day and Laufer. See also Harry Dammer III, *Prisoners, Prisons and Religion*. Ph.D. dissertation, Rutgers University, 1992.

64. Daniel Glaser, *The Effectiveness of a Prison and Parole System* (Indianapolis: Bobbs-Merrill, 1964).

65. Walter C. Bailey, "Correctional Outcome: An Evaluation of 100 Reports," *Journal of Criminal Law, Criminology, and Police Science*, **57** (1966): 153–160, at p. 157.

66. Roger Hood, "Research on the Effectiveness of Punishments and Treatments," in *Collected Studies in Criminological Research*, Council of Europe, European Committee on Crime Problems (Strasbourg: 1967).

67. James Robison and Gerald Smith, "The Effectiveness of Correctional Programs," *Crime and Delinquency*, **17** (1971): 67–80.

68. Freda Adler, Arthur D. Moffett, Frederick B. Glaser, John C. Ball, and Diane Horwitz, *A Systems Approach to Drug Treatment* (Philadelphia: Dorrance, 1974).

69. Douglas Lipton, Robert Martinson, and Judith Wilks, *The Effectiveness of Correctional Treatment: A Survey of Treatment Evaluation Studies* (New York: Praeger, 1975); Robert Martinson, "What Works?: Questions and Answers about Prison Reform," *Public Policy*, **35** (1974): 22–54.

70. Carl B. Klockars, "The True Limits of the Effectiveness of Correctional Treatment," *Prison Journal*, **55** (1975): 53–64; Ted Palmer, "Martinson Revisited," *Journal of Research in Crime and Delinquency*, **12** (1975): 133–152.

71. Robert Martinson, "New Findings, New Views: A Note of Caution Regarding Sentencing Reform," *Hofstra Law Review*, **7** (1979): 254–258. It appears that wardens had never really given up on the rehabilitative idea; see Francis T. Cullen, Edward J. Latessa, Velmer S. Burton, Jr., and Lucien X. Lombardo, "The Correctional Orientation of Prison Wardens: Is the Rehabilitative Ideal Supported?" *Criminology*, **31** (1993): 69–92.

72. Paul Gendreau and Robert R. Ross, "Effective Correctional Treatment: Bibliotherapy for Cynics," *Crime and Delinquency*, **25** (1979): 463–489. See also Michael R. Gottfredson, "Treatment Destruction Techniques," *Journal of Research in Crime and Delinquency*, **16** (1979): 39–54.

73. Paul Gendreau and Robert R. Ross, "Revivification of Rehabilitation: Evidence from the 1980s," *Justice Quarterly*, **4** (1987): 395; Francis T. Cullen and Paul Gendreau, "The Effectiveness of Correctional Rehabilitation: Reconsidering the 'Nothing Works' Debate," in *The American Prison: Issues in Research and Policy*, ed. Lynn Goodstein and Doris Layton Mackenzie (New York: Plenum, 1989), pp. 23–44.

74. Carol J. Garrett, "Effects of Residential Treatment on Adjudicated Delinquents: A Meta-Analysis," *Journal of Research in Crime and Delinquency*, **22** (1985): 287–308; Alexander B. Smith and Louis Berlin, *Treating the Criminal Offender*, 3d ed. (New York: Plenum, 1988); Cullen and Gendreau, "The Effectiveness of Correctional Rehabilitation."

75. Nathaniel J. Pallone and James J. Hennessy, *Criminal Behavior—A Process Psychology Analysis* (New Brunswick, N.J.: Transaction, 1991), pp. 362–363.

76. Francis T. Cullen and Karen E. Gilbert, *Reaffirming Rehabilitation* (Cincinnati, Ohio: Anderson, 1982), p. 247.

77. Caroline Wolf Harlow, *HIV in U.S. Prisons and Jails*, Bureau of Justice Statistics, U.S. Department of Justice, September 1993. See also Sherwood E. Zimmerman and Randy Martin, "AIDS Knowledge and Risk Perceptions among Pennsylvania Prisoners," *Journal of Criminal Justice*, **19** (1991): 239–256.

78. John O'Brien, "Record Award in HIV Needle Case," *New York Law Journal*, July 14, 1992, p. 1.

79. Lisa Belkin, "23% of State Prisoners Test Positive for TB," *New York Times*, Mar. 31, 1992, p. B4; Mireya Navairro, "As Suspects Wait, the Fear of Tuberculosis Rises," *New York Times*, Jan. 30, 1992, pp. B1, B2.

80. Imogene L. Moyer, "Differential Social Structures and Homosexuality among Women in Prison," *Virginia Social Science Journal*, **13** (1978): 13–14, 17–19.

81. Edna Erez, "The Myth of the New Female Offender: Some Evidence from Attitudes toward Law and Justice," *Journal of Criminal Justice*, **16** (1988): 499–509.

82. Peter Appleborne, "U.S. Prisons Challenged by Women behind Bars," *New York Times*, Nov. 30. 1992, p. A10.

83. For a general overview, see "Privatization of Corrections," special issue of *Corrections Today*, **50** (1988), with articles by Samuel F. Saxton, Bob Turner, T. Don Hulto and James D. Henderson, Edward J. Loughran, Merle E. Springer, and Michael J. Mahoney.

84. On the development of private penal institutions in the United States, see Douglas C. McDonald, "Private Penal Institutions" in *Crime and Justice: A Review of Research*, vol. 16, ed. Michael Tonry (Chicago: University of Chicago Press, 1993), pp. 361–419. For the lesson to be learned from our experience with private prisons in the nineteenth and early twentieth centuries (namely, caution), see Alexis M. Durham III, "Origins of Interest in the Privatization of Punishment: The Nineteenth and Twentieth Century American Experience," *Criminology*, **27** (1989): 107–139.

85. Quoted in Kevin Krajick, "Punishment for Profit," *Across the Road*, **21** (1984): 25.

86. Charles W. Thomas and Suzanna L. Foard, "Private Adult Correctional Facility Census," private corrections project, Center for Studies in Criminology and Law, University of Florida, Gainesville, December

1992.

87. Ira P. Robbins, "Privatization of Corrections: Defining the Issues," *Federal Probation*, **50** (1986): 24–30.

88. Ira P. Robbins, *The Legal Dimensions of Private Incarceration* (Washington, D.C.: American Bar Association, 1988), including a model contract form and a model statute.

89. See Harold Demone, Jr., and Margaret Gibelman, "Privatizing the Treatment of Criminal Offenders," *Clinical Treatment of the Criminal Offender*, **15** (1990): 7–26. For a general overview, see "Privatization of Corrections," special issue of *Corrections Today*, **50** (1988). See also Byron R. Johnson and Paul P. Ross, "The Privatization of Correctional Management: A Review," *Journal of Criminal Justice*, **18** (1990): 351–358.

90. Barbara J. Auerbach et al., *Work in American Prisons: The Private Sector Gets Involved*, for National Institute of Justice (Washington, D.C.: U.S. Government Printing Office, 1988).

91. Samuel Jan Broker, "Prison Management, Private Enterprise Style: The Inmates' Evaluation," *New England Journal on Criminal and Civil Confinement*, **14** (1988): 175–244.

92. Sheldon Glueck, Introduction to *John Augustus, First Probation Officer* (New York: National Probation Association, 1939), p. xvi.

93. Harry Allen, Chris Eskridge, Edward Latessa, and Gennaro Vito, *Probation and Parole in America* (New York: Free Press, 1985).

94. Gennaro F. Vito, "Developments in Shock Probation: A Review of Research Findings and Policy Implications," *Federal Probation*, **48** (1984): 22–27.

95. Camp and Camp, *The Corrections Yearbook, 1991*, p. 9. For a study of the effectiveness of probation with felons, see John T. Whitehead, "The Effectiveness of Felony Probation: Results from an Eastern State," *Justice Quarterly*, **8** (1991): 525–543.

96. Associated Press, "43% of Probationers Arrested," *New York Times*, Feb. 11, 1992, p. 16, but only 20 percent were rearrested for violent crimes.

97. Robert L. Spangenberg et al., *Assessment of the Massachusetts Probation System* (Newton, Mass.: Spangenberg Group, 1987). For a discussion of "social worker" versus "law enforcer," see Todd R. Clear and Edward J. Latessa, "Probation Officers' Roles in Intensive Supervision: Surveillance versus Treatment," *Justice Quarterly*, **10** (1993): 441–462.

98. Robert L. Thomas, "Stress Perception among Select Federal Probation and Pretrial Services Officers and Their Supervisors," *Federal Probation*, **52** (1988): 48–58. See also Charles Lindner, "The Refocused Probation Home Visit: A Subtle but Revolutionary Change," *Journal of Contemporary Criminal Justice*, **7** (1991): 115–127; and Thomas Ellsworth, "Identifying the Actual and Preferred Goals of Adult Probation," *Federal Probation*, **54** (1990): 10–15. With increased emphasis on the control function there may arise the need to arm probation officers. See Richard D. Sluder, Robert A. Shearer, and Dennis

W. Potts, "Probation Officers' Role Perceptions and Attitudes toward Firearms," *Federal Probation*, **55** (1991): 3–11.

99. Alexander Maconochie as quoted in Barnes and Teeters, *New Horizons in Criminology*, p. 548.

100. Don M. Gottfredson, M. G. Neithercutt, Joan Nuffield, and Vincent O'Leary, *Four Thousand Lifetimes: A Study of Time Served and Parole Outcomes* (Davis, Calif.: National Council on Crime and Delinquency, Research Center, 1973).

101. U.S. Department of Justice, Bureau of Justice Statistics, *Corrections Populations in the United States, 1990* (Washington, D.C.: U.S. Government Printing Office, 1991), p. 120.

102. M. K. Harris, "Disquisition on the Need for a New Model for Criminal Sanctioning Systems," *West Virginia Law Review*, **77** (1975): 263–301.

103. Andrew von Hirsch and Kathleen J. Hanrahan, *The Question of Parole: Retention, Reform, or Abolition?* (Cambridge, Mass.: Ballinger, 1979).

104. U.S. Department of Justice, Bureau of Justice Statistics, *Parole Today* (Washington, D.C.: U.S. Government Printing Office, 1980), p. 11. It is noteworthy, however, that though parole releases declined from 72 to 43 percent of prison discharges between 1977 and 1985, they rose again by 47 percent from August 1983 through 1987; see Bureau of Justice Statistics, *Annual Report, Fiscal 1988* (Washington, D.C.: U.S. Government Printing Office, 1989), p. 59.

105. Norval Morris and Michael H. Tonry, *Between Prison and Probation* (New York: Oxford University Press, 1990); David Weisburd and Ellen F. Chayet, "Good Time: An Agenda for Research," *Criminal Justice and Behavior*, **16** (1989): 183–195.

106. Sandra Evans Skovron, Joseph E. Scott, and Francis T. Cullen, "Prison Crowding: Public Attitudes toward Strategies of Population Control," *Journal of Research in Crime and Delinquency*, **25** (1988): 150–169.

107. This section is based on Edna McConnell Clark Foundation, *Overcrowded Time: Why Prisons Are So Crowded and What Can Be Done* (New York: Edna McConnell Clark Foundation, 1982). For a discussion of the proportion of all offenses committed by persons on probation and parole, see Michael R. Geerken and Hennessey D. Hayes, "Probation and Parole: Public Risk and the Future of Incarceration Alternatives," *Criminology*, **31** (1993): 549–564.

108. See William B. Lawless and Gerhard O. W. Mueller, *Report of the Commission to Advise the Nevada Legislature on the Question of Prison Overcrowding* (Reno, Nev.: National Judicial College, 1989).

109. New Jersey Criminal Disposition Commission, "Report to the Governor and Legislature, 1987," on file at NCCD Library, Rutgers University.

110. Susan B. Noonan and Edward J. Latessa, "Intensive Probation: An Examination of Recidivism and Social Adjustment for an Intensive Supervision Program," *American Journal of Criminal Justice*, **12** (1987): 45–61.

111. Edward Latessa and Gennaro F. Vito, "Effects of Intensive Supervision on Shock Probationers," *Jour-*

nal of Criminal Justice, **16** (1988): 319–330.

112. Virginia Department of Corrections, Research and Evaluation Unit, "Intensive Supervision Program: Final Evaluation Report; Client Characteristics and Supervision Outcomes: A Caseload Comparison" (Richmond, 1988).

113. Camp and Camp, *The Corrections Yearbook, 1991,* p. 49.

114. Joan Petersilia, *Expanding Options for Criminal Sentencing* (Santa Monica, Calif.: Rand Corporation, 1987), p. 32; and see Joan Petersilia, *Exploring the Option of House Arrest* (Santa Monica, Calif.: Rand Corporation, 1986).

115. See Barton L. Ingraham and Gerald W. Smith, "The Use of Electronics in the Observation and Control of Human Behavior and Its Possible Use in Rehabilitation and Parole," *Issues in Criminology,* **7** (1972): 35–53; and George E. Rush, "Electronic Surveillance: An Alternative to Incarceration," *American Journal of Criminal Justice,* **12** (1989): 219–242. For a detailed discussion of psycholegal effects of home confinement, see Dorothy K. Kagehiro and Ralph Taylor, "A Social Psychological Analysis of Home Electronic Confinement," in *Handbook of Psychology and Law,* ed. D. K. Kagehiro and W. S. Laufer (New York: Springer Verlag, in press). See also James F. Quinn and John E. Holman, "Electronic Monitoring and Family Control in Probation and Parole," *Journal of Offender Rehabilitation,* **17** (1992): 77–87; Ronald Corbett and Gary T. Marx, "Critique: No Soul in the New Machine: Technofallacies in the Electronic Monitoring Movement," *Justice Quarterly,* **8** (1991): 399–414.

116. For a pilot study on a limited number of home confinement offenders, see Paulette Hatchett, *The Home Confinement Program: An Appraisal of the Electronic Monitoring of Offenders in Washtenaw County, Michigan* (Lansing: Community Programs Evaluation Unit, Michigan Department of Corrections, 1987).

117. Doris Layton MacKenzie and James Shaw, "The Impact of Shock Incarceration on Technical Violations and New Criminal Activities," *Justice Quarterly,* **10** (1993): 463–487; Dale Parent, *Shock Incarceration: An Overview of Existing Programs* (Washington, D.C.: National Institute of Justice, 1989), p. 9. See also Jody Klein-Saffran, "Shock Incarceration: Bureau of Prisons Style," *Research Forum,* Federal Bureau of Prisons, Office of Research and Evaluation (July 1992): 1–9; Doris Layton MacKenzie, Larry Gould, Lisa Riechers, and James Shaw, "Shock Incarceration: Rehabilitation or Retribution?" *Journal of Offender Counseling, Services and Rehabilitation,* **14** (1989): 25–40; and Doris Layton MacKenzie and James W. Shaw, "Inmate Adjustment and Change during Shock Incarceration: The Impact of Correctional Boot Camp Programs," *Justice Quarterly,* **7** (1990): 125–150.

118. See Günther Kaiser, *Kriminologie,* 2d ed. (Heidelberg: C. F. Müller Jur. Verlag, 1988).

119. Criminal Law Education and Research Center, *International Conference of Correctional Policy Makers* (New York: New York University School of Law, 1973).

120. Burt Galaway, "Restitution as Innovation or Unfulfilled Promise?" *Federal Probation,* **52** (1988): 3–14.

121. Joe Hudson and Burt Galaway, "Financial Restitution: Toward an Evaluable Program Model," *Canadian Journal of Criminology,* **31** (1989): 1–18.

122. James Byrne, "Assessing What Works in the Adult Community Corrections System," paper presented to the Academy of Criminal Justice Sciences, Denver, March 1990. See also M. Kay Harris, Peter R. Jones, and Gail S. Funke, *The Kansas Community Corrections Act: An Assessment of a Public Policy Initiative* (Philadelphia: Temple University—Edna McConnell Clark Foundation, 1990). For an overview of the effectiveness of community corrections, see Thomas Ellsworth, *Contemporary Community Corrections* (Prospect Heights, Ill: Waveland, 1992).

Glossary

Accomplice   A person who helps another to commit a crime.

Aggravated assault   An attack on another person in which the perpetrator inflicts serious harm on the victim or uses a deadly weapon.

Aging-out phenomenon   A concept which holds that offenders commit less crime as they get older because they have less strength, initiative, stamina, and mobility.

Anomic suicide   A suicide that occurs in a time of economic change when the individual experiences a dramatic change in lifestyle and is thrown into an unfamiliar and personally unsatisfying way of life.

Anomie   A societal state marked by "normlessness," in which disintegration and chaos have replaced social cohesion.

Arraignment   First stage of the trial process, at which the indictment or information is read in open court and the defendant is requested to respond.

Arson   At common law, the malicious burning of the dwelling house of another. This definition has been broadened by state statutes and criminal codes to cover the burning of other structures or even personal property.

Assault   At common law, an unlawful offer or attempt with force or violence to do a corporal hurt to another or to frighten another.

Atavistic stigmata   Physical features of a human being at an earlier stage of development, which—according to Cesare Lombroso—distinguish a born criminal from the general population.

Attachment   The bond between individuals and their family, friends, and school.

Bankruptcy fraud   A scam in which an individual falsely attempts to claim bankruptcy (and thereby erase financial debts) by taking advantage of existing laws.

Battery   A common law crime consisting of the intentional touching of or inflicting of hurt on another.

Behavioral modeling   Learning how to behave by fashioning one's behavior after that of others.

Belief   The extent to which an individual subscribes to society's values.

Biocriminology   The subdiscipline of criminology that investigates biological and genetic factors and their relation to criminal behavior.

Birth cohort   A group consisting of all individuals born in the same year.

Boiler room   An operation run by one or more stock manipulators who, through deception and misleading sales techniques, seduce the unsuspecting and uninformed public into buying stocks in obscure and often poorly financed corporations.

Born criminal   According to Lombroso, persons born with features resembling an earlier, more primitive form of human life, destined to become criminals.

Burglary   A common law felony, the nighttime breaking and entering of the dwelling house of another, with the intention to commit a crime (felony or larceny) therein.

Case study An analysis of all pertinent aspects of one unit of study.

Certiorari, writ of A writ issued by a higher court directing a lower court to prepare the record of a case and send it to the higher court for review.

Challenge for cause A challenge to remove a potential juror because of his or her inability to render a fair and impartial decision in a case. *See also* Peremptory challenges; Voir dire.

Check forging The criminal offense of making or altering a check with intent to defraud.

Chromosomes Basic cellular structures containing genes, i.e., biological material that creates individuality.

Churning Frequent trading, by a broker, of a client's shares of stock for the sole purpose of generating large commissions.

Classical school of criminology A criminological perspective suggesting that (1) people have free will to choose criminal or conventional behavior; (2) people choose to commit crime for reasons of greed or personal need; and (3) crime can be controlled by criminal sanctions, which should be proportionate to the guilt of the perpetrator.

Commitment A person's support of and participation in a program, cause, or social activity, which ties the individual to the moral or ethical codes of society.

Communal consensus model *See* Consensus model.

Community policing A strategy that relies on public confidence and citizen cooperation to help prevent crime and make the residents of a community feel more secure.

Comparative criminology The study of crime in two or more cultures in an effort to gain broader information for theory construction and crime control modeling.

Computer espionage Any activity by which unauthorized computer access yields information from data bases belonging to government or private parties, for purposes of exploitation.

Computer fraud Falsification of stored data or deception in legitimate transactions by manipulation of data or programming, including the unlawful acquisition of data or programs for purposes of financial gain.

Computer hacking In criminology, any activity that includes the gaining of unauthorized access to data banks for malicious, though not necessarily destructive, purposes and for neither financial gain nor purposes of espionage.

Computer sabotage The tampering with or destruction or scrambling of data or software through unlawful access to data banks.

Conditioning The process of developing a behavior pattern through a series of repeated experiences.

Conduct norms Norms that regulate the daily lives of people and that reflect the attitudes of the groups to which they belong.

Confidence game A deceptive means of obtaining money or property from a victim who is led to trust the perpetrator.

Conflict theory A model of crime in which the criminal justice system is seen as being used by the ruling class to control the lower class. Criminological investigation of the conflicts of society is emphasized.

Conformity Correspondence of an individual's behavior to society's patterns, norms, or standards.

Conjugal visits A program that permits prisoners to have contact with their spouses or significant others in order to maintain positive relationships.

Consensus model A model of criminal lawmaking that assumes that members of society agree on what is right and wrong and that law is the codification of agreed-upon social values.

Constable An officer, established by the Statute of Winchester in 1285, who was responsible for suppressing riots and violent crimes in each county; later, a local law enforcement officer, lowest rank in some police hierarchies.

Consumer fraud An act that causes a consumer to surrender money through deceit or a misrepresentation of a material fact.

Containment theory A theory which posits that every person possesses a containing external structure and a protective internal structure, both of which provide defense, protection, or insulation against delinquency.

Corporate crime A crime attributed to a corporation, but perpetrated by or on the authority of an officer or high managerial agent.

Corrections Implementation and execution of sentences imposed by the courts; also, the system that administers those sentences.

Cortical arousal Activation of the cerebral cortex, a structure of the brain which is responsible for higher intellectual functioning, information processing, and decision making.

Crime An act in violation of law that causes harm, is identified by law, committed with criminal intent, and subject to punishment.

Crimes against the person Crimes violative of life or physical integrity. *See* Crime.

Crimes against property Crimes involving the illegal acquisition or destruction of property. *See* Crime.

Criminal attempt An act or omission constituting a substantial step in a course of conduct planned to culminate in the commission of a crime.

Criminal careers A concept that describes the onset of criminal activity, the types and amount of crime committed, and the termination of such activity.

Criminology The body of knowledge regarding crime as a social phenomenon. It includes within its scope the process of making laws, of breaking laws, and of reacting toward the breaking of laws (Sutherland). Thus, criminology is an empirical, social–behavioral science which investigates crime, criminals, and criminal justice.

Cultural deviance theories Theories which posit that crime results from cultural values which permit, or even demand, behavior in violation of the law.

Cultural transmission A theory that views delinquency as a socially learned behavior transmitted from one generation to the next in disorganized urban areas.

Culture conflict theory A theory which posits that two groups may clash when their conduct norms differ, resulting in criminal activity.

Culture of poverty A culture characterized by helplessness, cynicism, and mistrust of authority as represented by schools and police.

Customs Social conventions carried on by tradition, not subject to legal sanctions.

Data Collected facts, observations, and other pertinent information from which conclusions can be drawn.

Defense counsel A lawyer retained by an individual accused of a crime, or assigned by the court if the individual is unable to pay.

Deterrence The theory of punishment which envisages that potential offenders will refrain from committing crimes out of fear of punishment (sometimes called *general prevention*).

Deviance A broad concept encompassing both illegal behavior and behavior that departs from the social norm.

Differential association–reinforcement A theory of criminality based on the incorporation of psychological learning theory and differential association with social learning theory. Criminal behavior, the theory claims, is learned through associations and is contained or discontinued as a result of positive or negative reinforcements.

Differential association theory A theory of criminality based on the principle that an individual becomes delinquent because of an excess of definitions learned that are favorable to violation of law over definitions learned that are unfavorable to violation of law.

Differential opportunity theory A theory that attempts to join the concept of anomie and differential association by analyzing both legitimate and illegitimate opportunity structures available to individuals. It posits that illegitimate opportunities, like legitimate opportunities, are unequally distributed.

Direct control An external control that depends on rules, restrictions, and punishments.

Dizygotic (DZ) twins Fraternal twins, who develop from two separate eggs fertilized at the same time. *See also* Monozygotic twins.

Drift According to David Matza, a state of limbo in which youths move in and out of delinquency and in which their lifestyles can embrace both conventional and deviant values.

Due process According to the Fourteenth Amendment of the U.S. Constitution, a fundamental mandate that a person should not be deprived of life, liberty, or property without reasonable and lawful procedures.

Ego The part of the psyche that, according to psychoanalytic theory, governs rational behavior. The moderator between the superego and the id.

Embezzlement The crime of withholding or withdrawing (conversion or misappropriation), without consent, funds entrusted to an agent (e.g., a bank teller or officer).

Employment prison   A prison for low-risk offenders. Prisoners work at jobs outside the prison during the day but return to prison after work.

Equal protection   A clause of the Fourteenth Amendment to the U.S. Constitution that guarantees equal protection of the law to everyone, without regard to race, origin, economic class, gender, or religion.

Eugenics   A science, based on the principle of heredity, that has for its purpose the improvement of the race.

Exclusionary rule   A rule prohibiting use of illegally obtained or otherwise inadmissible evidence in a court of law.

Experiment   A research technique in which an investigator introduces a change into a process in order to make measurements or observations that evaluate the effects of the change.

Extraversion   According to Hans Eysenck, a dimension of the human personality; describes individuals who are sensation-seeking, dominant, and assertive.

False pretenses, obtaining property by   Leading a victim to part with property on a voluntary basis through trickery, deceit, or misrepresentation.

Federal Witness Protection Program   A program, established under the Organized Crime Control Act of 1970, designed to protect witnesses who testify in court by relocating them and assigning to them new identities.

Fee system   A system, used in some rural areas, in which the county government pays a modest amount of money for each prisoner per day as an operating budget.

Felony   A severe crime, subject to punishment of 1 year or more in prison or to capital punishment.

Felony murder   The imposition of criminal liability for murder upon one who participates in commission of a felony that is dangerous to life and that causes the death of another.

Fence   A receiver of stolen property who resells the goods for profit.

Field experiment   An experiment conducted in a real-world setting, as opposed to one conducted in a laboratory.

Frankpledge   An ancient system whereby members of a tithing, an association of ten families, were bound together by a mutual pledge to keep the peace. Every male over age 12 was part of the system.

Fraud   An act of trickery or deceit, especially involving misrepresentation.

Good-time system   A system under which time is deducted from a prison sentence for good behavior within the institution.

Habeas corpus   A writ requesting that a person or an institution that is detaining a named prisoner bring him or her before a judicial officer and give reasons for the prisoner's capture and detention so that the lawfulness of the imprisonment may be determined.

Homicide   The killing of one person by another.

Hypoglycemia   A condition that may occur in susceptible individuals when the level of blood sugar falls below an acceptable range, causing anxiety, headaches, confusion, fatigue, and aggressive behavior.

Hypothesis   A proposition set forth as an explanation for some specified phenomenon.

Id   The part of the personality that, according to psychoanalytic theory, contains powerful urges and drives for gratification and satisfaction.

Index crimes   The eight major crimes included in Part One of the Uniform Crime Reports: criminal homicide, forcible rape, robbery, aggravated assault, burglary, larceny-theft, auto theft, and arson.

Indictment   Accusation against a criminal defendant rendered by a grand jury on the basis of evidence constituting a prima facie case.

Indirect control   A behavioral influence that arises from an individual's identification with noncriminals and his or her desire to conform to societal norms.

Information   Accusation against a defendant prepared by a prosecuting attorney.

Inmate code   An informal set of rules that reflects the values of the prison society.

Insider trading   The use of material nonpublic financial information to obtain an unfair advantage in trading securities.

Intensive-supervision probation (ISP)   An alternative to prison for convicted nonviolent offenders who do not qualify for routine probation.

Internalized control Self-regulation of behavior and conformity to societal norms as a result of guilt feelings arising in the conscience.

International crimes The major criminal offenses so designated by the community of nations for the protection of interests common to all humankind.

Involuntary manslaughter Homicide in which the perpetrator unintentionally but recklessly causes the death of another person by consciously taking a grave risk that endangers the person's life.

Involvement An individual's participation in conventional activities.

Just deserts A philosophy of justice which asserts that the punishment should fit the crime and the culpability of the offender. *See also* Retribution.

Justice of the peace Originally (established in 1326), an untrained man, usually of the lower nobility, who was assigned to investigate and try minor cases; presently, a judge of a lower local or municipal court with limited jurisdiction.

Justifiable homicide A homicide, permitted by law, in defense of a legal right or mandate.

Kidnapping A felony consisting of the seizure and abduction of a person by force or threat of force and against the victim's will. Under federal law, the victim of a kidnapping is one who has been taken across state lines and held for ransom.

Labeling theory A theory that explains deviance in terms of the process by which a person acquires a negative identity, such as "addict" or "ex-con," and is forced to suffer the consequences of outcast status.

Larceny The trespassory (unconsented) taking and carrying away of personal property belonging to another with the intent to deprive the owner of the property permanently.

Laws of imitation An explanation of crime as learned behavior. Individuals are thought to emulate behavior patterns of others with whom they have contact.

Longitudinal study An analysis that focuses on studies of a particular group conducted repeatedly over a period of time.

Macrosociological study The study of overall social arrangements, their structures, and their long-term effects.

Mafia The entirety of those Sicilian families which, in both the United States and Sicily, are loosely associated with one another in operating organized crime.

Malice aforethought The mens rea requirement for murder, consisting of the intention to kill with the awareness that there is no right to kill. *See also* Mens rea.

Manslaughter Criminal homicide without malice, committed intentionally after provocation (voluntary manslaughter) or recklessly (involuntary manslaughter).

Mass murder The killing of several persons, in one act or transaction, by one perpetrator or a group of perpetrators.

Mens rea (Latin, "guilty mind") Awareness of wrongdoing; the intention to commit a criminal act or behave recklessly.

Microsociological study The study of everyday patterns of behavior and personal interactions.

Minimal brain dysfunction (MBD) An attention-deficit disorder that may produce such asocial behavior as impulsivity, hyperactivity, and aggressiveness.

Miranda warning A warning that explains the rights of an arrestee. An arresting officer is required by law to recite the warning at the time of the arrest.

Misdemeanor A crime less serious than a felony and subject to a maximum sentence of 1 year in jail or a fine.

Money laundering The process by which money derived from illegal activities (especially drug sales) is unlawfully taken out of the country, placed in a numbered account abroad, and then transferred as funds no longer "dirty."

Monozygotic (MZ) twins Identical twins, who develop from a single fertilized egg that divides into two embryos. *See also* Dizygotic twins.

Motion An oral or written request to a judge that asks the court to make a specified ruling, finding, decision, or order. It may be presented at any appropriate moment from arrest until the end of the trial.

Murder The unlawful (usually intentional) killing of a human being with malice aforethought.

Neuroticism A personality disorder marked by low self-esteem, excessive anxiety, and wide mood swings (Eysenck).

Night watchman Originally, a thirteenth-century

untrained citizen who patrolled at night on the lookout for disturbances.

Nonparticipant observation A study in which investigators observe closely but do not become participants.

Occupational crime A crime committed by an individual for his or her own benefit, in the course of performing a profession.

Parens patriae (Latin, "father of the fatherland") Assumption by the state of the role of guardian over children whose parents are deemed incapable or unworthy.

Parole Supervised conditional release of a convicted prisoner before expiration of the sentence of imprisonment.

Participant observation Collection of information through involvement in the social life of the group a researcher is studying.

Penitentiary A prison or place of confinement and correction for persons convicted of felonies; originally, a place where convicts did penance.

Penologist A social scientist who studies and applies the theory and methods of punishment for crime.

Peremptory challenges Challenges (limited in number) by which a potential juror may be dismissed by either the prosecution or the defense without assignment of reason. *See also* Challenge for cause; Voir dire.

Phrenology A nineteenth-century theory based on the hypothesis that human behavior is localized in certain specific brain and skull areas. According to this theory, criminal behavior can be determined by the "bumps" on the head.

Physiognomy The study of facial features and their relation to human behavior.

Pimp A procurer or manager of prostitutes who provides access to prostitutes and protects and exploits them, living off their proceeds.

Plea bargaining An agreement made between defense and prosecution for certain leniencies in return for a guilty plea.

Plead To respond to a criminal charge. Forms of pleas are guilty, not guilty, and nolo contendere.

Police subculture The result of socialization and bonding among police officers due to the stress and anxiety produced on the job.

Population A large group of persons in a study.

Pornography The portrayal, by whatever means, of lewd or obscene (sexually explicit) material prohibited by law.

Positivist school of criminology A criminological perspective that uses the scientific methods of the natural sciences and suggests that human behavior is a product of social, biological, psychological, or economic forces.

Preliminary hearing A preview of a trial held in court before a judge, in which the prosecution must produce sufficient evidence of guilt for the case to be bound over for the grand jury or to proceed to trial.

Prima facie case A case in which there is as much evidence as would warrant the conviction of the defendant if properly proved in court, unless contradicted; a case that meets evidentiary requirements for grand-jury indictment.

Primary data Facts and observations that researchers gather by conducting their own measurements for a study.

Principals Perpetrators of a criminal act.

Prisonization A socialization process in which new prisoners learn the ways of prison society, including rules, hierarchy, customs, and culture.

Probable cause A set of facts that would induce a reasonable person to believe that an accused person committed the offense in question; the minimum evidence requirement for an arrest, according to the Fourth Amendment to the U.S. Constitution.

Probation An alternative to imprisonment, allowing a person found guilty of an offense to stay in the community, under conditions and with supervision.

Problem-oriented policing A strategy to enhance community relations and to improve crime prevention whereby police work with citizens to identify and respond to problems in a given community.

Prosecutor An attorney and government official who represents the people in proceedings against persons accused of criminal acts.

Prostitution The practice of engaging in sexual activities for hire.

Psychoanalytic theory In criminology, a theory of criminality that attributes delinquent and criminal behavior to a conscience that is either so overbearing that it arouses excessive feelings of guilt or so weak that it cannot control the individual's impulses.

Psychopathy A condition in which a person appears to be psychologically "normal" but in reality has no sense of responsibility, shows disregard for truth, is insincere, and feels no sense of shame, guilt, or humiliation (also called Sociopathy).

Psychosis A mental illness characterized by a loss of contact with reality.

Psychoticism A dimension of the human personality describing individuals who are aggressive, egocentric, and impulsive (Eysenck).

Racketeer Influenced and Corrupt Organizations (RICO) Act A federal statute that provides for forfeiture of assets derived from a criminal enterprise.

Radical criminology A criminological perspective that studies the relationships between economic disparity and crime, avers that crime is the result of a struggle between owners of capital and workers for the distribution of power and resources, and posits that only when capitalism is abolished crime will disappear.

Random sample A sample chosen in such a way as to ensure that each person in the population to be studied has an equal chance of being selected. *See also* Sample.

Rape At common law, a felony consisting of the carnal knowledge (intercourse), by force and violence, by a man of a woman (not his wife) against her will. The stipulation that the woman not be the man's wife is omitted in modern statutes.

Rational-choice perspective A theory which states that crime is the result of a decision-making process in which the offender weighs the potential penalties and rewards of committing a crime.

Reaction formation An individual response to anxiety in which the person reacts to a stimulus with abnormal intensity or inappropriate conduct.

Reasonable suspicion Warranted suspicion (short of probable cause) that a person may be engaged in the commission of a crime.

Rehabilitation A punishment philosophy which asserts that through proper correctional intervention, a criminal can be reformed into a law-abiding citizen.

Retribution An "eye for an eye" philosophy of justice. *See also* Just deserts.

Robbery The taking of the property of another, or out of his or her presence, by means of force and violence or the threat thereof.

Routine-activities perspective A theory which states that an increase or decrease in crime rates can be explained by changes in the daily habits of potential victims; based on the expectation that crimes will occur where there is a suitable target unprotected by guardians.

Sample A selected subset of a population to be studied. *See also* Random sample.

Secondary data Facts and observations that were previously collected for a different study.

Selective incapacitation The targeting of high-risk and recidivistic offenders for rigorous prosecution and incarceration.

Self-report survey A survey in which respondents answer in a confidential interview or, most often, by completing an anonymous questionnaire.

Serial murders Killings of several victims over a period of time by the same perpetrator(s).

Sheriff The principal law enforcement officer of a county.

Sherman Antitrust Act An act (1890) of Congress prohibiting any contract, conspiracy, or combination of business interests in restraint of foreign or interstate trade.

Shock incarceration (SI) Short-time, high intensity, confinement intended to shock convicts into disciplined lifestyles.

Shoplifting Stealing goods from stores or markets.

Simple assault An attack that inflicts little or no physical harm on the victim.

Social control theory An explanation of criminal behavior which focuses on control mechanisms, techniques, and strategies for regulating human behavior, leading to conformity or obedience to society's rules, and which posits that deviance results when social controls are weakened or break down, so that individuals are not motivated to conform to them.

Social disorganization theory A theory of criminality in which the breakdown of effective social bonds, primary-group associations, and social controls in neighborhoods and communities is held to result in development of high-crime areas.

Social interactionists Scholars who view the human self as formed through a process of social interaction.

Social learning theory A theory of criminality which maintains that delinquent behavior is learned through the same psychological processes as nondelinquent behavior, e.g., through reinforcement.

Sociopath A person who has no sense of responsibility; shows disregard for truth; is insincere; and feels no sense of shame, guilt, or humiliation.

Sociopathy *See* Psychopathy.

Sodomy Sexual intercourse by mouth or anus; a felony at common law.

Somatotype school of criminology A criminological perspective that relates body build to behavioral tendencies, temperament, susceptibility to disease, and life expectancy.

Statutory rape Sexual intercourse with a person incapable of giving legally relevant consent, because of immaturity (below age), mental, or physical condition.

Sting operation An undercover operation in which police officers attract likely perpetrators by posing as criminals.

Stock manipulation An illegal practice of brokers in which clients are led to believe that the price of a particular stock will rise, thus creating an artificial demand for it.

Strain theory A criminological theory positing that a gap between culturally approved goals and legitimate means of achieving them causes frustration which leads to criminal behavior.

Stranger homicide Criminal homicide committed by a person unknown and unrelated to the victim.

Strict liability Liability for a crime or violation imposed without regard to the actor's guilt; criminal liability without mens rea. *See also* Mens rea.

Subculture A subdivision within the dominant culture that has its own norms, beliefs, and values.

Subculture of violence A subculture with values that demand the overt use of violence in certain social situations.

Superego In psychoanalytic theory, the conscience, or those aspects of the personality that threaten the

person or impose a sense of guilt or psychic suffering and thus restrain the id.

Survey The systematic collection of information by asking questions in questionnaires or interviews.

Synnomie A societal state, opposite of anomie, marked by social cohesion achieved through the sharing of values.

Target hardening A crime-prevention technique that seeks to make it more difficult to commit a given offense, by better protecting the threatened object or person.

Team policing A strategy for improving contacts between citizens and police, whereby a team of officers is responsible for a specific neighborhood on a 24-hour basis.

Terrorism The use of violence against a target to create fear, alarm, dread, or coercion for the purpose of obtaining concessions or rewards or commanding public attention for a political cause.

Theft of computer time, software, and hardware The unauthorized use of computer time and software services, unauthorized copying of software programs, or outright theft of computer equipment.

Theory A coherent group of propositions used as principles in explaining or accounting for known facts or phenomena.

Tithing In Anglo-Saxon law, an association of ten families bound together by a frankpledge, for purposes of crime control. *See also* Frankpledge.

Tort An injury or wrong committed against a person's property, subject to compensation; an infringement of the rights of an individual that is not founded on either contract or criminal law prohibition.

Transnational crime A criminal act or transaction violating the laws of more than one country, or having an impact on a foreign country.

Utilitarianism A criminological perspective positing that crime prevention and criminal justice must serve the end of providing the greatest good for the greatest number; based on the rationality of lawgivers, law enforcers, and the public at large.

Variables Changeable factors.

Victim precipitation Opening oneself up, by either direct or subliminal means, to a criminal response.

Victimization survey A survey that measures the extent of crime by interviewing individuals about their experiences as victims.

Victimology A criminological subdiscipline that examines the role played by the victim in a criminal incident and in the criminal process.

Violations Minor criminal offenses, usually under city ordinances, commonly subject only to fines.

Voir dire A process in which lawyers and a judge question potential jurors in order to select those who are acceptable, i.e., those who are unbiased and objective in relation to the particular trial. *See also* Challenge for cause; Peremptory challenges.

Voluntary manslaughter Homicide in which the perpetrator intentionally, but without malice, causes the death of another person, as in the heat of passion, in response to strong provocation, or possibly under severe intoxication.

White-collar crime A sociological concept encompassing any violation of the law committed by a person or group of persons in the course of an otherwise respected and legitimate occupation or business enterprise.

Photo Credits

2　　Top, Andy Levin/Photo Researchers Center, Figaro Magazine/Gamma Liaison; bottom, Jeff Christensen/Reuters/Bettmann

3　　Top left, Greg Mellis/The State Journal-Register; top right, Alon Reininger/Contact Press Images; bottom, Al Grillo/Saba

4　　Top, Wide World Photos; bottom, Sygma

America's Changing Ethnic Gangs

1　　Top, Douglas Burrows/Gamma Liaison; bottom, Ohlinger's

2　　Left, D. Kuroda/Sygma; right, Riha/Gamma Liaison

3　　Both, Alon Reininger/Contact Press Images

4　　Brian Palmer/Impact Visuals

Drugs: A Continuing Problem

1　　Top, John Coletti/The Picture Cube; bottom, High Patrick Brown/Sygma

2　　Top, John Chiasson/Gamma Liaison; bottom, J. Griffin/Image Works

2-3　　NEWSWEEK, December 13, 1993

4　　Top, Les Stone/Sygma; center, Boroff/Texa-Stock; bottom, Miami Herald

Police Activities: From Shootouts to Social Service

1　　Left, Michael Ginsberg/© 1994 Capital Cities/ABC, Inc.; right, Greg Mellis/The State Journal-Register

2　　Top, M. Richards/Photos Edit; bottom, Richard Pasley/Stock, Boston

3　　Left, Bob Daemmrich/Stock, Boston; right, Steve McCurry/Magnum

4　　Top, Paul S. Howell/Gamma Liaison; bottom, Yvvone Hemsey/Gamma Liaison

Illustration and Text Credits

Chapter 1

16 Figure 1.1: From *The Sociology of Deviance* by Jack D. Douglas and Frances C. Waksler, Little, Brown and Company, 1982. Reprinted by permission of the authors.

10 Criminological Focus: From Gerhard O. W. Mueller, "The Criminological Significance of the Grimms' Fairy Tales," in *Fairy Tales and Society: Illusion, Allusion, and Paradigm,* edited by Ruth B. Bottigheimer, University of Pennsylvania Press, 1986, pp. 217–227. Reprinted by permission.

Chapter 2

28 Figure 2.1: From *Surveying Victims: A Study of the Measurement of Criminal Victimization, Perceptions of Crime, and Attitudes to Criminal Justice* by R. F. Sparks, H. G. Genn, and D. J. Dodd. Copyright © 1977. Reprinted by permission of John Wiley & Sons, Ltd.

29 Box 2.1 (table): "States with Laws against Stalking," *The New York Times,* February 8, 1993. Copyright © 1993 by The New York Times Company. Reprinted by permission.

Chapter 3

61 Criminological Focus: From Jim Miller, "The Mismeasure of Man," From *Newsweek,* November 9, 1981. © 1981, Newsweek, Inc. All rights reserved. Reprinted by permission. Three figures from *Varieties of Delinquent Youth* by William H. Sheldon, Emil M. Hartl and Eugene McDermott. Copyright 1949 by Harper & Brothers, renewed © 1977 by William H. Sheldon, Emil M. Hartl and Eugene McDermott. Reprinted by permission of HarperCollins Publishers, Inc.

55 Windows to the World: Excerpted and adapted from Gerhard O. W. Mueller and Freda Adler, "The Emergence of Criminal Justice: Tracing the Route to Neolithic Times," in *Festskrift til Jacob W. F. Sundberg* edited by Erik Nerep and Wiweka Warnling Nerep (Stockholm: Juristforlaget, 1993), pp. 151–170.

Chapter 4

82–83 Table 4.1: From *Understanding Psychology* by Robert S. Feldman. Copyright © 1981. Reprinted by permission of McGraw-Hill Inc.

84 At Issue (table): From *Why Kids Kill Parents* by Kathleen M. Heide, Ohio State University Press, 1992, pp. 40–41. Reprinted by permission.

85 Table 4.2: From *Television and Aggression: A Panel Study* by J. Ronald Milavsky, H. H. Stipp, R. C. Kessler, and W. S. Rubens, Academic Press, 1982. Reprinted by permission.

87 Window to the World (table): Chart from "Networks Under the Gun" from *Newsweek,* July 12, 1993. © 1993, Newsweek, Inc. All rights reserved. Reprinted by permission.

94 Cartoon: Drawing by Chas. Addams; © 1981 The New Yorker Magazine, Inc.

Chapter 5

112 Table 5.1: Reprinted with the permission of The Free Press, a division of Macmillian, Inc. from *Social Theory and Social Structure* by Robert K. Merton. Copyright © 1957 by The Free Press, renewed 1977, 1985 by Robert K. Merton.

117 Figure 5.2: "A Profile of Job Corps Members," *The New York Times,* February 17, 1992. Copyright © 1992 by The New York Times Company. Reprinted by permission.

119 Figure 5.3: From *Theories of Delinquency* by Donald J. Shoemaker, Oxford University Press, 1984, p. 73.

120 Figure 5.4: From *The Chi* by Robert E. Park, Ernest W. Burgess, and R. D. McKenzie, The University of Chicago Press, 1925, p. 55. Reprinted by permission.

Chapter 6

138, 140, 148 Figures 6.1, 6.2, and 6.4: From *Theories of Delinquency* by Donald J. Shoemaker, Oxford University Press, 1984, pp. 105, 114, and 122.

142 Cartoon: From *Investigating Deviance* by Stephen Moore. Reprinted by permission of HarperCollins Ltd.

145 Figure 6.3: From *Business Week*, May 18, 1992, pp. 40–41.

150 Criminological Focus: Adapted from *The Girls in the Gang* by Anne Campbell, Blackwell Publishers, Ltd., 1984. Reprinted by permission.

152 At Issue: Excerpts from Seth Mydans, "Not Just the Inner City: Well-to-Do Join Gangs," *The New York Times*, July 10, 1990. Copyright © 1990 by The New York Times Company. Reprinted by permission. Excerpt from Melinda Henneberger, "Gang Membership Grows in Middle-Class Suburbs," *The New York Times*, July 24, 1993. Copyright © 1993 by The New York Times Company. Reprinted by permission.

Chapter 7

162 Figure 7.1: From *Causes of Delinquency* by Travis Hirschi, University of California Press, 1969. Copyright © 1969 The Regents of the University of California.

170 Table 7.1: Adapted from Walter C. Reckless, "A Non-causal Explanation: Containment Theory," *Excerpta Criminologia* 2(1962), pp. 131–132.

Chapter 8

185 Criminological Focus: Excerpts from D. L. Rosenhan, "On Being Sane in Insane Places," *Science*, Vol. 179, 1973, pp. 253–254. Copyright 1973 by the American Association for the Advancement of Science.

Chapter 9

209 Figure 9.1: © 1962 *The Saturday Evening Post*.

210 Criminological Focus: From Martin Gansberg, "38 Who Saw Murder Didn't Call Police," *The New York Times*, March 27, 1964. Copyright © 1964 by The New York Times Company. Reprinted by permission.

219 Window to the World: From *Outlaws of the Ocean: The Complete Book of Contemporary Crime on the High Seas* by Gerhard O. W. Mueller and Freda Adler, Hearst Marine Books, 1985. pp. 217–218.

222 At Issue: From *The Battered Woman Syndrome* by Lenore E. Walker, Springer Publishing Company, Inc., New York 10012, 1984, pp. 142–143. Used by permission.

Chapter 10

237 Figure 10.2: Table and Map from "Crime: A Deadly Neighborhood," *The New York Times*, October 13, 1992. Copyright © 1992 by The New York Times Company. Reprinted by permission.

245 Criminological Focus: From "Hate Crimes: 'Litany of Shame'—Incidents on rise in California," *USA Today*, March 13, 1992. Copyright 1992, USA Today. Reprinted with permission.

252 Cartoon: © 1993 by Sidney Harris, from *So Sue Me!*, Rutgers University Press. Reprinted by permission of Sidney Harris.

Chapter 11

275 Figure 11.3: "Out of the Woodwork," *The New York Times*, August 18, 1993. Copyright © 1993 by The New York Times Company. Reprinted by permission.

276 Criminological Focus: Excerpt from Kirk Johnson, "One Less Thing to Believe In: High-Tech Fraud at an ATM," *The New York Times*, May 13, 1993. Copyright © 1993 The New York Times Company. Reprinted by permission.

281 Figure 11.4: "Residential Security Systems in Use in the United States, 1986–1992 (in millions)," *The New York Times*, February 9, 1992. Copyright © 1992 by The New York Times Company. Reprinted by permission.

Chapter 12

287–288: Excerpts from Steve Yozwiak, "Big Fines for Lake Powell Dumping Exceed $1.3 Million," *The Arizona Republic*, May 13, 1993, p. Al. © 1993 The Arizona Republic. Used with permission.

288: Excerpts from "Mafia Chief Tied to Crime-Busting Judges Murder" Reuters Information, August 1, 1993. Reprinted by permission.

300–301: From Jim Mayer, "Confection Maker Indicted in Dumping," *Sacramento Bee*, July 10, 1993. Copyright, *The Sacramento Bee, 1994*.

303 At Issue: Excerpt from *Dangerous Ground: The World of Hazardous Waste Crime* by Donald J. Rebovich. Copyright © 1992. Reprinted by permission of Transaction Publishers.

307 Cartoon: © 1993 by Sidney Harris, from *So Sue Me!*, Rutgers University Press. Reprinted by permission of Sidney Harris.

309 Figure 12.2: From *Chinese Subculture and Criminality* by Ko-lin Chin. Copyright © 1990. Reprinted with permission of Greenwood Press, an imprint of Greenwood Publishing Group, Inc., Westport, CT.

Chapter 14

354 Criminological Focus: From *The Cheyenne Way: Conflict and Case Law in Primitive Jurisprudence* by Karl N. Llewellyn and E. Adamson Hoebel. Copyright © 1941 by the University of Oklahoma Press. Reprinted by permission.

Chapter 15

391 Table 15.3: From Simon I. Singer and David McCowall, "Criminalizing Delinquency: The Deterrent Effects of the New York Juvenile Offender Law," *Law and Society Review*, 22, 1988, pp. 512–535. Reprinted by permission of the Law and Society Association.

392 Table 15.4: From Barry C. Feld, "The Juvenile Court Meets the Principle of the Offense: Legislative Changes in Juvenile Waiver Statutes." Reprinted by special permission of Northwestern University School of Law, Volume 78, Issue 3, *Journal of Criminal Law and Criminology*, pp. 512–514, (1987).

Chapter 16

417 Figure 16.1: From *Introduction to Security*, Fifth Edition, by Robert J. Fisher and Gion Green, Butter-worth-Heinemann, 1992. Reprinted by permission.

419 Cartoon: The Far Side, Copyright 1985 FarWorks, Inc. Distributed by Universal Press Syndicate. Reprinted with permission. All rights reserved.

421 Figure 16.3: From Jack R. Greene and Carl B. Klockars, "What Police Do," in *Thinking About Police,* Second Edition, edited by Carl B. Klockars and Stephen D. Mastrofski. Copyright © 1991. Reprinted by permission of McGraw-Hill, Inc.

Chapter 17

445 Figure 17.1: Adapted from *Criminal Justice: Issues and Ironies* by Abraham S. Blumberg, New Viewpoints, 1979, p. 150.

460: Drawing by Dana Fradon; © 1992 The New Yorker Magazine, Inc.

Chapter 18

486–487 Table 18.2: From *New Horizons in Criminology,* Revised Edition, by Elmer Barnes and Negley K. Teeters, Prentice Hall, Inc., 1945, pp. 640–643.

488 Figure 18.1: From *Americans Behind Bars: A Comparison of International Rates of Incarceration*, The Sentencing Project, 1991. Reprinted by permission.

505 Figure 18.3: From *Expanding Options for Criminal Sentencing* by Joan Petersilia, The Rand Corporation, 1987, p. 32.

Name Index

Subject Index